ISBN 978-1-397-19358-2
PIBN 11368498

1 MONTH OF
FREE
READING

at

www.ForgottenBooks.com

By purchasing this book you are eligible for one month membership to ForgottenBooks.com, giving you unlimited access to our entire collection of over 1,000,000 titles via our web site and mobile apps.

To claim your free month visit:

www.forgottenbooks.com/free1368498

SOPHOCLES

THE PLAYS AND FRAGMENTS

WITH CRITICAL NOTES, COMMENTARY, AND
TRANSLATION IN ENGLISH PROSE,

BY

R. C. JEBB, Litt. D.,

REGIUS PROFESSOR OF GREEK AND FELLOW OF TRINITY COLLEGE IN THE
UNIVERSITY OF CAMBRIDGE :
HON. LL.D. EDINBURGH, HARVARD AND DUBLIN;
HON. DOCT. PHILOS., BOLOGNA.

PART III.

THE ANTIGONE.

SECOND EDITION.

EDITED FOR THE SYNDICS OF THE UNIVERSITY PRESS.

CAMBRIDGE:

AT THE UNIVERSITY PRESS.

1891

𝕮𝖆𝖒𝖇𝖗𝖎𝖉𝖌𝖊:

PRINTED BY C. J. CLAY, M.A. AND SONS,
AT THE UNIVERSITY PRESS.

PREFACE.

THE *Antigone*, one of the earliest of its author's extant plays,—the *Ajax* alone having a rival claim in this respect,—belongs by time, as by spirit, to the very centre of the age of Pericles. At the probable date of its composition, the Parthenon was slowly rising on the Acropolis, but was still some years from completion; Pheidias, a few years older than Sophocles, and then about sixty, was in the zenith of his powers. The traditional, and best, reading of a verse in the ode to Dionysus (v. 1119) suggests the fresh interest .in Southern Italy which Athenians had lately acquired by the foundation of Thurii[1], and recalls the days, then recent, when one of the new colonists, Herodotus, had been in the society of Sophocles. The figure of Antigone, as drawn by the poet, bears the genuine impress of this glorious moment in the life of Athens. It is not without reason that moderns have recognised that figure as the noblest, and the most profoundly tender, embodiment of woman's heroism which ancient literature can show; but it is also distinctively a work of Greek art at the highest. It is marked by the singleness of motive, and the

---

[1] In his able work, *The Age of Pericles* (vol. II. p. 132), Mr Watkiss Lloyd makes an interesting remark with reference to the *Antigone*. Thurii stood near the old site of Sybaris. Télys was despot of Sybaris when it was destroyed by Croton (*circ.* 510 B.C.). Shortly before that event, he had put some Crotoniat envoys to death, and exposed their unburied bodies before the walls, according to the historian Phylarchus (*circ.* 220 B.C.) in Athen. p. 521 D. Callias, the soothsayer of Télys, afterwards forsook him,—alarmed by the omens (Her. 5. 44). This story may well have been brought into notoriety at Athens by the keen interest felt just then in Thurii. Creon's part would thus suggest a striking reminiscence.

J. S. III.²   b

self-restraint, which belonged to such art; it deserves to be studied sympathetically, and as a whole; for there could be no better example of ideal beauty attained by truth to human nature.

Such a study of the play, as a work of art, stands here in a more than usually intimate relation with that study of language and of detail which it is the secondary office of an interpreter to assist. The poetical texture of the work is, even for Sophocles, remarkably close and fine; it is singularly rich in delicate traits which might easily escape our observation, but which are nevertheless of vital consequence to a just apprecia- tion of the drama in larger aspects. The *Antigone* is thus a peculiarly exacting subject for a commentator. In estimating the shortcomings of an attempt to illustrate it, it may at least be hoped that the critic will not altogether forget the difficulties of the task.

A reference to the works chiefly consulted will be found at p. liv. The editor has been indebted to Mr W. F. R. Shilleto, formerly Scholar of Christ's College, for his valuable assistance in reading the proof-sheets; and must also renew his acknow- ledgments to the staff of the Cambridge University Press.

The present edition has been carefully revised.

R. C. JEBB.

CAMBRIDGE, *December*, 1890.

CONTENTS.

INTRODUCTION.

§ 1. THE *Oedipus Tyrannus* is concerned with the fall of the Theban king; the *Coloneus*, with the close of his life; and the *Antigone*, with a later episode in the fortunes of his children. But the order of composition was, *Antigone, Tyrannus, Coloneus;* and the first was separated from the last by perhaps more than thirty years of the poet's life. The priority of the *Antigone* admits of a probable explanation, which is not without interest. There is some ground for thinking that the subject—though not the treatment—was suggested by Aeschylus.

The sisters Antigone and Ismene are not mentioned by Homer, Hesiod, or Pindar[1]. Antigone's heroism presupposes a legend that burial had been refused to Polyneices. Pindar knows nothing of such a refusal. He speaks of the seven funeral-pyres provided at Thebes for the seven divisions of the Argive army[2]. Similarly Pausanias records a Theban legend that the corpse of Polyneices was burned on the same pyre with that of Eteocles, and that the very flames refused to mingle[3]. The refusal of burial was evidently an Attic addition to the story. *Earliest trace of the story.*

---

[1] Salustius, in his Argument to this play (p. 5), notices that the fortunes of the sisters were differently related by other writers. Mimnermus (c. 620 B.C.) spoke of Ismene having been slain at Thebes by Tydeus, one of the Argive chiefs. Ion of Chios (c. 450 B.C.) said that both sisters were burned in the Theban temple of Hera by Laodamas, son of Eteocles, when Thebes was taken in the later war of the Epigoni. Here, then, we have an Ionian contemporary of Sophocles who did not know the legend of Antigone's deed,—another indication that the legend was of Attic growth.

[2] Pind. *Ol.* 6. 15; *Nem.* 9. 24.

[3] Paus. 9. 18. 3.

It served to contrast Theban vindictiveness with Athenian humanity; for it was Theseus who ultimately buried the Argives at Eleusis. If Creon's edict, then, was an Attic invention, it may be conjectured that Antigone's resolve to defy the edict was also the conception of an Attic poet. Aeschylus is the earliest author who refers to the edict against burial, and he is also the first who tells of Antigone's resolve. His Theban trilogy consisted of the *Laïus*, the *Oedipus*, and the *Seven against Thebes*[1]. At the end of the last play a herald proclaims an edict just published by the Council of Thebes; sepulture shall be given to Eteocles, but denied to Polyneices. Antigone at once declares her resolve; she will bury Polyneices. The Theban maidens who form the Chorus are divided. One half of their number goes to attend the funeral of Eteocles; the other half accompanies Antigone to her task. There the play ends.

§ 2. The situation, as it is thus left by the *Seven against Thebes*, is essentially different from that in the play of Sophocles. The Antigone of Aeschylus is not isolated in her action, but is escorted by a band of maidens who publicly avow their sympathy. Though the herald enters a formal protest, and hints that the rulers are likely to be 'severe,' yet he does not say that death is to be the price of disobedience, nor, indeed, does he specify any penalty. The Chorus represents average civic opinion; and one half of the Chorus openly defies the decree. A plot which began thus could scarcely end in the Council taking the heroine's life. It rather foreshadows a final solution which shall be favourable to her; and we might surmise that, in loosing the knot, Aeschylus would have resorted to a divine mandate or intervention. But the Antigone of Sophocles stands alone; the penalty of a dreadful death is definitely set before her; and, whatever the Thebans may think of Creon's edict, no one dares to utter a word of disapproval. Taking the two primary facts—the veto, and Antigone's resolve— Sophocles has worked in a manner which is characteristically his own.

---

[1] With regard to this trilogy, see Introd. to the *Oedipus Tyrannus*, p. xvi (2nd ed.).

§ 3. Let us first trace the outline of the action. Analysis of the play.

The scene is laid before the palace of Creon,—once that of Oedipus,—at Thebes. The city has just been delivered from a great peril. It had been besieged by an Argive army, the allies of the exile Polyneices, whom his brother Eteocles had driven out of Thebes, that he himself might be sole king. But on the day before that with which the play begins, the two brothers had slain each other in single fight. Besides Polyneices, six other leaders of the besiegers had been killed by as many Theban chiefs. Thus deprived of its commanders, the besieging host had fled, panic-stricken, in the night. I. Pro- logue: 1 —99.

It is the moment of dawn. Antigone has asked her sister Ismene to come forth with her from the house, in order that they may converse alone. Creon, their uncle, is now king. He has put forth an edict,—that Eteocles, the champion of Thebes, shall be honourably buried; but the body of Polyneices, the country's foe, shall be left on the plain outside the walls of Thebes, for dogs and birds to mangle at their will. If any citizen dares to disobey, he shall be stoned to death. Antigone tells her sister that she is resolved to defy this edict, and to bury their brother Polyneices. Ismene vainly seeks to dissuade her; and Antigone goes forth, alone, to do the deed.

The Chorus of fifteen Theban elders now enters. Creon has summoned them to meet him,—they do not yet know wherefore. They greet the rising sun, and, in a splendid ode, describe the danger from which Thebes has been saved. The dramatic effect of the ode is to make us feel how grievous, from a Theban point of view, had been the act of Polyneices. Parodos: 100—161.

Creon comes forth. Declaring his resolve that patriotism and treason shall never miss their due rewards, he acquaints the Chorus with the purport of his edict,—that Eteocles shall be honoured, and Polyneices dishonoured. The elders receive the decision with unquestioning respect; though their words are more suggestive of acquiescence than of approval. II. First episode: 162—331.

A guard arrives, with the startling news that unknown hands have already paid burial-rites to Polyneices, by the symbolical act of sprinkling dust on the corpse. Creon dismisses the man with threats of a terrible death, which the other guards shall share, if they fail to discover the men who have thus broken the edict.

First stasimon: 332—375. Anapaests, 376—383.

The choral ode which follows is a beautiful treatment of a theme which this mysterious deed suggests,—human inventiveness,—its audacity and its almost infinite resource, save for the limits set by fate. As these strains cease, anapaests spoken by the leader of the Chorus express sudden amazement and pain.—Antigone, the royal maiden, the niece of the king, is led in, a prisoner in the hands of the guard.

III. Second episode: 384—581.

Questioned by Creon, Antigone replies that she knew the edict, but nevertheless paid funeral-rites to her brother because she held that no human law could supersede the higher law of the gods. She is ready to die.

Creon, still more incensed by her demeanour, vows that she shall indeed perish by a shameful death. He suspects Ismene also; and she is presently brought in. Agonised by grief for her sister's impending doom, Ismene entreats that she may be considered as sharing the responsibility of the deed; she wishes to die with her sister. Antigone firmly and even sternly, though not bitterly, rejects this claim, which 'justice will not allow' the deed has been hers only. Ismene vainly seeks to move Creon; he is not touched by her despair, or by the thought—to which Ismene also appeals—that his son Haemon is betrothed to Antigone. He orders that both sisters shall be taken into the house, and closely guarded; for his present purpose is that both shall die.

Second stasimon: 582—625. Anapaests, 626—630.

Moved by the sentence which has just been passed, the Chorus speaks of the destiny which has pursued the royal line of Thebes: 'When a house hath once been shaken from heaven, there the curse fails nevermore.' The sisters were the last hope of the race; and now they too must perish. The ode closes with a strain of general reflection on the power of Zeus and the impotence of human self-will. There is no conscious reference to Creon; but, for the spectators, the words are suggestive and ominous.

IV. Third episode: 631—780.

Haemon enters. He has come to plead with his father for the life of his betrothed Antigone. This scene is one of the finest in the play. A lesser dramatist would have been ap to depict Haemon as passionately agitated. The Haemon of Sophocles maintains an entire calm and self-control so long as a ray of hope remains; his pleading is faultless in tone and in tact; he knows Creon, and he does not intercede with him as a lover for his betrothed; he speaks as a son solicitous for his father's reputation, and as a subject concerned for the authority of his king; he keeps his temper under stinging taunts; it is only when Creon is found to be inexorable that the pent-up fire at last flashes out. Then, when Haemon rushes forth,—resolved, as his latest words hint, not to survive his beloved,—he leaves with the spectators a profound sense of the supreme effort which he has made in a cause dearer to him than life, and has made without success.

Haemon having quitted the scene, Creon announces, in reply to a question of the Chorus, the mode of death which he designs for Antigone. As for Ismene, he will spare her; her entire innocence has been proved, to his calmer thoughts, by the words which passed between the sisters in his presence. Antigone is to be immured in a sepulchral chamber,—one of the rock-tombs in the low hills that fringe the plain of Thebes,—and there she is to be left, with only the formal dole of food which religion prescribes, in order to avert the pollution which the State would otherwise incur through the infliction of death by starvation.

A choral song celebrates the power of Love,—as seen in Haemon, who has not feared to confront a father's anger in pleading for one who had broken the law. While implying that Haemon has acted amiss, the ode also palliates his action by suggesting that the deity who swayed him is irresistible. At the same time this reference to Haemon's passion serves to deepen the pathos of Antigone's fate. *Third stasimon 781—800 Anapaest 801—805*

She is now brought out of the house by Creon's servants, who are to conduct her to her living tomb. At that sight, the Theban elders cry that pity constrains them, even as love constrained Haemon, to deplore the sentence. Antigone speaks to them of her fate, and they answer not unkindly; yet they say plainly that the blame for her doom rests with herself alone; the king could not grant impunity to a breach of his edict. Creon enters, and reproves the guards for their delay. In her *V. Fourth episode: 806—943* latest words, Antigone expresses her confidence in the love which awaits her beyond the grave; and also the trouble which overclouds her trust in the gods, who knew her deed, and yet have permitted her to suffer this doom. Then she is led forth, and is seen no more.

Fourth stasimon: 944—987.

The rocky tomb to which she is passing suggests the theme of a choral ode, commemorating three other sufferers of a cruel imprisonment,—Danaë, Lycurgus, and Cleopatra.

VI. Fifth episode: 988— 1114.

As the choral strains cease, the blind and aged prophet Teiresias is led in by a boy. He comes with an urgent warning for the king. The gods are wroth with Thebes; they will no longer give their prophet any sign by the voice of birds, or through the omens of sacrifice. The king is himself the cause, by his edict. Carrion-creatures have defiled the altars of Thebes with the taint of the unburied dead. Let burial-rites be at once paid to Polyneices. He speaks for Creon's own good.

Here we pause for a moment to answer a question which naturally occurs to the modern reader. Why is Polyneices said to be still unburied? Has not Antigone already rendered burial-rites to him; is it not precisely for that action that she is dying? Antigone had, indeed, given symbolical sepulture to Polyneices by sprinkling dust upon the corpse, and pouring libations. The performance of that act discharged her personal duty towards the dead and the gods below; it also saved her dead brother from the dishonour (which would else have been a reproach to him in the other world) of having been neglected by his nearest kinsfolk on earth. But Antigone's acts did not clear Creon. Creon's duty to the dead and to the gods below was still unperformed. So far as Creon was concerned, Polyneices was still unburied. And Creon's obligation could not be discharged, as Antigone's had been, merely by the symbolical act, which religion accepted only when a person was unavoidably hindered from performing regular rites. There was nothing to hinder Creon from performing such rites. These were still claimed from him. After Antigone's tribute had been rendered, birds and dogs had been busy with the corpse. Creon' duty to the dead and to the gods below was now also a duty towards the polluted State, from which his impiety had alienated the gods above.

In reply to the friendly and earnest warning of Teiresias, Creon angrily accuses the seer of mercenary complicity in a disloyal plot; malcontent Thebans wish to gain a triumph over their king by frightening him into a surrender. Never will he grant burial-rites to Polyneices.

Teiresias, angered in his turn, then declares the penalty which the gods reserve for such obduracy. With the life of his own son shall Creon atone for his twofold sin,—the detention of the dead among the living, and the imprisonment of the living in the abode of the dead. The seer then departs.

Creon is deeply moved. In the course of long and eventful years he has learned a lesson which is present also to the minds of the Theban elders. The word of Teiresias has never failed to come true.

After a hurried consultation with the Chorus, Creon's resolve is taken. He will yield. He immediately starts, with his servants, for the upper part of the Theban plain, where the body of Polyneices is still lying,—not very far, it would seem, from the place of Antigone's prison.

At this point an objection might suggest itself to the spectator. Is there not something a little improbable in the celerity with which Creon,—hitherto inflexible,—is converted by the threats of a seer whom he has just been denouncing as a venal impostor? Granting that experience had attested the seer's infallibility when speaking in the name of the gods, has not Creon professed to believe that, in this instance, Teiresias is merely the mouthpiece of disloyal Thebans? The answer will be found by attentively observing the state of mind which, up to this point, has been portrayed in Creon. He has, indeed, been inflexible; he has even been vehement in asserting his inflexibility. But, under this vehemence, we have been permitted to see occasional glimpses of an uneasy conscience. One such glimpse is at vv. 889 f., where he protests that *his* hands are clean in regard to Antigone;—he had given her full warning, and he has not shed her blood,—'but at any rate' (δ' οὖν,—*i.e.*, wherever the guilt rests)—'she shall die.' Another such trait occurs at v. 1040, where he says that he will not bury Polyneices, though the throne of Zeus in heaven should be defiled,—quickly adding, 'for I know that no mortal can pollute the gods.'[1] It may further be remarked that a latent self-mistrust is suggested by the very violence of his rejoinder to the Chorus, when they venture, with timid respect, to hint the possibility that some divine agency may have been at work in the mysterious tribute paid to Polyneices (278 f.). A like remark applies to the fury which breaks out at moments in his interviews with Haemon and with Teiresias. The delicacy of the dramatic tact which forbids these touches to be obtrusive is such as Sophocles, alone of the Attic masters, knew how to use. But they suffice to indicate the secret trembling of the balance behind those protestations of an unconquerable resolve; the terrible prophecy of Teiresias only turns the scale.

Hypor-heme: taking the place of the fifth stasimon) 115— 154. The Chorus is now gladdened by the hope that Creon's re-pentance, late though it is, may avail to avert the doom threatened by Teiresias. This feeling is expressed in a short and joyous ode, which invokes the bright presence of Dionysus. May the joyous god come with healing virtue to his favourite Thebes! The substitution of this lively dance-song ('hyporcheme') for a choral ode of a graver cast here serves the same purpose of contrast as in the *Oedipus Tyrannus*, the *Ajax*, and the *Trachiniae*. The catastrophe is approaching[2].

7II. Exo-los: 1155 —1352. A Messenger now enters,—one of the servants who had accompanied Creon to the plain. The words in which he briefly intimates the nature of his tidings (v. 1173) are overheard, within the house, by Eurydicè, then in the act of going forth with offerings to Pallas; and she swoons. On recovering consciousness, she comes forth, and hears the full account from the Messenger. He says that, when they reached the plain, Creon's first care was for the funeral rites due to Polyneices. After prayer to Pluto and Hecatè, the remains—lacerated by birds and dogs—were washed, and solemnly burned; a high funeral-mound was then raised on the spot. Creon and his followers then repaired to the tomb of Antigone. They found her already dead; she

---

[1] See note on v. 1044.			[2] See note on v. 1115.

had used her veil to hang herself. Haemon, in a frenzied state, was embracing her corpse. He drew his sword upon his father, who fled. Then, in a swift agony of remorse, the son slew himself.

Having heard this news, Eurydicè silently retires into the house.

She has hardly withdrawn, when Creon enters, with attendants, carrying Haemon's shrouded corpse[1] upon a bier. He bewails his own folly as the cause of his son's death. Amid his laments, a Messenger from the house announces that Eurydicè has stabbed herself at the household altar, with imprecations on the husband. Wholly desolate and wretched, Creon prays for death; nor has the Chorus any gentler comfort for him than the stern precept of resignation,—'Pray thou no more; mortals have no escape from destined woe.' As he is conducted into the house, the closing words of the drama are spoken by the leader of the Chorus: 'Wisdom is the supreme part of happiness, and reverence towards the gods must be inviolate. Great words of prideful men are ever punished with great blows, and in old age teach the chastened to be wise.'

§ 4. This sketch may serve to illustrate the powerful unity of the play. The issue defined in the opening scene,—the conflict of divine with human law,—remains the central interest throughout. The action, so simple in plan, is varied by masterly character-drawing, both in the two principal figures, and in those lesser persons who contribute gradations of light and shade to the picture. There is no halting in the march of the drama; at each successive step we become more and more keenly interested to see how this great conflict is to end; and when the tragic climax is reached, it is worthy of such a progress. It would not, however, be warrantable to describe the construction of the play as faultless. No one who seeks fully to comprehend and enjoy this great work of art can be content to ignore certain questions which are suggested by one part of it,—the part from v. 998 to 1243, which introduces and developes the catastrophe.

Unity of motive.

The mode of the catastrophe.

[1] *i.e.*, an effigy. The deuteragonist, who had acted Haemon, had been on the stage, as Messenger, up to v. 1256, and had still to come on as Second Messenger at v. 1278.

Teiresias, as we saw, came with the benevolent purpose of warning Creon that he must bury Polyneices. Creon was stubborn, and Teiresias then said that the gods would punish him. Haemon would die, because his father had been guilty of two sins,—burying Antigone alive[1], and dishonouring the corpse of Polyneices. This prophecy assumed that Creon would remain obdurate. But, in the event, he immediately yielded; he buried Polyneices, and attempted, though too late, to release Antigone. Now suppose that he had been in time to save Antigone. He would then have cancelled both his offences. And then, we must infer, the divine punishment predicted by Teiresias would have been averted; since the prediction does not rest on any statement that a specific term of grace had expired. Otherwise we should have to suppose that the seer did not know the true mind of the gods when he represented that Creon might still be saved by repentance (1025 ff.). But the dramatic function of Teiresias obviously requires us to assume that he was infallible whenever he spoke from 'the signs of his art'; indeed, the play tells us that he was so (1094).

Everything depended, then, on Creon being in time to save Antigone. Only a very short interval can be imagined between the moment at which she is led away to her tomb and that at which Creon resolves to release her; in the play it is measured by 186 verses (928—1114). The Chorus puts Creon's duties in the natural order; 'free the maiden from her rocky chamber, and make a tomb for the unburied dead' (1100); and Creon seems to feel that the release, as the more urgent task, ought to have precedence. Nevertheless, when he and his men arrive on the ground, his first care is given to Polyneices. After the rites have been performed, a high mound is raised. Only then does he proceed to Antigone's prison,—and then it is too late. We are not given any reason for the burial being taken in hand before

---

[1] In his first, or friendly, speech to Creon (998—1032) Teiresias says not a word concerning Antigone. Possibly he may be conceived as thinking that the burial of Polyneices would imply, as a consequence, the release of Antigone; though it is obvious that, from Creon's point of view, such an inference would be illogical: Antigone was punished because she had broken the edict; not because the burying of Polyneices was intrinsically wrong.

the release. The dramatic fault here has nothing to do with
any estimate of the chances that Creon might actually have
saved Antigone's life, if he had gone to her first. The poet
might have chosen to imagine her as destroying herself immediately after she had been left alone in her cell. In any case,
the margin for Creon must have been a narrow one. The The dramatic blemish.
dramatic fault is that, while we, the spectators, are anxious that
Antigone should be saved, and while every moment is precious,
we are left to conjecture why Creon should be spending so many
of these moments in burial rites which could have been rendered
equally well after Antigone had been rescued: nay, when the
rites have been finished, he remains to build a mound. The
source of pathos contained in the words 'too late' is available
for Tragedy, but evidently there is one condition which must be
observed. A fatal delay must not seem to be the result merely
of negligence or of caprice. As Bellermann has justly said,
modern drama has obeyed this rule with a heedfulness not
always shown by the ancients. Shakespeare took care that
there should be a good reason for the delay of Lorenzo to
resuscitate Juliet; nor has Schiller, in the 'Death of Wallen-
stein,' left it obscure why Octavio arrived only after Buttler's
deed had been done. Euripides, on the other hand, is content
that the prolixity of a Messenger's speech should detain Iocasta
until the sons whom she longed to reconcile had killed each
other.

§ 5. With regard to Creon's delay in the *Antigone*, I ven- A suggest-ed explan-ation.
ture to suggest that the true explanation is a simple one. If
it seems inadequate when tried by the gauge of modern drama,
it will not do so (I think) to those who remember two characteristics of old Greek drama,—first, the great importance of
the rhetorical element, more particularly as represented by the
speeches of messengers; secondly, the occasional neglect of
clearness, and even of consistency, in regard to matters which
either precede the action of the drama (τὰ ἔξω τῆς τραγῳδίας),
or, though belonging to the drama itself, occur off the stage.
The speech of the first Messenger in the *Antigone* (1192—1243)
relates the catastrophe with which the tragedy culminates. Its
effect was therefore of the highest importance. Now, if this

speech had first related the terrible scene in Antigone's tomb, and had then passed on to the quiet obsequies of Polyneices, its rhetorical impressiveness would have been destroyed. It was indispensable that the latter part of the recital should correspond with the climax of tragic interest. This, I believe, was the motive present to the poet's mind when, after indicating in the dialogue that the release was to precede the burial, he reversed that order in composing the Messenger's speech. He knew that his Athenian audience would be keenly susceptible to the oratorical quality of that speech, while they would be either inattentive, or very indulgent, to the defect in point of dramatic consistency. The result is a real blemish, though not a serious one; indeed, it may be said to compensate the modern reader for its existence by exemplifying some tendencies of the art, which admitted it.

§ 6. The simplicity of the plot is due,—as the foregoing sketch has shown,—to the clearness with which two principles are opposed to each other. Creon represents the duty of obeying the State's laws; Antigone, the duty of listening to the private conscience. The definiteness and the power with which the play puts the case on each side is a conclusive proof that the question had assumed a distinct shape before the poet's mind. It is the only instance in which a Greek play has for its central theme a practical problem of conduct, involving issues, moral and political, which might be discussed on similar grounds in any age and in any country of the world. Greek Tragedy, owing partly to the limitations which it placed on detail, was better suited than modern drama to raise such a question in a general form. The *Antigone*, indeed, raises the question in a form as nearly abstract as is compatible with the nature of drama. The case of Antigone is a thoroughly typical one for the private conscience, because the particular thing which she believes that she ought to do was, in itself, a thing which every Greek of that age recognised as a most sacred duty,— viz., to render burial rites to kinsfolk. This advantage was not devised by Sophocles; it came to him as part of the story which he was to dramatise; but it forms an additional reason for thinking that, when he dramatised that story in the precise

manner which he has chosen, he had a consciously dialectical
purpose[1]. Such a purpose was wholly consistent, in this instance,
with the artist's first aim,—to produce a work of art. It is
because Creon and Antigone are so human that the controversy
which they represent becomes so vivid.

§ 7. But how did Sophocles intend us to view the result? What is
What is the drift of the words at the end, which say that the moral
'wisdom is the supreme part of happiness'? If this wisdom, intended?
or prudence (τὸ φρονεῖν), means, generally, the observance of
due limit, may not the suggested moral be that both the parties
to the conflict were censurable? As Creon overstepped the due
limit when, by his edict, he infringed the divine law, so Antigone
also overstepped it when she defied the edict. The drama
would thus be a conflict between two persons, each of whom
defends an intrinsically sound principle, but defends it in a
mistaken way; and both persons are therefore punished. This
view, of which Boeckh is the chief representative, has found
several supporters. Among them is Hegel:—' In the view of
the Eternal Justice, both were wrong, because they were one-
sided; but at the same time both were right[2].'

Or does the poet rather intend us to feel that Antigone is
wholly in the right,—*i.e.*, that nothing of which the human
law-giver could complain in her was of a moment's account
beside the supreme duty which she was fulfilling;—and that
Creon was wholly in the wrong,—*i.e.*, that the intrinsically sound
maxims of government on which he relies lose all validity when
opposed to the higher law which he was breaking? If that
was the poet's meaning, then the 'wisdom' taught by the issue

---

[1] This point might be illustrated by contrast with an able romance lately published,
of which the title is borrowed from this play of Sophocles. 'The New Antigone'
declined the sanction of marriage, because she had been educated by a father who
had taught her to regard that institution as wrongful. Such a case was not well
suited to do dramatically what the *Antigone* of Sophocles does,—to raise the question
of human law against private conscience in a general form, —because the institution
concerned claims to be more than a human ordinance, and because, on the other hand,
the New Antigone's opinion was essentially an accident of perverted conscience.
The author of the work was fully alive to this, and has said (*Spectator*, Nov. 5,
1887) that his choice of a title conveyed 'a certain degree of irony.'

[2] *Religionsphilosophie*, ii. 114.

of the drama means the sense which duly subordinates human to divine law,—teaching that, if the two come into conflict, human law must yield.

This question is one which cannot be put aside by merely suggesting that Sophocles had no didactic purpose at all, but left us to take whichever view we pleased. For, obviously, according as we adopt one or other of the views, our estimate of the play as a work of art must be vitally affected. The punishments meted out to Creon and Antigone respectively require us to consider the grounds on which they rest. A difference will be made, too, in our conception of Antigone's character, and therefore in our judgment as to the measure of skill with which the poet has portrayed her.

A careful study of the play itself will suffice (I think) to show that the second of the two views above mentioned is the true one. Sophocles has allowed Creon to put his case ably, and (in a measure from which an inferior artist might have shrunk) he has been content to make Antigone merely a nobly heroic woman, not a being exempt from human passion and human weakness; but none the less does he mean us to feel that, in this controversy, the right is wholly with her, and the wrong wholly with her judge.

The character of Creon's edict.

§ 8. In the first place it is necessary to appreciate the nature of Creon's edict against burying Polyneices. Some modern estimates of the play have seemed to assume that such refusal of sepulture, though a harsh measure, was yet one which the Greek usage of the poet's age recognised as fairly applicable to public enemies, and that, therefore, Creon's fault lay merely in the degree of his severity. It is true that the legends of the heroic age afford some instances in which a dead enemy is left unburied, as a special mark of abhorrence. This dishonour brands the exceptionally base crime of Aegisthus[1]. Yet these same legends also show that, from a very early period, Hellenic feeling was shocked at the thought of carrying enmity beyond the grave, and withholding those rites on which the welfare of the departed spirit was believed to depend. The antiquity of

[1] Soph. *El.* 1487 ff.

the maxim that, after a battle, the conquerors were bound to allow the vanquished to bury their dead, is proved by the fact that it was ascribed either to Theseus[1] or to Heracles[2]. Achilles maltreated the dead Hector. Yet, even there, the *Iliad* expresses the Greek feeling by the beautiful and touching fable that the gods themselves miraculously preserved the corpse from all defacement and from all corruption, until at last the due obsequies were rendered to it in Troy[3]. The Atreidae refused burial to Ajax; but Odysseus successfully pleaded against the sentence, and Ajax was ultimately buried with all honour[4]. In giving that issue to his play, Sophocles was doing what the general feeling of his own age would strongly demand. Greeks of the fifth century B.C. observed the duty towards the dead even when warfare was bitterest, and when the foe was barbarian. The Athenians buried the Persians slain at Marathon, as the Persians buried the Lacedaemonians slain at Thermopylae. A notable exception may, indeed, be cited; but it is one of those exceptions which forcibly illustrate the rule. The Spartan Lysander omitted to bury the Athenians who fell at Aegospotami; and that omission was remembered, centuries later, as an indelible stigma upon his name[5].

Thus the audience for which Sophocles composed the *Antigone* would regard Creon's edict as something very different from a measure of exceptional, but still legitimate, severity. They would regard it as a shocking breach of that common piety which even the most exasperated belligerents regularly respected.

§ 9. The next point to be considered is, In what sense, and how far, does Creon, in this edict, represent the State? He is the lawful king of Thebes. His royal power is conceived as having no definite limit. The words of the Chorus testify that he is acting within the letter of his right; 'thou hast power, I ween, to take what order thou wilt, both for the dead, and for all us who live' (211 f.). On the other hand, he is acting

The edict in its political aspect.

---

[1] Plut. *Thes.* 29.

[2] *Il.* 24. 411 ff.

[3] Aelian *Var. Hist.* XII. 27.

[4] Soph. *Ai.* 1332 ff.

[5] Paus. 9. 32. 6.

against the unanimous, though silent, sense of Thebes, which, as
his son Haemon tells him, held that Antigone had done a
glorious deed (695). Creon replies: 'Shall Thebes prescribe to
me how I shall rule?' His son rejoins : 'That is no city (πόλις),
which belongs to one man' (737). Where the unanimous
opinion of the community was ignored, the Athenians of the
poet's day would feel that, as Haemon says, there was no
'city' at all. Indeed, when Creon summoned 'the conference
of elders,' that summons was itself an admission that he was
morally bound to take account of other judgments besides his
own. We may often notice in the Attic drama that the
constitutional monarchy of the legendary heroic age is made
to act in the spirit, and speak in the tone, of the unconstitutional *tyrannis*, as the historical age knew it. This was most
natural; it gave an opening for points sure to tell with a
'tyrant-hating' Athenian audience, and it was perfectly safe
from objection on the ground of anachronism,—an objection
which was about the last that Athenian spectators were likely
to raise, if we may judge by the practice of the dramatists.
Now, the Creon of the *Antigone*, though nominally a monarch
of the heroic age, has been created by the Attic poet in the
essential image of the historical *tyrannus*. The Attic audience
would mentally compare him, not to an Agamemnon or an
Alcinous, but to a Hippias or a Periander. He resembles the
ruler whose absolutism, imposed on the citizens by force,
is devoid of any properly political sanction. Antigone can
certainly be described, with technical correctness, as acting
'in despite of the State,' since Creon is the State, so far
as a State exists. But the Greeks for whom Sophocles wrote
would not regard Creon's edict as having a constitutional
character, in the sense in which that character belonged to
laws sanctioned (for instance) by the Athenian Ecclesia. They
would liken it rather to some of the arbitrary and violent acts
done by Hippias in the later period of his 'tyranny.' To take a
modern illustration, they would view it in a quite different light
from that in which we should regard the disobedience of a
Russian subject to a ukase of the Czar.

If, then, we endeavour to interpret Creon's action by the

standards which the poet's contemporaries would apply, we find, first, that he is doing a monstrous act; secondly, that, in doing it, he cannot, indeed, be said to exceed his prerogative, since this is indefinite; but he is exceeding his moral right in such a manner that he becomes the counterpart of the *tyrannus* who makes a cruel use of an unconstitutional power.

§ 10. Antigone, on the other hand, is fulfilling one of the most sacred and the most imperative duties known to Greek religion; and it is a duty which could not be delegated. She and her sister are the nearest kinsfolk of the dead. It is not to be expected that any stranger should brave the edict for the dead man's sake. As the Chorus says, 'no man is so foolish that he is enamoured of death' (220). Creon is furious when the Chorus suggests that the rites so mysteriously paid to the corpse may have been due to the agency of the gods (278 f.) That very suggestion of the Chorus shows how impossible it seemed to the Theban mind that Polyneices could receive the ministration of any human hand. A modern critic, taking the view that Antigone was wrong, has observed (not ironically) that she ought to have left the gods to provide the burial. It would have been ill for the world if all who have done heroic deeds had preferred to await miracles. As to another suggestion,—that Antigone ought to have tried persuasion with Creon,—the poet has supplied the answer in his portraiture of Creon's character,—a character known to Antigone from long experience. The situation in which Antigone was placed by Creon's edict was analogous to that of a Christian martyr under the Roman Empire. It was as impossible for Antigone to withhold those rites, which no other human being could now render, as it was impossible for the Christian maiden to avoid the torments of the arena by laying a grain of incense on the altar of Diana[1]. From both alike those laws which each believed to be 'the unfailing statutes of Heaven' claimed an allegiance which no human law could cancel, and it was 'by the human

Antigone's position. 1.

---

[1] Mr Long's beautiful picture, 'Diana or Christ,' will be remembered by many,—and the more fitly, since it presents a counterpart, not only for Antigone, but also for Creon and for Haemon.

ruler, not by his victim, that the conflict of loyalties had been made inevitable.

§ 11. One of the main arguments used to show that Sophocles conceived Antigone as partly censurable has been drawn from the utterances of the Chorus. It is therefore important to determine, if we can, what the attitude of these Theban Elders really is. Their first ode (the Parodos) shows how strongly they condemn Polyneices, as having led a hostile army against his country. We might have expected, then, that, when Creon acquainted them with his edict, they would have greeted it with some mark of approval. On the contrary, their words are confined to a brief utterance of submission: 'Such is thy pleasure, Creon, son of Menoeceus, touching this city's foe, and its friend; and thou hast power, I ween, to take what order thou wilt, both for the dead, and for all us who live' (211 ff.). We can see that they are startled by such a doom, even for a man whom they hold deeply guilty. Their words suggest a misgiving. Just afterwards, they significantly excuse themselves from taking any part in the enforcement of the edict (216). But it is otherwise when the edict, having been published, is broken. Then they range themselves on Creon's side. They refer to the disobedience as a daring offence (371). When Antigone is brought in, they speak of her folly (383). Nevertheless, Antigone is convinced that, in their hearts, they sympathise with her (504). And, indeed, it is plain that they do so, to this extent,—that they consider the edict to have been a mistake; though they also hold that it was wrong to break the edict. Hence they speak of Antigone's act as one prompted by 'frenzy at the heart' (603). The clearest summary of their whole view—up to this point of the drama—is given in verses 872—875, and amounts to this:—Antigone's act was, in itself, a pious one; but Creon, as a ruler, was bound to vindicate his edict. Her 'self-willed temper' has brought her to death.

So far, then, the view taken by the Chorus is very much Boeckh's:—the merits are divided; Creon is both right and wrong; so, too, is Antigone. But then Teiresias comes (v. 988), and convinces the Chorus that Creon has been wholly wrong; wrong in refusing burial to Polyneices; wrong in punishing

Antigone. It is at the urgent advice of the Chorus that Creon
yields. And when, a little later, Creon blames himself as the
cause of all the woe, the Chorus replies that now at last he sees
the truth (v. 1270). Thus the Theban Elders entertain two
different opinions in succession. Their first opinion is overthrown by Teiresias. Their second opinion—which they hold
from verse 1091 onwards—is that which the poet intends to be
recognised as the true one.

§ 12. After thus tracing the mind of the Chorus, we can see ^{Why the}
more clearly why it is composed of Theban elders. When the ^{Chorus is}
^{so consti-}
chief person of a Greek tragedy is a woman, the Chorus usually ^{tuted.}
consists of women, whose attitude towards the heroine is more
or less sympathetic. Such is the case in the *Electra* and the
Trachiniae, and in seven plays of Euripides,—the *Andromache*,
Electra, *Hecuba*, *Helena*, both *Iphigeneias*, and *Medea*. The Chorus
of the *Alcestis*, indeed, consists of Pheraean elders : but then
Alcestis is withdrawn from the scene at an early moment, and
restored to it only at the end : during the rest of the play, the
interest is centred in Admetus. In the *Antigone*, Sophocles had
a double reason for constituting the Chorus as he did. First, the
isolation of the heroine would have been less striking if she had
been supported by a group of sympathetic women. Secondly,
the natural predisposition of the Theban nobles to support their
king heightens the dramatic effect of their ultimate conversion.

§ 13. The character of Antigone is a separate question from ^{Character}
the merit of the cause in which she is engaged. She might be ^{of An-}
^{tigone.}
doing right, and yet the poet might have represented her as
doing it in such a manner as to render her heroism unattractive.
We may now turn to this question, and consider what manner
of woman she is.

Two qualities are at the basis of her character. One is an
enthusiasm, at once steadfast and passionate, for the right, as
she sees it,—for the performance of her duty. The other is
intense tenderness, purity, and depth of domestic affection ;
manifested here in the love of sister for brother, a love which
death has not weakened, but only consecrated ; as in the *Oedipus
Coloneus*—where the portraiture of her is entirely in unison with
that given here—it is manifested in the tender anxiety to recon-

cile her living brothers, and in the fearless, completely selfless devotion—through painful wanderings, through all misery and all reproach—to the old age of her blind and homeless father. In the opening scene of the play, we find her possessed by a burning indignation at the outrage done to her dead brother; the deep love which she feels for him is braced by a clear sense of the religious duty which this edict lays upon her, and by an unfaltering resolve to do it; it never occurs to her for an instant that, as a true sister, she could act otherwise; rather it seems wonderful to her that the author of the edict should even have expected it to prove deterrent—for *her* (ver. 32).

With her whole heart and soul dominated by these feelings, she turns to her sister Ismene, and asks for her aid; not as if the response could be doubtful—she cannot imagine its being doubtful; it does not enter her mind that one whom she has just addressed by so dear a name, and with whom her tie of sister-hood is made closer still by the destiny which has placed them apart, can be anything but joyful and proud to risk life in the discharge of a duty so plain, so tender, and so sacred. And how does Ismene meet her? Ismene reminds her that other members of their house have perished miserably, and that, if Antigone acts thus, Antigone and she will die more miserably still: they are women, and must not strive with men; they are subjects, and must not strive with rulers: Ismene will ask the dead to excuse her, since she is constrained, and will obey the living: 'for it is witless to *be over-busy*' (περισσὰ πράσσειν, v. 68). Ismene is amiable enough; she cannot be called exceptionally weak or timid; she is merely the average woman; her answer here is such as would have been made by most women—and perhaps by a still larger proportion of men, as the Chorus afterwards forcibly reminds us. But, given the character and the present mood of Antigone, what must be the effect of such a reply to such an appeal? It is the tenderness, quite as much as the strength, of Antigone's spirit that speaks in her answer:—' I will not urge thee,—no, nor, if thou yet should'st have the mind, would'st thou be welcome as a worker with me.' And the calmest reason thoroughly approves that answer; for the very terms in which Ismene had repulsed her sister proved a nature which could never rise to the height of such a task, and which would be more dangerous as an ally than as a neutral.

When the sisters next meet, it is in Creon's presence, and the situation is this:—Antigone has done the deed, unaided; and Creon has said that both sisters shall die—for he suspects Ismene of complicity. Ismene's real affection is now quickened by a feverish remorse, and by an impulse towards self-immolation,— an impulse·of a sentimental and almost hysterical kind: she will say that she helped Antigone; she will die with her; she will yet make amends to the dead. Was Antigone to indulge Ismene's impulse, and to allow Ismene's words to confirm Creon's suspicions? Surely Antigone was bound to do what she does,—namely, to speak out the truth: 'Nay, Justice will not suffer thee to do that; thou didst *not* consent to the deed, neither did I·give thee part in it.' But it will be said that her tone towards Ismene is too stern and hard. The sternness is only that of truth; the hardness is only that of reality: for, among the tragic circumstances which surround Antigone, this is precisely one of the most tragic, that Ismene's earlier conduct, at the testing-point of action, *has* made a spiritual division which no emotional after-impulse can cancel. One more point may be raised: when Ismene says, 'What life is dear to me, bereft of thee?'—Antigone replies, 'Ask Creon—all thy care is for him' (v. 549): is not this, it may be asked, a needless taunt? The answer is found in Antigone's wish to save Ismene's life. Thus far in the dialogue, Ismene has persisted—even after Antigone's denial—in claiming a share in the deed (vv. 536—547). Creon might well think that, after all, the fact was as he suspected. It was necessary for Antigone to make him see—by some trenchant utterance—that she regarded Ismene as distinctly ranged on his side. And she succeeded. Later in the play, where Creon acknowledges Ismene's innocence, he describes it in the very phrase which Antigone had impressed upon his memory; he speaks of Ismene as one '*who has not touched*' the deed (v. 771: cp. v. 546). It is with pain (v. 551), it is not with scorn or with bitterness, that Antigone remains firm. Her attitude is prescribed equally by regard for truth and right, and by duty towards her sister.

J. S. III.² *d*

Her rela-
ion to
Haemon. Antigone is betrothed to Haemon; the closeness of the
affection between them is significantly marked by the words of
Ismene (v. 570); it is expressed in the words, the deeds, and the
death, of Haemon. If verse 572 is rightly assigned to Antigone
(as, in my opinion, it is), that brief utterance tells much : but let
us suppose that it belongs to Ismene, and that Antigone never
once refers directly to Haemon: we say, 'directly,' because more
than once she alludes to sweet hopes which life had still to offer
her. It is evident that, if Sophocles had given greater prominence to Antigone's love for Haemon, he could have had
only one aim, consistently with the plan of this play,—viz., to
strengthen our sense of the ties which bound her to life,
and, therefore, of her heroism in resigning it. But it is also
evident that he could have done this, with any effect, only at
the cost of depicting a mind divided between the desire of
earthly happiness and the resolve to perform a sacred duty.
Sophocles has preferred to portray Antigone as raised above
every selfish thought, even the dearest, by the absorbing and
inspiring sense of her duty to the dead, and to the gods; silent,
not through apathy, concerning a love which could never be hers,
and turning for comfort to the faith that, beyond the grave, the
purest form of human affection would reunite her to those whom
she had lost. It is no blame to later dramatists that they found
it necessary to make more of the love-motive ; but, if our
standard is to be the noblest tragic art, it is a confession of their
inferiority to Sophocles. There is a beautiful verse in the play
which might suggest how little he can have feared that his
heroine would ever be charged with a cold insensibility. Creon
has urged that the honour which she has shown to Polyneices
will be resented by the spirit of Eteocles. Antigone answers,
' It is not my nature to join in hating, but in loving.' As she
had sought to reconcile them while they lived, so now she will
have no part in their feud—if feud there be where they have
gone,—but will love each, as he loves her.

The re-
action in
Antigone's
mind. So long as her task lies before Antigone, she is sustained
by the necessity for action. Nor does she falter for a moment,
even after the deed has been done, so long as she is in the
presence of Creon. For, though she has no longer the stimulus

of action, there is still another challenge to her fortitude; she, who is loyal to the divine law, cannot tremble before the man who is its embodied negation. It is otherwise when Creon is gone, and when there are only the Theban elders to see and hear her, as she is led to death. The strain on her mind is relaxed; the end is near; she now feels the longing for some word of pity as she passes to the grave,—for some token of human kindness. But, while she craves such sympathy, the Theban nobles merely console her with the thought of post-humous fame. She compares her doom to Niobe's; and they reply that it is a glory for her to be as Niobe, a daughter of the Tantalidae,—

> the seed of gods,
> Men near to Zeus; for whom on Ida burns,
> High in clear air, the altar of their Sire,
> Nor hath their race yet lost the blood divine[1].

Few things in tragedy are more pathetic than this yearning of hers, on the brink of death, for some human kindness of farewell, thus 'mocked'[2], as she feels it to be, by a cold assurance of renown. She turns from men to invoke 'the fount of Dircè and the holy ground of Thebes'; these, at least, will be her witnesses. In her last words, she is thinking of the dead, and of the gods; she feels sure of love in the world of the dead; but she cannot lift her face to the gods, and feel sure that they are with her. If they are so, why have they allowed her to perish for obeying them? Yet, again, they *may* be with her; she will know beyond the grave. If she has sinned, she will learn it there; but if she is innocent, the gods will vindicate when she is gone. How infinitely touching is this supreme trouble which clouds her soul at the last,—this doubt and per-plexity concerning the gods! For it is not a misgiving as to the paramount obligation of the 'unwritten laws' which she has obeyed: it is only an anguish of wonder and uncertainty as to the mysterious ways of the powers which have laid this

---

[1] From the *Niobe* of Aeschylus (fr. 157): οἱ θεῶν ἀγχίσποροι, | οἱ Ζηνὸς ἐγγύς· οἷς κατ' Ἰδαῖον πάγον | Διὸς πατρῴου βωμός ἐστ' ἐν αἰθέρι, | κοὔπω νιν ἐξίτηλον αἷμα δαιμόνων.

[2] v. 839.

obligation on mortals,—a surmise that, as gods and men seem alike without pity for her, there has perhaps been something wrong in her way of doing the duty which was so clear and so binding.

§ 14. The psychology of Sophocles is so excellent in the case of Antigone because he has felt that in a truly heroic nature there is the permanent strength of deep convictions, but there is also room for what superficial observers might think a moral anticlimax. So long as such a nature has to meet antagonism in word or deed, its permanent strength is heightened by a further support which is necessarily transient, —the strength of exaltation. But a mind capable of heroism is such as can see duties in their true proportions, and can sacrifice everything to the discharge of the highest : and it is such a mind, too, which, in looking back on a duty done, is most liable—through very largeness of vision, and sense of human limitations—to misgivings like those which vex the last moments of Antigone. The strength of exaltation has passed away; her clear intelligence cannot refuse to acknowledge that the actual results of doing right are in seeming conflict with the faith which was the sanction of the deed. It is worthy of notice that only at one moment of the drama does Antigone speak lightly of the penalty which she has deliberately incurred. That is at the moment when, face to face with Creon, she is asserting the superiority of the divine law. Nor does she, even then, speak lightly of death in itself; she only says that it is better than a life like hers; for at that moment she feels the whole burden of the sorrows which have fallen upon her race,—standing, as she does, before the man who has added the last woe. The tension of her mind is at the highest. But nowhere else does she speak as one who had sought death because weary of life; on the contrary, we can see that that life was dear to her, who must die young, 'without a portion in the chant that brings the bride.' It is a perfectly sane mind which has chosen death, and has chosen it only because the alternative was to neglect a sacred duty.

A comparison with other dramatists may serve to illustrate what Sophocles has gained by thus allowing the temporary strength of excitement to pass off before the end, leaving the permanent strength of the character to wrestle with this pain and doubt. In Alfieri's play of the same name, Antigone. shows no touch of human weakness; as death approaches, she seems more and more impatiently eager for it; she says to Creon's guards, who are leading her to her doom,—

> Let us make better speed; so slow a step
> Ill becomes her who has at length just reach'd
> The goal so long desired... Perhaps ye, O guards,
> May feel compassion for my fate?... Proceed.
> Oh terrible Death, I look thee in the face,
> And yet I tremble not[1].

In Massinger's *Virgin Martyr*, again, consider the strain in which Dorothea addresses Theophilus, the persecutor of the Christians, who has doomed her to torture and death :—

> Thou fool !
> That gloriest in having power to ravish
> A trifle from me I am weary of,
> What is this life to me? Not worth a thought;
> Or, if it be esteem'd, 'tis that I lose it
> To win a better : even thy malice serves
> To me but as a ladder to mount up
> To such a height of happiness, where I shall
> Look down with scorn on thee and on the world.

The dramatic effect of such a tone, both in Alfieri's Antigone and in Massinger's Dorothea, is to make their fate not more, but less, pathetic; we should feel for them more if they, on their part, seemed to feel a little 'what 'tis to die, and to die young,'— as Theophilus says to Dorothea. On the other hand, M. Casimir Delavigne, in his *Messéniennes*, is Sophoclean where he describes the last moments of Joan of Arc :—

> Du Christ, avec l'ardeur, Jeanne baisait l'image ;
> Ses longs cheveux épars flottaient au gré des vents :
> Au pied de l'échafaud, sans changer de visage,
>   Elle s'avançait à pas lents.

---

[1] C. Taylor's translation.

> Tranquille elle y monta ; quand, debout sur le faîte,
> Elle vit ce bûcher, qui l'allait dévorer,
> Les bourreaux en suspens, la flamme déja prête,
> *Sentant son cœur faillir, elle baissa la tête,*
> *Et se prit à pleurer*[1].

So it is that the Antigone of Sophocles, in the last scene
of her life, feels her heart fail, bows her head, and weeps; but
the first verse of the passage just quoted suggests a difference
which makes the Greek maiden the more tragic figure of the
two: when Antigone looked to heaven, she could find no certain
comfort.

Thus has Sophocles created a true heroine; no fanatic
enamoured of martyrdom, no virago, but a true woman, most
tender-hearted, most courageous and steadfast; whose sense of
duty sustains her in doing a deed for which she knows that she
must die ;—when it has been done, and death is at hand, then,
indeed, there is a brief cry of anguish from that brave and loving
spirit; it is bitter to die thus: but human sympathy is denied to
her, and even the gods seem to have hidden their faces. Nowhere
else has the poetry of the ancient world embodied so lofty or so
beautiful an ideal of woman's love and devotion. The Macaria
of Euripides resigns her life to save the race of the Heracleidae;
his Iphigeneia, to prosper the course of the Greek fleet; his
Alcestis, to save the life of her husband. In each of these cases,
a divine voice had declared that some one must die; in each,
the heroism required was purely passive; and in each a definite
gain was promised,—for it was at least a pious opinion in the
wife of Admetus (when all his other friends had declined his
request that some of them would oblige him by dying for him [2])
to think that his survival would be a gain. Not one of these
Euripidean heroines, pathetic though they be, can for a moment
be ranked with Fedalma in George Eliot's *Spanish Gypsy,* when

---

[1] Quoted by M. Patin in his *Études sur les Tragiques grecs*, vol. II., p. 271.

[2] Has the total absence of the sense of humour, in its disastrous effect upon tragic
pathos, ever been more wonderfully illustrated than by Euripides in those lines of the
Alcestis?—πάντας δ' ἐλέγξας καὶ διεξελθὼν φίλους, | πατέρα, γεραιάν θ' ἥ σφ' ἔτικτε
μητέρα, | οὐχ ηὗρε πλὴν γυναικὸς ὅστις ἤθελε | θανεῖν πρὸ κείνου μηδ' ἔτ' εἰσορᾶν φάος.
(vv. 15 ff.)

she accepts what seems worse than death for the sake of benefits to her race which are altogether doubtful;—

> 'my soul is faint—
> Will these sharp pains buy any certain good?'

But Antigone is greater than Fedalma. There was no father, no Zarca, at Antigone's side, urgently claiming the sacrifice,— on the contrary, there was a sister protesting against it; Antigone's choice was wholly free; the heroism which it imposed was one of doing as well as suffering; and the sole reward was to be in the action itself.

§ 15. The character of Creon, as Sophocles draws it in this Creon. play, may be regarded in somewhat different lights. It is interesting, then, to inquire how the poet meant it to be read. According to one view, Creon is animated by a personal spite against both Polyneices and Antigone; his maxims of state-policy are mere pretexts. This theory seems mistaken. There is, indeed, one phrase which might suggest previous dissensions between Creon and Antigone (v. 562). It is also true that Creon is supposed to have sided with Eteocles when Polyneices was driven into exile. But Sophocles was too good a dramatist to lay stress on such motives in such a situation. Rather, surely, Creon is to be conceived as entirely sincere and profoundly earnest when he sets forth the public grounds of his action. They are briefly these. Anarchy is the worst evil that can befall a State: the first duty of a ruler is therefore to enforce law and maintain order. The safety of the individual depends on that of the State, and therefore every citizen has a direct interest in obedience. This obedience must be absolute and unquestioning. The ruler must be obeyed 'in little things and great, in just things *and unjust*' (v. 667). That is, the subject must never presume to decide for himself what commands may be neglected or resisted. By rewarding the loyal and punishing the disloyal, a ruler will promote such obedience.

Creon puts his case with lucidity and force. We are reminded Comparison with Plato's of that dialogue in which Plato represents Socrates, on the eve Crito. of execution, as visited in prison by his aged friend Crito, who comes to tell him that the means of escape have been provided,

and to urge that he should use them. Socrates imagines the
Laws of Athens remonstrating with him: 'Do you imagine that
a State can subsist, in which the decisions of law are set aside
by individuals?' And to the plea that 'unjust' decisions may
be disobeyed, the Laws rejoin,—'Was *that* our agreement with
you? Or were you to abide by the sentence of the State?'
When Antigone appeals to the laws of Hades (v. 451), might
not Creon's laws, then, say to her what the laws of Athens say
with regard to the hypothetical flight of Socrates:—'We shall
be angry with you while you live, and our brethren, the Laws in
the world below, will receive you as an enemy; for they will
know that you have done your best to destroy us'?

Plato, it has been truly said, never intended to answer the
question of casuistry, as to when, if ever, it is right to break the
city's law. But at least there is one broad difference between the
cases supposed in the *Crito* and the *Antigone*. Antigone had
a positive religious duty, about which there was no doubt at all,
and with which Creon's law conflicted. For Socrates to break
prison might be justifiable, but could not be described as a
positive religious duty; since, however much good he might feel
confident of effecting by preserving his life, he was at least
morally entitled to think that such good would be less than the
evil of the example. Creon is doing what, in the case of
Socrates, Athens did not do,—he is invading the acknowledged
province of religion. Not that he forgets the existence of the
gods: he reveres them in what he believes to be the orthodox
way[1]. But he assumes that under no imaginable circumstances
can the gods disapprove of penalties inflicted on a disloyal
citizen. Meanwhile his characteristic tendency 'to do everything too much' has led him into a step which renders this
assumption disastrous. He punishes Polyneices in a manner
which violates religion.

Creon's
attitude
towards
Antigone. In Antigone, again, he sees anarchy personified, since, having
disobeyed, she seems to glory therein (v. 482). Her defence is
unmeaning to him, for her thoughts move in a different region
from his own. Sophocles has brought this out with admirable

---

[1] See especially the note on 1044.

skill in a short dialogue between Creon and Antigone (508—525): we see that he cannot get beyond his principle of State rewards and punishments; she is speaking foolishness to him—as, indeed, from the first she had felt the hopelessness of their understanding each other (469 f., 499 f.). As this dialogue serves to show Creon's unconsciousness of the frontier between divine and human law, so his scene with Haemon brings out his incapacity to appreciate the other great motive of Antigone's conduct,—sisterly piety. Creon regards the Family almost exclusively in one aspect; for him it is an institution related to the State as the gymnasium to the stadium; it is a little State, in which a man may prove that he is fit to govern a larger one.

Creon's temper is hasty and vehement. He vows that Haemon 'shall not save those two girls from their doom'; but, when the Chorus pleads for Ismene, he quickly adds that he will spare *her*,—' thou sayest well ' (770 f.). We also notice his love of hyperbole (1039 ff.). But he is not malevolent. He represents the rigour of human law,—neither restricted by the sense of a higher law, nor intensified by a personal desire to hurt. He has the ill-regulated enthusiasm of a somewhat narrow understanding for the only principle which it has firmly grasped.

§ 16. Such, then, are the general characteristics which mark the treatment of this subject by Sophocles. In a drama of rare poetical beauty, and of especially fine psychology, he has raised the question as to the limit of the State's authority over the individual conscience. It belongs to the essence of the tragic pathos that this question is one which can never be answered by a set formula. Enough for Antigone that she finds herself in a situation where conscience leaves her no choice but to break one of two laws, and to die.

These distinctive qualities of the play may be illustrated by a glance at the work of some other poets. The *Antigone* of Euripides is now represented only by a few small fragments, Euripides. and its plot is uncertain. It would seem, however, that, when Antigone was caught in the act of burial, Haemon was assisting her, and that the play ended, not with her death, but with her

marriage[1]. Some of the fragments confirm the belief that the
Attius. love-motive was prominent[2]. The Roman poet Attius (*c.* 140 B.C.)
also wrote an *Antigone*. The few remaining verses—some of
which have lived only because Vergil imitated them—indicate

[1] All that we know as to the plot is contained in the first Argument to this
play (see p. 3 below, and notes on p. 4): 'The story has been used also by Euripides
in his *Antigone*; only there she is detected with Haemon, and is given in marriage,
and bears a son Maion.' In the scholia at the end of L we also read, 'this play
differs from the *Antigone* of Euripides in the fact that, there, she was detected
through the love of Haemon, and was given in marriage; while here the issue is the
contrary' (*i.e.* her death). That this is the right rendering of the scholiast's words—
φωραθεῖσα ἐκείνη διὰ τὸν Αἵμονος ἔρωτα ἐξεδόθη πρὸς γάμον—seems probable from
a comparison with the statement in the Argument; though others have understood,
'she was detected, and, owing to the love of Haemon, given in marriage.' She was
detected, not, as in the play of Sophocles, directly by Creon's guards, but (in some
way not specified) through the fact that Haemon's love for her had drawn him to
her side.

Welcker (*Griech. Trag.* II. pp. 563 ff.) has sought to identify the *Antigone* of
Euripides with the plot sketched by Hyginus in *Fab.* 72. Antigone having been
detected, Haemon had been commissioned by Creon to slay her, but had saved her,
conveying her to a shepherd's home. When Maion, the son of their secret marriage,
had grown to man's estate, he visited Thebes at a festival. This was the moment
(Welcker thinks) at which the *Antigone* of Euripides began. Creon noted in Maion
a certain mark which all the offspring of the dragon's seed (σπαρτοί) bore on their
bodies. Haemon's disobedience was thus revealed; Heracles vainly interceded with
Creon; Haemon slew his wife Antigone and then himself.

But surely both the author of the Argument and the scholiast clearly imply that
the marriage of Antigone was contained in the play of Euripides, and formed its conclusion. I therefore agree with Heydemann (*Ueber eine nacheuripideische Antigone*,
Berlin, 1868) that Hyginus was epitomising some otherwise unknown play.

M. Patin (*Études sur les Tragiques grecs*, vol. II. p. 277) remarks that there is
nothing to show whether the play of Euripides was produced before or after that
of Sophocles. But he has overlooked a curious and decisive piece of evidence.
Among the scanty fragments of the Euripidean *Antigone* are these lines (Eur. fr.
165, Nauck);—ἄκουσον· οὐ γὰρ οἱ κακῶς πεπραγότες | σὺν ταῖς τύχαισι τοὺς λόγους
ἀπώλεσαν. This evidently glances at the *Antigone* of Sophocles, vv. 563 f., where
Ismene says, οὐδ' ὃς ἂν βλάστῃ μένει | νοῦς τοῖς κακῶς πράσσουσιν, ἀλλ' ἐξίσταται.
(For similar instances of covert criticism, see n. on *O. C.* 1116.)

[2] Eur. fr. 160, 161, 162 (Nauck). The most significant is fr. 161, probably spoken
by Haemon:—ἤρων· τὸ μαίνεσθαι δ' ἄρ' ἦν ἔρως βροτοῖς.—Another very suggestive
fragment is no. 176, where the speaker is evidently remonstrating with Creon:—
'Who shall pain a rock by thrusting at it with a spear? And who can pain the dead
by dishonour, if we grant that they have no sense of suffering?' This is characteristic
of the difference between the poets. Sophocles never urges the *futility* of Creon's
vengeance, though he does touch upon its ignobleness (v. 1030).

eloquence and spirit, but give no clue to the plot[1]. Statius, in Statius. his epic *Thebaid*, departs widely from the Attic version of the story. Argeia, the widow of Polyneices, meets Antigone by night at the corpse. Each, unknown to the other, has come to do the same task ; both are put to death by Creon,—'ambae hilares et mortis amore superbae[2].' This rapturous welcoming of death is, as we have seen, quite in the manner of Massinger and Alfieri, but not at all in that of Sophocles.

Alfieri's *Antigone* (published in 1783) follows Statius in asso- Alfieri. ciating Argeia with Antigone; besides whom there are only two other actors, Creon and Haemon. The Italian poet has not improved upon the Greek. There are here two heroines, with very similar parts, in performing which they naturally utter very similar sentiments. Then Alfieri's Creon is not merely a perverse despot of narrow vision, but a monster of wickedness, who, by a thought worthy of Count Cenci, has published the edict for the express purpose of enticing Antigone into a breach of it. Having doomed her to die, he then offers to pardon her, if she will marry his son (and so unite the royal line with his own); but Antigone, though she esteems Haemon, declines to marry the son of such a parent. So she is put to death, while Argeia is sent back to Argos ; and Haemon kills himself. It is not altogether unprofitable to be reminded, by such examples, what the theme of Sophocles could become in other hands.

§ 17. A word may be added regarding treatments of the Vase-subjects in works of art, which are not without some points of paintings. literary interest. Baumeister reproduces two vase-paintings, both curious[3]. The first[4] represents a group of three figures,—the

[1] Only six fragments remain, forming, in all, ten (partly incomplete) lines: Ribbeck, *Trag. Rom. Frag.* p. 153 (1871). The Ismene of Attius said to her sister (fr. 2), *quanto magis te isti modi esse intellego, | Tanto, Antigona magis me par est tibi consulere et parcere:* with which Macrobius (*Sat.* 6, 2. 17) compares Verg. *Aen.* 12. 19 *quantum ipse feroci | Virtute exsuperas, tanto me impensius aecum est | Consulere atque omnes metuentem expendere casus.* Again, he notes (*Sat.* 6. 1. 59) fr. 5, *iam iam neque di regunt | Neque profecto deûm supremus rex* [res] *curat hominibus,* as having an echo in *Aen.* 4. 371 *iamiam nec maxima Iuno | Nec Saturnius haec oculis pater aspicit aequis.* This latter fragment of Attius is well compared by Ribbeck with Soph. *Ant.* 921 ff.: the words were doubtless Antigone's.
[2] Stat. *Theb.* 12. 679.
[3] *Denkmäler*, pp. 83 f.   [4] From Gerhard, *Ant. Bildw.* Taf. 73.

céntral figure being an old man who has just doffed the mask
of a young maiden,—while a guard, spear in hand, seizes him by
the neck. This is explained as a comic parody of Antigone's
story; she has sent an old servant to perform the task in her
stead, and he, when confronted with Creon, drops his disguise.
The other vase-painting[1],—of perhaps c. 380—300 B.C.,—represents Heracles interceding with Creon, who is on the hero's right
hand, while Antigone and Haemon are on his left. Eurydicè,
Ismene, and a youth (perhaps Maion, the offspring of Antigone's
marriage with Haemon) are also present. Klügmann[2] refers
this picture to the lost play of Euripides. Heydemann[3] (with
more probability, I think) supposes it to represent a scene from
an otherwise unknown drama, of which he recognises the plot in
Hyginus (Fab. 72). It is briefly this:—Haemon has disobeyed
Creon by saving Antigone's life; Heracles intercedes with Creon
for Haemon, but in vain; and the two lovers commit suicide.
Professor Rhousopoulos, of Athens, in a letter to the French
Academy[4] (1885), describes a small fragment of a ceramic vase
or cup, which he believes to have been painted in Attica, about
400—350 B.C., by (or after) a good artist. The fragment shows
the beautiful face of a maiden,—the eyes bent earnestly on some
object which lies before her. This object has perished with
the rest of the vase. But the letters EIKHΣ remain; and it is
certain that the body of Polyneices was the sight on which the
maiden was gazing. As Prof. Rhousopolous ingeniously shows,
the body must have been depicted as resting on sloping ground,—
the lowest slope, we may suppose, of the hill upon which the
guards sat (v. 411). The moment imagined by the artist may have
been that at which Antigone returned, to find that the body had
been again stripped of dust (v. 426). The women of ancient
Thebes are said to have been distinguished for stature no less
than beauty; and the artist of the vase appears to have given
Antigone both characteristics.

[1] Mon. Inst. x. 27.
[2] Ann. Inst. 176, 1876.
[3] See footnote above, p. xxxviii, note 1 (3rd paragraph).
[4] Περὶ εἰκόνος Ἀντιγόνης κατὰ ἀρχαῖον ὄστρακον, μετὰ ἀπεικονίσματος. I am indebted to the kindness of Professor D'Ooge, late Director of the American School at
Athens, for an opportunity of seeing this letter.

§ 18. It is not, however, in the form of painting or of sculpture that Art has furnished the *Antigone* with its most famous and most delightful illustration. Two generations have now been so accustomed to associate this play with the music of Mendelssohn that at least a passing notice is due to the circumstances under which that music was composed; circumstances which, at a distance of nearly half a century, possess a peculiar interest of their own for these later days of classical revivals. After Frederick William IV. had come to the Prussian throne in June, 1840, one of his first acts was to found at Berlin the Academy of Arts for Painting, Sculpture, Architecture, and Music; Mendelssohn, who was then thirty-two, became the first Director of the department of Music, in the spring of 1841. The King had conceived the wish to revive some of the masterpieces of Greek Tragedy,— a project which the versatile poet Tieck, then on the confines of old age, encouraged warmly; none the less so, it would seem, because his own youth had been so vigorously identified with the protests of the Romantic school against classical restraint. Donner had recently published his German translation of Sophocles, 'in the metres of the original,' and the *Antigone* was chosen for the experiment. Mendelssohn accepted with enthusiasm the task of writing the music. The rapidity with which he worked may be estimated from the fact that Sept. 9, 1841, seems to have been about the date at which Tieck first broached the idea to him, and that the first full stage rehearsal took place some six weeks later,—on October 22nd. The success of the music in Germany seems to have been immediate and great; rather more than could be said of the first performance in London, when the *Antigone*, with the new music, was brought out at Covent Garden, on Jan. 2, 1845. The orchestra on that occasion, indeed, had a conductor no less able than the late Sir G. Macfarren; but the Chorus was put on the stage in a manner of which a graphic memorial has been preserved to us[1]. It may be added that the Covent

Mendelssohn.

---

[1] On March 25, 1845, Mendelssohn wrote to his sister:—'See if you cannot find *Punch* for Jan. 18 [1845]. It contains an account of Antigone at Covent Garden, with illustrations,—especially a view of the Chorus which has made me laugh for

Garden stage-manager improved the opportunity of the joyous 'dance-song' to Dionysus (vv. 1115—1154) by introducing a regular ballet.

To most lovers of music Mendelssohn's *Antigone* is too familiar to permit any word of comment here; but it may perhaps be less superfluous to remark a fact which has been brought under the writer's notice by an accomplished scholar[1]. For the most part, the music admits of having the Greek words set to it in a way which shows that Mendelssohn, while writing for Donner's words, must have been guided by something more than Donner's imitation of the Greek metres; he must also have been attentive, as a general rule, to the Greek text.

Date of the play. § 19. The question as to the date of the *Antigone* has a biographical no less than a literary interest. It is probable that the play was first produced at the Great Dionysia towards the end of March, 441 B.C. This precise date is, indeed, by no means certain; but all the evidence indicates that, at any rate, the years 442 and 441 B.C. give the probable limits. According to the author of the first Argument to the play[2], the success of the *Antigone* had led to Sophocles obtaining the office of general, which he held in an expedition against Samos. Athens sent two expeditions to Samos in 440 B.C. (1) The occasion of the first expedition was as follows. Samos and Miletus had been at war for the possession of Prienè, a place on the mainland not far from Miletus. The Milesians, having been worsted, denounced the Samians to the Athenians; who required that both parties should submit their case at Athens. This the Samians refused to do. The Athenians then sent forty ships to Samos,—put down the oligarchy there,—and established a democracy in its place[3]. (2) The second expedi-

three days.' In his excellent article on Mendelssohn in the *Dictionary of Music*, Sir G. Grove has justly deemed this picture worthy of reproduction.

[1] Mr George Wotherspoon, who has practically demonstrated the point by setting the Greek words to the music for the Parodos (vv. 100—161). It is only in the last antistrophe, he observes, that the 'phrasing' becomes distinctly modern, and less attentive to the Greek rhythms than to harmonic effects.

[2] See below, p. 3.

[3] The Greek Life of Sophocles says that he served as general 'in the war against the Anaeans' (Ἀναίους). Anaea was a place on the mainland, near Prienè. Boeckh

tion had to deal with Samos in open rebellion. The Samian oligarchs had come back,—overthrown the new democracy,—and proclaimed a revolt from Athens, in which Byzantium joined. Pericles was one of the ten generals for the year. He sailed at once to Samos, with sixty ships. All his nine colleagues went with him. When they reached Samos, sixteen of the sixty ships were detached on special service,—partly to watch the Carian coast, partly to summon aid from the two great islands to the north, Chios and Lesbos. Sophocles, who was one of the ten generals, was sent on the mission to these islands.

'I met Sophocles, the poet, at Chios, when he was sailing as general to Lesbos.' These are the words of Ion, the poet and prose-writer—who was only some twelve years younger than Sophocles—in a fragment preserved by Athenaeus[1]. The occasion of the meeting was a dinner given to Sophocles at Chios by Hermesilaus, a friend of his who acted as Athenian 'proxenus' there. Now, there is not the smallest real ground for questioning the genuineness of this fragment[2]. And its genuineness is confirmed by internal evidence. Sophocles said at the dinner-party,—alluding to a playful *ruse* by which he had amused the company,—that he was practising generalship, as Pericles said that he was a better poet than general. The diplomatic mission to Chios and Lesbos was a service in which

The strat gia of Sophocle:

supposes that the first expedition was known as 'the Anaean war,' and that Sophocles took part in it as well as in the second expedition. To me, I confess, there seems to be far more probability in the simple supposition that ἀναίους is a corruption of σαμίους.

[1] p. 603 E. Müller, *Frag. Hist.* II. 46.

[2] Arguments against the genuineness have been brought, indeed, by Fr. Ritter (*Vorgebliche Strategie d. Sophokles gegen Samos:* Rhein. Mus., 1843, pp. 187 ff.). (1) Ion represents Sophocles as saying,—Περικλῆς ποιεῖν με ἔφη, στρατηγεῖν δ' οὐκ ἐπίστασθαι. Sophocles (Ritter argues) would have said φησί, not ἔφη, if Pericles had been alive. The forger of the fragment intended it to refer to the revolt of Lesbos in 428 B.C.,—forgetting that Sophocles would then be 78. But we reply:—The tense, ἔφη, can obviously refer to the particular occasion on which the remark was made: 'Pericles *said* so [when I was appointed, or when we were at Samos together].' (2) Ion says of Sophocles, οὐ ῥεκτήριος ἦν. This (says Ritter) implies that Sophocles was dead; who, however, long survived Ion. [Ion was dead in 421 B.C., Ar. *Pax* 835.] But here, again, the tense merely refers to the time at which the writer received the impression. We could say of a living person, 'he was an agreeable man'—meaning that we found him so when we met him.

Pericles might very naturally utilize the abilities of his gifted,
though unmilitary, colleague. There is another trait which has
not (to my knowledge) been noticed, but which seems worth
remarking, as the coincidence is one which is not likely to have
been contrived by a forger. It is casually mentioned that, at
this dinner-party, an attendant was standing 'near the fire,' and
the couch of Sophocles, the chief guest, was also near it. The
warm season, then, had not begun. Now we know that Pericles
sailed for Samos early in 440 B.C., before the regular season for
navigation had yet opened[1].

If the fragment of Ion is authentic, then it is certain that
Sophocles held the strategia, and certain also that he held it in
440 B.C.: for Ion's mention of Lesbos cannot possibly be referred
to the revolt of that island from Athens in 428 B.C. Apart from
the fragment of Ion, however, there is good Attic authority for
the tradition. Androtion, whose *Atthis* was written about 280
B.C., gave the names of the ten generals at Samos on this occasion.
His list[2] includes Pericles, and 'Sophocles, the poet, of Colonus.'

[1] See Curtius, *Hist. Gr.* II. 472 (Eng. tr.).

[2] This fragment of Androtion has been preserved by the schol. on Aristeides,
vol. 3, p. 485 (Dind.). Müller, *Frag. Hist.* IV. 645. The names of two of the ten
generals are wanting in the printed texts, but have since been restored, from the
MS., by Wilamowitz, *De Rhesi Scholiis*, p. 13 (Greifswald, 1877).

I have observed a remarkable fact in regard to Androtion's list, which ought
to be mentioned, because it might be urged against the authenticity of the list, though
(in my opinion) such an inference from it would be unfair.

Androtion gives (1) the names, (2) the demes of the Generals, but *not* their
tribes. The regular order of precedence for the ten Cleisthenean tribes was this:—
1. Erectheis. 2. Aegeis. 3. Pandionis. 4. Leontis. 5. Acamantis. 6. Oeneis.
7. Cecropis. 8. Hippothontis. 9. Aeantis. 10. Antiochis. Now take the demes
named by Androtion. His list will be found to follow this order of the ten tribes,—
with one exception, and it is in the case of Sophocles. His deme, Colonus, belonged
to the Antiochis, and therefore his name ought to have come last. But Androtion
puts it second. The explanation is simple. When the ten tribes were increased to
twelve, by the addition of the Antigonis and Demetrias (in or about 307 B.C.), some
of the demes were transferred from one tribe to another. Among these was the deme
of Colonus. It was transferred from the Antiochis, the tenth on the roll, to the
Aegeis, the second on the roll. Hence Androtion's order is correct for his own time
(c. 280 B.C.), but not correct for 440 B.C. It is quite unnecessary, however, to infer
that he invented or doctored the list. It is enough to suppose that he re-adjusted
the order, so as to make it consistent in the eyes of his contemporaries.

Later writers refer to the poet's strategia as if it were a generally accepted fact[1].

§ 20. We have next to ask,—What ground is there for con- Had the necting this strategia of Sophocles with the production of his play any bearing *Antigone?* The authority for such a connection is the first upon the Argument to the play. This is ascribed to Aristophanes of pointment Byzantium (*c.* 200 B.C.), but is more probably of later origin (see p. 3). It says;—'They say (φασί) that Sophocles was appointed to the strategia which he held at Samos, because he had distinguished himself by the production of the *Antigone*.' Here, as so often elsewhere, the phrase, 'they say,' is not an expression of doubt, but an indication that the story was found in several writers. We know the names of at least two writers in whose works such a tradition would have been likely to occur. One of them is Satyrus (*c.* 200 B.C.), whose collection of biographies was used by the author of the Life of Sophocles[2]; the other—also quoted in the Life—is Carystius of Pergamum, who lived about 110 B.C., and wrote a book, Περὶ διδασκαλιῶν—'Chronicles of the Stage'—which Athenaeus cites. At the time when these works —and there were others of a similar kind—were compiled, old and authentic lists of Athenian plays, with their dates, appear to have been extant in such libraries as those of Alexandria and Pergamum. When, therefore, we meet with a tradition,—dating at least from the second century B.C.,—which affirms that the strategia of Sophocles was due to his *Antigone*, one inference, at least, is fairly secure. We may believe that the *Antigone* was known to have been produced earlier than the summer of 441 B.C. For, if Sophocles was strategus in the early spring of 440 B.C., he must have been elected in May, 441 B.C. The election of the

---

[1] The Argument to this play, and the Βίος Σοφοκλέους, have already been cited. See also (1) Strabo 14. p. 638 Ἀθηναῖοι δὲ...πέμψαντες στρατηγὸν Περικλέα καὶ σὺν αὐτῷ Σοφοκλέα τὸν ποιητὴν κακῶς διέθηκαν ἀπειθοῦντας τοὺς Σαμίους. (2) Schol. on Ar. *Pax* 696 λέγεται δὲ ὅτι ἐκ τῆς στρατηγίας τῆς ἐν Σάμῳ ἡγυρίσατο (ὁ Σοφοκλῆς). (3) Suidas *s. v.* Μέλητος [but referring to the Samian Μέλισσος: cp. Diog. L. 9. 24] ὑπὲρ Σαμίων στρατηγήσας ἐναυμάχησε πρὸς Σοφοκλῆν τὸν τραγικόν, ὀλυμπιάδι πδ΄ (Ol. 84 = 444—441 B.C.).—The theory that Sophocles the poet was confused with Sophocles son of Sostratides, strategus in 425 B.C. (Thuc. 3. 115), is quite incompatible with the ancient evidence.

[2] See Introduction to the *Oed. Col.*, § 18, p. xli.

J. S. III.[2]   e

ten strategi was held annually, at the same time as the other
official elections (ἀρχαιρεσίαι), in the month of Thargelion, at
the beginning of the ninth prytany of the civic year. Further,
we may conclude that the *Antigone* had not been produced at
any long interval before May, 441 B.C. Otherwise the tradition
that the play had influenced the election—whether it really did
so or not—would not have seemed probable.

Assuming, then, that the *Antigone* was brought out not long
before Sophocles obtained the strategia, we have still to consider whether there is any likelihood in the story that his election
was influenced by the success of the play. At first sight, a
modern reader is apt to be reminded of the man of letters who,
in the opinion of his admirer, would have been competent, at
the shortest notice, to assume command of the Channel Fleet.
It may appear grotesque that an important State should have
rewarded poetical genius by a similar appointment. But here, as
in other cases, we must endeavour to place ourselves at the old
Athenian point of view. The word 'general,' by which we
render 'strategus,' suggests functions purely military, requiring,
for their proper discharge, an elaborate professional training.
Such a conception of the Athenian strategia would not, however,
be accurate. The ten strategi, chosen annually, formed a board
of which the duties were primarily military, but also, in part,
civil. And, for the majority of the ten, the military duties were
usually restricted to the exercise of control and supervision at
Athens. They resembled officials at the War Office, with some
added functions from the province of the Home Office. The
number of strategi sent out with an army or a fleet was, at this
period, seldom more than three. It was only in grave emerg-
encies that all the ten strategi went on active service together.
In May, 441 B.C.,—the time, as it seems, when Sophocles was
elected,—no one could have foreseen the great crisis at Samos.
In an ordinary year Sophocles, as one of the strategi, would not
necessarily have been required to leave Athens. Among his
nine colleagues there were doubtless, besides Pericles, one or two
more possessed of military aptitudes, who would have sufficed
to perform any ordinary service in the field. Demosthenes—in
whose day only one of the ten strategi was ordinarily commis-

sioned for war—describes the other nine as occupied, among
other things, with arranging the processions for the great religious festivals at Athens[1]. He deplores, indeed, that they should
be so employed; but it is certain that it had long been one duty
of these high officials to help in organising the great ceremonies.
We are reminded how suitable such a sphere of duty would have
been for Sophocles,—who in his boyhood is said to have led the
Chorus that celebrated the victory of Salamis,—and we seem to
win a new light on the meaning of his appointment to the strategia. In so far as a strategus had to do with public ceremonies
and festivals, a man with the personal gifts of Sophocles could
hardly have strengthened his claim better than by a brilliant
success at the Dionysia. The mode of election was favourable
to such a man. It was by show of hands in the Ecclesia. If
the *Antigone* was produced at the Great Dionysia, late in March,
441 B.C., it is perfectly intelligible that the poet's splendid dramatic triumph should have contributed to his election in the
following May. It is needless to suppose that his special fitness
for the office was suggested to his fellow-citizens by the special
maxims of administration which he ascribes to Creon,—a notion
which would give an air of unreality,—verging, indeed, on
comedy,—to a result which appears entirely natural when it is
considered in a larger way[2].

§ 21. The internal evidence of the *Antigone* confirms the Internal
belief that it is the earliest of the extant seven. Certain traits evidence
for an
of composition distinguish it. (1) The division of an iambic early date
trimeter between two or more speakers—technically called ἀντι-
λαβή—is avoided, as it is by Aeschylus. It is admitted in the ·

---

[1] Dem. or. 4. § 26.

[2] One of Aelian's anecdotes (*Var. Hist.* 3. 8) is entitled, ὅτι ὁ Φρύνιχος διά τι
ποίημα στρατηγὸς ᾑρέθη. Phrynichus, he says, 'having composed suitable songs for
the performers of the war-dance (πυρριχισταῖς) in a tragedy, so captivated and enrap-
tured the (Athenian) spectators, that they immediately elected him to a military
command.' Nothing else is known concerning this alleged strategia. It is possible
that Phrynichus, the tragic poet of *c.* 500 B.C., was confounded by some later anec-
dote-monger with the son of Stratonides, general in 412 B.C. (Thuc. 8. 25), and that
the story was suggested by the authentic strategia of Sophocles. At any rate, the
vague and dubious testimony of Aelian certainly does not warrant us in using the case
of Phrynichus as an illustration.

other six plays. (2) An anapaest nowhere holds the first place of the trimeter. It may further be noticed that the resolution of any foot of the trimeter is comparatively rare in the *Antigone.* Including the proper names, there are less than 40 instances. A considerably higher proportion is found in later plays. (3) The use made of anapaestic verse is archaistic in three points. (*a*) The Parodos contains regular anapaestic systems (see p. 27, note on vv. 100—61). (*b*) The Chorus uses anapaests in announcing the entrance of Creon, Antigone, Ismene, Haemon. In the case of Ismene, these anapaests do not follow the stasimon, but occur in the midst of the epeisodion (see vv. 526—530). (*c*) Anapaests are also admitted, for purposes of dialogue, within an epeisodion (vv. 929—943, where the Chorus, Creon, and Antigone are the speakers). Aeschylus allowed this; but elsewhere it occurs only in the *Ajax* of Sophocles (another comparatively early play), and in the *Medea* of Euripides (431 B.C.).

'lace of
ie play in
ie series of
ie poet's
'orks.

§ 22. The first Argument (p. 3) ends by saying that the play 'has been reckoned as the thirty-second[1].' This statement was doubtless taken from authentic διδασκαλίαι—lists of performances, with their dates—which had come down from the 5th century B.C. to the Alexandrian age. The notice has a larger biographical interest than can often be claimed for such details. In 441 B.C. Sophocles was fifty-five: he died in 405 B.C., at ninety or ninety-one. More than 100 lost plays of his are known by name: the total number of his works might be roughly estimated at 110. It appears warrantable to assume that Sophocles had produced his works by tetralogies,—*i.e.*,

[1] λέλεκται δὲ τὸ δρᾶμα τοῦτο τριακοστὸν δεύτερον. Bergk (*Hist. Gr. Lit.* III. p. 414) proposes to read, δεδίδακται δὲ τὸ δρᾶμα τοῦτο τριακοστόν· δεύτερος ἦν. He assumes that Sophocles gained the second prize, because, according to the Parian Chronicle (60), the first prize was gained by Euripides in the archonship of Diphilus (442—1 B.C.). He adds that the word εὐδοκιμήσαντα, applied to Sophocles in the Argument, would suit the winner of the second prize,—as Aristophanes says of his own Δαιταλεῖς, which gained the second prize, ἄριστ' ἠκουσάτην (*Nub.* 529). But two things are wanting to the probability of Bergk's conjecture, viz., (1) some independent reason for thinking that the *Antigone* was the 30th, rather than the 32nd, of its author's works; and (2) some better ground for assuming that it gained the second prize.

three tragedies and one satyric drama on each occasion. If the number 32 includes the satyric dramas, then the *Antigone* was the fourth play of the eighth tetralogy, and Sophocles would have competed on seven occasions before 441 B.C. He is recorded to have gained the first prize at his first appearance, in 468 B.C., when he was twenty-eight. The production of 28 plays in the next 27 years would certainly argue a fair measure of poetical activity. If, on the other hand, this 32 is exclusive of satyric dramas, then the *Antigone* was the second play of the eleventh trilogy, and the whole number of plays written by the poet from 468 to 441 B.C. (both years included) was 44.

On either view, then, we have this interesting result,—that the years of the poet's life from fifty-five to ninety were decidedly more productive than the years from twenty-eight to fifty-five. And if we suppose that the number 32 includes the satyric dramas—which seems the more natural view—then the ratio of increased fertility after the age of fifty-five becomes still more remarkable. We have excellent reason, moreover, for believing that this increase in amount of production was not attended by any deterioration of quality. The *Philoctetes* and the *Coloneus* are probably among the latest works of all. These facts entitle Sophocles to be reckoned among the most memorable instances of poetical genius prolonging its fullest .vigour to extreme old age, and—what is perhaps rarer still—actually increasing its activity after middle life had been left behind.

§ 23.   Nothing is known as to the plays which Sophocles may have produced along with the *Antigone*. Two forms of trilogy were in concurrent use down at least to the end of the fifth century,—that in which the three tragedies were parts of one story,—and that in which no such link existed. The former was usually (though doubtless not always) employed by Aeschylus; the latter was preferred by his younger rival. Thus it is possible,—nay, probable,—that the two tragedies which accompanied the *Antigone* were unrelated to it in subject. Even when the Theban plays of Sophocles are read in the order of the fable, they do not form a linked trilogy in the Aeschylean sense. This is not due merely to discrepancy of detail or incompleteness of

[margin note: The Theban plays—not a connected trilogy]

juncture. The perversely rigorous Creon of the *Antigone* is, indeed, an essentially distinct character from the ruthless villain of the *Coloneus;* the *Coloneus* describes the end of Oedipus in a manner irreconcileable with the allusion in the *Antigone* (v. 50). But, if such differences existed between the *Choephoroe* and the *Eumenides*, they would not affect the solidarity of the 'Oresteia.' On the other hand, it does not suffice to make the triad a compact trilogy that the *Tyrannus* is, in certain aspects, supplemented by the *Coloneus*[1], and that the latter is connected with the *Antigone* by finely-wrought links of allusion[2]. In nothing is the art of Sophocles more characteristically seen than in the fact that each of these three masterpieces—with their common thread of fable, and with all their particular affinities—is still, dramatically and morally, an independent whole.

[1] See Introd. to *Oed. Col.* p. xxi. § 3.
[2] See *Oed. Col.* 1405—1413, and 1770—1772.

Manuscripts. Editions and Commentaries.

§ 1. In this play, as in the *Oedipus Coloneus* and in the second The Laurentian ms. (L). edition of the *Oedipus Tyrannus*, the editor has used the Autotype Facsimile of L (published by the London Hellenic Society in 1885); and, with its aid, has endeavoured to render the report of that manuscript as complete and exact as possible. In some instances, where discrepancies existed between previous collations, the facsimile has served to resolve the doubt; in a few other cases, it has availed to correct errors which had obtained general currency: the critical notes on 311, 375, 770, 1098, 1280 will supply examples.

The MSS., besides L, to which reference is made, are:—A (13th Other MSS. cent.), E (ascribed to 13th cent., but perhaps of the 14th), T (15th cent.), V (late 13th or early 14th), V² (probably 14th), with the following 14th century MSS.,—V³, V⁴, Vat., Vat. b, L², R. Some account of these has been given in the Introduction to the *Oedipus Tyrannus;* cp. also the Introd. to the *Oed. Col.* p. xlix. A few references are also made to an Augsburg MS. (Aug. b, 14th cent.), to Dresd. a (cod. 183, 14th cent.), and to M⁴ (Milan, Ambrosian Library, cod. C. 24 sup., 15th cent.). The symbol 'r' is occasionally used in the critical notes to denote 'one or more of the MSS. other than L'. The advantages of such a symbol are twofold: (1) the note can often be made shorter and simpler; (2) the paramount importance of L is thus more clearly marked, and, so far, the relative values of the documents are presented to the reader in a truer perspective. But this symbol has been employed only in those cases where no reason existed for a more particular statement.

§ 2. The *Antigone* supplies three instances in which the older scholia Readings due to the Scholia. do what they rarely do for the text of Sophocles,—give a certain clue to a true reading which all the MSS. have lost. One is 'φάπτουσα in v. 40; another, φονώσαισιν in v. 117; the third, δεδραγμένος in v. 235.

oints
aring on
e rela-
on of L
, the
her
ss.

§ 3. Again, this play presents some points of curious interest in regard to the much-discussed question whether L is the source from which all other known MSS. of Sophocles have been derived.

(1) There are two places in which an apparently true reading has been preserved by some of the later MSS., while L has an apparently false one. The first example is in v. 386, where L has εἰς μέσον, while A and others have εἰς δέον. Some editors, indeed, prefer εἰς μέσον: but A's reading seems far preferable (see comment.). The other example is clearer. In v. 831 L has τάκει, a manifest error, occasioned by τακομέναν shortly before. The true reading, τέγγει, is in A and other of the MSS. later than L.

(2) Verse 1167, ζῆν τοῦτον, ἀλλ' ἔμψυχον ἡγοῦμαι νεκρόν, is in none of the MSS. It is supplied by Athenaeus 7. 280 C, who quotes vv. 1165—1171. The earliest printed edition which contains it is that of Turnebus (Paris, 1553 A.D.). Now Eustathius (p. 957. 17) quotes v. 1165 (partly) and v. 1166,—remarking that, after v. 1166, 'the careful copies' (τὰ ἀκριβῆ ἀντίγραφα) give the verse ζῆν τοῦτον, ἀλλ' ἔμψυχον ἡγοῦμαι νεκρόν. Eustathius wrote in the second half of the 12th century: L was written in the first half of the eleventh century. It would be a very forced explanation to suppose that Eustathius, in speaking of τὰ ἀκριβῆ ἀντίγραφα, meant those MSS. of Sophocles on which Athenaeus, some 1000 years before, had relied for his quotation; or, again, those MSS. of Athenaeus in which Eustathius found it. According to the natural (or rather, the necessary) sense of the words, Eustathius is referring to MSS. of Sophocles extant in his own time. But did his memory deceive him, leading him to ascribe to MSS. of Sophocles what he had seen in Athenaeus? This, again, would be a very bold assumption. His statement has a *prima facie* claim to acceptance in its plain sense. And if his statement is accepted, it follows that, when L was written (in the first half of the eleventh century), two classes of MSS. of Sophocles could be distinguished by the presence or absence of verse 1167. But that verse is absent from every MS. of Sophocles now known. If, therefore, L was not the common parent of the rest, at any rate that parent (or parents) agreed with L in this striking defect, which (according to Eustathius) could have been corrected from other MSS. known in the twelfth century. There is no other instance in which a fault, now universal in the MSS. of Sophocles, is thus alleged to have been absent from a MS. or MSS. extant after the date at which L was written. Whatever construction may be placed on the statement of Eustathius, it is certain that it deserves to be carefully noted.

§ 4. Another noteworthy fact is the unusually large number of The MSS. passages in which the MSS. of the *Antigone* vary from the quotations *versus* ancient made by ancient writers. In every one of these instances (I think) our citations. MSS. are right, and the ancient citation is wrong: though there are some cases in which modern scholars have thought otherwise. See the critical notes on vv. 186, 203, 223 (with commentary), 241, 292 (with note in Appendix), 324, 456, 457, 563, 564, 678, 742, 911 f., 1037, 1167.

§ 5. Among the interpolations which modern criticism has suspected, Inter- there is one which is distinguished from the rest alike by extent and by polation. importance. This is the passage, founded on Herodotus 3. 119, in Antigone's last speech. I concur in the opinion of those who think that this passage,—*i.e.*, vv. 904—920,—cannot have stood in the text as Sophocles left it. The point is one of vital moment for our whole conception of the play. Much has been written upon it; indeed, it has a small literature of its own; but I am not acquainted with any discussion of it which appears to me satisfactory. In a note in the Appendix I have attempted to state clearly the reasons for my belief, and to show how the arguments on the other side can be answered.

This is the only passage of the play which seems to afford solid ground for the hypothesis of interpolation. It is right, however, to subjoin a list of the verses which have been suspected by the critics whose names are attached to them severally. Many of these cases receive discussion in the notes; but there are others which did not require it, because the suspicion is so manifestly baseless. It will be seen that, if effect were given to all these indictments, the *Antigone* would suffer a loss of nearly 80 verses.

Verses 4—6 rejected by Paley.—5 Bergk.—6 Nauck.—24 Wunder.—30 Nauck.— 46 Benedict.—203 Herwerden.—212 Kvičala.—234 Göttling.—287 f. Nauck.—313 f. Bergk.—393 f., to be made into one verse, Nauck.—452 Wunder.—465-468 Kvičala and Wecklein.—495 f. Zippmann.—506 f. Jacob.—570 and 573, with a rearrangement of 569-574, Nauck.—652-654, to be made into two verses, Nauck.—671 f., to be made into one verse, Heiland.—679 f. Heimreich.—680 Meineke and Bergk.—687 Heimreich, with δή for μή in 685.—691 Nauck.—838 Dindorf.—851 Hermann.— 1045-1047, 1053-1056, 1060 f., Morstadt.—1080-1083 Jacob.—1092-1094 and 1096 f. Morstadt.—1111-1114 Bergk.—1159 Nauck.—1167 Hartung.—1176 f. Jacob.—1215 Dindorf.—1232 Nauck.—1242 f. Jacob.—1250 Meineke.—1256 Nauck.—1279 Bothe. —1280 Wex.—1281 Heiland.—1301 Dindorf.—1347-1353 F. Ritter.

§ 6. In v. 125 f., where the MSS. have ἀντιπάλῳ...δράκοντι (with Emenda- indications of correction to ἀντιπάλου...δράκοντος), I propose with tions.

some confidence the simple emendation ἀντιπάλῳ...δράκοντος. In v 606 I give πάντ᾽ ἀγρεύων for πανταγήρως. In 966, πελάγει for L's πελάγεων (*sic*). In 1102, δοκεῖ for δοκεῖς. In 1124, ῥεῖθρόν τ᾽ for ῥέεθρον. The note on v. 23 f., suggesting δίκης | χρῆσαι as a correction of δίκῃ | χρησθείς, had been printed before I learned that Gerh. H. Müller had already suggested the same, though without forestalling my arguments for it. I am glad that the conjecture should have the re-commendation of having occurred independently to another. If the admission of it into the text is deemed too bold, it may be sub-mitted that the barbarous character of the traditional reading, and the absence of any emendation which can claim a distinctly higher pro-bability, render the passage one of those in which it is excusable to adopt a provisional remedy.

With regard to οὐκ ἄτης ἄτερ in v. 4, I would venture to invite the attention of scholars to the note in the Appendix. My first ob-ject has been to bring out what seems the essential point,—viz., that the real difficulty is the palaeographical one,—and to help in defining the conditions which a solution must satisfy before it can claim more than the value of guess-work. By the kind aid of Mr E. M. Thompson, I have been enabled to give a transcript of the words οὐκ ἄτης ἄτερ as they would have been written in an Egyptian papyrus of *circ.* 250 —200 B.C.

Editions, tc.

§ 7. Besides the various complete editions of Sophocles (*Oed. Tyr.*, p. lxi, 2nd ed.), these separate editions of the *Antigone* have been consulted.—Aug. Boeckh. With a German translation, and two Dissertations. (Berlin, 1st ed. 1843; new ed. 1884.)—John William Donaldson. With English verse translation, and commentary. (Lon-don, 1848).—Aug. Meineke. (Berlin, 1861.)—Moriz Seyffert. (Berlin, 1865.)—Martin L. D'Ooge. On the basis of Wolff's edition. (Boston, U.S.A., 1884.)—A. Pallis. With critical notes in Modern Greek. (Athens, 1885.)—D. C. Semitelos. With introduction, critical notes, and commentary, in Modern Greek. (Athens, 1887.)—Selected pas-sages of this play are discussed by Hermann Schütz, in the first part of his *Sophokleische Studien*, which deals with the *Antigone* only (Gotha, 1886, pp. 62). Many other critics are cited in connection with par-ticular points of the play which they have treated. Lastly, reference may be made to the list of subsidia, available for Sophoclean study generally, which has been given in the Introduction to the *Oedipus Tyrannus*, 2nd ed., p. lxii.

METRICAL ANALYSIS.

THE unit of measure in Greek verse is the short syllable, ◡, of which the musical equivalent is the quaver, ♪. The long syllable, –, has twice the value of ◡, being musically equal to ♩.

Besides ◡ and –, the only signs used here are the following.

(1) ⌐ for –, when the value of – is increased by *one half*, so that it is equal to ◡◡◡, – ◡, or ◡ –.

(2) >, to mark an 'irrational syllable' (συλλαβὴ ἄλογος), *i.e.*, bearing a metrical value to which its proper time-value does not entitle it; viz. ◡ for –, or – for ◡. Thus ἐργῶν means that the word serves as a choree, – ◡, not as a spondee, – –.

(3) ◡̑◡, instead of – ◡ ◡, in logaoedic verses. This means that the dactyl has not its full time-value, but only that of – ◡. This loss is divided between the long syllable, which loses ¼th of its value, and the first short, which loses ½. Thus, while the normal dactyl is equivalent to ♩ ♫, this more rapid dactyl is equivalent to ♪·♫. Such a dactyl is called 'cyclic.'

(4) – ♦, instead of – ◡ ◡, in choreic verses. Here, again, the dactyl has the value only of – ◡. But in the cyclic dactyl, as we have seen, the loss of ◡ was divided between the long syllable and the first short. Here, in the choreic dactyl, the long syllable keeps its full value; but each of two short syllables loses half its value. That is, the choreic dactyl is equivalent to ♩ ♬.

The choreic dactyl is used in two passages of this play: (1) First Stasimon, 1st Strophe, period III., vv. 1, 2 (vv. 339 f.), ἄφθιτον...ἔτος εἰς ἔτος : and *ib*. 2nd Strophe, per. I., vv. 1, 2 (vv. 354 f.) καὶ φθέγμα...καὶ ἐδιδάξατο. (2) First Kommos (No. V. in this Analysis), Epode, per. II., v. 1 (v. 879) οὐκέτι μοι τόδε λαμπάδος. Here, as elsewhere, the effect of such a dactyl is to give vivacity, relieving the somewhat monotonous repose of a choreic series. Other examples will be found in Schmidt's *Rhythmic and Metric*, p. 49, § 15. 3.

The last syllable of a verse is common (ἀδιάφορος, *anceps*). It is here marked ◡ or – according to the metre: *e.g.*, ἐργῶν, if the word represents a choree, or ἐργᾱ, if a spondee.

Pauses. At the end of a verse, ⋏ marks a pause equal to ◡, ⋏̄ a pause equal to –, and ⋏̣ a pause equal to – ◡.

The *anacrusis* of a verse (the part preliminary to its regular metre) is marked off by three dots placed vertically, ⁚ If the anacrusis consists of two short syllables with the value of only one, ◡ is written over them. In v. 1115 the first two syllables of πολυώνυμε form such an anacrusis. (Analysis, No. VII., first v.)

Metres used in this play.   The lyric elements of the *Antigone* are simple. Except the dochmiacs at the end (1261—1347), all the lyric parts are composed of logaoedic and choreic verses, in different combinations.

1. *Logaoedic*, or *prose-verse* (λογαοιδικός),—so called by ancient metrists because, owing to its apparent irregularity, it seemed something intermediate between verse and prose,—is a measure based on the choree, – ◡, and the cyclic dactyl, metrically equivalent to a choree, –◡ ◡. The following forms of it occur in the *Antigone*.

(*a*) The logaoedic verse of four feet, or tetrapody. This is called a Glyconic verse, from the lyric poet Glycon. It consists of one cyclic dactyl and three chorees. According as the dactyl comes first, second, or third, the verse is a First, Second, or Third, Glyconic. Thus the first line of the First Stasimon (v. 332) consists of a First Glyconic

$$-\!\smile\ \smile \quad -\ \smile \quad -\ \smile \quad \underset{}{\sqsubset} \quad \rightarrow$$

followed by a Second Glyconic: πολλα τα | δεινα | κουδεν | ανθρ ‖ ωπου |

$$-\!\smile\ \smile \quad -\ \smile \quad -$$

δεινοτερ | ον πελ | ει ⋏. Glyconic verses are usually shortened at the end ('catalectic'), as in this example.

(*b*) The logaoedic verse of three feet, or tripody,—called 'Pherecratic,' from the poet of the Old Comedy. It is simply the Glyconic verse with one choree taken away, and is called 'First' or 'Second' according as the dactyl comes first or second. Thus the fourth line of the Third Stasimon (vv. 788 f.) consists of a Second, followed by a First, Pherecratic: –   >   –◡ ◡   ⋏̄   –◡ ◡   ⋏̄   –

και σ οντ | αθανατ | ων ‖ φυξιμος | ουδ | εις ⋏.

(*c*) Logaoedic verses of six feet (hexapodies) are also frequent in this play. Such is the first line of the second Strophe of the Parodos

$$\overset{\smile}{-}\smile\quad\overset{\smile}{-}\smile\quad\overset{\smile}{-}\smile\quad-\smile\quad\llcorner\;-$$

(v. 134), αντιτυπ | ος δ επι | γα πεσε | ταυταλ | ωθ | εις Λ.

(*d*) The logaoedic verse of two feet (dipody) occurs once in this

$$\overset{\smile}{-}\smile\quad-\smile$$

play, as an ἐπῳδός, or postlude, to a choral strophe, v. 140 δεξιο | σειρος (= 154 Βάκχιος | ἀρχοι); Parodos, Second Strophe, period III. This is the '*versus Adonius,*' which closes the Sapphic stanza.

2. *Choreic* measures are those based simply on the choree (or ' trochee '), – ◡. They usually consist either of four or of six feet. In this play we have both tetrapodies and hexapodies. Thus in vv. 847 ff. a choreic hexapody is followed by a choreic tetrapody: see Analysis, No. V., Second Strophe, period III., vv. 1, 2 οἷα φίλων ἄκλαυτος...τάφου ποταινίου. As the Analysis will show, choreic measures are often combined with logaoedic in the same strophe. The first Strophe of the First Stasimon affords an instance.

3. *Dochmiacs* occur in the closing kommos (1261—1347, No. VIII. in the Analysis). A dochmiac has two elements, viz. a bacchius, – – ◡ (= 5 short syllables), and a shortened choree, –, (= 2 short syllables). Thus odd and even were combined in it. The name δόχμιος, 'slanting,' expressed the resulting effect by a metaphor. The rhythm seemed to diverge side-ways from a straight course.

The regular type of dochmiac dimeter (with anacrusis) is ◡ : – – ◡| –, ◡ ‖. The comma marks the ordinary caesura. As Dr Schmidt has noticed, the dochmiacs of the *Antigone* are remarkable for frequent neglect of the regular caesura. The dochmiac measure may be remembered by this line, in which '*serfs*' and '*wrongs*' must receive as much stress as the second syllable of '*rebel*' and of '*resent*':

Rebél! Sérfs, rebél! Resént wróngs so díre.

This is a dochmiac dimeter, with anacrusis, written ◡ : – – ◡ | –, ◡ ‖ – – ◡ | – ∧ ‖.

The diagrams added to the metrical schemes are simply short ways of showing how the verses are put together in rhythmical wholes. Thus the first diagram (No. I., First Str., per. I.) is merely a symbol of the following statement. 'There are here two verses. Each contains three rhythmical groups or 'sentences' (κῶλα); and each 'sentence' contains four feet. The first verse, as a whole, corresponds with the second, as a whole. And the three parts of the first verse correspond consecutively

Rhythm. —The diagrams

with the three parts of the second verse. These two verses together form a rhythmical structure complete in itself,—a rhythmical 'period' (περίοδος).' Some simple English illustrations have been given in the *Oed. Coloneus* (p. lx).—The end of a rhythmical sentence is marked by ‖, and that of a period by ⟧.

I. Parodos, vv. 100—154.

FIRST STROPHE.—Logaoedic. The second Glyconic is the main theme.

I., II., denote the *First* and *Second Rhythmical Periods*. The sign ‖ marks the end of a *Rhythmical Sentence;* ⟧ marks that of a *Period*.

I. 1. ακτις | αελι | ου το | καλλ ‖ ιστον | επταπυλ | ῳ φαν | εν ‖
στας δ υπ | ερ μελαθρ | ων φον | ωσ ‖ αισιν | αμφιχαν | ων κυκλ | ῳ ‖

θηβᾳ | των προτερ | ων φα | ος Λ ‖
λογχας | επτα πυλ | ον στομ | α Λ

2. ε ⫶ φανθ | ης ποτ | ω χρυσε | ας ‖ αμερ | ας βλεφαρ | ον Διρκ | αι ‖
ε ⫶ βα | πριν ποθ | αμετερ | ων ‖ αιματ | ων γεννσ | ιν πλησθ | ην ‖

ων υπ | ερ ρεεθρ | ων μολ | ουσα ⟧
αι τε | και στεφαν | ωμα | πυργων

II. 1. τον λευκ | ασπιν | αργοθεν | εκ ‖ βαντα | φωτα | πανσαγι | ᾳ Λ ‖
πευκα | ενθ ηφ | αιστον ελ | ειν ‖ τοιος | αμφι | νωτ εταθ | η

2. φυγαδα | προδρομον | οξυτερ | ῳ ‖ κινησ | ασα χαλ | ιν | ῳ Λ ⟧
παταγος | αρεος | αντιπαλ | ῳ ‖ δυσχειρ | ωμα δρακ | οντ | ος

I.   II.

$$\left(\begin{cases}4\\4\\4\\ \vdots \\4\\ \end{cases}\middle\} \begin{cases}4\\4\end{cases}\right)$$

$$\left(\begin{cases}4\\4\\ \vdots \\ 4 \\ 4\end{cases}\right)$$

After the first Strophe follows the first system of Anapaests (110 ὅς...116 κορύθεσσι): after the first Antistrophe, the second system (127 Ζεὺς...133 ἀλαλάξαι).

SECOND STROPHE.—Logaoedic, in sentences of varying lengths, viz. :
—I. two hexapodies : II. two tetrapodies, with one tripody between
them : III. two tetrapodies, followed by a *versus Adonius* ($\smile\smile \mid -\smile$)
as epode.

I. 1.
$$\overset{\smile\smile}{\quad} \quad \overset{-\;\smile}{\quad} \quad \overset{\smile\;\smile}{\quad} \quad \overset{-\;\smile}{\quad} \quad \overset{\mathrel{L}}{\quad}$$

αντιτυπ | ᾳ δ επι | γᾳ πεσε | τανταλ | ωθ | εις Λ ‖
αλλα γαρ | α μεγαλ | ωνυμος | ηλθε | νικ | α

2.
$$\overset{\smile\smile}{\quad} \quad \overset{\smile\;\smile}{\quad} \quad \overset{\smile\smile}{\quad} \quad \overset{-\;\smile}{\quad} \quad \overset{\mathrel{L}}{\quad}$$

πυρφορος | ος τοτε | μαινομεν | ᾳ ξυν | ορμ | ᾳ Λ]
τᾳ πολυ | αρματῳ | αντιχαρ | εισα | θηβ | ᾳ

II. 1.
$$\overset{-\;>}{\quad}\; \overset{\smile\smile}{\quad}\; \overset{-\;>}{\quad}\; \overset{\mathrel{L}\;-\;>}{\quad}\; \overset{\smile\smile}{\quad}$$

βακχευ | ων επεπν | ει ριπ | αις ‖ εχθιστ | ων ανεμ | ων Λ ‖
εκ μεν | δη πολεμ | ων των | νιν ‖ θεσθαι | λησμοσιν | αν

2.
$$\overset{-\;\smile}{\quad}\; \overset{\mathrel{L}}{\quad}\; \overset{-\;\smile}{\quad}$$

ειχε δ | αλλ | ᾳ τα | μεν Λ]
θεων δε | να | ουτ χορ | οις

$$\overset{\smile\smile\;\mathrel{L}}{\quad} \overset{\smile\smile\;\mathrel{L}}{\quad} \overset{\smile\;\smile\;\mathrel{L}}{\quad} \overset{\smile\smile\;-\;>}{\quad} \overset{\smile\smile}{\quad} \overset{-\;\smile}{\quad}$$

αλλα δ επ|αλλ | οις επε |νωμ‖α στυφελ | ιζ |ων μεγας|αρης ‖ δεξιο|σειρος]
παννυχι | οις | παντας επ| ελθ ‖ ωμεν ο |θηβ| ας δ ελελ |ιχθων‖βακχιος|αρχοι

I.	II.	III.
$\left.\begin{matrix}6\\6\end{matrix}\right)$	$\left.\begin{matrix}4\\3\\4\end{matrix}\right)$	$\left.\begin{matrix}4\\4\\2\end{matrix}\right) = ἐπ.$

After the second Strophe follows the third system of Anapaests (141 ἑπτὰ...147
ἀμφω): after the second Antistrophe, the fourth system (155 ἀλλ' ὅδε...161 πέμψαι).

II. First Stasimon, vv. 332—375.

FIRST STROPHE.—Period I. is logaoedic. It consists of one First
Glyconic verse, followed by three Second Glyconics. Periods II. and
III. are choreic. But the first verse of Period II. is logaoedic (a Second
Glyconic), and thus smooths the transition from logaoedic to choreic

I. 1.   πολλα τα | δεινα | κουδεν | ανθρ ‖ ωπου | δεινοτερ | ον πελ | ει ∧ ‖
        κουφονο | ων τε | φυλον | ορν ‖ ιθων | αμφιβαλ | ων εγ | ει

 2.   τουτο | και πολι | ου περ | αν ‖ ποντου | χειμερι | φ νοτ | φ ∧]
        και θηρ | ων αγρι | ων εθν | η ‖ τουτου τ | ειναλι | αν φυσ | ιν ∧

II. 1.   χωρ ⋮ ει περ | ιβρυχι | οισ | ιν ∧ ‖
        σπειρ ⋮ αισι | δικτυο | κλωστ | οις

 2.   περ ⋮ ων υπ | οιδμασ | ιν ∧ ‖
        περ ⋮ ι φραδ | ης αν | ηρ

 3.   θε ⋮ ων τε | ταν υπ | ερτατ | αν γαν]]
        κρατ ⋮ ει δε | μηχαν | αις αγρ | αυλου

III. 1.   αφθιτον | ακαματ | αν απο | τρυεται ‖
        θηρος ορ | εσσιβατ | α λασι | αυχενα θ

 2.   ιλλομεν | ων αροτρ | ων ετος | εις ετος ‖
        ιππον οχμ | αζεται | αμφι λοφ | ον ζυγων

 3.   ιππ | ει | φ γεν | ει πολ | ευ | ων ∧]]
        ουρ | ει | ον τ α | κμητα | ταυρ | ον

I. $\left.\begin{cases} 4 \\ 4 \\ 4 \\ 4 \end{cases}\right\rangle$ II. $\left.\begin{matrix} 4 \\ 3 \\ 4 \end{matrix}\right)$ III. $\left.\begin{matrix} 4 \\ 4 \\ 6 \end{matrix}\right.$ = ἐπῳδός

SECOND STROPHE.—Choreic.

I. 1.   και ⋮ φθεγμα και | ανεμο | εν ∧ ‖
        σοφ ⋮ ον τι το | μηχανο | εν

 2.   φρον ⋮ ηματα και | αστυνομ | ους οργ | ας εδι ‖ δαξατο | και δυσ | αυλ | ων ∧]]
        τεχν ⋮ ας υπερ | ελπιδ εχ | ων τοτε | μεν κακον ‖ αλλοτ επ | εσθλον | ερπ | ει

$$\smile \quad - \smile \quad \llcorner \quad - \smile \quad - \smile \quad - \smile \quad \llcorner \quad - \smile \quad -$$

I. 1. παγ : ων εν | αιθρ | εια | και δυσ ‖ ομβρα | φευγ | ειν βελ | η ∧ ‖

   νομ : ους γερ | αιρ | ων χθον | οι θε ‖ ων τ εν | ορκ | ον δικ | αν

$$- \smile \quad \smile \smile \smile \quad \smile \smile \smile \quad - \smile \quad - \smile \quad -$$

2. παντο | πορος α | πορος επ | ουδεν | ερχετ | αι ∧ ‖

   υψι | πολις α | πολις ο | τω το | μη καλ | ον

$$\smile \quad - \smile \quad \llcorner \quad - \smile \quad \llcorner \quad - \smile \quad > \smile \quad - \smile \quad -$$

3. το : μελλον | αιδ | α μον | ον ‖ φευξιν | ουκ επ | αξετ | αι ∧ ‖

   ξυν : εστι | τολμ | ας χαρ | ω ‖ μητ εμ | οι γαρ | εστι | οι

$$\smile \quad - \smile \quad - \smile \quad - \smile \quad \llcorner \quad - \smile \quad - \smile \quad -$$

4. νοσ : ων δ α | μηχαν | ων φυγ | ας | ξυμπε | φρασται]

   γερ : οιτο | μητ ισ | ον φρον | ων | οι ταδ | ερδει

Note.—In Period III. of the first Strophe, and in Period I. of the second, the apparent dactyls (marked $- \smile\smile$) are choreic dactyls; *i.e.*, the two short syllables, $\smile\smile$, have the time-value of one short, $\smile$. This is proved by the caesura after ὀργάς in verse 2 of the second Strophe. The choreic dactyl is usually found, as here, in a transition from (or into) logaoedic verse. Cp. Schmidt, *Rhythmic and Metric*, § 15. 3.

I. $\dfrac{\cdot}{3} = \pi\rho o\omega\delta\acute{v}s.$

$\left. \begin{matrix} 4) \\ 4) \end{matrix} \right.$

II. $\left\{ \begin{matrix} \cdot \\ 4 \\ 4 \\ \cdot \\ 6 \\ \cdot \\ 4 \\ 4 \\ \cdot \\ 6 \end{matrix} \right.$

III. Second Stasimon, vv. 582—625.

FIRST STROPHE.—Period I. is logaoedic (two hexapodies). Periods II. and III. are choreic. Just as in the first strophe of the first Stasimon, the first verse of Period II. is logaoedic, forming a transition. The remaining verses are choreic tetrapodies.

$$> \quad \smile\smile \smile \quad \smile\smile \smile \quad - \stackrel{?}{-} \quad - \smile \quad \llcorner \quad -$$

I. 1. ευ : δαιμονες | οισι κακ | ων α | γευστος | αι | ων ∧ ‖

   αρχ : αια τα | λαβδακιδ | αν οικ | ων ορ | ωμ | αι

$$- \quad \smile \quad - \quad > \quad \smile\smile \smile \quad \smile\smile \smile \quad \llcorner \quad -$$

2. οις γαρ | αν σεισ | θη θεο | θεν δομος | ατ | ας ∧]

   πηματ | α φθιτ | ων επι | πημασι | πιπτ | οντ

$$- \cup \quad - \quad > \quad\quad \cup\cup\quad \cup \quad\quad \cup\cup\quad \cup \quad\quad - \cup \quad -$$

II. 1. ουδεν | ελλειπ | ει γενε | ας επι | πληθος | ερπον ‖

      ουδ απ | αλλασσ | ει γενε | αν γενος | αλλ ερ | ειπει

$$\cup \quad\quad - \cup \quad - \quad - \quad\quad - \cup \quad L \quad\quad - \quad\cup \quad - \quad\quad - \quad \cup \quad -$$

   2. ομ ⋮ οιον | ωστε | ποντι | αις ‖ οιδμα | δυσπνο | οις οτ | αν ∧ ‖

      θε ⋮ ων τις | ουδ εχ | ει λυσ | ιν ‖ νυν γαρ | εσχατ | ας υπ | ερ

$$> \quad\quad - \cup \quad \cup\cup\cup \quad \cup\cup\cup \quad \overline{\cup\cup} \quad \cup \quad - \quad \cup \quad -$$

   3. θρησσ ⋮ αισιν | ερεβος | υφαλον | επιδραμ | η πνο | αις ∧ ⟧

      ριξ ⋮ ας ο | τετατο | φαος εν | οιδιπ | ου δομ | οις

$$\cup \quad\quad L \quad\quad L \quad\quad - \quad \cup \quad\quad - \quad \cup \quad L \quad\quad L \quad\quad - \cup \quad -$$

III. 1. κυλ ⋮ ινδ | ει | βυσσο | θεν κελ ‖ αιν | αν | θινα | και ∧ ‖

      κατ ⋮ αν | νυν | φοινι | α θε ‖ ων | των | νερτερ | ων

$$\cup \quad\quad - \cup \quad - \quad - \quad - \cup \quad - \quad\quad - \cup \quad L \quad -$$

   2. δυσ ⋮ ανεμ | οι στον | φ βρεμ | ουσιν ‖ αντι | πληγες | ακτ | αι ∧ ⟧

      αμ ⋮ φ κοπ | ις λογ | ου τα | νοια ‖ και φρεν | ων ερ | ιν | υς

      I. $\begin{matrix} \dot{6} \\ \dot{6} \end{matrix})$ II. $\begin{matrix} \dot{6} \\ 4 \\ 4 \\ \dot{6} \end{matrix})$ III. $\left\{\begin{matrix} 4 \\ 4 \\ 4 \\ 4 \end{matrix}\right\}$

SECOND STROPHE.—Logaoedic.—In Period III., the first and third
verses are choreic.

$$\overset{\frown}{\gtrless} \quad L \quad\quad \cup \quad \cup \quad\quad - \cup \quad\quad L \quad\quad - \overset{\frown}{\gtrless} \quad\quad \cup\cup\quad \cup \quad - \cup \quad\quad - \cup$$

I. 1. τε ⋮ αν | ζευ δυνασ | ιν τις | ανδρ ‖ ων υπ | ερβασι | α κατ | ασχοι ‖

      α ⋮ γαρ | δη πολυ | πλαγκτος | ελπ ‖ ις πολλ | οις μεν ορ | ασις | ανδρων

$$> \quad\quad - \cup \quad\quad \cup\cup\quad \cup \quad\quad - \cup \quad -$$

   2. ταν ⋮ ουθ υπνος | αιρ | ει ποθ ο | παντ αγρ | ευ | ων ∧ ⟧

      πολλ ⋮ οις δ απατ | α | κουφονο | ων ερ | ωτ ⋮ ων

$$\cup\cup\quad \cup \quad - \cup \quad\quad L \quad\quad L \quad\quad \cup\cup\quad \cup \quad\quad L \quad\quad - \cup \quad \cup$$

II. 1. ουτε θε | ων α | κματ | οι ‖ μηνες α | γηρ | ως δε χρον | φ ∧ ‖

      ειδοτι δ | ουδεν | ερπ | ει ‖ πριν πυρι | θερμ | φ | ποδα | τις

$$\cup \quad\quad L \quad\quad \cup\cup\quad \cup \quad - \cup \quad - \quad > \quad\quad \cup\cup\quad \cup \quad - \cup \quad\quad L \quad -$$

   2. δυν ⋮ αστ | ας κατεχ | εις ολ | υμπου ‖ μαρμαρο | εσσαν | αιγλ | αν ∧ ⟧

      προσ ⋮ αυσ | η σοφι | φ γαρ | εκ του ‖ κλεινον επ | ος πε | φαν | ται

[. 1. το τ επ : ειτα | και το | μελλ | ον Λ ‖
     το κακ : ον δοκ | ειν ποτ | εσθλ | ον

2. και : το πριν επ | αρκεσ | ει Λ ‖
     τῳδ : εμμεν ο | τῳ φρεν | ας

3. νομος οδ | ουδεν | ερπ | ει Λ ‖
     θεος αγ | ει προς | ατ | αν

4. θνατ : ων βιοτ | ῳ | παμπολυ γ | εκτος | ατ | ας Λ]]
     πρασσ : ει δ ολιγ | ιστ | ον χρονον | εκτος | ατας

I.
   4
   4
   6 = ἐπῳδός.

II.
  $\left(\begin{cases} 4 \\ 4 \\ 4 \\ 4 \end{cases} \right)$

III.
  $\left. \begin{array}{c} 4 \\ 3 \\ 4 \\ 6 = \text{ἐπ}. \end{array} \right)$

IV. Third Stasimon, vv. 781—800.

STROPHE.—Logaoedic.—(Period I., Glyconic verses : II., Glyconics varied by Pherecratic verses.)

I. 1. ερ : ως α | νικ | ατε μαχ | αν ερ ‖ ως ος | εν | κτημασι | πιπτεις ‖
     συ : και δικ | αι | ων αδικ | ους φρεν ‖ ας παρ | α | σπᾳς επι | λωβᾳ

2. ος : εν μαλακ | αις παρ | ει | αις νε ‖ ανιδος | εννυχ | ευ | εις Λ]
     συ : και τοδε | νεικος | ανδρ | ων ξυν ‖ αιμον εχ | εις ταρ | αξ | ας

[I. 1. φοιτ : ᾳς δ υπ | ερ | ποντιος | εν τ ‖ αγρονομ | οις | αυλ | αις Λ ‖
     νικ : ᾳ δ εν | αργ | ης βλεφαρ | ων ‖ ιμερος | ευ | λεκτρου

2. και σ ουτ | αθανατ | ων ‖ φυξιμος | ουδ | εις Λ ‖
     νυμφας | των μεγαλ | ων ‖ παρεδρος εν | αρχ | αις

3. ουθ : αμερι | ων σε γ | ανθρ | ωπ ‖ ων ο δ εχ | ων με | μην | εν Λ]
     θεσμ : ων αμαχ | ος γαρ | εμ | παις ‖ ει θεος | α φροδ | ιτ | α

f 2

In Period II., v. 2, φίξιμος = πάρεδρος ἐν : but the words πάρεδρος ἐν ἀρχαῖς are of doubtful soundness. As the text stands, πάρεδρος requires us to suppose that the arsis of the logaoedic dactyl is resolved into ⏑⏑. See Appendix on v. 797 f. Prof. D'Ooge writes ⏑⏑ ⏂ : *i.e.*, φύξιμος is a choreic dactyl, in which ⏑⏑ has the time-value only of ⏑. This suits the resolution of πάρεδρος, for it means that the syllables -δρος ἐν are uttered very rapidly. On the other hand, in this otherwise purely logaoedic strophe we hardly look for a choreic dactyl.

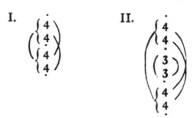

V. Kommos, vv. 806—882.

First Strophe.—Logaoedic (Glyconics).

I. 1. ορ ⋮ ατ εμ | ω | γας πατρι | ας πολ ‖ ιται | ταν νεατ | αν οδ | ον ⋀ ‖
     ηκ ⋮ ουσα | δη | λυγροτατ | αν ολ ‖ εσθαι | ταν φρυγι | αν ξεν | αν

2. στειχουσ | αν νεατ | ον δε | φεγγος ‖ λευσσ | ουσαν | αελι | ου ⋀ ‖
     τανταλ | ου σιπυλ | ῳ προς | ακρῳ ‖ ταν | κισσος | ως ατεν | ης

3. κουποτ | αυθις | αλλα μ ο | παγ ‖ κοιτας | αιδας | ζωσαν αγ | ει ⋀ ‖
     πετραι | α βλαστ | α δαμασ | εν ‖ και νιν | ομβροι | τακομεν | αν

4. ταν αχερ | οντος]
     ως φατις | ανδρων

II. 1. ακτ ⋮ αν | ουθ υμεν | αιων | εγ ‖ κληρον | ουτ επι | νυμφει | ος ⋀ ‖
     χι ⋮ ων τ | ου δαμα | λειπει | τεγγ ‖ ει δ υπ | οφρυσι | παγκλαυτ | οις

2. πω με τις | υμνος | υμν | ησεν ‖ αλλ αχερ | οντι | νυμφευσ | ω ⋀]
     δειραδας | ᾳ με | δαιμ | ων ομ ‖ οιοτατ | αν κατ | ευναξ | ει

The First Strophe is followed by the first system of Anapaests (vv. 817—822); the first Antistrophe, by the second system (vv. 834--838).

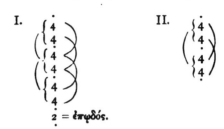

$$2 = \text{ἐπῳδός.}$$

SECOND STROPHE.—Period I. is logaoedic.   Period II., while mainly logaoedic, introduces choreics (v. 1), which are continued in III.

I. 1. οιμ ⋮ οι γελ | ωμ | αι τι με | προς θε | ων πατρ | φων ‖
        ε ⋮ ψαυσας | αλγ | ειυοτατ | α; εμ | οι μερ | ιμνας

2. ουκ ⋮ οιχομεν | αν υβρ | ιζεις | αλλ επι | φαντ | ον Λ ‖
        πατρ ⋮ ος τριπολ | ιστον | οικτον | του τε προ | παντ | ος

3. ω πολις | ω πολ | εως πολ | υ | κτημονες | ανδρες]
        αμετερ | ου ποτμ | ου κλεω | οις | λαβδακιδ | αισιν

I. 1. ι ⋮ ω διρκ | αιαι | κρην | αι Λ ‖
        ι ⋮ ω ματρ | φαι | λεκτρ | ων

2. θηβ ⋮ ας τ ευ | αρματου | αλσος | εμ ‖ πας ξυμ | μαρτυρας | υμμ επ | ι |
        ατ ⋮ αι κοιμ | ηματα τ | αυτο | γενν ‖ ητ εμ | ω πατρι | δυσμορ | ου |

        κτωμ | αι Λ]
        ματρ | ος

I. 1. οι ⋮ α φιλ | ων α | κλαυτος | οι | οις νομ | οις Λ ‖
        οι ⋮ ων εγ | ω ποθ | α ταλ | αι | φρων ε | φυν

‿ — ‿ — ‿ ‿ ‿̆‿̆ ‿ — ‿ — ‿ — ‿ —‿ —

2. προς ⋮ εργμα | τυμβο | χωστον | ερχομ ‖ αι ταφ | ου ποτ | αινι | ου Λ ‖
   προς ⋮ ους αρ | αιος | αγαμος | αδ εγ ‖ ω μετ | οικος | ερχομ | αι

‿ ∟ — ⋛ — ‿ ∟ ‿̆‿ ‿ — ‿ ∟ —

3. ι ⋮ ω | δυσταν | ος βροτ | οις ‖ ουτε νεκρ | οις κυρ | ουσ | α Λ ‖
   ι ⋮ ω | δυσποτμ | ων κασ | ι ‖ γνητε γαμ | ων κυρ | ησας

‿ — ‿ ∟ — ‿ — ‿ ∟ —

4. μετ ⋮ οικος | ου | ζωσιν | ου θαν | ουσ | ιν Λ]
   θαν ⋮ ων ετ | ουσ | αν κατ | ηναρ | ες | με

I. $\begin{matrix}\overset{\cdot}{6}\\\overset{\cdot}{6}\\\overset{\cdot}{6}\\\cdot\end{matrix}\Big)$ II. $\begin{matrix}\overset{\cdot}{4}\\\overset{\cdot}{4}\\6 = \text{ἐπ.}\\\cdot\end{matrix}\Big)$ III. $\begin{matrix}\overset{\cdot}{6}\\4\\4\\4\\4\\6\\\cdot\end{matrix}$

THIRD STROPHE.—A single period.   Choreic.

‿ — ‿ — ‿ — ‿ —

1. προ ⋮ βασ επ | εσχατ | ον θρασ | ους Λ ‖
   σεβ ⋮ ειν μεν | ευσεβ | εια | τις

⋛ — ‿ ‿ — ‿ — ‿ —

2. υψ ⋮ ηλον | ες δικ | ας βαθρ | ον Λ ‖
   κρατ ⋮ ος δ ο | τῳ κρατ | ος μελ | ει

‿ ‿ ‿ ‿ — ‿ — ‿ —

3. προσ ⋮ επεσες | ω τεκν | ον πολ | υ Λ ‖
   παρ ⋮ αβατον | ουδαμ | ᾳ πελ | ει

‿ ∟ ∟ — ‿ — ‿ ∟ ‿

4. πατρ ⋮ ῳ | ον δ | εκτιν | εις τιν | αθλ | ον Λ]
   σε δ ⋮ αυτ | ο | γνωτος | ωλεσ | οργ | α

$\begin{matrix}\overset{\cdot}{4}\\\overset{\cdot}{4}\\4\\6 = \text{ἐπ.}\end{matrix}\Big)$

EPODE (vv. 876—882).—Choreic.   The choreic dactyls (– ⏑) serve to vary and enliven the movement.

I. 1. ᾰ ⁝ κλαυτος | αφιλος | ανυμεν | αι ‖ ος ταλ | αι | φρων αγομ | αι ⋀ ‖

2. τανδ ετ | οιμ | αν οδ | ον ⋀ ⟧

II. 1. ουκετι | μοι τοδε | λαμπαδος | φον ‖

2. ομμα | θεμις ορ | αν ταλ | αινᾳ ‖

3. τον δ εμ | ον ποτμ | ον αδακρ | υτον ‖

4. ουδ ⁝ εις φιλ | ων στεν | αζ | ει ⋀ ⟧

I.   ·
     4
     4 *m.*⎰[*m.* = mesode.]
     ·
     4
     ·

II. ·
     4
     ·⎫
     4⎬
     ·⎭
     4⎫
     ·⎬
     4⎭
     ·

VI.   Fourth Stasimon, vv. 944—987.

FIRST STROPHE.—Periods I. and II. are logaoedic (Pherecratic verses in I., and Pherecratic and Glyconic in II.).   Period III. is choreic.

I. 1. ετλα | και δανα | ας ‖ ουρανι | ον | φως ⋀ ‖
      ζευχθη δ | οξυχολ | ος ‖ παις ο δρυ | αντ | ος

2. αλλαξ | αι δεμας | εν ‖ χαλκοδετ | οις αυλ | αις ⋀ ⟧
      ηδων | ων βασιλ | ευς ‖ κερτομι | οις οργ | αις

II. 1. κρυπτομεν | α δ εν | τυμβηρ ‖ ει θαλαμ | ῳ κατ | εζευχθ | η ⋀ ‖
       εκ διο | νυσου | πετρωδ ‖ ει κατα | φαρκτος | εν δεσμ | ῳ ⋀ ‖

– >   ‿ ‿ ⌣ L   ‿‿⌣ – >   –

2. καιτοι | και γενε | ᾳ ‖ τιμιος | ω παι | ται ∧ ‖

     ουτω | τας μανι | ας ‖ δεινον απ | ο σταξ | ει

– >   ‿ ‿ ⌣ L   ‿ ‿ ⌣ L   ‿ ‿ ⌣ –

3. και ζην | ος ταμι | ευ ‖ εσκε γον | ας | χρυσορυτ | ους ∧ ‖

     ανθηρ | ον τε μεν | ος ‖ κεινος επ | εγν | ω μανι | αις

– >   ‿ ‿ L   ‿ ‿   –⌣> –

4. αλλ α | μοιριδι | α ‖ τις δυνασ | ις δειν | α ∧]

     ψαυων | τον θεον | εν ‖ κερτομι | οις γλωσσ | αις

>   – ‿   – ⌣   – ⌣   – >   – ‿   – ⌣   – ⌣   –

III. 1. ουτ : αν νιν | ολβος | ουτ αρ | ης ου ‖ πυργος | ουχ αλ | ικτυπ | οι ∧ ‖

      ταυ : εσκε | μεν γαρ | ενθε | ους γυν ‖ αικας | ενι ι | ον τε | πυρ

‿   L   L   ‿‿   – ⌣   L   –

2. κελ : αιν | αι | ναες | εκφυγ | οι | εν ∧]

     φιλ : αυλ | ους τ | ηρεθ | ιξε | μου | σας

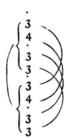

I. $\left\{\begin{array}{c} \cdot \\ 3 \\ 3 \\ \cdot \\ 3 \\ 3 \\ \cdot \end{array}\right.$ II. $\left\{\begin{array}{c} \cdot \\ 3 \\ 4 \\ \cdot \\ 3 \\ 3 \\ \cdot \\ 3 \\ 4 \\ \cdot \\ 3 \\ 3 \\ \cdot \end{array}\right.$ III. $\left.\begin{array}{c} \cdot \\ 4 \\ 4 \\ \cdot \\ 6 \end{array}\right) = \dot{\epsilon}\pi.$

SECOND STROPHE.—Periods I. and II. are logaoedic : III. is choreic.

‿ ‿ ‿   ‿‿ ⌣   ‿‿ ⌣   ‿‿ ⌣   – ‿   –

I. 1. παρα δε | κυανε | αν πελαγ | ει διδυμ | ας αλ | ος ∧ ‖

     κατα δε | τακομεν | οι μελε | οι μελε | αν παθ | αν

– >   ‿ ‿ ⌣   ‿‿ ⌣   – >   – ‿   –

2. ακται | βοσπορι | αι ιδ ο | θρηκων | αξεν | ος ∧]

     κλαιον | ματρος εχ | οντες α | νυμφευτ | ον γον | αν

$$\quad - \cup \quad \cup \cup \quad \llcorner \quad \smile\!\smile \cup \cup \; -$$

[. 1. σαλμυδ | ησσος ιν | αγχ ‖ ιπολις αρ | ης ∧ ‖

    α δε | σπερμα μεν | αρχ ‖ αιογον | ων

$$\quad > \quad - \cup \quad \cup \cup \; -$$

2. δισσ : οισι | φινεῖδ | αις ∧ ‖

    αντ : ασ ερ | εχθεῖ δ | αν

$$\quad \smile \cup \quad - \cup \quad \llcorner \quad -$$

3. ειδεν αρ | ατον | ελκ | ος ∧]

    τηλεπορ | οις δ εν | αντρ | οις

$$\quad \cup \quad - \cup \quad \llcorner \quad - \cup \quad - \cup \quad \llcorner \quad -$$

[I. 1. τυφλ : ωθεν | εξ | αγρι | ας δαμ | αρτ | ος ∧ ‖

    τραφ : η θυ | ελλ | αισιν | εν πατρ | ῳ | αις

$$\quad \cup \quad \cup\cup \cup \quad - \cup \quad - \cup \quad \smile\!\smile \cup \quad - \cup \quad -$$

2. α : λαον α | λαστορ | οισιν | ομματ | ων κυκλ | οις ∧ ‖

    βορ : εας αμ | ιππος | ορθο | ποδος υπ | ερ παγ | ου

$$\quad \cup \quad \llcorner \quad \llcorner \quad - \cup \quad - \cup \quad \llcorner \quad -$$

3. αρ : αχθ | εν | των υφ | αιματ | ηρ | αις ∧ ‖

    θε : ων | παις | αλλα | καπ εκ | ειν | ᾳ

$$\quad > \quad - \cup \quad \llcorner \quad - \cup \quad - \cup \quad \llcorner \quad -$$

4. χειρ : εσσι | και | κερκιδ | ων ακμ | αισ | ιν ∧]

    μοιρ : αι μακρ | αι | ωνες | εσχον | ω | παι

I.		II.		III.	
	6 ⎫		3		6 ⎫
	6 ⎭		2 *m.* ⎫ [*m.* = mesode.]		6 ⎬
			3 ⎭		6 ⎬
			4 = ἐπ.		6 ⎭

VII. Hyporcheme (taking the place of a Fifth Stasimon),
vv. 1115—1154.

FIRST STROPHE.—Period I. is logaoedic, except that vv. 3 and 6 have a choreic character. Per. II. is logaoedic (Pherecratics). Per. III. consists of one logaoedic and one choreic tetrapody.

$$\quad \omega \quad \smile \cup \quad - \; \breve{\;} \; - \; \breve{\;} \quad - \cup \quad \llcorner \quad -$$

I. 1. πολυ : ωνυμε | καδμει | ας νυμφ | ας αγ | αλμ | α ∧ ‖

    σε δ υπ : ερ διλοφ | ου πετρ | ας στερ | οψ οπ | ωπ | ε

$$- \cup - \cup \quad \smile\smile \cup \ -$$

2. και δι | ος βαρ | υβρεμετ | α ∧ ||

     λιγνυς | ενθα | κωρυκι | αι

$$\gtrless - \cup - \gtrless - \cup -$$

3. γεν ⁚ ος κλυτ | αν ος | αμφεπ | εις ∧ ||

     στειχ ⁚ ουσι | νυμφαι | βακχιδ | ες

$$\smile\cup - \cup \quad \llcorner -$$

4. ιταλι | αν μεδ | εις | δε ∧ ||

     κασταλι | ας τε | ναμ | α

$$- \gtrless - \cup \quad \smile\smile \cup -$$

5. παγκοιν | οις ελ | ευσινι | ας* ∧ ||

     και σε | νυσαι | ων ορε | ων

$$> \llcorner \llcorner - > \llcorner -$$

6. δη ⁚ ους | εν | κολποις | βακχευ | βακχ | αν ∧]

     κισσ ⁚ ηρ | εις | οχθαι | χλωρα τ | ακτ | α

II.

$$\cup \quad \smile\smile \cup - > -$$

1. ο ⁚ ματροπολ | ιν θηβ | αν ∧ ||

     πολ ⁚ υσταφυλ | ος πεμπ | ει

$$- \cup \quad \smile\smile \cup \ -$$

2. ναιετ | ων παρ υγρ | ον ∧]

     αβροτ | ων επε | ων

III.

$$- > - > \smile\smile \cup - \cup - \cup - \cup \llcorner -$$

ισμην | ου ρειθρ | ον τ αγρι | ου τ επ || ι σπορ | ᾳ δρακ | οντ | ος /

     εναξ | οντων | θηβαϊ | ας επ || ισκοπ | ουντ αγ | υι | ας

* The first ι of Ἐλευσινίας is here shortened, as in *Hom. hymn. Ce*
Ἐλευσῖνίδαο θύγατρες, *ib.* 266 παῖδες Ἐλευσινίων. The metre forbids us to su
that the ι is long, and that ιας form one syll. by synizesis. Vergil avoids th
using the form *Eleusinus* (*G.* 1. 163).

SECOND STROPHE (forming a single period).—Logaoedic and Choreic.

$$\overset{\geq}{\underset{\smile}{}} \; \llcorner \; \llcorner \quad \llcorner \quad \llcorner \quad - \smile \quad - \overset{\smile}{} \quad \overset{\smile}{\smile} \smile \; -$$

1. ταν ⋮ εκ | πασ | αν | τιμ ‖ ας υπ | ερτατ | αν πολε | ων Λ ‖
   ι ⋮ ω | πυρ | πνει | οντ ‖ ων χορ | αγ αστρ | ων νυχι | ων

$$- \smile \quad - \smile \quad - \smile \; -$$

2. ματρι | συν κερ | αυνι | ᾳ Λ ‖
   φθεγματ | ων επ | ισκοπ | ε

$$- \overset{\smile}{} \quad \overset{\smile}{\smile} \smile \quad \overset{\smile}{\smile} \smile \; -$$

3. και νυν | ως βιαι | ας εχετ | αι Λ ‖
   ται δι | ος γενεθλ | ον προφαν | ηθ

$$- \; > \quad \overset{\smile}{\smile} \smile \quad \smile \smile \smile \; -$$

4. πανδαμ | ος πολις | επι νοσ | ου Λ ‖
   ωναξ | σαις αμα | περιπολ | οις

$$\overset{\geq}{} \; - \smile \quad - \smile \quad \overset{\smile}{\smile} \smile \; \llcorner \quad - \smile \quad - \smile \quad - \; > \; -$$

5. μολ ⋮ ειν καθ | αρσι | ῳ ποδι | παρν ‖ ασι | αν υπ | ερ κλιτ | υν Λ ‖
   θυι ⋮ αισιν | αι σε | μαινομεν | αι ‖ παννυχ | οι χορ | ευουσ | ι

$$\overset{\smile}{\smile} \smile \; - \smile \quad \llcorner \quad -$$

6. η στονο | εντα | πορθμ | ον Λ ‖
   τον ταμι | αν ι | ακχ | ον

[The brackets on the left side show that the group formed by verses 1 and 2 corresponds with the group formed by vv. 5 and 6, while v. 3 corresponds with v. 4. Parts of vv. 1 and 2 correspond with parts of 5 and 6, as shown by the curves on the right.]

VIII. Kommos, vv. 1261—1347.

FIRST STROPHE.—Dochmiac.

$$-\,-$$

, 1. ιω
    ιω

2. φρεν ⋮ ων δυσφρον | ων αμ ‖ αρτηματ | α ⋀ ‖
     ι ⋮ ω δυσκαθ | αρτος ‖ αιδου λιμ | ην

3. στερ ⋮ εα θανατο | εντ ⋀ ‖
     τι μ ⋮ αρα τι μ ολεκ | εις

4. ω κτανοντ | ας τε και ‖
     ω κακαγγ | ελτα μοι

5. θαν ⋮ οντας βλεπ | οντες ‖ εμφυλι | ους ⋀ ⟧
     προ ⋮ πεμψας αχ | η τιν ‖ α θροεις λογ | ον

II. 1. ω ⋮ μοι εμων αν | ολβα ‖ βουλευματ | ων ⋀ ‖
      αι ⋮ αι ολωλοτ | ανδρ επ ‖ εξειργασ | ω

2. ι ⋮ ω παι νε | ος νε ‖ ῳ ξυν μορ | ῳ ⋀ ⟧
     τι ⋮ φης ω παι* | τινα λεγ ‖ εις μοι νε | ον

3. αιαι αιαι
    αιαι αιαι

III. 1. ε ⋮ θανες απελυθ | ης ⋀ ‖
      σφαγ ⋮ ιον επ ολεθρ | ῳ

2. εμ ⋮ αις ουδε | σαισι ‖ δυσβουλι | αις ⋀ ⟧
     γυν ⋮ αικειον | αμφι ‖ κεισθαι μορ | ον

---

* παῖ is here an 'irrational' long syllable, substituted for the normal short, as was sometimes allowed in this place of the dochmiac: cp. Fourth Strophe, v. 3: Aesch.

Eum. 266 φὲρ ⋮ οῑμᾶν βοσκ | ᾶν, and see Schmidt's *Rhythmic and Metric*, p. 77. Here, some read conjecturally, τί φής, ὦ τίν' αὖ λέγεις μοι νέον. See cr. n. on 1289.

I.

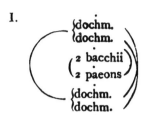

The exclamation Ἰώ, at the beginning, is marked (for clearness sake) as verse 1, but is outside of the rhythmical structure, as οἴμοι in the Second Strophe, and αἶαῖ αἶαῖ in the Third. Verse 2, a dochmiac dimeter, answers to verse 5. Verse 3 answers to v. 4. Hence, as Schmidt points out (*Rhyth. and Metr.*, p. 190), verse 3 must be regarded as a bacchic dipodia (the bacchius = ⏑ – –), shortened at the end (or 'catalectic'). The symbol ‾‿ denotes a pause equal in time-value to – ⏑. Verse 4 consists of two paeons of the 'cretic' form (cp. *Rhythm. and Metric*, p. 27).

II.

$\left.\begin{matrix} \text{{dochm.} \\ \text{{dochm.} \\ \text{{dochm.} \\ \text{{dochm.} \end{matrix}\right)$

III.

$\left.\begin{matrix} \text{dochm.} \\ \text{dochm. } m. \\ \text{dochm.} \end{matrix}\right)$ [*m.* = mesode.]

SECOND STROPHE (forming a single period).—Dochmiac, varied by iambic trimeters.

1.   — —
    οἰμοι

    οιμοι

2.   ⏑ — ⏑ — ⏑̲   — ⏑ —   ⏑   — ⏑ —
   εχ ⋮ ω μαθων δειλ | αιος εν δ εμ | ῳ καρᾳ ‿ ‖
   κακ ⋮ ον τοδ αλλο | δευτερον βλεπ | ω ταλας

3.   ⏑ ⏝̲ ⏝   ⏝ ⏑   ⏝ ⏑̲ ⏑   —
   θε ⋮ ος τοτ αρα | τοτε μεγ ‖ α βαρος μ εχ | ων ‿ ‖
   τις ⋮ αρα τις με | ποτμος ‖ ετι περιμεν | ει

4.   — ⏑ — ⏝̆   — ⏑ — ⏑   —
   ε ⋮ παισεν εν δ ε | σεισεν αγρι | αις οδοις ‿ ‖
   εχ ⋮ ω μεν εν χειρ | εσσιν αρτι | ως τεκνον

5.   ⏝̆ ⌐   — ⏑   — ⏑   — ⏑   — ⏑   —
   οιμ ⋮ οι | λακπατ | ητον | αντρεπ | ων χαρ | αν ‿ ‖
   ταλ ⋮ ας | τον δ εν | αντα | προσβλεπ | ω νεκρ | ον

6.   >   — — ⏑   — ⏑   — ⏑   —
   φευ ⋮ φευ ω πον | οι βροτ ‖ ων δυσπον | οι ‿]
   φευ ⋮ φευ ματερ | αθλι ‖ α φευ τεκν | ον

Schmidt observes that verse 5 cannot be regarded as a dochmius followed by a choreic tripody, *i.e.*, > ⁚ – – ◡ | – ◡ ‖ – ◡ | – ◡ | – ◡ | – ⋏ ‖. Such a verse would be wholly unrhythmical. Nor, again, can it be a dochmiac dimeter, since the second dochmius (ἀντρέπων χαράν) would be of an unexampled form, ◡ – – ◡ | – ⋏ ‖. He considers it, then, to be simply an iambic trimeter, with one lyric feature introduced, viz., the pause (equiv. to – ◡) on the second syllable of οἴμοι. This 'melic iambic trimeter' forms a mesode, while the dochmiac dimeters (vv. 3 and 6) correspond. The two regular iambic trimeters (vv. 2 and 4) do not belong to the lyric structure.

$$\left(\begin{array}{l} \text{\{dochm.} \\ \text{\{dochm.} \\ \quad\dot{6} \\ \text{\{dochm.} \\ \text{\{dochm.} \end{array} \right)$$

THIRD STROPHE.—Dochmiac.

I. 1. αιαι αιαι

     ιτω ιτω

     ◡   –   –   ◡   – ◡   –   –   ◡   –

2. αν ⁚ επταν φοβ | ῳ τι μ ‖ ουκ ανται | αν ⋏ ‖

   φαν ⁚ ητω μορ | ων ο ‖ καλλιστ εχ | ων

     ◡   –   –   ◡   –   ◡   –   – ◡   –

3. ε ⁚ παισεν τις | αμφι ‖ θηκτῳ ξιφ | ει ⋏ ⟧

   εμ ⁚ οι τερμι | αν αγ ‖ ων αμερ | αν

      >   ◡◡ ◡◡ ◡   –

II. 1. δειλ ⁚ αιος εγω αι | αι ⋏ ‖

     υπ ⁚ ατος ιτω ιτ | ω

      >   – –   ◡   – ◡   – – ◡ –

2. δειλ ⁚ αιᾳ δε | συγκε ‖ κραμαι δυ | ᾳ ⋏ ⟧

   οπ ⁚ ως μηκετ | αμαρ ‖ αλλ εισιδ | ω

I.   II.

$$\left(\begin{array}{l} \text{\{dochm.} \\ \text{\{dochm.} \\ \text{\{dochm.} \\ \text{\{dochm.} \end{array} \right)$$ $$\left. \begin{array}{l} \text{dochm.} \\ \text{dochm. } m. \\ \text{dochm.} \end{array} \right)$$ [*m.* = mesode.]

FOURTH STROPHE.—A single period.   Dochmiac.

1. ω ⋮ μοι μοι ταδ | ουκ επ ‖ αλλον βροτ | ων ⋀ ‖
    αγ ⋮ οιτ αν ματ | αιον ‖ ανδρ εκποδ | ων

2. ε ⋮ μας αρμοσ | ει ποτ ‖ εξ αιτι | ας ⋀ ‖
    ος ⋮ ω παι σε τ | ουχ εκ ‖ ων κατεκαν | ον

3. εγ ⋮ ω γαρ σ εγ | ω ε | κανον ω μελ | εος ⋀ ‖
    σε τ ⋮ αυ τανδ ω* | μοι μελ | εος ουδ εχ | ω

4. εγ ⋮ ω φαμ ετ | υμον ι ‖ ω προσπολ | οι ⋀ ‖
    προς ⋮ ποτερον ιδω* | πᾳ κλιθ ‖ ω ταντα | γαρ

5. αγ ⋮ ετε μ οτι ταχ | ιστ αγ ‖ ετε μ εκποδ | ων ⋀ ‖
    λεχρ ⋮ ια ταν χερ | οιν τα δ ‖ επι κρατι | μοι

6. τον ⋮ ουκ οντα | μαλλον ‖ η μηδεν | α ⋀]
    ποτμ ⋮ ος δυσκομ | ιστος ‖ εισηλατ | ο

Thus each of the six verses is a dochmiac dimeter.   In each verse the first and second dochmius answer respectively to the first and second dochmius of the next verse.

* Cp. n. on παῖ in First Strophe, Per. II., v. 2.

ΣΟΦΟΚΛΕΟΥΣ

ΑΝΤΙΓΟΝΗ

ΣΟΦΟΚΛΕΟΥΣ

ΑΝΤΙΓΟΝΗ

I.

ΑΡΙΣΤΟΦΑΝΟΥΣ ΓΡΑΜΜΑΤΙΚΟΥ ΥΠΟΘΕΣΙΣ.

'Αντιγόνη παρὰ τὴν πρόσταξιν τῆς πόλεως θάψασα τὸν Πολυνείκην
ἐφωράθη, καὶ εἰς μνημεῖον κατάγειον ἐντεθεῖσα παρὰ τοῦ Κρέοντος ἀνή-
ρηται· ἐφ' ᾗ καὶ Αἵμων δυσπαθήσας διὰ τὸν εἰς αὐτὴν ἔρωτα ξίφει ἑαυτὸν
διεχειρίσατο. ἐπὶ δὲ τῷ τούτου θανάτῳ καὶ ἡ μήτηρ Εὐρυδίκη ἑαυτὴν
ἀνεῖλε.   5

κεῖται ἡ μυθοποιία καὶ παρὰ Εὐριπίδῃ ἐν 'Αντιγόνῃ· πλὴν ἐκεῖ φωραθεῖσα μετὰ τοῦ Αἵμονος δίδοται πρὸς γάμου κοινωνίαν καὶ τέκνον τίκτει
τὸν Μαίονα.

ἡ μὲν σκηνὴ τοῦ δράματος ὑπόκειται ἐν Θήβαις ταῖς Βοιωτικαῖς. ὁ
δὲ χορὸς συνέστηκεν ἐξ ἐπιχωρίων γερόντων. προλογίζει ἡ 'Αντιγόνη· ὑπό-   10
κειται δὲ τὰ πράγματα ἐπὶ τῶν Κρέοντος βασιλείων. τὸ δὲ κεφάλαιόν
ἐστι τάφος Πολυνείκους, 'Αντιγόνης ἀναίρεσις, θάνατος Αἵμονος καὶ μόρος
Εὐρυδίκης τῆς Αἵμονος μητρός. φασὶ δὲ τὸν Σοφοκλέα ἠξιῶσθαι τῆς ἐν
Σάμῳ στρατηγίας εὐδοκιμήσαντα ἐν τῇ διδασκαλίᾳ τῆς 'Αντιγόνης. λέλεκται
δὲ τὸ δρᾶμα τοῦτο τριακοστὸν δεύτερον.   15

2 ἀνῄρηται] An aorist, not a perfect, is required: ἐφωράθη precedes, διεχειρίσατο follows. Nauck conjectures ἀνῃρέθη, Wecklein ἀνῄρησεν ἑαυτήν, which
Bellermann approves. But ἀνῄρηται, though a solecism, may nevertheless be genuine,
if the ascription of this Argument to Aristophanes is erroneous, as is now generally
held to be the case with regard to some other ὑποθέσεις which bear his name. The
use of the perfect in place of the aorist is not rare in scholia of the later age. Thus
on Thuc. 3. 68, τὴν δὲ γῆν δημοσιώσαντες ἀπεμίσθωσαν, the schol. has ἐπὶ μισθῷ
δεδώκασιν. As here we have ἐφωράθη—ἀνῄρηται—διεχειρίσατο, so on Thuc.
1. 20 the schol. gives ἐλιμωξέ ποτε ἡ 'Αττική, καὶ λύσις ἦν τῶν δεινῶν, παίδων σφαγή.
Λεὼς οὖν τις τὰς ἑαυτοῦ κόρας ἐπιδέδωκε καὶ ἀπήλλαξε τοῦ λιμοῦ τὴν πόλιν. So,
too, on Thuc. 2. 95 the schol. has ὡς δὲ οὐδὲν ἀποδέδωκε πρὸς αὐτὸν ὁ Περδίκκας
ἅπερ ὑπέσχετο, ἐστράτευσε κατ' αὐτοῦ. More on this subject may be seen in my

I—2

4   ΣΟΦΟΚΛΕΟΥΣ

Appendix to Vincent and Dickson's *Handbook of Modern Greek*, 2nd ed., p. 328 (Macmillan, 1881).   4 διεχειρίσατο L, and so most recent edd.: διαχειρίζεσθαι is thus used by Polybius, Plutarch, and others. The commoner reading here was διεχρήσατο, as in the Argument to the *Ajax* διαχρήσασθαι (where now διαχειρίσασθαι is usually read); and in the same Argument ἑαυτὸν διαχρῆται (*v.l.* διαχειρίζεται) is still generally retained.   7 μετὰ τοῦ Αἵμονος L: τῷ Αἵμονι cod. Dresd. D. 183, which may be a corruption of μετὰ τοῦτο Αἵμονι, as Bellermann thinks.   8 Μαίονα Nauck, comparing *Il.* 4. 394 Μαίων Αἱμονίδης.—αἵμονα L, and so Dindorf, who says that L has μαίδονᵃ in the margin; but it seems rather to be μαίμονᵃ.

ΑΡΙΣΤΟΦΑΝΟΥΣ ΓΡΑΜΜΑΤΙΚΟΥ] Aristophanes of Byzantium, librarian at Alexandria (flor. 200 B.C.), to whom the metrical argument for the *Oedipus Tyrannus* is also ascribed in the MSS., but incorrectly: see *Oed. Tyr.* p. 4. Though the genuineness of this prose ὑπόθεσις has not such a *prima facie* case against it as exists against that of all the metrical arguments ascribed to Aristophanes, it must at least be regarded as very doubtful. If the perfect ἀνῄρηται in line 2 is sound, it is an indication of much later age, as has been shown in the critical note above. Another such indication, I think, is the phrase εἰς μνημεῖον κατάγειον ἐντεθεῖσα παρὰ (instead of ὑπὸ) τοῦ Κρέοντος (l. 2),—a later (and modern) use of the prep. which does not surprise us in Salustius (Arg. II. l. 11 παρὰ τοῦ Κρέοντος κωλύεται), but which would be strange in the Alexandrian scholar of *circ.* 200 B.C. In the Laurentian MS. this Argument precedes, while the other two follow, the play.   6 ἐν Ἀντιγόνῃ] Only some 21 small fragments remain (about 40 verses in all), and these throw no light on the details of the plot.   8 τὸν Μαίονα. This reading is made almost certain by the mention of 'Maion, son of Haemon' in *Il.* 4. 394, coupled with the fact that L has Μαίμονα in the margin (see cr. n.). But the reading μετὰ τοῦ Αἵμονος just before is doubtful. If it is sound, then we must understand: 'having been discovered in company with Haemon, she was given in marriage (to him).' But I am strongly inclined to think that the conjecture μετὰ τοῦτο τῷ Αἵμονι (which would explain the *v.l.* τῷ Αἵμονι) is right. Dindorf differs from other interpreters in supposing that it was not Haemon, but someone else—perhaps a nameless αὐτουργός, as in the case of the Euripidean Electra—to whom Euripides married Antigone: and he reads τίκτει τὸν Αἵμονα. We have then to suppose that Antigone marked her affection for her lost lover by giving his name to her son by the αὐτουργός. At the end of the scholia in L we find these words:—Ὅτι διαφέρει τῆς Εὐριπίδου Ἀντιγόνης αὕτη, ὅτι φωραθεῖσα ἐκείνη διὰ τὸν Αἵμονος ἔρωτα ἐξεδόθη πρὸς γάμον· ἐνταῦθα δὲ τοὐναντίον. The contrast meant is between her marriage in Euripides and her death in Sophocles: but the words obviously leave it doubtful whether the person to whom Euripides married her was Haemon or not.
13 τῆς ἐν Σάμῳ στρατηγίας] The traditional στρατηγία of Sophocles, and its relation to the production of the *Antigone*, are discussed in the Introduction.   15 τριακοστὸν δεύτερον] Written λβ̄ in L. The statement seems to have been taken from Alexandrian διδασκαλίαι which gave the plays in chronological order. Sophocles is said to have exhibited for the first time in 468 B.C., *aet.* 28. See Introd.

II.

ΣΑΛΟΥΣΤΙΟΥ ΥΠΟΘΕΣΙΣ.

Τὸ μὲν δρᾶμα τῶν καλλίστων Σοφοκλέους. στασιάζεται δὲ τὰ περὶ τὴν ἡρωΐδα ἱστορούμενα καὶ τὴν ἀδελφὴν αὐτῆς Ἰσμήνην· ὁ μὲν γὰρ Ἴων ἐν τοῖς διθυράμβοις καταπρησθῆναί φησιν ἀμφοτέρας ἐν τῷ ἱερῷ τῆς Ἥρας ὑπὸ Λαοδάμαντος τοῦ Ἐτεοκλέους· Μίμνερμος δέ φησι τὴν μὲν Ἰσμήνην προσομιλοῦσαν Θεοκλυμένῳ ὑπὸ Τυδέως κατὰ Ἀθηνᾶς ἐγκέλευσιν τελευτῆσαι. 5 ταῦτα μὲν οὖν ἐστι τὰ ξένως περὶ τῶν ἡρωΐδων ἱστορούμενα. ἡ μέντοι κοινὴ δόξα σπουδαίας αὐτὰς ὑπείληφεν καὶ φιλαδέλφους δαιμονίως, ᾗ καὶ οἱ τῆς τραγῳδίας ποιηταὶ ἑπόμενοι τὰ περὶ αὐτὰς διατέθεινται. τὸ δὲ δρᾶμα τὴν ὀνομασίαν ἔσχεν ἀπὸ τῆς παρεχούσης τὴν ὑπόθεσιν Ἀντιγόνης. ὑπό-κειται δὲ ἄταφον τὸ σῶμα Πολυνείκους, καὶ Ἀντιγόνη θάπτειν αὐτὸ πειρω- 10 μένη παρὰ τοῦ Κρέοντος κωλύεται. φωραθεῖσα δὲ αὐτὴ θάπτουσα ἀπόλ-λυται. Αἵμων τε ὁ Κρέοντος ἐρῶν αὐτῆς καὶ ἀφορήτως ἔχων ἐπὶ τῇ τοιαύτῃ συμφορᾷ αὐτὸν διαχειρίζεται· ἐφ' ᾧ καὶ ἡ μήτηρ Εὐρυδίκη τελευτᾷ τὸν βίον ἀγχόνῃ.

4 Λαοδάμαντος Brunck (cp. Apollod. 3. 7. 3): Λαομέδοντος MSS.
9 τὴν ὀνομασίαν L: τὴν ἐπιγραφὴν cod. Paris.   †χούσης L (i.e. περιεχούσης): παρεχούσης Par.

ΣΑΛΟΥΣΤΙΟΥ] A rhetorician of the 5th cent. A.D.: see on *Oed. Col.*, p. 6.— In the Laurentian MS., which alone records him as the writer, this Argument stands at the end of the play, immediately after the anonymous Argument (our III.).

1 στασιάζεται, pass., 'are made subjects of dispute,' *i.e.* are told in conflicting ways, are 'discrepant': a late use of the word, which cannot be deduced from the older, though rare, active use of στασιάζω (τὴν πόλιν, etc.) as 'to involve in party strife.'   2 Ἴων] Of Chios, the poet and prose-writer, flor. *circ.* 450 B.C. His dithyrambs are occasionally mentioned (schol. on Ar. *Pax* 835 and on Apollon. Rhod. 1. 1165): it is probably from them that Athenaeus quotes (35 E): but only a few words remain.   4 Μίμνερμος] Of Smyrna, the elegiac poet, flor. *circ.* 620 B.C.   5 Θεοκλυμένῳ] The only persons of this name in Greek mythology seem to be the soothsayer in the *Odyssey* (*Od.* 15. 256 etc.), and a son of Proteus (Eur. *Helen.* 9): Wecklein suggests Ἐτεόκλῳ, an Argive who was one of the seven leaders against Thebes (*O. C.* 1316 n.).   6 ξένως] *i.e.* in a way foreign to the version followed by Sophocles.   14 ἀγχόνῃ] Eurydice kills herself with a sword (1301). Possibly ἀγχόνῃ should follow ἀπόλλυται in l. 11 (cp. Arg. III. l. 10 ἀπολομένη ἀγχόνη): but more probably it is due to a slip of memory, or to a confusion with the case of Iocasta in the *Oed. Tyr.*

III.

Ἀποθανόντα Πολυνείκη ἐν τῷ πρὸς τὸν ἀδελφὸν μονομαχίῳ Κρέων
ἄταφον ἐκβαλὼν κηρύττει μηδένα αὐτὸν θάπτειν, θάνατον τὴν ζημίαν ἀπει-
λήσας. τοῦτον Ἀντιγόνη ἡ ἀδελφὴ θάπτειν πειρᾶται. καὶ δὴ λαθοῦσα
τοὺς φύλακας ἐπιβάλλει χῶμα· οἷς ἐπαπειλεῖ θάνατον ὁ Κρέων, εἰ μὴ τὸν
5 τοῦτο δράσαντα ἐξεύροιεν. οὗτοι τὴν κόνιν τὴν ἐπιβεβλημένην καθάραντες
οὐδὲν ἧττον. ἐφρούρουν. ἐπελθοῦσα δὲ ἡ Ἀντιγόνη καὶ γυμνὸν εὑροῦσα
τὸν νεκρὸν ἀνοιμώξασα ἑαυτὴν εἰσαγγέλλει. ταύτην ὑπὸ τῶν φυλάκων παρα-
δεδομένην Κρέων καταδικάζει καὶ ζῶσαν εἰς τύμβον καθεῖρξεν. ἐπὶ τούτοις
Αἵμων, ὁ Κρέοντος υἱός, ὃς ἐμνᾶτο αὐτήν, ἀγανακτήσας ἑαυτὸν προσεπισφάζει
10 τῇ κόρῃ ἀπολομένῃ ἀγχόνῃ, Τειρεσίου ταῦτα προθεσπίσαντος· ἐφ' ᾧ λυπη-
θεῖσα Εὐρυδίκη, ἡ τοῦ Κρέοντος γαμετή, ἑαυτὴν ἀποσφάζει. καὶ τέλος θρηνεῖ
Κρέων τὸν τοῦ παιδὸς καὶ τῆς γαμετῆς θάνατον.

1 τῷ...μονομαχίῳ L: τῇ...μονομαχίᾳ vulg.

5 καθάραντες vulg., καθαίροντες L, and so most recent edd. But the present partic.
cannot stand here; the removal of the dust was not a continued or repeated act (cp.
v. 409). The form ἐκάθαρα has earlier epigraphic evidence (347 B.C.) than ἐκάθηρα:
see Meisterhans, *Gramm. Att. Inschr.* p. 86.   9 προσεπισφάζει L: ἐπισφάζει
vulg.   11 ἀποσφάζει L: κατασφάζει vulg.

---

4 ἐπιβάλλει χῶμα, because the strewing of dust on the corpse was a symbolical
sepulture: see v. 256, and n. on 10. The phrase is strange, but no emendation
seems probable.   7 ἑαυτὴν εἰσαγγέλλει, 'denounces herself': see v. 435.
10 προθεσπίσαντος: alluding to vv. 1064 ff.

ΤΑ ΤΟΥ ΔΡΑΜΑΤΟΣ ΠΡΟΣΩΠΑ.

ΑΝΤΙΓΟΝΗ.	ΑΙΜΩΝ.
ΙΣΜΗΝΗ.	ΤΕΙΡΕΣΙΑΣ.
ΧΟΡΟΣ ΘΗΒΑΙΩΝ ΓΕΡΟΝΤΩΝ.	ΑΓΓΕΛΟΣ.
ΚΡΕΩΝ.	ΕΥΡΥΔΙΚΗ.
ΦΥΛΑΞ.	ΕΞΑΓΓΕΛΟΣ.

The parts may have been cast as follows :

    1. *Protagonist.* Antigone. Teiresias. Eurydice.

    2. *Deuteragonist.* Ismene. Watcher. Haemon. Messenger. Second Messenger.

    3. *Tritagonist.* Creon.

Schneidewin gives Eurydice to the second actor, and the two Messengers to the first actor. But, as the part of Eurydice is much lighter than the combined parts of the Messengers, it is more naturally assigned to the first actor, who already bears the heaviest burden. From Demosthenes *De Falsa Legat.* § 247 it is known that the third actor played Creon.

It is a general rule of Greek Tragedy that, when the protagonist represents a woman, the Chorus represent women. The dramatic motive for the exception in this play is noticed in the Introduction.

STRUCTURE OF THE PLAY.

    1. πρόλογος, verses 1—99.
    2. πάροδος, 100—161.

    ———————

    3. ἐπεισόδιον πρῶτον, 162—331.
    4. στάσιμον πρῶτον, 332—375. Anapaests, 376—383.

    ———————

    5. ἐπεισόδιον δεύτερον, 384—581.
    6. στάσιμον δεύτερον, 582—625. Anapaests, 626—630.

    ———————

    7. ἐπεισόδιον τρίτον, 631—780.
    8. στάσιμον τρίτον, 781—800. Anapaests, 801—805.

    ———————

    9. ἐπεισόδιον τέταρτον, 806—943, beginning with a κομμός, 806—882.
    10. στάσιμον τέταρτον, 944—987.

    ———————

    11. ἐπεισόδιον πέμπτον, 988—1114.
    12. ὑπόρχημα, 1115—1154, taking the place of a fifth stasimon.

    ———————

    13. ἔξοδος, 1155—1352, including a κομμός, 1261—1347.

ΑΝΤΙΓΟΝΗ.

· Ὦ ΚΟΙΝΟΝ αὐτάδελφον Ἰσμήνης κάρα,
· ἆρ᾽ οἶσθ᾽ ὅ τι Ζεὺς τῶν ἀπ᾽ Οἰδίπου, κακῶν
· ὁποῖον οὐχὶ νῷν ἔτι ζώσαιν τελεῖ;
· οὐδὲν γὰρ οὔτ᾽ ἀλγεινὸν οὔτ᾽ ἄτης ἄτερ
· οὔτ᾽ αἰσχρὸν οὔτ᾽ ἄτιμόν ἐσθ᾽, ὁποῖον οὐ   5
· τῶν σῶν τε κἀμῶν οὐκ ὄπωπ᾽ ἐγὼ κακῶν.

L=cod. Laur. 32. 9 (first half of eleventh century). r=one or more of the
later MSS. This symbol is used where a more particular statement is unnecessary.
'MSS.,' after a reading, means that it is in all the MSS. known to the editor.
1 κοινόν] κλεινὸν Wecklein *Ars Soph. em.* 52: μοῦνον M. Schmidt.
2 ἆρ᾽ οἶσθ᾽ ὅ, τι L. For the emendations proposed here and in v. 3, see Appendix.

Scene:—*The same as in the* Oedipus
Tyrannus,—*viz., an open space before
the royal palace (once that of Oedipus) at
Thebes. The back-scene represents the
front of the palace, with three doors, of
which the central and largest (the βασί-
λειος θύρα) is that which in v. 18 is called
αὔλειοι πύλαι, as being the principal entrance to the αὐλή of the house.*

1—99 Prologue. At daybreak (v.
100) on the morning after the fall of the
two brothers and the flight of the Argives,
Antigone calls Ismene forth from the
house, in order to speak with her apart.
She tells her that Creon has forbidden the
burial of Polyneices, and declares her
resolve to perform it herself. Ismene
declines to assist, and endeavours to dissuade her. Antigone then goes alone to
the task.

1 The words κοινόν (kindred) αὐτάδελφον (very sister) form a single emphatic expression ('my sister, mine own
sister'), not a climax ('kinswoman, and
sister')—κοινόν strengthening αὐτάδελφον
much as in *O. C.* 535 κοιναί γε πατρὸς
ἀδελφεαί ('yea, very sisters of their sire').
κοινόν refers simply to birth from the same
parents (cp. 202): it will not bear the added
moral sense, 'having common interests
and feelings': that is only implied, in so far
as it may be a result of kinship. αὐτάδελφον (subst. below, 503, 696) is merely a
poetical strengthening of ἀδελφός, and
does not necessarily imply (as it might
here) what prose expresses by ἀδελφὸς ὁμο-
πάτριος καὶ ὁμομήτριος (Lys. or. 42 § 4):
thus Apollo, son of Zeus and Leto, can
address Hermes, son of Zeus and Maia,
as αὐτάδελφον αἷμα καὶ κοινοῦ πατρὸς

(Aesch. *Eum.* 89).—κάρα: the periphrasis
(as with κεφαλή) usu. implies respect,
affection, or both (cp. Horace's *tam cari
capitis*).—The pathethic emphasis of this
first line gives the key-note of the drama.
The origin which connects the sisters also
isolates them. If Ismene is not with her,
Antigone stands alone.

2 f. ἆρ᾽ οἶσθ᾽... τελεῖ; For the
various interpretations and emendations,
see Appendix. The soundness of the text
is doubtful, but no proposed correction is
probable. I read ὅ τι, pron., not ὅτι,
conjunction, and supply ἐστί. In the
direct question, τί ὁποῖον οὐ τελεῖ; we
understand ἐστί with τί. In the indirect
form, it is simplest to say οὐκ οἶδ᾽ ὅ τι οὐ
τελεῖ: and we certainly could not say,
οὐκ οἶδ᾽ ὅ τι [ἐστὶν] ὁποῖον οὐ τελεῖ, if ὅ τι
came immediately before ὁποῖον. Here,
however, the separation of ὅ τι from ὁποῖον
by Ζεὺς τῶν ἀπ᾽ Οἰδίπου κακῶν makes a
vital difference. The sentence begins as
if it were to be, ἆρ᾽ οἶσθ᾽ ὅ τι Ζεὺς οὐ
τελεῖ; But when, after an interval, ὁποῖον
comes in, the Greek hearer would think
of the direct form, τί ὁποῖον οὐ τελεῖ;
and so his ear would not be offended.
This, too, suggests the answer to the objection that Ζεύς ought to follow ὁποῖον.
Certainly Eur. *I. A.* 525, οὐκ ἔστ᾽ Ὀδυσ-
σεὺς ὅ τι σὲ κἀμὲ πημανεῖ, would be
parallel only if here we had ἆρ᾽ οἶσθα,
Ζεύς (without ὅ τι). Nor could we have
(*e.g.*) ἆρ᾽ οἶσθ᾽ ἥτις Ζεὺς τῶν νόσων ὁποίαν
οὐ τελεῖ; But, since ὅ τι might be *acc.*,
Ζεύς seems to follow it naturally; and
when, afterwards, the sentence takes a
shape which makes ὅ τι *nom.*, the ear
does not return on Ζεύς as on a misplaced

ΑΝΤΙGONE.

ISMENE, my sister, mine own dear sister, knowest thou what ill there is, of all bequeathed by Oedipus, that Zeus fulfils not for us twain while we live? Nothing painful is there, nothing fraught with ruin, no shame, no dishonour, that I have not seen in thy woes and mine.

4 2. οὔτ' ἄτης ἄτερ MSS. For the proposed emendations, see Appendix.—Paley regards vv. 4—6 as interpolated: v. 6 is suspected by Nauck.—οὐκ ὅπωπ'] εἰσόπωπ' B. Todt. The 1st hand in L wrote οὐχί (thinking of v. 3), but the letters

word, because the whole is felt as = τί Ζεὺς ὁποῖον οὐ τελεῖ;—The main objection to reading ὅτι, and taking ὁποῖον as substituted for the direct ποῖον ('that he fulfils—what not?') is the shortness of the sentence.

τῶν ἀπ' Οἰδ. κακῶν, the ills derived from Oed. (cp. Ph. 1088 λύπας τᾶς ἀπ' ἐμοῦ): i.e. the curse upon the Labdacidae (594) which he had inherited, and which be bequeathed to his children in a form intensified by his own acts,—the parricide, the incest, the imprecation upon his sons. That imprecation finds a further fulfilment in Creon's edict. ἔτι ζώσαιν does not mean, 'living wearily on,' but simply, 'still living' (not yet dead), so that ἔτι is almost pleonastic, as in 750 ἔτι ζῶσαν, and so Tr. 305. Sometimes, indeed, the use of ἔτι with ζῆν is more emphatic, as in Ai. 990 ἔτι ζῶν...ἐφίετο (while yet alive), Eur. Bacch. 8 πυρὸς ἔτι ζῶσαν φλόγα (still smouldering).

4—6 Paley (Journ. Ph. 10. 16) regards these three verses as interpolated, because (1) Antigone, like Ismene, should have only seven verses: (2) the words only repeat vv. 2, 3: (3) the double negative offends. But we have no warrant for requiring such a correspondence; and this is not repetition, but development. On (3), see below.

4 οὔτ' ἄτης ἄτερ. I translate as if οὔτ' ἄτης ἄγος (or the like) stood in the text, since there can be no doubt that such was the general sense; but I leave the traditional words, οὔτ' ἄτης ἄτερ, thinking no emendation sufficiently probable to be admitted. A discussion will be found in the Appendix. Here, the following points may be noted. (1) This seems to have been the only reading known to Didymus of Alexandria, circ. 30 B.C. (2) It certainly does not yield any tolerable sense. (3) But the phrase

ἄτης ἄτερ is not, in itself, at all suspicious: cp. Tr. 48 πημονῆς ἄτερ: Aesch. Suppl. 377 βλάβης ἄτερ, 703 ἄτερ πημάτων: Ag. 1148 κλαυμάτων ἄτερ: Th. 683 αἰσχύνης ἄτερ: Ch. 338 τί δ' ἄτερ κακῶν; Eur. Her. 841 οὐκ ἄτερ πόνων. (4) The gentlest remedy would be οὐδ' for the second οὔτ': 'nothing painful and not-free from calamity' (= nothing painful and calamitous). The mental pain was accompanied by ruin to their fortunes. I think this possible, but not quite satisfactory. (5) One word, instead of ἄτης ἄτερ, might seem desirable: I had thought of ἀτηφόρον (cp. δικηφόρος). (6) Donaldson's ἄτην ἄγον can be supported by fr. 325 ὅτῳ δ' ὄλεθρον δεινὸν ἀλήθει' ἄγει, and fr. 856. 5 ἐν κείνῃ τὸ πᾶν, | σπουδαίον, ἡσυχαῖον, ἐς βίαν ἄγον. (7) But no emendation has yet been made which, while giving a fit sense, also accounts palaeographically for ἄτης ἄτερ being so old. We cannot assume marginal glosses (as ἀτηρ) in MSS. of 30 B.C.

5 2. αἰσχρόν, shocking the moral sense: ἄτιμον, attended by outward marks of dishonour,—as Oedipus imagines his daughters exposed to slights at the public festivals (O. T. 1489 ff.). Thus αἰσχρόν in a manner balances the subjective ἀλγεινόν, as the external ἀτιμία corresponds with the ἄτη. Cp. O. T. 1283 ff.—ὁποῖον οὐ...οὐκ ὅπωπα. The repetition of the negative is warranted by the emphasis: cp. Ph. 416 οὐχ ὁ Τυδέως γόνος, | οὐδ' οὑμπολητὸς Σισύφου Λαερτίῳ, | οὐ μὴ θάνωσι: Tr. 1014 οὐ πῦρ, οὐκ ἔγχος τις ὀνήσιμον οὐκ ἐπιτρέψει; Aesch. Ag. 1634 ὃς οὐκ, ἐπειδὴ τῷδ' ἐβούλευσας μόρον, | δρᾶσαι τόδ' ἔργον οὐκ ἔτλης αὐτοκτόνως: and so oft. after οὐ μά, as El. 626. We need not, then, change οὐ (in v. 5) to ὃν, with Blaydes, nor οὐκ ὅπωπ' to εἰσόπωπ' with B. Todt.—τῶν...κακῶν, sc. ὄν, possessive (or 'partitive') gen. with

· καὶ νῦν τί τοῦτ' αὖ φασὶ πανδήμῳ πόλει
' κήρυγμα θεῖναι τὸν στρατηγὸν ἀρτίως;
' ἔχεις τι κεἰσήκουσας; ἤ σε λανθάνει
· πρὸς τοὺς φίλους στείχοντα τῶν ἐχθρῶν κακά;　　10

ΙΣΜΗΝΗ.

· ἐμοὶ μὲν οὐδεὶς μῦθος, Ἀντιγόνη, φίλων,
' οὔθ' ἡδὺς οὔτ' ἀλγεινός, ἵκετ', ἐξ ὅτου
· δυοῖν ἀδελφοῖν ἐστερήθημεν δύο,
· μιᾷ θανόντοιν ἡμέρᾳ διπλῇ χερί·
· ἐπεὶ δὲ φροῦδός ἐστιν Ἀργείων στρατὸς　　15
· ἐν νυκτὶ τῇ νῦν, οὐδὲν οἶδ' ὑπέρτερον,
· οὔτ' εὐτυχοῦσα μᾶλλον οὔτ' ἀτωμένη.

χὶ were afterwards erased.—For οὐ, Blaydes conject. ὄν.　　**10** τῶν] τάξ Blaydes.

ὄπωπα,—'which I have not seen as belonging to, being in the number of,' our woes. For the omission of ὄν cp. *O. C.* 694 ἔστιν δ' οἷον ἐγὼ γᾶς Ἀσίας οὐκ ἐπακούω.

7 αὖ is oft. thus joined with the interrogative τίς ('what *new* thing?'); cp. 1172, 1281: *O. C.* 357 νῦν δ' αὖ τίν' ἥκεις μῦθον... | φέρουσα...; *ib.* 1507 τί δ' ἐστίν...—νέορτον αὖ;—**πανδήμῳ πόλει**, the whole body of the citizens: so 1141, *El.* 982: πανδήμου στρατοῦ *Ai.* 844. For the adj. compounded with a noun cognate in sense to the subst., cp. βίος μακραίων (*O. T.* 518), εὐήρετμος πλάτα (*O. C.* 716 n.).

8 θεῖναι, not θέσθαι. τίθημι νόμον denotes simply the legislative act as such; hence it is fitting when the lawgiver is supreme or absolute; as Athena says, θεσμὸν...θήσω (Aesch. *Eum.* 484). τίθεμαι νόμον further implies the legislator's personal concern in the law; hence it is said of legislative assemblies (Ar. *Pol.* 4. 1. 9): but it can be said also of the despot, if his interest is implied: Plat. *Rep.* 338 E τίθεται δέ γε τοὺς νόμους ἑκάστη ἡ ἀρχὴ πρὸς τὸ αὑτῇ ξυμφέρον, δημοκρατία μὲν δημοκρατικούς, τυραννὶς δὲ τυραννικούς. τὸν στρατηγόν. Creon is already βασιλεὺς χώρας (155), having become so by the fact of Eteocles falling (173). She calls him στρατηγός because that was the special capacity in which, as king, he had first to act; but the title serves also to suggest rigour. The poets sometimes speak of the δῆμος as στρατός (Pind. *P.* 2. 87, Aesch. *Eum.* 566).

9 ἔχεις, *cognitum habes*: *Tr.* 318 οὐδ' ὄνομα πρός του τῶν ξυνεμπόρων ἔχεις;—κεἰσήκουσας, simply 'heard' (not, 'given heed to'), as *O. C.* 1645, *Ai.* 318, *Tr.* 351, 424.

10 τῶν ἐχθρῶν κακά, 'that evils belonging to (proper for) our enemies are coming upon our friends'; *i. e.* that our brother Polyneices is to share the doom of the Argive dead, by being left unburied. As appears from vv. 1081 ff., Soph. supposes that burial was denied to the slain foemen generally, and not to Polyneices alone. No legend was more familiar at Athens than that of Theseus recovering the Argive corpses from Creon (Eur. *Suppl.*). Cp. 1162, where, as here, ἐχθρῶν are the Argives,—the πολέμιοι in their relation to individuals. Ismene, too, seems to understand the Argives; in her reply verses 11—14 refer to φίλους, and vv. 15—17 to ἐχθρῶν. It is rare that ἐχθρῶν should have the art., while κακά has none; but cp. 365: *O. T.* 1530 τέρμα τοῦ βίου.—We might take τῶν ἐχθρῶν κακά as 'evils planned by our foes' (*i. e.* by Creon): cp. *Ph.* 422 τά γε | κείνων κάκ' ἐξήρυκε: *ib.* 512 τὸ κείνων κακόν. So schol., τὰ τῶν ἐχθρῶν μηχανήματα ἐπὶ τοὺς φίλους ἰόντα. But (*a*) the authorship of the decree having been already named, we now expect a hint of its purport: and (*b*) ἐχθροί being the natural persons to hurt φίλοι, the antithesis loses point. Some join στείχοντα τῶν ἐχθρῶν, 'coming from foes'; which is open to the objec-

And now what new edict is this of which they tell, that our Captain hath just published to all Thebes? Knowest thou aught? Hast thou heard? Or is it hidden from thee that our friends are threatened with the doom of our foes?

ISMENE.

No word of friends, Antigone, gladsome or painful, hath come to me, since we two sisters were bereft of brothers twain, killed in one day by a twofold blow; and since in this last night the Argive host hath fled, I know no more, whether my fortune be brighter, or more grievous.

13 δύο has been made from δύω in L, o being also written above.　　**14** θανόντοιν

---

tions just mentioned, and also to this, that, after such a verb as στείχειν, the simple gen. ought to denote place (*O.T.* 152 Πυθῶνος ἔβας), not agent.

11 f. μέν does not answer to the δέ in 15, but merely gives a slight emphasis to ἐμοί; cp. Xen. *Cyr.* 1. 4. 12 ἐγὼ μὲν οὐκ οἶδα (though others may know).—Ἀντιγόνη, placed as in *O. C.* 1 n., 1415; while once (*O. C.* 507) the anapaest is in the 4th place.—φίλων, objective gen. with μῦθος, tidings *about* them: cp. *Ai.* 221 ἀνδρὸς αἴθονος ἀγγελίαν: *ib.* 998 δέξαι γάρ σου βάξις. In *O. C.* 1161 f. σοῦ...μῦθον (where the gen. is objective) = 'speech *with* thee.'—ἐξ ὅτου, referring to a definite time, as 1092, *O. C.* 345, *Tr.* 326, *Ph.* 493, like ἐξ οὗ (*O. T.* 1201, *Tr.* 38, *Ai.* 661, 1337). It refers to an indefinite time below, 457. The brothers had fallen on the preceding day.

δυοῖν...δύο. The addition of δύο would have more point if two pairs were in question, each consisting of one brother and one sister (as, *e.g.*, one might say, 'the two husbands were taken from the two wives'): yet it is not pointless, since it helps to suggest the isolation of the sisters. As Greek (esp. tragic) idiom loves to mark reciprocity by a repeated word (73 φίλη...φίλου, *Ai.* 267 κοινὸς ἐν κοινοῖσι), so it also loves to mark coincidence or contrast of number, whether this is, or is not, especially relevant (cp. 14, 55, 141).

14 θανόντοιν is clearly required here, though our MSS. have θανόντων. So in *El.* 1397, where νῷν ἐπελθόντοιν is certainly right, L has ἐπελθόντων (with οι written over ω as a correction). A plur. noun can stand with δύο (*Od.* 12. 73), and in

Il. 16. 428 we have αἰγυπιοὶ γαμψώνυχες ...κλάζοντε. But I have been able to find only one proper parallel for such a combination as δυοῖν ἀδελφοῖν θανόντων, viz., a verse of an unknown poet, fr. adesp. 153 in Nauck *Trag. Frag.* p. 679 Αἴαντε δ' ὁρμήσαντες ἐκ συνωρίδος: and this has survived because Herodian cited it as a solecism (*Anecd. Boiss.* 3. 244): ἔδει γὰρ ἐπενεχθῆναι δυϊκῷ δυϊκόν. In that verse, too, the license had an obvious metrical motive, which did not exist here. Cp. 55 f. ἀδελφὼ δύο...αὐτοκτονοῦντε; 58 λελειμμένα; 62 μαχουμένα.— διπλῆ χειρί, *i.e.* each by the other's right hand (as in *O. C.* 1425 θάνατον ἐξ ἀμφοῖν = ἐξ ἀλλήλοιν): so 170 διπλῆς μοίρας, a doom given by each to the other. Cp. *El.* 206 θανάτους...διδύμαιν χειροῖν, a murder done by two right hands (that of Clytaemnestra and that of Aegisthus). Distinguish the use of the plur. διπλοῖ for δύο, as 51, 1233.

15 f. ἐπεί, temporal, 'since' (like ἐξ οὗ), as oft. in Her. and the poets. So also ὅτε (Thuc. 1. 13 ἔτη δ' ἐστί...τριακόσια...ὅτε...ἦλθε).—ἐν νυκτὶ τῇ νῦν, last night: so νυκτὸς τῆσδε *Ai.* 21 (cp. *ib.* 209): νυκτὶ τῇδε *El.* 644: while 'tonight' is τῆς ἐπιούσης νυκτός (Plat. *Crito* 46 A). The Argives, having on the preceding day lost all their leaders except Adrastus, fled shortly before dawn (cp. 100).—ὑπέρτερον here simply = πλέον (cp. *nihil supra*).—As οἶδ' εὐτυχοῦσα = οἶδ' ὅτι εὐτυχῶ, so the participles εὐτυχοῦσα and ἀτωμένη are epexegetic of οὐδὲν ὑπέρτερον, = οὔθ' ὅτι εὐτυχῶ οὔθ' ὅτι ἀτῶμαι. Of ἀτᾶσθαι we find only this pres. part. (below, 314, *Ai.* 384, Eur. *Suppl.* 182) and ἀτώμεσθα *Ai.* 269.

ΣΟΦΟΚΛΕΟΥΣ

ΑΝ. ἤδη καλῶς, καί σ' ἐκτὸς αὐλείων πυλῶν
· τοῦδ' οὕνεκ' ἐξέπεμπον, ὡς μόνη κλύοις.
ΙΣ. ' τί δ' ἔστι ; δηλοῖς γάρ τι καλχαίνουσ' ἔπος.   20
ΑΝ. ' οὐ γὰρ τάφου νῶν τὼ κασιγνήτω Κρέων
· τὸν μὲν προτίσας τὸν δ' ἀτιμάσας ἔχει ;
Ἐτεοκλέα μέν, ὡς λέγουσι, σὺν · δίκης
· *χρήσει δικαίᾳ καὶ νόμου, κατὰ χθονὸς
· ἔκρυψε, τοῖς ἔνερθεν ἔντιμον νεκροῖς·   25

Blaydes: θανόντων MSS.   18 ἤδειν L: ᾔδη Pierson.   Schol., ἀντὶ τοῦ ᾔδεα;
he therefore read ᾔδη in the text, though in his own note he writes, καὶ ᾔδειν σε

---

18 £. ᾔδη: see on *O. T.* 1525. **καλῶς** has a slightly ironical tone (*O. T.* 1008), glancing at Ismene's apathy. —**αὐλείων πυλῶν**, the outer door (or gate) of the court-yard, the αὔλειοι (or αὐλῆς) θύραι of the Homeric house (*Od.* 18. 239), in distinction from the θύραι μεγάρου, or inner door from the court into the men's hall. This was the αὔλειος θύρα, or front door, of the later Greek house, in distinction from the μέταυλος θύρα leading from the court to the inner part. The tragedians commonly use the more stately word πύλαι, rather than θύραι, for these outer doors of the palace: cp. Eur. *Helen.* 431 πύλας τε σεμνὰς ἀνδρὸς ὀλβίου τινὸς | προσῆλθον: *ib.* 438 πρὸς αὐλείοισιν ἑστηκὼς πύλαις. **ἐξέπεμπον**, 'sought to bring thee forth': the act., since she had herself fetched or called Ismene; the midd. meaning to summon by a messenger, *O. T.* 951 τί μ' ἐξεπέμψω δεῦρο τῶνδε δωμάτων; cp. on 161, 165. The imperf., because she speaks of the motive present to her mind while the act was being done: cp. *O. C.* 770 τότ' ἐξεώθεις κἀξέβαλλες, n. **20 τί δ' ἔστι;** marking surprise (*O. T.* 319 n.). **δηλοῖς** is not intransitive, the thing shown being expressed by the partic. in the nomin., just as below, 242 (cp. on 471), Thuc. 1. 21 ὁ πόλεμος οὗτος ...δηλώσει...μείζων γεγενημένος. There is a really intransitive use of δηλόω in [Andoc.] or. 4. § 12 δηλώσει δὲ ἡ τῶν συμμάχων ἔχθρα πρῶτον, etc., unless δηλώσεται should be read there; but the speech is a work of the later rhetoric (see *Attic Orators,* 1. 137). Not one of the few instances adduced from classical Greek requires δηλόω to be intransitive: Her. 2. 117 (subject τόδε): 5. 78 (ἡ

ἰσηγορίη): Plat. *Gorg.* 483 D (ἡ φύσις). In Her. 9. 68 δηλοῖ τέ μοι ὅτι πάντα... ἤρτητο..., εἰ καὶ τότε...ἔφευγον, the real subject is the clause with εἰ (the fact of their flight shows me). · **καλχαίνουσ' ἔπος τι** (for the enclitic τις placed before its noun, see on *O. C.* 280 f.), 'that thou art troubled by some tidings.' The verb is intrans., ἔπος being the 'internal,' or cognate, accus. (*Ph.* 1326 νοσεῖς τόδ' ἄλγος): for its sense cp. *O. C.* 302 τίς δ' ἔσθ' ὁ κείνῳ τοῦτο τοὖπος ἀγγελῶν; From κάλχη, the purple limpet (perh. connected with κόχλος, κόγχη), comes καλχαίνω, to make, or to be, purple: then fig., to be darkly troubled in mind: Eur. *Her.* 40 ἀμφὶ τοῖσδε καλχαίνων τέκνοις. Hence perh. **Κάλχας,** the seer who darkly broods on the future. The descent of this metaphor is curious. φυρ, the root of πορ-φύρ-ω, signified 'to be agitated,'—like heaving water, for instance (Skt. *bhur,* Lat. *ferv-ere,* Curt. § 413). In *Il.* 14. 16 ff. a man's troubled hesitation is likened to the trouble of the sea just *before* a storm, while as yet the waves are not driven either way: ὡς δ' ὅτε πορφύρῃ πέλαγος μέγα κύματι κωφῷ (not yet breaking in foam)...ὣς ὁ γέρων ὥρμαινε δαϊζόμενος κατὰ θυμόν. The Homeric image is thus subtler than that of a storm in the soul (*Volvere curarum tristes in pectore fluctus,* Lucr. 6. 34). (2) Then πορφύρω is said of the mind itself: *Il.* 21. 551 ἔστη, πολλὰ δέ οἱ κραδίη πόρφυρε μένοντι, 'was troubled.' (3) From πορφύρω, as = 'to be turbid,' came πορφύρα as = simply '*the dark*' (purple-fish and dye): and then in later Greek the verb took on the specific sense, 'to be *purple.*' (4) κάλχη = πορφύρα: and hence καλχαίνω

AN. I knew it well, and therefore sought to bring thee
beyond the gates of the court, that thou mightest hear alone.

IS. What is it? —'Tis plain that thou art brooding on some
dark tidings. ·

AN. What, hath not Creon destined our brothers, the one
to honoured burial, the other to unburied shame? Eteocles,
they say, with due observance of right and custom, he hath
laid in the earth, for his honour among the dead below.

καλῶς κ.τ.λ.   **28 f.** σὺν δίκῃ | χρησθεὶς δικαίᾳ καὶ νόμῳ MSS. (δίκαια for δικαίᾳ
R).   In the margin of L the first corrector has written δικαία (sic) κρίσει χρησάμενος.

---

is figuratively used like the Homeric πορφύρω. In πορφύρω the idea of trouble
precedes that of colour: in καλχαίνω, vice
versa.

21 f. οὐ γάρ, 'what, has not,' etc.,
introducing an indignant question, as *Ai.*
1348, *Ph.* 249. τὼ κασιγνήτω...τὸν μὲν
...τὸν δέ, partitive apposition (σχῆμα καθ'
ὅλον καὶ μέρος), the whole, which should
be in the genitive, being put in the same
case as the part,—a constr. freq. in nom.,
but rare in accus.: cp. 561: Thuc. 2. 91
δύο ὑποσχέσεις τὴν μὲν βουλόμενος ἀνα-
πρᾶξαι, τὴν δὲ αὐτὸς ἀποδοῦναι.—The
place of τάφου before τὼ κασιγνήτω
shows the first thought to have been,—
'*of a tomb*, he has deemed our two
brothers, the one *worthy*, the other
unworthy': but προτίσας, which has
taken the place of a word in the sense of
ἀξιώσας, substitutes the idea of preferring
one brother to the other. Thus τάφου is
left belonging, in strict grammar, to
ἀπροτίσας only; for the genit. with
which, cp. *O. C.* 49.—ἀτιμάσας ἔχει = a
perfect, *O. T.* 577.

28 f. σὺν δίκῃ | χρησθεὶς δικαίᾳ καὶ
νόμῳ, the reading of our MSS., was a
clumsy attempt to mend a corrupt text,
in the sense: 'having treated (him) in
accordance with righteous judgment and
usage.' The lateness of the corruption
is shown by χρησθεὶς as = χρησάμενος,
since in classical Greek χρησθῆναι is
always pass., Her. 7. 144 (the ships) οὐκ
ἐχρήσθησαν, Dem. or. 21 § 16 ἕως ἂν χρησθῇ
(ἡ ἐσθής); of oracles being delivered,
Ai. T. 604, *O. C.* 355: in Polyb. 2. 32
ἐβούλοντο συγχρήσθαι ταῖς...δυνάμεσι, συγ-
χρησθῆναι is found, indeed, in some MSS.,
but is manifestly corrupt. Several conjectures are discussed in the Appendix.
It is most improbable that vv. 23, 24
have grown out of one verse, either by
the interpolation of v. 24, or by the

expansion of v. 23. For it is evidently
essential to the contrast with vv. 26—30
that the honours paid to Eteocles should
be described with emphasis. Were v. 23
immediately followed by v. 25, the effect
would be too bald and curt. I con-
jecture σὺν δίκης | χρήσει δικαίᾳ καὶ
νόμου, 'with righteous observance of justice and usage' (νόμῳ could be retained,
but would be harsh; and the corruption
of δίκης would have caused that of νόμου].
δίκης, following σύν, was changed to
δίκῃ, and then χρήσει became χρησθείς,
in an attempt to mend the sense. σὺν
χρήσει δικαίᾳ δίκης καὶ νόμου = δίκῃ καὶ
νόμῳ δικαίως χρώμενος. For the latter,
cp. Antiphon or. 5 § 87 χρῆσθαι τῇ δίκῃ καὶ
τῷ νόμῳ. Eur. *I. A.* 316 οὐδὲν τῇ δίκῃ
χρῆσθαι θέλει. The substantival periphrasis (σὺν χρήσει τινὸς for χρώμενος τινι)
is of a common kind; *e.g.* Thuc. 2. 39
διὰ...τὴν ἐν τῇ γῇ ἐπὶ πολλὰ ἡμῶν αὐτῶν
ἐπίπεμψιν: 5. 8 ἄνευ προόψεως...αὐτῶν
(= εἰ μὴ προΐδοιε αὐτούς).—Schütz (1876,
Jahr. f. kl. Phil. p. 176) proposed
χρῆσθαι δικαίων, 'deeming it right to treat
(him) in accordance with justice,' etc.:
where, however, to supply αὐτῷ is most
awkward: I should prefer τῷ (instead of
καὶ) νόμῳ. *O. T.* 1526 is an instance in
which καὶ seems to have supplanted an
article (ταῖς) after the sense had become
obscured. But χρῆσθαι δικαίων τῷ νόμῳ
appears somewhat too prosaic and cold,
and, in so lucid a phrase, would δικαιῶν
have been likely to become δικαίᾳ?—
νόμου, of funeral rites, cp. 519: so νόμιμα
(Thuc. 3. 58), τὰ νομιζόμενα ποιεῖν (*iusta
facere*): Plut. *Sull.* 38 κηδείας τῆς νενομισ-
μένης, the usual obsequies.

26 τοῖς ἔνερθεν ἔντιμον νεκροῖς, ethic
dat., in eir sight (*O. T.* 8 πᾶσι κλεινός,
cp. *O. Ah1*446). The dead repelled the
spirit of the unburied from their converse:
Il. 23. 71 (the shade of the unburied

· τὸν δ' ἀθλίως θανόντα Πολυνείκους νέκυν,
· ἀστοῖσί φασιν ἐκκεκηρῦχθαι τὸ μὴ
· τάφῳ καλύψαι μηδὲ κωκῦσαί τινα,
· ἐᾶν δ' ἄκλαυτον, ἄταφον, οἰωνοῖς γλυκὺν
· θησαυρὸν εἰσορῶσι πρὸς χάριν βορᾶς.   30
· τοιαῦτά φασι τὸν ἀγαθὸν Κρέοντα σοὶ
· κἀμοί, λέγω γὰρ κἀμέ, κηρύξαντ' ἔχειν,
· καὶ δεῦρο νεῖσθαι ταῦτα τοῖσι μὴ εἰδόσιν
· σαφῆ προκηρύξοντα, καὶ τὸ πρᾶγμ' ἄγειν

For conjectures see comment. and Appendix. **27** φασὶν made from φησὶν L. **29** ἄταφον ἄκλαυτον (which a late hand sought to change into ἄκλαυστον) L : ἄκλαυστον ἄταφον r. **30** θησαυρὸν] ἑρμαιον Heimreich, from schol. (*Beitr.* p. 9).—εἰσορῶσι] εἰσορμῶσι is an anonymous conject. mentioned by Burton. ὡς φέρωσι Semitelos. Nauck would omit the verse. **33** τοῖς

Patroclus to Achilles) θάπτε με ὅττι τάχιστα, πύλας Ἀΐδαο περήσω. | τῆλέ με εἴργουσι ψυχαί, εἴδωλα καμόντων, | οὐδέ μέ πω μίσγεσθαι ὑπὲρ ποταμοῖο ἐῶσιν. **26 θανόντα ... Πολυνείκους νέκυν,** by enallage for θανόντος, but also with a reminiscence of the Homeric νεκύων κατατεθνηώτων: cp. 515 ὁ κατθανὼν νέκυς. **27 2. ἐκκεκηρῦχθαι** = προκεκηρῦχθαι, as in 203. The compound with ἐκ usu. ='to banish by proclamation' (*O. C.* 430 n.).—**τὸ μὴ...καλύψαι,** instead of the ordinary μὴ καλύψαι: cp. 443: *O. C.* 1739 ἀπέφυγε... | ...τὸ μὴ πίτνειν κακῶς. Though τὸ μὴ καλύψαι might be viewed as subject to ἐκκεκηρῦχθαι, the latter was probably felt as an impersonal pass. The addition of the art. to the infin. is freq. in drama: cp. 78, and *O. C.* 47 n. **29 ἐᾶν δ'.** Since τινά can mean πάντα τινά, it is not necessary to supply πάντας as subject for ἐᾶν, though in *O. T.* 238 ff. we have μήτ' ἐσδέχεσθαι μήτε προσφωνεῖν τινα,...ὠθεῖν δ' ἀπ' οἴκων πάντας.—L has ἄταφον ἄκλαυτον. For this order it may be said, that a tribrach contained in one word forms the second foot in *Ph.* 1235 πότερα, ib. 1314 πατέρα, Aesch. *Ch.* 1 χθόνιε. Also, ἄταφον thus gains a certain abrupt force, and the order corresponds with καλύψαι...κωκῦσαι. But against it we may urge:—(1) The other order was the usual one: *Il.* 22. 386 κεῖται γὰρ νήεσσι νέκυς ἄκλαυτος ἄθαπτος: Eur. *Hec.* 30 | ἄκλαυτος, ἄταφος. (2) On

such a question of order no great weight belongs to L, in which wrong transpositions of words certainly occur; *e.g. Ph.* 156, 1332: *O. C.* 1088. Here some MSS. give ἄκλαυτον ἄταφον. There is no ground for distinguishing ἄκλαυστος, as 'not to be wept,' from ἄκλαυτος, 'not wept' (see *O. T.* 361 note in Appendix on γνωτός and γνωστός). L gives the form without sigma here, as below, 847, 876, and in *O. C.* 1708; but the sigmatic form in *El.* 912. **30 θησαυρόν:** schol. ἑρμαιον, εὔρημα, taking it as merely 'treasure trove'; but here 'treasure' evidently implies 'store' (cp. *Ph.* 37 θησαύρισμα); the carrion-birds can return again and again to their feast.—**εἰσορῶσι,** when they look down upon it from the air. There is no ground for saying that εἰσορᾶν was specially 'to eye *with desire*': in Xen. *Cyr.* 5. 1. 15 οὔτε πυρὸς ἅπτομαι οὔτε τοὺς καλοὺς εἰσορῶ, it is simply 'look at.' The conjecture εἰσορμῶσι, to be taken with πρὸς χάριν βορᾶς, 'swooping *to* the joy of the feast,' is not only needless, but bad. Far finer is the picture of the birds pausing in their flight at the moment when they first *descry* the corpse below.

Take **πρὸς χάριν βορᾶς** with γλυκὺν θησαυρόν, not with εἰσορῶσι: lit., a *welcome store* to the birds, when they look upon it, *with a view to pleasure in feeding.* For the sensual use of χάρις cp. Plat. *Phaedr.* 254 A τῆς τῶν ἀφροδισίων χάριτος. **πρὸς χάριν** is used either adverbially or with a genitive. (1) As

But the hapless corpse of Polyneices—as rumour saith, it hath been published to the town that none shall entomb him or mourn, but leave unwept, unsepulchred, a welcome store for the birds, as they espy him, to feast on at will.

Such, 'tis said, is the edict that the good Creon hath set forth for thee and for me,—yes, for *me*,—and is coming hither to proclaim it clearly to those who know it not ; nor counts the matter

---

MSS.: τοῖσι Heath. **84** προκηρύξαντα L, made from προκηρύσσοντα: the first of the two σσ almost erased. προκηρύξαντα ι.—ἄγειν] ἔχειν ι, probably a mere oversight.

---

an adverb, it means literally, 'with a view to gratification': hence (a) when the χάρις is one's own, '*at pleasure*,' as Philoctetes calls the birds (*Ph.* 1156) κορέσαι στόμα πρὸς χάρω, to glut their beaks on him 'as they will': (b) when the χάρις is another's, 'so as to *give* pleasure,' '*graciously*,' as *O. T.* 1152 σὺ πρὸς χάρω μὲν οὐκ ἐρεῖς. (2) A genitive after πρὸς χάρω can denote (a) that *in which* the χάρις consists, as βορᾶς here: or (b) the person or thing *whose* the χάρις is, as below, 908, τίνος νόμου...πρὸς χάρω; 'in deference to what law?' Eur. *Med.* 538 νέμοιεν τε χρῆσθαι μὴ πρὸς ἰσχύος χάρω, 'not at the pleasure of force,'—*i.e.* not so that force can do what it pleases. Here, πρὸς χάρω βορᾶς differs from a simple χάρω βορᾶς by implying the same notion as the adverbial πρὸς χάρω in *Ph.* 1156 quoted above: 'to feast on at *their pleasure*.'—Eustathius on *Il.* 8. 379 (p. 719. 9) defines carrion-birds as τοὺς πρὸς χάρω ὁρῶσι βορᾶς τῆς ἀπὸ τῶν σαρκῶν. It cannot be doubted that he was thinking of our passage, and that his text, like ours, had εἰσορῶσι: but, using the simple ὁρῶσι, he has made a new phrase, '*looking to* pleasure in food,' and his words afford no argument for joining πρὸς χάρω with εἰσορῶσι here.

88 ἔ. σοί, like κἀμοί, depends on κηρύξαντ' ἔχειν (for which see 21). Creon's edict, addressed to all Thebans, touches the sisters first, since, as the nearest relatives of the dead, they were most concerned to see that he received burial. Antigone speaks with burning indignation. She says, in effect:—'Thus hath Creon forbidden thee and me to render the last offices to our brother.' The parenthesis λέγω γὰρ κἀμέ is prompted by the intense consciousness of a resolve.

To her, who knows her own heart, it seems wonderful that Creon should even have imagined her capable of obeying such an edict. It is a fine psychological touch, and one of the most pathetic in the play.—τὸν ἀγαθόν, ironical, as *O. T.* 385 Κρέων ὁ πιστός, *Ph.* 873 ἀγαθοὶ στρατηλάται.—λέγω γὰρ κἀμέ (instead of κἀμοί), a constr. most freq. when the acc. is a proper name, as Dem. or. 24 § 6 προσέκρουσ' ἀνθρώπῳ πονηρῷ...'Ανδροτίωνα λέγω. So *Tr.* 9, *Ph.* 1261, Aesch. *Th.* 609, Eur. *Her.* 642. On the other hand cp. Dem. or. 8 § 24 παρ' ὧν ἂν ἕκαστοι δύνωνται, τούτων τῶν τὴν 'Ασίαν ἐνοικούντων λέγω, χρήματα λαμβάνουσιν: Aesch. fr. 169 ἀλλ' 'Αντικλείας ἄσσον ἦλθε Σίσυφος, | τῆς σῆς λέγω τοι μητρός. In *Ai.* 569 where L has 'Εριβοία (*sic*) λέγω, most edd. now give the dat.

Two other explanations may be noticed. Both make σοι enclitic. (1) Taking σοι as ethic dat. with τοιαῦτα: 'There is the good Creon's proclamation for you,—aye, and for *me* too, for I count myself also amongst those forbidden' (Campbell). Thus κἀμοί is not, like σοι, a mere ethic dat., but rather a dat. of interest. Such a transition seems hardly possible. (2) Taking σοι as ethic dat. with ἀγαθόν: 'your good Creon, aye and mine, for I own I too thought him so' (Kennedy). But Antigone is too much occupied with the edict itself to dwell with such emphasis at such a moment on the disappointment which she has experienced as to Creon's amiability.

32 νείσθαι pres. (*Od.* 15. 88): Eur. has νεῖσθε (*Alc.* 737) and νεόμενος (in lyr. *El.* 723): otherwise the word is not tragic. —τοῖσι μὴ εἰδόσιν, synizesis, as 263, 535, *O. C.* 1155 ὡς μὴ εἰδότ' αὐτόν, *Tr.* 321 καὶ ξυμφορᾷ τοι μὴ εἰδέναι.

· οὐχ ὡς παρ' οὐδέν, ἀλλ' ὃς ἂν τούτων τι δρᾷ,   35
· φόνον προκεῖσθαι δημόλευστον ἐν πόλει.
οὕτως ἔχει σοι ταῦτα, καὶ δείξεις τάχα
· εἴτ' εὐγενὴς πέφυκας εἴτ' ἐσθλῶν κακή.
ΙΣ. · τί δ', ὦ ταλαῖφρον, εἰ τάδ' ἐν τούτοις, ἐγὼ
· λύουσ' ἂν ἢ 'φάπτουσα προσθείμην πλέον;   40
ΑΝ. · εἰ ξυμπονήσεις καὶ ξυνεργάσει σκόπει.
ΙΣ. · ποῖόν τι κινδύνευμα; ποῦ γνώμης ποτ' εἶ;
ΑΝ. · εἰ τὸν νεκρὸν ξὺν τῇδε κουφιεῖς χερί.
ΙΣ. · ἦ γὰρ νοεῖς θάπτειν σφ', ἀπόρρητον πόλει;

40 ἢ θάπτουσα MSS. The true ἢ 'φάπτουσα is indicated by the schol. in L, who first explains the vulgate, λύουσα τὸν νόμον καὶ θάπτουσα τὸν ἀδελφόν: and then proceeds, εἰ δὲ γρ. ἢ θάπτουσα (the θ in an erasure), ἀντὶ τοῦ, λύουσα τὸν νόμον ἢ ἐπιβεβαιοῦσα αὐτόν. Brunck restored ἢ 'φάπτουσα·—λύουσ' ἂν εἴθ'

---

35 παρ' οὐδέν: cp. 466: O. T. 983 ταῦθ' ὅτῳ | παρ' οὐδέν ἐστι. The addition of ὡς serves to mark Creon's point of view more strongly: cp. O. C. 732 ἥκω γὰρ οὐχ ὡς δρᾶν τι βουληθείς, n.—ὃς ἂν... δρᾷ, the antecedent τούτῳ being suppressed, = a dat., τῷ δρῶντι: cp. Isocr. or. 18 § 37 προσήκει βοηθεῖν ὑμᾶς οὐχ οἵτινες ἂν δυστυχεστάτους σφᾶς αὐτοὺς ἀποδείξωσιν ἀλλ' οἵτινες ἂν δικαιότερα λέγοντες φαίνωνται. That such a relative clause was felt as practically equivalent to a noun-case may be seen from Thuc. 2. 62, where it is co-ordinated with a dative: αὔχημα μὲν...καὶ δειλῷ τινι ἐγγίγνεται, καταφρόνησις δέ, ὃς ἂν καὶ γνώμῃ πιστεύῃ. Thuc. uses this constr. esp. in definitions, as 6. 14, τὸ καλῶς ἄρξαι τοῦτ' εἶναι, ὃς ἂν τὴν πατρίδα ὠφελήσῃ.

36 δημόλευστον = λευσθέντα ὑπὸ τοῦ δήμου, the epith. of the victim being transferred to the doom: Tr. 357 ὁ μιστὸς Ἰφίτου μόρος. Cp. Aesch. Ag. 1616 δημορριφεῖς...λευσίμους ἀράς. Death by public stoning would mean that the transgressor was execrated as a traitor to the commonweal: see n. on O. C. 435.—προκεῖσθαι: cp. 481: O. T. 865 νόμοι πρόκεινται.

37 f. σοι ethic dat.: so O. C. 62 and El. 761 τοιαῦτά σοι ταῦτ' ἐστίν.—ἐσθλῶν, gen. of origin with πέφυκας, from a good stock: O. T. 1062 ἐὰν τρίτης ἐγὼ | μητρὸς φανῶ τρίδουλος n. Cp. fr. 601 (race cannot be relied upon, since often) τελεται |

οὔτ' ἀπ' εὐγενέων ἐσθλὸς οὔτ' ἀχρείων | τὸ λίαν κακός.

39 ὦ ταλαῖφρον, 'my poor sister': cp. ἄνολβος (1026), δύσποτμος (O. T. 888), μέλεος, etc.—εἰ τάδ' ἐν τούτοις: cp. O. C. 1443 ταῦτα... | ...τῇδε φῦναι. The plur. ἐν τούτοις means either (1) 'in these circumstances,' as here, and Plat. Phaed. 101 C: or (2) 'meanwhile,' inter haec, as Plat. Symp. 220 B. The sing. ἐν τούτῳ usually = 'meanwhile'; more rarely 'in this case' (Thuc. 1. 37), or 'at this point' (id. 2. 8).

40 λύουσ'...ἢ 'φάπτουσα, 'by seeking to loose or to tighten the knot,'—a phrase, perhaps proverbial, for 'meddling in any way.' She can do no good by touching the tangled skein. The Greek love of antithesis naturally tended to expressions like our 'by hook or by crook,' 'by fair means or foul,' 'for love or money,' 'good or bad,' etc. Cp. 1109 οἵ τ' ὄντες οἵ τ' ἀπόντες (n.): Eur. Bacch. 800 ἀπόρῳ γε τῷδε συμπεπλέγμεθα ξένῳ, | ὃς οὔτε πάσχων οὔτε δρῶν σιγήσεται, which is plainly colloquial,—meaning 'who will not hold his peace on any terms'; for though πάσχων suits the recent imprisonment of Dionysus, δρῶν could not mean definitely, 'as a free agent.' Similarly we may suppose that some such phrase as οὔτε λύων οὔτε ἅπτων (Plat. Crat. 417 E τὸ δὲ ἅπτειν καὶ δεῖν ταὐτόν ἐστι) was familiar as = 'by no possible means.' If ἐφάπτουσα is sound,

light, but, whoso disobeys in aught, his doom is death by stoning before all the folk. Thou knowest it now; and thou wilt soon show whether thou art nobly bred, or the base daughter of a noble line.

IS. Poor sister,—and if things stand thus, what could I help to do or undo?

AN. Consider if thou wilt share the toil and the deed.

IS. In what venture? What can be thy meaning?

AN. Wilt.thou aid this hand to lift the dead?

IS. Thou wouldst bury him,—when 'tis forbidden to Thebes?

ἀττουσα Porson.   **42** τοῖ L: τοῦ r.   **48** χερί] ἄθρει or ὅρα Meineke.
44 ἦ] εἰ L, which an early hand sought to change into ἦ: η is also written above.

---

the poet has refined a colloquialism by modifying ἀττουσα into ἐφάπτουσα, just as τί δρῶν ἢ τί λέγων (cp. Aesch. *P. V.* 660) appears in *O. T.* 71 as ὅ τι | δρῶν ἢ τί φωνῶν. Some find a reference to weaving;—'by loosening the web, or fast- ening a new thread'; but, though the phrase may have been first suggested by the loom, it was probably used without any such conscious allusion. Quite different from our passage is *Ai.* 1317 εἰ μὴ ξυνά- ψων ἀλλὰ συλλύσων πάρει, 'not to em- broil the feud, but to help in solving it': cp. Eur. *Hipp.* 670 τίνας νῦν τέχνας ἔχομεν ἢ λέγους | σφαλεῖσαι κάθαμμα λύειν λόγου; 'to loose the knot of controversy.'— Another view makes the phrase refer to Creon's edict: 'seeking to undo it, or to tighten it,'—i.e. to break it, or to make it more stringent than it already is (schol. λύουσα τὸν νόμον, ἢ βεβαιοῦσα αὐτόν). But, though Antigone has not yet revealed her purpose, too great callousness is as- cribed to Ismene if she is supposed to doubt whether her sympathy is invited against or *for* such an edict.—The *act.* ἐφάπτειν is rare: *Tr.* 933 τοὔργον ὡς ἐφάψειεν, that he had imposed the deed on her (by his fierce reproaches): Pind. *O. 9.* 60 μὴ καθέλοι νιν αἰὼν πότμον ἐφά- ψαις | ὀρφανὸν γενεᾶς. Was Porson right in conjecturing εἰθ' ἀττουσα? For it, we may observe:—(1) An opposition of the simple λύειν and ἅπτειν suits a proverbial phrase: (2) ἦ and εἰ are else- where confused, as *O. C.* 980 (n.): (3) the single εἴτε is found in *O. T.* 517 λόγοισιν εἴτ' ἔργοισιν, *Tr.* 236 πατρῴας εἴτε βαρ- βάρου; Against the conjecture is the fact that εἰθ' ἀττουσα would have been much less likely to generate the ἢ θάπτουσα

of our MSS., since the intermediate εἰ θάπτουσα, being obviously unmeaning, would have been likely to cure itself.— προσθέμην: cp. *O. C.* 767 προσθέσθαι χάριν, n.—πλέον, 'for thine advantage': *O. T.* 37 οὐδὲν ἐξειδὼς πλέον, n.

41 f. ξυμπονήσεις is the more gene- ral word,—'co-operate'; ξυνεργάσει, the more explicit,—'help to accomplish the deed.'—ποῖόν τι κ., cognate acc. to the verbs in 41: cp. *O. C.* 344 κακὰ | ὑπερ- πονεῖτον, n.—Read ποῦ γνώμης...εἶ (from εἶναι): cp. *El.* 390 τοῦ ποτ' εἶ φρενῶν. The question between ποῦ and ποῖ here is one of sense, not of idiom. ποῖ γνώμης ...εἶ (from ἰέναι) would mean, 'to what thought will you have recourse?' Cp. *O. C.* 170 ποῖ τις φροντίδος ἔλθῃ; (n.), *Tr.* 705 οὐκ ἔχω...ποῖ γνώμης πέσω. But the meaning here is, 'what can you be think- ing of?'

43 f. εἰ *sc.* σκότει.—Join ξὺν τῇδε χερί: she lifts her hand.—κουφιεῖς, take up for burial: cp. *Ai.* 1410 πλευρὰς σὺν ἐμοὶ | τάσδ' ἐπικούφιζ' (the dead Ajax): and the common phrase ἀναιρεῖσθαι νεκρούς. —ἢ γὰρ marks surprise (*O. C.* 64). The absence of caesura in the first three feet allows each of the two important words (νοεῖς θάπτειν) to fall slowly from the astonished speaker's lips.—ἀπόρρητον, acc. neut. in appos. with θάπτειν σφε: Plat. *Gorg.* 507 E ἐπιθυμίας...πληροῦν, ἀνήνυτον κακόν.—πόλει, 'to' or 'for' (dat. of interest), not 'by' (dat. of agent), though the latter might be supported by Eur. *Phoen.* 1657 ἐγώ σφε θάψω, κἂν ἀπεν- νέπῃ πόλις.—σφε = αὐτόν, as 516, 1226. σφε can be s. or pl., m. or f.: νιν, s. or pl., m., f. or n.

ΑΝ. τὸν γοῦν ἐμόν, καὶ τὸν σόν, ἢν σὺ μὴ θέλῃς, 45
· ἀδελφόν· οὐ γὰρ δὴ προδοῦσ᾽ ἁλώσομαι.
ΙΣ. · ὦ σχετλία, Κρέοντος ἀντειρηκότος ;
ΑΝ. · ἀλλ᾽ οὐδὲν αὐτῷ τῶν ἐμῶν μ᾽ εἴργειν μέτα.
ΙΣ. · οἴμοι· φρόνησον, ὦ κασιγνήτη, πατὴρ
· ὡς νῷν ἀπεχθὴς δυσκλεής τ᾽ ἀπώλετο, 50
· πρὸς αὐτοφώρων ἀμπλακημάτων διπλᾶς
· ὄψεις ἀράξας αὐτὸς αὐτουργῷ χερί·
· ἔπειτα μήτηρ καὶ γυνή, διπλοῦν ἔπος,
· πλεκταῖσιν ἀρτάναισι λωβᾶται βίον·
· τρίτον δ᾽ ἀδελφὼ δύο μίαν καθ᾽ ἡμέραν 55

45 f. L points thus: τὸν γοῦν ἐμόν καὶ τὸν σόν· ἢν σὺ μὴ θέλῃς ἀδελφόν, etc.—
Benedict (*Observ. in Soph.*, Leipsic, 1820, p. 104) is followed by several edd. in
rejecting v. 46, which was already suspected in antiquity: see comment. In v. 45

---

45 f. τὸν γοῦν ἐμὸν κ.τ.λ. To the
question—'Do you really mean to bury
him?'—the simple answer would have
been, τὸν γοῦν ἐμὸν ἀδελφόν, 'I certainly
mean to bury my own brother.' But the
word ἐμόν—reminding her that he is
equally *Ismene's* brother—prompts the
insertion of the reproachful clause, καὶ
τὸν σόν, ἢν σὺ μὴ θέλῃς. Thus the contrast between τὸν ἐμόν and τὸν σόν anticipates the emphasis on the word ἀδελφόν. The whole thought is,—'I will
certainly do *my* duty,—and *thine*, if thou
wilt not,—to a *brother*.' Since ὁ ἐμός is
the same person as ὁ σός, this thought
can be poetically expressed by saying,
'I will certainly bury *my* brother,—and
thine, if thou wilt not': for the tribute
rendered to him by one sister represents
the tribute *due* from both. Remark
that γοῦν often emphasises a pers. or
possessive pron. (as here ἐμόν): 565 σοὶ
γοῦν: *Ai.* 527 πρὸς γοῦν ἐμοῦ: *O. T.*
626 τὸ γοῦν ἐμόν: *El.* 1499 τὰ γοῦν
σ᾽.—Two other versions are possible, but
less good. (1) Taking τὸν...ἐμὸν καὶ τὸν
σόν as='him who is my brother and
thine,' and ἢν as='*even* if.' But for this
we should expect τὸν γοῦν ἐμόν τε καὶ
σόν, and κἄν. (2) Taking καὶ with ἢν,
'I will bury my brother, even if thou wilt
not bury thine.' But (i) the separation
of καὶ from ἢν is abnormal: (ii) the mode
of expression would be scarcely natural
unless ὁ ἐμός and ὁ σός were different
persons.

ἀδελφόν...ἁλώσομαι. Didymus (*circ.*
30 B.C.) said this verse was condemned as
spurious 'by the commentators' (ὑπὸ τῶν
ὑπομνηματιστῶν). I believe it to be undoubtedly genuine. One modern argument against it is that Antigone should
here speak only one verse. But these
two verses express the resolve on which
the action of the play turns: it is
an important moment in the dialogue.
And, at such a moment, Soph. often
allows a stichomuthia to be broken by
two or more verses for the same speaker.
See the stichomuthia in 401—406, broken
by 404 f.: *O. T.* 356—369, broken by
366 f.: *ib.* 1000—1046, broken by 1002
f. and 1005 f.: *O. C.* 579—606, broken
by 583 f. and 599 ff. Further, verse 46 is
Sophoclean in three traits: (*a*) ἀδελφόν
emphasised by position as first word, with
a pause after it: cp. 72, 525: *O. T.* 278
δεῖξαι: *O. C.* 1628 χωρεῖν. (*b*) οὐ γὰρ δή
in rejecting an alternative: *O. T.* 576
ἐκμάνθαν᾽· οὐ γὰρ δὴ φονεὺς ἁλώσομαι.
Cp. *O. C.* 110 n. (*c*) The phrase with
the aor. part.: *Ai.* 1267 χάρις διαρρεῖ
καὶ προδοῦσ᾽ ἁλίσκεται. Lastly, v. 45.
if alone, would be too bald and
curt.

47 ὦ σχετλία, 'over-bold.' The word
primarily means 'enduring' (√σχε, σχεθ-
εῖν). Hence: (1) Of *persons*, (*a*) 'un-
flinching,' in audacity or cruelty,—the
usu. Homeric sense, as *Od.* 9. 494 σχέτλιε,
τίπτ᾽ ἐθέλεις ἐρεθιζέμεν ἄγριον ἄνδρα; So
Ph. 369, 930 ὦ σχέτλιε, Eur. *Alc.* 741

AN. I will do my part,—and thine, if thou wilt not,—to a brother. False to him will I never be found.

IS. Ah, over-bold! when Creon hath forbidden?

AN. Nay, he hath no right to keep me from mine own.

IS. Ah me! think, sister, how our father perished, amid hate and scorn, when sins bared by his own search had moved him to strike both eyes with self-blinding hand; then the mother wife, two names in one, with twisted noose did despite unto her life; and last, our two brothers in one day,—

Dindorf conject. κού τὸν σόν: M. Schmidt, τὸν καὶ σόν: Nauck, ἔγωγε τὸν ἐμόν, τὸν σόν. **48** μ' was added by Brunck, from the schol., εἴργειν με ἀπὸ τῶν ἐμῶν. **53** ἔτος] πάθος was a variant. L has ἔτος in the text, with πάθος written above by the first corrector (S). Other MSS. (as A) read πάθος in the text, with γρ. ἔτος.

σχέτλια τόλμης. (b) 'Suffering,' = τλή-μων, as Aesch. P. V. 644 (of Io), Eur. Hec. 783. Neither Homer nor Soph. has this use. (2) Of things, 'cruel,' 'wretched,'—a use common to all the poets: so Ai. 887 σχέτλια γάρ ('tis cruel'), Tr. 879.

48 οὐδέν, adv.: μέτα = μέτεστι: τῶν ἡμῶν (masc.) with ἔργειν only: cp. El. 536 ἀλλ' οὐ μετῆν αὐτοῖσι τήν γ' ἐμήν κτανεῖν. Plat. Apol. 19 c ἐμοὶ τούτων... οὐδέν μέτεστι. For the plur. cp. O. T. 1448 ὀρθῶς τῶν γε σῶν τελεῖς ὕπερ ('thou wilt meetly render the last rites to thine own,'—Iocasta).

50 νῷν ethic dat. with ἀπώλετο (cp. O. C. 81 βέβηκεν ἡμίν). ἀπεχθής, hateful to mankind for his involuntary crimes. ἀπώλετο, 'died,' not merely 'was disgraced' (cp. 59 ὀλούμεθ'): she is speaking of the deaths which had left them alone. But ἔπειτα in 53 is merely 'then,' 'in the next place,' and need not mean that Oedipus died before Iocasta. Here Soph. follows the outline of the epic version, acc. to which Oed. died at Thebes: see Introd. to Oed. Tyr. pp. xvi ff. The poet of the Odyssey (11. 275) makes him survive his consort's suicide, and no version appears to have assumed the contrary. The Antigone knows nothing of his exile from Thebes, or of the sacred honour which surrounded the close of his life, as the story is told in the later Oedipus at Colonus.

51 f. πρὸς...ἀμπλακημάτων...δράξας, 'impelled by them to strike his eyes': cp. O. T. 1236 (ἔθνηκε) πρὸς τίνος ποτ' αἰτίας:—αὐτοφώρων = ἃ αὐτὸς ἐφώρασεν (cp. fr. 768 τὰ πλεῖστα φωρῶν αἰσχρὰ

φωράσεις βροτῶν), detected by himself, when he insisted on investigating the murder of Laïus (cp. O. T. 1065). Elsewhere αὐτόφωρος = φωραθεὶς ἐπ' αὐτῷ τῷ ἔργῳ, 'taken in the act': Thuc. 6. 38 κολάζων, μὴ μόνον αὐτοφώρους (χαλεπὸν γὰρ ἐπιτυγχάνειν), ἀλλὰ καὶ ὧν βούλονται μέν, δύνανται δ' οὔ: and so in the adv. ἐπ' αὐτοφώρῳ λαμβάνειν etc.—δράξας, with the golden brooches (περόναι): O. T. 1276 ἤρασσ' ἐπαίρων βλέφαρα. — αὐτὸς αὐτουργῷ χερί, emphatic, like αὐτὸς πρὸς αὐτοῦ (1177), but not strictly pleonastic, since αὐτός = 'by his own act,' i.e. 'of his free will,' while αὐτ. χερί refers to the instrument, 'with hand turned against himself.' Cp. on 56.

53 f. διπλοῦν ἔτος, a two-fold name (for the same person): as conversely Aesch. P. V. 209 ἐμοὶ δὲ μήτηρ...Θέμις | καὶ Γαῖα, πολλῶν ὀνομάτων μορφὴ μία. Valckenär on Eur. Phoen. p. 153 cites Heracleitus Alleg. Hom. 21 (of Hera) διπλοῦν ὄνομα φύσεως καὶ συμβιώσεως, 'a name signifying at once birth and marriage' (since she was coniunx Iovis et soror). Seneca Oed. Tyr. 389 mixtumque nomen coniugis, nati, patris. (The feeble v. l. πάθος for ἔτος meant, 'a double calamity,' since both mother and wife perished.)—ἀρδάναις: cp. O. T. 1264 πλεκταῖσιν αἰώραισιν ἐμπεπλεγμένην.

55 f. δύο...μίαν: see on 13.—αὐτοκτονοῦντε is not literally, 'slaying themselves,' or 'slaying each other,' but, 'slaying with their own hands': the context explains that the person whom each so slew was his own brother. So either (1) suicide, or (2) slaying of kinsfolk, can be expressed by αὐθέντης, αὐτοκτόνος, αὐ-

αὐτοκτονοῦντε τὼ ταλαιπώρω μόρον
κοινὸν κατειργάσαντ' ἐπαλλήλοιν χεροῖν.
νῦν δ' αὖ μόνα δὴ νὼ λελειμμένα σκόπει ✓
ὅσῳ κάκιστ' ὀλούμεθ', εἰ νόμου βία
ψῆφον τυράννων ἢ κράτη παρέξιμεν.   60
ἀλλ' ἐννοεῖν χρὴ τοῦτο μὲν γυναῖχ' ὅτι
ἔφυμεν, ὡς πρὸς ἄνδρας οὐ μαχουμένα·
ἔπειτα δ' οὕνεκ' ἀρχόμεσθ' ἐκ κρεισσόνων,
καὶ ταῦτ' ἀκούειν κἄτι τῶνδ' ἀλγίονα.
ἐγὼ μὲν οὖν αἰτοῦσα τοὺς ὑπὸ χθονὸς   65
ξύγγνοιαν ἴσχειν, ὡς βιάζομαι τάδε,

56 αὐτοκτενοῦντε L, αὐτοκτενοῦντες Γ: αὐτοκτονοῦντε (sic) Coraës ad Heliod. vol. 2, p. 7.   **57** ἐπ' ἀλλήλοιν MSS.: ἐπαλλήλοιν Hermann.   In L the ' after ἐπ' and the breathing on ἁ are either from the first hand or from S.—Nauck conject. δαίοιν:

τοσφαγής, αὐτοφόνος, etc. The compound merely expresses that the deed is done with one's own hand, implying that such a use of one's own hand is unnatural. The object of the deed may be one's own life, or another's. This ambiguity of the compound is illustrated by 1175 f. αὐτόχειρ δ' αἱμάσσεται.—ΧΟ. πότερα πατρῴας ἢ πρὸσδικείας χερός; 'by his father's hand, or by is own?'

57 κατειργάσαντ', plur. verb with dual subject, as oft., even when another verb with the same subject is dual, as Xen. Cyr. 6. 1. 47 ὡς εἰδέτην...ἡσπάσαντο: Plat. Euthyd. 294 E ὅτε παιδία ἤστην ...ἠπίστασθε: see O. C. 343 n.—ἐπαλλήλοιν χεροῖν, 'with mutual hands,'—each brother lifting his hands against the other. It is hard to believe that Soph. would here have written ἐπ' ἀλλήλοιν, 'against each other,' when χεροῖν would seem a weak addition, and the double οιν would be brought into harsh relief by the independence of the two words. The verse is in every way better if we can read ἐπαλλήλοιν as an epithet of χεροῖν. Now we know that the word ἐπάλληλος was in common use at least as early as the 2nd century B.C. In the extant literature it seems always to correspond with ἐπ' ἀλλήλοις as = 'one on top of another' (Od. 23. 47 κεῖατ' ἐπ' ἀλλήλοισι), being used to mean, 'in close order' or 'in rapid sequence' (as Polyb. 11. 11 ἐν ἐπαλλήλοις τάξεσι, in close ranks: Alciphro Epp. 3. 6 τὰς ἐπαλλήλους πληγάς, the showers

of blows). An exception might, indeed, be supposed in Philo Judaeus De Mose 3. p. 692, where he is saying that the continuity of human record has been broken διὰ τὰς ἐν ὕδασι καὶ πυρὶ γενομένας συνεχεῖς καὶ ἐπαλλήλους φθοράς: which Adrian Turnebus rendered, 'propter illas eluvionum et exustionum continuas et alternas ('mutual') interneciones.' But Philo was evidently (I think) using ἐπάλληλοι in its ordinary sense, and meant merely, 'owing to the continuous and rapid succession of calamities by flood and fire.' It by no means follows, however, that a poet of the 5th cent. B.C. could not have used ἐπάλληλος in a sense corresponding with ἐπ' ἀλλήλοις as = 'against each other,'—the more frequent and familiar sense of the words, as in the Homeric ἐπ' ἀλλήλοισιν ἰόντες, ἐπ' ἀλλήλοισι φέρον πολύδακρυν Ἄρηα (Il. 3. 132): cp. Ar. Lys. 50 ἐπ' ἀλλήλοισιν αἴρεσθαι δόρυ. The use of ἐπάλληλος here may have been partly prompted by a reminiscence of Aesch. Theb. 931 ἐτελεύτασαν ὑπ' ἀλλαλοφόνοις χερσὶν ὁμοσπόροισιν (cp. Xen. Hier. 3. 8 ἀδελφοὺς... ἀλληλοφόνους).

58 νῦν δ' αὖ. Though in L δ' has been inserted by a later hand, it is found in A, and its omission by the first hand in L (which has made other such oversights) cannot weigh much against it. Some of the recent edd. omit it: but the effect of νῦν αὖ without it would here be intolerably abrupt. For αὖ ('in our

each shedding, hapless one, a kinsman's blood,—wrought out with mutual hands their common doom. And now *we* in turn—we two left all alone—think how we shall perish, more miserably than all the rest, if, in defiance of the law, we brave a king's decree or his powers. Nay, we must remember, first, that we were born women, as who should not strive with men; next, that we are ruled of the stronger, so that we must obey in these things, and in things yet sorer. I, therefore, asking the Spirits Infernal to pardon, seeing that force is put on me herein,

Semitelos, πολεμίαιν. 58 In L the first hand wrote νῦν αὖ: a later inserted δ': νῦν δ' αὖ r. 60 ἡ κράτη] καὶ κράτη Axt. 63 ἔπειτα δ' οὕνεκ'] ἐπειθ' ὁθούνεκ' Wecklein.—κρειττόνων L, with σσ written above by an early hand. 63 ℓ In

turn ') cp. 7.—μόνα δή, 'all alone': Tr. 1063 μόνη με δὴ καθεῖλε: Ai. 992 ἀπάντων δή: so esp. with superlatives, ib. 858 παρύστατον δή; Thuc. 1. 50 μεγίστη δή.

60 ψῆφον, the pebble used in voting, then, the vote; here (as below, 632) applied to the resolve or decree of an absolute monarch. Cp. O. T. 606 μή μ' ἁπλῇ κτάνῃς | ψήφῳ, διπλῇ δέ, i.e. not by thine own royal voice alone, but by mine also.—τυράννων, i.e. Creon: allusive plur., as 67: O. T. 366 n.—κράτη, the powers of the king, as 173 (cp. O. C. 392 n.). The disjunctive ἤ (for which Axt proposed καί) means: 'if we offend against this edict, or (in any way) against the royal powers.' It could not mean: 'if we infringe his edict, or (by persistence after warning) come into conflict with his power.'

61 ℓ τοῦτο μέν is not governed by ἐννοεῖν, but is adv., 'on the one hand,' answered by ἔπειτα δ' (63) instead of τοῦτο δέ, as elsewhere by τοῦτ' αὖθις (167), τοῦτ' ἄλλο (O. T. 605), εἶτα (Ph. 1346), or δέ (O. C. 441).—ὡς, with οὐ μαχουμένα, marks the intention of nature as expressed in sex,—'showing that we were not meant to strive with men.' This might be illustrated by Arist.'s phrase, βούλεται ἡ φύσις ποιεῖν τι, in regard to nature's intention or tendency (De Anim. Gen. 4. 10, etc.).

63 ℓ οὕνεκ', 'that' (as O. T. 708, O. C. 1395, and oft.): not, 'because,' as some take it, supplying χρή with ἀκούειν—ἔκ, as from the head and fount of authority; so El. 264 κἀκ τῶνδ' ἀρχόμεθ: cp. O. C. 67 n.—ἀκούειν, infin. expressing consequence ('so that we should hearken'), without ὥστε, as 1076

ληφθῆναι. We find ἀκούω τινός, 'to obey a person,' but not ἀκούω τι, as 'to hear (and obey) a command.' Here ταῦτα and ἀλγίονα are accusatives of respect, 'in regard to these things,' as πάντα in El. 340, τῶν κρατούντων ἐστὶ πάντ' ἀκουστέα, 'I must obey the rulers in all things.' If the accusatives were objective, the sense would be, 'to hear these taunts' (or, 'to be called these names'): cp. Ph. 607, Ai. 1235.

63 ℓ ἐγὼ μὲν οὖν. μέν (with no answering δέ) emphasises ἐγώ (see on 11), while οὖν has its separate force, 'therefore,' as in O. T. 483, O. C. 664. The composite μὲν οὖν ('nay rather') would be unfitting here.—τοὺς ὑπὸ χθονός, the gods below (451), and also the departed spirit of Polyneices,—which, like the spirit of the unburied Patroclus (Il. 23. 65), can have no rest till sepulture has been given to the corpse. Cp. O. C. 1775 τῷ κατὰ γῆς (Oedipus): for the allusive plur., El. 1419 ζῶσιν οἱ γᾶς ὑπαὶ κείμενοι (Agamemnon). In ref. to the nether world, Attic writers regularly join ὑπό with gen., not dat.: El. 841 ὑπὸ γαίας... ἀνάσσει: Tr. 1097 τὸν θ' ὑπὸ χθονὸς | Ἅιδου...σκύλακα: Plat. Phaedr. 249 A τὰ ὑπὸ γῆι δικαστήρια. Indeed ὑπό with dat. is altogether rare in Attic prose, except as meaning (a) under an authority, as ὑπὸ νόμοις, or (b) under a class, as Plat. Symp. 205 B αἱ ὑπὸ πάσαις ταῖς τέχναις ἐργασίαι. In poetry, Attic and other, it is freq. also in the local sense: cp. 337 ὑπ' οἰδμασιν.—βιάζομαι τάδε, pass. with cogn. acc., as 1073 βιάζονται τάδε. Cp. Ph. 1366 κἄμ' ἀναγκάσεις τάδε; and below, 219.

· τοῖς ἐν τέλει βεβῶσι πείσομαι· τὸ γὰρ
· περισσὰ πράσσειν οὐκ ἔχει νοῦν οὐδένα.
ΑΝ. οὔτ' ἂν κελεύσαιμ', οὔτ' ἄν, εἰ θέλοις ἔτι
' πράσσειν, ἐμοῦ γ' ἂν ἡδέως δρῴης μέτα.　　　70
· ἀλλ' ἴσθ' ὁποία σοι δοκεῖ· κεῖνον δ' ἐγὼ
· θάψω· καλόν μοι τοῦτο ποιούσῃ θανεῖν.
' φίλη μετ' αὐτοῦ κείσομαι, φίλου μέτα,
· ὅσια πανουργήσασ'· ἐπεὶ πλείων χρόνος
, ὃν δεῖ μ' ἀρέσκειν τοῖς κάτω τῶν ἐνθάδε.　　　75
· ἐκεῖ γὰρ ἀεὶ κείσομαι· σοὶ δ' εἰ δοκεῖ,

L the first hand wrote τὸ γὰρ | περισσὰ πράσσειν ἐμοῦ γ' ἂν ἡδέως δρῴης μέτα.
He then effaced περισσά, and added one of the omitted verses (68) in the margin, and
the other (69) in the text, between 67 and 70.　　　**70** ἐμοῦ γ'] ἐμοὶ γ' Meineke.
—ἡδέως] ἀσμένης Lehrs.—δρῴης] δρώῃς Mekler, understanding πράσσοις.　　　**71** ὁποῖά
σοι δοκεῖ L: ὁποία r.　The Schol. knew both readings: γίγνωσκε ὁποῖα σὺ θέλεις, τὸ

67 ί.　τοῖς ἐν τέλει βεβῶσι = τυράννων
in 60, i.e. Creon.　**βεβῶσι**, as *El.* 1094
μοίρα μὲν οὐκ ἐν ἐσθλᾷ | βεβῶσαν : *O. C.*
1358 ἐν πόνῳ | ταὐτῷ βεβηκώς.　Else-
where Soph. has the simple phrase : *Ai.*
1352 κλύειν...τῶν ἐν τέλει, and so *Ph.* 385,
925.　οἱ ἐν τέλει are 'those in authority,'
—τέλος meaning 'final or decisive power,'
as Thuc. 4. 118 τέλος ἔχοντες ἰόντων,
'let the envoys go as plenipotentiaries.'
Pindar's τέλος δωδεκάμηνον ('an *office* held
for a year'), *N.* 11. 10, is perh. poetical.
As synonyms for οἱ ἐν τέλει we find (1)
οἱ τὰ τέλη ἔχοντες, Thuc. 5. 47, and (2)
τὰ τέλη simply,—'the authorities,' sometimes with masc. part., as Thuc. 4. 15
ἔδοξεν αὐτοῖς...τὰ τέλη καταβάντας βουλεύειν.　Xen. *Hellen.* 6. 5 has τὰ μέγιστα τέλη, 'the highest magistrates'
(like Thuc. 1. 10 ἔξω τῶν βασιλέων καὶ
τῶν μάλιστα ἐν τέλει: cp. 2. 10).—**τὸ
γὰρ** | ...**πράσσειν**: for the art. in the
6th place, with its noun in the next v.,
cp. 78: *O. T.* 231: *O. C.* 265, 351:
Ph. 674.—**περισσά πρ.**: cp. 780: so
Tr. 617 περισσὰ δρᾶν, = πολλὰ πράττειν,
πολυπραγμονεῖν.—**οὐκ ἔχει νοῦν οὐδ.** =
ἀνόητόν ἐστι: prop. of persons, as *Tr.* 553
γυναῖκα νοῦν ἔχουσαν.

69 ί.　ἔτι, 'γα,'—at some future time:
so *El.* 66 (κἄμ' ἐπαυχῶ) ἄστρον ὣς λάμψειν ἔτι: *Tr.* 257 δουλώσειν ἔτι (he vowed
that he would *yet* enslave him).—**πράσσειν...δρῴης** (instead of πράσσοις): for
such substitution of a synonym cp. *O. T.*
54 ἄρξεις...κρατεῖς (n.): *O. C.* 1501 σαφὴς

...**ἐμφανής**.　With **δρῴης** we have a double
ἄν, the first after the negative, the second
after the emphatic **ἐμοῦ γ'**: cp. *O. T.* 339
n.—Objection has been made to **ἡδέως** 'with
the ground that it ought to mean, 'with
pleasure *to yourself.*'　Wecklein, indeed,
takes that to be the sense, supposing **γε**
to be misplaced ; *i.e.* the proper order
would have been, ἡδέως γε ἂν ἐμοῦ κ.τ.λ.:
but the position of **ἐμοῦ** in the verse sufficiently shows that **γε** must go with it.
ἐμοί γ' (Meineke) would leave **μέτα** awkward : and **ἀσμένης** (Lehrs) would not
have been displaced　y **ἡδέως**, which the
old scholia confirm.b All the difficulty
has arisen from failing to distinguish between (1) οὐκ ἂν ἡδέως δρῴης, and (2) οὐκ
ἂν μετὰ ἐμοῦ ἡδέως δρῴης.　In (1)
ἡδέως could mean only, 'agreeably to
yourself.'　But in (2) it is ambiguous ;
for the statement is equivalent to saying,
'your co-operation with me would not be
agreeable'; *i.e.* to you, or to me, or to
either of us,—as the context may imply.
Here, as the emphatic **ἐμοῦ γε** indicates,
she means ἡδέως ἐμοί.　Cp. Plat. *Rep.*
426 c ὅς...ἂν σφᾶς...ἥδιστα θεραπεύῃ,
i.e. 'whoever serves them *most acceptably*'
(not, '*most gladly*').　Ar. *Nub.* 79 πῶς
δῆτ' ἂν ἥδιστ' αὐτὸν ἐπεγείραιμι ; (*i.e.*
most pleasantly *for him*).

71　ἴσθ' from εἰμί: 'be such as thou
wilt,'—show what character thou wilt.
Cp. *Ph.* 1049 οὗ γὰρ τοιούτων δεῖ, τοιοῦτός
εἰμ' ἐγώ: ib. 1271 τοιοῦτος ἦσθα τοῖς λόγοισι:
El. 1024 ἄσκει τοιαύτη νοῦν δι' αἰῶνος μά-

will hearken to our rulers; for 'tis witless to be over-busy.

AN. I will not urge thee,—no, nor, if thou yet shouldst have the mind, wouldst thou be welcome as a worker with *me*. Nay, be what thou wilt; but I will bury him: well for me to die in doing that. I shall rest, a loved one with him whom I have loved, sinless in my crime; for I owe a longer allegiance to the dead than to the living: in that world I shall abide for ever. But if *thou* wilt,

πείθεσθαι τοῖς τυράννοις· ἢ τοιαύτη γενοῦ ὁποία βούλει. **76** aἰεί L., as in iambics *O. C.* 1530, 1532, *Tr.* 16, *El.* 305 (but made from ἀεί), 650, 917: in anapaests *Ph.* 148. But L has ἀεί (ᾱ) in iambics *O. T.* 786, 1513, *O. C.* 1584, in anapaests *El.* 218, in lyrics six times (*El.* 1242, *Ph.* 172, 717, *O. T.* 481, *O. C.* 682, *Ai.* 599).—σοὶ δ'] σὺ δ' Elms., Dindorf, Hartung.

νεω: *O. T.* 435 ἡμεῖς τοιοίδ' ἔφυμεν.—ὁποία σοι δοκεῖ = (τοιαύτη) ὁποίᾳ (or ὁποίαν) εἶναι δοκεῖ σοι, the relative being attracted into the case of the suppressed antecedent. This was the more natural since ὁποία σοι δοκεῖ, 'of any kind you please,' was felt as almost one word, ὁποιαδήποτε; just so ὅς βούλει (quivis), instead of οὗτος ὃν βούλει, Plat. *Gorg.* 517 A μήποτέ τις τῶν νῦν ἔργα τοιαῦτα ἐργάσηται οἷα τούτων ὃς βούλει εἴργασται: *Crit.* 432 A ὥσπερ αὐτὰ τὰ δέκα ἢ ὅστις βούλει ἄλλος ἀριθμός.—Those who read ἴσθ' (from οἶδα) ὁποῖά σοι δοκεῖ compare *El.* 1055 ἀλλ' εἰ σεαυτῇ τυγχάνεις δοκοῦσά τι | φρονεῖν, φρόνει τοιαῦτα. But εἰδέναι is not φρονεῖν. In Attic, ἴσθ' ὁποῖά σοι δοκεῖ could mean nothing but 'know such things as seem good to thee.' It could not mean (a) 'Have such sentiments as seem good to thee': nor (b) 'Be wise in thine own wisdom.' The Homeric phrases, πεπνυμένα εἰδώς ('wise of heart'), ἀθεμίστια εἰδώς, ἤπια οἶδε ('he has kindly feelings,' *Od.* 13. 405), etc., have no counterpart in the Attic usage of εἰδέναι. In 301 δυσσέβειαν εἰδέναι, and in *Ph.* 960 δοκοῦντος οὐδὲν εἰδέναι κακόν, the verb means simply 'to know.'

72 ξ. φίλη, emphatic by place and person: see on 46 ἀδελφόν.—φίλη...φίλον, loved by him, as he is loved by me: *Ai.* 267 ἐχθρὸς ἐν κακοῖσι: *ib.* 620 ἄφιλα παρ' ἀφίλοις.—μετ' αὐτοῦ κείσομαι, *i.e.* in the same world of the dead (76). The repetition of μετά serves to bring out the reciprocity of love more strongly: φίλη μετ' αὐτοῦ κείσομαι, μετὰ φίλου (κειμένη),— instead of the simpler φίλη μετὰ φίλου κείσομαι.

76 ξ. ὅσια πανουργήσασ': having

broken a human law in a manner which the gods permit,—viz., in order to observe a divine law. Creon uses the word πανουργίας below, 300. ὅσια is peculiarly appropriate since the word was familiar where duty to heaven was distinguished from duty to man: cp. Polyb. 23. 10 παραβῆναι καὶ τὰ πρὸς τοὺς ἀνθρώπους δίκαια καὶ τὰ πρὸς τοὺς θεοὺς ὅσια. The phrase is an ὀξύμωρον (a paradox with a point), like 'splendide mendax'; *i.e.* the qualification (ὅσια) seems contrary to the essence of the thing qualified. Cp. Milton (*Tetrachordon*), 'Men of the most renowned virtue have sometimes by transgressing most truly kept the law'; which is not an oxymoron, because the words, 'most truly,' suggest an explanation by showing that 'kept' is not used in its ordinary sense.—ἐπεὶ κ.τ.λ.: (I will obey gods rather than men), *for* the other world is more to me than this.—τῶν ἐνθάδε = ἢ τοῖς ἐνθάδε: *O. C.* 567 τῆς ἐς αὔριον | οὐδὲν πλέον μοι σοῦ (= ἢ σοί) μέτεστιν ἡμέρας (n.).

76 ξ. κείσομαι, though we have had the word in 73. For other examples of such repetition, see n. on *O. C.* 554, and cp. below 163 ὤρθωσαν, 167 ὤρθου: 207 ἐκ γ' ἐμοῦ, 210 ἐξ ἐμοῦ: 613, 618 (ἕρπει): 614, 625 (ἐκτὸς ἄτας).—σοὶ δ' is better than Elmsley's σὺ δ', since the primary contrast is between their points of view: 'if it seems right *to thee*, dishonour the dead,' rather than, 'do *thou*, if it seems right, dishonour the dead.' Remark, too, that the simple εἰ δοκεῖ (without dat. of pron.) is usually a polite formula, 'if it is pleasing to you (as well as to me)': *Ph.* 526 ἀλλ' εἰ δοκεῖ, πλέωμεν: *ib.* 645 ἀλλ' εἰ δοκεῖ, χωρῶμεν: *ib.* 1402 εἰ δοκεῖ, στείχωμεν.—τὰ τῶν θεῶν ἔντιμα, the honoured

τὰ τῶν θεῶν ἔντιμ' ἀτιμάσασ' ἔχε.

ΙΣ. ἐγὼ μὲν οὐκ ἄτιμα ποιοῦμαι, τὸ δὲ
βίᾳ πολιτῶν δρᾶν ἔφυν ἀμήχανος.

ΑΝ. σὺ μὲν τάδ' ἂν προύχοι'· ἐγὼ δὲ δὴ τάφον   80
χώσουσ' ἀδελφῷ φιλτάτῳ πορεύσομαι.

ΙΣ. οἴμοι ταλαίνης, ὡς ὑπερδέδοικά σου.

ΑΝ. μὴ 'μοῦ προτάρβει· τὸν σὸν ἐξόρθου πότμον.

ΙΣ. ἀλλ' οὖν προμηνύσῃς γε τοῦτο μηδενὶ
τοὔργον, κρυφῇ δὲ κεῦθε, σὺν δ' αὕτως ἐγώ.   85

ΑΝ. οἴμοι, καταύδα· πολλὸν ἐχθίων ἔσει
σιγῶσ', ἐὰν μὴ πᾶσι κηρύξῃς τάδε.

ΙΣ. θερμὴν ἐπὶ ψυχροῖσι καρδίαν ἔχεις.

ΑΝ. ἀλλ' οἶδ' ἀρέσκουσ' οἷς μάλισθ' ἀδεῖν με χρή.

---

78 Between μέν and οὐκ L has an erasure of some letters (οὖν?).   **83** μὴ μου προτάρβει MSS.   μὴ 'μοῦ Schaefer, Donaldson, M. Seyffert: μὴ ἐμοῦ Nauck, Wecklein.—πότμον] In L, S has written γρ. βίον above; some of the later MSS. read βίον.   **85** αὕτως MSS.: αὔτως Hermann, Bergk,

---

things of the gods; the laws which are *theirs* (454 θεῶν νόμιμα), held in honour (by them and by men). τὰ τοῖς θεοῖς ἔντιμα (25, *El.* 239 ἔντιμος τούτοις) would have presented the gods only as *observers*, not also as *authors*, of the laws.—ἀτιμάσασ' ἔχε (cp. 22), 'be guilty of dishonouring': cp. *Ai.* 588 μὴ προδοὺς ἡμᾶς γένῃ, and n. on *O. T.* 957.

78 f. ἐγώ is slightly emphasised by μέν (see on 11), which goes closely with it, and does not here answer to the following δέ.—ἄτιμα ποιοῦμαι = ἀτιμάζω: cp. *O. C.* 584 δι' οὐδενὸς ποιεῖ.—τὸ δὲ | ...δρᾶν: see on 67 τὸ γάρ | ...πράσσειν. The inf. with art. is strictly an acc. of respect ('as for the acting..., I am incapable of it'), but is practically equiv. to the simple inf., ἀμήχανος δρᾶν: see n. on *O. C.* 47 οὐδ' ἐμοί...τοὐξανιστάναι... | ...ἐστὶ θάρσος.

80 f. τάδ' ἂν προύχοιο, 'thou canst make these excuses' (sc. εἰ βούλοιο): Aesch. *Ag.* 1394 χαίροιτ' ἄν, εἰ χαίροιτ'· ἐγὼ δ' ἐπεύχομαι. For προέχεσθαι as = προφασίζεσθαι cp. Thuc. 1. 140 ὅπερ μάλιστα προύχονται. So πρόσχημα = πρόφασις (*El.* 525). —δή, 'now,' as the next thing to be done: cp. 173.—τάφον χώσουσ', prop. to raise a mound on the spot where the remains of the dead had been burned : *Il.* 7. 336 τύμβον δ' ἀμφὶ πυρὴν ἕνα χεύομεν. So *Il.* 24. 799 σῆμ' ἔχεαν,—after placing the

bones in an urn (λάρναξ), and depositing this in a grave (κάπετος). She speaks as if she hoped to give him regular sepulture. This is ultimately done by Creon's command (1203 τύμβον...χώσαντες), though the rites which Antigone herself is able to perform are only symbolical (255, 429).

82 f. Join οἴμοι ταλαίνης, 'alas for thee, unhappy one': *O. C.* 1399 οἴμοι κελεύθου τῆς τ' ἐμῆς δυσπραξίας, | οἴμοι δ' ἑταίρων: but the *nom.* when the ref. is to th° speaker, as *El.* 1143 οἴμοι τάλαινα τῆς ἐμῆς πάλαι τροφῆς.—μὴ 'μοῦ προτάρβει (or, as some write it, μὴ ἐμοῦ) is clearly right. If we read μὴ μου προτάρβει, then the emphasis is solely on the verbal notion. 'I fear for thee.'—'*Fear* not so: make thine own fate prosperous.' But the stress on τὸν σόν renders it certain that the poet intended a corresponding stress on the preceding pronoun: 'Fear not for *me*—make *thine own* fate prosperous.' And μὴ 'μοῦ is no more objectionable than μὴ 'γώ in *El.* 472. προτάρβει, as *Tr.* 89 (with gen. πατρός). Distinguish προδείσας, 'afraid beforehand,' *O. T.* 90 (n.).—ἐξόρθου here = 'straighten out,' *i.e.* guide in a straight course or prosperous course: cp. 167 ὤρθου πόλιν, 675 ὀρθουμένων.   Elsewhere ἐξορθόω is usu. 'to correct, amend' (Plat. *Tim.* 90 D); more rarely, like ἀνορθόω (*O. T.* 51), 'to set upright' (τὸ πεσόν,

be guilty of dishonouring laws which the gods have stablished in
honour.

Is. I do them no dishonour; but to defy the State,—I have
no strength for that.

— An. Such be thy plea:—I, then, will go to heap the earth
above the brother whom I love.

Is. Alas, unhappy one! How I fear for thee!

An. Fear not for me : guide thine own fate aright.

Is. At least, then, disclose this plan to none, but hide it
closely,—and so, too, will I.

An. Oh, denounce it! Thou wilt be far more hateful for thy
silence, if thou proclaim not these things to all.

Is. Thou hast a hot heart for chilling deeds.

An. I know that I please where I am most bound to please.

Ellendt, and others; see on *O. T.* 931.   **86** πολλόν] μᾶλλον Porson, and

Plat. *Legg.* 862 c). In the figurative uses
of ὀρθός and its derivatives the context
must always guide our choice between the
notion of 'upright' and that of 'straight.'
86 ξ. ἀλλ' οὖν...γε. In this combination ἀλλά is like our 'well'; οὖν = 'at
any rate' (*i.e.* if you *must* do it); and γε
emphasises the word which it follows.
Cp. *El.* 233 ἀλλ' οὖν εὐνοίᾳ γ' αὐδῶ,
'well, at any rate (*i.e.* though you will
not listen to me) it is with *good-will* that
I speak.' *Ph.* 1305.—κρυφῇ δέ: here
δέ = ἀλλά: Thuc. 4. 86 οὐκ ἐπὶ κακῷ, ἐπ'
ἐλευθερώσει δέ,—σὺν δ', adv., *sc.* κεῖσω:
cp. *Ai.* 1288 δ' ἦν ὁ πράσσων ταῦτα, σὺν
δ' ἐγὼ παρών.—αὔτως (adv. of αὐτός, see
on *O. T.* 931), in just that way—'like-
wise': *Tr.* 1040 ὧδ' αὔτως ὥς μ' ὤλεσε.
86 ξ. κατ᾽αύδα, *sc.* τὸ ἔργον, '*denounce
it.*' The word occurs only here, the pres.
used in this sense being καταγορεύω
(Thuc. 4. 68 καταγορεύει τις ξυνειδὼς τοῖς
ἐχθροῖς τὸ ἐπιβούλευμα): aor. κατεῖπον.—
πολλόν: this Ionic form occurs also *Tr.*
1196 πολλόν δ' ἀρσεν' ἐκτεμόνθ' ὁμοῦ |
ἄγριον ἔλαιον, though in no other places
of tragedy. And Soph. also used the
epic form πουλύπους in a trimeter, fr. 286
νόει πρὸς ἀνδρί, σῶμα πουλύπους ὅπως |
πέτρᾳ, κ.τ.λ. Porson on Eur. *Hec.* 618
wished to read in our verse either πλεῖον
(which is inadmissible, as Nauck observes,
Eur. Stud. 2. 27), or μᾶλλον, which some
add. receive. But πολλόν is manifestly
better than μᾶλλον.—σιγῶσ' is explained
by ἄν...τάδε, while the thought is
strengthened by πᾶσι: she is to tell the

news *to all.*

88 θερμὴν ἐπὶ ψυχροῖσι κ.τ.λ. : 'thou
hast a hot heart for chilling deeds'; *i.e.* in
thy rash enthusiasm thou art undertaking
deeds which might well chill thy soul
with a presage of death. ἐπί with dat.
here = 'with a view to' (Xen. *An.* 3. 5.
18 ἐπὶ τούτοις ἐθύσαντο): not 'in,' like
ἐπ' ἔργοις πᾶσι *O. C.* 1268 (n.). Cp. 157.
θερμήν has suggested ψυχρά, and the
thought of the *dead* has helped (cp. *O. C.*
621 νέκυς ψυχρός). In Aesch. *P. V.* 693
δείματα are said ἀμφάκει κέντρῳ ψύχειν
ψυχάν (to chill,—where Meineke's ψήχειν,
'to wear,' is improbable). Cp. Ar. *Ach.*
1191 στυγερὰ τάδε κρυερὰ πάθεα: Eur.
fr. 908 κρυερὰ Διόθεν | θανάτου πεμφθεῖσα
τελευτή. For the verbal contrast, Schütz
cp. *Ad Herenn.* 4. 15. 21 *in re frigidis-
sima cales, in ferventissima friges*, and
Hor. *A. P.* 465 *ardentem frigidus Aetnam
Insiluit.* He thinks that Ismene (hurt
by vv. 86 f.) implies, 'and a cold heart
for thy living sister,' to which Ant.
rejoins by v. 89. But θερμήν is not
'affectionate,' and Ant. seems to mean
simply, 'love and piety banish fear.'—
Some understand, 'with a view to *joyless*
things' (cp. on 650): but this would be
weak.
89 ξ. ἀδεῖν, an aor. inf. used in
Il. 3. 173, as also by Solon (fr. 7 ἔργμασιν
ἐν μεγάλοις πᾶσιν ἀδεῖν χαλεπόν), Her.,
and Pind. This is the only place in
classical Attic where any part of the aor.
ἔαδον occurs.

ΙΣ. ' εἰ καὶ δυνήσει γ'· ἀλλ' ἀμηχάνων ἐρᾷς.　　　90
ΑΝ. οὐκοῦν, ὅταν δὴ μὴ σθένω, πεπαύσομαι.
ΙΣ. ' ἀρχὴν δὲ θηρᾶν οὐ πρέπει τἀμήχανα.
ΑΝ. εἰ ταῦτα λέξεις, ἐχθαρεῖ μὲν ἐξ ἐμοῦ,
'ἐχθρὰ δὲ τῷ θανόντι προσκείσει δίκῃ.
· ἀλλ' ἔα με καὶ τὴν ἐξ ἐμοῦ δυσβουλίαν,　　　95
· παθεῖν τὸ δεινὸν τοῦτο· πείσομαι γὰρ οὐ
· τοσοῦτον οὐδὲν ὥστε μὴ οὐ καλῶς θανεῖν.
ΙΣ. · ἀλλ' εἰ δοκεῖ σοι, στεῖχε· τοῦτο δ' ἴσθ', ὅτι
· ἄνους μὲν ἔρχει, τοῖς φίλοις δ' ὀρθῶς φίλη.

---

so Nauck, Wecklein: see comment.
it.　　98 ἐχθαρεῖ] ἐχθρανῆ L, with
91 In L the first h. omitted μὴ: S added
γρ. ἐχθαρῇ from a later hand in marg.

---

90 εἰ καὶ δυνήσει γ', yes, if (besides having the wish to please them) you shall *also* have the power. καὶ goes closely with δυνήσει: cp. *O. T.* 283 εἰ καὶ τρίτ' ἐστί. Such cases must be carefully distinguished from those in which εἰ καὶ form a single expression; see *O. T.* p. 296.

91 Since οὐκοῦν ('well, then') precedes, δὴ is best taken as giving precision to ὅταν,—'so soon as.'—πεπαύσομαι, 'I will cease *forthwith*': so *Tr.* 587. Cp. the perf., *Ph.* 1279 εἰ δὲ μή τι πρὸς καιρὸν λέγων | κυρῶ, πέπαυμαι, 'I have done.'

92 ἀρχήν, adv., 'to begin with,' 'at all,'—in *negative* sentences; often placed, as here, before the negative word; *El.* 439 ἀρχὴν δ' ἂν...οὐκ ἂν...ἐπέστεφε: *Ph.* 1239 ἀρχὴν κλύειν ἂν οὐδ' ἅπαξ ἐβουλόμην: Her. 3. 39 ἔφη χαριεῖσθαι μᾶλλον ἀποδιδοὺς τὰ ἔλαβε ἢ ἀρχὴν μηδὲ λαβών. In *affirmative* sentences the art. is usu. added: Andoc. or. 3. § 20 ἐξῆν γὰρ αὐτοῖς καὶ τὴν ἀρχὴν ἐῶσιν Ὀρχομενίους αὐτονόμους εἰρήνην ἄγειν: so Isocr. or. 15 § 272.

93 ἐχθαρεῖ, pass.: so, from liquid stems, 230 ἀλγυνεῖ: *O. T.* 272 φθερεῖσθαι: *Ai.* 1155 σημανούμενος. The ' midd.' fut. in σ affords numerous examples, as below, 210, 637, 726: see n. on *O. T.* 672 and *O. C.* 1185.—ἐξ ἐμοῦ, 'on my part' (cp. 95), rather than simply ' by me ' (cp. 63).

94 ἐχθρά...τῷ θανόντι προσκείσει δίκῃ, 'thou wilt be subject to the lasting enmity of the dead.' The word προσκείσει means literally, '*wilt be attached to...*,' *i.e.*, '*wilt be brought into a lasting relation with*'; and ἐχθρά defines the nature of that rela-

tion. The sense is thus virtually the same as if we had, ὁ θανὼν ἐχθρός σοι προσκείσεται, 'the enmity of the dead will cleave to thee.' The convertible use of προσκεῖσθαι is illustrated by 1243 ἀνδρὶ προσκειται κακόν, as compared with *El.* 1040 ᾧ σὺ πρόσκεισαι κακῷ, and *ib.* 240 εἰ τῷ πρόσκειμαι χρηστῷ. Here, προσκείσει expresses merely the establishment of the permanent relation between the two persons. It does not mean, 'you will be brought, as his foe, *into dependence* on him' (*i.e.* under the power of his curse); as in Eur. *Tro.* 185 τῷ πρόσκειμαι δούλα τλάμων; 'to whom have I been assigned as a slave?' (*i.e.* by the casting of lots:— the answer is, ἐγγύς που κεῖσαι κλήρου). Nor, again, 'you will *press upon* the dead as his foe,' *i.e.* be hostile and grievous to him: for, as δίκῃ shows, the punishment is to be hers, not his. The idea might have been expressed in a converse form by τὸν θανόντα ἐχθρὸν προσθήσει (cf. Xen. *Cyr.* 2. 4. 12).

Lehrs proposed Δίκῃ, *i.e.* 'you will fall under the chastisement of justice.' Donaldson, following Emper, reads ἐχθρᾷ... δίκῃ, as *iure inimicorum apud mortuum eris: i.e.* on the part of the dead you will be deemed to have only the rights of a foe. This is impossible. The ordinary reading is sound.

95 f. ἔα, one syll. by synizesis, as *O. T.* 1451 (n.).—τὴν ἐξ ἐμοῦ δυσβ., the folly proceeding from me, the folly *on my part*, for which I bear the sole blame: *El.* 619 ἀλλ' ἡ γὰρ ἐκ σοῦ δυσμένεια καὶ τὰ σὰ | ἔργ' ἐξαναγκάζει με, 'it is the enmity on thy part,' etc. *Tr.* 631 μὴ

Is. Aye, if thou canst; but thou wouldst what thou canst not.

An. Why, then, when my strength fails, I shall have done.

Is. A hopeless quest should not be made at all.

An. If thus thou speakest, thou wilt have hatred from me, and wilt justly be subject to the lasting hatred of the dead. But leave me, and the folly that is mine alone, to suffer this dread thing; for I shall not suffer aught so dreadful as an ignoble death.

Is. Go, then, if thou must; and of this be sure,—that, though thine errand is foolish, to thy dear ones thou art truly dear.

[*Exit* ANTIGONE *on the spectators' left.* ISMENE *retires into the palace by one of the two side-doors.*

94 ἐχθρά] ἐχθρᾷ Emper, Donaldson. ἐχθρᾳ Kvičala.—δίκῃ] Δίκῃ Lehrs: κάσει Dindorf: κάτω L Dindorf. πρὸς δίκης ἐσει Herwerden (*Stud. crit.* p. 9). **96** οὐ] οὖν Elms. on Eur. *Med.* 804, M. Seyffert, Dindorf.

πρῷ λέγοις ἂν τὸν πόθον τὸν ἐξ ἐμοῦ, | πρὶν εἰδέναι τἀκεῖθεν εἰ ποθούμεθα. Cp. *O. C.* 453 n.—τὸ δεινὸν τοῦτο, ironical: cp. *El.* 376 (Electra in answer to her sister's warnings) φέρ᾽ εἰπὲ δὴ τὸ δεινόν.—πείσομαι γὰρ οὐ: for the position of the negative (which belongs to the verb, not to τοσοῦτον), cp. 223, *O. C.* 125 προσέβα γὰρ οὐκ ἄν. We still write οὐ here, not οὔ, because the sentence runs on without pause: but 255 τυμβήρης μὲν οὔ, *Ai.* 545 ταρβήσει γὰρ οὔ, since in each case a comma can follow the negative.—μὴ οὐ, not μή, because the principal verb πείσομαι is negatived: *O. T.* 283 n. She means, 'even if I have to die, at least I shall not suffer the worst of evils; which is not death, but an ignoble death.' Cp. frag. adesp. 61 οὐ κατθανεῖν γὰρ δεινόν, ἀλλ᾽ αἰσχρῶς θανεῖν.

99 τοῖς φίλοις δ᾽ ὀρθῶς φίλη, 'but truly dear to thy friends'—*i.e.* both to the dead brother and to the living sister. The words are especially a parting assurance (ἴσθι) that *Ismene's* love is undiminished. ὀρθῶς = ἀληθῶς, as Diphilus frag. incert. 20 τὸν ὀρθῶς εὐγενῆ. Others make φίλη active,—'a true friend to thy friends' (*i.e.* to Polyneices): which is certainly the fittest sense in Eur. *I. T.* 609 ὡς ἀπ᾽ εὐγενοῦς τινος | ῥίζης πέφυκας, τοῖς φίλοις τ᾽ ὀρθῶς φίλος (Orestes, when he devotes his life to save his friend's). But here the other view is decidedly preferable.

100—161 Parodos. For the metres

see Metrical Analysis. The framework is as follows. (1) *1st strophe,* 100 ἀκτὶς to 109 χαλινῷ = *1st antistrophe,* 117 στὰς to 133 ἀλαλάξαι. (2) *2nd strophe,* 134 ἀντιτύπᾳ to 140 δεξιόσειρος = *2nd antistrophe,* 148 ἀλλὰ γὰρ to 154 ἄρχοι. Each strophe and each antistrophe is followed by an anapaestic system (σύστημα) of seven verses, recited by the Coryphaeus alone, in the pauses of the choral dance. The fourth and last of these systems, following the second antistrophe, announces the approach of Creon.

The *Ajax* is the only play of Sophocles which has a Parodos beginning, in the older style, with a regular anapaestic march. But something of the same character is given to this ode by the regularity of the anapaestic systems. In the Parodos of the *O. C.*, on the other hand, though anapaests similarly divide each strophe from each antistrophe, the systems are of unequal lengths, and the general character is wholly different, being rather that of a κομμός: see n. on *O. C.* 117.

The fifteen Theban elders who form the Chorus have been summoned to the palace by Creon,—they know not, as yet, for what purpose (158). They greet the newly-risen sun, and exult in the flight of the Argives.

The ode vividly portrays the enormous sin of Polyneices against his country, and the appalling nature of the peril which Thebes has just escaped. We already

ΧΟΡΟΣ.

στρ. α΄. ἀκτὶς ἀελίου, τὸ κάλλιστον ἑπταπύλῳ φανὲν 100
· 2 Θήβᾳ τῶν προτέρων φάος,
· 3 ἐφάνθης ποτ᾽, ὦ χρυσέας
· 4 ἀμέρας βλέφαρον, Διρκαίων ὑπὲρ ῥεέθρων μολοῦσα,
· 5 τὸν λεύκασπιν, Ἀργόθεν *ἐκβάντα φῶτα πανσαγίᾳ 106
· 6 φυγάδα πρόδρομον ὀξυτέρῳ κινήσασα χαλινῷ·

100 ἀελίοιο L. The first hand wrote ἀελίου, which is also in the lemma of the scholium. An early hand then changed υ into ιο. Hence Bothe, ἀελίοιο κάλλιστον (omitting τὸ). **102** τῶν προτέρων L: τῶν πρότερον A, Brunck, Blaydes. **104** βλεφαρὶς Nauck. **106** ἀργόθεν | φῶτα βάντα MSS. A syllable is wanting (cp. 123). For Ἀργόθεν, Erfurdt

know Antigone's motive. This is a dramatic prelude to the announcement of Creon's.

100 f. ἀελίου, Dor. for the epic ἠελίου, with ᾱ as usu. (808, *O. C.* 1245), though it is sometimes used with ᾰ, as *Tr.* 835, Eur. *Med.* 1252.—τὸ κάλλιστον ...φάος. Two constructions are possible; I prefer the first. (1) Θήβᾳ φανὲν τὸ κάλλιστον φάος, the art. going with the superlative, which it emphasises,—'the very fairest,'—a common use, as Plat. *Hipp.* 289 B οὐχ ἡ καλλίστη παρθένος αἰσχρὰ φανεῖται; *Od.* 17. 415 οὐ μέν μοι δοκέεις ὁ κάκιστος Ἀχαιῶν. (2) τὸ Θήβᾳ φανὲν κάλλιστον φάος, the art. going with φανέν. This seems awkward. When a voc. is followed by a noun or partic. with art., this is normally in direct agreement with the voc., as ὦ ἄνδρες...οἱ παρόντες (Plat. *Prot.* 337 C), as if here we had ἡ φανεῖσα. The Schol., who prefers this constr., shirks the difficulty by his paraphrase, ὦ τῆς ἀκτῖνος τοῦ ἡλίου φῶς, τὸ φανὲν κ.τ.λ.— ἑπταπύλῳ; epithet of Θήβη in *Od.* 11. 263, Hes. *Op.* 161, as ἑκατόμπυλοι in *Il.* 9. 383 of Θῆβαι Αἰγύπτιαι.—τῶν προτέρων: cp. 1212 f.: Thuc. 1. 10 στρατείαν ... μεγίστην ... τῶν πρὸ αὐτῆς. Tacitus *Hist.* 1. 50 *solus omnium ante se principum.* Milton *P. L.* 4. 322 *Adam, the goodliest man of men since born, His sons, the fairest of her daughters Eve.* Goethe *Hermann und Dorothea* 5. 101 *Von ihren Schwestern die beste.*

103 f. ἐφάνθης with an echo of φανὲν (παρήχησις): cp. *O. C.* 794 στόμα, |...στόμωσιν.—χρυσέας, with ῠ as *O. T.* 157, 188. So Pind. *Pyth.* 4. 4 ἔνθα ποτὲ χρυσέων Διὸς αἰητῶν πάρεδρος. The ῠ was admitted by the lyrists, and from them borrowed by the dramatists, though only in lyrics,

and even there only occasionally. Homer never shortens the υ: for, as χρυσέῳ ἀνὰ σκήπτρῳ (*Il.* 1. 15) shows, the Homeric χρυσέῃ (etc.) must be treated as disyll. by synizesis.—βλέφαρον = ὄμμα: Eur. *Ph.* 543 νυκτὸς τ᾽ ἀφεγγὲς βλέφαρον (the moon). Cp. Job iii. 9 (Revised Version), 'neither let it behold the eyelids of the morning.'—Διρκαίων. The Dircè was on the w. of Thebes, the Ismenus on the E.: between them flowed the less famous Strophia: Callim. *Hymn Del.* 76 Δίρκη τε Στροφίη τε μελαμψήφιδος ἔχουσαι | Ἰσμηνοῦ χέρα πατρός (alluding to their common source S. of the town). Though the Ismenus, as the eastern stream, would have been more appropriately named here, the Dircè is preferred, as the representative river of Thebes: so Pindar, 'the Dircaean swan,' expresses 'at Thebes and at Sparta' by ῥεέθροισί τε Δίρκας... καὶ παρ᾽ Εὐρώτα (*Isthm.* 1. 29). Cp. 844.

106 τὸν λεύκασπιν...φῶτα, in a collective sense: so ὁ Πέρσης, the Persian army, Her. 8. 108, etc. Cp. Aesch. *Theb.* 90 ὁ λεύκασπις λεώς (Dind. λευκοπρεπής): Eur. *Phoen.* 1099 λεύκασπιν εἰσορῶμεν Ἀργείων στρατόν. The round shield, painted white, which the Argive soldier carried on his left arm, is the λευκῆς χιόνος πτέρυξ of 114. The choice of white as the Argive colour may have been prompted by a popular association of Ἄργος with ἀργός. The words τὸν λεύκασπιν Ἀργόθεν answer metrically to 123 πευκάενθ᾽ Ἥφαιστον ἑλεῖν. Instead of Ἀργόθεν (–�’–) we therefore require –˘˘–. The short final of λεύκασπιν is legitimate, the metre being Glyconic (see Metr. Analysis). In the antistrophic verse, the H of Ἥφαιστον is 'irrational,' *i.e.* is a long syllable doing

_chl_ⁿ

CHORUS.

Beam of the sun, fairest light that ever dawned on Thebè ¹ˢᵗ
of the seven gates, thou hast shone forth at last, eye of golden ˢᵗʳᵒᵖʰᵉ
day, arisen above Dircè's streams! The warrior of the white
shield, who came from Argos in his panoply, hath been stirred
by thee to headlong flight, in swifter career;

conject. ἀπ' Ἀργόθεν: Ahrens, Ἀπιόθεν: Boeckh, Ἀργεῖον: Wolff, Ἀργογενῆ:
Blaydes, Ἀργολίδος or Ἀργολικόν: Wecklein, γᾶς Πέλοπος: Mekler, Ἰναχόθεν:
Hermann, Ἀργόθεν ἐκ φῶτα βάντα: Feussner and Schütz, Ἀργόθεν ἐκβάντα φῶτα.
108 ὀξυτόρῳ L (with ὀξεῖ written above): ὀξυτέρῳ r, and Schol. Blaydes conject.

---

duty for a short: and Nauck is incorrect
in saying that the metre 'requires' (though
it admits) a choriambus beginning with a
consonant. The simplest remedy is to
read Ἀργόθεν ἐκ|βάντα φῶτα, and to
suppose that, after the loss of ἐκ, βάντα
and φῶτα were accidentally transposed.
Cp. _O. C._ 1088 where σθένει 'πινικείῳ is
certainly the right order, but the MSS.
reverse it. (See also above on v. 29.)
Dindorf reads ἐκ φῶτα βάντα, assuming
tmesis: but tmesis of ἐκ in Soph. occurs
elsewhere only before μέν (_Tr._ 1053) or
δέ, and there was no motive here for in-
terposing φῶτα. Hermann reads Ἀργόθεν ἐκ as = ἐξ Ἀργόθεν: but elsewhere ἐκ
comes before, not after, such forms (ἐξ
Αἰσύμηθεν, _Il._ 8. 304: ἐξ ἀλόθεν, ἐξ οὐ-
ρανόθεν, etc.). If Ἀργόθεν is not genuine,
then it was probably a gloss on some
other form in -θεν. Had γᾶς Ἡέλοπος
(or Λαπαοῦ) been in the text, a scholiast
would have been more apt to paraphrase
with ἀπ' or ἐξ Ἄργους. This is against
such conjectures as Ἀργεῖον, Ἀργογενῆ,
Ἀργολικόν, Ἰναχίδαν, Ἰνάχιον, as is also
the fact that βάντα suggests a mention of
'the place whence.' Ἀπιόθεν (Ahrens)
would mean 'from Ἄπιος,' but we require 'from Ἀπία' sc. (γῆ), the Pelopon-
nesus, _O. C._ 1303 n.), _i.e._ Ἀπίαθεν: cp
Ὀλυμπίαθεν. I had thought of Ἰναχόθεν, which Mekler, too, has lately suggested, though he has not supported it by
argument. The points in its favour are:
(a) the order φῶτα βάντα can be kept;
(b) after 'Dircè's streams' in v. 105 a reference to the Argive river would be appropriate: (c) Ἀργόθεν might have come
in either as a gloss, or a corruption of the
letters αχόθεν, if ω had dropped out after
Ἰσμηνοῦτον. But I hesitate to displace
Ἀργόθεν, esp. when a direct mention of
Argos here so naturally corresponds with
the direct mention of Thebes in v. 101.

107 ff. παντεγίᾳ (only here) = παν-

 οπλίᾳ, modal dat. σάγη (for accent,
. Chandler § 72) = 'what one carries,'
and so, generally, 'equipment' (Aesch
Cho. 560 ξένῳ γὰρ εἰκώς, παντελῆ σά-
γην ἔχων), or, specially, _body-armour:_
Aesch. _Pers._ 240 ἔγχη σταδαῖα καὶ
φεράσπιδες σάγαι (opp. to the _light_
equipment of the τοξότης). — φυγάδα
πρ., proleptic, with κινήσασα, 'having
stirred to flight,' etc. cp. _O. C._ 1292
ἐξελήλαμαι φυγάς. πρόδρομον, 'running _forward,_' _i.e._ 'in headlong haste':
Aesch. _Th._ 211 ἐπὶ δαιμόνων πρόδρομος
ἦλθον ἀριχαῖα βρέτη. In prose, always
of _precursors_ (as heralds, or an advanced
guard). — ὀξυτέρῳ...χαλινῷ, 'in swifter
career,' dat. of manner with φυγάδα
πρόδρομον. Cp. _O. C._ 1067 (where the
Attic horsemen are described rushing in
pursuit of the Thebans), πᾶς γὰρ ἀ-
στράπτει χαλινός, 'the steel of every
bridle flashes,'—as they gallop on with
slack reins. So here, the χαλινός, which
glitters as the horse rushes along, is
poetically identified with the career itself, and thus is fitly joined with ὀξύτερος.
The phrase seems happy in this context. The Argives began their retreat
in the darkness (16): when the sun
rises, the flashing steel of their bridles
shows them in headlong flight.—ὀξυτέρῳ
does not mean (1) 'in flight swifter than
their former approach'; nor (2) that the
reins are shaken ever faster on the horses'
necks. ὀξυτόρῳ (L) was a mere blunder:
it could only mean 'piercing' (the horse's
mouth), not, 'giving a sharp sound,' when
the reins are shaken.—Cp. Aesch. _Th._
122 (describing the Argive besiegers) διά-
δεται δέ τοι γενῦν ἱππίαν | κινύρονται (μι-
νύρονται L. Dind.) φόνον χαλινοί. _Ib._ 152
ὅτοβον ἁρμάτων ἀμφὶ πόλιν κλύω. Our
passage suggests horsemen rather than
drivers of war-chariots: perh. the poet
imagined both, as in _O. C._ 1062 πώλοισιν
ἢ ῥιμφαρμάτοις | φεύγοντες ἀμίλλαις.

σύστ. α.' *ὃς ἐφ᾽ ἡμετέρᾳ γᾷ *Πολυνείκους   110
· ἀρθεὶς νεικέων ἐξ ἀμφιλόγων·.
· ὀξέα κλάζων
· αἰετὸς εἰς γᾶν ὡς ὑπερέπτα,
· λευκῆς χιόνος πτέρυγι στεγανός,
' πολλῶν μεθ᾽ ὅπλων   115
' ξύν θ᾽ ἱπποκόμοις κορύθεσσι.

ἀντ. α.' στὰς δ᾽ ὑπὲρ μελάθρων, *φονώσαισιν ἀμφιχανὼν κύκλῳ
· 2 λόγχαις ἑπτάπυλον στόμα,

ὀξυτόνῳ or ὀξυτόμῳ: Nanek, ὀξυκρότῳ. **110 ff.** L. has ὃν ἐφ᾽ ἡμετέρα (the first hand
wrote ἡμερα, but added τέ above) γᾶι πολυνεικησο | ἀρθεὶσ νεικέων ἐξ ἀμφιλόγων | ὀξέα
κλάζων αἰετὸσ εἰσ γᾶν | ὡσ (sic) ὑπερέπτα. All MSS. have accus. ὃν and nom. Πολυνείκης.
Scaliger conject. ὃς...Πολυνείκους.—Dindorf gives γᾷ, γῆν, ὑπερέπτη instead of the
Doric forms.   **112** Before ὀξέα κλάζων, Erfurdt conjecturally supplies ἐπόρευσε·
θοῶς δ': J. F. Martin, ὦρσεν· κεῖνος δ': Pallis, ἤλασ᾽ ὁ δ': Nanek, ἤγαγεν· ἐχθρὸς δ',

---

110 f. The MSS. have ὃν...Πολυνεί-
κης. If this were sound, it would be
necessary to suppose that after ἀμφιλόγων
a dipodia has been lost, such as Nauck
supplies by < ἤγαγεν᾽ ἐχθρὸς δ' > ὀξέα
κλάζων. For (1) a verb is wanted to
govern ὃν, and (2) the description of the
eagle, beginning with ὀξέα κλάζων, clearly
refers to the Argive host, not to Polyneices
only. But if, with Scaliger, we read ὃς...
Πολυνείκους, no such loss need be assumed. The correspondence between
anapaestic systems is not always strict,
and the monometer ὀξέα κλάζων could
stand here, though the anti-system has a
dimeter in the same place (129). The
MS. reading ὃν ... Πολυνείκης probably
arose from a misunderstanding of the
scholium:—ὄντινα στρατὸν Ἀργείων, ἐξ
ἀμφιλόγων νεικέων ἀρθείς, ἤγαγεν ὁ
Πολυνείκης, οἷον ἀμφιλογίᾳ χρησάμενος
πρὸς τὸν ἀδελφόν· διὰ βραχέων δὲ
εἶπεν αὐτό, ὡς γνωρίμων οὔσης τῆς ὑπο-
θέσεως. The Schol. wrote ἀρθείς, to
agree with Πολυνείκης, and not ἀρθέντα,
to agree with στρατόν, because it suited
the form of his paraphrase, οἷον ἀμφιλογίᾳ
χρησάμενος πρὸς τὸν ἀδελφόν. By διὰ
βραχέων δὲ εἶπεν αὐτό, the Schol. meant
not merely the indefiniteness of νεικέων ἐξ
ἀμφιλόγων, but also the compactness of
Πολυνείκους | ἀρθεὶς ἐκ νεικέων for ὄντινα
στρατὸν ἤγαγεν ὁ Πολυνείκης. But a
transcriber, noticing that the Schol. joined
ἀρθείς with Πολυνείκης, might easily infer
that ὃν...Πολυνείκης ought to stand in the
text, and might take διὰ βραχέων as

meaning that the verb ἤγαγε could be
understood.—L has the Doric γᾷ, and
presently γᾶν, ὑπερέπτα, which I keep:
see Appendix.

Πολυνείκους...νεικέων, playing on the
name, like Aesch. (Th. 577, 658, 829):
as elsewhere on that of Ajax (Ai. 432
αἰάζειν), and of Odysseus (fr. 877, πολλοὶ
γὰρ ὠδύσαντο δυσμενεῖς ἐμοί, have been
bitter).—ἀρθείς, 'having set forth': so
Her. 1. 165 ἀερθέντες ἐκ τῶν Οἰνουσσέων
ἔπλεον: 9. 52 (of a land-force) ἀερθέντες
...ἀπαλλάσσοντο. Attic prose similarly
uses the act. ἄρας, either absolutely, or
with dat. (ταῖς ναυσί, τῷ στρατῷ), or,
more rarely, with acc. (τὰς ναῦς Thuc.
1. 52). Here the choice of the word
suits the image of an eagle soaring.—
νεικ. ἐξ ἀμφιλόγων, lit. in consequence
of contentious quarrels, i.e. his claims to
the Theban throne, against his brother
Eteocles. Eur. Med. 636 ἀμφιλόγους
ὀργὰς (contentious moods) ἀκόρεστά τε
νείκη: Ph. 500 ἀμφίλεκτος...ἔρις. The
prep. as O. C. 620 ἐκ σμικροῦ λόγου.

112 f. ὀξέα κλάζων: Homeric, Il. 17.
88 (of Hector) ὀξέα κεκληγώς: Il. 16. 429
μεγάλα κλάζοντε (of vultures fighting):
so Aesch. Ag. 48 (the Atreidae) μέγαν ἐκ
θυμοῦ κλάζοντες Ἄρη.—αἰετὸς εἰς γᾶν ὡς
ὑπερέπτα seems clearly right. If ὡς is
omitted, we have a metaphor instead of
a simile, with harsh effect. If we read
αἰετὸς ὥς, and omit εἰς, γᾶν ὑπερέπτα
could mean only, 'flew over the land,'
not, 'flew over the border into the land.'
Further, it is better that the flow

who set forth against our land by reason of the vexed claims of 1st ana-
Polyneices; and, like shrill-screaming eagle, he flew over into paestic
our land, in snow-white pinion sheathed, with an armèd throng, system.
and with plumage of helms.

He paused above our dwellings; he ravened around our 1st anti-
sevenfold portals with spears athirst for blood; strophe.

or ἤγαγε· κεῖνος δ'.   **113** εἰς γᾶν ὥς] ὥς is omitted by Hermann: εἰς by Blaydes,
who places ὥς before γᾶν.   **117** στὰς] πτὰς K. L. Struve, Nauck (referring to
Lobeck *Phryn.* p. 255).—φονίαισιν MSS.: Schol. ταῖς τῶν φόνων ἐρώσαις λόγχαις,
whence Bothe and Boeckh restored φονώσαισιν. In such a MS. as L, where φονί|αισιν
is thus divided between two verses, the corruption would have been easy.   **119** λόγ-
χαις] χηλαῖς Blaydes.—ἑπτάπυλον] ἑπταπύλῳ Semitelos.—στόμα] πόλισμ' Nauck.

of these descriptive verses should not
be broken by a paroemiac before v.
116. No argument either way can be
founded on v. 130 (where see n.), since,
even if it were a paroemiac, that would
not require a paroemiac here.—ὑπερέπτα.
The act. strong aor. ἔπτην (as if from
ἵπτημι) occurs simple only in the *Batra-
chomyomachia* (210. if sound) and the
Anthol.: compounded, only in the tragic
lyrics and in late prose. Cp. 1307.
    114 ff. λευκῆς χιόνος πτ., 'a wing
white as snow' (the white shield, see on
106); genitive of quality (or material),
equiv. to an epithet: cp. *O. T.* 533 τόλμης
πρόσωπον (a bold front): *El.* 19 ἄστρων εὐ-
φρόνη (starry night): Eur. *Ph.* 1491 στολί-
δα...τρυφᾶς (a luxurious robe): *ib.* 1526 γά-
λακτος...μαστοῖς (milky breasts).—στεγανός, pass. here, 'covered'; but act. in Aesch.
Ag. 358 στεγανὸν δίκτυον: cp. Xen. *Cyr.*
7. 1. 33 αἱ ἀσπίδες...στεγάζουσι τὰ σώματα.
—ἀπλῶν...κορύθεσσι. The image of the
eagle with white wings, which suited the
Argive descent on Thebes, here passes
into direct description of an invader who
comes with many ὅπλα and κόρυθες,—the
shield, spear, and helmet of heavy-armed
troops. For the dat. in -εσσι cp. 976
χάλκεσσι. ἱπποκόμοις, 'with horse-hair
crest' (*Il.* 13. 132 l. κόρυθες). For ξύν
denoting what one wears or carries, cp.
O. T. 207, *O. C.* 1258, *Ai.* 30 πηδῶντα
πεδία ξὺν νεορράπτῳ ξίφει. There is no
real difference here between μετά and
ξύν. Donaldson refines too much in suggesting that μετά means merely 'by their
sides,' while ξύν 'denotes a closer union'
(*i.e.* 'on their heads').
    127 ff. In στὰς δ' ὑπὲρ μελάθρων
there is a momentary return to the image
of the flying eagle,—'having stayed his

flight above my dwellings,'—before
swooping. The words do not mean that
the Argive army was posted on hills around
Thebes: the only hills available were
to the N. of the town. The Ἰσμήνιοι
λόφοι (Paus. 9. 10. 2), on which Donaldson places the Argives, was merely a low
eminence close to one of the city gates.
Thebes stood on a low spur of ground
projecting southward, and overlooking the
plain. Sophocles has elsewhere described
the Argive besiegers, with topographical
correctness, as having 'set their leaguer
round the plain of Thebes' (*O. C.* 1311 τὸ
Θήβης πεδίον ἀμφεστᾶσι πᾶν). Struve's
πτάς (a partic. not found elsewhere except
in composition with a prep.) seems improbable, and also less forcible.
    The words φονώσαισιν ἀμφιχανών...
λόγχαις once more merge the image of
the eagle,—as at v. 115,—in literal description of a besieging army, save in
so far as the figurative ἀμφιχανών suggests a monster opening its jaws. The
word was perh. suggested by *Il.* 23.
79 ἐμὲ μὲν κὴρ | ἀμφέχανε στυγερή
(hath gaped for me—*i.e.* 'devoured
me'). These transitions from clear
imagery to language in which the figure
is blurred by the thought of the object
for which it stands, are thoroughly Sophoclean: cp. n. on *O. T.* 866.—φονώσαισιν: the word is not rare in later writers,
bu in classical Greek occurs only
here and *Ph.* 1209 φονᾷ, φονᾷ νόος ἤδη.
Cp. τομάω (*Ai.* 582).—ἑπτάπυλον στόμα,
prop. the access afforded by seven gates:
fr. 701 Θήβας λέγεις μοι τὰς πύλας ἑπτα-
στόμους (seven-mouthed as to its gates).
Nauck changes στόμα to πόλισμ' to avoid
hiatus: but cp. *O. T.* 1202 βασιλεὺς καλεῖ
| ἐμός, n.

' 8 ἔβα, πρίν ποθ' ἀμετέρων　　　　　　　　　　120
' 4 αἱμάτων γένυσ'ιν πλησθῆναί τε καὶ στεφάνωμα πύργων
' 5 πευκάενθ' Ἥφαιστον ἑλεῖν. τοῖος ἀμφὶ νῶτ' ἐτάθη
' 6 πάταγος Ἄρεος, ἀντιπάλῳ δυσχείρωμα δράκοντος.　126

σύστ. β.' Ζεὺς γὰρ μεγάλης γλώσσης κόμπους
' ὑπερεχθαίρει, καί σφας ἐσιδὼν
' πολλῷ ῥεύματι προσνισσομένους,
· χρυσοῦ καναχῆς *ὑπεροπλίαις,　　　　　　130

122 πλησθῆναι καὶ MSS. A short syllable is wanting before καὶ, since the corresponding strophic words are Διρκαίων ὑπὲρ (v. 105). For καὶ, Triclinius gives τε καὶ : Blaydes ιω ἢ (suggesting also σφε καὶ, γε or τι καὶ, and τό τε). Supposing the syllable to be common, Wolff writes καὶ πρίν : while, keeping the simple καὶ, Boeckh changes πλησθῆναι to ἐμπλησθῆναι, and Semitelos to πληρωθῆναι. Naber's γένυιν (for γένυσιν) ἐμπλησθῆναι καὶ still leaves a syllable wanting. **125 f.** ἀντιπάλωι—δράκοντι L, with ου written above ωι, and οσ above ι, by an early hand. I read ἀντιπάλῳ—δράκοντος. One of the later MSS. (V, 13th or 14th cent.) has ἀντιπάλω—δράκοντος, but prob. by accident : the rest agree with L, some (as A) having the correction, ου—οσ, written above.—δυσχεί-

120 f. ἔβα, emphatic by place : cp. 46.—πρίν ποθ', 'or ever,' as Tr. 17.—αἱμάτων, streams of blood, as Aesch. Ag. 1293 αἱμάτων εὐθνησίμων | ἀπορρυέντων (with ref. to one person). Soph. has the plur. only here : Aesch. and Eur. use it several times each, either in this sense, or as = 'deeds of bloodshed' (once as = 'slain persons,' αἵματα σύγγονα, Eur. Ph. 1503).—γένυσιν might be locative dat., 'in'; but seems rather instrumental, 'with.' After πλησθῆναι the missing short syllable is best supplied by τε (Triclinius). The constr. is, πρίν (αὐτός) τε πλησθῆναι, καὶ Ἥφαιστον στεφάνωμα πύργων ἑλεῖν. For τε irregularly p ac , cp. O. T. 258 n.—στεφάνωμα: Eur. Hlk. 910 (of Troy) ἀπὸ δὲ στεφάναν κέκαρσαι | πύργων: cp. n. on O. C. 15.—πευκάενθ' Ἥφαιστον, the flame of pine-wood torches (Verg. Aen. 11. 786 pineus ardor). Cp. 1007, Il. 2. 426 σπλάγχνα δ' ἄρ' ἀμπείραντες ὑπείρεχον Ἡφαίστοιο.

124 f. τοῖος, introducing the reason ; O. C. 947 n.—ἐτάθη, lit. 'was made intense,' here suggesting both loud sound and keen strife. Cp. Il. 12. 436 ἐπὶ ἶσα μάχη τέτατο πτόλεμός τε : 23. 375 ἵπποισι τάθη δρόμος: Aesch. Pers. 574 τεῖνε δὲ δυσβάυκτον | βοᾶτιν τάλαιναν αὐδάν.—πάταγος, clatter of arms (a word expressive of the sound), as distinguished from βοή, a human cry ; cp. Her. 7. 211 οἱ δὲ βάρβαροι ὁρέοντες φεύγοντας βοῇ τε καὶ πατάγῳ ἐπήϊσαν. The Argives began to

retreat in the night : at dawn, the Thebans made a sally in pursuit of them, and turned the retreat into a rout.

ἀντιπάλῳ δυσχείρωμα δράκοντος, a thing hard to vanquish for him who was struggling against the (Theban) dragon, —i.e. for the Argive eagle. The two readings between which the MSS. fluctuate, viz., ἀντιπάλῳ...δράκοντι and ἀντιπάλου...δράκοντος, arose, I feel sure, from ἀντιπάλῳ...δράκοντος (V has ἀντιπάλω...δράκοντος). For the gen. after this adj., cp. Pind. O. 8. 94 μένος γήραος ἀντίπαλον, a spirit that wrestles with old age: Eur. Alc. 922 ὑμεναίων γόος ἀντίπαλος, wails contending with marriage-songs.

The interpretation of the passage turns primarily on two points.

(1) The δράκων certainly means the Thebans,—the σπαρτοί (O.C. 1534) sprung from the dragon's teeth sown by Cadmus, and thence called δρακοντογενεῖς (schol.), Ovid's anguigenae (Met. 3. 531): cp. 1125 ἐπὶ σπορᾷ δράκοντος. Poetry often represented a struggle between an eagle and a dragon or snake (δράκων could mean either, the 'dragon' being conceived as a sort of huge python); as Il. 12. 201, Hor. Od. 4. 4. 11.

(2) The δυσ in δυσχείρωμα must refer to difficulty experienced by the vanquished Argives, not by the victorious Thebans. The word must mean, then, '*a thing hard to overcome,*' not, '*a victory won with diffi-*

but he went hence, or ever his jaws were glutted with our gore, or the Fire-god's pine-fed flame had seized our crown of towers. So fierce was the noise of battle raised behind him, a thing too hard for him to conquer, as he wrestled with his dragon foe.

For Zeus utterly abhors the boasts of a proud tongue; and when he beheld them coming on in a great stream, in the haughty pride of clanging gold, 2nd ana·paestic system.

ρωμα] Keeping ἀντιπάλῳ—δράκοντι, Blaydes conject. δυσχείρωτα: M. Schmidt, δοὺς χείρωμα. Reading ἀντιπάλου . . δράκοντος, Herwerden conject. σωτείραμα, Gleditsch τε σπείραμα. 128 εἰσιδὼν L, ἐσιδὼν r: ἐπιδὼν conject. Nauck. 129 πολλῷ ῥεύματι] ῥεύματι πολλῷ Blaydes.—προσνισσομένους L (the fut. part., cp. Eusth. 1288. 56): προσνισσομένους r. 180 χρυσοῦ καναχῆς ὑπεροπτίας L (with ὑπερόπτας written above by an early hand): ὑπεροπτίας and ὑπερόπτα r. Dorville conject. ὑπεροπλίας: Vauvilliers, ὑπεροπλίαις, which is now received by several edd.—Other conjectures are: Emper, καναχᾷ θ' ὑπερόπτας (others, καναχᾷς with ὑπερόπτας or ·ηι, or ὑπέροπτα as adv.): Donaldson, καναχᾷ θ' ὑπερόπλους: Boeckh, καναχῇ ὑπεροπτείαις:

culty.' So δυσχείρωτος is 'hard to subdue' (Her. 7. 9), as ἀχείρωτος is 'unsubdued' (Thuc. 6. 10), and εὐχείρωτος 'easy to subdue' (Xen. Hellen. 5. 3. 4). Cp. δυσπάλαιστος, δυσπάλαμος, δύσμαχος, etc., used with poetical irony to express the irresistible. In O. T. 560 θανάσιμον χείρωμα is a deed of deadly violence: in Aesch. Th. 1022 τυμβοχόα χειρώματα are works of the hand in mound-making. In itself, δυσχείρωμα might mean 'a thing achieved with difficulty'; but here the irony is clearly pointed against the routed Argives: the poet does not mean that the Thebans won with difficulty. Thus δυσχείρωμα is here the opposite of what Aesch. calls εὔμαρὲς χείρωμα, a thing easily subdued: Ag. 1326 δούλης θανούσης, εὐμαροῦς χειρώματος. The Theban πτάγος Ἄρεος was a thing which the Argives could not overcome.

Those who read ἀντιπάλῳ...δράκοντι explain either (a) 'a hard-won victory for the dragon foe': but this gives a wrong sense to δυσχείρωμα: or (b) join the dat. with body: 'a din was raised by the dragon foe (cp. Il. 22. 55 'Αχιλῆι δαμασθείς), a thing hard (for the Argive) to subdue.' But δυσχείρωμα, placed as it is, cannot be thus dissociated from the dat. ἄντ. δράκοντι and mentally referred to another dat. which is left to be understood.

Those who read ἀντιπάλου...δράκοντος understand (a) a thing on the part of the dragon foe which was hard (for the Argive) to overcome; i.e. 'an irresistible onset of the dragon foe.' But such a

construction of δυσχείρωμα with the gen. seems impossible, esp. when there is no dat. to help it out. Or (b) 'a hard-won victory of the dragon foe'; which gives a wrong sense to δυσχείρωμα.—The form of the word is in one respect unique. Every similar neuter noun compounded with δυσ is from a verb so compounded: as δυσείργημα, δυσημέρημα, δυσπράγημα, δυσσέβημα, δυστύχημα, δυσφήμημα, δυσχέρασμα, δυσχρήστημα, δυσώπημα. But there is no such verb as δυσχειρόω, 'to subdue with difficulty.' The noun has been boldly coined to express δυσχείρωτον πρᾶγμα.

127 ff. μεγάλης: 1350 μεγάλοι... λόγοι: Plato Phaed. 95 B μὴ μέγα λέγε: Verg. Aen. 10. 547 Dixerat ille aliquid magnum.—ῥεύματι: Aesch. Pers. 88 μεγάλῳ ῥεύματι φωτῶν (so ib. 412 ῥεῦμα Περσικοῦ στρατοῦ). Eur. I. T. 1437 παῦσαι διώκων ῥεῦμά τ' ἐξορμῶν στρατοῦ. The transposition ῥεύματι πολλῷ is unnecessary. In the same dipodia an anapaest must not precede a dactyl, nor a dactyl an anapaest; but a spondee can be followed by a dactyl, as O. C. 146 δηλῶ δ'. οὐ γὰρ ἂν ὧδ' ἀλλοτρίοις.

180 χρυσοῦ καναχῆς ὑπεροπλίαις, 'in the haughty pride of clanging gold.' ὑπεροπλίαις seems a certain correction of ὑπεροπτίας (see cr. n.), and has justly won its way with recent edd. The word is fitting, since ὑπεροπλία is prop. 'overweening confidence in arms'; and Soph. has used the epic plur. with the epic ῑ, Il. 1. 205 ἧς ὑπεροπλίῃσι: so too Theocr. ῑ, 25. 138 σθένεϊ ᾧ | ἠδ' ὑπεροπλίη Φαέθων

· παλτῷ ῥιπτεῖ πυρὶ βαλβίδων
· ἐπ' ἄκρων ἤδη
· νίκην ὁρμῶντ' ἀλαλάξαι.

στρ. β'. · ἀντιτύπᾳ δ' ἐπὶ γᾷ πέσε τανταλωθεὶς
, 2 πυρφόρος, ὃς τότε μαινομένᾳ ξὺν ὁρμᾷ   135
, 8 βακχεύων ἐπέπνει
· 4 ῥιπαῖς ἐχθίστων ἀνέμων.
, 5 εἶχε δ' ἄλλα τὰ μέν,
, 6 ἄλλα δ' ἐπ' ἄλλοις ἐπενώμα στυφελίζων μέγας Ἄρης

Hartung, κavaχῆs ὑπερηφανίαιs.   **184** ἀντίτυπα L, which a later hand wished to make into ἀντιτύπωs (not ἀντίτυπος, as the accent shows). The later MSS. read with L, except those which have the conject. of Triclinius, ἀντίτυπος. Porson restored ἀντιτύπα. Bergk and Wieseler conject. ἀντιτυπάς (cp. ἐντυπάς).   **188** εἶχε δ' ἄλλαι τὰ μέν ἄλλαι τὰ δ' ἐπ' ἄλλοισ | L. The first hand wrote ἄλλα—ἄλλα: the first corrector added ι to each. The word μέν is represented by μ in an erasure, with < above it.

μέγαs. In post-Homeric poetry ὑπέρ-οπλοs is a freq. epith. of overweening strength (ἠνορέη, βίη, ἤβη, etc.).—Other readings are :—(1) χρυσοῦ κaναχῇ θ' ὑπερόπταs, 'and haughty in the clang of gold.' This involves an improbable change; the subst. ὑπερόπτηs, too, is un-suitable here, and cannot be defended by Theocr. 22. 58 πρὸs πάντα παλίγκοτοs ἠδ' ὑπερόπτηs. Wecklein, reading ὑπερόπταs, keeps κaναχῆs in the sense, 'hoffärtig auf': but a genit. after ὑπερόπτηs could not denote that in which one takes pride. (2) χρυσοῦ κaναχῇ ὑπερόπτηs, or -όπτα, i.e., 'Zeus, a despiser of the clang of gold.' (3) χρυσοῦ κaναχῆs ὑπέροπτα, adv. neut. plur. (as O. T. 883), 'advancing haughtily in a great stream of clanging gold.' But the adv. comes weakly at the end, and χρυσοῦ κ. is harshly joined with π. ῥεύματι.—Aesch., too, gives pro-minence to gold in picturing the Argive chiefs: Capaneus has golden letters on his shield (Th. 434), Polyneices has the image of a warrior in golden armour, with a golden legend (644, 660).—κανα-χῆs, of metal, as Il. 16. 105 πήληξ βαλ-λομένη κaναχὴν ἔχε.

131 ff. παλτῷ πυρί, i.e. with the thunderbolt which Zeus brandishes in his hand before hurling it: Ar. Av. 1714 πάλ-λων κεραυνόν, πτεροφόρον Διὸς βέλοs.—βαλβίδων ἐπ' ἄκρων, at his topmost goal, i.e. at his goal on the top of our walls. ἄκρων might mean merely 'utter-most,' but is rather associated in the poet's mind with the object meant by

βαλβίδων. In Eur. Ph. 1180 Capaneus is struck by Zeus at the moment that he is surmounting the γεῖσα τειχέων, the coping of the walls. The βαλβῖδες were the posts, to which a rope was attached, marking the point from which runners in the double foot-race (δίαυλος) set out, and to which they returned: hence both starting-point and goal.—ὁρμῶντα: for the partic. as subst., without either art. or τις, cp. El. 697 δύναιτ' ἂν οὐδ' ἂν ἰσχύων φυγεῖν: Plat. Gorg. 498 A ΚΑΛ. εἶδον. ΣΩ. τί δέ; νοῦν ἔχοντα λυπούμενον καὶ χαίροντα; The name of Capaneus could be left unmentioned, since the story was so famous. No leader of the Argive host, except Polyneices, is named in this play. The attack of Capaneus was said to have been made at the Ἠλέκτραι πύλαι on the s. side of Thebes (Aesch. Th. 423, Paus. 9. 9. 8). His fall from the scaling-ladder, as the lightning struck him, was often repre-sented in art.—νίκην, cogn. acc. with ἀλαλάξαι, to raise the cry ἀλαλαί for v ry: Ar. Av. 1763 ἀλαλαί, ἰὴ παιήων, | ἰὴ μέλλα καλλίνικος.

184 ἀντιτύπᾳ, restored by Porson (Adv. p. 169) for ἀντίτυπα, is certainly right. Adjectives in οs, compounded with a prep., are oft. of three terminations in epic poetry, as ἀμφιέλισσα, ἀμφιρύτη, ἀντιθέη (Od. 13. 378), ἀμφιβρότη (Il. 2. 389), ὑποδεξίη (Il. 9. 73), etc. The dra-matists could admit some such forms, esp. in lyrics; thus they have ἡ ἐναλία as well as ἡ ἐνάλιος, ἡ ἐννυχία as well as ἡ ἐννύχιος.

he smote with brandished fire one who was now hasting to shout victory at his goal upon our ramparts.

Swung down, he fell on the earth with a crash, torch in band, 2nd strop he who so lately, in the frenzy of the mad onset, was raging against us with the blasts of his tempestuous hate. But those threats fared not as he hoped ; and to other foes the mighty War-god dispensed their several dooms, dealing havoc around,

The scribe had written τὰ δ' ἄλλα (his eye running on to τὰ δ' ἄλλοις): then, on perceiving the error, he deleted δ', but, in the narrow space between τά and ἄλλα, could not write μέν at full length. With regard to the last word of the v., Campbell thinks that the first hand wrote ἄλλους, and that the corrector made this into ἄλλοις: but I doubt whether the ι was ever υ.—The only noteworthy variation in the later MSS. is that, instead of L's second ἄλλαι, V has δεινά, prob. a grammarian's conjecture.—For

As regards the sense, ἀντίτυπος was regularly used of hard surfaces, which, as it were, *repel* that which strikes them (for the accent ἀντίτυπος, not ἀντιτύπος, though the sense is act., see on *O. T.* 460). Arist. *Probl.* 5. 40 οἱ...ἐν ἀντιτύποις περίπατοι. Lucian *Amor.* 13 τὴν ἀντίτυπον οὕτω καὶ καρτερὰν τοῦ λίθου φύσιν. So, fig., Plat. *Crat.* 420 D τὸ...ἀναγκαῖον καὶ ἀντίτυπον, what is necessary, and what *resists* us.—τανταλωθείς, '*swung*,' that is, sent flying through the air from the edge of the wall on which he was just setting foot. The word expresses the force with which the thunderbolt struck him, just as ἀντιτύπᾳ expresses the crash when he struck earth. This form of the verb occurs only here. Arist. uses both ταλαντεύομαι (pass.) and ταλαντεύω (act. intr.) as 'to sway to and fro.' The Schol., explaining by διασεισθείς (*i.e.* 'with a rude shock,' which is substantially right) quotes Anacreon 78 [δ'] μελαμφύλλῳ δάφνᾳ χλωρᾷ τ' ἐλαίᾳ ταντάλίζει (where the subject was perh. a god, or the wind).

133 ff. πυρφόρος, 'torch in hand': so of Prometheus (*O. C.* 55, where see n.) and Artemis (*O. T.* 207). Aesch. *Th.* 433 φλέγει δὲ λαμπὰς διὰ χερῶν ὡπλισμένη | χρυσοῖς δὲ φωνεῖ γράμμασιν, πρήσω πόλιν.—βακχεύων: so oft. Eur. as *H. F.* 898 Ἄδουσα βακχεύσει: but this is the only place where Soph. connects *evil* frenzy with the name of a god whom this same Ode invokes (154).—ῥιπαῖς...ἀνέμων. Capaneus, breathing fury and slaughter, is likened to a deadly tempest. For ῥιπαί, 'blasts,' cp. 929 and *O. C.* 1248 n. So Aesch. *Th.* 63 πρὶν καταιγίσαι πνοὰς | Ἄρεως.

136 ff. εἶχε δ' ἄλλα τὰ μέν, 'but

those things indeed' (the threats of Capaneus) 'went otherwise' (than he had expected): ἄλλα δ' ἐπ' ἄλλοις μέγας Ἄρης ἐπενώμα, 'while to others great Ares assigned various dooms,' etc. The poet has described how *Zeus* smote the most formidable foe. As to the other Argive chiefs, he briefly adds that *Ares* struck them down by various deaths: *i.e.* they perished, not by a stroke from heaven, but in the course of battle. In L's reading, εἶχε δ' ἄλλαι τὰ μέν ἄλλαι τὰ δ' ἐπ' ἄλλοις, one cause of corruption has evidently been a confusion between alternative modes of expressing 'some' and 'other,' viz. (1) by doubled ἄλλος, (2) by τὰ μέν, τὰ δέ. It is in favour of our reading (Erfurdt's) that it helps to account for this, since it supposes that τὰ μέν was answered by ἄλλα δέ. Cp. *O. C.* 1671 οὐ τὸ μέν, ἄλλο δὲ μή: *Il.* 6. 147 τὰ μέν τ' ἄνεμος χαμάδις χέει, ἄλλα δέ θ' ὕλη | τηλεθόωσα φύει. It is immaterial that, here, τὰ μέν means, not, '*some* things,' but, '*those* things'; since the latter is its first sense also where we render it by 'some.' Further, with regard to ἄλλα, remark that this form of adverb is used elsewhere also in ref. to the course ordained by *gods or fate:* *O. C.* 1443 ταῦτα δ' ἐν τῷ δαίμονι, | καὶ τῇδε φῦναι χἀτέρᾳ: Aesch. *P. V.* 511 οὐ ταῦτα ταύτῃ μοῖρά πω τελεσφόρος | κρᾶναι πέπρωται. For other proposed readings, see Appendix.—ἐπενώμα. Aesch. *Eum.* 310 λάχη τὰ κατ' ἀνθρώπους | ὡς ἐπινωμᾷ στάσις ἁμά, apportions.—στυφελίζων (στύφελός, 'firm,' στύφω, to compress), 'striking heavily': *Il.* 1. 581 ἐξ ἑδέων στυφελίξαι.

· ἢ δεξιόσειρος.   140

συστ. γ΄.' ἑπτὰ λοχαγοὶ γὰρ ἐφ' ἑπτὰ πύλαις
· ταχθέντες ἴσοι πρὸς ἴσους ἔλιπον
· Ζηνὶ τροπαίῳ πάγχαλκα τέλη,
" πλὴν τοῖν στυγεροῖν, ὣ πατρὸς ἑνὸς
' μητρός τε μιᾶς φύντε καθ' αὑτοῖν   145
' δικρατεῖς λόγχας στήσαντ' ἔχετον
· κοινοῦ θανάτου μέρος ἄμφω.

ἀντ. β΄. · ἀλλὰ γὰρ ἁ μεγαλώνυμος ἦλθε Νίκα

emendations, see Appendix.   140 In L the first σ of δεξιόσειροσ has been altered
from χ either by the first hand itself or by the first corrector.   The latter has written
in the right-hand margin, ὁ γενναῖος· οἱ γὰρ ἰσχυροὶ ἵπποι εἰς τὴν δεξιὰν σειρὰν ζεύγνυνται

δεξιόσειρος, 'right-hand trace-horse,'
here means a vigorous ally, who does
more than his own share of the work.
Ares has brought the Theban chariot vic-
toriously through the crisis of the race
against its Argive rival. In the four-
horse chariot-race the four horses were
harnessed abreast : the two in the middle
were under the yoke (ζύγιοι), being called
ὁ μέσος δεξιός and ὁ μέσος ἀριστερός (schol.
Ar. *Nub.* 122): the two outside horses
drew in traces (σειραῖοι). The chariot
went down the right-hand side of the
course, turned sharply from right to left
at the distance-post (καμπτήρ, νύσσα), and
came back down the left side. Hence,
at the turning-point, the right-hand trace-
horse had most work to do; and the best
horse was put in that place. Cp. *El.*
721 (at the turning-post) δεξιὸν τ' ἀνεὶς |
σειραῖον ἵππον εἶργε τὸν προσκείμενον.
Xen. *Symp.* 4. 6 ἁρματηλατοῦντα δεῖ ἐγγὺς
μὲν τῆς στήλης κάμψαι, quoting from *Il.*
23. 336 the precept τὸν δεξιὸν ἵππον |
κένσαι ὁμοκλήσαντ', εἶξαί τέ οἱ ἡνία χερσίν.
Cp. Aesch. *Ag.* 842 ζευχθεὶς ἕτοιμος ἦν
ἐμοὶ σειραφόρος (said by Agam. of Odysseus): and cp. *ib.* 1640.—The old *v. l.*
δεξιόχειρος, explained by the schol. γεν-
ναῖος καὶ παραδέξιος, is read by Musgrave,
Hartung, and A. Pallis. Hartung renders it 'der Starke,'—understanding it as
'the strong and deft striker.' Neither
δεξιόχειρος nor δεξιόχειρ seems to occur,
though ἀριστερόχειρ (left-handed) is found
in late Greek.
   141 ff. ἑπτὰ λοχαγοί. In *O. C.* 131
ff. the list agrees with that of Aesch.,—

Amphiaraus, Tydeus, Eteoclus, Hippo-
medon, Capaneus, Parthenopaeus, Polyneices. (Adrastus, who escaped, is not
counted as one of the seven.) Capaneus,
though not slain by human hand, is included, since he was vanquished. Amphiaraus, according to the legend which
Soph. recognises in *El.* 837, was swallowed up by the earth, but seems here to be
reckoned among those who fell in fight
(cp. n. on *O. C.* 1313).—ἴσοι πρὸς ἴσους,
instead of saying simply πρὸς ἑπτά,—a
common idiom : Eur. *Ph.* 750 ἴσους ἴσοισι
πολεμίοισιν ἀντιθείς : Her. 1. 2 ἴσα πρὸς
ἴσα: 9. 48 ἴσοι πρὸς ἴσους: Plat. *Legg.* 774
C ἴσα ἀντὶ ἴσων.
   Ζηνὶ τροπαίῳ, to Zeus who makes a
τροπή, or rout, of enemies. Eur. *El.*
671 ὣ Ζεῦ πατρῷε καὶ τροπαῖ' ἐχθρῶν
ἐμῶν. So he is invoked after a victory, *Her.* 867. (In *Tr.* 303 ὣ Ζεῦ
τροπαῖε is usu. taken as = ἀποτρόπαιε,
'averting.') In his relation to war, Zeus
was worshipped also as Ἀγήτωρ (esp. at
Sparta), Ἄρειος (at Olympia, etc.), Στρά-
τιος, Χρυσάωρ (in Caria), Στήσιος or Ἐπι-
στάσιος (the Roman *stator*, stayer of
flight).—πάγχαλκα τέλη, 'tributes of
panoplies,' as *Tr.* 238 Heracles dedicates
βωμοὺς τέλη τ' ἔγκαρπα Κηναίῳ Διί, *i. e.*
'dues of fruits,'—alluding to the τέμενος
of which the produce was given to the
god (*ib.* 754). Not, (1) 'complete suits
of armour' : nor (2) ὁπλιτικὰ τάγματα,
'troops of warriors,' as Eustath. took it
(p. 686. 16), led perh. by Aesch. *Pers.*
47 δίρρυμά τε καὶ τρίρρυμα τέλη.—It was
the ordinary practice to set up a τρό-

a mighty helper at our need.

For seven captains at seven gates, matched against seven, left the tribute of their panoplies to Zeus who turns the battle; save those two of cruel fate, who, born of one sire and one mother, set against each other their twain conquering spears, and are sharers in a common death. 3rd ana-paestic system.

But since Victory of glorious name hath come to us, 2nd anti-strophe.

τοῦ ἅρματος. Another schol., in the left-hand marg., has δεξιόχειρος in its lemma, and explains both readings. The later MSS. have δεξιόσειρος. Blaydes conject. δεξιόγυιος.

ταιον (old Att. τροπαῖον) after a victory, on the spot where it had been won, or, in the case of a sea-fight, on the nearest land (Thuc. 2. 92). Such a trophy ordinarily consisted of shields, helmets, and weapons, conspicuously displayed on wooden supports, and dedicated, with an inscription, to a deity. Cp. Eur. *Ph.* 1473 (of the Thebans after the victory) οἱ μὲν Διὸς τροπαῖον ἵστασαν βρέτας (*i.e.* a wooden image of Ζεὺς Τροπαῖος), | οἱ δ' ἀσπίδας συλλῶντες Ἀργείων νεκρῶν | σκυλεύματ' εἴσω τειχέων ἐπέμπομεν. Part of the armour would be affixed to the walls of Theban temples (cp. Aesch. *Ag.* 577, *Th.* 276).

144 ff. πλὴν τ. στυγεροῖν, 'wretched' (as *Ph.* 166): not, 'hateful,' nor, 'filled with hate.' Of the seven Argive leaders, Polyneices was the only one who could not properly be said to have been van-quished, since he was not more vanquish-ed than victorious. But, in excepting him, the poet associates him with the brother who was his victim as well as his conqueror. Thus ἑπτὰ...ἔλιπον..., πλὴν τοῖν στυγεροῖν, is a lax way of saying, 'defeat befell each of the seven Argive leaders, except *in the case of* the two brothers,'—in which an Argive leader and a Theban leader slew *each other.*—πατρός, etc., gen. of origin (38).—καθ' αὑτοῖν = κατ' ἀλλήλοιν. Cp. Dem. or. 40 § 29 ὧν ἂν ἐν αὑτοῖς διενεχθῶσι γυνὴ καὶ ἀνήρ. Plat. *Prot.* 347 D λέγοντάς τε καὶ ἀκούοντας ἐν μέρει ἑαυτῶν.—δικρατεῖς λόγχας, two spears, each of which was victorious over the wielder of the other. So *Ai.* 251 δικρατεῖς Ἀτρεῖδαι, two Atrei-dae, each of whom is a king. That is, δικρατεῖς is equiv. to two distinct epithets (δύο and κρατοῦσαι): cp. *O.C.* 1055 δισ-

τόλους...ἀδελφάς, two journeying sisters: *ib.* 17 πυκνόπτεροι = many, and feathered (n.): see *O.T.* 846 n.—στήσαντε, having set in position, *levelled*, against each other. The Homeric δόρυ was chiefly a missile; here the λόγχη is used for thrust-ing.

148 f. ἀλλὰ γάρ, like ἀλλ' οὐ γάρ (*O.C.* 988 n.), can be used with or with-out an ellipse. Here there is no ellipse, since ἐπέλθωμεν follows (153), and γάρ, introducing the reason given by ἦλθε, = 'since.' Below, 155, there is an ellipse, —'But (let us cease), for Creon comes'; where γάρ might be rendered '*indeed.*' —μεγαλώνυμος: schol. ἡ μεγάλην περι-ποιοῦσα δόξαν: the personified Νίκη is 'of great name,' because victory is glori-ous. πολυάρματψ implies warlike re-nown, as well as wealth and splendour (cp. 845). Already in *Il.* 4. 391 the Cadmeans are 'urgers of horses' (κέν-τορες ἵππων): so *Scut. Herc.* 24 Βοιωτοὶ πλήξιπποι: Pindar *Ol.* 6. 85 has πλάξιπ-πον...Θήβαν, *Isthm.* 7. 20 φιλαρμάτου πόλιος (as elsewhere χρυσάρματος, εὐάρ-ματος). Critias, speaking of the inven-tions for which various cities were famous, says (fr. 1. 10) Θήβη δ' ἁρματόεντα δίφρον συνεπήξατο πρώτη.—ἀντιχαρεῖσα, with gladness responsive to that of Thebe. The goddess Νίκη has come to meet the victors, and their joy is reflected in her radiant smile. (We can imagine her descending towards them from the sky, like the winged Νίκη of Paeonius found at Olympia.) The doubts which have been felt as to ἀντιχαρεῖσα disappear if it is observed that χαρεῖσα here refers to the *outward manifestation* of joy, not merely to the feeling in the mind. Thus ἀντί expresses the *answer* of smile to

2 τᾷ πολυαρμάτῳ ἀντιχαρεῖσα Θήβᾳ,
3 ἐκ μὲν δὴ πολέμων   150
4 τῶν νῦν θέσθαι λησμοσύναν,
5 θεῶν δὲ ναοὺς χοροῖς
6 παννυχίοις πάντας ἐπέλθωμεν, ὁ Θήβας δ᾽ ἐλελίχθων
7 Βάκχιος ἄρχοι.

ἀλλ᾽ ὅδε γὰρ δὴ βασιλεὺς χώρας,   155
Κρέων ὁ Μενοικέως, ∞ - νεοχμὸς
νεαραῖσι θεῶν ἐπὶ συντυχίαις
χωρεῖ, τίνα δὴ μῆτιν ἐρέσσων,
ὅτι σύγκλητον τήνδε γερόντων   160
προὔθετο λέσχην,

---

149 ἀντιχαρεῖσα] M. Schmidt conject. ἄρτι φανεῖσα, which Nauck adopts. Blaydes, ἄρτι χαρεῖσα. **151** θέσθε L. The second ε has been made either from ω (as Dübner thinks), or from αι (as Campbell). Almost all the later MSS. (including A) have θέσθε: but one (V) has θέσθαι, with ε written above. Hence conject. πᾶι νῦν θέσθω: Nauck, χρὴ νῦν θέσθαι.—λησμοσύνην L, -αν Brunck. **158** παννύχοιο L: παννυχίοις Γ.—

---

smile, as in ἀντιλάμπω of light to light, or in ἀντιφθέγγομαι of sound to sound. I do not take ἀντί here to mean *merely* 'over against,' as when Pind. *Ol.* 3. 19 says ἤδη γὰρ αὐτῷ... | ...ὀφθαλμὸν ἀντέφλεξε Μήνα, the (mid-month) moon showed the light of her eye over against him. —Not (1) ἴσον αὐτῇ χαρεῖσα (schol.), *i.e.* merely, 'rejoicing as Thebes does,' which extenuates ἀντιχαρεῖσα into συγχαρεῖσα. Nor (2) ἀντὶ τῶν κακῶν χαρεῖσα, *i.e.* rejoicing in requital of past troubles.

150 ff. ἐκ...πολέμων τῶν νῦν, 'after the recent wars.' For ἐκ, cp. *Ph.* 271 ἐκ πολλοῦ σάλου | εὕδοντ᾽, sleeping, after long tossing on the sea. For νῦν referring to the recent past (='just now'), cp. Dem. or. 18 § 13 ἡλίκα νῦν ἐτραγῴδει καὶ διεξῄει: Xen. *An.* 7. 1. 26 ἀναμνησθέντας τὰ νῦν ἤδη γεγενημένα (*i.e.* the events of the Peloponnesian war, which had ended four years before).—θέσθαι (L), as infin. for imperative (*O. C.* 481 n.), has a certain solemnity which seems to make it better here than θέσθε, though the latter is not excluded by ἐπέλθωμεν. The last syll. of θέσθαι answers to the second of ἐχθίστων in 137; each is an 'irrational' syllable (- for ⏑): see Metr. Anal.—θεῶν, monosyll. by synizesis (*O. C.* 964 n.).— παννυχίοις, since a παννυχίς was esp. grateful to the city's tutelar god Dionysus (1147), whose rites are νύκτωρ τὰ πολλά

(Eur. *Bacch.* 486).—ὁ Θήβας (gen. sing.) ἐλελίχθων, = ὁ τὴν Θήβης χθόνα ἐλελίζων, shaking the ground of Thebes (with his dances): for the objective gen., cp. *O. C.* 333 λόγων αὐτάγγελος.—Βάκχιος = Βάκχος, as Eur. *Bacch.* 235 τὴν δ᾽ Ἀφροδίτην πρόσθ᾽ ἄγειν τοῦ Βακχίου, and oft.—ἄρχοι sc. τῆς χορείας (schol.). Cp. 1146.

155 ff. ἀλλά...γάρ: see on 148.— Κρέων, monosyll. by synizesis, as πλέων *Od.* 1. 183; in Aesch. *Ag.* 1493 ἰαπνέων is a spondee. Cp. *O. C.* 1073 'Ρέαι, a monosyll.—Μενοικέως, =⏑--, as *O. C.* 1003 Θησέως (--), and so oft.—νεοχμὸς νεαραῖσι. Neither adj. is suspicious; *new* events have made a *new* ruler; and the doubled adj. is quite in the poet's manner. Cp. 1266 νέος νέῳ ξὺν μόρῳ: *Ai.* 735 νέας | βουλὰς νέοισιν ἐγκαταζεύξας τρόποις: *O. C.* 475 οἰὸς...νεαρᾶς νεοσπόρῳ μαλλῷ: *ib.* 1259 γέρων γέροντι συγκατῴκηκεν πίνος: *Tr.* 613 καινῷ καινὸν ἐν πεπλώματι, etc. Though νεαρός usu. = 'young,' it occurs also in the sense of 'novel,' as in Pindar's νεαρὰ ἐξευρών (*N.* 8. 20). Three views of the metre have been taken. (1) That v. 156 should be enlarged to a dimeter by supplying one anapaest or its equivalent. (2) That v. 156 should be reduced to a monometer by omitting νεοχμὸς or Μενοικέως. (3) That both v. 156 and v. 160 should be made dimeters by supplying three anapaests or

with joy responsive to the joy of Thebè whose chariots are many, let us enjoy forgetfulness after the late wars, and visit all the temples of the gods with night-long dance and song; and may Bacchus be our leader, whose dancing shakes the land of Thebè.

But lo, the king of the land comes yonder, Creon, son of Menoeceus, our new ruler by the new fortunes that the gods have given; what counsel is he pondering, that he hath proposed this special conference of elders,

ἐλελίζων L, with γρ. ἐλελίχθων written above by S: ἐλελίχθων r. The Aldine has ἐλελίζων, which Heath, Vauvilliers, and Brunck preferred: but nearly all later edd. read ἐλελίχθων. Musgrave conject. ἐλελιχθείς (as = 'invoked with cries'). **154** βακχεῖοσ MSS.: Βάκχιοσ Bothe. **156 f.** κρέων ὁ μενοικέωσ νεοχμὸσ | νεαραῖσι θεῶν ἐπὶ συντυχίαισ | MSS. **159** ἐρέσσων] ἐλίσσων Johnson.

their equivalents. See Appendix. I prefer the first of these views. An anapaest or spondee, meaning 'ruler,' has probably dropped out before νεοχμός. Seyffert's κρέων is at first sight attractive, as accounting for its own disappearance; but, since it is the same word as Κρέων—which had an epic form Κρείων, as conversely Pind. and Aesch. use κρέων—this would be rather a feeble pun than a strong παρήχησις. Either ἄρχων or ταγός is possible.—θεῶν...συντυχίαις, fortunes sent by the gods,—the possessive gen. denoting the authors, just as it can denote the parents: cp. Ph. 1116 πότμος...δαιμόνων: Eur. Aeol. fr. 37 τὰς δὲ δαιμόνων τύχας | ὅστις φέρει κάλλιστ', ἀνὴρ οὗτος σοφός. (In O. T. 34 δαιμόνων σωαλλαγαῖς is different.) ἐπὶ συντυχίαις means that the fortunes are the conditions which have made Creon king: this ἐπί with dat. of attendant circumstance sometimes = our 'in,' as O. C. 1268 ἐπ' ἔργοις πᾶσι (n.), sometimes 'for,' as Ar. Eq. 406 τὶν' ἐπὶ συμφοραῖς (i.e. to celebrate them), cp. El. 1230: here we could say, 'under the new dispensations of the gods.' (Distinguish 88 ἐπὶ ψυχροῖσι as = 'for' in the sense 'with a view to.')

158 f. μῆτιν ἐρέσσων, consilium animo volutans, 'turning it over' busily in the mind. ἐρέσσειν, to ply the oar, is fig. said of putting a thing in lively motion, as Eur. I. A. 139 ἐρέσσων σὸν πόδα. Then also of activity in s , as Ai. 251 ἐρέσσουσιν ἀπειλάς, 'they both threats' (utter them repeatedly and loudly): or, as here, in thought. Cp. 231.—(Not, 'speeding his counsel hitherward,' i. e. coming to disclose it: 'advolvens, i.e.

patefacturus,' Ellendt.)—σύγκλητον, specially convoked;—implying that there were other and regularly appointed seasons at which the king met the γέροντες in council. At Athens four meetings of the ἐκκλησία were regularly held in each πρυτανεία (a period of 35 or 36 days): these were κύριαι (though the term may once have been restricted to the first of them), or νόμιμοι. An extraordinary meeting was σύγκλητος or κατάκλητος. Pollux 8. 116 σύγκλητος ἐκκλησία ἦν ἐξαίφνης ἐποίουν μείζονος χρείας ἐπιλαβούσης· ἐκαλεῖτο δὲ καὶ κατάκλησία, ὅτι καὶ τοὺς ἐκ τῶν ἀγρῶν κατεκάλουν (down to the ἄστυ). Arist. Pol. 3. 1. 10 ἐνίαις γὰρ οὐκ ἔστι δῆμος, οὐδ' ἐκκλησίαν νομίζουσιν ἀλλὰ σύγκλητους· 'in some States there is no popular body, and they have no regular assembly, but only meetings on special occasions.' σύγκλητος is one of those words which, though a technical term at Athens, could still be used by Attic poets without any prosaic local allusion being felt,—just as they used πρύτανις, ἐπιστάτης, ἄρχων, ψήφισμα, etc.—προὔθετο is another example. The presidents of the ecclesia were said γνώμας προθεῖναι when they invited a discussion. Thuc. 6. 14 ὦ πρύτανι...γνώμας προτίθει αὖθις Ἀθηναίοις, 'lay the question again before the assembly.' Id. 3. 42 τοὺς προθέντας τὴν διαγνώμην. Cp. Xen. Mem. 4. 2. 3 τῆς πόλεως λόγον περὶ τινος προτιθείσης. Lucian Menipp. 19 has προθεσαν οἱ πρυτάνεις ἐκκλησίαν, 'gave notice of': but for this the usual phrase was that of Aeschin. or. 2 § 60 προγράψαι τοὺς πρυτάνεις ἐκκλησίας δύο. Here, λέσχην is

· κοινῷ κηρύγματι πέμψας;

ΚΡΕΩΝ.

ἄνδρες, τὰ μὲν δὴ πόλεος ἀσφαλῶς θεοὶ,
πολλῷ σάλῳ σείσαντες, ὤρθωσαν πάλιν·
ὑμᾶς δ' ἐγὼ πομποῖσιν ἐκ πάντων δίχα
ἔστειλ' ἱκέσθαι, τοῦτο μὲν τὰ Λαΐου   165
σέβοντας εἰδὼς εὖ θρόνων ἀεὶ κράτη,
τοῦτ' αὖθις, ἡνίκ' Οἰδίπους ὤρθου πόλιν,
κἀπεὶ διώλετ', ἀμφὶ τοὺς κείνων ἔτι
παῖδας μένοντας ἐμπέδοις φρονήμασιν.

162 πόλεωσ L (it was never πόλεοσ): πόλεος r.   167 τοῦτ'] εἶτ' Reisig.
Wecklein suspects the loss of a verse after 167, such as τούτῳ βεβαίους ὄντας

not the meeting, but the discussion which is to take place there: thus the poet's phrase, true to Attic usage, corresponds with γνώμας προθεῖναι rather than with ἐκκλησίαν προθεῖναι. Herod. uses λέσχη of a public discussion (9. 71): cp. *O. C.* 167. The midd. προὔθετο suggests Creon's personal interest in the question: the active would denote the mere act (see on 8 θεῖναι). Cp. 1249. προτίθεσθαι more oft. denotes what one proposes *to* oneself.—κοινῷ κ. πέμψας, lit. having sent (notice of the meeting) by means of a summons addressed to each of us. The κήρυγμα is the mandate which κήρυκες carried to each of the fifteen elders,—not, of course, a public proclamation: cp. 164. For the absolute πέμπω, cp. Thuc. 5. 43 πέμπει εὐθὺς ἐς Ἄργος ἰδίᾳ: and so oft. (Not, 'having sent for us,' μεταπεμψάμενος: cp. on 19.)

162—331 First ἐπεισόδιον. Creon, the new king, enters from the central door of the palace. Recognising the loyalty which the Elders had shown to his predecessors, he expresses his own conception of the duty which a king owes to the State. He then announces the edict which, in accordance with that conception, he has published concerning the two brothers. The Chorus submissively acknowledge his right to do so, but express no approval. A guard now arrives (223), and announces that the king's edict has already been violated by an unknown hand, which has strewn dust upon the corpse of Polyneices. Creon dis-

misses him with threats of a dreadful death for him and for his fellows, if they fail to discover and produce the offender.

162—210 There is a general dramatic analogy between this speech and that of Oedipus in *O. T.* 216—275. In each case a Theban king addresses Theban elders, announcing a stern decree, adopted in reliance on his own wisdom, and promulgated with haughty consciousness of power; the elders receive the decree with a submissive deference under which we can perceive traces of misgiving; and as the drama proceeds, the elders become spectators of calamities occasioned by the decree, while its author turns to them for comfort.

162 ff. τὰ μὲν δὴ πόλεος .. ὑμᾶς δ'. The perils of the war are now over; the affairs of civil government claim my next care; and I have therefore sent for you, the nearest supporters of my throne.—πόλεος occurs only here in Soph., but twice in the trimeters of Aesch. (*Th.* 218, *Suppl.* 344), and thrice in those of Eur. (*Or.* 897, *El.* 412, *Ion* 595). Eur. has also in trimeters ὄφεος (*Bacch.* 1027, 1331, *Suppl.* 703), and κόρεος (*Cycl.* 641). In Comedy we find ὕβρεος (Ar. *Th.* 465, *Plut.* 1044), and φόσεος (*Vesp.* 1282, 1458). Such forms, which metrical convenience recommended to Attic poets, must not be confounded with the Ionic genitives in ι, such as πόλιος. The gen. πόλευς, contracted from πόλεος, is used by Theogn. 776 etc.—πολλῷ σάλῳ σείσαντες. Cp. *O. T.* 22.

summoned by his general mandate?

Enter CREON, *from the central doors of the palace, in the garb of king; with two attendants.*

CR.   Sirs, the vessel of our State, after being tossed on wild waves, hath once more been safely steadied by the gods: and ye, out of all the folk, have been called apart by my summons, because I knew, first of all, how true and constant was your reverence for the royal power of Laïus; how, again, when Oedipus was ruler of our land, and when he had perished, your steadfast loyalty still upheld their children.

αὖ παραστάτας (*Ars Soph. cm.* 40).   169 ἐμπέδοις] ἐμπέδους Reiske.

The image of the State as a ship dates in Greek literature from Alcaeus (whom Horace copied, *Carm.* 1. 14), fr. 18. The ship of Alcaeus is labouring in the trough of a wild sea,—water is coming in,—the sail is torn,—the anchor will not hold: ναῖ φορήμεθα σὺν μελαίνᾳ | χείμωνι μοχθεῦντες μεγάλῳ μάλα, κ.τ.λ. It is only through Heracleides *Alleg. Homer.* 5 that we know the meaning of Alcaeus to have been figurative and political. Aesch. often uses the image (*Th.* 2, 62, 208 etc.). Creon returns to it at 189. It is peculiarly well suited to his point,—the unity of the public interest.—ἄρθωσαν, made *upright*, 'righted': but below 167, ὦρθου = was keeping *straight:* cp. on 83.

164 f. ἐκ πάντων, (chosen) out of all, δίχα *adv.* (with ἱκέσθαι) apart from them: cp. 656 πόλεως..ἐκ πάσης μόνην, 1137 τὰν ἐκ πασᾶν τιμᾷς! *El.* 1351 ὅν ποτ' ἐκ πολλῶν ἐγὼ | μόνον προσηῦρον πιστόν. In other places, where δίχα is *prep.* with gen., we find it similarly connected with another expression of like purport, as *Ai.* 749 ἐκ..κύκλου | ..μεταστὰς οἷος 'Ατρειδῶν δίχα.—ἔστειλ' ἱκέσθαι: lit., by means of messengers I *caused* you *to set forth*, so that you should come (epexeg. inf.): *Ph.* 60 οἵ σ' ἐν λιταῖς στείλαντες ἐξ οἴκων μολεῖν. But στέλλεσθαι (midd.) 'to summon *to oneself*' (*O. T.* 434): cp. n. *O. T.* 860.— τοῦτο μὲν, answered by τοῦτ' αὖθις: see ὅτι π.—σέβοντας, like μένοντας (169), part. of the imperf., = ὅτι ἐσέβετε: so 1192: *O. T.* 835 τοῦ φαρόντος (n.): and cp. on *O. C.* 1565 f.—θρόνων..κράτη, powers belonging to the throne: cp. 60, 173.

167 ff. ἡνίκ' Οἰδίπους κ.τ.λ. The only obscurity arises from the use of the plur. κείνων in 168. κείνων παῖδας ought to mean, 'the descendants of Laïus and Oedipus,' viz. Eteocles and Polyneices. But, as the sentence stands, it must mean, 'the offspring of Laïus and of Oedipus *respectively';* viz. Oedipus, the son of Laïus; Eteocles and Polyneices, the sons of Oedipus. The relative clause, ἡνίκ'..ὤρθου πόλιν, induced the poet to add immediately the other relative clause to which the same person is subject, viz. ἐπεὶ διώλετο, instead of inserting, after ὤρθου πόλιν, words expressing their loyalty to Oedipus. We might, indeed, suppose that, after ὤρθου πόλιν, we were intended to supply mentally, καὶ τὰ ἐκείνου θρόνων κράτη σέβοντας. But against this is the fact that, after τοῦτο μέν .. τοῦτ' αὖθις,—'in the first place' .. 'in the second place,'—καὶ (in κἀπεὶ) would scarcely have been thus used to introduce a distinct third clause. Evidently καὶ links ἡνίκα ὤρθου to ἐπεὶ διώλετο.—ἐμπέδοις φρονήμασιν, with steadfast sentiments (of loyalty), modal dat., as oft. προθυμίᾳ, εὐνοίᾳ, φρονήματι (Thuc. 2. 62), etc. Hartung, whom some recent editors follow, adopts ἐμπέδους on the strange ground that Soph. must otherwise have written ἐμμένοντας. But μένοντας ἀμφὶ τοὺς κείνων παῖδας = 'remaining around them,' and the modal dat. is added no less legitimately than the causal dat. in Eur. *Her.* 701 δειλίᾳ μένειν, 'to remain through cowardice.' Soph. could have said ἐμπέδους φρονήμασιν, as he has said συντρόφοις | ὀργαῖς ἔμπεδος (*Ai.* 639): but ἐμπέδοις is better here, both (*a*) be-

'ὅτ' οὖν ἐκεῖνοι πρὸς διπλῆς μοίρας μίαν   170
'καθ' ἡμέραν ὤλοντο παίσαντές τε, καὶ
πληγέντες αὐτόχειρι σὺν μιάσματι,
'ἐγὼ κράτη δὴ πάντα καὶ θρόνους ἔχω
'γένους κατ' ἀγχιστεῖα τῶν ὀλωλότων.
'ἀμήχανον δὲ παντὸς ἀνδρὸς ἐκμαθεῖν   175
ψυχήν τε καὶ φρόνημα καὶ γνώμην, πρὶν ἂν
'ἀρχαῖς τε καὶ νόμοισιν ἐντριβὴς φανῇ.
'ἐμοὶ γὰρ ὅστις πᾶσαν εὐθύνων πόλιν
'μὴ τῶν ἀρίστων ἅπτεται βουλευμάτων,

171 παίσαντες] In L the letters αισ are small and cramped, having been substituted by the first corrector (S) for two erased letters. I suppose that the first hand

---

cause a series of accusatives has preceded, and (*b*) because, as μένοντας has already marked their constancy, we now want an epithet for their φρονήματα.

170 f. ὅτι causal, *O. T.* 918 n.—πρὸς διπλῆς μ.: cp. 14 n.: for πρὸς, 51 n.: for διπλῆς.. μίαν, 13 n.—παίσαντες.. πληγέντες. In Attic prose the verb 'to strike' usu. had as pres. τύπτω (or παίω), fut. τυπτήσω (or πατάξω), aor. ἐπάταξα, aor. pass. ἐπλήγην. The aor. of παίω is mainly a poetical word, used in tragedy, more rarely in comedy, and by Xen. In Attic prose ἔπαισα is usu. the aor. of παίζω. Meineke proposed πλήξαντες here, but that aor. (except in comp. with a prep.) is almost unknown to classical Attic. παισθέντες, again, though that aor. pass. occurs twice in Aesch., is very rare. —αὐτόχειρι.. μιάσματι, the stain of a kinsman's murder (see on 52, and cp. 1176): cp. Aesch. *Th.* 849 κακὰ | αὐτοφόνα. σύν, as 1266 νέῳ ξὺν μόρῳ: *O. C.* 1663, σὺν νόσοις : Pind. *O.* 2. 42 σὺν ἀλλαλοφονίᾳ.

173 f. ἐγὼ.. δή, I *now*: where δή nearly = ἤδη, *O. T.* 968 n. Aesch. *Eum.* 3 (after Gaia came Themis) ἣ δὴ τὸ μητρὸς δευτέρα τόδ' ἕζετο | μαντεῖον.—κράτη: cp. 166.—γένους κατ' ἀγχιστεῖα τῶν ὀλ., by nearness of kinship to the dead, γένους ἀγχιστεῖα forming one notion, on which the genit. τῶν ὀλ. depends, as on words meaning 'near.' The neut. plur. ἀγχιστεῖα (only here) would most properly mean 'rights' or 'privileges' of such nearness (cp. ἀριστεῖα, πρωτεῖα, etc.), but seems here to be merely a poetical equiv. for the abstract ἀγχιστεία. In Attic law ἀγχιστεία was any degree of

relationship on which a claim to an inheritance could be founded in the absence of a will otherwise disposing of it. To claim an inheritance under a will was ἀμφισβητεῖν κατὰ διαθήκην: to claim on the ground of relationship, ἀμφισβητεῖν κατ' ἀγχιστείαν. συγγένεια, consanguinity, might, or might not, constitute ἀγχιστεία: *e.g.* Isaeus says of the relationship of mother to son that it is συγγενέστατον μὲν τῇ φύσει πάντων, ἐν δὲ ταῖς ἀγχιστείαις ὁμολογουμένως οὐκ ἔστιν (or. 11 § 17), since a mother could not inherit from her son. (See *Selections from the Attic Orators*, pp. 331, 344.) Creon succeeds as the nearest male relative. Aesch., Soph., and Eur. ignore the Boeotian legend which gave a son, Laodamas, to Eteocles (Her. 5. 61), and a son, Thersander, to Polyneices (id. 4. 147, etc.). The sisters represent the λοχάτη ῥίζα (599).

175 ἀμήχανον δέ. 'You were loyal to the kings whose successor I am. Now (δέ) a man cannot be really known until he has been tried in office. (I do not, therefore, ask you to pledge your loyalty to me until I have been so tested.) I will, however, tell you the principles which I intend to observe.' Thus δέ merely marks the transition to a new topic. It is not directly adversative, as if he meant: 'You were loyal to my predecessors, *but* I do not yet ask you to be loyal to me.' On that view, however, the general connection of thoughts would remain the same. Demosthenes, in his speech on the Embassy (343 B.C.), quotes this passage (vv. 175—190) as illustrating maxims

Since, then, his sons have fallen in one day by a twofold doom,
—each smitten by the other, each stained with a brother's blood,
—I now possess the throne and all its powers, by nearness of
kinship to the dead.

No man can be fully known, in soul and spirit and mind, until he hath been seen versed in rule and law-giving. For if any,
being supreme guide of the State, cleaves not to the best counsels,

had by a mere oversight written πᾳσαντες (πείσαντες). The erasure of the original
σ was necessary in order to make room for αι.　　　**178** πᾶσαν] Nauck con-

---

which Aeschines had violated, though,
accustomed as he had been to play
tritagonist's parts, he ought to have
known them by heart (or. 19 § 247).

176 ψυχήν, 'soul,' the man's moral
nature generally: φρόνημα, the 'spirit'
of his dealing in public affairs, according as his aims are lofty or mean,
his policy bold or timid (cp. 207 τοιόνδ'
ἐμὸν φρόνημα): γνώμην, the intellectual aspect of the man, his ability and
judgment. In Her. 5. 124 ψυχὴν οὐκ
ἄκρος, 3. 14 διεπειρᾶτο αὑτοῦ τῆς ψυχῆς,
the word = 'fortitude.' But the usage of
Soph. favours the more general sense here:
cp. 227, 929, Ai. 1361 σκληρὰν...ψυχήν,
El. 219 σᾷ δυσθύμῳ τίκτους' ἀεὶ | ψυχᾷ
πολέμους. Plato has the phrase τῆς ψυχῆς
τὴν γνώμην for 'the intellect' (Legg.
672 B).

177 ἀρχαῖς, duties of administration.
It might be explained as a generic plur.
of ἀρχή, in the sense of 'sovereignties,'
as Isocr. or. 3 § 15 αἱ μοναρχίαι, § 16 τὰς
τυραννίδας, etc.: but it seems truer to say
that the Athenian poet was thinking of
public offices or magistracies. νόμοισιν
has a general sense: the king is concerned
with νόμοι both as νομοφύλαξ and as νο-
μοθέτης: but, as the context suggests, it is
of law-giving that Creon is more particularly thinking. Tournier has suggested ἀρχῇ τε καὶ θρόνοισιν, but we must
recollect how largely the language of
Attic tragedy is tinged with democratic
associations.—ἐντριβής, exercitatus: Plat.
Legg. 769 B ἐντριβής γε οὐδαμῶς γέγονα
τῇ τοιαύτῃ τέχνῃ. φανῇ 'be found,'
without ὤν, as Pind. P. 5. 107 πέφανταί
θ' ἁρμαπηλάτας σοφός: Thuc. 1. 8 Κᾶρες
ἐφάνησαν (were found to be). Not: 'be
revealed,' by being conversant.' Cp.
Arist. Eth. N. 5. 3 πολλοὶ γὰρ ἐν μὲν
τοῖς οἰκείοις τῇ ἀρετῇ δύναται χρῆσθαι, ἐν δὲ τοῖς πρὸς ἕτερον ἀδυνατοῦ-

σιν. καὶ διὰ τοῦτο εὖ δοκεῖ ἔχειν τὸ τοῦ
Βίαντος, ὅτι ἀρχὴ ἄνδρα δείξει· πρὸς
ἕτερον γὰρ καὶ ἐν κοινωνίᾳ ἤδη ὁ ἄρχων.
Besides Bias of Priene, others of the
ἑπτὰ σοφισταί,—as Chilon, Pittacus, Solon,—had this saying ascribed to them.
Plut. Sull. 30 (Sulla) εἰκότως προσετρίψατο
ταῖς μεγάλαις ἐξουσίαις διαβολὴν ὡς τὰ ἤθη
μένειν οὐκ ἐώσαις ἐπὶ τῶν ἐξ ἀρχῆς
τρόπων (as not allowing characters to
be constant under the influence of habits
formed in office), ἀλλ' ἔμπληκτα καὶ χαῦνα
καὶ ἀπάνθρωπα ποιούσαις. Shaksp. Jul.
Caes. ii. 1. 12 He would be crown'd:—
How that might change his nature, there's
the question....The abuse of greatness is,
when it disjoins | Remorse from power.

178 ff. ἐμοὶ γάρ. A ground for the
preceding statement is introduced by γάρ,
though the compression of the thought
slightly obscures the connection. 'A man
cannot be known until he has been tested
in power. For (γάρ) a man in power
may easily be deterred, by fear of unpo-
pularity, from pursuing the counsels best
for the State: and if he is so deterred,
I think him worthless.' πᾶσαν...πόλιν,
the whole city, as 656 πόλεως...ἐκ
πάσης, 776 πᾶσα...πόλις, Ai. 851 ἐν
πάσῃ πόλει (in the hearing of all the
city). In prose the art. would have
been added (cp. Thuc. 7. 29 τῇ πόλει
πάσῃ, 4. 87 ξυμπάσῃ τῇ πόλει, 2. 65 ἡ
ξύμπασα πόλις); but its omission in
poetry being so common, it is strange
that πᾶσαν should have been suspected
here.—μὴ...ἅπτεται, not οὐ, since the
relative clause is general ('such an one as
does not...,' Lat. qui with subjunct.): cp.
O. C. 1175 ἃ μὴ | χρῄζεις. Instead of
ὅστις μὴ ἅπτεται we should more often
find ὅστις ἂν μὴ ἅπτηται: yet the instances of the indic. after ὅστις in general
statement are not rare even in prose; cp.
Thuc. 2. 64 οἵτινες...ἥκιστα λυποῦνται,

44 ΣΟΦΟΚΛΕΟΥΣ

ʼἀλλʼ ἐκ φόβου του γλῶσσαν ἐγκλῄσας ἔχει, 180
ʼκάκιστος εἶναι νῦν τε καὶ πάλαι δοκεῖ·
ʼκαὶ μεῖζον· ὅστις ἀντὶ τῆς αὑτοῦ πάτρας
ʼφίλον νομίζει, τοῦτον οὐδαμοῦ λέγω.
ʼἐγὼ γάρ, ἴστω Ζεὺς ὁ πάνθʼ ὁρῶν ἀεί,
ʼοὔτʼ ἂν σιωπήσαιμι τὴν ἄτην ὁρῶν 185
ʼστείχουσαν ἀστοῖς ἀντὶ τῆς σωτηρίας,
ʼοὔτʼ ἂν φίλον ποτʼ ἄνδρα δυσμενῆ χθονὸς
ʼθείμην ἐμαυτῷ, τοῦτο γιγνώσκων ὅτι
ʼἥδʼ ἐστὶν ἡ σῴζουσα, καὶ ταύτης ἔπι
ʼπλέοντες ὀρθῆς τοὺς φίλους ποιούμεθα. 190

ject. ταγὸς: Blaydes, πρύμναν . . πόλεως.   **180** ἐγκλείσασ L: ἐγκλῄσας Elmsley.
Cp. on *O. T.* 1388.   **182** μεῖζον·] In L the first hand wrote μεῖζον: another hand
added ʼ after ν, indicating μεῖζον·, but left the circumflex unchanged. μεῖζον, which
Wakefield conjectured, is read by Nauck and others.—αὑτοῦ] αὑτοῦ L.   **184** [ἴστω]
Nauck conject. ἴστωρ.   **186** ἀστοῖς] ἆσσον is conjectured by Dobree (*Adv.* I. 436)

ἔργῳ δὲ μάλιστα ἀντέχουσιν: *ib.* ὅστις
λαμβάνει.—**ἐκ φ. του**: cp. 111 νεικέων ἐξ
ἀμφιλόγων.—**ἐγκλῄσας ἔχει** (cp. 22), = a
perf., in the sense 'has shut once for all,'
'keeps shut.' Distinguish the prose idiom,
Dem. or. 9 § 12 Φεράς...ἔχει καταλαβών,
has seized, and keeps.—νῦν τε καὶ πάλαι,
an emphatic formula ('seems, and has
always seemed'), *El.* 676, *Ph.* 966: cp.
El. 1049 πάλαι δέδοκται ταῦτα κοὐ νεωστί
μοι: *Il.* 9. 105 οἷον ἐγὼ νοέω, ἠμὲν πάλαι
ἠδʼ ἔτι καὶ νῦν.

182 f. μεῖζον: whoever recognises
a friend *more important* than his country,
—*i.e.* with stronger claims upon him:
ἀντὶ τῆς...πάτρας instead of the simple
gen., or ἤ with accus., as *Tr.* 576 ὥστε
μήτινʼ εἰσιδὼν | στέρξει γυναῖκα κεῖνος
ἀντὶ σοῦ πλέον. Cp. 638 (γάμος) μείζων
φέρεσθαι, more important to win: *O. T.*
772 τῷ γὰρ ἂν καὶ μείζονι | λέξαιμʼ ἂν ἤ
σοί..., 'to whom more important,' *i.e.*
with a better claim on my confidence,—
nearer and dearer. μεῖζον (which was
written by the first hand in L) is specious,
—'a more important thing,' a greater
good: cp. Eur. *Or.* 784 μέγα γὰρ ἡ γέ-
νεια σου, *Andr.* 209 ἢ Λάκαινα μὲν πό-
λις | μέγʼ ἐστί. But Demosthenes, at
least, seems to have read μεῖζον: for,
in applying the verses to Aeschines,
he paraphrases thus (or. 19 § 248):
τούτων οὐδὲν Αἰσχίνης εἶπε πρὸς αὑτὸν
ἐν τῇ πρεσβείᾳ, ἀλλʼ ἀντὶ μὲν τῆς πόλεως
τὴν Φιλίππου ξενίαν καὶ φιλίαν πολλῷ

μείζονα ἡγήσατο αὑτῷ καὶ λυσιτελε-
στέραν, ἐρρῶσθαι πολλὰ φράσας τῷ
σοφῷ Σοφοκλεῖ.—οὐδαμοῦ λέγω: Aesch.
Pers. 497 θεοὺς δέ τις | τὸ πρὶν νομίζων
οὐδαμοῦ, τότʼ ηὔχετο. Eur. *Andr.* 210
Σκῦρον οὐδαμοῦ τίθης (*nullo in numero
habes*). Xen. *Mem.* 1. 2. 52 ὥστε μηδα-
μοῦ παρʼ αὑτοῖς τοὺς ἄλλους εἶναι πρὸς
αὑτόν, 'so that the rest *were nowhere* with
them in comparison to him.' So οὐδενὸς
λόγου (or ἐν οὐδενὶ λόγῳ) ποιεῖσθαι, ἐν οὐ-
δεμιᾷ μοίρᾳ ἄγειν, etc.

184 ἐγὼ γάρ. Here, as in ἐμοὶ γάρ
above (178), γάρ introduces a reason;
but here, again, the connection is obscured by the form of the sentence. The
reason is contained in τοῦτο γιγνώσκων
κ.τ.λ. (188). 'I have no esteem for a
man who prefers popularity or private
friendship to the good of the State (178—
183); *for* (184) I well know that all private welfare depends on the welfare of
the State; and so I should never commit
the faults which I have just condemned
in others.'—ἴστω is confirmed against the
conjecture ἴστωρ (or ἴστωρ) by those passages in which it is joined with an accus.,
as *Il.* 7. 411 ὅρκια δὲ Ζεὺς ἴστω, 15. 36
ἴστω νῦν τόδε Γαῖα, etc.

185 οὔτʼ ἂν σιωπήσαιμι. Applied
to the actual case, Creon's words mean,
'I should never be deterred by fear of
popular murmurs (cp. 692 ff.) from pub-
lishing such an edict as this against
burying Polyneices, when I clearly saw

but, through some fear, keeps his lips locked, I hold, and
have ever held, him most base; and if any makes a friend of
more account than his fatherland, that man hath no place in
my regard. For I—be Zeus my witness, who sees all things
always—would not be silent if I saw ruin, instead of safety,
coming to the citizens; nor would I ever deem the country's foe
a friend to myself; remembering this, that our country is the
ship that bears us safe, and that only while she prospers in our
voyage can we make true friends.

and Shilleto (Dem. *De Falsa Legat.* p. 146): but see comment. **187** χθονόs] L
has πόλεωs written above by S (not by the first band). It was prob. a mere conjecture
suggested by the schol., οὐκ ἄν κτησαίμην φίλον τῆs ἐμῆs πόλεωs δυσμενῆ: Nauck,
however, places πόλεωs in the text.—Lugebil conject. οὔτ' ἄν ποτ' ἄνδρα δυσμενῆ πόλει
φίλον. **190** τοὺs φίλουs] Gomperz suspects these words: Mekler conject. πλοῦs

that otherwise a disastrous precedent
would be set. And though Polyneices
was my nephew, I should never allow
myself to recognise as friend or kinsman
a man who had borne arms against the
country.'

186 στείχουσαν ἀστοῖς. Demosthenes paraphrases this by στείχουσαν
ὁμοῦ (or. 19 § 248); whence Dobree
and Shilleto surmised that he read ἄσσον
(cp. *O. C.* 312 στείχουσαν ἡμῶν ἄσσον).
Now I think that I can explain why
Demosthenes so paraphrased. He is
applying the verses to Aeschines (see
above, n. on 182): τὴν δὲ ἄτην ὁρῶν στείχουσαν ὁμοῦ, τὴν ἐπὶ Φωκέας στρατείαν, οὐ προεῖπεν οὐδὲ προεξήγγειλεν.
The ἄτη which Aeschines saw approaching was the interference of Philip in the
Sacred War,—his action against the
Phocians. If Demosthenes had said στείχουσαν ἀστοῖς, this must have seemed to
refer to the fellow-citizens of Aeschines,
—the Athenians. The orator therefore
modified the poet's phrase by substituting
ὁμοῦ,—a word vague enough to suggest
the concern of other Greek states besides
Phocis in the peril.—ἀντὶ τῆs σωτηρίαs,
added for emphasis: 'ruin, *and not*
welfare, which a king is bound to promote.' (The art. τῆs is merely generic, as
in τὴν ἄτην.) So *Tr.* 267 φανεὶς δὲ
δοῦλος ἀνδρὸς ἀντ' ἐλευθέρου, a slave, and
not a free man (as he ought to be): *O. T.*
1490 κεκλαυμέναι | πρὸς οἶκον ἵξεσθ' ἀντὶ
τῆs θεωρίας.

187 ἄνδρα δυσμενῆ χθονός; cp.
Plat. *Lysis* 213 B τὸ φίλον ἄν εἴη φίλον τοῦ
φιλουμένου...τὸ μισοῦν ἄρα πάλιν ἐχθρὸν

τοῦ μισουμένου. Andoc. or. 1 § 96 (in
a νόμος) πολέμιος ἔστω Ἀθηναίων.—ἐμαυτῷ with φίλον. Some MSS. of Dem. (or.
19 § 247) give ἐμαυτοῦ in the quotation,
but here the dat. is clearly better. θείμην
'hold' (rather than 'make'): cp. Tyrt.
12. 1 οὔτ' ἄν μνησαίμην οὔτ' ἐν λόγῳ ἄνδρα
τιθείμην.

189 l. ἡ σῴζουσα, 'who bears us
safe.' σῴζειν was esp. said of a ship or
its captain: cp. Plat. *Gorg.* 511 D ἐὰν ..
ἐξ Αἰγίνης δεῦρο σώσῃ, if she (ἡ κυβερνη-
τική) has carried us safely from Aegina
to Athens.—ταύτης κ.τ.λ. It is only
while she remains upright, as we sail
on board of her, that we can make
real friends. ὀρθῆς (like ὤρθωσαν in
163) refers to the ship maintaining a
safe stability, as opposed to capsizing:
the contrast is given by ὑπτίοις .. σέλμασιν .. ναυτίλλεται in 716 (where see
n.). So Cic. *Ep. ad Fam.* 12. 25. 5
ut rectam teneamus (navem).—τοὺς
φίλους ποιούμεθα, we make the friends
(whom we really make): since friends
made at the cost of endangering or
wrecking the ship of the State cannot
properly be considered friends at all: they
are φίλοι ἄφιλοι. For the use of the art.,
cp. Thuc. 2. 40 οὐ .. πάσχοντες εὖ ἀλλὰ
δρῶντες κτώμεθα τοὺς φίλους. The
thought is like that ascribed to Pericles
by Thuc. 2. 60, ἐγὼ γὰρ ἡγοῦμαι πόλιν
πλείω ξύμπασαν ὀρθουμένην ὠφελεῖν
τοὺς ἰδιώτας ἤ καθ' ἕκαστον τῶν πολιτῶν
εὐπραγοῦσαν ἀθρόαν δὲ σφαλλομένην.
καλῶς μὲν γὰρ φερόμενος ἀνὴρ τὸ καθ' ἑαυτὸν διαφθειρομένης τῆς πατρίδος οὐδὲν
ἦσσον ξυναπόλλυται, κακοτυχῶν δὲ ἐν

·τοιοῖσδ' ἐγὼ νόμοισι τήνδ' αὐξω πόλιν·
ⁱκαὶ νῦν ἀδελφὰ τῶνδε κηρύξας ἔχω
·ἀστοῖσι παίδων τῶν ἀπ' Οἰδίπου πέρι·
·Ἐτεοκλέα μέν, ὃς πόλεως ὑπερμαχῶν
·ὄλωλε τῆσδε, πάντ' ἀριστεύσας δορί,   195
·τάφῳ τε κρύψαι καὶ τὰ πάντ' ἐφαγνίσαι
·ἃ τοῖς ἀρίστοις ἔρχεται κάτω νεκροῖς·
ⁱτὸν δ' αὖ ξύναιμον τοῦδε, Πολυνείκην λέγω,
·ὃς γῆν πατρῴαν καὶ θεοὺς τοὺς ἐγγενεῖς
ⁱφυγὰς κατελθὼν ἠθέλησε μὲν πυρὶ   200
ⁱπρῆσαι κατ' ἄκρας, ἠθέλησε δ' αἵματος
·κοινοῦ πάσασθαι, τοὺς δὲ δουλώσας ἄγειν,

καλούς.   191 αὔξω] Schneidewin conj. ἄξω, or τῆσδ' ἄρξω πόλεως.   198 τῶν ρ,
τῶνδ' L.   195 δορί L, with χε (i.e. χερί) written above by S.   196 ἐφαγνίσαι

εὐτυχούσῃ πολλῷ μᾶλλον διασψζεται. 'Pericles Thucydidis II. 60 Sophoclem videtur respexisse, vel eum Sophocles,' is Dobree's remark (*Adv*. 2. 37); but there is no adequate ground for such a view. The verbal coincidence of ὀρθῆς with ὀρθουμένην may well have been accidental. What is really common to poet and historian is the general sentiment of Periclean Athens. For another example of this, cp. *O. C.* 116 n.

191 νόμοισι, here, rules of conduct, principles, as *El.* 1043; cp. *O. C.* 907.—αὔξω, pres. (used also in Attic prose): the Attic fut. was αὐξήσω. The pres. here expresses purpose ('I intend to make Thebes prosperous'). Cp. Plat. *Legg.* 731 A φιλονεικείτω δὲ ἡμῖν πᾶς πρὸς ἀρετήν· ὁ γὰρ τοιοῦτος αὔξει τὰς πόλεις.

192 f. ἀδελφά τῶνδε, the more usu. constr.: but *O. C.* 1262 ἀδελφὰ τούτοισιν (n.). This use of the word is freq. in Attic prose, as Plat. *Phaedr.* 276 D ὅσα τούτων ἀδελφά.—τῶν ἀπ' Οἰδίπου. In regard to origin, ἐκ is properly said of parents, ἀπό of ancestors: Isocr. or. 12 § 81 τοὺς μὲν ἀπὸ θεῶν τοὺς δ' ἐξ αὐτῶν τῶν θεῶν γεγονότας. Cp. 466, 471, 1066; *Ph.* 260 ταῖ πατρὸς ἐξ Ἀχιλλέως. *Ai.* 202 χθονίων ἀπ' Ἐρεχθειδᾶν. But poetry oft. has ἀπό of the parent, as *O. C.* 571 κἀφ' ὅτου πατρὸς γεγώς: while, again, ἐκ oft. denotes merely the stock (including progenitors above the parent): cp. 1056:

so ἀγαθοὶ καὶ ἐξ ἀγαθῶν (Plat. *Phaedr.* 246 A), etc. The poetical indifference on this point is well seen in fr. 104, where τοὺς μὲν δυσσεβεῖς κακῶν τ' ἄπο | βλαστόντας is opposed to τοὺς δ' ὄντας ἐσθλοὺς ἔκ τε γενναίων ἅμα | γεγῶτας.

193 f. δορί was the ordinary Attic form, occurring in prose (as Thuc. 1. 128, 4. 98), and was prob. used by Soph. as well as δόρα, which metre requires in *O. C.* 620 (n.), 1314, 1386: cp. n. on *O. C.* 1304.—τὰ πάντ' ἐφαγνίσαι, to perform all due rites over the grave; *i.e.* to make the proper offerings to the dead (ἐναγίσματα, *O. C.* 402 n.), esp. libations, χοαί. For ἐπί in the compound cp. *El.* 440 χοὰς | οὐκ ἄν ποθ', ὃν γ' ἔκτεινε, τῷδ' ἐπέστεφε: *O.C.* 484 τάσδ' ἐπεύχεσθαι λιτάς, *i.e.* 'over' the rite. ἐφαγνίσαι is the reading of L; the force of the prep. is rightly given in the glosses, ἐπὶ τῷ τάφῳ ἁγνίσαι τὰ πάντα, and ἐπὶ τῷ τάφῳ ὁσίως ποιῆσαι. Though ἐφαγνίζειν is not elsewhere extant, there seems no reason to question it. ἀφαγνίσαι has been preferred by some, merely because that compound is recognised by the old grammarians (Suid., Hesych., Phrynichus in Bekk. *Anecd.* 26). But ἀφαγνίζειν meant esp. to purify from guilt (*expiare*): Paus. 2. 31. 8 (of Orestes at Troezen) ἐκάθαιρον καὶ εἱστίων, ἐς ὁ ἀφήγνισαν, 'until they had purged him.' Similarly in midd., Eur. *Alc.* 1145 πρὶν ἄν θεοῖσι τοῖσι νερτέροις | ἀφαγνίσηται, until

Such are the rules by which I guard this city's greatness. And in accord with them is the edict which I have now published to the folk touching the sons of Oedipus;—that Eteocles, who hath fallen fighting for our city, in all renown of arms, shall be entombed, and crowned with every rite that follows the noblest dead to their rest. But for his brother, Polyneices,—who came back from exile, and sought to consume utterly with fire the city of his fathers and the shrines of his fathers' gods,—sought to taste of kindred blood, and to lead the remnant into slavery;

L, ἀφαγνίσαι r.　　197 ἔρχεται] Ludw. Dindorf conject. ἔρδεται.　　201 πρῆσαι]

she has made expiatory offerings to them. So ἀφαγνεύω in Plut. *Mor.* 943 C (the souls of the good are to suffer only so long) ὅσον ἀφαγνεῦσαι καὶ ἀποπνεῦσαι τοὺς ἀπὸ τοῦ σώματος..μιασμούς ('to purge away': perh. we should read ἀφαγνίσαι). The force of ἀπό is thus the same as in ἀφοσιοῦσθαι, and in ἀφιερώμεθα as used by Aesch. *Eum.* 451 ('I have been hallowed,' *i.e.* purified). The case of κἀφαγιστεύσας below (247) is different from that of ἐφαγνίσαι here: it is, I think, for καὶ ἀφαγιστεύσας.

197 τοῖς ἀρίστοις, implying that, in his case, the αὐτόχειρ μίασμα (172) is to make no difference. Cp. *Ai.* 1379, where Odysseus offers to join in funeral honours to Ajax (notwithstanding his offence), μηδὲν ἐλλείπων, ὅσον | χρὴ τοῖς ἀρίστοις ἀνδράσιν πονεῖν βροτούς.—ἔρχεται κάτω: the χοαί were supposed to pass through the earth, and to be drunk by the spirits of the dead: Aesch. *Ch.* 164 ἔχει μὲν ἤδη γαποτοὺς χοὰς πατήρ: cp. *Od.* 10. 94, Eur. *Hec.* 535 ff. The dat., as *O. T.* 711 χρησμὸς..ἦλθε Λαΐῳ.

198 L has Πολυνείκην here, but Πολυνείκη in *O. C.* 375. Both forms are sound. From about 400 B.C. the Attic tendency of proper names in -ης was to pass from the 3rd to the 1st declension. Attic inscriptions of *circ.* 410–350 B.C. give the acc. in -ην more often than that in -η. From *c.* 350 to 30 B.C. the gen. in -ου is far more frequent than that in -ους. Even proper names in -κλέης, which kept the acc. in -κλέα to *c.* 300 B.C., afterwards formed it in -κλῆν. (No Attic inscript. gives -κλῆ.)—λέγω: see n. on 32 λέγω γὰρ κἀμέ.

199 Ω. γῆν πατρῴαν..καὶ θεοὺς.. πρῆσαι: cp. Aesch. *Th.* 582 (of Polynei-

ces) πόλιν πατρῴαν καὶ θεοὺς τοὺς ἐγγενεῖς | πορθεῖν, στράτευμ' ἐπακτὸν ἐμβεβληκότα. But πέρσαι, for πρῆσαι, would be a needless change here. 'To burn his country' means 'to burn his native city': so *O. C.* 1421 πάτραν κατασκάψαντι, when thou hast laid thy native city in ruins. θεοὺς πρῆσαι is to burn the gods' temples and the ancient wooden images (βρέτη) therein: cp. Her. 8. 109 ἐμπιμπράς τε καὶ καταβάλλων τῶν θεῶν τὰ ἀγάλματα. Aesch. *Pers.* 809 οὐ θεῶν βρέτη | ᾐδοῦντο συλᾶν οὐδὲ πιμπράναι νεώς.—θ. τοὺς ἐγγενεῖς, of the *race*, here in a large sense, of the Cadmean stock: while θεοὶ πατρῷοι are usu. rather the gods of one's own *family* (*O. C.* 756 n.). Cp. *El.* 428 πρός νιν θεῶν σε λίσσομαι τῶν ἐγγενῶν.—κατελθών, not καταχθεὶς ὑπὸ τῆς πόλεως: on the shield of Polyneices, Dikè was portrayed saying, κατάξω δ' ἄνδρα τόνδε (Aesch. *Th.* 647).—ἠθέλησε μέν ..ἠθέλ. δέ, rhetor. epanaphora (*O. C.* 610 φθίνει μέν..φθίνει δέ). Since πάσασθαι cannot govern γῆν..καὶ θεούς, ἠθέλησε μέν should in strictness have preceded γῆν.—πρῆσαι. Prose would have used ἐμπρῆσαι, though Thuc. has the pres. part. of the simple form (6. 94 πίμπραντες).—κατ' ἄκρας, here in its proper sense, of a town being sacked 'from top to bottom' (*Il.* 13. 772): cp. *O. C.* 1241 n.—αἵματος κ. πάσασθαι (πατέομαι), denoting the extreme of savage hatred; *Il.* 4. 35 ὠμὸν βεβρώθοις Πρίαμον: 24. 212 τοῦ ἐγὼ μέσον ἧπαρ ἔχοιμι | ἐσθέμεναι: Theogn. 349 τῶν εἴη μέλαν αἷμα πιεῖν.—τοὺς δέ..ἄγειν, as if τῶν μέν had preceded αἵματος. *O. T.* 1228 ὅσα | κεύθει, τὰ δ' αὐτίκ' εἰς τὸ φῶς φανεῖ. *Tr.* 117 στρέφει, τὸ δ' αὔξει. *Il.* 22. 157 παραδραμέτην, φεύγων, ὁ δ' ὄπισθε διώκων.

· τοῦτον πόλει τῇδ᾽ *ἐκκεκήρυκται τάφῳ
· μήτε κτερίζειν μήτε κωκῦσαί τινα,
· ἐὰν δ᾽ ἄθαπτον, καὶ πρὸς οἰωνῶν δέμας   205
· καὶ πρὸς κυνῶν ἐδεστὸν αἰκισθέντ᾽ ἰδεῖν.
· τοιόνδ᾽ ἐμὸν φρόνημα, κοὔποτ᾽ ἔκ γ᾽ ἐμοῦ
· *τιμῇ προέξουσ᾽ οἱ κακοὶ τῶν ἐνδίκων·
· ἀλλ᾽ ὅστις εὔνους τῇδε τῇ πόλει, θανὼν
· καὶ ζῶν ὁμοίως ἐξ ἐμοῦ τιμήσεται.   210
ΧΟ.· σοὶ ταῦτ᾽ ἀρέσκει, παῖ Μενοικέως Κρέον,

Musgrave conject. τέρσαι.   **203** ἐκκεκρύχθαι (sic) τάφῳ MSS., and so Wolff, understanding λέγω. Musgrave's ἐκκεκήρυκται τάφῳ has been received by most later edd.
But Nauck gives ἐκκεκηρῦχθαι λέγω from the parody by Carneades in Diog. L. 4.64,
τοῦτον σχολῇ τῇσδ᾽ ἐκκεκηρῦχθαι λέγω, and so Wecklein.   **206** αἰ κι σθέν τ᾽ L,
where the final a has been added by S, lest αἰκισθέν τ᾽ should be read. The spaces
left by the scribe (as often) between other letters in the word show that the space

---

203 f. The traditional ἐκκεκηρῦχθαι
τάφῳ can be explained only by supplying λέγω or the like. But in 196
κρύψαι and ἐφαγνίσαι depended on κηρύξας ἔχω in 192 (I have proclaimed to
the people). It would be intolerably
awkward to communicate the second
part of the proclamation in an oblique
form with the principal verb unexpressed :
—'(I tell you that) it has been proclaimed.' The choice lies between (1) Musgrave's ἐκκεκήρυκται τάφῳ, and (2)
Nauck's ἐκκεκηρῦχθαι λέγω. In favour
of (1) remark:—(a) τάφῳ is not, indeed, necessary with κτερίζειν, which
can be used absolutely; as Il. 11. 455
αὐτὰρ ἐπεί κε θάνω, κτεριοῦσί με δῖοι
Ἀχαιοί, 'will give me funeral honours':
but, as the main point is that a τάφος is
given to one brother and refused to the
other, the addition of τάφῳ to the more
general term κτερίζειν is plainly desirable
here. (b) The misplacement of μήτε is
due to the thought of κωκῦσαι having
come only after τάφῳ had been uttered
(μήτε κτερίζειν μήτε having been preferred to μὴ κτερίζειν μηδέ), and is not
bolder than (e.g.) the misplacement of τε
in Ph. 1411 f. αὐδὴν τὴν Ἡρακλέους | ἀκοῇ
τε κλύειν λεύσσειν τ᾽ ὄψιν. (c) The MS.
error may have arisen from a reminiscence
of ἐκκεκηρῦχθαι in 27. The line of Carneades (Diog. L. 4. 64), τοῦτον σχολῇς
τῇσδ᾽ ἐκκεκηρῦχθαι λέγω, is no argument
for λέγω in the text of Sophocles. What

could the parodist have made of τάφῳ?
The tragic solemnity of the decree was the
point of the parody, which uses ἐκκεκ. in
a different sense from the poet's ('I proclaim that he is banished from this
school': see on 27).
205 ff. ἐὰν δ᾽: see on 29. Construe, ἄθαπτον, αἰκισθέντ᾽ ἰδεῖν, mangled for all to see, δέμας καὶ πρὸς οἰωνῶν καὶ πρὸς κυνῶν ἐδεστόν, in the
body (acc. of respect) which birds and
dogs devour. L favours αἰκισθέν τ᾽: but
this is a point on which our MSS. have
little weight. Reading αἰκισθέντ᾽, it
would be also possible to take ἐδεστόν
as masc., with a slight pause after it; but
this seems less good. With αἰκισθέν τ᾽,
δέμας is accus. in appos.: leave him unburied, a body eaten (etc.), and mangled.
Some recent edd. prefer this.—δέμας of a
corpse, as 903, El. 756, Eur. Or. 40 etc.:
in Hom. always of the living, who has
σῶμα only of the dead: in Attic σῶμα is
said of either.—ἰδεῖν: the aor. inf., as in
the epic θαῦμα ἰδέσθαι, since the aor.
suggests the moment at which the startling
sight catches the eye, whereas the pres.
inf. would suggest continued gazing.
207 f. φρόνημα: on 176.—ἔκ γ᾽ ἐμοῦ,
by an act of mine (cp. 63, 93), while ἐν
γ᾽ ἐμοί in a negative sentence=(not) if I
can help it (O. C. 153).
208 The MSS. have τιμὴν προέξουσ᾽
. . τῶν ἐνδ., shall have honour before the
just, schol. ἕξουσι πρὸ τῶν δικαίων. Such

—touching this man, it hath been proclaimed to our people that none shall grace him with sepulture or lament, but leave him unburied, a corpse for birds and dogs to eat, a ghastly sight of shame.

Such the spirit of my dealing; and never, by deed of mine, shall the wicked stand in honour before the just; but whoso hath good will to Thebes, he shall be honoured of me, in his life and in his death.

CH. Such is thy pleasure, Creon, son of Menoeceus,

---

between ν and τ is consistent with his having meant ἀκισθέντ'.—αἰκισθέν τ' r. *207 ἐκ γ' ἐμοῦ L., with γρ. ἐξ ἐμοῦ written in the marg. by S. 208 τιμήν MSS.: τιμῇ Pallis. 211 Κρέον] L has κρέον, but the ο has been made from ω by erasure. Cp. on O. T. 637. For Κρέον, Seyffert conject. κυρεῖν: Martin, ποιεῖν: Bellermann, τὸ δρᾶν. Keeping Κρέον, Nauck would alter σοὶ ταῦτ' ἀρέσκει to σὺ ταῦτα δράσεις: Hartung would write σοὶ ταῦτ' ἀρέσκει δρᾶν, Μενοικέως παῖ Κρέον (and so Blaydes, with ταῦτ' for

---

a constr. of προέχω occurs nowhere else. But the objection to rendering, 'shall have the advantage of the just in honour' (τιμήν as acc. of respect) is that, after προέχειν in this sense, the point of advantage was regularly expressed by the dat.: see examples on O. C. 1007. τιμῇ (A. Pallis) is most probable, since either ΤΙΜΗΙ or τιμῃ might easily have become the accus. before the verb. Hermann read προσήξουτ' (which I do not understand) because of the hiatus (but cp. O. T. 351 προεῖπας, ib. 107 αὐτοέντας); and because the honours claimed for Polyneices are only equal, not superior. But Creon's meaning is explained by vv. 514 ff.: the honour is greater for a public foe than for a patriot.—τιμήσεται: cp. on 93.

211 f. I print Dindorf's κἀς for καὶ in v. 212, not as thinking it certain, but because, with the least change, it gives a satisfactory construction. Soph. has this crasis in fr. 428 φίλων τε μέμψιν κεἰς θεοὺς ἁμαρτάνειν. Cp. Plat. Rep. 538 B παράνομόν τι δρᾶσαι ἢ εἰπεῖν εἰς αὐτούς ('with regard to them'). For the place of the prep., cp. 367, O. T. 734 Δελφῶν κἀπὸ Δαυλίας. With the MS. reading, the accusatives in v. 212 must be governed by σοὶ ταῦτ' ἀρέσκει as = σὺ ταῦτα δράσαι δεινοῖ. Greek was bold in constructions κατὰ σύνεσιν, and might possibly have tolerated this: but it seems improbable. In the apparently similar instances the periphrasis for the transitive verb always contains a noun di-

rectly suggestive of that verb: as Eur. Ion 572 τοῦτο κἄμ' ἔχει πόθος = τοῦτο κἀγὼ ποθῶ: Aesch. Ag. 814 φθορὰς... ψήφους ἔθεντο: Suppl. 533 γένος...νέωσον αἷνον: Theb. 289 ζωπυροῦσι τάρβος ...λεών: Dem. or. 19 § 81 τεθνάναι τῷ φόβῳ...ξένους. Nor can the accusatives in v. 212 be explained as mere accus. 'of respect'; nor as if, by a euphemism, παθεῖν were understood.—There is much in favour of the view that Κρέον in v. 211 has displaced an infin., such as παθεῖν, λαβεῖν, λαχεῖν, ποιεῖν, or τὸ δρᾶν. In v. 1098 L has εὐβουλίας δεῖ, παῖ Μενοικέως, λαβεῖν, where later MSS. have Κρέον in place of λαβεῖν: see n. there. If Κρέον is not genuine in v. 211, then it is much more likely to have been a mere gloss on παῖ Μενοικέως than a corruption of a similar word. The conjecture κυρεῖν, then, merits no preference; though the acc. ταῦτα could stand with it (Aesch. Ch. 714 κυρούντων...τὰ πρόσφορα, Eur. Hec. 699 ἐπ' ἀκταῖς νιν κυρῶ).—Brunck wrote ταῦτ', understanding ἀρέσκει (με) ταυτὰ σοί, 'my view is the same as yours.' But ταῦτ' is right. The Chorus say—'Such is my lord's pleasure. And, of course, he can do as seems him good.' Their tone is sufficiently interpreted by vv. 216, 220, 278. Cp. Her. 1. 119 (Harpagus to Astyages) ἔφη... ἀρεστὸν εἶναι πᾶν τὸ ἂν βασιλεὺς ἔρδῃ. The Chorus do not oppose Creon; but they feel a secret misgiving; they wish at least to remain passive.

΄τὸν τῇδε δύσνουν *κἀς τὸν εὐμενῆ πόλει·
΄ νόμῳ δὲ χρῆσθαι παντί πού γ' ἔνεστί σοι
΄ καὶ τῶν θανόντων χὠπόσοι ζῶμεν πέρι.
ΚΡ.΄ ὡς ἂν σκοποὶ νῦν ἦτε τῶν εἰρημένων.   215
ΧΟ.΄ νεωτέρῳ τῳ τοῦτο βαστάζειν πρόθες.
ΚΡ.΄ ἀλλ' εἰσ' ἕτοιμοι τοῦ νεκροῦ γ' ἐπίσκοποι.
ΧΟ.΄ τί δῆτ' ἂν ἄλλο τοῦτ' ἐπεντέλλοις ἔτι;
ΚΡ.΄ τὸ μὴ 'πιχωρεῖν τοῖς ἀπιστοῦσιν τάδε.
ΧΟ.΄ οὐκ ἔστιν οὕτω μῶρος ὃς θανεῖν ἐρᾷ.   220
ΚΡ.΄ καὶ μὴν ὁ μισθός γ' οὗτος· ἀλλ' ὑπ' ἐλπίδων
΄ ἄνδρας τὸ κέρδος πολλάκις διώλεσεν.

ΦΥΛΑΞ.

΄ ἄναξ, ἐρῶ μὲν οὐχ ὅπως τάχους ὕπο

ταῦτ'). **212** Leaving v. 211 unchanged, M. Schmidt and Todt conject. ὁρᾶν τόν τε δύσνουν: Wecklein, ἐς τόν τε δύσνουν. Dindorf would merely change καὶ to κἀς. **213** παντί πουτ (sic) ἔνεστί σοι L. The later MSS. have πού τ' or ποτ' ἔνεστί σοι. Erfurdt conject. πού γ': C. Winckelmann, σοί γ' ἔνεστί που: Dindorf, formerly που μέτεστί σοι, then που πάρεστί σοι. **215** ὡς ἂν σκοποὶ νῦν ἦτε MSS. Schneidewin conject. ὡς οὖν . . ἦτε: Dindorf, πῶς ἂν . . εἶτε: Todt, ὅπως σκοποὶ δ' ἔσεσθε: Nauck, καλῶς· σκοποὶ νῦν ἐστε: Semitelos, ὡς οὖν σκοποὶ μενεῖτε. **217** νεκροῦτ' L: the τ' is somewhat like τ, but the first hand certainly did not mean γ', as may be seen by comparing 207 (ἐκ γ'), and 221 (μισθός γ'). The error is like πουτ' in 213.—νεκροῦ γ'

213 f. In **παντί πού γ'** the enclitic που closely adheres to παντί, and γε emphasises the whole expression; as in *El.* 1506, ὅστις πέρα πράσσειν γε τῶν νόμων θέλει, the γε emphasises the whole phrase πέρα πράσσειν. The transposition σοί γ'...που is open to the objection that παντί, not σοί, claims the chief emphasis. παντί που πάρεστι has also been proposed. But ἔνεστι is slightly more suitable to this context, because more suggestive of *tacit disapproval*. 'It is *possible* for you' ('but we doubt whether it is expedient'). πάρεστί σοι is generally said rather when the speaker means, 'it is easy for you,' or 'it is open to you,'—in seconding a wish of the other person, or in making an offer to him. *Ph.* 364 τἄλλα μὲν πάρεστί σοι | πατρῷ' ἑλέσθαι. Cp. *O. T.* 766.—παντί που μέτεστί σοι, which some prefer, is still less suitable here. It would imply a right shared by the King with some other man or men (cp. on 48).—Though the antecedent (ἡμῶν) to χὠπόσοι ζῶμεν is understood, πέρι can stand at the end of the verse, since such a relative clause was felt almost as a noun-case: see on 35. Cp. Eur. *Ion* 560 ἦ θίγω δῆθ' οἵ μ' ἔφυσαν; (=τῶν φυσάντων).

215 ὡς ἂν...ἦτε can be explained only by an ellipse of ἐπιμελεῖσθε or the like. After verbs of 'taking care,' the usu. constr. is ὅπως with fut. indic.; but ὡς ἂν with subj. is sometimes found, as Xen. *Hipparch.* 9. 2 ἐπιμελεῖσθαι ὡς ἂν πραχθῇ...ἢν μή τις ἐπιμελῆται ὡς ἂν ταῦτα περαίνηται. In elliptical phrases, where a precept or charge is given (ὅρα, etc., being understood), the regular constr. is ὅπως with fut. ind., as Lys. or. 1. 21 ὅπως τοίνυν ταῦτα μηδεὶς ἀνθρώπων πεύσεται. The elliptical ὅπως μή with subjunct. is different,—'take care *lest*,' —a deferential way of hinting an objection (Plat. *Crat.* 430 D), like the simple elliptical μή with subjunct. *O. C.* 1180. Since, however, ἐπιμελεῖσθαι could be followed by ὡς ἂν with subjunct., it is conceivable that Soph. should write ὡς ἂν σκοποὶ ἦτε instead of the usual ὅπως σκοποὶ ἔσεσθε. I cannot think, with Wecklein, that the sentence is broken off, as though Creon said,—'*In order that* ye

touching this city's foe, and its friend; and thou hast power,
I ween, to take what order thou wilt, both for the dead, and for
all us who live.

CR.   See, then, that ye be guardians of the mandate.
CH.   Lay the burden of this task on some younger man.·
CR.   Nay, watchers of the corpse have been found.
CH.   What, then, is this further charge that thou wouldst
give?
CR.   That ye side not with the breakers of these commands.
CH.   No man is so foolish that he is enamoured of death.
CR.   In sooth, that is the meed; yet lucre hath oft ruined
men through their hopes.

Enter GUARD.

My liege, I will not say that I come breathless from

Brunck.   **216** ἄλλωι L, with o written over ω by the first hand. ἄλλω and ἄλλο r.
Brunck conject. ἄλλο τοῦδ': Pallis, ἀλλ' ἐκ τοῦδ' (or ἐκ τῶνδ').   **219** 'πιχωρεῖν L first
hand, but an early hand has changed ω to ει. Schol., μὴ ἐπιτρέπειν μηδὲ συγχωρεῖν
τοῖς ἀπειθοῦσιν,—showing that he, too, read 'πιχωρεῖν, which almost all the later MSS.
have.   L² has ἐπιχειρεῖν, but with the gloss ἐπιτρέπειν (see Campbell).   **223 ΦΥΛΑΞ**]
In L the designation of the speaker is ἀγγ, with ε written above (ἄγγελος): below, at
v. 384, it is αγ, but with φύλαξ in the margin.   In L's list of the Dramatis Personae
(prefixed to the play) it is φύλαξ ἄγγελος.   τάχους MSS.: σπουδῇ Arist. *Rhet.* 3. 14.

---

may be watchers of my mandate,'—being
about to add, μὴ ἐπιχωρεῖτε.—Dindorf's
τάς ἄν...εἶτε is supported by usage, as
O. T. 765 πῶς ἄν μόλοι δῆθ' ἡμὶν ἐν
τάχει πάλιν; Nauck (*Cur. Eur.* II. 79)
refuses οἶμεν and εἶτε to tragedy, but is
not convincing. In *O. T.* 1046 εἰδεῖτ'
(for εἰδείητε) is certain: and εἶτε for εἴητε
is strictly parallel.   εἶτε occurs in *Od.* 21.
195 τοῦ κ' εἴη 'Οδυσῆι ἀμυνέμεν, εἰ ποθεν
ἔλθοι; In Eur. *Alc.* 921 ἦμεν might replace εἶμεν: though in *Hipp.* 349, at least,
the opt. εἶμεν seems required. But πῶς
ἄν εἶτε is here less fitting than ὡς ἄν
ἔντε, because a request is less suitable
than an injunction.—σκοποί, φύλακες,
who watch to see that no one breaks the
edict.—νυν is better than νῦν.—τῶν εἰρ.,
the commands: cp. Aesch. *Ag.* 1620 σωφρονεῖν εἰρημένον, Her. 7. 16 εἴρητο συλ-
λέγεσθαι...στρατόν.
   216 f. πρόθες τοῦτο, set him this as a
task (cp. 1249), βαστάζειν, for him to
take in hand (*suscipiendum*); the act. inf.
as *O. C.* 231 πόνον...ἀντιδιδῶσιν ἔχειν.
For the lit. sense of the verb cp. *Ai.* 827
ὥς με βαστάσῃ | πεπτῶτα (raise me).—
τοῦ νεκροῦ γ': but ἐπίσκοποι τῶν ἀστῶν
are still needed.

218 f. τί δῆτ' ἄν...ἐπεντέλλοις = τί
δῆτ' ἄν εἴη...ὃ ἐπεντέλλεις; cp. *O. C.* 647
μέγ' ἄν λέγοις δώρημα: *Ph.* 26.—The reading ἄλλῳ is a bad one, for the contrast is
between commands, not persons; and an
awkward ambiguity would arise, since
τοῦτο might then seem to mean the
watching of the corpse.—ἐπιχωρεῖν, ac-
cedere, to join their side: Thuc. 4. 107
δεξάμενος τοὺς ἐθελήσαντας ἐπιχωρῆσαι...
κατὰ τὰς σπονδάς. Arist. *Mirab.* 133
τούτῳ τῷ ἐπιγράμματι ἐπεχώρησε καὶ ὁ
τόπος ἐκεῖνος (corroborated it).—ἀπιστοῦσιν = ἀπειθοῦσιν: 381, 656.—τάδε,
cogn. acc.: cp. 66.
   220 ff. ὃς (instead of ὥστε) φρᾷ, a
constr. most freq. in negative sentences,
usu. with ὅστις (Dem. or. 1 § 15 τίς οὕτως
εὐήθης ἐστίν...ὅστις ἀγνοεῖ), or ὃς ἄν and
opt. (Plat. *Rep.* 360 B οὐδεὶς ἄν γένοιτο
οὕτως ἀδαμάντινος, ὃς ἄν μείνειεν). But it
occurs also in affirmative sentences, as
Eur. *Andr.* 170 ἐς τοῦτο δ' ἥκεις ἀμαθίας
...ἤ...τολμᾷς. Cp. Her. 4. 52.—καὶ μὴν
(lit., 'and verily') here confirms the last
speaker's remark by adding an assurance
that disobedience does indeed mean
death; while γε after μισθός emphasises
that word.   'And I can tell you that the

· δύσπνους ἱκάνω, κοῦφον ἐξάρας πόδα·
·πολλὰς γὰρ ἔσχον φροντίδων ἐπιστάσεις,   225
·ὁδοῖς κυκλῶν ἐμαυτὸν εἰς ἀναστροφήν·
·ψυχὴ γὰρ ηὔδα πολλά μοι μυθουμένη·
·τάλας, τί χωρεῖς οἷ μολὼν δώσεις δίκην;
·τλήμων, μένεις αὖ; κεἰ τάδ' εἴσεται Κρέων
·ἄλλου παρ' ἀνδρός, πῶς σὺ δῆτ' οὐκ ἀλγυνεῖ;   230
· τοιαῦθ' ἑλίσσων ἥνυτον σχολῇ βραδύς,
·χοὕτως ὁδὸς βραχεῖα γίγνεται μακρά.
· τέλος γε μέντοι δεῦρ' ἐνίκησεν μολεῖν

§ 11, and so Dindorf, Hartung, Nauck, Wecklein.   **225** ἔσχον L: εὗρον r.—φροντίδων] Nauck conj. δεῦρ' ἰών.   **229** μένεις αὖ;] In L the first hand seems to have written μὲν εἰ σαῦ (μὲν εἰς αὖ): a corrector has wished to make this into μενεῖς αὖ, the reading of most of the later MSS. (including A), but has left the accent on μὲν (cp. n.

requital of disobedience is that.' For καὶ μήν so used, cp. O. T. 836, 1004 f., El. 556.—**τὸ κέρδος**, 'gain,' i.e., as ἐλπίδων shows, the prospect of gain, with the generic art. (cp. 1242): so fr. 749 τὸ κέρδος ἡδύ, κἂν ἀπὸ ψευδῶν ἴῃ.—**διώλεσεν**, gnomic aor.

223 ἐρῶ μὲν οὐχ: cp. on 96.—**ὅπως** = ὅτι, as O. T. 548: cp. El. 963 μηκέτ' ἐλπίσῃς ὅπως | τεύξει. This use is rare in Attic prose (for after θαυμάζω, etc., ὅπως = 'how'), though freq. in Her., as 2. 49 οὐδὲ φήσω ὅκως...ἔλαβον. Yet cp. Plat. Euthyd. 296 E οὐκ ἔχω ὑμῖν πῶς ἀμφισβητοίην...ὅπως οὐ πάντα ἐγὼ ἐπίσταμαι.—**τάχους ὕπο** is the reading of the MSS. Aristotle quotes this verse as an example of a προοίμιον used by the speaker to avert a danger from himself, and gives it thus:—ἄναξ, ἐρῶ μὲν οὐχ ὅπως σπουδῆς ὕπο (Rhet. 3. 14 § 10). Hence some edd. adopt σπουδῆς, as coming from a source older than our MSS. But, since τάχους is free from objection, such a change is unwarrantable. Aristotle's quotations seem to have been usually made from memory, and his memory was not infallible. To take only three examples cited by Bellermann, we find: (1) El. 256 ἀλλ' ἡ βία γὰρ ταῦτ' ἀναγκάζει με δρᾶν, quoted Metaphys. 4. 5 ἀλλ' ἡ βία με ταῦτ' ἀναγκάζει ποιεῖν: (2) O. T. 774 ἐμοὶ πατὴρ μὲν Πόλυβος ἦν, quoted Rhet. 3. 14 § 6 ἐμοὶ πατὴρ ἦν Πόλυβος: (3) Ant. 911 μητρὸς δ' ἐν Ἅιδου καὶ πατρὸς κεκευθότοιν, quoted Rhet. 3. 16 § 9 with βεβηκότων as last word. So Il. 9. 592 κήδε' ὅσ' ἀνθρώποισι πέλει τῶν ἄστυ ἀλώῃ· |

ἄνδρας μὲν κτείνουσι, is quoted Rhet. 1. 7 § 31 with ὅσσα κάκ' substituted for the first two words, and λαοὶ μὲν φθινύθουσι for the last three.

224 ff. ἐξάρας (ά), aor. part., not pres., because, as ἐξ- shows, the notion is, 'having set in nimble movement' (at starting). Cp. Eur. Tro. 342 μὴ κοῦφον αἴρῃ βῆμ' ἐς Ἀργείων στρατόν.—**φροντίδων**, possessive gen. with **ἐπιστάσεις**, halts belonging to thoughts, i.e. caused by them. Others understand, 'halts for thought' (made in order to reflect),—which is less simple. Cp. Arist. De Anim. 1. 3 (p. 407ᵃ 32) ἡ νόησις ἔοικεν ἠρεμήσει τινὶ καὶ ἐπιστάσει (halt) μᾶλλον ἢ κινήσει.—**ὁδοῖς**, locative dat.; cp. O. C. 553 ὁδοῖς | ἐν ταῖσδ', 'in this my coming.'—**κυκλῶν** = περιστρέφων.

227 ψυχὴ γὰρ ηὔδα κ.τ.λ. The naïveté consists in the direct quotation of what his ψυχή said, rather than in the statement that it spoke; thus Hor. Sat. 1. 2. 68 (quoted by Schneid.) is really similar,—Huic si...Diceret haec animus. Take **πολλὰ** with **μυθουμένη** only. I do not think that ηὔδα...μυθουμένη was meant to mark garrulity; the language is not homely enough: rather it is simply,—'found a voice, speaking many things.' ἔφη λέγων is not similar (Ai. 757).—Cp. Launcelot Gobbo in Shaksp. Merch. 2. 2: Certainly my conscience will serve me to run from this Jew my master. The fiend is at mine elbow and tempts me...My conscience says, 'Launcelot, budge not.' 'Budge,' says the fiend. 'Budge not,' says my conscience.

speed, or that I have plied a nimble foot; for often did my thoughts make me pause, and wheel round in my path, to return. My mind was holding large discourse with me ; ' Fool, why goest thou to thy certain doom?' 'Wretch, tarrying again? And if Creon hears this from another, must not thou smart for it?' So debating, I went on my way with lagging steps, and thus a short road was made long. At last, however, it carried the day that I should come hither—to

on 182). This accent suggests that the scribe of L had μένεις in his archetype.—κεί L, but by correction, prob. from καί, which some of the later MSS. (as A) have, while others have εί. **231** σχολῇ βραδύς MSS. : schol. in marg. of L. γρ. ταχύς. Seyffert

228 f. τάλας...τλήμων, nom., not voc., because each is rather a comment ('hapless that thou art !') than properly an address: so *O. C.* 185 ὦ τλάμων, *ib.* 753 ὦ τάλας ἐγώ, Eur. *Med.* 61 ὦ μῶρος. —μένεις is better than μενεῖς, since, '*are you* tarrying again?' (his halts hāving been frequent, 225) is more graphic than, '*will you* tarry again?'— αὖ cannot mean here, 'on the contrary' (*i.e.* instead of going on).—πῶς...οὐκ, as *O. T.* 937, 976, etc.—ἀλγυνεῖ, pass.: cp. on 93 ἐχθαρεῖ.
231 ἑλίσσων, turning over and over in the mind: cp. on 158 ἐρέσσων.— ἤνυτον (*sc.* τὴν ὁδόν), gradually made my way (impf.); whereas ἤνυσα would have suited a quick journey. Cp. this impf. in Plat. *Symp.* 127 c οὐδαμῇ ταύτῃ ἤνυτον, 'they could make no progress by that means.' Soph. has this tense also in *Tr.* 319 (ἔργον ἤνυτον): cp. below, 805. In Dem. or. 21 § 104 our MSS. give οὐδὲν ἤνυε. For the use of the verb in ref. to journeys, cp. Thuc. 2. 97 (ὁδὸς) ἡμερῶν ἀνδρὶ εὐζώνῳ τριῶν καὶ δέκα ἀνύσαι. The Attic *pres.* seems to have been ἀνύτω as='to accomplish,' or 'to make way,' but ἀνύειν as='to hasten.' Ar. *Plut.* 413 μή νυν διατρίβ' ἀλλ' ἄνυε: *Ran.* 606 ἀνύετον: though in *Plut.* 606 οὐ μᾶλλον | χρῆ σ', ἀλλ' ἀνύειν, some MSS. have ἀνύτειν (see Pors. on *Phoen.* 463). This is the distinction meant by the grammarian in Bekk. *Anecd.* 411. 28 ἀνύτειν (*sic*) οἱ Ἀττικοὶ ὅπερ ἡμεῖς. ἀνύειν δὲ τὸ σπεύδειν. (The aspirated forms lack good evidence.) Cp. ἀρύω, Attic ἀρύτω.
σχολῇ βραδύς, reluctantly and slowly ; the opposite of σὺν σπουδῇ ταχύς (*Ph.* 1223), with eagerness and speed. σχολῇ oft. ='at a slow pace' (πορεύεσθαι, Xen. *An.* 4. 1. 16; ὑποχωρεῖν, Thuc. 3. 78).

As βραδύς could mean 'sluggish' (*O. C.* 306), we might here refer σχολῇ to pace, and βραδύς to reluctance; but, though the common use of σχολῇ in regard to pace helps to make it suitable here, it is better, in this context, to give σχολῇ the moral and βραδύς the physical sense. For σχολῇ combined with another word in such an expression, cp. Polyh. 8. 30 σχολῇ καὶ βάδην ποιεῖσθαι τὴν πορείαν. There is no lack of point. Such a messenger ought to have come σπουδῇ ταχύς.—The conjecture σπουδῇ βραδύς is (I think) not only wrong but bad. It would mean, 'slow in my haste'; eager to arrive, yet moving slowly. σπεῦδε βραδέως, to which it is supposed to allude, meant, 'never remit your efforts, but advance circumspectly towards your aim': *festina lente* (on which see Erasmus in the *Adagia*); *Eile mit Weile*; Goethe's *Ohne Hast, ohne Rast.* (σπεῦδε βραδέως was a favourite maxim of Augustus, Suet. *Aug.* 25; Gellius 10. 11 § 5, on whom, as often, Macrobius has drawn, *Sat.* 6. 8. 9.) The frightened and irresolute φύλαξ, —sent, sorely against his will, on a hateful errand,—had no more σπουδή than Mr Facing-both-ways. Wecklein, keeping σχολῇ, supposes the Guard to mean, 'th's was a case of σχολῇ βραδύς, not σπουδῇ βραδύς,'—an improbably obscure and feeble jest at such a critical moment. The variant given by the schol., σχολῇ ταχύς, would be an oxymoron, designedly comic; 'I took my time about hurrying,' ''twas but a laggard haste that I made.' A cheerful epigram of this sort would better suit a mind more at ease.
233 τέλος γε μέντοι, *at last*, however ; γε emphasizing the word before it : *O. T.* 442 n.—ἐνίκησεν, impers., as Thuc. 54 ἐνίκησε δὲ...λοιμὸν εἰρῆσθαι (the opinio² prevailed that...): Her. 6. 101 ἐνίκα μὴ

.σοί· κεἰ τὸ μηδὲν ἐξερῶ, φράσω δ' ὅμως.

·τῆς ἐλπίδος γὰρ ἔρχομαι δεδραγμένος,   235

·τὸ μὴ παθεῖν ἂν ἄλλο πλὴν τὸ μόρσιμον.

ΚΡ.·τί δ' ἐστὶν ἀνθ' οὗ τήνδ' ἔχεις ἀθυμίαν;

ΦΥ.·φράσαι θέλω σοι πρῶτα τἀμαυτοῦ· τὸ γὰρ

'πρᾶγμ' οὔτ' ἔδρασ' οὔτ' εἶδον ὅστις ἦν ὁ δρῶν,

·οὐδ' ἂν δικαίως ἐς κακὸν πέσοιμί τι.   240

ΚΡ.·εὖ γε στοχάζει κἀποφράγνυσαι κύκλῳ

'τὸ πρᾶγμα· δηλοῖς δ' ὥς τι σημανῶν νέον.

conject. σπονδῇ βραδύς.   **234** σοί κ' εἰ L (the apostrophe after κ from a later hand). Erfurdt, κεί σοι: Hartung, σοὶ δ' οὖν.—φράσω δ'] φράσαι δ' Wunder; φράσων (without δ') Wecklein.   **235** πεπραγμένος L, with schol. ὑπὸ γὰρ τῆς ἐλπίδος νενικημένος ἐλήλυθα. ἢ οὕτως· ἀντειλημμένος τῆς ἐλπίδος ἐλήλυθα. We have here two commentators: the first was attempting to explain πεπραγμένος: the second read δεδραγμένος, which is in E (with φαρ written above) and V³: while in Aug. b and V⁴ is the gl., γρ. δὲ καὶ δεδραγμένος. The rest of the later MSS. have either πεπραγμένος (as A, L³), or πεφραγμένος (as Aug. b, Vat., V⁴).—Dindorf wrote πεφαργμένος.—Semitelos conject.

ἐκλιπεῖν τὴν πόλιν. That μολεῖν should not be regarded as the subject to ἐνίκησε, is shown by such an example as Her. 8. 9 ἐνίκα τὴν ἡμέρην ἐκείνην αὐτοῦ μείναντάς τε καὶ αὐλισθέντας μετέπειτα νύκτα μέσην παρέντας πορεύεσθαι, where the length of the interval excludes such a view. The personal constr. occurs below, 274; cp. Thuc. 2. 12 ἦν...Περιγνώμη...νενικηκυῖα.

κλέους σοί with μολεῖν. In Attic prose a case of the person after ἔρχομαι is freq., and oft. can be rendered (as here) only by 'to,' though it is properly rather a dat. of interest. Thus Thuc. 1. 13 Ἀμεινοκλῆς Σαμίοις ἦλθε = 'A. came to the Samians,' though the primary notion is, 'the Samians enjoyed the advantage of A.'s coming' (to build triremes for them). So id. 1. 27 ὡς αὐτοῖς...ἦλθον ἄγγελοι: Plat. Prot. 321 C ἀπορῦντι δὲ αὐτῷ ἔρχεται Προμηθεύς. In poetry this dat. is freely used after verbs of motion, but the idea of interest is always traceable; cp. 186 n. Aesch. P. V. 358 ἀλλ' ἦλθεν αὐτῷ Ζηνὸς ἄγρυπνον βέλος. So here, μολεῖν σοί is not strictly a mere equiv. for μολεῖν πρὸς σέ, but implies Creon's interest in the news. The notion is, 'to come and place myself at your disposal.' For the emphatic place of σοί, cp. 273 (and 46 n.): for the pause after the first syllable of the verse, 250, 464.—κεἰ, 'and if': not, 'even if.' If καί were taken

as = 'even,' there would be a very harsh asyndeton, whether the stop were at σοί, or (as Nauck places it) after μολεῖν. It is true that καί could mean 'even,' without causing an asyndeton, if we adopted Wecklein's tempting φράσων for φράσω δ': but the latter is confirmed by O. T. 302 εἰ καὶ μὴ βλέπεις, φρονεῖς δ' ὅμως (where see n.),—δέ introducing the apodosis after a concessive protasis. For κεἰ as = 'and if,' cp. Ai. 447, 1057. The transposition κεί σοι is improbable, as destroying the significant emphasis and pause on σοί.—τὸ μηδέν, what is as nought,—a tale of simple discomfiture: since he can only report the deed, without giving any clue to the doer. Cp. Tr. 1107 κἂν τὸ μηδὲν ὦ: Ai. 1275 ἤδη τὸ μηδὲν ὄντας ἐν τροπῇ δορός.

235 f. τῆς ἐλπίδος, not 'hope,' but 'the hope'—defined in next v.—δεδραγμένος is certain. Il. 13. 393 κόνιος δεδραγμένος (and 16. 486). D¹od. 12. 67 δράξασθαι καιροῦ. (Cp. Shaks. Per. 1. 1. 49 Gripe not at earthly joys.) Here the phrase is meant to be homely. The v. l. πεφραγμένος was simply an attempt to mend L's πεπραγμένος. We should require the dat. with it. The gen. cannot be justified by instances in which poetry uses a gen. of the agent without ὑπό, after pass. part., as Ai. 807 φωτὸς ἠπατημένη, Eur. Or. 497 πληγεὶς θυγατρός, etc.—τὸ μὴ παθεῖν ἄν = ὅτι οὐ

thee; and, though my tale be nought, yet will I tell it; for I
come with a good grip on one hope,—that I can suffer nothing
but what is my fate.

CR. And what is it that disquiets thee thus?

GU. I wish to tell thee first about myself—I did not do the
deed—I did not see the doer—it were not right that I should
come to any harm.

CR. Thou hast a shrewd eye for thy mark; well dost thou
fence thyself round against the blame:—clearly thou hast some
strange thing to tell.

δεδραμένοις ('on account of my deeds'). **238** πρῶτα L: πάντα r. **241** στοχάζει
MSS.: Hartung conject. στιχάζει (others, στιχίζει): Emper, σκεπάζει: F. Jacobs,
στεγάζει.—From Arist. *Rhet.* 3. 14. 11 Bergk and others adopt τί φροιμάζει; Wecklein
suggests εὖ φροιμάζει.—κάποφράγνυσαι MSS.: κάποφάργνυσαι Dindorf. **242** ση-
μαίνων L: σημανῶν r. Didymus (*circ.* 30 B.C.) read the latter, as appears from the
schol. on *Ai.* 1225 Δίδυμος· καὶ δῆλός ἐστιν ὥς τι σημανῶν νέον, a verse composed by a
slip of memory, as Dindorf saw, from this verse and *Ai.* 326 καὶ δῆλός ἐστιν ὥς τι δρα-

πάθοιμι ἄν, depending on ἐλπίδος...δεδρ.
as = ἐλπίζων: for the art. with infin., cp.
78 n.—τὸ μόρσιμον: i.e. if you do kill
me, then it was my destiny to be killed.
237 f. ἀνθ' οὗ, on account of which:
O. T. 264 ἀνθ' ὧν: El. 585 ἀνθ' ὅτου.—
τὸ γάρ | πρᾶγμ': cp. on 67. γάρ pre-
faces the statement: O. T. 277 n.: cp.
below, 478, 999.
241 f. εὖ γε στοχάζει κ.τ.λ.: 'yes,
you take your aim well, and seek to
fence yourself round against the charge.'
The mark at which the man aims is his
own safety; and this is explained by the
next phrase. Commentators have made
difficulties by assuming that the metaphors
of στοχάζω and ἀποφράγνυσαι must be
harmonised into a single picture,—as of
an archer shooting from covert. But in
fact there is a rapid transition from one
to the other; the second interprets the
first; and all that is common to them is
their military source. στοχάζομαι was
familiar in a sense akin to that which
it has here: cp. Plat. *Lach.* 178 B στοχα-
ζόμενοι τοῦ συμβουλευομένου ἄλλα λέγουσι
παρὰ τὴν αὐτῶν δόξαν (trying to hit the
thought of the person who consults
them): Polyb. 6. 16 ὀφείλουσι δὲ ἀεὶ
ποιεῖν οἱ δήμαρχοι τὸ δοκοῦν τῷ δήμῳ καὶ
μάλιστα στοχάζεσθαι τῆι τούτου βου-
λήσεως. So here the verb suggests a
designing person, whose elaborate pre-
amble covers a secret aim. Creon is
quick to suspect bribery (221). Cp.

1033 ὥστε τοξόται σκοποῦ | τοξεύετ' ἀνδρὸς
τοῦδε. Schneidewin thought that στοχάζει
might here be a term of hunting or war,
with ref. to the erecting of nets on poles,
or of palisades. στοιχίζειν was so used,
of nets in hunting (Xen. *cyneg.* 6. 8). But
στοῖχος is from rt στιχ, while στόχος is
from a probably distinct rt σταχ (στάχυς),
στεχ (perhaps lengthened from στα).
In Ar. *Rhet.* 3. 14 § 10 the citation of
v. 223 is immediately followed by the
words τί φροιμάζῃ; which Nauck (with
Bergk) substitutes for εὖ γε στοχάζει here.
But, though the schol. there says that
Creon spoke them, they evidently belonged to some other passage, which
Arist. cites as a second example: perh.
to Eur. *I. T.* 1162 τί φροιμάζει νεοχμόν;
ἐξαύδα σαφῶς. A schol. on Arist. *l. c.*
says, τὸ δὲ τί φροιμάζῃ ἐν τισὶ τῶν
ἀντιγράφων οὐ κεῖται (i.e. in some MSS.
of Arist.); which looks as if the words
had been deleted, in such copies, by
readers who could not find them in Soph.
—κἀποφράγνυσαι. Inscriptions of the
5th cent. B.C. show φάρξαι (not φράξαι) to
have been the old Attic aor. (Meisterhans
p. 89), and so ναύφαρκτος, etc.: but the
analogy of the pres. φράττω recommends
φράγνυμι rather than φάργνυμι. For the
constr., cp. Thuc. 8. 104 ἐβούλοντο ἀπο-
φάρξασθαι αὐτοὺς οἱ ἐναντίοι (to shut them
off).—τὸ πρᾶγμα, so soon after 239: cp.
on 76.—δηλοῖς δ' ὥς τι σ.: see on 20.

ΦΥ. τὰ δεινὰ γάρ τοι προστίθησ᾽ ὄκνον πολύν.

ΚΡ. οὔκουν ἐρεῖς ποτ᾽, εἶτ᾽ ἀπαλλαχθεὶς ἄπει;

ΦΥ. καὶ δὴ λέγω σοι. τὸν νεκρόν τις ἀρτίως   245
θάψας βέβηκε κἀπὶ χρωτὶ διψίαν
κόνιν παλύνας κἀφαγιστεύσας ἃ χρή.

ΚΡ. τί φῄς; τίς ἀνδρῶν ἦν ὁ τολμήσας τάδε;

ΦΥ. οὐκ οἶδ᾽· ἐκεῖ γὰρ οὔτε του γενῆδος ἦν
πλῆγμ᾽, οὐ δικέλλης ἐκβολή· στύφλος δὲ γῆ   250
καὶ χέρσος, ἀρρὼξ οὐδ᾽ ἐπημαξευμένη
τροχοῖσιν, ἀλλ᾽ ἄσημος οὑργάτης τις ἦν.
ὅπως δ᾽ ὁ πρῶτος ἡμὶν ἡμεροσκόπος
δείκνυσι, πᾶσι θαῦμα δυσχερὲς παρῆν.
ὁ μὲν γὰρ ἠφάνιστο, τυμβήρης μὲν οὔ,   255
λεπτὴ δ᾽ ἄγος φεύγοντος ὡς ἐπῆν κόνις.

σείων κακόν.   **249** In L του has been made from του by an early hand (perh.

---

243 f. τὰ δεινά, dangers,—*i.e.* the κακὰ ἔπη (277) which he brings: γάρ (yes, I am cautious) for, etc.—ποτ᾽, *tandem aliquando*, *O. T.* 335 n.—ἀπαλλαχθείς, 'having been removed,' *i.e.* 'having taken yourself off'; cp. Ar. *Vesp.* 484 ἆρ᾽ ἄν, ὦ πρὸς τῶν θεῶν, ὑμεῖς ἀπαλλαχθεῖτέ μου;

245 ff. καὶ δή, without more ado: *O. C.* 31 n.—θάψας, because the essential rite was the throwing of earth on the body: cp. on 80, and below, 256.—The καί in κἀπί is 'and' (rather than 'both,' answering to καί in 247); it introduces an explanation of θάψας, as Aesch. *Ag.* 495 πηλοῦ ξύνουρος διψία κόνις: Lucr. 2. 376 *bibula...arena.*—κἀφαγιστεύσας (καὶ ἀ.) ἃ χρή, *i.e.* having made the due offerings, perh. flowers (*El.* 896), or στέφη of wool. We may doubt whether the poet thought of any χοαί as having been poured by Antigone at this first visit: see n. on 429.—ἀφαγιστεύσας and ἐφαγιστεύσας are equally possible; but I prefer the former, because here, as v. 256 suggests, the idea is that of ἀφοσιωσάμενος,—having avoided an ἄγος by satisfying religion: see on 196 ἐφαγνίσαι.

248 ff. ἀνδρῶν: he does not think of women.—οὔτε του γενῆδος ...οὐ δικέλλης. For the enclitic του so placed, cp. 20 n.: for οὔτε ..οὐ, *O. C.* 972 n. γενῆς, γενῆς (only here), is prop. an adj., an

implement with a γένυς (jaw), or blade: *El.* 485 ἀμφάκης γένυς, the two-edged blade (of a bronze axe). Hesych. γενῆδα· ἀξίνην, πέλεκυν (referring, as the acc. shows, to some other passage): and here the γενῆς is prob. the same as the ἀξίνη below (1109), which was to be used in raising the mound (1203). We may render 'pickaxe,' since this properly has a blade as well as a point. The γενῆς would break the hard surface. Then the earth would be thrown up (ἐκβολή) with the δίκελλα, which was a sort of heavy two-pronged hoe, used, like the Roman *ligo* or *bidens*, in hoeing up soil: the μάκελλα (μία, κέλλω to drive forward) being a like tool with one prong. The σμινύη was like the δίκελλα, a two-pronged hoe. 'Mattock' is the nearest word for it. 'Spade' would better suit ἅμη (or the Homeric λίστρον), though this was prop. rather a shovel. For the combination cp. Shaks. *Tit. Andr.* 5. 3. 11 '*Tis you must dig with mattock and with spade.*—δικ. ἐκβολή, throwing up of earth by mattock (possessive gen. denoting the subject, γῆ ἦν ἣ δ. ἐκβάλλει): ἐκβ., abstract for concrete, like τροφή for θρέμμα (*O. T.* 1 n.). In Mod. Greek ἐκβολάδες is a mining term, 'out-put.'—The epithets στύφλος ('hard,' cp. 139), and χέρσος 'dry,' tell something which the preceding words, and the following ἀρρώξ, would not alone have told; viz.

GŮ. Aye, truly; dread news makes one pause long.

CR. Then tell it, wilt thou, and so get thee gone?

GU. Well, this is it.—The corpse—some one hath just given it burial, and gone away,—after sprinkling thirsty dust on the flesh, with such other rites as piety enjoins.

CR. What sayest thou? What living man hath dared this deed?

GU. I know not; no stroke of pickaxe was seen there, no earth thrown up by mattock; the ground was hard and dry, unbroken, without track of wheels; the doer was one who had left no trace. And when the first day-watchman showed it to us, sore wonder fell on all. The dead man was veiled from us; not shut within a tomb, but lightly strewn with dust, as by the hand of one who shunned a curse.

by S). **251** ἀρώξ L: ἀρρώξ r. **254** θαῦμα] Nauck conject. φάσμα.

why no foot-prints were traceable.—ἀπημαξευμένη, lit. 'traversed (*i.e.* furrowed) by a carriage' with its (four) wheels, =τροχοῖς ἀμάξης κεχαραγμένη: ἀπ-, not ἐφ-, since as Eusth. says (on *Il.* 18. 485) τὸ...ἄμαξα οἱ μὲν παλαιοὶ ψιλοῦσι, οἱ μέντοι νεώτεροι Ἀττικοὶ ἐδάσυναν. (Cp. n. on ἀπήνη, *O. T.* 753.)—ἀλλ' ὁ ἐργάτης ἀσημός τις ἦν: for τις added to the predicate, where the subject has the art., cp. *O. T.* 618, Aesch. *Theb.* 491 ὁ σηματουργὸς δ' οὔ τις εὐτελὴς ἄρ' ἦν: Ar. *Pl.* 726 ὡς φιλόπολις τις ἔσθ' ὁ δαίμων καὶ σοφός. Not: ὁ ἐργάτης τις (the doer, whoever he is) ἄσημος ἦν, like ὁ κύριός τις (*O. C.* 288 n.).

253 f. It is still the early morning of the day on which the drama opens. The Argives having fled in the night, Creon had published his edict shortly before dawn. Antigone had done her deed in the short interval between the publication of the edict and the beginning of the watch over the corpse. ὁ πρῶτος ἡμεροσκόπος, the man who took the first watch of this day, was the first who had watched at all. If a sentinel had been near the body, Ant. must have been seen. The other men were somewhere near. (Afterwards, they all watched, 435.) ἡμεροσκ., in prose ἡμεροφύλαξ (Xen. *H.* 7. 2. 6), as opp. to νυκτοφύλαξ (id. *An.* 7. 2. 18).—δείκνυσι...παρῆν: historic pres. combined with past tense; cp. Lys. or. 1 § 6 ἐπειδὴ δέ μοι παιδίον γίγνεται, ἐπίστευον ἤδη καὶ πάντα τὰ ἐμαυτοῦ ἐκείνῃ παρέδωκα.—δυσχερές,

not merely 'perplexing,' but 'distressing' (*Ai.* 1395), since they foreboded punishment. So δυσχέρεια, *molestia* (*Ph.* 473).

255 f. ὁ μὲν answered by σημεῖα δ' (257).—τυμβήρης μὲν οὔ (cp. on 96), not entombed: *i.e.* there was no τύμβος, indicating that the ashes had been buried beneath it (1203): the body itself lay there, though covered over with dust. τυμβ., prop., 'provided with a mound,' but below, 946, merely = 'tomblike'; and so in Ar. *Th.* 889 Euripides says τυμβήρεις ἕδρας, 'seat on a tomb.'—λεπτῇ δ'...ἀγει, instead of λέπτη δὲ κόνει κεκαλυμμένος (as in *Ph.* 545 δοξάζων μὲν οὔ, | τύχῃ δὲ...ὁρμωθείς): for this introduction of a new finite verb, where a participial clause was expected, cp. 813 ff.—ἄγος φεύγοντος ὥς *sc.* τινος (*O. T.* 619 οὗτος κακῶς γ' ἄρχοντος, n.): the gen. is not absol., but possessive, denoting the author: 'as of (*i.e.* from) one avoiding.' ἄγος, the guilt incurred by one who passed by an unburied corpse without throwing earth on it: οἱ γὰρ νεκρὸν ὁρῶντες ἄταφον, καὶ μὴ ἐπαμησάμενοι κόνιν, ἐναγεῖς εἶναι ἐδόκουν. Aelian *Var. Hist.* 5. 14 νόμος καὶ οὗτος Ἀττικός, ὃς ἂν ἀτάφῳ περιτύχῃ σώματι ἀνθρώπου πάντως ἐπιβάλλειν αὐτῷ γῆν· θάπτειν δὲ πρὸς δυσμὰς βλέποντας. So, too, Aelian says of the hawk. *Hist. Anim.* 2. 49, νεκρὸν δὲ ἄνθρωπον ἰδὼν ἱέραξ, ὥς λόγος, πάντως ἐπιβάλλει γῆν τῷ ἀτάφῳ· καὶ τοῦτο μὲν αὐτῷ οὐ κελεύει Σόλων, ὡς Ἀθηναίους ἐπαίδευσε δρᾶν (though our schol. ascribes the precept to a prehistoric

· σημεῖα δ' οὔτε θηρὸς οὔτε του κυνῶν
· ἐλθόντος, οὐ σπάσαντος ἐξεφαίνετο.
· λόγοι δ' ἐν ἀλλήλοισιν ἐρρόθουν κακοί,
· φύλαξ ἐλέγχων φύλακα· κἂν ἐγίγνετο   260
· πληγὴ τελευτῶσ', οὐδ' ὁ κωλύσων παρῆν.
· εἷς γάρ τις ἦν ἕκαστος οὑξειργασμένος,
· κοὐδεὶς ἐναργής, ἀλλ' ἔφευγε μὴ εἰδέναι.
· ἦμεν δ' ἕτοιμοι καὶ μύδρους αἴρειν χεροῖν,

258 ἐλθόντος] Naber conject. ἕλκοντος.   **263** ἔφευγε τὸ μὴ εἰδέναι MSS.: Erfurdt
deleted τό. Blaydes reads πᾶς δ' ἔφευγε μὴ εἰδέναι: Dindorf, ἀλλ' ἔφευγε πᾶς τὸ μή:

Βουζύγης): and of the elephant, *H. A.* 5. 49 τὸν ἐλέφαντα θεασάμενος ἐλέφας νεκρὸν οὐκ ἂν παρέλθοι, μὴ τῇ προβοσκίδι γῆν ἀρυσάμενος καὶ ἐπιβαλών, ὁσίαν τινὰ ἀπόρρητον ὑπὲρ τῆς κοινῆς φύσεως τελῶν ('fulfilling some mysterious law of piety imposed by Nature'), καὶ φεύγων ἄγος· εἶναι γὰρ τὸ μὴ δρᾶσαι τοῦτο ἐναγές. It was remembered as a disgrace to Lysander that, having put to death some prisoners of war, οὐδὲ ἀποθανοῦσιν ἐπήνεγκε γῆν (Paus. 9. 32. 6). Cp. id. 1. 32. 5 πάντως ὅσιον ἀνθρώπου νεκρὸν γῇ κρύψαι. Hor. *Carm.* 1. 28. 33 *precibus non linquar inultis, Teque piacula nulla resolvent...licebit Iniecto ter pulvere curras.*

257 f. θηρός, here a wild beast, as dist. from domesticated animals (cp. 1081): more often the term excludes only birds and fishes.—του with θηρός also: Eur. *Hec.* 370 οὔτ' ἐλπίδος γὰρ οὔτε του δόξης ὁρῶ | θάρσος παρ' ἡμῖν.—οὐ σπάσαντος. The negatives in 257 affect ἐλθόντος: and οὐ stands with σπάσαντος as if we had simply οὐκ ἐλθόντος, οὐ σπάσαντος, σημεῖα ἦν. οὐ is not here an irregular substitute for οὔτε, as in 250: this would be so only if we had οὔτ' ἐλθόντος. Either οὐδὲ σπ. or οὔτε σπ. would be correct, but the latter would suppose an οὔτε understood before ἐλθόντος. For σπάσαντος of rending, cp. 1003. It could not mean, 'having cast up earth' over the body (as Triclinius took it). The point is that the body must have been covered before the beasts had had time to come. The poet has preferred this order to σπάσαντος οὐδ' ἐλθόντος (*i.e.* 'or even having come'), because, εἰ ἦλθον, καὶ ἔσπασαν ἄν.

259 ff. λόγοι δ'...φύλακα. The regular form would be, λόγοις κακοῖς ἐρρο-θοῦμεν ἐν ἀλλήλοις, ἐλέγχοντες φύλαξ φύλακα (or ἄλλος ἄλλον), φύλαξ being the part in apposition with the whole (ἡμεῖς). The irregularity of the form in the text is threefold. (1) For λόγοις κακοῖς ἐρρο-θοῦμεν we have an equiv. in sense, though not in grammar, λόγοι κακοὶ ἐρρόθουν. (2) In spite of this, ἐν ἀλλήλοισιν is retained, whereas ἐν ἡμῖν is now needed. (3) As a *plur.* part. would have been awkward after λόγοι, we have φύλαξ ἐλέγχων φύλακα, which thus is virtually equiv. to a gen. absol., φύλακος ἐλέγχοντος φύλακα. Remark that, even in regular examples of partitive apposition, a participle, describing what all do, is sometimes thus made singular: Xen. *An.* 7. 3. 47 οἱ ἱππεῖς οἴχονταί μοι ἄλλος ἄλλῃ διώκων (instead of διώκοντες). It is only the first of these three points that this passage has in common with others to which it has been compared. 'They disputed, some saying this, some that,' often appears in Greek as 'there was a dispute,' etc., without causing οἱ μὲν...οἱ δέ to be changed into the gen. absol. Her. 8. 74 πολλὰ ἐλέγετο,...οἱ μὲν ὡς...χρεὸν εἴη ἀποπλεῖν, Ἀθηναῖοι δέ etc. Thuc. 4. 23 ὑπ' ἀμφοτέρων...ἐπολεμεῖτο, Ἀθηναῖοι μὲν περιπλέοντες..., Πελοποννήσιοι δέ etc. Aesch. *P. V.* 200 στάσις τ' ἐν ἀλλήλοισιν ὡροθύνετο, | οἱ μὲν θέλοντες...οἱ δέ etc. (This illustrates the use of ἐν ἀλλήλ. here, but is less bold, since the noun is sing.) Eur. *Ph.* 1462 ἦν δ' ἔρις στρατηλάταις, | οἱ μὲν πατάξαι...οἱ δέ etc. *Bacch.* 1131 ἦν δὲ πᾶσ' ὁμοῦ βοή, | ὁ μὲν στενάζων...αἱ δέ etc. For ἐρρόθουν, of a confused noise of angry tongues, cp. 290. ῥόθος (onomatop.) is said of a rushing noise of waves, or of oars dashed into them, etc.: then, fig., Aesch. *Pers.* 406 Περσίδος

And no sign met the eye as though any beast of prey or any
dog had come nigh to him, or torn him.

Then evil words flew fast and loud among us, guard accusing
guard ; and it would e'en have come to blows at last, nor
was there any to hinder. Every man was the culprit, and no
one was convicted, but all disclaimed knowledge of the deed.
And we were ready to take red-hot iron in our hands ;—

Seyffert, ἀλλ' ἔφη τὸ μὴ εἰδέναι.   **264** αἴρειν] ἔχειν L, with γρ. αἴρειν written above

---

γλώσσης ῥόθος, of an unintelligible jargon. ('ἔλεγχων, questioning (434, O. T.
333, 783: El. 1353), here, in the sense of
'accusing.'—κἂν ἐγίγνετο : and blows
would have come at last,—had not the
matter been settled by the proposal mentioned at 268. (Not, 'blows would
come,' i.e. were often exchanged, as
Nauck takes it.)—τελευτῶσ', 'at last,' the
adverbial use, found even with another
partic., as Thuc. 6. 53 τυραννίδα χα-
λεπὴν τελευτῶσαν γενομένην.—ὁ κωλύσων : cp. O. T. 297.

262 f. ἦν...οὔργ., was the doer
(in the belief of his comrades).—ἐναργής,
manifestus facti: O. T. 535 λῃστής τ'
ἐναργής.—ἀλλ' (ἕκαστος), evolved from
οὐδείς: fr. 327 ἐμοὶ δ' οὐδεὶς δοκεῖ | εἶναι,
πένης ὢν, ἄνοσος, ἀλλ' ἀεὶ νοσεῖν. Dem.
or. 20 § 74 μηδεὶς φθόνῳ τὸ μέλλον
ἀκούσῃ, ἀλλ', ἂν ἀληθὲς ᾖ, σκοπείτω.—
ἔφευγε μὴ εἰδέναι, 'pleaded in defence
that he knew nothing of it.' For this
pregnant use of φεύγειν cp. Aesch. Suppl.
390, where the Argive king says to
the Danaides, whose cousins threaten
to seize them under Egyptian law, δεῖ
τοι σε φεύγειν κατὰ νόμους τοὺς οἴκοθεν |
ὡς οὐκ ἔχουσι κῦρος οὐδὲν ἀμφὶ σοῦ: you
must plead, in accordance with Egyptian law, that they have no right over
you. So defendere, Cic. In Pison. 10.
5 si triumphum non cupiebas, cuius
tandem rei te cupiditate arsisse defen-
das? ('will you plead?') Note that
this use (like the absol. legal sense, 'to
be a defendant,' from which it comes)
was necessarily restricted to pres. and
impf. Hence we must not cite, with
Donaldson, Dem. or. 27 § 1 οὗτοι τοὺς
μὲν σαφῶς εἰδότας τὰ ἡμέτερα ἔφυγε μηδὲν διαγνῶναι περὶ αὐτῶν, εἰς δ' ὑμᾶς τοὺς
οὐδὲν τῶν ἡμετέρων ἀκριβῶς ἐπισταμένους
ἐλήλυθεν (which means: 'he has avoided
any decision on the case being given by

those who knew our affairs thoroughly,
but has come to you,' etc.): nor, with
Paley, Xen. Hellen. 1. 3. 19 ὑπαγό-
μενοι θανάτου...ἀπέφυγεν, ὅτι οὐ προ-
δοίη τὴν πόλιν ἀλλὰ σώσαι, i.e. 'being put
on trial for his life, he was acquitted, (on
the plea) that he had not betrayed the
city,' etc.—μὴ (not οὐκ) εἰδέναι, as after
verbs of denying, Ar. Eq. 572 ἠρνοῦντο μὴ
πεπτωκέναι.—Only one other version is
tenable, viz., 'shrunk from knowing it';
but this could hardly be said in the
sense, 'shrunk from confessing that he
knew it.'—Others understand τοὺς ἄλλους
as subject to εἰδέναι, 'shrunk from (the
others) knowing it' ('entzog sich dem
Wissen der anderen'), which is impossible. So also is Campb.'s version, 'always escaped, so that we could not know
him,' which would, in the first place,
require ἔφυγε.

264 μύδρους, lumps of red-hot iron.
μύδρος = a molten mass, from rt μυδ,
whence μύδος, 'moisture,' μυδάω, etc.
Cyril Adv. Iulian. 359 quotes this verse,
after referring to a Chaldean custom of
making an oath more solemn by causing
those who took it to pass between the
severed portions of a victim (διὰ μέσων...
διχοτομημάτων). It is probably the oldest
trace in Greek of ordeals analogous to
the medieval 'judgments of God.' The
word μύδρος occurs elsewhere in connection with a solemn sanction for an oath.
In Her. 1. 165 the Phocaeans μύδρον
σιδήρεον κατεπόντωσαν, swearing not to
return till it should float. Plut. Aristid.
25 ὁ δ' Ἀριστείδης ὥρκισε μὲν τοὺς Ἕλληνας
καὶ ὤμοσεν ὑπὲρ τῶν Ἀθηναίων (to observe the defensive league against Persia,
479 B.C., Grote 5. 257), μύδρους ἐμ-
βαλὼν ἐπὶ ταῖς ἀραῖς (in sanction of
the curses on traitors) εἰς τὴν θάλατταν.
I conceive that in these passages, as
elsewhere, μύδρος has its proper sense,

· καὶ πῦρ διέρπειν, καὶ θεοὺς ὁρκωμοτεῖν   265
· τὸ μήτε δρᾶσαι μήτε τῳ ξυνειδέναι
· τὸ πρᾶγμα βουλεύσαντι μήτ᾽ εἰργασμένῳ.
· τέλος δ᾽, ὅτ᾽ οὐδὲν ἦν ἐρεύνωσιν πλέον,
· λέγει τις εἷς, ὃς πάντας ἐς πέδον κάρα
· νεῦσαι φόβῳ προύτρεψεν· οὐ γὰρ εἴχομεν   270
· οὔτ᾽ ἀντιφωνεῖν οὔθ᾽ ὅπως δρῶντες καλῶς
· πράξαιμεν. ἦν δ᾽ ὁ μῦθος ὡς ἀνοιστέον
· σοὶ τοὔργον εἴη τοῦτο κοὐχὶ κρυπτέον.
· καὶ ταῦτ᾽ ἐνίκα, κἀμὲ τὸν δυσδαίμονα
· πάλος καθαιρεῖ τοῦτο τἀγαθὸν λαβεῖν.   275
· πάρειμι δ᾽ ἄκων οὐχ ἑκοῦσιν, οἶδ᾽ ὅτι·
· στέργει γὰρ οὐδεὶς ἄγγελον κακῶν ἐπῶν.
ΧΟ. · ἄναξ, ἐμοί τοι, μή τι καὶ θεήλατον

by S: αἱρεῖν r.   **267** μήτ᾽] μηδ᾽ Blaydes.   **269** εἷς, ὃς] εἷς ὃ Nauck.   Blaydes

---

a *red-hot mass* of metal, and that the custom was symbolical of an older use of the μύδρος in ordeals by fire. This would explain how the Alexandrian poets of the 3rd cent. B.C. (Lycophron, Callimachus) came to use the word μύδρος, in defiance of its etymology, as simply 'a lump' (or even 'a stone'). They supposed that the μύδροι had been cold masses.

265 ff. πῦρ διέρπειν must here refer to a definite ordeal, by walking through a fire. The idea, at least, of such an ordeal appears in the familiar Attic phrase διὰ πυρὸς ἰέναι ('to go through fire and water'); Xen. *Symp.* 4. 16 ἐγὼγ᾽ οὖν μετὰ Κλεινίου κἂν διὰ πυρὸς ἰοίην, Ar. *Lys.* 133 διὰ τοῦ πυρὸς | ἐθέλω βαδίζειν. But it is doubtful whether the actual use of any such ordeal in the historical age can be inferred from Dem. or. 54 § 40 ἀξιοπιστότερος τοῦ κατὰ τῶν παίδων (by the lives of one's children, cp. or. 29 § 26) ὀμνύοντος καὶ διὰ τοῦ πυρός, i.e. swearing that one is ready to undergo the test by fire. It has been suggested that ἰόντος has fallen out after πυρός, which seems improbable. But the phrase may be rhetorical. Cp. Verg. *Aen.* 11. 787 (the Hirpi): *medium freti pietate per ignem Cultores multa premimus vestigia pruna.*—Becker *Char.* 183 notices some other ordeals. There was a temple in Achaia, the priestess of which, before election, was proved by drinking bull's

blood; if impure, she died (Paus. 7. 25. 13). Perjury, and some other crimes, were assayed by the accused mounting the steps of an altar for burnt sacrifice (ἐσχάρα): if he was guilty, flames appeared (Heliod. *Aeth.* 10. 8). Incontinence was tried by the test of entering a grotto of Pan at Ephesus (Achilles Tatius 8. 6).—θεοὺς ὁρκ., to swear by the gods; the acc. is cognate (the god being identified with the oath), like ὅρκον ὀμνύναι:. Xen. *Cyr.* 5. 4. 31 ταῦτα...ὄμνυμί σοι θεούς.—τὸ μήτε δρ.: for the art., cp. 236.—μήτ᾽ εἰργασμένῳ: the conjecture μηδ᾽ is needless, since μήτε can be understood before βουλεύσαντι: see *O. T.* 239 n.

268 f. πλέον: cp. 40.—λέγει, between two past tenses: cp. 254.—τις εἷς. It is at first sight tempting to write τις, εἷς δὲ πάντας. But such emphasis on the idea of 'one against all' seems hardly appropriate here. And τις εἷς sometimes =εἷς τις: Thuc. 6. 61 καί τινα μίαν νύκτα καὶ κατέδαρθον: Plat. *Soph.* 235 B (οὐκέτ᾽ ἐκφεύξεται) τὸ μὴ οὐ τοῦ γένους εἶναι τοῦ τῶν θαυματοποιῶν τις εἷς: *Parm.* 145 D ἔν τινι γὰρ ἐνὶ μὴ ὂν οὐκ ἂν ἔτι που δύναιτο ἔν γε ἅπασιν εἶναι.

270 ff. προύτρεψεν, impelled, here =ἠνάγκασε: cp. *O. T.* 358 n.—οὐ γὰρ εἴχομεν κ.τ.λ.: 'for we did not know how to gainsay him, nor how, *if we did the thing* (advised by him), we could prosper.'

to walk through fire;—to make oath by the gods that we had not done the deed,—that we were not privy to the planning or the doing.

At last, when all our searching was fruitless, one spake, who made us all bend our faces on the earth in fear; for we saw not how we could gainsay him, or escape mischance if we obeyed. His counsel was that this deed must be reported to thee, and not hidden. And this seemed best; and the lot doomed my hapless self to win this prize. So here I stand,— as unwelcome as unwilling, well I wot; for no man delights in the bearer of bad news.

CH. O King, my thoughts have long been whispering, can

conject. *ἔπος δ.*   **278** XO.] L omits this indication, which Triclinius added.

As **ἀντιφωνεῖν** means *opposing* his suggestion, so **δρῶντες** means acting on it. Others join **ὅπως δρῶντες**, 'by what course of action.' Since, however, a definite proposal was before them—viz., reference to Creon—we must then understand, 'by what *other* course' (than the proposed one). But the sense is, 'We could not refute him, and, on the other hand, we dreaded your anger if we followed his advice.' **εἴχομεν** has the same sense in both clauses. **ἔχω**, as = '*to know how*,' takes (1) an infin., or (2) a relat. clause with subjunct., as 1342, *Tr.* **702** *οὐκ ἔχω...ποῖ γνώμης πέσω.* This is merely an indirect form of the deliberative subjunct., *ποῖ γνώμης πέσω*; So here, **πράξαιμεν** would be **πράξωμεν** if the principal verb were in a primary tense. The direct question would be, *πῶς καλῶς πράξωμεν*; Carefully distinguish **ὅπως** (or **πῶς**) **ἄν** with optat. after this *οὐκ ἔχω*, as *Tr.* 991 *οὐ γὰρ ἔχω πῶς ἄν | στέρξαιμι,* I know not how I *could*. The two constructions are combined again in *Ai.* 428 *οὔτοι σ' ἀπείργειν οὐδ' ὅπως ἐῶ λέγειν | ἔχω.*

278 f. **σοί** (cp. 234), rare for *εἰς σέ*. After *ἀναφέρω τι* the pers. is usu. expressed by *εἴς τινα* (less oft. by *ἐπί* or *παρά τινα*). But Lysias has the dat. in or. 12. 84 *οἷς τὰς ἀπολογίας ἀνοίσει,* 'to whom he will carry back his defensive pleas' (*i.e.* 'on whom he will lay the blame,' and so, again, in or. 7 § 17): yet *ib.* § 64 *τὰς... ἀπολογίας εἰς ἐκεῖνον ἀναφερομένας.* In Mod. Greek *ἀναφορά* is used of an official 'report.'—**ταῦτ' ἡνίκα**: see on 233: the impf. differs from the aor. only as *ἐδόκει*

('seemed good') from *ἔδοξε* ('was resolved').— **πάλος**, perh. taken by shaking lots in a helmet (cp. 396, *Ai.* 1285): **καθαιρεῖ**, reduces, *i.e.* 'condemns': Lys. or. 13 § 37 *τὴν ..ψῆφον...τὴν...καθαιροῦσαν,* the vote of condemnation.— **τἀγαθόν**, iron., whereas his second errand is a true *ἕρμαιον* (397).— **ἄκων οὐχ ἑκοῦσιν**: cp. *Tr.* 198 (the herald detained against his will by a throng of questioners) *οὐχ ἑκών ἑκοῦσι δὲ | ξύνεστιν.*— **οἶδ' ὅτι**, adverbial ('doubtless'), like *δῆλον ὅτι*, cp. 758: so used even in the middle of a clause, as Dem. or. 9 § 1 *πάντων, οἶδ' ὅτι, φησάντων γ' ἄν* ('when all, I know, would certainly admit,' etc.).

278 f. **ἐμοί**, ethic dat., 'for me,' rather than dat. with *βουλεύοι* as = 'advises'; the latter dat. is rare (Aesch. *Eum.* 697 *ἀστοῖς...βουλεύω σέβειν*); in *Tr.* 807, *Ai.* 1055 the dat. with *βουλεύω* is a dat. of interest (to plot *against* one). In poetry the act. can mean, not only 'to form a plan' (*O. T.* 619), or to *give* counsel (*ib.* 1417), but also, like the midd., to deliberate.—With **μή** supply *ἐστί*: cp. 1253; Plat. *Theaet.* 145 C *ὅρα μὴ παίζων ἔλεγεν,* look *whether he did not* speak (*i.e.* I suspect that he spoke) in jest. To supply **ἦ** is also possible (cp. *O. C.* 1180), but less fitting here.—**τι**, adv., 'perchance': *O. T.* 969.—**θεήλατον**, sent by gods (*O. T.* 992 *θεήλατον μάντευμα*), *i.e. wrought* by them (cp. 285), since there was no trace of human agency (249): not, imposed upon a human agent by a divine commission (as *O. T.* 255 *πρᾶγμα θεήλατον*). So in *Il.* 16. 667 Zeus provides supernaturally for the

· τοὔργον τόδ᾽, ἡ ξύννοια βουλεύει πάλαι.

ΚΡ.· παῦσαι, πρὶν ὀργῆς καί με μεστῶσαι λέγων, 280
· μὴ ᾽φευρεθῇς ἄνους τε καὶ γέρων ἅμα.
· λέγεις γὰρ οὐκ ἀνεκτά, δαίμονας λέγων
· πρόνοιαν ἴσχειν τοῦδε τοῦ νεκροῦ πέρι.
· πότερον ὑπερτιμῶντες ὡς εὐεργέτην
· ἔκρυπτον αὐτόν, ὅστις ἀμφικίονας 285
· ναοὺς πυρώσων ἦλθε κἀναθήματα
᾽ καὶ γῆν ἐκείνων, καὶ νόμους διασκεδῶν;
· ἦ τοὺς κακοὺς τιμῶντας εἰσορᾷς θεούς;
· οὐκ ἔστιν. ἀλλὰ ταῦτα καὶ πάλαι πόλεως
· ἄνδρες μόλις φέροντες ἐρρόθουν ἐμοί, 290
· κρυφῇ κάρα σείοντες, οὐδ᾽ ὑπὸ ζυγῷ
λόφον δικαίως εἶχον, ὡς στέργειν ἐμέ.

279 τόδ᾽, ἡ ξύννοια] Nauck has now withdrawn his former conjecture, τόδ᾽ ᾖ, ξύννοια.
280 καί με] καμέ (sic) L.   **284** ὑπερτιμῶντασ L, ὑπερτιμῶντες r.   Nauck would
delete vv. 287 f., and re-write thus:—πότερον ὑπερτιμῶντας ὡς εὐεργέτην, | ναοὺς
ἐκείνων ὅστις ἀμφικίονας | καὶ γῆν πυρώσων ἦλθε κἀναθήματα; | οὐκ ἔστιν κ.τ.λ.
287 καὶ γῆν] Schneidewin conject. δίκην: Pallis, τιμάς.—ἐκείνων L: ἐκείνην r.

burial of Sarpedon. Cp. O. C. p. xxxv.
—ἡ ξύννοια, the art. being equiv. to a
possessive pron., as 1089 f. τὴν γλῶσσαν,
τὸν νοῦν. Cp. Plat. Rep. 571 E εἰς
σύννοιαν αὐτὸς αὑτῷ ἀφικόμενος.—πάλαι,
i.e. ever since the φύλαξ spoke (249).
Cp. 289.

280 πρὶν ὀργῆς καί με μεστῶσαι,
'before thou hast actually filled me with
anger': καί has nothing to do with πρὶν,
but belongs solely to μεστῶσαι, a strong
word, the stress on which makes it easier
for the force of καί to pass over the
enclitic με. Cp. O. T. 772 τῷ γὰρ ἂν
καὶ μείζονι | λέξαιμ᾽ ἄν: ib. 989 ποίας
δὲ καὶ γυναικὸς ἐκφοβεῖσθ᾽ ὕπερ; where
in each case καί goes with the verb.
We must distinguish the ordinary combination πρὶν καί, 'before even,' which
would be in place here only if Creon
meant, 'Cease, before you have so much
as angered me': cp. Tr. 396 ἅσσεις, πρὶν
ἡμᾶς κἀννεώσασθαι λόγους (before we have
even renewed our talk): Ar. Av. 1033
πέμπουσιν ἤδη 'πισκόπους | ἐς τὴν πόλιν,
πρὶν καὶ τεθύσθαι τοῖς θεοῖς: Plat. Gorg.
458 B πάλαι..., πρὶν καὶ ὑμᾶς ἐλθεῖν,...
ἐπεδειξάμην.—κἀμέ would be unmeaning:
no one else is angry.—μεστῶσαι: Plat.
Rep. 330 E ὑποψίας...καὶ δείματος μεστός,

and so often.

284 ff. πότερον κ.τ.λ. Did they
think him good? Or, thinking him bad,
did they yet honour him?—Ἔκρυπτον (sc.
γῇ)= ἔθαπτον: the word is specially suitable here to the covering with dust (256).
Cp. O. C. 621 κεκρυμμένος νέκυς: El.
838 κρυφθέντα (of Amphiaraus swallowed
up by the earth). Bellermann cites an
inscr. from Smyrna (Rhein. Mus. 1872,
27 p. 465) παίδων σε φίλαι χέρες, ὡς θέμις
ἐστί, | κρύψαν. The impf. ('were for bury-
ing') refers to the motive present to the
agent's mind when the act was under-
taken: cp. 19 ἐξέπεμπον n.—ἀμφικίονας
ναούς, temples surrounded by columns,
an epith. marking their stateliness and
splendour, as Eur. Andr. 1099 ἐν περι-
στύλοις δόμοις (of a temple), I. T. 406
περικίονας ναούς. The ναὸς περίστυλος
or περίπτερος (so called because the
ceiling of the colonnade projected like a
wing, from the cella) had a colonnade on
each of its four sides: the ναὸς ἀμφι-
πρόστυλος, only on two (front and back):
but, t ou   the latter would satisfy the
word ἀμφικίονας, the poet doubtless meant
the former.—κἀναθήματα, votive offerings, such as gold and silver vessels of all
kinds; statues; bronze tripods, etc. (Cp.

this deed, perchance, be e'en the work of gods?

CR. Cease, ere thy words fill me utterly with wrath, lest thou be found at once an old man and foolish. For thou sayest what is not to be borne, in saying that the gods have care for this corpse. Was it for high reward of trusty service that they sought to hide his nakedness, who came to burn their pillared shrines and sacred treasures, to burn their land, and scatter its laws to the winds? Or dost thou behold the gods honouring the wicked? It cannot be. No! From the first there were certain in the town that muttered against me, chafing at this edict, wagging their heads in secret; and kept not their necks duly under the yoke, like men contented with my sway.

M. Schmidt conject. κενώσιν.—νόμους] Herwerden conject. δόμους. 291 κρυφῇ] σιγῇ Meineke, from Plut. *Mor.* 170 E : see comment. 292 For λόφον δικαίως εἴχον, Hartung writes νῶτ᾽ εὐλόφως ἔχοντες: for ὡς στέργειν ἐμέ, Nauck, εὐλόφως φέρειν : see comment.—ὡς] In L the σ has been added by S : but the scribe's oversight obviously arose through the next word beginning with σ, and in no way warrants

Her. 1. 50; Thuc. 6. 46; Isae. or. 7 § 41.) The wealth of Delphi in ἀναθήματα is already proverbial in *Il.* 9. 404: at Thebes the Ἰσμήνιον (*O. T.* 21) also seems to have been rich in them. After ἀνάθημα the gen. denotes either ὁ ἀναθείς (as more oft.), or, as here, the divine owner.—γῆν ἰκάνων (depending on πυρώσων), *i.e.* the territory of Thebes (cp. on 199), since the land belongs to the θεοὶ ἐγχώριοι and πολιοῦχοι: not merely the τεμένη attached to their shrines.—νόμους διασκεδῶν, to scatter the laws abroad, *i.e.* to shatter the fabric of civil order: cp. Tennyson, *Red ruin, and the breaking up of laws.* Cic. *Agr.* 2. 37 *disturbare... legem.* So διασκεδ. of breaking up a treaty (*O. C.* 620), or a king's peace (*ib.* 1341).—διασκεδῶν would suit ἀναθήματα, but could not possibly be joined with γῆν (as if the latter meant 'State'): hence it must be taken with νόμους only.

288 τοὺς κακοὺς τιμῶντας...θεούς; owing to the natural emphasis on τοὺς κακούς, the ambiguity is only grammatical. Cp. Her. 7. 150 ἐπεὶ δέ σφεας παραλαμβάνειν τοὺς Ἕλληνας, oblique for ἐπεὶ δέ σφεας παρελάμβανον οἱ Ἕλληνες.

289 ἐ. ταῦτα, the edict, depending on μόλις φέροντες (*aegre ferentes*): καὶ πάλαι, even from the moment when it was proclaimed; cp. 279, where πάλαι only refers back to 249.—πόλεως ἄνδρες, like γῆν τῆσδέ τις (*O. T.* 236 n.).—ἐρρόθουν, muttered: 259 n.—ἐμοί, against me, dat. of object, as after χαλεπαίνω, μέμ-

φομαι, etc.—κάρα σείοντες, 'tossing the head,' in defiant menace (so *caput quassans*, Verg. *Aen.* 12. 894), instead of going quietly under the yoke. Plut. *Mor.* 170 E τοὺς τυράννους ἀσπάζονται,...ἀλλὰ μισοῦσι σιγῇ κάρα σείοντες (alluding to this v.). So, acc. to Suidas, *s.v.*, Soph. used ἀναχαιτίζειν (prop. said of a horse *throwing the mane back*, rearing) as = ἀπειθεῖν καὶ ἀντιτείνειν, 'to be restive.'—ὑπὸ ζυγῷ. Cp. Aesch. *Ag.* 1639 ζεύξω βαρείαις (ζεύγλαις).—λόφον, the back of the neck, a word used of draught-animals (of the *human* nape, perh. only once, *Il.* 10. 573): hence, fig., Eur. fr. 175 ὅστις δὲ πρὸς τὸ πῖπτον εὐλόφως φέρει | τὸν δαίμον᾽, οὗτος ἧσσόν ἐστ᾽ ἀνόλβιος. id. *Tro.* 302 κάρτα τοι τοὐλεύθερον | ἐν τοῖς τοιούτοις δυσλόφως φέρει κακά, 'impatiently.' (Shaksp. *Henry VI.* Pt. III. 3. 1. 16 *yield not thy neck To fortune's yoke.*)—Nauck writes the verse thus, νῶτον δικαίως εἴχον εὐλόφως φέρειν, because Eustathius, in alluding to it, once represents it by νῶτον εὐλόφως εἴχον (on *Od.* 5. 285), and twice by νῶτον εὐλόφως φέρειν (on *Il.* 10. 573, *Od.* 10. 169). But Eustath. was quoting, or rather paraphrasing, from memory, and confused our verse with Eur. fr. 175 (quoted above); also, perhaps, with Lycophron 776 εὐλόφῳ νώτῳ φέρειν. His references to Sophocles are often loose and inexact. See Appendix.—δικαίως, loyally. Donaldson had a too ingenious view that the word here meant, 'with

· ἐκ τῶνδε τούτους ἐξεπίσταμαι καλῶς
, παρηγμένους μισθοῖσιν εἰργάσθαι τάδε.
· οὐδὲν γὰρ ἀνθρώποισιν οἷον ἄργυρος   295
· κακὸν νόμισμ᾽ ἔβλαστε. τοῦτο καὶ πόλεις
· πορθεῖ, τόδ᾽ ἄνδρας ἐξανίστησιν δόμων·
· τόδ᾽ ἐκδιδάσκει καὶ παραλλάσσει φρένας
· χρηστὰς πρὸς αἰσχρὰ πράγμαθ᾽ ἵστασθαι βροτῶν·
πανουργίας δ᾽ ἔδειξεν ἀνθρώποις ἔχειν   300
· καὶ παντὸς ἔργου δυσσέβειαν εἰδέναι.
ὅσοι δὲ μισθαρνοῦντες ἤνυσαν τάδε,
· χρόνῳ ποτ᾽ ἐξέπραξαν ὡς δοῦναι δίκην.
· ἀλλ᾽ εἴπερ ἴσχει Ζεὺς ἔτ᾽ ἐξ ἐμοῦ σέβας,
· εὖ τοῦτ᾽ ἐπίστασ᾽, ὅρκιος δέ σοι λέγω,   305
· εἰ μὴ τὸν αὐτόχειρα τοῦδε τοῦ τάφου

Mekler's theory that L's archetype had εἶχον...εισφέρειν, and that the letters εὔλοφ had become illegible.   **296** κακὸν νόμισμ᾽] Nauck conject. κακῶν ἔναυσμ᾽ ('incitement'):

equal poise' (*New Crat.* 371).—ὡς = ὥστε (*O. T.* 84): στέργων, *tolerare*: *Tr.* 486 (Lichas advising Deianeira with regard to Iolè) στέργε τὴν γυναῖκα, *be patient of her*.

293 f. τῶνδε, masc., the malcontents (for ἐκ, cp. 63).—τούτους, the watchers of the corpse: the pronouns joined as in 39 (n.).—εἰργάσθαι is best taken with ἐξανίσταμαι: cp. 1092 ἐπιστάμεσθα...αὐτὸν...λακεῖν. The inf., instead of the partic., with ἐπίσταμαι, seems unknown in Attic prose, except, of course, where the sense is 'to know how.' Cp. 472. The inf. might, indeed, depend on παρηγμένους, as ἐπάγω (to induce) oft. takes an inf.: but (*a*) as a matter of fact, an infin. seems not to occur after παράγω in this sense: and (*b*) it may be noticed that Attic idiom often prefers the form, 'induced by them, he did it,' to, 'he was induced by them to do it': *e.g.* Xen. *Mem.* 4. 8. 5 πολλοὺς...λόγῳ παραχθέντες ἀπέκτειναν: Dem. or. 5 § 10 οἱ ἐπαχθέντες ὑμεῖς...προείσθε Φωκέας. For this participial expression of the leading idea, see n. on *O. C.* 1038.

296 f. νόμισμ᾽, *institutum*. This primary and general sense of the word was almost confined to poetry (Aesch. *Th.* 269 Ἑλληνικὸν νόμισμα θυστάδος βοῆς), the special sense, 'current coin,' being the ordinary one. For the other sense, the usual word was νόμιμον (or νόμος). Hence in Ar. *Nub.* 247, when So-

crates says, θεοὶ | ἡμῖν νόμισμ᾽ οὐκ ἔστι, Strepsiades rejoins, τῷ γὰρ ὄμνυτ᾽; ἦ | σιδαρέοισιν, ὥσπερ ἐν Βυζαντίῳ (*i.e.* if gods are not *current* with you, do you swear by iron coin?): where the schol. remarks that νόμισμα meant ποτὲ μὲν τὸ νόμιμον ἔθος, ποτὲ δὲ τὸ κόμμα τοῦ τετυπωμένου χαλκοῦ.—ἔβλαστε: cp. *O. C.* 611 βλαστὼσι δ᾽ ἀπιστία.—πορθεῖ, 'sacks' (not merely, in a general sense, 'ruins'): money invites attack, and often purchases betrayal: cp. Hor. *Carm.* 3. 16. 13 *diffidit urbium Portas vir Macedo et subruit aemulos Reges muneribus.*—τόδ᾽ (after τοῦτο: cp. 39) ἄνδρας, individual citizens, as distinguished from πόλεις. ἐξ-ανίστ. δόμων, drives them from their cities by corrupt intrigue,—for which the στάσεις of democrat and oligarch in Greek cities gave many openings. The phrase is strikingly illustrated by the verses in which Timocreon of Rhodes, when an exile, assailed Themistocles (Plut. *Them.* 21), as τοὺς μὲν κατάγων ἀδίκως, τοὺς δ᾽ ἐκδιώκων, τοὺς δὲ καίνων, | ἀργυρίων ὑπόπλεως.

298 f. τόδ᾽ ἐκδ. καὶ παραλλάσσει, this trains and perverts good minds of men, ἵστασθαι πρὸς αἰσχρ. πράγμ., to address themselves to base deeds. παραλλάσσει='alters sideways'; *i.e.* causes to turn out of a straight course into an oblique course; hence, like παράγω, παραστρέφει, perverts. Cp. Arist. *Pol.* 8.

'Tis by them, well I know, that these have been beguiled
and bribed to do this deed. Nothing so evil as money ever
grew to be current among men. This lays cities low, this drives
men from their homes, this trains and warps honest souls till
they set themselves to works of shame ; this still teaches folk to
practise villanies, and to know every godless deed.
But all the men who wrought this thing for hire have
made it sure that, soon or late, they shall pay the price. Now,
as Zeus still hath my reverence, know this—I tell it thee on
my oath :—If ye find not the very author of this burial,

Pallis, κακὸν νόημ'. **299** βροτοῦσ L (accentless) with ω written above.
300 ἔχειν] Wecklein conject. ἄγειν : Pallis, τέχνην (or -αι).

---

7 § 7 αἱ ψυχαὶ παρεστραμμέναι τῆι
κατὰ φύσιν ἕξεωι (their minds being
warped from their natural condition).
Since παραλλάσσει implies a bad training, it can be followed, like ἐθίζει and
like words, by an infin. : it is unnecessary, then, to make ἵστασθαι, in its relation to παραλλάσσει, merely epexegetic
('so that they set themselves'); though
it might, of course, be so. Wecklein
takes καὶ παραλλάσσει as parenthetic
= παραλλάσσουσα : but this, too, is needless, nor is it supported by 537 (where
see n.).—ἵστασθαι πρός τι means here,
'to set oneself facing it,' so 'to turn to it,
address oneself to it,' just like τρέπεσθαι
πρός τι: cp. Plat. Rep. 452 E πρὸς ἄλλον τινὰ σκοπὸν στησάμενος ἢ τὸν
τοῦ ἀγαθοῦ, 'having set himself to some
other aim,' etc. Distinguish some other
phrases with ἵστασθαι and πρός which are
not really similar: Thuc. 3. 11 πρὸς ὅ τι
χρὴ στῆναι (a power to which they could
rally): 4. 56 πρὸς τὴν ἐκείνων γνώμην
ἀεὶ ἕστασαν (they had always sided with
the Athenian policy): 6. 34 πρὸς τὰ λεγόμενα καὶ αἱ γνῶμαι ἵστανται (men's minds
adapt their attitudes to what is said).
300 l. πανουργίας...ἔχειν: showed
men how to practise villanies. For ἔχειν
of the moral habit, cp. Od. 1. 368 μνη-
στῆρες ὑπέρβιον ὕβριν ἔχοντες: Il. 9. 305
λύσσαν ἔχων ὀλοήν. The inf. might be
epexegetic, but really depends on ἔδειξεν
as implying 'taught': cp. Eur. Med. 195
οὐδεὶς λύπας | ηὕρετο... | ᾠδαῖς παύειν
(has found out how to...). δείκνυμι of invention, as Ai. 1195 ὃς στυγερῶν ἔδειξεν
ὅπλων | Ἕλλασι κοινὸν Ἄρη: fr. 396.
ὁ στρατοῦ φρυκτωρίαν | ἔδειξε, κἀνέφηνεν
οὐ δεδειγμένα (Palamedes).—εἰδέναι, 'to
know,' i.e. to be conversant with (cp.

on 71) παντὸς ἔργου δυσσέβ., impiety of
(shown in) any deed, = πᾶν δυσσεβὲς ἔργον
(cp. 603 λόγου τ' ἄνοια) : for πᾶς, cp. O. C.
761 n. Note παντὸς ἔργ. after πανουργίας: the familiar use of πανουργία ex-
tenuates the force to which etymology
entitles it, while in πᾶν ἔργον that whole
force is felt: so πᾶν ποιεῖν is stronger
than πανουργεῖν, and πᾶν λέγειν than
παρρησιάζεσθαι (Plat. Apol. 39 A ἐὰν τις
τολμᾷ πᾶν ποιεῖν καὶ λέγειν). Cp. Ph.
407 παντὸς ἂν λόγου κακοῦ | γλώσσῃ
θιγόντα καὶ πανουργίας, where πᾶσης
must be supplied, showing how πανουργία
could be used without direct reference to
its derivation.
302 f. ἤνυσαν: cp. 231.—χρόνῳ
ποτέ, at some time or other: i.e. they
will be caught sooner or later. With
δοῦναι δίκην: Ph. 1041 τίσασθε, τίσασθ'
ἀλλὰ τῷ χρόνῳ ποτέ.—ἐξέπραξαν ὡς (= ὥστε, 292), as Aesch. Pers. 723 καὶ τόδ' ἐξέ-
πραξεν, ὥστε Βόσπορον κλῆσαι μέγαν; The
verb is here ironical; cp. Plat. Gorg. 479 A
τὸ αὐτὸ διαπεπραγμένοι εἰσὶν ὥσπερ ἂν εἰ
τις τοῖς μεγίστοις νοσήμασι συνισχόμενος
διαπράξαιτο μὴ διδόναι δίκην .. τοῖς
ἰατροῖς, μηδὲ ἰατρεύεσθαι.
304 f. Ζεύς, in his quality of Βασιλεύς (Xen. An. 3. 1. 12), is fitly invoked
by a king who vows that he will uphold
the royal authority. Cp. 487.—ὅρκιος,
adverbial: O. C. 1637 κ...ἤγγεισεν τάδ'
ὅρκιος (n.). Cp. 823 (ξυγηρότατα).—τὸν
αὐτόχειρα, the very man (248) whose
hand strewed the dust, said with an
emphasis corresponding to that with
which the Guard had insisted on the
absence of any clue (249). For αὐτο-,
cp. 56, 172. τάφου = ταφῆς, as 490, 534,
O. T. 1447 : in a symbolical sense like
that of θάψας (246).

J. S. III.² 5

-εὑρόντες ἐκφανεῖτ' ἐς ὀφθαλμοὺς ἐμούς,
- οὐχ ὑμῖν Ἀιδης μοῦνος ἀρκέσει, πρὶν ἂν
- ζῶντες κρεμαστοὶ τήνδε δηλώσηθ' ὕβριν,
- ἵν' εἰδότες τὸ κέρδος ἔνθεν οἰστέον   310
  τὸ λοιπὸν ἁρπάζητε, καὶ μάθηθ' ὅτι
  οὐκ ἐξ ἅπαντος δεῖ τὸ κερδαίνειν φιλεῖν.
  ἐκ τῶν γὰρ αἰσχρῶν λημμάτων τοὺς πλείονας
  ἀτωμένους ἴδοις ἂ ἢ σεσωσμένους.

ΦΥ.-εἰπεῖν τι δώσεις, ἢ στραφεὶς οὕτως ἴω;   315
ΚΡ.-οὐκ οἶσθα καὶ νῦν ὡς ἀνιαρῶς λέγεις;
ΦΥ.-ἐν τοῖσιν ὠσὶν ἢ 'πὶ τῇ ψυχῇ δάκνει;
ΚΡ.-τί δὲ ῥυθμίζεις τὴν ἐμὴν λύπην ὅπου;
ΦΥ.-ὁ δρῶν σ' ἀνιᾷ τὰς φρένας, τὰ δ' ὦτ' ἐγώ.
ΚΡ.-οἴμ' ὡς λάλημα δῆλον ἐκπεφυκὸς εἶ.   320

311 L has ἁρπάζητε, not (as has been stated) ἁρπάξητε. The mistake was easy, because the ς begins low down, being a continuation of the down stroke of the α. But the difference between αζ and αξ, as the scribe of L writes them, can be seen by comparing this word with ἐξέπραξαν in 303, or (e.g.) ἄξω in O. C. 819 with θαύμαζε ib. 1119. 312 L ἐκ τῶν . . σεσωσμένους. Bergk rejects these two verses ; M. Schmidt would spare them, but place them after v. 326.—Wecklein writes σεσωσμένους (Curae epigraph. p. 60). 315 τι δώσεις] δεδώσεις L (no accent on δε): δὲ δώσεις Γ. Over δε an early hand in L (the first, as Dübner thinks) has written . τι. 317 ἐν τοῖσιν ὠσὶν

308 f. μοῦνος: c.?. O. T. 304 n.—'Death alone shall not suffice for you,' already implies a threat of torture. To make this threat explicit, πρὶν ἄν . . δηλώσητε is added, as if merely οὐ θανεῖσθε had preceded. '(You shall not die,) until you have first been hung up alive, and have revealed (the authorship of) this outrage.' They are to be suspended by the hands or arms, and flogged. Cp. Ai. 106 θανεῖν γὰρ αὐτὸν οὔ τί πω θέλω . . πρὶν ἂν δεθεὶς πρὸς κίον' ἑρκείου στέγης . . μάστιγι πρῶτον νῶτα φοινιχθεὶς θάνῃ. Ter. Phorm. 1. 4. 43 ego plectar pendens. In Plat. Legg. 872 B a slave who has slain a free man is to be flogged, and then (if he does not die under the lash, ἐάνπερ βιῷ παιόμενος) put to death by other means. Other views of κρεμαστοί refer it to (1) mere suspension, as a torture, like that of Melanthius in Od. 22. 175: (2) stretching on a cross-like frame; cp. Alexis ap. Athen. 134 A ἥδιστ' ἀναπήξαιμ' αὐτὸν ἐπὶ ξύλου λαβών. Impalement (ἀνασταυρόω, ἀνασκολοπίζω) is certainly not meant.— ζῶντες κρεμαστοί, 'suspended alive,' as

ζῶν is oft. joined with another partic.: Xen. An. 2. 6. 29 οὐχ ὥσπερ οἱ ἄλλοι . . ἀποτμηθέντες τὰς κεφαλάς, ὥσπερ τάχιστος θάνατος δοκεῖ εἶναι, ἀλλὰ ζῶν αἰκισθεὶς ἐνιαυτόν.—δηλώσηθ': as to the belief that torture was sure to wring the truth from slaves, cp. Isae. or. 8. 12 ὁπόταν δοῦλοι καὶ ἐλεύθεροι παραγένωνται, . . οὐ χρῆσθε ταῖς τῶν ἐλευθέρων μαρτυρίαις, ἀλλὰ τοὺς δούλους βασανίζοντες οὕτω ζητεῖτε εὑρεῖν τὴν ἀλήθειαν τῶν γενομένων. (Cp. Selections from the Attic Orators, p. 358 n.)—ὕβριν, in concrete sense (O. C. 1029).

310 ff. ἵν' . . ἁρπάζητε, with grim irony, since they are to die before they can apply the lesson. So O. C. 1377 (Oed. calls down destruction upon his sons) ἵν' ἀξίωτον τοὺς φυτεύσαντας σέβειν, where see n. Cp. below, 716.—τὸ κέρδος, accus. (cp. 1242): ἔνθεν οἰστέον (ἐστί).— μάθηθ', aor., learn once for all: but ἁρπάζητε, pres., go on stealing.—ἐξ ἅπαντος, from every source, with τὸ κερδαίνειν: Xen. Mem. 2. 9. 4 οὐ γὰρ ἦν οἷος ἀπὸ παντὸς κερδαίνειν: Ar. Th. 735 ὦ ποτίσταται | κἀκ παντὸς ὑμεῖς μηχανώμεναι

and produce him before mine eyes, death alone shall not be
enough for you, till first, hung up alive, ye have revealed this
outrage,—that henceforth ye may thieve with better knowledge
whence lucre should be won, and learn that it is not well to
love gain from every source.   For thou wilt find that ill-gotten
pelf brings more men to ruin than to weal.

GU.   May I speak?   Or shall I just turn and go?
CR.   Knowest thou not that even now thy voice offends?
GU.   Is thy smart in the ears, or in the soul?
CR.   And why wouldst thou define the seat of my pain?
GU.   The doer vexes thy mind, but I, thine ears.
CR.   Ah, thou art a born babbler, 'tis well seen.

L, with an erasure of three or four letters after τοι, in which ι has been made from υ:
i.e. the scribe had first written ἐν τούτοισ.   **318** δαί L, δέ r.   **320** οἴμ' ὡς λάλημα δῆλον] L has λάλημα, with an α erased before it: either, then, the scribe wrote
ἀλάλημα, or he had begun to write ἄλημα, but perceived the error before he had
written η.   The later MSS. have λάλημα.   The schol. has λάλημα in the lemma, but
interprets ἄλημα,—τὸ περίτριμμα τῆς ἀγορᾶς, οἷον πανοῦργοι.—M. Schmidt writes
οἴμοι, λάλημ' ὡς: Gleditsch, ἴσθ' ὡς λάλημα: for δῆλον, Burges δεινόν.

πιεῖν. In *O. C.* 807 ἐξ ἅπαντος εὖ λέγει
=speaks well on any theme (starting from
anything).

315 ἴ. τι suits a timid appeal: cp.
O. C. 1414 ἱκετεύω σε πεισθῆναί τί μοι.
δί (Boeckh), though favoured by L, could
not be justified as an expostulatory 'now.'
δώσεις: *O. C.* 1287 διδοὺς ἐμοὶ | λέξαι.—
οὕτως, 'without more ado,' ὥσπερ ἔχω:
Ph. 1066 οὐδὲ σοῦ φωνῆς ἔτι | γενήσομαι
προσφθεγκτός, ἀλλ' οὕτως ἄπει; Plat.
Phaedr. 237 C νῦν μὲν οὕτως οὐκ ἔχω εἰπεῖν ('off-hand').—ἰω, delib. subjunct.,
somewhat rare in pres. (*O. T.* 651).—καὶ
νῦν δε = ὡς καὶ νῦν: for the hyperbaton of
ὡς, cp. *Ai.* 590, *El.* 949, 1243, etc.—
ἀναρός, with ῑ: but Eur., like Ar., has
ἀναρός (*Or.* 230 etc.): Aesch. does not
use the adj., though he has ἄνοος. ἀνία (ῑ)
is used by Soph., but not by Aesch. or
Eur.

317 ἐν with ἐσίν, through association with such phrases as Aesch. *Pers.*
605 βοᾷ δ' ἐν ὠσὶ κέλαδος.—ἐπί with τῇ
ψυχῇ denotes the seat, and, equally with
ἐν, here=our 'in': cp. *Il.* 1. 55 τῷ γὰρ
ἐπὶ φρεσὶ θῆκε θεά.

318 τί δή is right, not τί δαί (L): see
Appendix.—ῥυθμίζεις, bring under ῥυθμός,
i.e. reduce to a clear form, define, ὅπου
(ἐστί), *with respect to its seat,* (*i.e.* whether
it is in the ears or in the mind.) Cp.
Arist. *Metaphys.* 11. 10 ἐὰν μὴ ῥυθμίσῃ

τις, unless one reduce (the opinions) to a
clear form, or method.   So he oft. associates ῥυθμός with σχῆμα, as *Phys. Ausc.*
8. 3 τὸ σχηματιζόμενον καὶ ῥυθμιζόμενον,
what is being reduced to form and system.
For the epexegetic ὅπου cp. *Ai.* 103 ἦ
τοὐπίτριπτον κίναδος ἐξήρου μ'' ὅπου; *ib.*
890 ἄνδρα μὴ λεύσσειν ὅπου.—Cp. Shaksp.
Troil. 4. 5. 244 *That I may give the local
wound a name, And* make distinct *the
very breach whereout Hector's great spirit
flew.*

319 ἴ. τὰς φρένας ... τὰ δ' ἀτ', acc.
defining σε: *Ph.* 1301 μέθες με χεῖρα: cp.
on *O. C.* 113.—οἴμ' ὡς, impatient, as Ar.
Ach. 590 οἴμ' ὡς τεθνήξεις: elsewhere in
Soph. it expresses pity or grief (1270, *Ai.*
354, 587).—λάλημα suits Creon's contemptuous impatience.   The schol. (see
crit. n.) prob. read ἄλημα ('a knave,' lit.,
'fine meal,' from ἀλέω): cp. Ar. *Av.* 430
παιπάλημ' ὅλον.   But if Creon used that
word, he would seem to give the man
credit for real subtlety: he would be
taking him too seriously.   Thus ἄλημα is
the word applied by Ajax to his mortal
foe, Odysseus (*Ai.* 381, 389), who is similarly called πάνσοφον κρότημα in fr. 827:
cp. *Ph.* 927 πανουργίας | δεινῆς τέχνημ'
ἔχθιστον (Neoptolemus).   Cp. 756 δούλευμα: *O. T.* 85 κήδευμα (n.).—δῆλον,
like ἐναργές cp. on 263).

ΦΥ. οὔκουν τό γ᾽ ἔργον τοῦτο ποιήσας ποτέ.

ΚΡ.- καὶ ταῦτ᾽ ἐπ᾽ ἀργύρῳ γε τὴν ψυχὴν προδούς.

ΦΥ.- φεῦ.

-ἦ δεινόν, ᾧ δοκεῖ γε, καὶ ψευδῆ δοκεῖν.

ΚΡ.- κόμψευέ νυν τὴν δόξαν· εἰ δὲ ταῦτα μὴ
    φανεῖτέ μοι τοὺς δρῶντας, ἐξερεῖθ᾽ ὅτι   325
    τὰ δειλὰ κέρδη πημονὰς ἐργάζεται.

ΦΥ.- ἀλλ᾽ εὑρεθείη μὲν μάλιστ᾽· ἐὰν δέ τοι
    ληφθῇ τε καὶ μή, τοῦτο γὰρ τύχη κρινεῖ,
    οὐκ ἔσθ᾽ ὅπως ὄψει σὺ δεῦρ᾽ ἐλθόντα με·
    καὶ νῦν γὰρ ἐκτὸς ἐλπίδος γνώμης τ᾽ ἐμῆς   330
    -σωθείς, ὀφείλω τοῖς θεοῖς πολλὴν χάριν.

στρ. α΄. ΧΟ.- πολλὰ τὰ δεινὰ, κοὐδὲν ἀνθρώπου δεινότερον πέλει·

321 τό γ᾽ Reiske: τόδ᾽ MSS. **323** φεῦ in the verse L.—ἦ] ἦ᾽ L.—ᾧ δοκεῖ] L has ἦν and η written above ὦ and εἰ, by the first hand. ἦν δοκῇ r (including A).—δοκεῖν] δοκεῖ L.—Vauvilliers conject. ἦν δοκῇ γε καὶ ψευδῆ, δοκεῖν: Kvičala, ἦν δοκῇ γε, κεὶ ψευδῆ δοκεῖ: Hartung. ᾧ δόκησις ᾖ, ψευδῆ δοκεῖν: Anonym. in Class. Journ. xvii. 57 ᾧ δοκεῖ γε, τὸ ψευδῆ δοκεῖν: Pallis, ὃς δοκεῖ γε καὶ ψευδῆ δοκεῖν ('that a man of repute should have false opinions'). **324** νιν] νῦν L.—For τὴν δόξαν, one late MS. (Aug. b, 14th

---

321 'At any rate (οὖν—babbler or not) I certainly have not done this deed.' εἰμί is supplied with ποιήσας. For οὔκουν . . γε cp. 993, Ph. 907 ΝΕ. αἰσχρὸς φανοῦμαι . . Φι. οὔκουν ἐν οἷς γε δρᾷς· ἐν οἷς δ᾽ αὐδᾷς, ὀκνῶ: and so oft., as O. T. 565, 1357, O. C. 848.

322 'Yes, (you have done it,) and that, too, at the cost of betraying,' etc. The particle γε implies the contradiction, ἐποίησας: καὶ ταῦτα goes with the participle (προδούς): cp. O. T. 37, El. 614 τὴν τεκοῦσαν ὕβρισεν, | καὶ ταῦτα τηλικοῦτος. So Lat., hominem . . studiis optimis dedi- tum, idque a puero (Cic. Fam. 13. 16).

323 ἦ δεινόν. Creon has pronounced the Guard guilty on mere δόξα, without proof. The Guard says, 'It is grievous that, when a man does harbour suspicions (ᾧ δοκεῖ γε), those suspicions should at the same time (καὶ) be false.' γε means that, in such a matter, hasty δόξα should be avoid- ed altogether. It is always bad to assume a man guilty without proof; it is worse when the rash assumption is also erroneous. Cp. δόκησις ἀγνώς, 'a blind suspicion' (O. T. 681), and ib. 608 γνώμῃ δ᾽ ἀδήλῳ μή με χωρὶς αἰτιῶ. Eur. Bacch. 311 μηδ᾽ ἢν δοκῇς μέν, (ἡ δὲ δόξα σου νοσεῖ,) | φρονεῖν δόκει τι.—Nauck supposes a play on two senses of δοκεῖν, ᾧ δοκεῖ (or, as he reads,

δοκῇ) having been suggested by ἔδοξε τῷ δήμῳ, etc.: ''Tis monstrous that he who decides should have false views.' But, even if the absolute ᾧ δοκεῖ could be thus used, the colloquial frequency of δοκεῖ (μοι ποιεῖν τι) in Aristophanes suffices to show that ᾧ δοκεῖ could not, to an Athenian ear, have suggested 'the ruler' or 'the judge': it would have seemed to mean merely one who 'proposes,' not 'dis- poses.'—Schütz makes δοκεῖν depend on δοκεῖ: ''Tis grievous when a man is re- solved to believe even what is false' (if only he wishes to believe it). A bold speech for the Guard to Creon; nor does it satisfy either γε or καὶ.

324 κόμψευε . τὴν δόξαν, make neat sayings about it,—referring to the rhetori- cal form of the last verse, with its παρή- χησις, δοκεῖ...δοκεῖν. Not necessarily, 'quibble upon it,'—as if δοκεῖν had been used in two different senses,—a view of κόμψευε which has been brought to sup- port the interpretations of v. 323 men- tioned above. The verb is usually midd., often with acc., as Eur. I. A. 333 εὖ κεκόμψευσαι πονηρά ('thou hast given subtle form to wicked pleas'): Plat. Lach. 197 D πρέπει...σοφιστῇ τὰ τοιαῦτα μᾶλλον κομψεύεσθαι.—τὴν δόξαν, that δόξα of yours: cp. 96: El. 1110 οὐκ οἶδα τὴν σὴν

GU. May be, but never the doer of this deed.

CR. Yea, and more,—the seller of thy life for silver.

GU. Alas! 'Tis sad, truly, that he who judges should misjudge.

CR. Let thy fancy play with 'judgment' as it will;—but, if ye show me not the doers of these things, ye shall avow that dastardly gains work sorrows. [*Exit.*

GU. Well, may he be found! so 'twere best. But, be he caught or be he not—fortune must settle that—truly thou wilt not see me here again. Saved, even now, beyond hope and thought, I owe the gods great thanks. [*Exit.*

CHORUS.

Wonders are many, and none is more wonderful than man; 1st strophe.

cent.) has τὸ δόξαν.—Moschopulus περὶ σχεδῶν p. 20 reads κόμψευε τὴν δόκησιν: prob., as Dindorf says, by a confusion with the schol. here, σεμνολόγει· τὴν δόκησιν περιλάλει. **326** δεινά] δεινὰ L, which Seyffert and others prefer: schol. γρ. τὰ δειλά· ἀντὶ τοῦ κακά· ἀπὸ τοῦ τοὺς δειλοὺς εἶναι ἀχρείους. Wecklein conject. τἀδηλα. **327** τοι] σοι L, with τ above from first hand. **328** καὶ] Blaydes conject. κἂν. **332** πολλὰ τά] Neue conject. πολλά τε.

κληδόν' (the κληδών of which you speak), not merely, 'the word δόξα.' If the *v. l.* τὸ δόξαν (see cr. n.) was intended to mean the latter, it should have been τὸ δόξα (= 'very well,' like οὖν) is better than νῦν, which would mean 'for the present' (as opposed to the near future).— ταῦτα...τοὺς δρῶντας = τοὺς ταῦτα δρῶντας: cp. 384: the pron. gains emphasis by its place.

326 δειλά, as involving mean treachery towards king and city. Theognis 835 ἀλλ' ἀνδρῶν τε βίῃ καὶ κέρδεα δειλὰ καὶ ὕβρις | πολλῶν ἐξ ἀγαθῶν ἐς κακότητ' ἔβαλεν (*sc.* ἡμᾶς).—δεινά (L) is defended by Seyffert as = 'flagitious,' by Whitelaw as = 'clever' (*ironically.*), 'your wondrous winnings.' In some forms of minuscule writing λ and ν could easily be confused: cp. *O. T.* 1130 ξυναλλάξας, where the first λ has been made from ν: and *O. T.* 1164, where μόνον has been restored from μολόντ'.

327 f. ἀλλ' prefacing the wish (*O. C.* 421): εὑρεθείη *sc.* ὁ δρῶν (319): μάλιστ', denoting the best thing that could happen (*O. T.* 926 n.).—κἂν for καὶ is needless. We find καὶ ἐάν...καὶ ἐάν: ἐάν τε...ἐάν τε: but, as a rule, ἐάν (or ἐάν τε)...καὶ [not καὶ ἐάν] μή: *e.g.* Eur. *Hec.* 751 κἂν τύχω κἂν μὴ τύχω: Plat. *Legg.* 660 E ἐάν τε μέγας...ἐάν τε σμικρὸς...ἢ, καὶ ('and') ἐὰν πλουτῇ καὶ μή. For the conjunctive

form in stating alternatives, cp. *O. C.* 488 n.

330 καὶ with νῦν, not with γάρ.— γνώμης, of reasonable forecast, cp. *O. T.* 1087.

332—375 First στάσιμον. 1st strophe (332—342) = 1st antistrophe (343—353): 2nd strophe (354—364) = 2nd antistr. (365—375). For the metres see Metrical Analysis.

The Chorus had not thought it possible that any one should brave death to bury the corpse (220). But the deed has been done, and without leaving a trace (252). And Creon has silenced the suggestion that gods did it (278). The train of thought is continued in this ode. Its theme is man's daring,—his inventiveness, and the result to his happiness.

Man is master of sea and land; he subdues all other creatures; he has equipped his life with all resources, except a remedy against death. His skill brings him to prosperity, when he observes divine and human laws, but to ruin when he breaks them.—At that moment Antigone is led in, and the coryphaeus speaks the closing anapaests (376—383).

332 πολλὰ...κοὐδέν. Schol. ἐν σχή- ματι εἶπεν, ἀντὶ τοῦ, πολλῶν ὄντων τῶν δεινῶν, οὐδέν ἐστιν ἀνθρώπου δεινότερον. The σχῆμα is the rhetorical parataxis,

-2 τοῦτο καὶ πολιοῦ πέραν πόντου χειμερίῳ νότῳ   335
-3 χωρεῖ, περιβρυχίοισιν
-4 περῶν ὑπ᾽ οἴδμασιν·
-5 θεῶν τε τὰν ὑπερτάταν, Γᾶν
-6 ἄφθιτὸν, ἀκαμάταν ἀποτρύεται,
-7 ἰλλομένων ἀρότρων ἔτος εἰς ἔτος,   340
-8 ἱππείῳ γένει πολεύων.

335 πόντου made from πόντωι by the first hand in L.   **338** θεῶν τε] τ has been corrected from θ (or δ) by an early hand in L. After τὰν a point has been erased.   **339** f. ἀκαμάταν] ἀκαμάτων Semitelos (as Triclinius read), joining it with ἀρότρων, which he substitutes for ἀρότρων.—ἀποτρύετ᾽ ἀπλομένων L, the ο after λ made from ω: schol. in marg., γρ. ἀποτρύεται Πλομένων. A mis-writing of the latter, with λ for λλ, caused the error, ΑΠΟΤΡΥΕΤΑΠΛΟΜΕΝΩΝ (Π for ΙΙ). The

καί being equiv. to 'and yet': cp. *Tr.* 1046 ὦ πολλὰ δὴ καὶ θερμὰ κοὐ λόγῳ κακά |...μοχθήσας ἐγώ | κοὔπω τοιοῦτον οὔτ᾽ ἄκοιτις ἡ Διὸς | προὔθηκεν κ.τ.λ. It is stronger to say, 'they are great; and he is greater': than, 'though they are great, he is greater.'—τὰ δεινά, not 'dread,' nor 'able,' but 'wonderful.' There is a certain resemblance to Aesch. *Ch.* 585 ff. πολλὰ μὲν γᾶ τρέφει | δεινὰ δειμάτων ἄχη...ἀλλ᾽ ὑπέρτολμον ἀνδρὸς φρόνημα τίς λέγοι; but there δεινά = 'dread,' and the scope is limited to the violence of human passion.

334 τοῦτο, *sc.* τὸ δεινόν, this wondrous power, man. The schol. quotes Theocr. 15. 83 σοφόν τοι χρῆμ᾽ ἄνθρωπος. Not adverbial with χωρεῖ, 'so' (in a way corresponding with his δεινότης), as Bellermann takes it, comparing *O. T.* 1005 (τοῦτ᾽ ἀφικόμην), where see n.— πέραν, properly, 'to the further side of' (*trans*). The point here is that man dares to cross the sea. πέρα (*ultra*), which Blaydes prefers, would imply wanderings (not merely over, but) beyond sea. A European visitor to New York goes πέραν πόντου: to San Francisco, πέρα. Cp. *O. C.* 885 and p. 279.

335 χειμερίῳ νότῳ with χωρεῖ, goes (driven) by it: cp. *Od.* 14. 253 ἐπλέομεν Βορέῃ ἀνέμῳ, and *ib.* 299 (of the ship) ἡ δ᾽ ἔθεεν Βορέῃ ἀνέμῳ. The dat. might be merely 'with' (dat. of circumstance), but is better taken as instrumental. Cp. 588 πνοαῖς. Some make χειμερίῳ νότῳ a temporal dat., like ὥρα χειμῶνος, which it can hardly be.—Soph. is thinking of the Aegean, where the prevailing winds were from the N. or N.W. in spring and

summer, while stormy south winds were associated with winter: Hesiod warns a man with a voyage before him not to await χειμῶν᾽ ἐπιόντα νότοιό τε δεινὰς δήτας, | ὅς τ᾽ ὤρινε θάλασσαν ὁμαρτήσας Διὸς ὄμβρῳ | πολλῷ ὀπωρινῷ, χαλεπὸν δέ τε πόντον ἔθηκεν. The epithet χειμερίῳ aptly distinguishes this wintry νότος from that gentle south breeze (now called the 'embates') which regularly sets in at sunset in the fair season (cp. Curt. *Hist. Gr.* 1. 14).

336 f. περιβρ...ὑπ᾽ οἴδμασιν, passing under swelling waters which open depths around: *i.e.* he is in the trough of a heavy sea, while on each side the waves rise above his ship, threatening to engulf it. Verg. *Aen.* 1. 106 *his unda dehiscens Terram inter fluctus aperit.* βρύχιος, 'of the depths' (βρύχια...ἰχὼ βροντᾶς, Aesch. *P. V.* 1082), is formed as if from βρόξ, of which Oppian uses acc. βρόχα ('depth of the sea,' *Hal.* 2. 588). ὑποβρόχιος = 'under water,' and so neut. pl. adv. ὑπόβρυχα (*Od.* 5. 319 etc.). περιβρόχιος occurs only here. For the ῑ before βρ cp. 348, 1104, 1117. The schol.'s ἠχώδεις means that περιβρύχιος was taken as 'roaring around' (βρῑχάομαι), where the υ would be long, against metre (cp. 347). The Homeric ἀμφὶ δὲ κῦμα | βέβρυχεν ῥόθιον (*Od.* 5. 411) might suggest this view.

338 ὑπερτάταν, highest, as eldest, παμμήτωρ (Aesch. *P. V.* 90), and παμβῶτις (*Ph.* 391): Plat. *Tim.* 40 c γῆν... πρώτην καὶ πρεσβυτάτην θεῶν ὅσοι ἐντὸς οὐρανοῦ γεγόνασι.

339 ἀκαμάταν: this form of the fem. occurs only here, unless ἀκαμάτησι (and

the power that crosses the white sea, driven by the stormy
south-wind, making a path under surges that threaten to
engulf him ; and Earth, the eldest of the gods, the immortal,
the unwearied, doth he wear, turning the soil with the offspring
of horses, as the ploughs go to and fro from year to year.

later MSS. have ἀπλωμένων (as V), εἰλομένων (as Vat.), or παλλομένων (as A).—ἔτος
εἰς ἔτος L.. Some later MSS. have ἔτους εἰς ἔτος. Musgrave conject. ἔτος ἐξ ἔτους,
from the schol., περικυκλούντων τῶν ἀρότρων ἔτος ἐξ ἔτους. **841** πολεύων (corrected
from πόλευον) L: πολεύων r.

---

not ἀκαμάτοισι) χέρεσσιν be right in
Hes. *Th.* 747, but is warranted by similar
epic forms in tragedy, as ἀθανάτας (gen.)
Aesch. *Ch.* 619, Eur. *Ph.* 235: ἀδ-
μήταν Soph. *El.* 1238 (and -ης in dial.
O. C. 1321). For the initial ἀ, cp. the
epic ἀθάνατος, ἀγοράασθε, etc. (and see
Introd. to Homer, Appendix, note 5, p.
195): but in *El.* 164 we find 'ἀκάμαρτα.—
ἀποτρύεται, prop., wears away for his
own purposes (midd.),—*fatigat*, vexes
(with constant ploughing). Earth is
'immortal,' and not to be exhausted; but
man's patient toil subdues it to his use.
Cp. *Tr.* 124 ἀποτρύει ἐλπίδα, to wear it
out.—Not, 'wearies himself by tilling' the
soil.
  840 ἰλλομένων ἀρότρων, as the
ploughs go backwards and forwards,—
turning at the end of one furrow, and
going down the next. Cp. Nicander
Ther. 478 φεῦγε δ' ἀεὶ σκολιήν τε καὶ οὐ
μίαν ἀτραπὸν ἴλλων, 'in flying (from the
snake), always *make your course wind*
(ἴλλων) from side to side, instead of keeping it straight.' Xen. *Cyn.* 6. 15 κύνες
ἰλλοῦσαι τὰ ἴχνη, 'puzzling out the
tracks,' *i.e.* going backwards and forwards
till they have found a clue. As to the
spelling ἴλλω *versus* εἴλλω, see Appendix.
It is needless to write ἀρότρων, 'ploughing-
seasons' (*Tr.* 825), and to take ἰλλομένων
as = περιτελλομένων. The picture of the
ploughs at work is more vivid; and, with
ἀρότρων, ἔτος εἰς ἔτος would be feebly redundant.—ἔτος εἰς ἔτος, an adverbial
phrase, like 'year in, year out': for the
use of the simple acc. in temporal adverbs
(like αὔριαν) see *O. T.* 1138 n.; for εἰς,
Od. 9. 134 μάλα κεν βαθὺ λήϊον αἰεὶ | εἰς
ὥρας ἀμῷεν ('as each year comes round'):
Theocr. 18. 15 κἠς ἔτος ἐξ ἔτεος: so εἰς
νέωτα (next year), and the Mod. Gk

χρόνῳ σὲ (= εἰς) χρόνῳ, 'year after year.'
  841 ἱππείῳ γένει, 'the offspring of
horses,' meaning 'mules'; which are 'far
better than oxen to drag the jointed
plough through the deep fallow' (*Il.* 10.
352). Arist. *Rhet.* 3. 2 § 14 ὁ Σιμωνίδης,
ὅτε μὲν ἐδίδου μισθὸν ὀλίγον αὐτῷ ὁ νικήσας
τοῖς ὀρεῦσιν, οὐκ ἤθελε ποιεῖν ὡς δυσχε-
ραίνων εἰς ἡμιόνους ποιεῖν· ἐπεὶ δ' ἱκανὸν
ἔδωκεν, ἐποίησε, χαίρετ', ἀελλοπόδων
θύγατρες ἵππων. As this story suggests, the very fact that the ordinary Attic
word for 'mule' was ἡμίονος (adj. ὀρικός)
might lead an Attic poet to prefer such a
periphrasis as ἵππειον γένος. The objections to taking ἱππείῳ γένει as simply
= ἵπποις are, that (1) Greek ploughmen used
oxen or mules more than horses, and (2)
the achievement of taming the horse (350)
is thus anticipated. Some understand
both horses and mules, giving γένει a double sense—rather awkwardly, I think.—
πολεύων, κατὰ σύνεσιν after τοῦτο. Cp.
Od. 11. 90 ἦλθε δ' ἐπὶ ψυχὴ Θηβαίου Τειρε-
σίαο, | χρύσεον σκῆπτρον ἔχων: 16. 476
μείδησεν δ' ἱερὴ ἲς Τηλεμάχοιο, | ἐς πατέρ'
ὀφθαλμοῖσιν ἰδών: *Il.* 11. 690 ἐλθὼν γὰρ
ἐκάκωσε βίη Ἡρακληείη. But as Soph.
would write ΠΟΛΕΤΟΝ, it was the easier
to read πόλευον.
  342—352 Man's conquests over the
animal world are here taken in two
groups. First, those of which the primary aim is to kill or to capture. Here
the means is netting (ἀμφιβαλὼν σπείραισι
δικτυοκλώστοις), in its threefold sporting
use, as applied to fowling (ὀρνίθων), hunting (θηρῶν), and fishing (πόντου φύσιν).
Secondly, those conquests which aim at
reducing wild animals to man's service.
These are effected by μηχαναί (349),—
arts of taming and training. And their
result is aptly expressed by the word

ἀντ. αʹ. - κοῦφονόων τε φῦλον ὀρνίθων ἀμφιβαλὼν ἄγει   343
          - 2 καὶ θηρῶν ἀγρίων ἔθνη πόντου τ᾽ εἰναλίαν φύσιν   345
          - 3 σπείραισι δικτυοκλώστοις,
          - 4 περιφραδὴς ἀνήρ·
          5 κρατεῖ δὲ μηχαναῖς ἀγραύλου
          6 θηρὸς ὀρεσσιβάτα, λασιαύχενά θ᾽   350
          7 ἵππον *ὀχμάζεται *ἀμφὶ λόφον ζυγῶν,
          8 οὔρειόν τ᾽ ἀκμῆτα ταῦρον.

στρ. βʹ.   καὶ φθέγμα καὶ ἀνεμόεν   354

342 κουφονέωντε L, the ω from o. The first hand seems to have written κοῦφον ἐόντε. κουφονέων τε or κουφονέον τε Γ: κουφονόων τε Brunck.   344 ἀμφιβαλὼν, with o above ω from the first hand (for the sake of consistency with πολεύων in 341).—The first hand in L wrote ἔχει ἄγει: another early hand erased the second word, and changed the first into ἄγει.   345 εἰναλίαν] ἐναλίαν L.   350 ὀρεσσιβάτᾱ L: a letter erased

κρατεῖ: here, man is not merely the slayer or captor; he becomes the master of docile toilers. The horse and the bull are types.

Thus, in this ode, the scale of achievement ever ascends: man (1) conquers inanimate nature: (2) makes animals his captives: (3) trains them to be his servants: (4) develops his own social and intellectual life.

343 κουφονόων is merely a general epithet, 'light-hearted,' 'blithe and careless'; Theognis 580 σμικρῆς ὄρνιθος κοῦφον ἔχουσα νόον: cp. the proverbial phraseology of Athens, ἄνθρωπος ὄρνις, ἀστάθμητος, πετόμενος, | ἀτέκμαρτος, οὐδὲν οὐδέποτ᾽ ἐν ταὐτῷ μένων (Ar. Av. 169). The epithet is given to ἔρωτες below (617), and to εὐηθία in Aesch. P. V. 383.—Not, 'quick-witted' (and therefore harder to catch).—ἀμφιβαλὼν with σπείραισι δ.: it can precede the dat. by so much, because its meaning is already clear, and the dat. is merely a poet. amplification.

345 f. πόντου...εἰναλίαν φύσιν, a brood living in the waters of the sea, the tautology being only of the same order as in πόντος ἁλός, ἁλὸς ἐν πελάγεσσιν, πέλαγος θαλάσσης, etc.—σπείραισι δικτυοκλ., instr. dat. with ἀμφιβαλὼν, in the coils of woven nets: for the adj. compounded with a subst. (δίκτυον) cognate in sense to σπεῖρα, see n. on O. C. 716 εὐήρετμος πλάτα.—Ar. Av. 528 mentions ἔρκη, νεφέλας, δίκτυα, πηκτάς as nets used by the fowler (ὀρνιθευτής). In hunting the lion, bear, boar, deer, hare, etc., various

nets were used; the δίκτυον, to enclose large spaces; the ἐνόδιον, to close passages; the ἄρκυς (cassis) or tunnel-net. The chief fishing-nets were the ἀμφίβληστρον (casting-net), and the σαγήνη (drag-net, whence seine, sean).

348 περιφραδής. Eustath. p. 135, 25 φραδής...ὅθεν σύνθετον ὁ παρὰ Σοφοκλεῖ ἀριφραδὴς ἀνήρ. This was evidently a mere slip of memory. Neither Soph. nor Eur. uses any compound with ἀρι or ἐρι, though Aesch. has ἀρίδακρυς, ἐρίδματος, ἐρικύμων.

349 f. μηχαναῖς. μαχαναῖς in Ai. 181 and μαχανά in Aesch. Th. 133 are the only instances in which Tragedy gives a Doric form to words from this stem.—ἀγραύλου, having his αὐλή, or dwelling, in the open country, as opposed to a domesticated animal: Eur. Bacch. 1187 πρέπει γ᾽ ὥστε θὴρ ἄγραυλος φόβῃ. For the combination with ὀρεσσιβάτα cp. Plat. Crat. 394 E τὸ θηριῶδες τῆς φύσεως καὶ τὸ ἄγριον αὐτοῦ καὶ τὸ ὀρεινόν.

350 λασιαύχενά θ᾽. The elision at the end of the verse (ἐπισυναλοιφή) is comparatively rare in lyrics, as in dialogue (1031); but cp. 595 πίπτοντ᾽, 864 αὐτογέννητ᾽.

351 ὀχμάζεται, he tames, ἀμφὶ λόφον ζυγῶν, putting the yoke about its neck. ὀχμάζω (prop., 'to get a firm hold upon') was esp. used of breaking horses: Eur. El. 816 (Thessalians honour a man) ὅστις ταῦρον δραμεῖ (cuts to pieces) καλῶς, | ἵππους τ᾽ ὀχμάζει. Schol. on Apollon.

And the light-hearted race of birds, and the tribes of savage 1st anti
beasts, and the sea-brood of the deep, he snares in the meshes strophe
of his woven toils, he leads captive, man excellent in wit.
And he masters by his arts the beast whose lair is in the wilds,
who roams the hills; he tames the horse of shaggy mane, he
puts the yoke upon its neck, he tames the tireless mountain
bull.

And speech, and wind-swift 2nd
strophe

after ᾱ, perhaps ν. **351** λασιαύχενά θ' ἵππον ἔξεται ἀμ|φίλοφον ζυγόν L. Schol.
in marg. (on 352) ἀπὸ κοινοῦ τὸ ὑπὸ ζυγὸν ἕξεται, with ά written over ἔ. The later MSS.
have ἄξεται (A), ἄξετ', ἕξεται, ἕξετ'. See comment. and Appendix. **352** ἀκμῆτα
L, ἀδμῆτα r.

Rhod. 1. 743 κυρίωϲ ἐστὶν ὀχμάσαι τὸ
ἵππον ὑπὸ χαλινὸν ἀγαγεῖν ἢ ὑπὸ ζυγόν.
The midd. voice does not occur elsewhere;
but this cannot be regarded as an objection, when we remember how many
rare middle forms occur in the dramatists.
Thus προσορωμένα in *O. C.* 244 is a solitary example of that verb in the midd.,
and if the license could be taken with so
common a word, much more might it be
allowed with a comparatively rare one.
Blaydes writes ὀχμάζει ὑπ' ἀμφίλοφον
ζυγόν: but the MS. ἔξεται indicates that
the verb, whatever it was, was of the
midd. form. ὀχμάζεται was published
by G. Schöne in 1833, and by Franz in
1846: they appear to have made the conjecture independently. Donaldson (1848)
printed ὀχμάζεται ἀμφὶ λόφον ζυγῶν, and
seems to ascribe ζυγῶν to Franz and
Schöne; though Franz, at least, proposed
ἀμφὶ λόφον ζυγῷ. ζυγῶν has lately been
revived (seemingly without knowledge of
a predecessor) by H. Schütz (1886). Sophocles would write ΑΜΦΙΛΟΦΟΝΖΥΓΟΝ,
and thus ζυγῶν changes no letter. Aesch.
used the fut. ζυγώσω (fr. 110), and Soph.
has the verbal ζυγωτόν (*El.* 702). To
ἀμφιλόφῳ ζυγῷ it may be objected that,
being clear, it was not likely to become
-ον -ον: but, when ἀμφίλοφον had once
been written, ζυγὸν (or ζυγῷ) would easily
become ζυγόν. As to the schol. on ἀμφίλοφον,—ἀντὶ τοῦ, περιβαλὼν αὐτῷ ζυγὸν
περὶ τὸν λόφον, ὑπάγει,—it cannot fairly
be urged for ζυγῶν (or for any partic.),
since it may be merely a paraphrase of
ἀμφίλοφον.—Schütz's ἐφέζεται is attractive; for the acc. he cp. Aesch. *Eum.* 409
βρέτας...ἐφημένῳ, Eur. *Helen.* 1493 Εὐρώ-
ταν ἐφεζόμεναι. Add Aesch. *Ag.* 664
ναῦν θέλουσ' ἐφέζετο. The sense would
be, 'seats himself behind the horse' (in a
chariot): cp. *Il.* 5. 46 ἵππων ἐπιβησόμενον,
etc. But, though oxen were used for
draught, ἐφέζεται suits ταῦρον less well.
The sense, 'tames,' is clearly that which
we require. See Appendix.
354 φθέγμα κ.τ.λ. The phrase, 'man
has taught himself speech,' should not
be pressed as if the poet was thinking of
a theory on the origin of language. It
was the Eleatic view that language came
θέσει, not φύσει, and Soph. may have
known that; but by his ἐδιδάξατο he meant
simply, 'developed for his own benefit,
by his own effort.' So Isocrates (or. 3 § 6)
conceives primitive man as living in a
brutal state, and emerging from it by the
development of speech and thought,—
λόγος being one of the human faculties
(τῶν ἐνόντων ἐν τῇ τῶν ἀνθρώπων φύσει),
and the distinctive one:—ἐγγενομένου δ'
ἡμῖν τοῦ πείθειν ἀλλήλους καὶ δηλοῦν πρὸς
ἡμᾶς αὐτοὺς περὶ ὧν ἂν βουληθῶμεν, οὐ
μόνον τοῦ θηριωδῶς ζῆν ἀπηλλάγη-
μεν, ἀλλὰ καὶ συνελθόντες πόλεις ᾠκί-
σαμεν καὶ νόμους ἐθέμεθα καὶ τέχνας
εὕρομεν. Cp. Hor. *Sat.* 1. 3. 103 (men
fought,) *Donec verba, quibus voces sen-
susque notarent, Nominaque invenere:
dehinc absistere bello, Oppida coeperunt
munire et ponere leges.* The Aeschylean
Prometheus (*P. V.* 444) claims to have
made men ἔννους...καὶ φρενῶν ἐπηβόλους,
but not (like Shelley's Prometheus) to
have also given them language. Cp.
Peile's chapter 'On the Nature of Language' (*Primer of Philology*), p. 156: 'In
this way then we may conceive of the

2 φρόνημα καὶ ἀστυνόμους ὀργὰς ἐδιδάξατο, καὶ δυσ-
αύλων
3 πάγων ἐναίθρεια καὶ δύσομβρα φεύγειν βέλη,
4 παντοπόρος· ἄπορος ἐπ' οὐδὲν ἔρχεται 360
5 τὸ μέλλον· Ἄιδα μόνον φεῦξιν οὐκ ἐπάξεται·

355 φρόνημα] φώνημα Scaliger (so, too, Valckenaer and Bergk). φρούρημα Semitelos. ἀμερόφρον νόημα Schneidewin.—ὀργὰς] One of the later MSS., V (13th cent.), has ὁρμὰς, prob. a late conjecture, if not a mere error. Valckenaer conject. ἀρχὰς: Musgrave, ὀρχμὰς ('bounds,' Hesych., ὀρχμαί· φραγμοί): Mekler and Semitelos, ἀγορὰς: Gleditsch, ἀρετὰς (and ἀστυνόμων σοφίαν). **356** ἐδιδάξατο L, with ι over the first a from the first hand. **357** αἴθρια MSS. (marg. gloss in L, ψυχρά). ἐναίθρεια Helmke: ὑπαίθρεια Boeckh. Musgrave had already proposed αἴθρεια, which, however, does not satisfy the metre (cp. 368). Blaydes would prefer ὑπαίθρῖα or δυσαίθρῖα. **359** ταντ' ὁποροσ L first hand (πάντ' ἄπορος?): a later hand has accented the second o. L has a point after βέλη, and none after παντοπόρος. **361** Ἄιδα L, with ι over the second a from the first hand: the

---

beginnings of speech...Speech is the development, through imitation, of a capacity of man—the capacity of making a noise.' This is quite compatible with ἐδιδάξατο.—ἀνεμόεν φρόνημα: cp. *Il.* 15. 80 ὡς δ' ὅτ' ἂν ἀίξῃ νόος ἀνέρος...| ὡς κραιπνῶς μεμαυῖα διέπτατο: *Od.* 7. 36 τῶν νέες ὠκεῖαι ὡσεὶ πτερὸν ἠὲ νόημα: *O. C.* 1081 ἀελλαία ταχύρρωστος πελειάς: fr. 621 ἀελλάδες φωναί. Not 'lofty,' in which sense ἀνεμόεν could be said only of a high place. Cp. Shelley, *Prometheus:* 'He gave man speech, and speech created thought, Which is the measure of the universe.' Soph. does not imply that speech created thought; he is rather thinking of them as developed (in their riper forms) together. **355** ἀστυνόμους ὀργὰς, 'such dispositions as regulate cities'; *i.e.* those feelings which lead men to organise social life, and to uphold the social order by their loyalty. For ὀργὰς, cp. *Ai.* 639 συντρόφοις | ὀργαῖς, the dispositions that have grown with his growth: Eur. *Tro.* 53 ἐπήνεσ' ὀργὰς ἠπίους. The relation of φθέγμα to ἀστυνόμοι ὀργαί is illustrated by Arist. *Pol.* 1. 2 § 12, where he is showing that man, more than any other ἀγελαῖον ζῷον, is πολιτικόν: 'Speech is intended to explain what is expedient and what is hurtful,—and so also what is just and unjust. It is characteristic of man, as compared with other animals, that he alone has a sense of good and evil, just and unjust; and it is the association of beings with this sense that make a Family and a State.' **356** ἐδιδάξατο here = simply αὐτὸς ἑαυτὸν ἐδίδαξε. The notion, 'men taught

each other,' 'learned by mutual converse,' cannot be extracted from it. The passive διδάσκομαι as = μανθάνειν is freq., but I can find no parallel for the use of the aor. midd. here. For the ordinary use, cp. Plat. *Meno* p. 93 D τὸν υἱὸν ἱππέα...ἐδιδάξατο (*had* his son *taught* to ride): so Plat. *Rep.* 467 E (διδαξαμένους, 'when we have had them taught'); [Plat.] *Theag.* 122 E, *De Virt.* 377 H; Xen. *Cyr.* 1. 6. 2, *Mem.* 4. 4. 5, Ar. *Nub.* 1338. Once or twice ἐδιδαξάμην is merely ἐδίδαξα with the idea of the teacher's interest superadded: Pind. *O.* 8. 59 τὸ διδάξασθαι | εἰδότι φατερον: so Simonides fr. 145 (of himself) διδαξάμενος χορόν (unless he meant, 'caused to be trained'). In Ar. *Nub.* 783 διδάξαιμ' ἂν (Elmsley) should prob. be read. It is rare for any midd. form, without a reflexive pron., to denote that the subject acts *on* (and not for) himself: thus, 'he kills himself' is not ἀποκτείνεται, but ἀποκτείνει ἑαυτόν (Plat. *Phaed.* 61 E). The exceptions are chiefly words of the toilet, as λούομαι. The dative of the reflexive can be more easily understood, as Thuc. 6. 40 πόλις...οὐκ...αὐθαίρετον δουλείαν ἐπιβαλεῖται, *sibi imponet.* **358** πάγων κ.τ.λ. Construe: καὶ (ἐδιδάξατο) φεύγειν ἐναίθρεια βέλη δυσαύλων πάγων, καὶ δύσομβρα βέλη. He learned to build houses, to shelter himself from frost and rain. πάγοι δύσαυλοι = frosts which make it unpleasant to bivouac in the open: cp. Aesch. *Ag.* 555 δυσαυλίας. ἐναίθρεια = under a clear (frosty) sky: cp. fr. 154 ὅταν πάγου φαντέντος αἰθρίου ('a clear frost') χεροῖν | κρύσταλλον ἁρπάσωσι. Nauck takes δυσαύλων πάγων as 'inhos-

thought, and all the moods that mould a state, hath he taught himself; and how to flee the arrows of the frost, when 'tis hard lodging under the clear sky, and the arrows of the rushing rain; yea, he hath resource for all; without resource he meets nothing that must come: only against Death shall he call for aid in vain;

dots on the first ι have been erased.—μόνον L, with ον (not ου) over ων from the first hand. **362** ἐπάξεται] Heindorf conject. ἐπεύξεται. Schneidewin, ἐπάσεται (so Semitelos, placing a stop at ἔρχεται, and reading τὸ μέλλον "Αιδαν μόνον | θέλξειν οὐκ ἐπάσεται, 'only he will not find the spell which can charm Hades'). Rauchenstein, οὐκ ἐπαρκέσει. Pallis, ἐπίσταται. M. Schmidt, ἔπραξέ πα. Seyffert, διδάξεται. Wecklein, πεπάσεται.

---

pitable *hills*,' citing Moschion fr. 7. 5 (*Frag. Trag.* p. 633), who describes primitive man as inhabiting ὀρειγενῆ σπήλαια: but the context is against this. As corrections of the MS. αἰθρια, there is little to choose between ἐναίθρεια and ὑπαίθρεια: Aesch. *Ag.* 335 has ὑπαιθρίων πάγων: but after πάγων the loss of ἐν would be easier than that of ὑπ. The ι of αἰθρία could be long (as Solon 13. 22): but ῑ is not elsewhere found in the derivatives; for in Cratinus Δηλιάδες fr. 5 we must read Ὑπερβορέους αἰθρια τιμῶντας στέφη (not, as Blaydes gives it, Ὑπερβορέους αἰθρίᾳ). The spelling ἐναίθρεια is conjectural, but in *O. C.* 1088 L has ἐπινικείῳ, as metre requires, for ἐπινικίῳ. Below, v. 814, ἐπινύμφειος has been conjectured: see n. there.—βέλη, the 'shafts' of piercing cold, or of lashing rain. Cp. Plat. *Legg.* 873 Ε κεραυνός, ἤ τι παρὰ θεοῦ τοιοῦτον βέλος ἰόν (some such swift and sudden visitation): Aesch. *P. V.* 371 βέλεσι πυρπνόου ζάλης (sent forth from Aetna); *Il.* 1. 53 κῆλα θεοῖο (of the pestilence).

360 παντοπόρος is at once a comment on the achievements already enumerated (cp. περίφραδὴς in 348), and a general expression absolving the poet from further detail: 'yes, there is nothing that he cannot provide.' Isocr. may have had this passage in mind in or. 3 § 6 (quoted on 354), where an enumeration parallel with that of Soph. is closed by a phrase answering to παντοπόρος,—καὶ σχεδὸν ἅπαντα τὰ δι' ἡμῶν μεμηχανημένα λόγος ἡμῖν ἐστιν ὁ συγκατασκευάσας. We must not point thus: βέλη· παντοπόρος, ἄπορος κ.τ.λ., when the sense would be weakened, and the construction perplexed ('all-providing, and in no case without resource, he meets the future').

οὐδὲν...τὸ μέλλον = οὐδὲν ὃ μέλλει

(ἔσεσθαι), nothing that is to be (cp. the absolute τὸ μέλλον, τὰ μέλλοντα). So Plat. *Lach.* 197 Α ἔγωγε ἀνδρεῖα καλῶ οὔτε θηρία οὔτε ἄλλο οὐδὲν τὸ τὰ δεινὰ ὑπὸ ἀγνοίας μὴ φοβούμενον = οὐδὲν ὃ μὴ φοβεῖται. This negative form is as correct as (though actually rarer than) the positive πᾶν τὸ καλῶς ἔχον (Plat. *Rep.* 381 Α) for πᾶν ὃ καλῶς ἔχει. Donaldson took τὸ μέλλον adverbially: 'in regard to the future, he comes to nothing without resources.' Cp. 728, μηδὲν τὸ μὴ δίκαιον, where μηδέν is subst., not adv.

361 f. μόνον and μόνου are alike admissible; μόνον means, 'the only thing that he will not achieve is to escape death'; μόνου, 'the only thing that he will not escape is death.' In this general view of human achievement, μόνον seems a little the better. φεύξιν ἐπάξεται, procure means of escape from death. ἐπάγεσθαι, prop. 'to bring into one's own country'; usu. said of calling in allies to help one; or of importing foreign products: Thuc. 4. 64 ξυμμάχους δὲ οὐδέποτε ...ἐπαξόμεθα: id. 1. 81 ἐκ θαλάσσης ὧν δέονται ἐπάξονται. Then often fig., of calling in anything to one's aid: Plat. *Legg.* 823 Α τὸ δὲ δὴ παρὸν ἡμῖν τὰ νῦν οἷον μάρτυρα ἐπαγόμεθα· δηλοῖ μὲν ἂν ὃ βουλόμεθα: 'we call to our help, as a witness, the example which is actually present with us; it will show what we mean.' *Gorg.* 492 Β αὐτοὶ ἑαυτοῖς δεσπότην ἐπαγάγοιντο τὸν τῶν πολλῶν ἀνθρώπων νόμον τε καὶ λόγον καὶ ψόγον ('call in to rule them'). Menander 'Υδρία fr. 2 γέροντα δυστυχοῦντα, τῶν θ' αὑτοῦ κακῶν | ἐπαγόμενον λήθην, ἀνέμνησα πάλιν ('seeking to procure forgetfulness of his troubles'). The word is admirably suitable and vivid here: man looks to every side for succour against the foe that is ever in the land,—Death; but from no

6 νόσων δ' ἀμηχάνων φυγὰς ξυμπέφρασται.

ἀντ. β'.　σοφόν τι τὸ μηχανόεν　　　　　　　　　　　　365
2 τέχνας ὑπὲρ ἐλπίδ' ἔχων τοτὲ μὲν κακόν, ἄλλοτ'
ἐπ' ἐσθλὸν ἕρπει·
3 νόμους *γεραίρων χθονὸς θεῶν τ' ἔνορκον δίκαν,
4 ὑψίπολις· ἄπολις, ὅτῳ τὸ μὴ καλὸν　　　　　　　370
5 ξύνεστι τόλμας χάριν. μήτ' ἐμοὶ παρέστιος
- 6 γένοιτο μήτ' ἴσον φρονῶν, ὃς τάδ' ἔρδει.　　　375

363 ἀμηχάνων L, with ουσ written over ων by a late hand. (Dübner says, ' ων ex
ουσ factum a m. rec.'; but ων is from the first hand, and has not been touched.)
365 σοφόν τι] Heimsoeth conject. δεινόν τι: Schmidt, τοῖόν τι: Gleditsch, τοσόνδε.
366 ὑπερ ἐλπίδ' L (not ὑπερελπίδ').—ἔχων] ἔχον r: cp. 344.　　**367** τοτὲ L, ποτὲ r.
368 γεραίρων MSS. (with glosses πληρῶν, τηρῶν, στέργων).—Reiske conject. γεραίρων.
Dindorf, παραιρῶν. Schaefer, γὰρ αἴρων. Schneidewin, τ' ἀείρων. Pallis, τε τηρῶν.

quarter can he find help. It is surprising
that so many recent critics should have
confidently condemned ἐπάξεται, and
sought to replace it by conjectures (see
cr. n.).

363 f. ἀμηχάνων, such as seem to baffle
all treatment: El. 140 ἀμήχανον | ἄλγος:
Simonides ap. Plat. Prot. 344 C ἀμήχανος
συμφορά.—φυγάς, like φεύξιν: Eur. Helen.
799 λέκτρων...φυγάς, means of escape from
the union; cp. Ar. Eq. 759 κἀκ τῶν
ἀμηχάνων πόρους εὐμηχάνους πορίζων.—
ξυμπέφρασται, here midd., as Aesch.
Suppl. 438 καὶ δὴ πέφρασμαι: cp. O. C.
1016 n.

365—375 The ode closes with a
more direct reference to the incident
which suggested its theme. The daring
ingenuity shown by the unknown breaker
of Creon's edict is an instance of the
subtlety which leads to ruin. The implied contrast with Creon—ὑψίπολις by
his care for the laws—is effective in view
of the destined περιπέτεια.

365 f. σοφόν τι...ἔχων: lit., possessing, in his resourceful skill, a thing subtle
beyond belief: σοφόν τι is predicate, and
in apposition with τὸ μηχανόεν τέχνας.
Cp. Thuc. 2. 89 μέγα τι τῆς διανοίας τὸ
βέβαιον ἔχοντες ἀντιτολμῶσιν: 'they are
strong in the confidence of their spirit
when they confront the foe.' There is
no ground for altering σοφόν into δεινόν,
τοῖον, or the like.—τὸ μηχανόεν τ., the
inventive quality in his skill: for τέχνας,
cp. O. T. 380 n.; for the absence of τᾶς,
cp. above, 10 (κακά). Cp. Thuc. 1. 90

τὸ...βουλόμενον καὶ ὕποπτον τῆς γνώμης:
2. 61 ἐν τῷ ὑμετέρῳ ἀσθενεῖ τῆς γνώμης.

367 τοτὲ μὲν...ἄλλοτ'. L has τοτὲ
here: cp. El. 739 τότ' (i.e. τοτὲ) ἄλλος,
ἄλλοθ' ἄτερος: Plat. Phaedr. 237 E τοτὲ
μὲν ἡ ἑτέρα, ἄλλοτε δὲ ἡ ἑτέρα κρατεῖ. Cp.
O. C. 1745 n. There is no reason, then,
for reading ποτὲ μὲν here with inferior
MSS., though it is equally good (Plato has
ποτὲ μὲν answered by ποτὲ δέ, by ἐνίοτε δέ,
or by αὖθις δέ).—ἐπ' with κακόν as well as
ἐσθλόν: cp. 212 n. on κάς.

368 γεραίρων, 'honouring,' is in my
belief a certain correction of the MS.
παραίρων. The latter = 'weaving in,' as
a thread into a texture, or a flower into a
wreath: for the genuine fig. use of it, see
Xen. Symp. 6. 2 μεταξὺ τοῦ ὑμᾶς λέγειν
οὐδ' ἂν τρίχα, μὴ ὅτι λόγον, ἄν τις παραί-
ρειε: 'while you are speaking, one could
not put in a hair, much less a speech'
(so close and continuous is the texture
of your speaking). Here, παραίρων has
been explained as, 'weaving the laws
(etc.) into the texture of his life'; but,
even if we grant that so strange a phrase
would be possible with words added to
express 'the texture of his life,' it is certainly impossible without them. Dindorf
proposed παραιρῶν as = 'wresting,' 'vio-
lating' (a strange sense), and pointed at
δίκαν· 'he comes to evil (though at other
times to good) when he violates the
laws,' etc. ΓΕΡΑΙΡΩΝ could easily
generate ΠΑΡΕΙΡΩΝ. γεραίρειν, prop. to
distinguish by gifts of honour, is also a
general poet. synonym for τιμᾶν: cp. Her.

but from baffling maladies he hath devised escapes.

Cunning beyond fancy's dream is the fertile skill which brings him, now to evil, now to good. When he honours the laws of the land, and that justice which he hath sworn by the gods to uphold, proudly stands his city: no city hath he who, for his rashness, dwells with sin. Never may he share my hearth, never think my thoughts, who doth these things! *2nd antistrophe.*

Semitelos, παροίκων ('dwellers' in the land), with εὐορκῶν (='φυλάττων εὐσεβῶς') for ἔνορκον. **370** ὑψίπολις] ῥυσίπολις Iernstedt. **373** μή τέ μοι (not μήτε μοι) L: μήτ' ἐμοὶ r. **374** μήτ' ἴσον] In L more than one letter has been erased after τ' (Dübner suggests ισ, Campb. εγ). **375** ἔρδει L (not ἔρδοι: the ε is clear, and has not been touched).

5. 67 ἐτίμων τὸν Ἄδρηστον καὶ δὴ πρὸς τὰ πάθεα αὐτοῦ τραγικοῖσι χοροῖσι ἐγέραιρον. Ar. *Th.* 960 γένος Ὀλυμπίων θεῶν | μέλπε καὶ γέραιρε φωνῇ.

369 θεῶν τ' ἔνορκον δίκαν, Justice, which men swear to observe, taking oaths by the gods (ὅρκοι θεῶν: *O. T.* 647 n.): =ὅρκοις θεῶν κεκυρωμένην.

370 f. ὑψίπολις seems best taken as =ὑψηλὴν πόλιν ἔχων: cp. Pind, *P.* 8. 22 ἁ δικαιόπολις...νᾶσος (Aegina). In *O. 2.* 8 Theron, tyrant of Acragas, is called ὀρθόπολις in an active sense, as=ὀρθῶν τὴν πόλιν. In *O. T.* 510 ἀδύπολις=ἀνδάνων τῇ πόλει: but it is harder to suppose that ὑψίπολις could have been intended to mean, 'standing high in his city.' Nor would that be the fittest sense. The loyal citizen makes the prosperous city; and her prosperity is his. See on 189. In this clause the Chorus thinks especially of Creon (191 τοιοῖσδ' ἐγὼ νόμοισι τήνδ' αὔξω πόλιν).—ἄπολις. Where the typical citizen is a law-breaker, the city is ruined, and the evil-doer is left citiless. So Creon had described law-breaking as ἄνω...ἄστοῖς (185). The contrast with ὑψίπολις shows that the sense is not merely, 'when a man breaks the law he becomes an exile' (Lys. or. 21 § 35 ἀντὶ ...πολιτῶν ἀπόλιδας). The central thought is the power of human wit to make or mar the πόλις, according as the man is moral or immoral.—τὸ μὴ καλόν, the generic μή, such a mood as is not good.— τόλμας χάριν, by reason of ('thanks to') his audacity; with ξύνεστι, not with ἄπολις (ἔστι). In *O. T.* 888 δυσπότμου χάριν χλιδᾶς is not precisely similar, since it goes with κακά νιν ἔλοιτο μοῖρα. Others

point at ξύνεστι, taking τόλμας χάριν with μήτ' ἐμοὶ κ.τ.λ.: but μήτ' should clearly be the first word in that sentence.

372 ff. παρέστιος. Cp. *O. T.* 249 n., where Oed. invokes a curse on himself, should the murderer become ξυνέστιος with him: also *ib.* 240 n. Hor. *Carm.* 3. 2. 26 *vetabo, qui Cereris sacrum Vulgarit arcanae, sub isdem Sit trabibus, fragilemve mecum Solvat phaselon.* Schneidewin cp. also Eur. fr. 848 (the dishonourer of parents) μή μοι γένοιτο μήτε συνθυτὴς ποτε, κ.τ.λ., and Callim. *Hymn.* 6. 117 (to Demeter) μή τῆνος ἐμὶν φίλος, ὅς τοι ἀπεχθής, | εἴη, μηθ' ὁμότοιχος.—Ἴσον φρονῶν, 'may he not become like-minded with me,' is another way of saying, 'may I never come to share his sentiments.' Cp. *Il.* 15. 50 ἴσον ἐμοὶ φρονέουσα, 'like-minded with me': Ar. *Av.* 634 ἐμοὶ φρονῶν ξυνῳδά. In a narrower sense (not intended here) τὰ αὐτὰ φρονεῖν was said of agreement in politics, *idem sentire de republica*: Her. 1. 60 τὠυτὸ φρονήσαντες, 'having made common cause' (the στασιῶται of Megacles and Lycurgus).

375 ἔρδει, L's reading, should be kept. The indic. is, of course, compatible with generality: for such an indic. after an optative, cp. Dem. or. 4. 51 νικῴη δ' ὅ τι πᾶσιν ὑμῖν μέλλει συνοίσειν. It is also rather in favour of the indic. that the speaker is here thinking of an actual case. The optat. ἔρδοι would be abstract, 'any one who should conceivably do these things,' and would be equally correct: cp. on 666.

376 The choral ode has closed with an allusion to the unknown *man* (ὅς: cp. 248 τίς ἀνδρῶν, 319 ὁ δρῶν). At this mo-

ἐς δαιμόνιον τέρας ἀμφινοῶ
τόδε· πῶς εἰδὼς ἀντιλογήσω
τήνδ' οὐκ εἶναι παῖδ' Ἀντιγόνην;
ὦ δύστηνος
καὶ δυστήνου πατρὸς Οἰδιπόδα,   380
-τί ποτ'; οὐ δή που σέ γ' ἀπιστοῦσαν
τοῖς βασιλείοισιν ἄγουσι νόμοις
καὶ ἐν ἀφροσύνῃ καθελόντες;

ΦΤ. ἥδ' ἐστ' ἐκείνη τοὔργον ἡ 'ξειργασμένη·
τήνδ' εἴλομεν θάπτουσαν. ἀλλὰ ποῦ Κρέων;   385
ΧΟ. ὅδ' ἐκ δόμων ἄψορρος ἐς δέον περᾷ.
ΚΡ. τί δ' ἔστι; ποίᾳ ξύμμετρος προὔβην τύχῃ;
ΦΤ. ἄναξ, βροτοῖσιν οὐδέν ἐστ' ἀπώμοτον·
√ ψεύδει γὰρ ἡ 'πίνοια' τὴν γνώμην· ἐπεὶ

376 ἐς] Reiske conject. εἰ [*i.e.* 'I marvel whether this portent is supernatural'], and presently πῶς δ'.—ἀμφινοῶ L, the first o blotted.   **378** τήνδ' οὐκ εἶναι] Hermann conject. μὴ οὐ τήνδ' εἶναι.   **380** καὶ δυστήνου] Meineke conject. κἀκ (or παῖ) δ.   **382** βασιλείοισ ἄγουσι L, βασιλείοισιν ἄγουσι Triclinius.   So in 931 L has τοῖσ for τοῖ-

---

ment Antigone is led in by the Guard.—
ἀμφινοῶ: cp. *O. C.* 316 (where Antigone can scarcely believe her eyes, on seeing Ismene,) ἆρ' ἔστιν; ἆρ' οὐκ ἔστιν; ἢ γνώμη πλανᾷ; For ἐs, cp. φοβεῖσθαι εἴς τι, *O. T.* 980 n.—**δαιμόνιον τέρας**, a portent sent by gods,—so astounding as to require a supernatural cause. Xen. *Mem.* 1. 3. 5 εἰ μή τι δαιμόνιον εἴη.

377 f. πῶς εἰδὼς κ.τ.λ.: 'How, when I know (that she *is* Antigone, κ. ὅτι ἐστί), shall I maintain that she is *not?*' (οὐκ εἶναι=ὅτι οὐκ ἐστί). A simple verb of 'saying' regularly takes οὐ with inf. in oratio obliqua: λέγω οὐκ εἶναι=ὅτι οὐκ ἐστί. If this verb of saying is negatived, the negative with the inf. is still οὐ: πῶς λέξω οὐκ εἶναι; Here, ἀντιλογέω has the construction of a simple verb of saying: πῶς ἀντιλογήσω οὐκ εἶναι; Hermann conjectured μὴ οὐ τήνδ' εἶναι (which is palaeographically very improbable). μὴ οὐκ εἶναι would be the normal constr. after πῶς ἀντιλογήσω, if ἀντιλογέω were viewed in its special quality as a verb of 'denying.' ἀρνοῦμαι μὴ εἶναι: πῶς ἀρνήσομαι μὴ οὐκ (or simply μή, *O. T.* 1388 n.) εἶναι; Cp. below, 443 n. It may be noted that, when ἀντιλέγω means to 'deny,' it is more often followed by ὡς (or ὅτι) οὐ with the finite

verb; when followed by μή and inf., it more often means 'to protest against' a measure; Thuc. 3. 41 ἀντέλεγε...μὴ ἀποκτεῖναι Μυτιληναίους: Xen. *Cyr.* 2. 2. 20 αἰσχρὸν ὄν (= οὐ δεῖ) ἀντιλέγειν τὸ μὴ οὐχὶ τὸν πλεῖστα πονοῦντα...μεγίστων ἀξιοῦσθαι.—**ἀντιλογήσω** might be deliberative aor., but is rather fut. ind. (cp. *O. T.* 1419, *O. C.* 310).

379 f. ὦ δύστηνος: nom. for voc., *O. C.* 185 n.—**δ. πατρός**, gen. of origin: *O. C.* 214 n.—Οἰδιπόδα occurs as gen. in *O. T.* 495, but as voc. *ib.* 1194.

381 f. τί ποτ'; Cp. *Ph.* 1210.—**οὐ δή που**: cp. *O. T.* 1472 οὐ δὴ κλύω που...;—**ἀπιστοῦσαν** = ἀπειθοῦσαν, cp. 219, 656.—**ἄγουσι**. It is far more probable that the final υ of βασιλείοισιν should have dropped out in L (see cr. n.) than that Soph. should have written ἀπάγουσι. At Athens ἀπάγω and ἀπαγωγή were technical terms for a process of summary arrest by which any citizen could bring before the magistrates a person taken in a criminal act (ἐπ' αὐτοφώρῳ). We have seen (on v. 158) that a word with a technical Attic sense was not necessarily excluded from Attic poetry. But ἀπάγω would surely jar here. Allowing for the difference between a technicality and a

Enter the Guard, on the spectators' left, leading in
ANTIGONE.

What portent from the gods is this?—my soul is amazed. Anap
I know her—how can I deny that yon maiden is Antigone?
O hapless, and child of hapless sire,—of Oedipus! What
means this? Thou brought a prisoner?—thou, disloyal to the
King's laws, and taken in folly?

GUARD.

Here she is, the doer of the deed :—we caught this girl
burying him :—but where is Creon?
CH. Lo, he comes forth again from the house, at our need.
CR. What is it? What hath chanced, that makes my
coming timely?
GU. O King, against nothing should men pledge their
word ; for the after-thought belies the first intent. I could

σιν.—βασιλεῖοιs ἀπάγουσι Boeckh (for which Wecklein suggests ἰσάγουσι or προσάγουσι).
384 In L the speaker is designated by ἀγ, before which S has written φύλαξ: cp.
223.—ἐξειργασμένη L (without art.): ἡ 'ξειργασμένη r and Brunck. **386** ἀψορροσ]
The d made from ῦ in L.—εἰs δέον r (including A): εἰs μέσον L. Nauck writes εἰs
καιρόν: Semitelos, αἰσίωs. Wecklein conject. ἐs καλόν. **387** ξύμμετροσ ἐξέβην L,
with προύβην written above by S. ποία ξύμμετροσ προύβη τύχη r.—Bergk conject.

colloquialism, it would be nearly as bad
as, 'Have they taken you up?'—καὶ
connects ἀπιστοῦσαν with καθελόντες
(not with ἐν ἀφροσύνη): cp. O. C. 737 n.
384—581 Second ἐπεισόδιον. Antigone, brought before Creon, avows and
justifies her deed. Creon declares that
she shall die. Ismene, when led in
(531), associates herself with the act,
but is not permitted by her sister to
claim any part in it. Creon orders that
both sisters shall be kept prisoners.
384 ἐκείνη, she whom we sought:
cp. O.C. 138 ὅδ' ἐκεῖνος ἐγώ, n.—τοὔργον
δ' ἐμόν.: for the order, cp. 324.
386 ἐs δέον: cp. O. T. 1416 ἐs δέον
πάρεσθ' ὅδε | Κρέων: so ib. 78 εἰς καλὸν
Ai. 1168 ἐs αὐτὸν καιρόν. L has εἰς μέσον,
i.e. 'he comes forth in public' (so that
you, and all, can speak with him).
The phrase occurs elsewhere in Soph.,
but never with ref. to entrance on the
stage: Ph. 609 ἔδειξ' Ἀχαιοῖς ἐς μέσον
(showed him publicly); Ai. 1285 τὸν
κλῆρον ἐς μέσον καθεὶς (i.e. among the
others); Tr. 514 ἴσαν ἐς μέσον (into the
arena). Here, ἐs δέον is not only far the
better phrase, but is confirmed by Creon's
question in the next v., ποία ξύμμετρος...

τύχῃ; A, and almost all the later MSS.,
have εἰς δέον, which may, doubtless, have
been a conjecture suggested by O. T. 1416,
—as is held by those who believe all our
MSS. to have come from L; but it looks
more like a true reading which L had
somehow missed. Cp. on 831.
387 ξύμμετρος, commensurate with,
i.e. here, opportune for. O. T. 84 ξύμμετρος γὰρ ὡς κλύειν: ib. 1113 ξινάδει τῷδε
τάνδρὶ σύμμετρος.
388 ἀπώμοτον, abiurandum : there
is nothing, the possibility of which men
ought to deny on oath: οὐκ ἔστιν ὅ τι
ἀπομύναι χρὴ βροτοὺς μὴ οὐκ ἂν γενέσθαι.
Archilochus fr. 76 χρημάτων ἄελπτον οὐδέν
ἐστιν οὐδ' ἀπώμοτον | οὐδὲ θαυμάσιον. Eu-
polis Πόλεις fr. 25 τί δ' ἐστ' Ἀθηναίοισι
πρᾶγμ' ἀπώμοτον;
389 ψεύδει = falsifies (like ψευδοποιεῖν):
Thuc. 3. 66 τὴν...ψευσθεῖσαν ὑπόσχεσιν.—
ἡ 'πίνοια, here, the after-thought, al
δεύτεραι φροντίδες. But usually the ἐπὶ
in ἐπινοέω, ἐπίνοια, denotes advance,—
'forming a design,' or 'inventing': Ar.
Eq. 90 οἶνον σὺ τολμᾷς εἰς ἐπίνοιαν λοιδο-
ρεῖν; Cp. Lucian Προμηθεὺς εἶ ἐν λόγοις
7 τό γε μεταβουλεύεσθαι Ἐπιμηθέως ἔργον,
οὐ Προμηθέως ἐστίν.

σχολῇ ποθ' ἥξειν δεῦρ' ἄν, ἐξηύχουν ἐγώ,   390
ταῖς σαῖς ἀπειλαῖς, αἷς ἐχειμάσθην τότε·
ἀλλ' ἡ γὰρ ἐκτὸς καὶ παρ' ἐλπίδας χαρὰ
ἔοικεν ἄλλῃ μῆκος οὐδὲν ἡδονῇ,
ἥκω, δι' ὅρκων καίπερ ὢν ἀπώμοτος,
κόρην ἄγων τήνδ', ἣ καθῃρέθη τάφον   395
κοσμοῦσα. κλῆρος ἐνθάδ' οὐκ ἐπάλλετο,
ἀλλ' ἔστ' ἐμὸν θοὐρμαῖον, οὐκ ἄλλου, τόδε.
καὶ νῦν, ἄναξ, τήνδ' αὐτός, ὡς θέλεις, λαβὼν
καὶ κρῖνε κἀξέλεγχ'· ἐγὼ δ' ἐλεύθερος
δίκαιός εἰμι τῶνδ' ἀπηλλάχθαι κακῶν.   400
ΚΡ. ἄγεις δὲ τήνδε τῷ τρόπῳ πόθεν λαβών;
ΦΥ. αὕτη τὸν ἄνδρ' ἔθαπτε· πάντ' ἐπίστασαι.
ΚΡ. ἦ καὶ ξυνίης καὶ λέγεις ὀρθῶς ἃ φής;

ξύμμετρ' ἐξέβην. **390** σχολῇ ποθ' ἥξειν (ἥξειν L) δεῦρ' ἂν ἐξηύχουν ἐγώ MSS. Wecklein conject. δεῦρό μ' for δεῦρ' ἄν. Meineke, ἥκειν for ἥξειν, or δεῦρό γ' for δεῦρ' ἄν. Blaydes, ποτ' ἐλθεῖν, or γ' ἂν ἐλθεῖν, for ποθ' ἥξειν. F. W. Schmidt, δεῦρ', ἄναξ, ἤῦχουν. **392** ἐκτὸς] Seyffert conject. ἄτοπος: Gleditsch, ἄλογος: Pallis, εἰκός.— ἐλπίδας] In L the first hand wrote ἐλπίδα, but σ has been added (by the first hand itself, I think) above the α. Some think that the ρά of χαρά was added by S: this seems

390 ἐξηύχουν ἄν, I could have vowed, σχολῇ ἥξειν ποτὲ δεῦρο, that it would be long before I ever came hither. Cp. Eur. *Helen.* 1619 οὐκ ἂν ποτ' ηὔχουν οὔτε σ' οὔθ' ἡμᾶς λαθεῖν | Μενέλαον, ὦναξ, ὡς ἐλάνθανεν ταρών: 'I should never have expected that he would escape us'; where (as the order of words shows) ἄν goes with ηὔχουν,—the suppressed protasis being, as here, εἰ ἠρώτα τις, 'if any one had asked me.' So Lys. or. 12 § 22 ἐγὼ δ' ἐβουλόμην ἂν αὐτοὺς ἀληθῆ λέγειν, 'I could wish' (the ref. there being to present time), sc. εἰ δυνατὸν ἦν. Cp. *Ph.* 869 n. The needless emendations of this verse have aimed at disjoining ἄν from ἐξηύχουν and attaching it to the infin., or else at removing it altogether. But, though the φύλαξ had actually said (in the 'aside' at 329) that he did not mean to come back, he was not therefore debarred from using this turn of phrase; 'I *could have* vowed that I would not come back.'—σχολῇ (cp. 231), here iron., 'not in a hurry' (*O. T.* 434 n.); Shaksp. *Tit. Andron.* 1. 2. 301 'I'll trust by leisure him that mocks me once.'

391 ταῖς σαῖς ἀπειλαῖς, 'by reason of thy threats': cp. 335 (νότῳ) n., 588

(πνοαῖς), 956 (ὀργαῖς). Here, the causal dat. seems also to suggest occasion ('at the time of your threats'): see on 691 λόγοις.—ἐχειμάσθην: *Ph.* 1460 χειμαζομένῳ (ἐμοί), in my sore trouble.

392 ἡ...ἐκτὸς (τῶν ἐλπίδων) καὶ παρὰ ἐλπίδας. I cannot parallel this zeugma of preps. with a case suited only to the second (in *Il.* 17. 760 περί τ' ἀμφί τε τάφρον both preps. take acc.): and yet it seems to be genuine, the phrase being so energetic and compact. ἐκτός is certainly supported by 330, while ἄτοπος, ἄλογος, and εἰκός are all very improbable substitutes. Nor can I think, with Schütz, that ἐκτός is here adverb: 'the outside joy' (*i.e.* outside of one's calculations).

393 f. οὐδὲν ἔοικε μῆκος, is not at all (adv.) like in greatness, ἄλλῃ ἡδονῇ, to any other pleasure; *i.e.* is vastly greater than any other. For the adv. οὐδέν, cp. Plat. *Lys.* 220 c τὸ φίλον...οὐδὲν τούτοις ἔοικε. For μῆκος = *amplitudo*, Empedocles 15 ἐξ οἵης τιμῆς τε καὶ ὅσσου μήκεος ὄλβου: so Pindar speaks of μακρὸς ὄλβος (*P.* 2. 26), μακροτέρα ἀρετά (*I.* 4. 21), Aristotle of μακρὰ τιμήματα (*Pol.* 3. 5. 6, opp. to βραχέα *ib.* 4. 4. 24), μακρὰ οὐσία

have vowed that I should not soon be here again,—scared by
thy threats, with which I had just been lashed : but,—since the
joy that surprises and transcends our hopes is like in fulness
to no other pleasure,—I have come, though 'tis in breach of
my sworn oath, bringing this maid ; who was taken showing
grace to the dead. This time there was no casting of lots ;
no, this luck hath fallen to me, and to none else. And now,
Sire, take her thyself, question her, examine her, as thou wilt ;
but I have a right to free and final quittance of this trouble.

CR. And thy prisoner here—how and whence hast thou
taken her ?

GU. She was burying the man ; thou knowest all.

CR. Dost thou mean what thou sayest ? Dost thou speak
aright ?

---

very doubtful. The ρ is somewhat small and fine ; but cp. the λ of ἐλπίδα, and the οσ
of ἀπώμοτοσ in 394. **393 f.** Nauck condenses these two verses into one, which he
places in the text: πέπεικεν, ἥκω καίπερ ὣν ἀπώμοτος. Mekler rejects vv. 392—394
as spurious.—ὅρκων] L has ον over ων from the first hand. **395** καθευρέθη L.—
καθῃρέθη an anonymous critic in *Class. Journ.* xvii. 58: and so many recent edd.
402 ἔθαπτε] ἔθαπτεν L. **403** ξυνίῃς] ξυνίεις L, as *O. T.* 628, *El.* 1347, and
ἵεις *El.* 596. Some hold, with Brunck, that the Attic 2nd sing. pres. was ἱεῖς,
and of τίθημι, τιθεῖς. But see Porson, *Eur. Or.* 141, and Ellendt *s.v.* ἵημι.

(μλ. 4. 4. 5), and Soph. himself of μακρὸς
πλοῦτος (*Ai.* 130). For ἔοικε Wolff-Bel-
lermann cp. Thuc. 7. 71 ὁ...φόβος ἦν...
οὐδενὶ ἔοικώς ('great beyond example'),
Xen. *De Vect.* 4. 31 οὐδενὶ τῶν παρεληλυ-
θότων ἔοικός ('far greater than any of the
past'); and for the sentiment, Eur. fr.
554 ἐκ τῶν ἀέλπτων ἡ χάρις μείζων βροτοῖς
| φανεῖσα μᾶλλον ἢ τὸ προσδοκώμενον.—
Nauck's treatment of this verse and the
next has no justification: see cr. n.

394 δι' ὅρκων...ἀπώμοτος, though I
had sworn with oaths (sworn solemnly)
not to come. Cp. *Ai.* 1113 ὅρκων οἶσιν
ἦν ἐνώμοτος: Ar. *Ran.* 150 ἐπίορκον ὅρκον
ὤμοσεν.

395 f. καθῃρέθη (cp. 383 καθελόντες)
is clearly better here than L's καθευρέθη :
and the compound καθευρίσκω is nowhere
found in classical Attic.—τάφον κοσμού-
σα, paying the due rites of burial (τάφον =
ταφάς, cp. 490), by sprinkling the dust and
pouring the libations on the corpse. κοσμέω
was specially said of obsequies: cp. 901,
El. 1139 λουτροῖς ἐκόσμησ'.—ἐπάλλετο, as
when lots were shaken in a helmet (*Ai.*
1285; cp. *El.* 710). His ἕρμαιον is the
luck of being the first to bring the glad
tidings,—as his former mission was ironically called τοῦτο τἀγαθόν (275). In the

discovery and seizure of Antigone he had
no greater share than his comrades (432).

399 f. κρῖνε=ἀνάκρινε, question : *Ai.*
586 μὴ κρῖνε, μὴ 'ξέταζε.—δίκαιός εἰμι :
the only certain instance in Tragedy of
the personal constr. (Thuc. 1. 40 δίκαιοί
γ' ἐστε...ἱέναι); for in Eur. *Hipp.* 1080
πολλῷ γε μᾶλλον σαυτὸν ἤσκησας σέβειν |
ἢ τοὺς τεκόντας ὅσια δρᾶν, δίκαιος ὤν, the
latter words are more pointed if ironical
('just man though thou art'): and Aesch.
Eum. 55 καὶ κόσμος οὔτε πρὸς θεῶν ἀγάλ-
ματα | φέρειν δίκαιος is different ('proper
to bring'). But Ar. has ὁμῖλος, *Nub.*
1283 ἀπολαβεῖν...δίκαιος εἶ, and ib. 1434.—
ἀπηλλάχθαι, perf., for good and all: *O.*
T. 1050.

401 f. Observe the order of the words
as marking his amazement. For the
double interrog. cp. *Il.* 21. 150 τίς πόθεν
εἶς ἀνδρῶν ; *Ph.* 243 τίνι | στόλῳ προσ-
έσχες τήνδε γῆν, πόθεν πλέων ;—πάντ'
ἐπίστασαι : one of the formulas which
often close a messenger's speech, as *Tr.*
484 πάντ' ἐπίστασαι λόγον : *Ai.* 480 πάντ'
ἀκήκοας λόγον : ib. 876 πάντ' ἀκήκοας : *Ph.*
241 οἶσθα δὴ τὸ πᾶν.

402 ἦ καί, *O. T.* 368 n. The first καί
here is not 'both.'—ὀρθῶς, 'rightly': *i.e.*
do your words express what you really

ΦΥ. ταύτην γ' ἰδὼν θάπτουσαν ὃν σὺ τὸν νεκρὸν
    ἀπεῖπας. ἆρ' ἔνδηλα καὶ σαφῆ λέγω;   405
ΚΡ. καὶ πῶς ὁρᾶται κἀπίληπτος ᾑρέθη;
ΦΥ. τοιοῦτον ἦν τὸ πρᾶγμ'. ὅπως γὰρ ἥκομεν,
    πρὸς σοῦ τὰ δείν' ἐκεῖν' ἐπηπειλημένοι,
    πᾶσαν κόνιν σήραντες ἣ κατεῖχε τὸν
    νέκυν, μυδῶν τε σῶμα γυμνώσαντες εὖ,   410
    καθήμεθ' ἄκρων ἐκ πάγων ὑπήνεμοι,
    ὀσμὴν ἀπ' αὐτοῦ μὴ βάλῃ πεφευγότες,
    ἐγερτὶ κινῶν ἄνδρ' ἀνὴρ ἐπιρρόθοις

---

404 ἰδών Brunck: ἴδον L: εἶδον r.   **406** κἀπίληπτος] κάπίλημπτος L.—ᾑρέθη] εὐρέθη, with η over ευ from the first hand. The correction meant was ᾑρέθη (not ηὑρέθη, for L regularly gives ευ in the aor., impf., and pf. of εὑρίσκω) which the schol., too, read: ποίῳ τρόπῳ αὐτὴν συνελάβεσθε καὶ κατειλήφατε;   **407** ἥκομεν] ἱκόμην Kvíčala.

---

mean to say? (Not, merely, 'truly,' *i.e.* in accordance with the fact: cp. 99 n.)

404 τὸν νεκρόν: antecedent with art. drawn into relative clause: *O. C.* 907 n. νῦν δ' ὥσπερ αὐτὸς τοὺς νόμους εἰσῆλθ' ἔχων, | τούτοισιν κ.τ.λ.

405 ἆρ' ἔνδηλα: said triumphantly: Aesch. *Ag.* 268 ΧΟ. πῶς φῄς...; ΚΛ. Τροίαν 'Αχαιῶν οὖσαν· ἦ τορῶς λέγω; Cp. *Ai.* 1158 οὐδεὶς ποτ' ἄλλος ἢ σύ. μῶν ἠνίξάμην;

406 ὁρᾶται...ᾑρέθη: historic pres. combined with aor., as *Ai.* 31 φράζει τε κἀδήλωσεν: cp. 419, *Tr.* 359 ff., *O. T.* 118 f.—ἐπίληπτος, seized in the act = ἐπ' αὐτοφώρῳ. Her. 3. 69 ἐπιλαμπτος... ἀφάσσουσα (τὰ ὦτα) ἔσται, 'will be caught feeling the ears.' [Dem.] or. 25 § 80 τοὺς ἐπιλήπτους (the epileptic) φησὶν ἰᾶσθαι, αὐτὸς ὢν ἐπίληπτος πάσῃ πονηρίᾳ.

407 ἥκομεν. The occupation of the guards was temporarily gone when they perceived that the burial, which they had been set to prevent, had been effected (255). Creon, speaking to their deputy, sent them back to their post, with orders to discover the culprit (306). ἥκομεν (imperf.) simply refers to their taking up their station again near the body. It need not imply that they had escorted their comrade on his way to Creon. We could not take ἥκομεν...ἐπηπειλημένοι as merely plur. for sing., and then refer σήραντες, etc., to the guards collectively. Nor is the conject. ἱκόμην needed.

408 f. τὰ δείν' ἐκεῖν'. Creon's threats

were addressed to all the guards: cp. 305 ff.—τὸν | νέκυν: so *O. C.* 351 τὰ τῆς | οἴκοι διαίτης: *Ph.* 263 ὃν οἱ | δισσοὶ στρατηγοί: *El.* 879 κἀπὶ τοῖς | σαυτῆς κακοῖσι. So Ar. *Eccl.* 452 οὐδὲ τὸν | δῆμον. Aesch. places the art. thus only when it is a *pronoun* (*Ag.* 7 τῶν: *Theb.* 385, *Eum.* 137 τῷ). In Eur. no instance seems to occur.

411 καθήμεθ' is better taken as plpf. than pf., for, though ἥκομεν is ambiguous, we have a series of historical tenses in 415—421. Ar. sometimes uses and sometimes omits the augment as *Ach.* 638 ἐκάθησθε, *Eccl.* 304 καθῆτο (both proved by metre); and if our MSS. can be trusted, classical prose, too, admitted both forms, as Aeschin. or. 2 § 89 ἐκαθήμην, Dem. or. 18 § 169 καθῆτο. In the five pluperfects furnished by Attic inscriptions of 428—325 B.C. the syllabic augment is always added, but there is no epigraphic evidence in the particular case of ἐκαθήμην (see Meisterhans, p. 77).—ἄκρων ἐκ πάγων, with καθήμεθα, 'on the hill-top.' The corpse lay on the highest part of the Theban plain (1110, 1197), with rising ground (πάγοι) behind or around it. The guards post themselves on this rising ground, facing the corpse, and with their backs to the wind. The use of ἐκ (or ἀπό) with a verb denoting *position*, occurs only in a few places of poetry; but it is certainly genuine, and deserves attention, for its true force has not (I think) been observed. (1) *Il.* 14. 153 Ἥρη δ' εἰσεῖδε χρυσόθρονος ὀφθαλμοῖσιν | στᾶσ'

GU. I saw her burying the corpse that thou hadst forbidden
to bury. Is that plain and clear?
CR. And how was she seen? how taken in the act?
GU. It befell on this wise. When we had come to the
place,—with those dread menaces of thine upon us,—we
swept away all the dust that covered the corpse, and bared
the dank body well; and then sat us down on the brow
of the hill, to windward, heedful ·that the smell from
him should not strike us; every man was wide awake,
and kept his neighbour alert with torrents of threats,

---

408 δεῖν'] δεῖν' L. 410 εὖ] Reiske conject. αυ. 411 ὑπήνεμοι] Keck and
Naber conject. ὑπήνεμον (to go with ὀσμήν): Tournier, ἀπήνεμοι: Semitelos, σκοπού-
μενοι. 412 βάληι L: βάλοι H. Stephanus. 413 κινῶν Γ: κεῖνον L. Nauck and

---

ἐξ Οὐλόμποιο ἀπὸ ρίου. Here, ἀπὸ ρίου
goes with εἰσεῖδε: but ἐξ Οὐλύμποιο, however much εἰσεῖδε may have influenced it,
at least cannot be disjoined from στᾶσ'.
(2) Eur. *Ph.* 1009 ἀλλ' εἶμι καὶ στὰς ἐξ
ἐπάλξεων ἄκρων | σφάξας ἐμαυτὸν σηκὸν
εἰς μελαμβαθῆ | δράκοντος, ἔνθ' ὁ μάντις
ἐξηγήσατο, | ἐλευθερώσω γαῖαν. It is im-
possible to sever στάς from ἐξ ἐπ., even
if we partly explain ἐξ by σφάξας. (3) *ib.*
1224 Ἐτεοκλέης δ' ὑπῆρξ' ἀπ' ὀρθίου
σταθεὶς | πύργου κελεύσαι σῖγα κηρῦξαι
στρατῷ. The position of σταθεὶς forbids
us to sever it from ἀπ' ὀρθ. π., even
though ὑπῆρξε or κελεῦσαι is used to explain ἀπό. (4) Eur. *Tro.* 522 ἀνὰ δ'
ἐβόασεν λεὼς | Τρωάδος ἀπὸ πέτρας
σταθείς. A similar case. In all these
passages, a picture is presented, and we
have to glance from a remoter to a nearer
object. The mental eye is required to
measure the space between Hera on
the peak of Olympus, and Poseidon on
the plain of Troy; between Megareus
on the walls of Thebes, and the cavern
into which his corpse is to fall. And, in
each case, ἐκ or ἀπό denotes the *quarter*
in which the remoter object is to be
looked for. This, which might be called
the 'surveying' use, is distinct from that
in which the prep. has a pregnant force,
as being directly suggestive of motion (οἱ
δὲ Σικελίας ἥξουσι); but it springs from
the same mental tendency,—viz., to take
a rapid glance over the dividing interval.
Cp. ἵστασθαι πρός τινος ('on his side').
So here: in the foreground of the picture
is the corpse, which they have ·just laid
bare. Now look to the hillocks behind
it; in that quarter you will see the guards

at their post.—I have not cited *Od.* 21.
419 τὸν ῥ' ἐπὶ πήχει ἑλὼν ἕλκεν νευρὴν
γλυφίδας τε | αὐτόθεν ἐκ δίφροιο καθήμε-
νος, because there ἐκ δίφροιο goes with
ἕλκεν, not with καθήμενος (he drew the
bow, just from the chair, where he sat).
—ὑπήνεμοι, under the wind, *i.e.*, so that
it blew from behind them, and not in their
faces, as the next v. explains., (At v. 421
the dust is blown in their faces, but that
is by the sudden, gusty σκηπτός.) The
idea of 'sheltered,' which ὑπήνεμοι usu.
implies, is less prominent here, yet quite
admissible, if we suppose them to sit just
below the summits of the πάγοι. Cp. Xen.
Oec. 18.6 ἐκ τοῦ προσηνέμου μέρους, on the
side *towards which* the wind blows, opp.
to ἐκ τοῦ ὑπηνέμου, to windward. Theophr.
Causs. Plantt. 3.6.9 opposes πνευματώδης
καὶ προσήνεμος τόπος to τὰ ὑπήνεμα: and
Arist. *Hist. An.* 9. 15 ἐν προσηνέμῳ to ἐν
ἐπισκεπεῖ.

412 βάλῃ, the 'vivid' subjunct. (instead of βάλοι), after a secondary tense;
while in v. 414 we have the normal optat.
(ἀκηθήσοι). For this combination cp.
Xen. *An.* 3. 5. 17 παρήγγειλαν, ἐπειδὴ
δειπνήσειαν,...ἀναπαύεσθαι, καὶ ἕπεσθαι
ἡνίκ' ἄν τις παραγγείλῃ.

413 ἐγερτί: see on ἄστακτί, *O. C.*
1251. Each man was careful to keep
wide awake, and also to see that his
comrades did so.—κινῶν, urging to vigi-
lance. Plat. *Rep.* 329 D βουλόμενος ἔτι
λέγειν αὐτὸν ἐκίνουν καὶ εἶπον, ὦ Κέφαλε,
κ.τ.λ. The conject. νεικῶν is needless.
For the sing. instead of the plur. (κινοῦν-
τες) in partitive apposition, see on φύλαξ
ἐλέγχων φύλακα, 260.—ἐπιρρόθοις κακοῖσιν, lit., with obstreperous taunts,

κακοῖσιν, εἴ τις τοῦδ' *ἀκηδήσοι πόνου.

χρόνῳ τάδ' ἦν τοσοῦτον, ἔστ' ἐν αἰθέρι   415
μέσῳ κατέστη λαμπρὸς ἡλίου κύκλος,
καὶ καῦμ' ἔθαλπε· καὶ τότ' ἐξαίφνης χθονὸς
τυφὼς ἀείρας σκηπτόν, οὐράνιον ἄχος,
πίμπλησι πεδίον, πᾶσαν αἰκίζων φόβην
ὕλης πεδιάδος, ἐν δ' ἐμεστώθη μέγας   420
αἰθήρ· μύσαντες δ' εἴχομεν θείαν νόσον.
καὶ τοῦδ' ἀπαλλαγέντος ἐν χρόνῳ μακρῷ,
ἡ παῖς ὁρᾶται, κἀνακωκύει πικρᾶς
ὄρνιθος ὀξὺν φθόγγον, ὡς ὅταν κενῆς
εὐνῆς νεοσσῶν ὀρφανὸν βλέψῃ λέχος·   425
οὕτω δὲ χαὕτη, ψιλὸν ὡς ὁρᾷ νέκυν,

Semitelos conject. νεικῶν: Hense, κεντῶν.   **414** ἀφειδήσοι MSS.: ἀκηδήσοι Bonitz.
Golisch proposed ἀφ' εὑδήσοι (*Jahr. Phil.* p. 176, 1878), and so, by an independent

---

the adj. expressing the loud, continuous noise of tongues. The ἐπι- does not mean 'bandied to and fro': see *Tr.* 263 πολλὰ μὲν λόγοις | ἐπερρόθησε. In fr. 521 ἐπίρροθα δώματα = 'open to reproach.' Elsewhere (as with Aesch.) ἐπίρροθος = 'helper' (ἐπιρροθέω, to come with shouts to the rescue). Cp. ἐρρόθουν 259 n., 290.

414 ἀκηδήσοι: fut. opt. in orat. obliqua; the direct form of the threat would be (κλαύσει) εἰ ἀκηδήσεις (or ἐὰν ἀκηδήσῃς). Cp. *Ph.* 374 ἤρασσον κακοῖς | τοῖς πᾶσιν... | εἰ τἀμὰ κεῖνος ὅπλ' ἀφαιρήσοιτό με: he said (ὅλοιο), εἰ ἀφαιρήσει. *Ai.* 312 δεῖν' ἐπηπείλησ' ἔπη, | εἰ μὴ φανοίην (he said, εἰ μὴ φανεῖς). ἀκηδέω had been used by Hom. *Il.* 14. 427, 23. 70, Aesch. *P. V.* 508, and recurs in later poetry. The MS. ἀφειδήσοι cannot be defended as = 'play the prodigal with,' *i.e.* 'be careless of.' ἀφειδεῖν πόνου could mean only to be unsparing of labour. In Thuc. 4. 26 ἀφειδὴς ὁ κατάπλους καθειστήκει is explained by the next words, ἐπώκελλον γὰρ τὰ πλοῖα τετιμημένα χρημάτων: they were 'unsparing' of their boats, since a value had been set on the latter. Bonitz, to whom ἀκηδήσοι is due, refers to Apoll. Rhod. 2. 98 οὐδ' ἄρα Βέβρυκες ἄνδρες ἀφείδησαν βασιλῆος, where Choeroboscus has preserved the true ἀκήδησαν. In the schol. on *Ai.* 204 φειδόμενοι occurs by error for κηδόμενοι.

415—421 The incident of the storm was a dramatic necessity, to account for Antigone reaching the corpse unobserved. A powerful picture is compressed into seven lines. (Cp. *O. C.* 1315 ff. for a like instance of self-restraint in description.)

416 f. κατέστη, prop., had taken its place. There is a Homeric echo here: *Il.* 8. 66 ὄφρα μὲν ἠὼς ἦν καὶ ἀέξετο ἱερὸν ἦμαρ, | τόφρα μάλ' ἀμφοτέρων βέλε' ἥπτετο, πῖπτε δὲ λαός | ἦμος δ' ἠέλιος μέσον οὐρανὸν ἀμφιβεβήκει, | καὶ τότε δὴ χρύσεια πατὴρ ἐτίταινε τάλαντα. — χθονὸς (*from* the ground) with ἀείρας: cp. *O. T.* 142 βάθρων | ἵστασθε, n.

418 τυφώς, the whirlwind: the σκηπτός is the storm of dust (κονιορτός) which it lifts from the ground. The word σκηπτός usu. = 'a thunderbolt,' and by its deriv. ought at least to mean a storm swooping on the earth from the sky; but the schol. attests its use in a larger sense: σκηπτὸς δὲ λέγεται πᾶν πνεῦμα θυελλῶδες, ὅταν συνερείδῃ τῇ γῇ, καὶ πάλιν ἄνω αἴρῃ· τὸ δὲ τοιοῦτο καὶ στροβῖλόν τινες καλοῦσι, παρὰ τὸ στροβεῖν. — οὐράνιον ἄχος, a trouble in the sky (cp. *O. C.* 1466 οὐράνια...ἀστραπή), since the cloud of dust darkened the sky: schol. τὸ λυποῦν τὸν αἰθέρα, καθὸ ταράσσει αὐτόν: only ἄχος is rather what annoys *us* than what annoys the (personified) οὐρανός. In these lines the poet describes the actual physical

if any one should be careless of this task.

So went it, until the sun's bright orb stood in mid heaven, and the heat began to burn: and then suddenly a whirlwind lifted from the earth a storm of dust, a trouble in the sky, and filled the plain, marring all the leafage of its woods; and the wide air was choked therewith: we closed our eyes, and bore the plague from the gods.

And when, after a long while, this storm had passed, the maid was seen; and she cried aloud with the sharp cry of a bird in its bitterness,—even as when, within the empty nest, it sees the bed stripped of its nestlings. So she also, when she saw the corpse bare,

conjecture, Semitelos reads (1887). **420** ἐν δ' τ: ἐνθ' L. **428** πικρᾶς] πικρῶς Bothe. **424** In L two letters have been erased before κενῆσ, perh. ἐκ.

effects produced by the storm. He mentions the destruction of foliage; and we need some reference also to the main point of all—the obscuring of the air. Therefore I should not take οὐράνιον ἄχος as='a *heaven-sent* plague'; that is presently said by θείαν νόσον (421). A third version—'a trouble rising *high as* heaven' (like οὐράνιον πήδημα, etc.)—is also possible, but less suitable here than either of the others. In Aesch. *Suppl.* 809 τύξε δ' ὀμφὰν οὐρανίαν, the adj. clearly=οὐρανομήκη, and so perh. in *Pers.* 572 ἀμβόασον οὐράνι' ἄχη, though there (as in *Ai.* 196 ἄτω οὐρανίαν φλέγων) 'heaven-sent' is at least equally fitting.—For the tribrach in the 5th place, see *O. T.* 719 n.

419 *f.* πίμπλησι (histor. pres., between ἔθαλπε and ἀνεμεστώθη, cp. 406), viz., with dust and scattered leaves.—αἰκίζων, maltreating, λυμαινόμενος, by breaking the branches and tearing off the leaves.—ἐν δ' ἐμεστ., tmesis: cp. 1274, *El.* 713 ἐν δὲ πᾶς ἐμεστώθη δρόμος. Distinguish the adv. ἐν δέ (and withal), *O. T.* 27 n.

421 *f.* μύσαντες. μύω (from μῦ, a sound made with closed lips)='to be shut,' said of the eyes, the lips, or any opening (*Il.* 24. 637 οὐ γάρ πω μύσαν ὄσσε): but the aor. part. regularly meant, 'with eyes shut': Plat. *Gorg.* 480 c ταρέχειν μύσαντα καὶ ἀνδρείως ὥσπερ τέμνειν καὶ κάειν ἰατρῷ. There was a proverb, μύσαντα φέρειν ('to grin and bear it'), Meineke *Com.* 3, p. 4.—νόσον, the scourge of the storm: cp. 1141.—ἐν χρ. μακρ.: for the prep. see *O. C.* 88 n.

423 πικρᾶς, in its bitterness. Else-

where πικρός, said of persons, means 'embittered,' and so 'hostile,' etc. (as *Ai.* 1359). But there is no reason why πικρός should not also mean 'embittered' in the sense, 'with a bitter feeling of anguish.' There is a pathos in this which is lost by reading πικρῶς, 'shrilly.' Nor could πικρᾶς mean merely 'piercing,' as if the epithet of the cry were given to the bird itself. In *O. C.* 1610 φθόγγος πικρός, and in *Ph.* 190 πικρὰ οἰμωγή, mean not merely a 'shrill,' but a 'bitter,' cry; and so conversely here, the epithet πικρά, while primarily denoting anguish, also suggests the shrill sound.

425 εὐνῆς...λέχος would be a weak pleonasm for 'nest'; it is better to take εὐνῆς as the nest, and λέχος as the resting-place of the young birds within it. The phrases λέκτρων εὐναί, λέκτρων κοῖται, κοίτης λέκτρον, etc., said of the *marriage*-bed, are not properly similar, meaning rather, 'the bed on which they slept,' etc.: *i.e.* εὐναί or κοῖται refer to the act of sleeping. κενῆς is certainly pleonastic with νεοσσῶν ὀρφανόν (cp. *Ph.* 31 κενὴν οἴκησιν ἀνθρώπων δίχα, and *O. T.* 57 n.), yet hardly anticipates it; the bird, approaching its nest, feels that it is κενή, then peeps in, and, sure enough, the λέχος is ὀρφανόν.

426 οὕτω δέ, 'so, I say, she': for δέ introducing the apodosis in a simile cp. *El.* 25 ὥσπερ γὰρ ἵππος εὐγενής...θυμὸν οὐκ ἀπώλεσεν | ..., ὡσαύτως δὲ σὺ | ἡμᾶς τ' ὀτρύνεις κ.τ.λ.: so *Tr.* 112 ff., πολλὰ γὰρ ὥστ'...οὕτω δὲ τὸν Καδμογενῆ.—ψιλόν, sc. κόνιος, stripped of the dust which she had sprinkled on it (409). Cp. *O. C.* p. 279.

γόοισιν ἐξώμωξεν, ἐκ δ' ἀρὰς κακὰς
ἠρᾶτο τοῖσι τοὔργον ἐξειργασμένοις.
καὶ χερσὶν εὐθὺς διψίαν φέρει κόνιν,
ἔκ τ' εὐκροτήτου χαλκέας ἀρδην πρόχου   430
χοαῖσι τρισπόνδοισι τὸν νέκυν στέφει.
χἠμεῖς ἰδόντες ἱέμεσθα, σὺν δέ νιν
θηρώμεθ' εὐθὺς οὐδὲν ἐκπεπληγμένην,
καὶ τάς τε πρόσθεν τάς τε νῦν ἠλέγχομεν
πράξεις· ἄπαρνος δ' οὐδενὸς καθίστατο,   435
*ἅμ' ἡδέως ἔμοιγε κἀλγεινῶς ἅμα.
τὸ μὲν γὰρ αὐτὸν ἐκ κακῶν πεφευγέναι
ἥδιστον· ἐς κακὸν δὲ τοὺς φίλους ἄγειν
ἀλγεινόν. ἀλλὰ πάντα ταῦθ' ἧσσω λαβεῖν
ἐμοὶ πέφυκε τῆς ἐμῆς σωτηρίας.   440
ΚΡ. σὲ δή, σὲ τὴν νεύουσαν ἐς πέδον κάρα,

429 εὐθὺς] αὖθις Reiske. διψὰν ἐκφέρει κόνιν L. ι had been written over ν; a later
hand erased it, and accented α. In the marg. S has written γρ. διψίαν φέρει, and so
A reads, with other later MSS. Dindorf conject. διψάδ' ἐμφέρει. But ἐκφέρει was a mere

427 ff. γόοισιν ἐξώμωξεν: cp. *O. T.*
65 ὕπνῳ γ' εὕδοντα, n.—ἐκ δ'...ἠρᾶτο,
tmesis: cp. n. on 106.—διψίαν: cp. 246.

429 φέρε κόνιν. A difficulty presents
itself. The essence of the symbolical
rite was the sprinkling of dust. She had
done that (245). Was it not, then, done
once for all? In Horace (*C.* 1. 28. 35) the
passer-by is free when the dust has been
thrown; he can go his way. I have
never seen this question put or answered.
The only answer which I can suggest is
that, at her first visit, she had not brought
the χοαί. (Cp. on 245 ff.) Perhaps the
rite was considered complete only if the
χοαί were poured while the dust still
covered the corpse.

430 f. The πρόχους, or 'out-pourer,'
was a jug, especially a water-jug, with a
handle, and had, of course, various forms;
some of the types given by Guhl and
Koner (p. 147, fig. 198, 26—31) resemble
modern water-jugs for washing.—εὐκρό-
τητος, 'well-hammered,' and so 'well-
wrought,' is the epith. of a knife (δωρὶς,
sc. κοπίς) in Eur. *El.* 819.—ἄρδην (for
ἀέρδην, from αἴρω) is found with πηδᾶν
(*Ai.* 1279) and φέρειν (Eur. *Alc.* 608), but is
usu. fig., as with ἀπολλύναι. Here, ἄρδην

ἐκ πρόχου στέφει=ἄρασα τὸν πρόχουν
στέφει.

431 χοαῖσι. In *Od.* 10. 519 the three
χοαί to the dead are of (1) hydromel, (2)
wine, (3) water: see *O. C.* 479 n.—τρι-
σπόνδ., instead of the simple τρισίν: cp.
on 346 στ. δικτυοκλώστοις. χοαί were to
the νέρτεροι, as σπονδαί to the ὕπατοι:
λοιβαί could mean either (*O. C.* 477).—
στέφει: *El.* 51 τύμβον... | λοιβαῖσι πρῶ-
τον καὶ καρατόμοις χλιδαῖς | στέψαντες.

432 f. ἱέμεσθα, pres.: for the ι, cp.
O. C. 1279 n.—σὺν δέ...θηρώμεθ', tmesis,
as *El.* 746 σὺν δ' ἑλίσσεται | τμητοῖς ἱμᾶσι.
But σύν is adv. ib. 299 σὺν δ' ἐποτρύνει:
cp. above, 85.

434 f. ἠλέγχομεν, proceeded to prove
against her, *i.e.* taxed her with, her
past and present deeds. We should
not supply αὐτήν: the verb governs τὰς
πράξεις only: cp. Plat. *Theaet.* 161 E
ἐλέγχειν τὰς ἀλλήλων φαντασίας τε καὶ
δόξας (examine into). It would be natural
to say, ταῦτα ἐλέγχω αὐτήν, but hardly
τὰς πράξεις ἐλέγχω αὐτήν.—ἄπαρνος...
οὐδενός = οὐδὲν ἀπαρνουμένη, the gen. with
the adj. corresponding to the acc. with
the verb; cp. κωλυτικός, ποιητικός τινος
etc.—καθίστατο, she did not take up the

lifted up a voice of wailing, and called down curses on the doers of that deed. And straightway she brought thirsty dust in her hands; and from a shapely ewer of bronze, held high, with thrice-poured drink-offering she crowned the dead.

We rushed forward when we saw it, and at once closed upon our quarry, who was in no wise dismayed. Then we taxed her with her past and present doings; and she stood not on denial of aught,—at once to my joy and to my pain. To have escaped from ills one's self is a great joy; but 'tis painful to bring friends to ill. Howbeit, all such things are of less account to me than mine own safety.

CR. Thou—thou whose face is bent to earth—

---

blunder like ἐξέβην in 387. **434** πρόσθεν] πρόσθε L. (Cp. 402, 462.)
436 ἁμ' Dindorf: ἀλλ' MSS. **439** ταῦθ'] τἀλλ' Blaydes. **440** πέφυκεν L.

---

position of denying anything. Her *attitude* towards the charge was one of simple confession. καθίστασθαι with a predicative adj. expresses definite assumption of a character, or complete attainment of a state; Thuc. 3. 102 ξύμμαχον καθεστήξει (will have definitely allied itself): 6. 15 πολέμιοι καθέστασαν: 4. 78 τοῖς πᾶσι...ὕποπτον καθεστήκει: 2. 59 ἄποροι καθεστῶτες: 4. 26 ἀφειδὴς...καθεστήκει: 6. 59 χαλεπωτέρα...ἡ τυραννὶς κατέστη. So Ai. 306 ἔμφρων...καθίσταται: O. T. 703 φονέα...καθεστάναι.

436 ἁμ' for the MS. ἀλλ' (AM for ΑΛΛ) is certain: καθίστ. would be unmeaning with the adverbs, and we cannot supply a new verb. (Cp. Arndt's conject. ἀλλη for ἡμή in O. T. 1463.) Besides ἅμα μέν...ἅμα δέ ('partly'...'partly'), we also find double ἅμα, (a) where the clauses are linked by καί, as here; Plat. *Gorg.* 496 B ὧν ἅμα τε ἀπαλλάττεται ἄνθρωπος καὶ ἅμα ἔχει (cp. ib. 497 A): (b) with partic. and finite verb: id. *Tim.* 38 B ἵνα ἅμα γεννηθέντες ἅμα καὶ λυθῶσιν. Verg. *G.* 3. 201 *simul arva fuga, simul aequora verrens.* Cp. Hor. S. 1. 7. 11 *Inter|Hectora Priamiden animosum atque inter Achillen.*

438 φίλους φησί, διὰ τὸ εἶναι τὴν Ἀντιγόνην τοῦ βασιλικοῦ γένους (schol.): he is a δοῦλος of the family. Cp. Eur. *Med.* 54 χρηστοῖσι δούλοις συμφορὰ τὰ δεσποτῶν | κακῶς πίτνοντα.

439 f. πάντα ταῦθ' refers to ἐς κακὸν δέ...ἀλγεινόν: 'all these things' = 'all such objects as the safety of friends.'

λαβεῖν, 'to obtain,' epexeg. of ἥσσω: cp. 638: *Ph.* 81: *El.* 1015 προνοίας οὐδὲν ἀνθρώποις ἔφυ | κέρδος λαβεῖν ἄμεινον: where, as here, we have a gen. depending on the comparat., instead of ἤ with non.—Semitelos takes λαβεῖν as = ὑπολαβεῖν: 'all these considerations are naturally lower in my estimate than my own safety.' Similarly Campbell; 'It is in my nature' (ἐμοὶ πέφυκε—a questionable sense) 'to take less account of all this than of my own safety.' But such a use of λαμβάνειν does not seem warranted by Thuc. 2. 42 τὴν τιμωρίαν...ποθεινοτέραν λαβόντες, or by such phrases as λαμβάνειν τι ἐν πόθῳ (O. C. 1679).—Blaydes's τἀλλ' for ταῦτ' is attractive, but unnecessary; and palaeographically it is not probable.

441 σὲ δή, κ.τ.λ. *sc.* καλῶ. Eur. *Helen.* 546 σὲ τὴν ὄρεγμα δεινὸν ἡμιλλωμένην | τύμβου 'πὶ κρηπῖδ' ἐμπύρους τ' ὀρθοστάτας, | μεῖνον. Ar. *Av.* 274 Eur. οὗτος, ὦ σέ τοι. ΠΕ. τί βωστρεῖ; The abrupt acc. calls the person's attention in a rough and harsh way. A governing verb is sometimes added, as *El.* 1445 σέ τοι, σὲ κρίνω, ναὶ σέ, τὴν ἐν τῷ πάρος | χρόνῳ θρασεῖαν. Ai. 1226 σὲ δὴ τὰ δεινὰ ῥήματ' ἀγγέλλουσί μοι | τλῆναι... | σέ τοι, τὸν ἐκ τῆς αἰχμαλωτίδος λέγω. Eur. *Med.* 271 σὲ τὴν σκυθρωπὸν καὶ πόσει θυμουμένην, | Μήδειαν, εἶπον, etc. Antigone has her eyes bent on the ground: she is neither afraid nor sullen, but feels that Creon and she can never come to terms. There is nothing in common between their thoughts. Cp. 499.

φής, ἢ καταρνεῖ μὴ δεδρακέναι τάδε;

AN. καὶ φημὶ δρᾶσαι κοὐκ ἀπαρνοῦμαι τὸ μή.

KP. σὺ μὲν κομίζοις ἂν σεαυτὸν ᾗ θέλεις

ἔξω βαρείας αἰτίας ἐλεύθερον·   445

σὺ δ᾽ εἰπέ μοι μὴ μῆκος, ἀλλὰ συντόμως,

*ᾔδησθα κηρυχθέντα μὴ πράσσειν τάδε;

AN. ᾔδη· τί δ᾽ οὐκ ἔμελλον; ἐμφανῆ γὰρ ἦν.

KP. καὶ δῆτ᾽ ἐτόλμας τούσδ᾽ ὑπερβαίνειν νόμους;

AN. οὐ γάρ τί μοι Ζεὺς ἦν ὁ κηρύξας τάδε,   450

οὐδ᾽ ἡ ξύνοικος τῶν κάτω θεῶν Δίκη

*τοιούσδ᾽ ἐν ἀνθρώποισιν ὥρισεν νόμους·

οὐδὲ σθένειν τοσοῦτον ᾠόμην τὰ σὰ

κηρύγμαθ᾽, ὥστ᾽ ἄγραπτα κἀσφαλῆ θεῶν

---

442 καταρνεῖ] καταρνῆι L.   448 τὸ μή] το ἡ L, with μ written above by the first hand, and a letter (σ?) erased before ἡ.—τὸ μὴ οὐ Hermann.   444 ᾗ L: οἱ r, and so Blaydes. 445 ἐλεύθερον] ἐλεύθεροι Pallis.   446 συντόμως L.   Some later MSS. have σύντομα (as A, V), or σύντομον (V⁴).   447 ᾔδει στά L: ᾔδησθα Cobet.   448 ᾔδη] ᾔδειν

---

442 φής δεδρακέναι, ἢ καταρνεῖ μὴ δεδρ., a zeugma. καταρνεῖ. In this compound (found only here) κατά gives the notion of 'downright,' 'explicit': cp. καταφάναι (to affirm), κατάδηλος. μή regularly precedes the inf. when ἀρνεῖσθαι means 'to deny,' but not when it means 'to refuse': Plat. Phaedr. 256 A ἀπαρνηθῆναι τὸ αὑτοῦ μέρος χαρίσασθαι.

443 καὶ......κοὐκ, corresponding with the alternatives in Creon's question: for the conjunctive form, cp. 1192: [Eur.] Rhes. 164 ναί, καὶ δίκαια ταῦτα κοὐκ ἄλλωι λέγω.—τὸ μή: for the art., cp. 78. τὸ μὴ οὐκ is unnecessary, though it would be normal: cp. O. T. 1387 οὐκ ἂν ἐσχόμην | τὸ μὴ ᾽ποκλῇσαι, n.

444 f. σὺ μέν. If she had denied the charge, the φύλαξ must have been detained; now, he can go. κομίζοις ἂν σ. gives a contemptuous permission. So in gentle command, Ph. 674 χωροῖς ἂν εἴσω, Tr. 624 στείχοις ἂν ἤδη. Cp. Eur. Ph. 1636 κόμιζε σαυτὴν...δόμων ἔσω.—ἔξω with β. αἰτίας, after which ἐλεύθερον is pleonastic: cp. Ai. 464 γυμνὸν φανέντα τῶν ἀριστείων ἄτερ: and see n. on κενῆς above, v. 424.

446 μῆκος, adv., 'at great length,' like μακράν, τέλος, etc. If we read σύντομον or σύντομα, μῆκος might be obj. acc. to εἰπέ, but συντόμως seems right. Cp. Aesch. Pers. 698 μή τι μακιστῆρα

μῦθον ἀλλὰ σύντομον λέγων | εἰπέ καὶ πέραινε πάντα.

447 ᾔδησθα, not ᾔδης τά, is certainly right. This 2nd pers. occurs in seven places of drama, two of which require it (Eur. El. 926, Cycl. 108), while the other five admit it (this v., Tr. 988, Ar. Nub. 329, Th. 554, Eccl. 551). Similarly ᾖσθα is either necessary or admissible whenever it occurs in Attic drama. Ar. Lys. 132 has ἔφησθα, and ἔφης nowhere: but the case for ἔφησθα as the sole classical form seems less strong than for ᾖσθα and ᾖσθα. ἔφησθα is required in four Homeric passages (Il. 1. 397, 16. 830: Od. 3. 357, 23. 71), but ἔφης in one, Il. 22. 331 Ἕκτορ, ἀτάρ που ἔφης Πατροκλῆ᾽ ἐξεναρίζων, and in another it is traditional, 22. 280 ἤτοι ἔφης γε (where ἔφησθα is unlikely). The ending is -σθα, not -θα, σ being an integral part of it: Curtius compares Lat. -sti (dedi-sti), and Gothic -st (saiso-st, thou sowedst), Gk Verb pp. 34 ff. Besides οἶσθα, ᾖσθα, ᾖσθα, and ἔφησθα, the forms which take σθα are the Hom. εἶσθα ('thou wilt go'); the presents indic. διδοῖσθα (Il. 19. 270) and τίθησθα (Od. 9. 404, 24. 476); and a few subjunctives and optatives (as βάλῃσθα, βάλοισθα).—κηρυχθέντα, the plur. partic. impersonal, as 570 ἡρμοσμένα, 576 δεδογμένα: a use more freq. with adjectives, as ἀδύνατα, δίκαια (cp. O. C. 485 n.), esp. verbals (below, 677).

dost thou avow, or disavow, this deed?

AN. I avow it; I make no denial.

CR. (*To Guard.*) Thou canst betake thee whither thou wilt, free and clear of a grave charge. [*Exit Guard.*

(*To* ANTIGONE.) Now, tell me thou—not in many words, but briefly—knewest thou that an edict had forbidden this?

AN. I knew it: could I help it? It was public.

CR. And thou didst indeed dare to transgress that law?

AN. Yes; for it was not Zeus that had published me that edict; not such are the laws set among men by the Justice who dwells with the gods below; nor deemed I that thy decrees were of such force, that a mortal could override the unwritten

L.—ἐκφανῆ L, with μ above κ from the first hand. **481** ξύνοικοι] ξύνεδροι Blaydes. **482** οἱ τούσδ᾽ .. ὥρισαν MSS. Semitelos, οἱ τούι γ᾽: Wakefield, ἢ τούσδ᾽ .. ὥρισεν: Valckenaer, τοιούσδ᾽ .. ὥρισεν. Wunder and others reject the verse.

448 ᾔδη: on the form cp. *O. T.* 1525 n.—τί δ᾽ οὐκ ἔμελλον, *sc.* εἰδέναι: 'why was I not likely to know it?'= 'of course I knew it.' Plat. *Rep.* 605 c τάνδεινόν του (ἐστί). τί δ᾽ οὐ μέλλει (*sc.* εἶναι), εἴπερ γε δρᾷ αὐτό; Xen. *H.* 4. 1. 6 τὸν δ᾽ υἱόν... ἑώρακας αὐτοῦ ὡς καλός ἐστι;—τί δ᾽ οὐ μέλλω (*sc.* ἑωρακέναι);—ἐμφανῆ. I prefer this to L's ἐκφανῆ, not because Soph. does not elsewhere use ἐκφανής, but because, in the two places where Aesch. has used it, it has the sense of *emerging into view* (*Pers.* 398, the Greeks going into action at Salamis), or of *standing out among* other objects which are less distinct (ἀνδρὸς ἐκφανὲς τέκμαρ, *Eum.* 244). The sense required here is simply, 'public.'

449 καὶ δῆτ᾽, 'And you *indeed* dared ...?' Not, 'And *then*' (*i.e.* with that knowledge), which would be κᾆτα.

450 Ζεύς is opposed to Creon's edicts, not only as supreme god and therefore guardian of all religious duty, but also in each of his two special qualities,—as χθόνιος (*O. C.* 1606 n.),—and as οὐράνιος, since the denial of burial pollutes the realm of οἱ ἄνω θεοί (1072).

451 f. τῶν κάτω θεῶν. For this rare gen. (instead of the regular dat.) with ξύνοικος, cp. Lycurgus *In Leocr.* § 145 οὗτος ἐν ταύτῃ τῇ χώρᾳ σύνοικος ὑμῶν γενήσεται. So *O. C.* 1382 Δίκη ξύνεδρος Ζηνός. 'The Justice that dwells with the gods below' is their personified right to claim from the living those religious observances which devote the dead to them. A person who

omits such observances is defrauding Hades of his own: see 1070. This Justice, then, 'has not ordained such laws' as Creon's; it has not *forbidden* kinsfolk to bury their dead; on the contrary, it has bound them to do so. τοιούσδ᾽...ὥρισαν is a certainly true correction of the MS. οἱ τούσδ᾽...ὥρισαν. With the latter, οἱ are either Zeus and Δίκη,—which would be the natural sense,—or οἱ κάτω θεοί: and τούσδε νόμους are the laws of sepulture. But, after τάδε in 450, referring to Creon's edicts, the demonstrative pronoun here also should refer to them. Creon has just called his own laws τούσδε νόμους (449). If Antigone, immediately afterwards, used τούσδε νόμους to describe the divine laws, the stress on τούσδε would be extremely awkward. Further, τοιούσδ᾽ ὥρισεν has a pathetic force which renders it incomparably finer here than the somewhat tame statement of fact, 'who have appointed the laws of burial among men.'

454 f. ἄγραπτα...νόμιμα. Arist. *Rhet.* 1. 13 § 2 distinguishes (1) ἴδιοι νόμοι, the particular law which each community defines for itself, which is partly written, partly (so far as consisting in custom) unwritten: (2) κοινὸς νόμος, the universal, unwritten law of nature (ὁ κατὰ φύσιν). ἔστι γάρ, ὃ μαντεύονταί τι πάντες, φύσει κοινόν δίκαιον καὶ ἄδικον, κἂν μηδεμία κοινωνία πρὸς ἀλλήλους ᾖ μηδὲ συνθήκη, οἷον καὶ ἡ Σοφοκλέους 'Αντιγόνη φαίνεται λέγουσα, ὅτι δίκαιον, ἀπειρημένον (= in spite of the edict), θάψαι τὸν Πολυνείκην, ὡς φύσει ὂν τοῦτο δίκαιον. (Here be

νόμιμα δύνασθαι θνητὸν ὄνθ᾽ ὑπερδραμεῖν·   455
οὐ γάρ τι νῦν γε κἀχθές, ἀλλ᾽ ἀεί ποτε
ζῇ ταῦτα, κοὐδεὶς οἶδεν ἐξ ὅτου 'φάνη.
τούτων ἐγὼ οὐκ ἔμελλον, ἀνδρὸς οὐδενὸς
φρόνημα δείσασ᾽, ἐν θεοῖσι τὴν δίκην
δώσειν. θανουμένη γὰρ ἐξῄδη, τί δ᾽ οὔ;   460
κεἰ μὴ σὺ προὐκήρυξας· εἰ δὲ τοῦ χρόνου
πρόσθεν θανοῦμαι, κέρδος αὔτ᾽ ἐγὼ λέγω.
ὅστις γὰρ ἐν πολλοῖσιν, ὡς ἐγώ, κακοῖς
ζῇ, πῶς ὅδ᾽ οὐχὶ κατθανὼν κέρδος φέρει;
οὕτως ἔμοιγε τοῦδε τοῦ μόρου τυχεῖν   465
παρ᾽ οὐδὲν ἄλγος· ἀλλ᾽ ἄν, εἰ τὸν ἐξ ἐμῆς

---

455 θνητὸν ὄνθ᾽] θνητὰ φύνθ᾽ Bothe.   **456** οὐ γάρ] οὐ μήν in Plutarch's quotation, *Mor.* 731 C, doubtless by a slip of memory.—νῦν γε κάχθές] Arist. twice quotes this v.: (1) *Rhet.* I. 13 § 2, where Q (=Marcianus 200) and Y^b (=Vat. 1340) have τε instead of γε, and Q has καὶ χθές. (2) *ib.* I. 15 § 6 where all have γε κάχθές.

---

quotes vv. 456 f.) Cp. *O. T.* 865 ff. νόμοι... | ὑψίποδες, οὐρανίαν | δι᾽ αἰθέρα τεκνωθέντες, with notes there. Thuc. 2. 37 (νόμοι) ὅσοι ἄγραφοι ὄντες αἰσχύνην ὁμολογουμένην φέρουσι. When 'the unwritten laws' are thus called νόμοι, the latter word is used figuratively. νόμιμα, observances sanctioned by usage, is the more correct word: so Plat. *Legg.* 793 A observes that τὰ καλούμενα ὑπὸ τῶν πολλῶν ἄγραφα νόμιμα cannot properly be called νόμοι, but still must be taken into account: δεσμοὶ γὰρ οὗτοι πάσης εἰσὶ πολιτείας, μεταξὺ πάντων ὄντες τῶν ἐν γράμμασι τεθέντων τε καὶ κειμένων καὶ τῶν ἔτι τεθησομένων.—ἀσφαλῆ, they stand fast for ever, like the θεῶν ἔδος ἀσφαλὲς αἰεί (*Od.* 6. 42).—θνητὸν ὄντ᾽, 'one who is a mortal,'—*i.e.* Creon; but it is needless to supply σέ from τὰ σά: the expression is the more forcible for being general. Cp. Eur. fr. 653 οὐ θαῦμ᾽ ἔλεξας, θνητὸν ὄντα δυστυχεῖν: *Alc.* 799 ὄντας δὲ θνητοὺς θνητὰ καὶ φρονεῖν χρεών. Bothe's θνητὰ φύνθ᾽, rashly adopted by Nauck, is a wanton change, which the ambiguity of the neut. pl. makes still worse.—ὑπερδραμεῖν, out-run, and so fig., prevail over: Eur. *Ph.* 578 ἢν δ᾽ αὖ κρατηθῇς καὶ τὰ τοῦδ᾽ ὑπερδράμῃ, and his cause prevail (Canter's certain corr. of ὑπεκδράμῃ): *Ion* 973 καὶ πῶς τὰ κρείσσω θνητὸς οὖσ᾽ ὑπερδράμω; (prevail against Apollo). It has been proposed to refer θνητὸν ὄνθ᾽ to

Antigone: but if she said, 'I did not think your edicts so strong that I, a mortal, could prevail over divine law,' δύνασθαι would rather imply that, if she had been able, she would have been willing to do so. Besides, ὑπερδραμεῖν is more naturally said of the law-giver who sets his law above the other law.

456 f. νῦν γε κάχθές. Cp. Her. 2. 53 μέχρι οὗ πρώην τε καὶ χθές. Plat. *Legg.* 677 D ὡς ἔπος εἰπεῖν, χθές καὶ πρώην γεγονότα (where the phrase is presently strengthened into τὸν ἀτεχνῶς χθές γενόμενον). The usu. Attic form was χθές καὶ πρώην, though πρώην καὶ χθές also occurs. Cp. Catullus 61. 137 *hodie atque heri*. So *heri et nudius tertius*. Tryphon, an Alexandrian grammarian of the Augustan age, is quoted by Apollonius *De Adverb.* p. 556, 32 as saying, χθές ἀττικώτερον τοῦ ἐχθές: but the reverse seems to be the case. Attic Comedy supports ἐχθές against χθές in a majority of cases; though χθές may have been preferred, even in prose, after a vowel.—ζῇ: cp. *O. T.* 482 ζῶντα (of the oracles which are operative, effectual), and *ib.* 45 n.— 'φάνη, with prodelision of the temporal augment in the 6th place, as ὡς ἐγὼ 'φάνην *O. C.* 974 n.

458 f. τούτων (sc. τῶν νομίμων)... τὴν δίκην, the penalty belonging to these laws: *i.e.* the penalty of breaking them. The emphasis on τούτων

and unfailing statutes of heaven.   For their life is not of to-day
or yesterday, but from all time, and no man knows when they
were first put forth.

Not through dread of any human pride could I answer to
the gods for breaking *these*.   Die I must,—I knew that well
(how should I not?)—even without thy edicts.   But if I am
to die before my time, I count that a gain: for when any one
lives, as I do, compassed· about with evils, can such an one
find aught but gain in death?

So for me to meet this doom is trifling grief; but if I had

---

457 ταῦτα] τοῦτο Arist. *Rh*. 1. 13 § 2.   Victorins supposed that Arist. thus
purposely altered ταῦτα, to suit his own words introducing the citation, ὡς φύσει
ὃν τοῦτο δίκαιον (see comment. on 454 f.).   Rather it was a mere slip: cp.
comment. on 223.—'φάνη] φάνη L.   **458** ἐγὼ οὐκ] ἐγ' οὐκ L.   **460** ἐξῄδη
Brunck: ἐξῄδειν L.   **462** πρόσθεν] πρόσθε I..—αὐτ' L, αὐτ' r.

---

shows that, like ταῦτα just before, it refers
to the νόμιμα: we cannot, therefore, render, 'the penalty of such an act' (*sc*. τοῦ
ὑπερδραμεῖν).—ἐν θεοῖσι, the forensic ἐν,
denoting the tribunal: Plat. *Legg*. 916 B
διαδικαζέσθω δὲ ἐν τισι τῶν ἰατρῶν: *Gorg*.
464 D εἰ δέοι ἐν παισὶ διαγωνίζεσθαι: Lys.
or. 13 § 35 ὁ δὲ δῆμος ἐν τῷ δικαστηρίῳ ἐν
δισχιλίοις ἐψηφίσατο (*sc*. ποιεῖν τὴν κρίσιν).
Cp. *O. T.* 677 ἐν...τοῖσδ', n.

460 f. θανεῖν.   The fut. inf. and
the pres. inf. are equally common after
μέλλω in Soph. (*O. T.* 967 n.).—θανουμένη γάρ introduces the reason for her
conduct.   'It was not likely that I should
obey your edicts, and thereby incur
punishment after death, for the sake of
avoiding immediate death.   *For*, as to
death, I knew already that I must die
some time or other; and if it is to be a
little sooner, so much the better.'—τί δ'
οὔ; *sc*. ἔμελλον ἐξειδέναι (448).

461 f. καὶ μὴ σὺ προὐκήρυξας: Even
if thou hadst not proclaimed death as the
penalty of infringing the edict.   The apodosis might be either (a) ἐξῄδη ἄν, implied
in τί δ' οὔ; or (b) ἔδει ἄν με θανεῖν, implied
in θανουμένη.   But (a) is best: 'I should
have known it, even if you had not brought
it publicly to my knowledge.'   For καὶ εἰ
cp. *O. T.* 305 n.—τοῦ χρόνου, the natural
term of life (cp. *O. T.* 963): expressed
below by πρίν μοι μοῖραν ἐξήκειν βίου (896).
—αὐτ', i.e. αὐτό.   Cp. *El.* 1267 εἴ σε θεὸς
ἐνόρισεν | ἀμέτερα πρὸς μέλαθρα, δαιμόνιον
| αὐτὸ τίθημ' ἐγώ: fr. 154 ἔχοιμ' ἂν αὐτὸ
μὴ κακῶς ἀπεικάσαι.   αὖτε (L) would mean,
'again,' 'on the other hand' (so far from

thinking it a loss).   The epic αὖτε is used
by Soph. in one lyric passage (*Tr.* 1010);
by Aesch. both in lyrics and in trimeters;
never by Eur.   The simpler αὐτό is more
probable here.

464 φέρει = φέρεται (*O. C.* 6 n.).—The
woman uses the masc. gender in putting
the general case.   Cp. Eur. *Med*. 1017
οὔτοι μόνη σὺ σῶν ἀπεζύγης τέκνων | κού-
φως φέρειν χρὴ θνητὸν ὄντα συμφοράς.

465—468 Kvičala and Wecklein reject these four verses, despairing of the
difficulties found in vv. 466, 467, which
have been variously amended; see Appendix.   The alleged difficulties are, (1)
παρ' οὐδὲν ἄλγος: (2) the mention of the
mother only: (3) the position of θανόντ',
which might suggest the sense, 'slain by
my mother': (4) ἠσχόμην (as L has it).
Before dealing with these points, I would
call attention to a trait which the im-
pugners of these verses have overlooked,
and which speaks strongly for the genuineness of the passage as a whole,· corrupt
though it be in certain words.   That trait
is the clause τοῖσδε δ' οὐκ ἀλγύνομαι in
468, returning upon the thought παρ' οὐδὲν ἄλγος in 466.   This series of three
clauses, in|which the second is opposed
to the first, and the third re-iterates the
sense of the first, is peculiarly Sophoclean:
cp. *Ai.* 1111 οὐ γάρ τι τῆς σῆς οὕνεκ' ἐ-
στρατεύσατο | γυναικός,... | ἀλλ' οὕνεχ' ὅρ-
κων οἷσιν ἦν ἐνώμοτος, | σοῦ δ' οὐδὲν
similar instances are *O. T.* 337 f., *Tr.*
431 ff.   This touch would hardly have
come from an interpolator.

466 ἄλγος, nom., *sc*. ἐστί: παρ' οὐδέν,

μητρὸς θανόντ᾽ ἄθαπτον ἠνσχόμην νέκυν,
κείνοις ἂν ἤλγουν· τοῖσδε δ᾽ οὐκ ἀλγύνομαι.
σοὶ δ᾽ εἰ δοκῶ νῦν μῶρα δρῶσα τυγχάνειν,
σχεδόν τι μώρῳ μωρίαν ὀφλισκάνω.   470
ΧΟ. δηλοῖ τὸ γέννημ᾽ ὠμὸν ἐξ ὠμοῦ πατρὸς
τῆς παιδός· εἴκειν δ᾽ οὐκ ἐπίσταται κακοῖς.
ΚΡ. ἀλλ᾽ ἴσθι τοι τὰ σκλήρ᾽ ἄγαν φρονήματα
πίπτειν μάλιστα, καὶ τὸν ἐγκρατέστατον·

---

467 ἠσχόμην νέκυν L: with marg. gloss by S, ἠνεσχόμην ὑπερεῖδον. The later MSS. have ἠσχόμην (L²), ἠνσχόμην (A, V²), ἠσχόμην (Vat. b), ἰσχόμην (E, V⁴), ἠνεσχόμην (R, Vat.), or ἠνειχόμην (V). See comment. **471 ἔ. δηλοῖ**]

---

adv.: 'is a pain in no appreciable degree,' is a pain not worth a thought: as he might have said, οὐδαμοῦ ἄλγος ἐστί. The normal use of παρ᾽ οὐδέν, 'of no account,' is either (a) with the verb εἶναι, as O. T. 982 ταῦθ᾽ ὅτῳ | παρ᾽ οὐδέν ἐστι, or (b) with a verb meaning 'to esteem,' as above, v. 34; τὸ πρᾶγμ᾽ ἄγειν | οὐχ ὡς παρ᾽ οὐδέν. The only peculiarity here is that, instead of a word in the general sense, 'is esteemed' (ἄγεται), we have a virtual equivalent, tinged with the special thought of the moment, viz., 'is a pain.' Exactly so in El. 1327 we have πότερα παρ᾽ οὐδὲν τοῦ βίου κήδεσθ᾽ ἔτι, instead of πότερα παρ᾽ οὐδὲν τὸν βίον ἄγετε. Thus the suspicions as to the genuineness of παρ᾽ οὐδὲν ἄλγος are illusory.

ἀλλ᾽ ἄν. For the position of ἄν (to which objection has been taken) cp. El. 333 ἀλγῶ 'πὶ τοῖς παροῦσιν· ὥστ᾽ ἄν, εἰ σθένος | λάβοιμι, δηλώσαιμ᾽ ἂν οἷ᾽ αὐτοῖς φρονῶ: ib. 439 ἀρχὴν δ᾽ ἄν, εἰ μὴ τλημονεστάτη γυνὴ | πασῶν ἔβλαστε, τάσδε δυσμενεῖς χοὰς | οὐκ ἄν ποθ᾽, ὃν γ᾽ ἔκτεινε, τῷδ᾽ ἐπέστεφε.

467 ἄθαπτον ἠνσχόμην νέκυν, had allowed him to be an unburied corpse. For ἄθαπτον without ὄντα, cp. Arist. Hist. An. 8. 8 δύναται δ᾽ ἄποτος ἀνέχεσθαι (sc. ὤν): and O. T. 412 n. L has ἠσχόμην, and ἠνσχόμην appears only as one of several readings in the later MSS.,—the other readings being manifestly impossible. The first question is, Could an Attic poet have used ἠνσχόμην for ἠνεσχόμην? We can only say that we find nothing really like it, and that no support for it can be drawn from the Homeric forms in which ἀνά suffers apocope, viz., ἄνσχεο = ἀνασχοῦ (Il. 23. 587

etc.), ἀνσχήσεσθαι (Il. 5. 104), ἀνσχετά (Od. 2. 63), ἀνσχεθέειν (Od. 5. 320). Still, there is force in Prof. Tyrrell's remark (Classical Review, vol. II. p. 140) that ἠνσχόμην is just the form in which an Attic poet would have applied apocope of ἀνά, inasmuch as he would have felt that he was only sacrificing the redandant augment.'

In my first edition I placed in the text the emendation of Semitelos (1887) ἠσχυναν κύνες. Cp. Il. 22. 74 ἀλλ᾽ ὅτε δὴ πολιόν τε κάρη πολιόν τε γένειον | αἰδῶ τ᾽ αἰσχύνωσι κύνες κταμένοιο γέροντος. If the ες of κύνες had been obliterated, νέκυν would easily have arisen (esp. after ν); and a change of υ into ο would have taken ἠσχυναν far towards ἠσχόμην. But, while I still hold that this brilliant conjecture has no small degree of probability, I also recognise the justice of the criticism that the context here decidedly favours a verb in the first person.

Other emendations will be found in the Appendix. Most of them assume that we must have ἠνεσχόμην (or ἀνεσχόμην), and therefore alter the words θανόντ᾽ ἄθαπτον and νέκυν in various ways, —usu. omitting νέκυν. The verses produced by these processes are wretched, while, from a palaeographical point of view, they are pure conjectures, which do not attempt to account for the tradition in L.—Two points remain. (1) τὸν ἐξ ἐμῆς | μητρός. This is like saying, 'the son of the same womb.' Cp. Eur. I. T. 497 πότερον ἀδελφῶ μητρός ἐστον ἐκ μιᾶς; Yet it has been seriously urged by many critics, as a ground for change, that a mention of the father was indispensable. ἐμῆς need not be altered to ὁμῆς (Seyffert)

suffered my mother's son to lie in death an unburied corpse, that would have grieved me; for this, I am not grieved. And if my present deeds are foolish in thy sight, it may be that a foolish judge arraigns my folly.

CH. The maid shows herself passionate child of passionate sire, and knows not how to bend before troubles.

CR. Yet I would have thee know that o'er-stubborn spirits are most often humbled; 'tis the stiffest iron, baked to

---

δῆλον Nauck.—τὸ γέννημ'] M. Schmidt gives τι γέννημ' (with ἡ παῖς ὃν for τῆς παιδός): Semitelos, γονὴν λῆμ'. For τῆς παιδός Mekler conject. πεφυκός.—ἐπίσταται] L has the second τ in an erasure, perh. from σ. The final ι had been omitted, and has been added above α by the first hand. **474** πίπτει Boeckh.

---

or μᾶς (Meineke). (2) τὸν ἐξ ἐμ. | μητρὸς θανόντ'. It is quite true that, when written, these words have an awkward ambiguity; bu they would have ad none when spoken, since a slight pause after μητρός would have been required to bring out θανόντ'. This is the right test to apply in the case of a play written to be acted.

470 σχεδόν τι, 'almost,' iron., 'it might perhaps be said that...': so El. 608 (also at the close of a defiant speech), εἰ γὰρ πέφυκα τῶνδε τῶν ἔργων ἴδρις, | σχεδόν τι τὴν σὴν οὐ καταισχύνω φύσιν. Cp. ib. 550 εἰ δὲ σοὶ δοκῶ φρονεῖν κακῶς | γνώμην δικαίαν σχοῦσα, τοὺς πέλας ψέγε (end of a speech): also Ai. 1038, O. C. 1665.—μόρῳ μορίαν: cp. 754. The παρήχησις gives bitterness (O. T. 371).—ὀφλισκάνω with dat., as Eur. Bacch. 854 γέλωτα Θηβαίοις ὀφλεῖν, etc.; but in this use it can also take πρός τινα or παρά τινι (Plato). Cp. O. T. 511.

471 f. These two verses give a moment of stillness before the storm breaks forth. So at O. T. 404 four verses of the chorus divide the angry speech of Oedipus from the retort of Teiresias.—τὸ γέννημα τῆς παιδός (the offspring consisting in the maiden) the maiden his offspring, δηλοῖ (sc. ὅν) ὠμόν, shows herself fierce, ἐξ ἀμοῦ πατρός, from a fierce sire (i.e. by the disposition inherited from him). Cp. 20 δηλοῖς...καλχαίνουσα (n.): the omission of ὅν is somewhat bold, but possible for poetry; 709 ὤφθησαν κενοί: Plat. Legg. 496 cp. δέδεικται ψυχὴ τῶν πάντων πρεσβυτάτη. B γέννημα occurs below, 628, O. T. 1167, and Tr. 315, meaning always 'that which is begotten,' the offspring. So in Plato the word always means the thing produced; for in Sophist. 266 D, τὸ δ' ὁμοιωμάτων τινῶν

γέννημα, where Ast takes it as = 'confectio,' the sense is, 'the other a product (consisting in) certain images.' In Aesch. P. V. 850 ἐπώνυμον δὲ τῶν Διὸς γεννημάτων | τέξεις κελαινὸν Ἔπαφον, the word, if genuine, would certainly mean 'begetting'; but Wieseler's correction, γέννημ' ἀφῶν ('an offspring called after the touch of Zeus'), is highly probable. For τὸ γέννημα τῆς παιδός as = ἡ γεννηθεῖσα παῖς, cp. 1164 τέκνων σπορᾷ, El. 1233 γοναὶ σωμάτων ἐμοὶ φιλτάτων (her brother), Eur. Med. 1098 τέκνων...βλάστημα. Here, the thought would have been complete without τῆς παιδός ('the offspring shows the father's fierceness'), which is added, as if by an after-thought, for the further definition of τὸ γέννημα. I cannot believe that Soph. intended τὸ γέννημα τῆς παιδός to mean, 'the inborn disposition of the maiden,'—an unexampled sense for γέννημα. On the other hand, all the emendations are unsatisfactory and improbable. The language, though somewhat peculiar, appears to be sound.

472 εἴκειν...κακοῖς, not 'to succumb' to them, but to bend before them (as trees before a storm, 713), with a prudent view to self-preservation. Cp. Aesch. P. V. 320 σὺ δ' οὐδέπω ταπεινός, οὐδ' εἴκεις κακοῖς, | πρὸς τοῖς παροῦσι δ' ἄλλα προσλαβεῖν θέλεις.

473 f. ἀλλ' ἴσθι τοι: so oft. in threatenings: cp. 1064: Tr. 1107 ἀλλ' εὖ γέ τοι τόδ' ἴστε: El. 298 ἀλλ' ἴσθι τοι τίσουσά γ' ἀξίαν δίκην.—πίπτειν, instead of the regular πίπτοντα: this inf. after οἶδα (as = 'I know that...', not, 'I know how to...') is not rare in poetry; cp. O. T. 691, Ph. 1329, Aesch. Pers. 173, 431, 435: so after ἐπίσταμαι above, 293, and 1092.

σίδηρον, ὀπτὸν ἐκ πυρὸς περισκελῆ,   475
θραυσθέντα καὶ ῥαγέντα πλεῖστ' ἂν εἰσίδοις·
σμικρῷ χαλινῷ δ' οἶδα τοὺς θυμουμένους
ἵππους καταρτυθέντας· οὐ γὰρ ἐκπέλει
φρονεῖν μέγ', ὅστις δοῦλός ἐστι τῶν πέλας.
αὕτη δ' ὑβρίζειν μὲν τότ' ἐξηπίστατο,   480
νόμους ὑπερβαίνουσα τοὺς προκειμένους·
ὕβρις δ', ἐπεὶ δέδρακεν, ἥδε δευτέρα,
τούτοις ἐπαυχεῖν καὶ δεδρακυῖαν γελᾶν.
ἦ νῦν ἐγὼ μὲν οὐκ ἀνήρ, αὕτη δ' ἀνήρ,
εἰ ταῦτ' ἀνατὶ τῇδε κείσεται κράτη.   485
ἀλλ' εἴτ' ἀδελφῆς εἴθ' ὁμαιμονεστέρα

476 ἐσίδοισ L, with ει over ε from the first hand. **482 f.** L inverts the order of these two vv., but S has corrected the error by writing β' before 483 and a' before 482 in the left-hand marg. **484** νῦν] τάρ' Elmsley. **485** ἀνατὶ L: ἀνατεὶ r.—κείσεται] πείσεται Semitelos (Blaydes had conjectured εἰ ταῦτά μου γυναικὶ πείσεται κράτη). Nauck proposes ἐάσεται. **486** ὁμαιμονεστέραισ

---

475 ὀπτὸν...περισκελῆ, m d to hardness: for the proleptic adje, quer'è huc. 2. 75 ᾔρετο τὸ ὕψος...μέγα, Eur. *El.* 376 (πενία) διδάσκει δ' ἄνδρα τῇ χρείᾳ κακὸν (to be bad).—περισκελῆς, dried or parched all round, fi m σκέλλω, *torrere*: cp. *Il.* 23. 190 μή σφιν μένος ἠελίοιο | σκήλει' ἀμφὶ περὶ χρόα ἴνεσιν: hence, fig., αἱ περισκελεῖς φρένες (*Ai.* 649): cp. *retorridus*. From the same rt come σκληρός, σκελετός (skeleton), and ἀσκελής (dried),—this last having a fig. sense in the Homeric ἀσκελὲς αἰεί ('stubbornly,' *Od.* 1. 68).—ἐκ πυρός, *by means of* fire; cp. 990: *Ph.* 710 ἐξ ὡκυβόλων τόξων...ἀνύσειε...φορβάν.

476 θραυσθέντα καὶ ῥαγέντα, 'broken and shivered.' ῥαγέντα is here the stronger word, in so far as it pictures the fragments of the ruptured iron flying asunder, while θραυσθέντα merely says that the iron is broken into pieces. As Heinrich Schmidt observes, the foremost idea in ῥήγνυμαι is that of the separation of the parts,—the *rent* or *rift* being brought before us; in θραύειν, that of a whole being broken into small pieces (*Synonymik der Gr. Sprache*, vol. III. pp. 304 ff.).

477 f. χαλινῷ δ'. Cp. *O. C.* 714 ἵππoισιν τὸν ἀκεστῆρα χαλινόν, n. For σμικρῷ cp. *Ai.* 1253 μέγας δὲ πλευρὰ βοῦς ὑπὸ σμικρᾶς ὅμως | μάστιγος ὀρθὸς εἰς ὁδὸν πορεύεται.—καταρτυθέντας, brought under discipline, made docile. καταρτύω = to equip, or prepare (*O. C.* 71): then,

like ἁρμόζω (*O. C.* 908), in a fig. sense, to bring into order, regulate, by a course of training: cp. Plat. *Legg.* 808 D (a child is the ὑβριστότατον θηρίων), ὅσῳ μάλιστα ἔχει πηγὴν τοῦ φρονεῖν μήπω κατηρτυμένην (not yet brought under discipline): Plut. *Mor.* 38 C (the sensuous impulses, αἱ ἐφ' ἡδονὴν ὁρμαί, are disastrous) ἂν ἐᾷ τις ἀφέτους, ᾗ πεφύκασι, χωρεῖν, καὶ μὴ...καταρτύῃ τὴν φύσιν (discipline the character). Plut. *Them.* 2 τοὺς τραχυτάτους πώλους ἀρίστους ἵππους γίνεσθαι φάσκων, ὅταν ἧς προσήκει τύχωσι παιδείας καὶ καταρτύσεως (education and discipline). In Aesch. *Eum.* 473 the act. perf. part. κατηρτυκὼς (ἱκέτης) is said to be a term applied to a horse whose mouth was 'fully furnished' with teeth (*i.e.* which had shed its foal's teeth), and hence, 'broken in,' 'tamed': at any rate, it must be kept distinct from the passive καταρτυθείς as used here.

478 f. Suspicion has fallen on ἐκπέλει, which occurs only here: Hesych. explains it by ἔξεστι, and ἐξέτελεν by ἐξεγένετο. He would hardly have invented the imperf., if he had not met with it in literature: and the metrical convenience of such a synonym for ἔξεστι is a further reason for believing that it was current.—ὅστις: for the omission of the anteced. τούτῳ, see on 35: for the gender, on 464.—τῶν πέλας: cp. fr. 83 ('tis better to conquer by any means) ἢ δοῦλον αὐτὸν ὄντα τῶν πέλας κλύειν.

hardness in the fire, that thou shalt oftenest see snapped and shivered; and I have known horses that show temper brought to order by a little curb; there is no room for pride, when thou art thy neighbour's slave.—This girl was already versed in insolence when she transgressed the laws that had been set forth; and, that done, lo, a second insult,—to vaunt of this, and exult in her deed.

Now verily I am no man, she is the man, if this victory shall rest with her, and bring no penalty. No! be she sister's child, or nearer to me in blood than

L first hand; but the letters ισ have been partially erased. ὁμαιμονεστέρας r (including A). The schol. in L read the gen.: εἴτε ἐξ ἀδελφῆς ἐμῆς εἴτε οἰκειοτέρας καὶ συγγενικωτέρας κ.τ.λ. The Roman ed., indeed, gives οἰκειοτέρα καὶ συγγενικωτέρα: but L's authority for the scholium is the better.

---

480 ff. αὕτη δ'. Creon began by addressing Antigone (473). He now denounces her to the Chorus. Cp. *O. T.* 1078 αὕτη δ' ἴσως, κ.τ.λ. (of Iocasta).—ὑβρίζειν μὲν...ὕβρις δ': epanaphora (*O. T.* 25 n.). The sense is, 'Her *disobedience* was an act of consummate insolence; and her *defiance* now makes it worse.' ἐξηπίστατο, 'knew thoroughly,' with bitterness; cp. 686; Eur. fr. 796 ὅστις σωφρονεῖν ἠπίσταται. τότ' is explained by ὑπερβαίνουσα.—τοὺς προκ., which had been set forth: cp. *O. T.* 865, Eur. *I. T.* 1189 τὸν νόμον...τὸν προκείμενον.—τούτοις, neut., these deeds: cp. 468 κείνοις ...τοῖσδε.—δεδρακυΐαν γελᾶν=to exult in having done it. For the partic., cp. Ar. *Vesp.* 1007 κοὐκ ἐγχανεῖταί σ' ἐξαπατῶν Ὑπέρβολος.

484 f. νῦν, 'now,' *i.e.* 'under these circumstances,' is better than νυν or τἄρ here.—εἰ ταῦτα...κράτη, if this victory shall remain on record for her, without bringing her any punishment. For κράτη, deeds of might, and so prevalence, victory, cp. *El.* 476 Δίκα δίκαια φερομένα χεροῖν κράτη: *ib.* 689 κοὐκ οἶδα τοιοῦθ' ἀνδρὸς ἔργα καὶ κράτη. For κείσεται, ep. Pind. *I.* 4. 17 τὶν δ' ἐν Ἰσθμῷ διπλόα θάλλοισ' ἀρετά, | Φυλακίδα, κεῖται, 'for thee, Phylacidas, a double glory of valour is *laid up* at the Isthmus.' So, here, κείσεται means, 'placed to her credit,' 'permanently secured to her'; cp. the colloquialism, 'to *score* a success.' Other interpretations are:—(1) 'If this royal power of mine shall have been instituted without penalty for her.' For the word κράτη, this sense is tenable (cp. 60, 166, 173, *O. T.* 237): it is the whole phrase that appears strained. And ταῦτ'

(said with bitter emphasis) evidently refers to Antigone's acts; cp. 483 τού-τοις. Semitelos reads κείσεται: 'If this sovereignty of mine' (here Creon lifts his sceptre) 'shall yield to her without punishing her.' The verb would, however, be strange, and somewhat weak. (2) 'If these edicts shall have been set forth without penalty for her.' This last gives an impossible sense to κράτη. Ar. *Ran.* 1126 ff. illustrates the poetical ambiguity of κράτη, the debate there being whether, by πατρῷα κράτη, Aesch. meant, 'a victory over a father,' or 'power derived from a father.'—For the form of ἀνατί, cp. *O. C.* 1251 n.: for ταῦτα without τά, *ib.* 471.

486 f. ἀδελφῆς, (child of) a sister, ἀδελφιδῆ: for the gen., cp. 380, 825.—εἴθ' ὁμαιμονεστέρα, 'or nearer in blood to me than any member of my family.' The gen. ὁμαιμονεστέρας (see cr. n.) would mean, 'or (child of) one nearer in blood to me,' etc. She could be the child of no one nearer than a sister, unless it were of a mother or of a daughter; and it is far-fetched to suppose that Creon means, 'my niece,—aye, my sister, or my grand-daughter.' All that he means is, 'my niece,—aye, or the nearest relation possible.' This is more simply and clearly said by the nom. ὁμαιμονεστέρα. If the comparative were here restricted to the regular Sophoclean sense of the positive ὅμαιμος and ὁμαίμων, as meaning brother or sister (see on *O. C.* 330), then the gen. could be explained in another way, viz., as a rhetorical hyperbole: 'sister's child, or child of one who was thrice my sister,'—like Plato *Lysis* 210 C ὁ πατὴρ καὶ ἡ μήτηρ καὶ εἴ τι τούτων οἰκειότερόν ἐστι.

τοῦ παντὸς ἡμῖν Ζηνὸς ἑρκείου κυρεῖ,
αὐτή τε χἠ ξύναιμος οὐκ ἀλύξετον
μόρου κακίστου· καὶ γὰρ οὖν κείνην ἴσον
ἐπαιτιῶμαι τοῦδε βουλεῦσαι τάφου.   490
καί νιν καλεῖτ'· ἔσω γὰρ εἶδον ἀρτίως
λυσσῶσαν αὐτὴν οὐδ' ἐπήβολον φρενῶν·
φιλεῖ δ', ὁ θυμὸς πρόσθεν ᾑρῆσθαι κλοπεὺς
τῶν μηδὲν ὀρθῶς ἐν σκότῳ τεχνωμένων.)
μισῶ γε μέντοι χὤταν ἐν κακοῖσί τις   495
ἁλοὺς ἔπειτα τοῦτο καλλύνειν θέλῃ.

487 ἑρκίου L: ἑρκείου r.   490 βουλεῦσαι] Keck conject. φροντίσαι: Mekler, ἐπι-
ψαῦσαι: Semitelos, συλλαβεῖν: Metzger, τόνδε κηδεῦσαι τάφον.   494 ὀρθῶς] ὀρθὸν

Hyperbole is congenial to Creon's excitement; cp. 1040. But the addition, τοῦ παντὸς Z. ἑρκείου, ill suits this, while, on the other hand, it agrees well with the nom. ὁμαιμονεστέρα. On the whole, then, I incline to prefer the nom.; but the point is a nice one, and the gen. is quite tenable.—κυρεῖ (οὖσα), =ἐστί: cp. O. T. 362 φονέα...κυρεῖν.

487 τοῦ παντὸς Ζηνὸς ἑρκείου = πᾶς τῶν τῶν οἰκείων (schol.): so Eustath. 1930, 30 ἑρκεῖον Δία ἐκεῖνος (Sophocles) τοὺς ἐν οἴκῳ πάντας δηλοῖ. The altar of Ζεὺς ἑρκεῖος stood in the court-yard (αὐλή) in front of the Greek house; ἕρκος denoting the buildings which enclose the αὐλή, or, sometimes, the space so enclosed, the αὐλή itself. In Od. 22. 334 Phemius thinks of passing from the μέγαρον into the αὐλή, Διὸς μεγάλου ποτὶ βωμὸν | Ἑρκείου. (Cp. my Introd. to Homer, p. 58.) This is the altar at which Peleus was sacrificing, αὐλῆς ἐν χόρτῳ (Il. 11. 774: cp. Athen. 5, p. 189 F): as in Plat. Rep. 328 C there is sacrifice in the αὐλή. So in Her. 6. 68 Demaratus supplicates his mother especially by τοῦ Ἑρκείου Διὸς τοῦδε (whose altar or image he is touching, καταπτόμενος): Priam is slain πρὸς...κρηπῖδων βάθροις...Ζηνὸς ἑρκείου (Eur. Tro. 16),—ἐπὶ τῇ ἐσχάρα τοῦ Ἑρκείου (Paus. 4. 17. 4): cp. Ovid Ibis 286, Cui nihil Hercei profuit ara Iovis. In Cratinus jun., Χείρων 1 ff. (c. 350 B.C.), a returned exile says, ξυγγενεῖς | καὶ φράτορας καὶ δημότας εὑρὼν μόλις | εἰς τὸ κυλικεῖον ἐνεγράφην (put on the feasting-list—παρὰ προσδοκίαν for εἰς τὸ γραμματεῖον)· Ζεὺς ἐστί μοι | ἑρκεῖος, ἔστι φράτριος: where ἑρκεῖος corresponds with ξυγγενεῖς. Dionysius 1. 67 expresses the attributes of the Roman Penates by the words πατρῷοι, γενέθλιοι, κτήσιοι, μύχιοι, ἑρκεῖοι (for ἑρκίους in his text should be ἑρκείους: so L has ἑρκίου here).—In relation to the family, Ζεὺς is also γενέθλιος (Pind. O. 8. 16: cp. ξύναιμος, 659), ὁμόγνιος, and ἐφέστιος (as presiding over household life: Ai. 492, Her. 1. 44).—For the god's name used to denote that which he protects, cp. Eur. Hec. 345 πέφευγας τὸν ἐμὸν ἱκέσιον Δία, = my supplication, with its consequences.

488 ἀλύξετον. The pres. ind. ἀλύσκω occurs in Apollon. Rhod., and the pres. part. in Od.; otherwise we find only the fut. (usu. ἀλύξω, but ἀλύξομαι, Hes. Op. 363) and aor. ἤλυξα (once midd., ἐξαλύξομαι Ai. 656). The gen. μόρου follows the analogy of ἀπολύεσθαι, ἀπαλλάττεσθαι, etc. The regular constr. of the verb is with the acc. (as in the Homeric κῆρας ἀλύξας), and so Eur. always has an acc. with ἐξήλυξα. In El. 627 θράσους | τοῦδ' οὐκ ἀλύξεις, the gen. is not like this, but causal ('for this boldness'). Oppian's ἐξήλυξα μόροιο (Hal. 3. 104) was obviously suggested by our verse. So in Ph. 1044 Soph. has ventured on τῆς νόσου πεφευγέναι, thinking, doubtless, of the Homeric πεφυγμένος ἦεν ἀέθλων.

489 f. καὶ γὰρ οὖν, for indeed: cp. 771 εὖ γὰρ οὖν, O. C. 980 οὐ γὰρ οὖν, ib. 985 ἀλλ' ἐν γὰρ οὖν.—ἐπαιτιῶμαι κείνην, I accuse her, βουλεῦσαι ἴσον τοῦδε τάφου, of having had an equal share in plotting this burial. For the inf. after ἐπαιτιᾶσθαι cp. El. 603 ἃν πολλὰ δή με σοὶ τρέφειν μιάστορα | ἐπητιάσω. Ar. Vesp. 1446 Αἴσωπον οἱ Δελφοί ποτε...φιάλην ἐπῃτιῶντο κλέψαι. Plat. Critias 120 C εἴ τίς τι παραβαίνειν αὐτῶν αἰτιῷτό τινα. For the substantival ἴσον with gen., cp.

any that worships Zeus at the altar of our house,—she and her kinsfolk shall not avoid a doom most dire ; for indeed I charge that other with a like share in the plotting of this burial.

And summon her—for I saw her e'en now within,—raving, and not mistress of her wits. So oft, before the deed, the mind stands self-convicted in its treason, when folks are plotting mischief in the dark. But verily this, too, is hateful,—when one who hath been caught in wickedness then seeks to make the crime a glory.

Nauck (ascribing it to Tournier, whose text, however, has ὀρθῶς).   **496** θέλῃ L, with ει deleted between λ and η.

Eur. *Ion.* 818 ὁμοῖοι εἶναι τῆς τύχης τ' ἴσον φέρειν: id. *Ph.* 547 δωμάτων ἔχων ἴσον.—Another construction is possible: ἴσον ἐπαιτιῶμαι κείνην τοῦδε τοῦ τάφου, βουλεῦσαι : 'I charge her equally with this burial,—*i.e.* with plotting it.' The constr. with the gen. is frequent (Aesch. *P. V.* 974 ἢ κἀμὲ γάρ τι ξυμφορᾶς ἐπαιτιᾷ ;): the objection here is that the epexegetic infin. βουλεῦσαι, requiring a case different from that governed by ἐπαιτιῶμαι, ought to come last: cp. Plat. *Crito* 52 B οὐδ' ἐπιθυμία σε ἄλλης πόλεως οὐδ' ἄλλων νόμων ἔλαβεν εἰδέναι : Eur. *Med.* 1399, χρῆξω στόματος | παίδων ὁ τάλας προσπτύξασθαι. In *O. T.* 644 εἴ σέ τι | δέδρακ', ὀλοίμην, ὧν ἐπαιτιᾷ με δρᾶν, ὧν might represent either (*a*) τούτων ὧν, δρᾶν being epexegetic, or (*b*) τούτων ἅ (acc. governed by δρᾶν); the latter is simplest. —βουλεῦσαι, of plotting mischief, as *Tr.* 807 τοιαῦτα...πατρὶ βουλεύσασ' ἐμῷ: *Ai.* 1055 στρατῷ...βουλεύσας φόνον.

491 καὶ νιν καλεῖτ', 'And now call her.' This is the καὶ so frequent in the orators, when the speaker turns to call for witnesses, documents, etc.: Lys. or. 16 § 13 καὶ μοι ἀνάβηθι, or. 13 § 35 καὶ μοι ἀνάγνωθι τὸ ψήφισμα.

492 λυσσῶσαν...οὐδ' ἐπ.: cp. *O. T.* 58 n.: Her. 9. 55 μαινόμενον καὶ οὐ φρενήρεα. — ἐπήβολον, 'in possession of' (*compos*), a word used by Aesch. (*P. V.* 444 φρενῶν, *Ag.* 542 νόσου), but not by Eur. It belonged to the diction of Ionian epos, appearing first in *Od.* 2. 319 (οὐ γάρ νηὸς ἐπήβολος οὐδ' ἐρετάων), and is used by Herod. ; Plato, too, admits it (as *Euthyd.* 289 B ἐπιστήμης ἐπηβόλους). Düntzer would derive it from ἐπί and ἄβολος ('meeting with'), assumed from the same verb ἀβολέω as = ἀντιβολέω (Ap. Rhod. 3. 1148); but it is more likely that it was simply an epic metrical license for

ἐπίβολος. The sense seems to come from ἐπιβάλλομαι as = 'to throw oneself on' a thing, and so take possession of it.

493 f. ὁ θυμὸς τῶν...τεχνωμένων, the mind of those who are planning nothing aright (planning utter mischief) in the dark, φιλεῖ κλοπεὺς ἠρῆσθαι, is apt to stand convicted of its treason, πρόσθεν, before ...nd,—*i.e.* before the treasonable deed ...s been done. For the order of words ὁ θυμὸς being divided from the attributive gen. by the predicate), cp. Thuc. 2. ἐ ἡ δὲ εὔνοια παρὰ πολὺ ἐποίει τῶν ἀνθρώπων μᾶλλον ἐς τοὺς Λακεδαιμονίους. *Ismene* has not yet been caught in a disloyal act ; but her guilty conscience has already shown itself. κλοπεύς here answers to κλέπτειν as = 'to do by stealth or fraud,' *Ai.* 1137 πόλλ' ἂν κακῶς λάθρᾳ σὺ κλέψειας κακά. It denotes the plotter's treachery towards the State, not the betrayal of the plotter by his own conscience (as some have taken it). ἠρῆσθαι κλοπεύς (without ὤν), as *O. T.* 576 φωρεὺς ἁλώσομαι: the perf. (expressing that the exposure is already decisive), like πυρήσεθαι *ib.* 1050.—τεχνωμένων midd., as usual; cp. *Ph.* 80 τεχνᾶσθαι κακά. This is better than to make it pass., as a gen. absol., ('when utter mischief is being contrived,') a constr. which seems to require the change of ὀρθῶς to ὀρθῶν, since τὰ μηδὲν ὀρθῶς could hardly mean, 'things which (are) in no wise well,' *sc.* ἔχοντα. οἱ μηδὲν ὀρθῶς τεχνώμενοι = those who plan nothing in such a way as to be right (the generic μή): cp. *Ph.* 407 παντὸς ἂν λόγου κακοῦ | γλώσσῃ θιγόντα καὶ πανουργίας, ἀφ' ἧς | μηδὲν δίκαιον ἐς τέλος μέλλοι ποιεῖν.

495 f. γε μέντοι: cp. *O. T.* 442 n. '(I hate such plotting in the dark :) however, I certainly hate this also,—when a detected traitor seeks to glorify the treason.' Is-

ΑΝ. θέλεις τι μεῖζον ἢ κατακτεῖναί μ' ἑλών;

ΚΡ. ἐγὼ μὲν οὐδέν· τοῦτ' ἔχων, ἅπαντ' ἔχω.

ΑΝ. τί δῆτα μέλλεις; ὡς ἐμοὶ τῶν σῶν λόγων
ἀρεστὸν οὐδέν, μηδ' ἀρεσθείη ποτέ·   500
οὕτω δὲ καὶ σοὶ τἄμ' ἀφανδάνοντ' ἔφυ.
καίτοι πόθεν κλέος γ' ἂν εὐκλεέστερον
κατέσχον ἢ τὸν αὐτάδελφον ἐν τάφῳ
τιθεῖσα; τούτοις τοῦτο πᾶσιν ἁνδάνειν
λέγοιτ' ἄν, εἰ μὴ γλῶσσαν ἐγκλήοι φόβος.   505
ἀλλ' ἡ τυραννὶς πολλά τ' ἄλλ' εὐδαιμονεῖ,
κἄξεστιν αὐτῇ δρᾶν λέγειν θ' ἃ βούλεται.

ΚΡ. σὺ τοῦτο μούνη τῶνδε Καδμείων ὁρᾷς.

---

497 L prefixes ΑΓ (by error for ΑΝ).—τι] τί L.   **500** ἀρεσθείη] ἀρέστ' εἴη Elmsley.
504 ἀνδάνει L, with most of the later mss., but A and V² have ἀνδάνειν.   **505** ἐγ-
κλείσαι L: ἐκκλείσαι or ἐγκλήσαι r: ἐγκλῆσαι Erfurdt: ἐγκλήοι Schaefer.   Cp. cr. n.
on O. T. 1388.   **506 f.** These two vv. are rejected as spurious by A. Jacob, who

---

mene's guilty terror is contrasted with
Antigone's impudent hardihood,—as
Creon deems it. μισῶ...ὅταν, like μέμ-
νησαι ὅτε...ἐποίησας (Xen. Occ. 2. 11),
οἶδ' ἶριζ Αἴας εἷλκε (Eur. Tro. 70) etc.—
ἔπειτα, like εἶτα, as Ai. 760 ὅστις ἀνθρώ-
που φύσιν | βλαστὼν ἔπειτα μὴ κατ' ἄνθρω-
πον φρονῇ.—καλλύνειν, to make καλός
(fr. 786 πρόσωπα καλλύνουσα, of the wax-
ing moon), here, to make specious: so
Plat. Legg. 944 B εὐδιάβολον κακὸν καλ-
λύνων (a soldier excusing himself for
ὅπλων ἀποβολή).
    497 f. θέλεις τι μεῖζον, sc. ποιεῖν,—
not that θέλω could not take a simple
acc., but a Greek would mentally supply
a general inf. to balance κατακτεῖναι: cp.
Thuc. 3. 85 ἀπόγνοια...τοῦ ἄλλο τι (sc.
ποιεῖν) ἢ κρατεῖν τῆς γῆς.—ἑλών: cp.
O. T. 641 κτεῖναι λαβών.—ἐγὼ μὲν οὐδέν.
He desires nothing more,—and will take
nothing less.—ἅπαντ' ἔχω: cp. Eur. Or.
749 τοῦτο πάντ' ἔχω μαθών ('tell me that,
and I am satisfied').
    500 ἀρεστὸν οὐδέν, not ἀρεστὸς οὐδείς:
cp. O. T. 1195 βροτῶν | οὐδέν.—μηδ'
ἀρεσθείη. Cp. 686· If sound (as it seems
to be), this is a solitary example of the
aor. pass. ἡρέσθην as='became pleasing,'
and must be defended by the pass. (or
midd.) ἀρέσκομαι as used by Herod., 6.
128 ἡρέσκοντο, 'they were approved' (or,
'they pleased'): 9. 79 μήτε Αἰγυπτηοι
ἄδοιμι μήτε τοῖσι ταῦτα ἀρέσκεται (those
who approve this course). Considering

the Ionic affinities of Attic Tragedy, this
use of ἀρέσκομαι in Ionic prose seems a
sufficient warrant for a corresponding use
of ἡρέσθην, whether we take it as properly
passive ('was approved'), or as a pass.
form used to supplement the middle
('pleased'). I do not add Eur. fr. 942
θεοῖς ἀρέσκου, because there I should read
θεοὺς ἀρέσκου, 'propitiate the gods,' the
Attic use of the midd.; cp. Xen. Mem. 4.
3. 16 νόμος δὲ δήπου πανταχοῦ ἐστι κατὰ
δύναμιν ἱεροῖς θεοὺς ἀρέσκεσθαι, 'to propitiate the gods with sacrifice.' The Attic
passive meant 'I am pleased,' Thuc. 1.
129 τοῖς λόγοις τοῖς ἀπὸ σοῦ ἀρέσκομαι,
5. 37 οἱ βοιωτάρχαι ἠρέσκοντο, but occurs
only in pres. and impf.: ἡρέσθην, as the
corresponding aor., appears only in later
Greek, as Paus. 2. 13. 8 οὐκ ἀρεσθεὶς τῷ
δοθέντι πώματι. The traditional ἀρεσθείη,
then, is at least not less probable than
Hermann's ἀρεσθείην, when the whole
question is viewed in the light of attested
usage. As to Elmsley's neat ἀρέστ' εἴη,
a fatal objection to it is the change to
the impers. plur.; as if one said, 'not one
of your words pleases me; and never may
I feel pleasure:' (without, 'in them.')
    501 τἀμά, a general phrase, 'my
views.' Cp. El. 1050 οὔτε γὰρ σὺ τἀμ'
ἔπη | τολμᾷς ἐπαινεῖν οὔτ' ἐγὼ τοὺς σοὺς
τρόπους.—ἔφυ with partic. ('are naturally
...'), cp. ... T. 9 πρέπων ἔφυς.
    502 καίτοι marks the transition to
another and higher point of view than

AN. Wouldst thou do more than take and slay me?

CR. No more, indeed; having that, I have all.

AN. Why then dost thou delay? In thy discourse there is nought that pleases me,—never may there be!—and so my words must needs be unpleasing to thee. And yet, for glory—whence could I have won a nobler, than by giving burial to mine own brother? All here would own that they thought it well, were not their lips sealed by fear. But royalty, blest in so much besides, hath the power to do and say what it will.

CR. Thou differest from all these Thebans in that view.

is followed by Dindorf, Meineke, Nauck, and M. Schmidt.—In L there has been an attempt to make πολλὰ τἆλλ' out of πολλά τ' ἀλλ'.—δρᾶν, omitted in the text of L, has been added above the line by an early corrector.

Creon's. '*Thou* wilt never approve my deed. *And yet* how could I have won a better claim to the approval of all who judge rightly?' In καίτοι πόθεν κλέος γ' the absence of caesura gives a slower movement, just as in v. 44: she communes with her own thought. κλέος... εὐκλεέστερον, like δύσπνοοι πνοαί (587), φρένες δύσφρονες (1261), πότοι δύσπονοι (1277): *Ph.* 894 ξύνηθες...ἔθος. Distinguish the case of the adj. compounded with a noun merely cognate in sense to the subst.; above, v. 7 n.

503 ff. ἐν τάφῳ τιθεῖσα, *i.e.* symbolically, by sprinkling dust and pouring χοαί: cp. 80, 395, and *O. C.* 1410 n.— τούτοις πᾶσιν λέγοιτο ἄν, by all these it would be said, τοῦτο ἀνδάνειν (αὐτοῖς), that this seems good to them: for dat. with pres. pass. (a constr. usually restricted to the pf. pass.) cp. Menander *Sentent.* 511 τἀληθὲς ἀνθρώποισιν οὐχ εὑρίσκεται. If the datives were taken with ἀνδάνειν, λέγοιτο ἄν would be too indefinite. At the same time the proximity of ἀνδάνειν has influenced the construction. ταὐτὸ has been suggested, but there is nothing suspicious in τούτοις τοῦτο, which Nauck groundlessly condemns.—The pres. ἐγκλῄει is required by the sense, since the act is a continuing one; ἐγκλῆ-σαι would refer to some given moment or particular occasion. The MSS. favour the aor., but most of the recent edd. rightly give the pres.

505 f. ἀλλ' ἡ τυραννίς. '(If these men dared to say what they think, they would applaud me.) *But* royalty has the advantage of being able to do and say what it pleases, without being opposed in word or deed':—and so these men are silent. These are two excellent and vigorous lines,—not only free from the slightest internal mark of spuriousness, but admirably suited to their place, both by thought and by expression. It was an extraordinary freak of arbitrary criticism to reject them. The reasons assigned for doing so deserve mention only for their curious weakness; as (a) ἀλλ' ἡ ought to be ἡ γάρ—Dindorf: (b) Antigone should not mention the *advantages* of the τυραννίς—A. Jacob: (c) Creon could not be reproached with δρᾶν λέγειν θ' ἃ βούλεται—Nauck: of which last objection Bellermann, in his simple and triumphant vindication of these verses, justly says that it is 'wholly unintelligible.' (d) Wecklein, too, has effectively defended them. We may add that Creon's reply in v. 508, which refers primarily to vv. 504 f., does not therefore ignore vv. 506 f., since these two vv. cohere closely with the former: vv. 504—507 express a single thought. For similar references in tragedy to the τυραννίς, as it was viewed by Greeks in the historical age, cp. Aesch. *P. V.* 224 f., Eur. *Ion* 621—632.

508 f. μούνη: τῶνδε refers to the Chorus: for the Ionic form, cp. 308, 705. —τοῦτο...ὁρᾷς, seest this, = 'takest this view'; viz., that thy deed is right, and that only my power prevents its being publicly approved. A very rare use of ὁρᾶν: indeed, I know no strictly similar instance, for we cannot compare *O. T.* 284, where see n.: still, it is natural enough. Cp. Plat. *Phaedr.* 276 A ἄλλον ὁρῶμεν λόγον. So we say, 'I do not see it,' = 'I cannot take that view.' μούνη τῶνδε: cp. 101 κάλλιστον...τῶν προτέρων, n.—ὑπίλλουσιν (for the spelling cp. n. in

7—2

ΑΝ. ὁρῶσι χοῦτοι· σοὶ δ' ὑπίλλουσιν στόμα.
ΚΡ. σὺ δ' οὐκ ἐπαιδεῖ, τῶνδε χωρὶς εἰ φρονεῖς;   510
ΑΝ. οὐδὲν γὰρ αἰσχρὸν τοὺς ὁμοσπλάγχνους σέβειν.
ΚΡ. οὔκουν ὅμαιμος χὠ καταντίον θανών;
ΑΝ. ὅμαιμος ἐκ μιᾶς τε καὶ ταὐτοῦ πατρός.
ΚΡ. πῶς δῆτ' ἐκείνῳ δυσσεβῆ τιμᾷς χάριν;
ΑΝ. οὐ μαρτυρήσει ταῦθ' ὁ κατθανὼν νέκυς.   515
ΚΡ. εἴ τοί σφε τιμᾷς ἐξ ἴσου τῷ δυσσεβεῖ.
ΑΝ. οὐ γάρ τι δοῦλος, ἀλλ' ἀδελφὸς ὤλετο.
ΚΡ. πορθῶν δὲ τήνδε γῆν· ὁ δ' ἀντιστὰς ὕπερ.
ΑΝ. ὅμως ὅ γ' Ἅιδης τοὺς νόμους τούτους ποθεῖ.
ΚΡ. ἀλλ' οὐχ ὁ χρηστὸς τῷ κακῷ λαχεῖν *ἴσους.   520
ΑΝ. τίς οἶδεν εἰ κάτωθεν εὐαγῆ τάδε;

509 ἰπίλλουσιν L: ὑπίλλουσι r (as A), or ὑπείλουσι (V⁴).   513 μιᾶς τε MSS.:
μιᾶς γε Hermann.—πατρός] Tournier conject. γεγώς.   514 δυσσεβῶ L, with
ῃ over ῶι: δυσσεβεῖ or δυσσεβῆ r.—τιμᾶις L, with gl. ἀντὶ τοῦ νέμεις.   516 εἰ
τοί σσφε L: εἰ τοί σφε r.   518 πορθῶν δε (without acc.) L. Most of the later

Appendix on 340), lit., 'turn' (or 'roll')
'under,' said of an animal putting its tail
between its legs; cp. Eur. fr. 544 (from
his Οἰδίπους,—referring to the Sphinx)
οὐρὰν δ' ὑπίλασ' ὑπὸ λεοντόπουν βάσιν | κα-
θίζετ'. Verg. Aen. 11. 812 (a terrified
wolf) caudamque remulcens Subiecit pavi-
tantem utero. Here, 'keep down' the
utterance of their thoughts; 'make their
lips subservient' to thee. Cp. σαίνειν,
adulari.—Euphony commends, though
metre does not require, the ν ἐφελκυστι-
κόν, which L gives. Cp. 571.

510 f. σὺ δ' οὐκ ἐπαιδεῖ; And art thou
not ashamed of it (cp. ἐπαισχύνομαι), if
thou thinkest otherwise than they do?—
thinkest, namely, that thou art free to act
on thy own views, regardless of thy king.
For the sake of argument, he concedes
their possible sympathy with her, but insists on their loyal behaviour. She answers, 'No, I am not ashamed, for I am
doing nothing shameful.'

512 f. ὅμαιμος always of brother and
sister in Soph.: O. C. 330 n.—ἐκ μιᾶς τε.
The soundness of the text is thoroughly
vindicated by Plat. Legg. 627 C (quoted
by Schneidewin), πολλοὶ ἀδελφοί που γέ-
νοιντ' ἂν ἑνὸς ἀνδρός τε καὶ μιᾶς υἱεῖς,
which also confirms the MS. τε against
the conjecture γε.

514 f. πῶς δῆτ': why, then, dost thou
render (to Polyneices) a tribute impious
in the sight of Eteocles?—i.e., which

places the latter on the same level with
the former.—ἐκείνῳ, ethic dat., 'in his
judgment': cp. 904, O. C. 1446 ἀνάξιαι…
πᾶσιν, and ib. 810 n., O. T. 40. We cannot well render, 'impious towards him,'
which would be πρὸς or εἰς ἐκεῖνον: nor
can the dat. be one of 'interest,' as though
δυσσεβῆ were equivalent to βλαβερὰν.
The next verse agrees well with ἐκείνῳ
being ethic dat.: 'he will not so testify,'
= 'he will not say that he thinks my act
impious.'—χάριν is usu. explained as acc.
of the inner object, like τιμᾷς τιμήν. But
it would evidently be awkward to have an
objective acc. added, as τιμῶ χάριν αὐτόν.
Rather τιμᾷς is here slightly deflected
from the sense, 'to honour by observance,'
'to observe duly,' as Eur. Tro. 1210 οὓς
Φρύγες νόμοισι | τιμῶσιν, Ion 1045 τὴν
εὐσέβειαν…τιμᾷς, and means, 'to render
duly,' as religious observance requires.
So I should take it also in the parallel
phrase, Eur. Or. 828 πατρῴαν | τιμῶν
χάριν, duly rendering grace to thy sire.—
ὁ κατθανὼν νέκυς: cp. 26.

516 εἴ τοι, siquidem: O. T. 549.—
σφε: cp. 44 n.—ἐξ ἴσου, only on a level
with, as O. T. 1019. So ἴσον = 'equally
little' (Her. 2. 3), or 'equally vain' (id.
8. 79): and id. 8. 109 τά τε ἱρὰ καὶ τὰ
ἴδια ἐν ὁμοίῳ ἐποιέετο, i.e. made sacred
things of (only) the same account as
things profane. Cp. 393.

517 οὐ γάρ τι δοῦλος. No, Eteocles

ANTIΓONH 101

AN. These also share it; but they curb their tongues for thee.
CR. And art thou not ashamed to act apart from them?
AN. No; there is nothing shameful in piety to a brother.
CR. Was it not a brother, too, that died in the opposite cause?
AN. Brother by the same mother and the same sire.
CR. Why, then, dost thou render a grace that is impious in his sight?
AN. The dead man will not say that he so deems it.
CR. Yea, if thou makest him but equal in honour with the wicked.
AN. It was his brother, not his slave, that perished.
CR. Wasting this land; while *he* fell as its champion.
AN. Nevertheless, Hades desires these rites.
CR. But the good desires not a like portion with the evil.
AN. Who knows but this seems blameless in the world below?

MSS. have δέ, but a few γε. The older edd. give γε: most of the recent, δέ. **519** ὁμῶς Mekler.—τοὺσ νόμουσ τούτουσ MSS.: schol. marg. of L. γρ. τοὺς νόμουσ ἴσουσ.—Semitelos writes ὁμοὺς (for ὅμως)...τούτοις. **520** λαχεῖν L: λαβεῖν Γ.— ἴσοι MSS. Bergk conject. ἴσα (which Nauck adopts), or ἴσον. Nauck also suggests ἴσους (if τούτους be kept in 519). **521** κάτω᾿στιν MSS. In L, γρ. κάτωθεν is written

cannot complain, for Polyneices was not his slave—his natural inferior—but his brother, and had the same claim on me that he had. Creon insists on the difference between the loyal man and the disloyal. Antigone dwells on the fact that both men had the same claim on her natural piety, and (519) on her sense of religious duty.

518 τορῶν δέ: for δέ introducing an objection, cp. *O. T.* 379: for the partic., *ib.* 1001, 1011.—ὁ δ᾽, but the other (perished) ἀντιστὰς ὑπὲρ τῆσδε γῆς, as this land's champion. ὑπερ is paroxytone as virtually following its case, since the gen. is supplied from τήνδε γῆν. Cp. *Ai.* 1231 τοῦ μηδὲν ἀντέστης ὑπερ.

519 τούτους, the reading of the MSS., has been rejected by nearly all modern editors in favour of ἴσους, which the Scholiast mentions as a variant. But the simple τούτους is perfectly suitable,— 'these laws,' the laws of sepulture (τὸ θάπτειν, as a schol. paraphrases); and everything that ἴσους would convey is already expressed by ὅμως. 'One was the country's foe, the other its champion— granted. *Nevertheless* Hades desires these laws,'—*i.e.* even in the case of the foe. A corruption of ἴσους into τούτους is

very improbable. Rather ἴσους was merely one of those conjectures which so often appear in the margin of the MSS., having for their object the supposed improvement of a point. The MS. ἴσοι in 520 does not strengthen the case for ἴσους here.

520 The MS. λαχεῖν ἴσος is usu. explained, 'equal in respect to obtaining (rites),' *i.e.* with an equal claim to rites. The phrase is not only without any parallel, but seems impossible. ἴσοι λαχεῖν νόμιμα would be very strange; ἴσοι λαχεῖν, absolutely, is stranger still. The train of thought strongly favours ἴσους (which Soph. would have written ΙΣΟΣ), as Nauck suggests and Semitelos reads. 'Hades may desire these rites; but the good man does not (desire) to receive only the same rites as the wicked': *i.e.* Eteocles will not be satisfied with the equality merely because Polyneices was his brother (517): he will think of the contrast between that brother's merits and his own. The dead can be said λαγχάνειν νόμους (of burial), in the sense of obtaining that which the νόμος give. Therefore we need not write ἴσον or ἴσα.

521 f. κάτωθεν, simply 'below': cp. 1070, Eur. *Alc.* 424 τῷ κάτωθεν ἀσπόνδῳ

ΚΡ. ˙οὔτοι ποθ᾽ οὑχθρός, οὐδ᾽ ὅταν θάνῃ, φίλος.

ΑΝ. ˙οὔτοι συνέχθειν, ἀλλὰ συμφιλεῖν ἔφυν.

ΚΡ. ˙κάτω νυν ἐλθοῦσ᾽, εἰ φιλητέον, φίλει
  κείνους· ἐμοῦ δὲ ζῶντος οὐκ ἄρξει γυνή.   525

ΧΟ. ˙καὶ μὴν πρὸ πυλῶν ἥδ᾽ Ἰσμήνη,
  ᵛφιλάδελφα κάτω δάκρυ᾽ *εἰβομένη·
  ᵛνεφέλη δ᾽ ὀφρύων ὕπερ αἱματόεν
  ᵛῥέθος αἰσχύνει,
  ᴵτέγγουσ᾽ εὐῶπα παρειάν.   530

ΚΡ. ᴵσὺ δ᾽, ἢ κατ᾽ οἴκους ὡς ἐχιδν᾽ ὑφειμένη

above. **528** οὔτοι συνέχθειν] In L the first hand seems to have written οὐ τοινυν εχειν, but added θ above χ, and S completed the correction. **524** νυν] νῦν L. **525** ἄρξει] L has ει in erasure, prob. from η. **527** δάκρυα λειβόμενα L, δάκρυα

θεῷ: Dem. or. 23 § 28 ὁ κάτωθεν νόμος, the law below (= the continuation of a law alread cited). We need not understand herey'if these things are approved *from* below.' κάτω᾽στιν has the MS. authority: but it is most improbable that Soph. would have given such a needlessly unpleasing verse, and the change is sufficiently explained by a later belief that the sense required κάτω.—εὐαγῆ, right in respect to ἄγος, i.e. free from it, pure (*O. T.* 921). She means: 'who can tell if Eteocles, in the world below, will not think it consonant with piety that Polyneices should be honoured?' Perhaps earthly feuds are made up there. Creon answers, 'No,—foe once, foe always,—even in death: Eteocles *will* resent it.' Cp. *Od.* 11. 543 where the spirit of Ajax in Hades will not speak to Odysseus—κεχολωμένη εἴνεκα νίκης | τήν μιν ἐγὼ νίκησα.—There would be far less point in Creon's words if we took them to mean, ' *my* dead foe is still my foe' (cp. *Ai.* 1348, 1372).
528 οὔτοι συνέχθειν. 'Even if my brothers hate each other still, my nature prompts me, not to join Eteocles in hating Po yneices, but to love each brother as he lloves me': cp. 73 φίλη...φίλου μέτα. Cp. Polybius 1. 14 φιλόφιλον δεῖ εἶναι τὸν ἀγαθὸν ἄνδρα καὶ φιλόπατρυν, καὶ συμμισεῖν τοῖς φίλοις τοὺς ἐχθροὺς καὶ συναγαπᾶν τοὺς φίλους. Eur. imitates our verse, *I. A.* 407 (Agam. to Menelaus) συσσωφρονεῖν γάρ, οὐχὶ συννοσεῖν ἔφυν, 'nay, my sympathies are with prudence, not with frenzy.'

524 f. νῦν, as *Ai.* 87, *Tr.* 92, *Ph.* 1196, but νῦν *O. T.* 658, and oft.—κείνους = τοὺς ἐκεῖ, the dead. Nauck proposes νεκρούς, which would be a deplorable change. For the pause after the emphatic word, cp. 46 n.
526 f. καὶ μὴν introducing the new person: *O. C.* 549 n. At Creon's command (491), two πρόσπολοι had gone to bring Ismene. The door from which she now enters is that by which she had left the stage (99). It is supposed to lead to the γυναικωνῖτις (cp. 578).—εἰβομένη, the correction of Triclinius for the MS. λειβομένη, enables us to keep δάκρυα, instead of changing it to δάκρυ, when φιλάδελφα must be taken as adv. (cp. *O. T.* 883 n.). The Schol. so took it (he paraphrases by φιλαδέλφως), and it would seem, therefore, that he read δάκρυ λειβομένη. But, though this constr. is quite admissible, it would be far more natural that φιλάδελφα should agree with δάκρυα. In *O. C.* 1251 we have λείβων δάκρυον: neither λείβω nor εἴβω occurs elsewhere in Soph.; and the only other place in Tragedy where εἴβω has good support is Aesch. *P. V.* 400, where Hermann, by reading δακρυσίστακτον ἀπ᾽ ὄσσων ῥαδινῶν δ᾽ εἰβομένα ῥέος, for the MS. δακρυσίστακτον δ᾽...λειβομένα, restores the metre. But κατὰ δάκρυον εἴβειν and δάκρυα λείβειν were equally familiar as Homeric phrases; and if an Attic poet could use the latter, there was certainly no reason why he should not use the former. I may remark, too, that κάτω points to a reminiscence of the phrase

CR. A foe is never a friend—not even in death.| Ν γ
AN. 'Tis not my nature to join in hating, but in loving.
CR. Pass, then, to the world of the dead, and, if thou must needs love, love them. While I live, no woman shall rule me.

Enter ISMENE *from the house, led in by two attendants.*

CH. Lo, yonder Ismene comes forth, shedding such tears as fond sisters weep; a cloud upon her brow casts its shadow over her darkly-flushing face, and breaks in rain on her fair cheek.
CR. And thou, who, lurking like a viper in my house,

λειβομένα or δάκρυα λειβομένη r. δάκρυ' εἰβομένη Triclinius: δάκρυ λειβομένη Wex.
528 αἱματόεν] ἱμερόεν M. Schmidt, adding the words ἱσταμένη | τὸ πρίν after ὑπερ.

with εἴβειν, for Homer never says κατὰ δάκρυα λείβειν. Nothing is more natural than that εἰβομένη should have become λειβομένη in the MSS., the latter word being much the commoner.—κάτω, adv., 'downwards': cp. 716, fr. 620 ὦτα κυλλαίνων κάτω. Nauck's objection, that κάτω εἰβομένη could not stand for κατειβομένη, would have force only if κάτω were necessarily a prep., substituted for κατά. He proposes κατal (cp. καταιβάτης).

528 f. νεφέλη δ' ὀφρύων ὕπερ, a cloud of grief (resting) on her brow,—as dark clouds rest on a mountain-summit: cp. Eur. *Hipp.* 173 στυγνὸν δ' ὀφρύων νέφος αὐξάνεται: Aesch. *Theb.* 228 τὰν ἀμηχανον | κἀκ χαλεπᾶς δύας ὑπερθ' ὀμμάτων | κρημναμέναν νεφέλαν: so συννεφὴς = συνωφρυωμένος. Cp. *Deme supercilio nubem* (Hor. *Ep.* 1. 18. 94). The cloud of sorrow is associated with the rain of tears: cp. Shaksp. *Ant.* 3. 2. 51 *Will Caesar weep?—He has a cloud in 's face.*—αἱματόεν, here, '*suffused with* blood,' darkly flushed. This application of αἱματόεις to the human face seems unparalleled, though in *Anthol. P.* 6. 154 Leonidas of Tarentum (c. 280 B.C.) has φύλλα τε πεφυσμένων αἱματόεντα ῥόδων. Eur. *Phoen.* 1487 was less daring when he called a dark blush τὰν ὑπὸ βλεφάροις | φοίνικ' ('crimson'), ἐρύθημα προσώπου. It recalls the well-known fragment of Ion in Athen. 603 E, where the schoolmaster objects to Phrynichus's ἐπὶ πορφυρέαις παρῇσι, on the principle, οὐ κάρτα δεῖ τὸ καλὸν τῷ μὴ καλῷ φαινομένῳ εἰκάζειν,—and Sophocles makes a lively defence of it. Shaksp. uses 'bloody' for 'blood-red': *Hen. V.* 1. 2. 101 *unwind your bloody flag.*—ῥέθος = πρόσωπον, as Eur. *H. F.* 1203 πάρες ἀπ' ὀμμάτων | πέπλον, ἀπόδικε, ῥέθος δελίῳ

δεῖξον. Cp. Eustathius 1090, 27 ἰστέον ὅτι ῥέθεα οἱ μὲν ἄλλοι τὰ μέλη φασίν, Αἰολεῖς δὲ μόνοι, κατὰ τοὺς παλαιούς, τὸ πρόσωπον ῥέθος καλοῦσιν. This suggests that the Attic dramatists had lyric precedent for this use of ῥέθος: as Lycophron (173) may also have had for using it as = σῶμα. The Homeric use is confined to the phrase ἐκ ῥεθέων (thrice in *Il.*, never in *Od.*).—αἰσχύνει, *i.e.* overcasts its sunny beauty: cp. Thomson, *Spring* 21, *Winter* ...*bids his driving sleets* Deform *the day delightless.*

531 σὺ δ' with φέρ', εἰπέ (534).—ὑφειμένη. *submissa*, 'lurking,' as a viper lurks under stones: Arist. *H. A.* 8. 15 αἱ δ' ἔχιδναι ὑπὸ τὰς πέτρας ἀποκρύπτουσιν ἑαυτάς. Eur. *H. F.* 72 σῴζω νεοσσοὺς ὄρνις ὡς ὑφειμένη, like a cowering hen (ὑφειμένοις Kirchhoff). The word may also suggest a contrast between Antigone's bolder nature and the submissive demeanour of Ismene (cp. *El.* 335 νῦν δ' ἐν κακοῖς μοι πλεῖν ὑφειμένη δοκεῖ, 'with shortened sail'). But we should not render it by 'submissive'; its primary reference is to the image of the ἔχιδνα. Others render, 'having crept in,' *clam immissa.* The act. can mean to 'send in secretly' (see on ὑφεὶς, *O. T.* 387), but the pass. ὑφίεσθαι does not seem to occur in a corresponding sense.—ἔχιδνα: cp. *Tr.* 770 (the poison works) φοινίας | ἐχθρᾶς ἐχίδνης ἰὸς ὤν. So of Clytaemnestra (Aesch. *Cho.* 249): Eur. *Andr.* 271 ἐχίδνης καὶ πυρὸς περαιτέρω: cp. *Ion* 1262. This image for domestic treachery is quaintly illustrated by the popular notions mentioned in Arist. *Mirab.* 165 (p. 846 *b* 18 Berl. ed.) τοῦ περκνοῦ ἔχεως τῇ ἐχίδνῃ συγγινομένου, ἡ ἔχιδνα ἐν τῇ συνουσίᾳ τὴν κεφαλὴν ἀποκόπτει. διὰ τοῦτο καὶ τὰ τέκνα,

λήθουσά μ' ἐξέπινες, οὐδ' ἐμάνθανον
τρέφων δύ' ἄτα κἀπαναστάσεις θρόνων.
φέρ', εἰπὲ δή μοι, καὶ σὺ τοῦδε τοῦ τάφου
φήσεις μετασχεῖν, ἢ 'ξομεῖ τὸ μὴ εἰδέναι; 535
ΙΣ. δέδρακα τοὔργον, εἴπερ ἥδ' ὁμορροθεῖ,
καὶ ξυμμετίσχω καὶ φέρω τῆς αἰτίας.
ΑΝ. ἀλλ' οὐκ ἐάσει τοῦτό γ' ἡ δίκη σ', ἐπεὶ
οὔτ' ἠθέλησας οὔτ' ἐγὼ 'κοινωσάμην.
ΙΣ. ἀλλ' ἐν κακοῖς τοῖς σοῖσιν οὐκ αἰσχύνομαι 540
ξύμπλουν ἐμαυτὴν τοῦ πάθους ποιουμένη.
ΑΝ. ὧν τοὔργον, Ἅιδης χοἰ κάτω ξυνίστορες·
λόγοις δ' ἐγὼ φιλοῦσαν οὐ στέργω φίλην.
ΙΣ. μήτοι, κασιγνήτη, μ' ἀτιμάσῃς τὸ μὴ οὐ
θανεῖν τε σὺν σοὶ τὸν θανόντα θ' ἁγνίσαι. 545
ΑΝ. μή μοι θάνῃς σὺ κοινά, μηδ' ἃ μὴ 'θιγες

531 ᾗ] ἢ L.—ὑφειμένη] ὑφημένη Brunck. Cp. schol., ἡ γὰρ ἔχιδνα λάθρᾳ καθεζομένη τῶν ἀνθρώπων ἐκπίνει τὸ αἶμα.—Semitelos conject. φονία. 532 ἄτα L, ἄται r. 535 ἢ ἐξομῇ τό μ' εἰδέναι L. The acc. on τό has been altered from τὸ: the latter

ὥσπερ τὸν θάνατον τοῦ πατρὸς μετερχόμενα, τὴν γαστέρα τῆς μητρὸς διαρρήγνυσιν. (Cp. Shaksp. *Per.* 1. 1. 64 *I am no viper, yet I feed On mother's flesh.*)

532 λήθουσά μ' ἐξέπινες. It seems unnecessary to suppose a confusion of images. The venom from the echidna's bite is here described as working insidiously, and, at first, almost insensibly. So Heracles says of the poison, which he has already (*Tr.* 770) compared to the echidna's, ἐκ δὲ χλωρὸν αἶμά μου | πέπωκεν ἤδη, *Tr.* 1055. Cp. *El.* 784 ἥδε γὰρ μείζων βλάβη | ξύνοικος ἦν μοι, τοὐμὸν ἐκπίνουσ' ἀεὶ | ψυχῆς ἄκρατον αἶμα.

533 ἄτα κἀπαναστάσεις. The dual is commended, as against ἄτας, by a certain scornful vigour; just as at 58 the dual has an emphasis of its own. And the combination with a plural is no harsher than (*e.g.*) Plat. *Laches* p. 187 A αὐτοὶ εὑρεταὶ γεγονότε. Cp. *O. C.* 530 αὗται δὲ δύ' ἐξ ἐμοῦ...παῖδε, δύο δ' ἄτα. ἀπαναστάσεις, abstract (like ἄτα) for concrete: so 646 πόνους (bad sons): κεῖνος ἢ πᾶσα βλάβη (*Ph.* 622), ὄλεθρος, etc. θρόνων, object. gen. (ἐπανίστασθαι θρόνοις). Creon suspects the sisters of being in league with malcontent citizens (cp. 289), who wish to overthrow his rule.

535 τὸ μή: cp. 443. [Dem.] or. 57

§ 59 οὐκ ἂν ἐξομόσαιτο μὴ οὐκ εἰδέναι. Plat. *Legg.* 949 A ἐξαρνηθέντι καὶ ἐξομοσαμένῳ.

536 f. ὁμορροθεῖ, concurs, consents: fr. 446 ὁμορροθῶ, συνθέλω, | συμπαραινέσας ἔχω. Schol. *ad* Ar. *Av.* 851 ὁμορροθεῖν δὲ κυρίως τὸ ἅμα καὶ συμφώνως ἐρέσσειν. So *Orphic Argonaut.* 254 ὁμορροθέοντες, 'rowing all together' (cp. above on 259). The image thus agrees with ξύμπλουν in 541. Ismene remembers her sister's words: 'even if you should change your mind, I could never welcome you now as my fellow-worker' (69). She says, then, 'I consider myself as having shared in the deed—if my sister will allow me.' Nauck sadly defaces the passage by his rash change, εἴπερ ἥδ'· ὁμορροθῶ.

537 τῆς αἰτίας depends on both verbs. ξυμμετίσχω having prepared the ear for a partitive gen., no harshness is felt in the reference of that gen. to φέρω also. We cannot take the gen. with the first verb only, and regard καὶ φέρω as parenthetic. Some real instances of such a parenthetic construction are given in the n. on 1279 f.: but the supposed examples often break down on scrutiny. Thus in *Ai.* 274, ἔληξε κἀνέπνευσε τῆς νόσου, the gen. goes with both verbs (cp. on *O. C.* 1113): or *O. C.* 1330, see n. there: in Aesch. *P. V.* 331 πάντων μετασχὼν καὶ

wast secretly draining my life-blood, while I knew not that I was nurturing two pests, to rise against my throne—come, tell me now, wilt thou also confess thy part in this burial, or wilt thou forswear all knowledge of it ?

Is. I have done the deed,—if she allows my claim,—and share the burden of the charge.

An. Nay, justice will not suffer thee to do that : thou didst not consent to the deed, nor did I give thee part in it.

Is. But, now that ills beset thee, I am not ashamed to sail the sea of trouble at thy side.

An. Whose was the deed, Hades and the dead are witnesses : a friend in words is not the friend that I love.

Is. Nay, sister, reject me not, but let me die with thee, and duly honour the dead.

An. Share not thou my death, nor claim deeds to which

---

points to the true reading. Cp. 544.   **536** εἴπερ ἥδ' ὁμορροθεῖ] εἴπερ ἥδ'· ὁμορροθῶ Nauck.   **538** σ' added in L by S.   **539** 'κοινωσάμην] κοινωσάμην L. Cp. 457, 546.   **541** τοιουμένην L, but a line has been drawn across the final ν. **544** τὸ μ' οὐ L, with η above μ from the first hand. Cp. 535.   **546** μηδ'] μὴ

τετολμηκὼς ἐμοί, the pron. might be dat. of interest with the second partic.; but we ought perhaps to read συντετολμηκὼς τ' ἐμοί.

538 f. ἀλλ' οὐκ ἐάσει σ': cp. O. C. 407 ἀλλ' οὐκ ἐᾷ τοὐμφύλον αἷμά σ', ὦ πάτερ.— 'κοινωσάμην: prodelision of the augment, as 457 (n.): cp. O. C. 1602 ταχεῖ πόρευσαν σὺν χρόνῳ.

541 ξύμπλουν: cp. Eur. H. F. 1225 καὶ τῶν καλῶν μὲν ὅστις ἀπολαύειν θέλει, | συμπλεῖν δὲ τοῖς φίλοισι δυστυχοῦσιν οὔ. I. T. 599 ὁ ναυστολῶν γάρ εἰμ' ἐγὼ τὰς συμφοράς, | οὗτος δὲ συμπλεῖ.

542 f. Cp. Ph. 1293 ὡς θεοὶ ξυνίστορες.—λόγοις, and not ἔργοις. Cp. Ph. 307 λόγοις | ἐλεοῦσι, they show compassion in word (only). Theognis 979 μή μοι ἀνὴρ εἴη γλώσσῃ φίλος ἀλλὰ καὶ ἔργῳ.

544 f. μή μ' ἀτιμάσῃς, do not reject me (the word used by the suppliant Oed., O. C. 49, 286), τὸ μὴ οὐ (cp. 443 n.), so as to hinder me from dying with thee, and paying due honour to the dead. ἁγνίσαι τὸν θ. is to make him ἁγνός, i.e. to give him the rites which religion requires; as, conversely, a corpse which is ἄμοιρος and ἀκτέριστος is also ἀνόσιος (1071). Eur. Suppl. 1211 ὧν αὐτῶν σώμαθ' ἡγνίσθη πυρί, where their corpses received the rites of fire, i.e. were burned. Cp. 196 n. If Ismene shares in the penalty of the deed,

she will share in the merit.

546 μή μοι, not μή 'μοι, since the main emphasis is on the verbal notion ('share not my death,' rather than, 'share not my death'): cp. 83 n. The combination μή μοι...σὺ has a scornful, repellent tone (cp. O. C. 1441 n.). κοινά, adv.: cp. Ai. 577: O. T. 883 ὑπέροπτα (n.).—μηδ' ἃ μὴ 'θιγες. If this were an instance of θιγγάνω with acc., it would be a solitary instance in Soph., who has θιγγάνω with genitive in nine passages; in Ph. 667 πάρεσται ταῦτά σοι καὶ θιγγάνειν, ταῦτα is nom. Nor is there any authentic instance of θιγγάνω with acc. in classical Greek. In Eur. H. F. 963, πατὴρ δέ νιν | θιγὼν κραταιᾶς χειρὸς ἐννέπει τάδε, νιν depends on ἐννέπει: cp. Ai. 764 ὁ μὲν γὰρ αὐτὸν ἐννέπει· τέκνον, etc. In Theocr. 1. 59 οὐδέ τί πα ποτὶ χεῖλος ἐμὸν θίγεν, the gen. αὐτοῦ is understood with προσέθιγεν, and τι is adv., 'at all.' Nor does ψαύω govern an acc. below in 859, 961 (where see notes). Krüger (II. § 47. 12. 2) treats ἃ here as a sort of adverb (ib. II. § 46. 6. 9), i.e., in a case where you did not put your hand (to the deed, sc. τοῦ ἔργου); but this is very awkward. Rather, I think, there is an unusual kind of attraction, due to the special form of the sentence. We could not say (e.g.) ἃ μὴ ἐρᾷ τις, οὐ θηρᾶται, (ἃ for ταῦτα ὧν). But here μηδ' ὧν μὴ

ⱽποιοῦ σεαυτῆς· ἀρκέσω θνήσκουσ' ἐγώ.

ΙΣ. ʼκαὶ τίς βίος μοι σοῦ λελειμμένῃ φίλος;

ΑΝ.ⱽΚρέοντ' ἐρώτα· τοῦδε γὰρ σὺ κηδεμών.

ΙΣ. ⱽτί ταῦτ' ἀνιᾷς μ', οὐδὲν ὠφελουμένη;   550

ΑΝ.ʼἀλγοῦσα μὲν δῆτ', εἰ *γελῶ γ', ἐν σοὶ γελῶ.

ΙΣ.ᵇʼτί δῆτ' ἂν ἀλλὰ νῦν σ' ἔτ' ὠφελοῖμ' ἐγώ;

ΑΝ.ʼσῶσον σεαυτήν· οὐ φθονῶ σ' ὑπεκφυγεῖν.

ΙΣ. ʼοἴμοι τάλαινα, κἀμπλάκω τοῦ σοῦ μόρου;

ΑΝ.ʼσὺ μὲν γὰρ εἵλου ζῆν, ἐγὼ δὲ κατθανεῖν.   555

ΙΣ. ʼἀλλ' οὐκ ἐπ' ἀρρήτοις γε τοῖς ἐμοῖς λόγοις.

ΑΝ.ʼκαλῶς σὺ μὲν τοῖς, τοῖς δ' ἐγὼ 'δόκουν φρονεῖν.

ΙΣ. ʼκαὶ μὴν ἴση νῷν ἐστιν ἡ 'ξαμαρτία.

ΑΝ.ʼθάρσει· σὺ μὲν ζῇς, ἡ δ' ἐμὴ ψυχὴ πάλαι

ⱽτέθνηκεν, ὥστε τοῖς θανοῦσιν ὠφελεῖν.   560

δ' L.—'θίγες] θίγες L. Cp. 457, 539.   **547** θνήσκουσ' L. For the ι subscript, see comment on *O. T.* 118.   **548** φίλος has been suspected. Wecklein conject. μόνῃ: Hense, μένει: M. Schmidt, δίχα: Nanek, σοῦ γ' ἄτερ λελειμμένη.   **551** δῆτ', εἰ MSS.   Dindorf conject. δή, κεί: Wolff, δή, τὸν.—γελῶ γ'] γελῶτ' L.   Heath conject. γελῶ γ'.   **552** σετ' L (without acc.): σ' ἔτ' τ (σ' ἐπ' E).   **557** καλῶς σὺ μὲν τοι...τοῖσδ' L.   The τ of τοι is in an erasure, which appears to show that τοι has not been made from τοῖς.   Dübner thinks that the first hand wrote μὲν γ' οὐ:

'θίγες ποιοῦ σεαυτῆς would have been intolerable, on account of the second gen. after ποιοῦ. For the sake of compactness, and of clearly marking the object to ποιοῦ, the poet has here allowed ἅ to stand for ταῦτα ὧν. I do not compare *O. C.* 1106, αἰτεῖς ἅ τεύξει, holding that ἅ there = ταῦτα ἅ (not ὧν): see n.

547 ποιοῦ σεαυτῆς, a somewhat rare phrase. Her. 1. 119 ἑαυτοῦ ποιέεται τὸ Κύρου ἔργον. [Plat.] *Hipp. min.* 372 C ἐμαυτοῦ ποιούμενος τὸ μάθημα εἶναι ὡς εὕρημα. Dem. or. 19 § 36 εἰ αὐτὸν ποιούμενος (taking on himself) τὰ τούτων ἁμαρτήματα. In Thuc. 8. 9 ἑαυτοῦ...τὸν στόλον ἴδιον ποιήσασθαι, the gen. goes with the adj.—ἀρκέσω in the pers. constr., cp. *Ai.* 76 ἔνδον ἀρκείτω μένων, and *O. T.* 1061 n.

548 σοῦ λελειμμένη, bereft of thee. λείπομαί τινος, to lag behind, then, fig., to be deprived of, as *El.* 474 γνώμας λειπομένα, Eur. *Alc.* 406 νέος ἐγώ, πάτερ, λείπομαι φίλας | ...ματρός.—φίλος has been groundlessly suspected, for no other reason, seemingly, than because it is masc.

549 κηδεμών, alluding esp. to v. 47.

Cp. Xen. *Anab.* 3. 1. 17 ἡμᾶς δέ, οἷς κηδεμών...οὐδεὶς πάρεστιν, who would have no one *to plead our cause* (no 'friend at court,' such as the younger Cyrus had in his mother Parysatis). In *Il.* 23. 163 κηδεμόνες are the chief mourners for the dead. In Attic, though sometimes poet. for κηδεστής, the word did not necessarily imply kinship.

551 ἀλγοῦσα μὲν δῆτ', yes, indeed, it is to my own pain that I mock *thee*,—if I do mock. δῆτα assents (*O. T.* 445 n.) to οὐδὲν ὠφελουμένη: there is, indeed, no ὄφελος in it, but only ἄλγος—ἐν σοί: cp. *Ai.* 1092 ἐν θανοῦσιν ὑβριστής, ib. 1315 ἐν ἐμοὶ θρασύς.—Heath's εἰ γελῶ γ', for εἰ γέλωτ', is supported by the accent γελῶτ' in L, and seems right. It smooths the construction; and εἰ γελῶ γ' better expresses that the taunt sprang from anguish, not from a wish to pain. Then γέλωτα γελῶ, without an epithet for the subst., is unusual.—Cp. *Ai.* 79 οὔκουν γέλως ἥδιστος εἰς ἐχθροὺς γελᾶν;

552 ἀλλὰ νῦν, now, at least: *O. C.* 1276 ἀλλ' ὑμεῖς γε, n.

554 κἀμπλάκω, and am I to miss the

thou hast not put thy hand : my death will suffice.

Is.   And what life is dear to me, bereft of thee ?

AN.   Ask Creon ; all thy care is for him.

Is.   Why vex me thus, when it avails thee nought ?

AN.   Indeed, if I mock, 'tis with pain that I mock thee.

Is.   Tell me,—how can I serve thee, even now ?

AN.   Save thyself : I grudge not thy escape.

Is.   Ah, woe is me ! And shall I have no share in thy fate ?

AN.   Thy choice was to live ; mine, to die.

Is.   At least thy choice was not made without my protest.

AN.   One world approved thy wisdom ; another, mine.

Is.   Howbeit, the offence is the same for both of us.

AN.   Be of good cheer ; thou livest ; but my life hath long been given to death, that so I might serve the dead.

---

but it seems equally possible that it was μέν σοι. There is no trace of erasure at the two dots after τοι. Of the later MSS., A and V³ have μὲν τοῖσ: others, μὲν θοῦ, μέν θ' οὖ, or μέν τ' οἴου: but none (I believe) μέντοι or μὲν σοί. The schol. in L has μέντοι in the lemma, but explains, σεαυτῇ καλῶς ἐδόκεις φρονεῖν, μὴ συμπράττουσά μοι· ἐγὼ δὲ τούτοις κ.τ.λ. Hence Martin, καλῶς σὺ μὲν σοί.   **560 ὥστε**] Wieseler conject. ὡς σε : Dobree, with the same view, proposed ὠφελεῖς ('and so you are helping a sister who is already as the dead': cp. 552).

---

fate? *i.e.* to be dissociated from it: delib. aor. subj., which can be used, not only in asking what one is *to do*, but also in expressions of despair as to what one must suffer (*Tr.* 973 τί πάθω ;). For ἀμπλακεῖν cp. 910, 1234.

555 ἐλον, alluding to v. 78 f.—ζῆν: for the emphatic pause, cp. *Ph.* 907 οὔκουν ἐν οἷς γε δρᾷς· ἐν οἷς δ' αὐδᾷς, ὀκνῶ.

556 ἐπ' ἀρρήτοις...τοῖς ἐμ. λ. (but you did not choose as) without my words (my arguments against that course) having been spoken,—referring to vv. 49—68. For ἐπί with the negative verbal (= πρὶν τοὺς ἐμοὺς λόγους ῥηθῆναι) cp. Eur. *Ion* 228 ἐπὶ δ' ἀσφάκτοις | μήλοισι δόμων μὴ πάριτ' ἐς μυχόν ('before sheep have been slain, pass not,' etc.).

557 σὺ μὲν τοῖς: 'you seemed wise to the one side (Creon); I, to the other' (to Hades and the dead). Nauck pronounces the text unsound, objecting to the use of τοῖς: but that it was good Attic is sufficiently shown by Plat. *Legg.* 701 E (cited by Wolff) οὐ συνήνεγκεν οὔτε τοῖς οὔτε τοῖς (it profited neither party). Cp. *O. C.* 742, p. on ἐκ δὲ τῶν.—σὺ μὲν σοί, the schol.'s reading, is very inferior.—For the rhetorical χιασμός cp. *O. T.* 538 n. (and *Ph.* 300).

558 καὶ μήν, and yet,—though I *did* shrink from breaking Creon's law,—I am now, morally, as great an offender as you, since I sympathise with your act.

559 f. θάρσει is not said with bitterness (that could hardly be, after 551): rather it means, 'Take heart to live,' as Whitelaw renders it. These two verses quietly express her feeling that their lots are irrevocably sundered, and exhort Ismene to accept the severance.—ἡ ἐμὴ ψυχή, my life, a periphrasis for ἐγώ, like *O. C.* 998 τὴν πατρὸς | ψυχήν...ζῶσαν (n.). —πάλαι, *i.e.* ever since she resolved to break the edict. (Cp. *O. T.* 1161.)—ὥστε τοῖς θ. ὠφελεῖν, so as to (with a view to) serving the dead. The dat., as with ἐπαρκεῖν : *Ph.* 871 ξυνωφελοῦντά μοι : Aesch. *Pers.* 842 ὡς τοῖς θανοῦσι πλοῦτος οὐδὲν ὠφελεῖ: Eur. *Or.* 665 τοῖς φίλοισιν ὠφελεῖν : Ar. *Av.* 419 φίλοισιν ὠφελεῖν ἔχειν. So ἐπωφελεῖν *O. C.* 441.—Dobree proposed to understand σε as subj. to the inf., 'so that (you) are helping the dead,' —*i.e.*, your offer of help (552) is made to one who is already as good as dead. But σέ could not be thus understood ; and this sense (which it has been sought to obtain by emendations, see cr. n.) would be frigid.

ΚΡ. τὼ παῖδε φημὶ τώδε τὴν μὲν ἀρτίως
    ἄνουν πεφάνθαι, τὴν δ' ἀφ' οὗ τὰ πρῶτ' ἔφυ.

ΙΣ. οὐ γάρ ποτ', ὦναξ, οὐδ' ὃς ἂν βλάστῃ μένει
    νοῦς τοῖς κακῶς πράσσουσιν, ἀλλ' ἐξίσταται.

ΚΡ. σοὶ γοῦν, ὅθ' εἵλου σὺν κακοῖς πράσσειν κακά.   565

ΙΣ. τί γὰρ μόνῃ μοι τῆσδ' ἄτερ βιώσιμον;

ΚΡ. ἀλλ' ἥδε μέντοι μὴ λέγ'· οὐ γὰρ ἔστ' ἔτι.

ΙΣ. ἀλλὰ κτενεῖς νυμφεῖα τοῦ σαυτοῦ τέκνου;

ΚΡ. ἀρώσιμοι γὰρ χἀτέρων εἰσὶν γύαι.

ΙΣ. οὐχ ὥς γ' ἐκείνῳ τῇδέ τ' ἦν ἡρμοσμένα.   570

ΚΡ. κακὰς ἐγὼ γυναῖκας υἱέσι στυγῶ.

563 οὐ γάρ ποτ'] ἀλλ' οὐ γὰρ Plutarch *Phoc.* 1, and *Mor.* 460 E. The grammarian Gregorius Corinthius (*c.* 1150 A.D.) p. 417 has ἀλλὰ γάρ.   564 πράσσουσιν] πρά-ξασιν Plut. *Mor.* 460 E. πράττουσιν Gregorius *l. c.*   565 σοὶ γοῦν] καὶ has been deleted before σοὶ in L.—κακοῖς] L has ·ἦ· written above by S. Some of the later MSS. have κακῇ or (as A) κακῷ.   567 μέν σοι L, and so nearly all the later MSS.;

561 L gives τὼ παῖδε φημὶ as in *O. C.* 317 καὶ φημί, and this may probably be taken as the traditional accentuation, though some modern edd. write τὼ παῖδέ φημι, καὶ φημι. The justification of the oxytone φημί is in the emphasis which falls on it. Similarly it has the accent when parenthetic, as Lucian *Deor. Conc.* 2 πολλοὶ γάρ, φημί, οὐκ ἀγαπῶντες κ.τ.λ. —τὼ παῖδε...τὴν] μὲν...τὴν δέ, partitive apposition: see on 21.—ἀρτίως, because Creon had hitherto regarded Ismene as being of a docile and submissive nature: cp. on 531 ὑφειμένη.

563 f. The apology is for her sister as well as for herself: even such prudence (cp. 68 νοῦν) as may have been inborn for-sakes the unfortunate under the stress of their misfortunes.—βλάστῃ: cp. *El.* 238 ἐν τίνι τοῦτ' ἔβλαστ' ἀνθρώπων; *O. C.* 804 φύσας...φρένας (n.).—τοῖς κ. πράσσουσιν, dat. of interest: *Tr.* 132 μένει γὰρ οὔτ' αἰόλα νὺξ | βροτοῖσιν.—ἐξίσταται, stands aside, gives place (*Ai.* 672); and so, leaves its proper place, becomes deranged: cp. Eur. *Bacch.* 928 ἀλλ' ἐξ ἕδρας σοι πλό-καμος ἐξέστηχ' ὅδε. The converse phrase is commoner, ἐξίσταμαι τῶν φρενῶν: cp. 1105.—Schneidewin cp. Eur. *Antigone* fr. 165 ἄκουσον· οὐ γὰρ οἱ κακῶς πεπρα-γότες | σὺν ταῖς τύχαισι τοὺς λόγους ἀπώλε-σαν,—which plainly glances at our passage. For similar allusions cp. *O. C.* 1116 n.

565 σοὶ γοῦν (cp. 45 n.) *sc.* ἐξέστη.— κακοῖς, *i.e.* Antigone: for the plur., cp. 10.

566 τῆσδ' ἄτερ explains μόνῃ: cp. on 445.—βιώσιμον is Ionic and poet.; the Attic word was βιωτός. It is needless to change τί (subst.) into πῶς. The more usual phrase was, indeed, impers., as Her. 1. 45 οὐδέ οἱ εἴη βιώσιμον: Plat. *Crito* 47 D ἆρα βιωτὸν ἡμῖν ἐστί; But, just as we can have ὁ βίος οὐ βιωτός ἐστι (cp. *O. C.* 1691), so also οὐδὲν βιωτόν ἐστι, no form of life is tolerable. Cp. *O. T.* 1337 τί δῆτ' ἐμοὶ βλεπτόν, ἢ | στερκτόν, ἢ προσήγορον | ἔτ' ἔστ', etc., where the only difference is that the subst. τί corresponds to an object. accus., and not as here to a cognate (βίον βιῶναι).

567 ἀλλὰ...μέντοι, 'nay, but...': cp.*Ph.* 524 ἀλλ' αἰσχρὰ μέντοι σοῦ γέ μ' ἐνδεέστε-ρον | ξένῳ φανῆναι.—ἥδε μὴ λέγε, say not 'ἥδε,' speak not of her as still with thee, for she is already numbered with the dead. οἵδε are οἱ ἐνθάδε, the living (75), as κεῖνοι (525) are οἱ ἐκεῖ, the dead (cp. 76). The peculiarity is that we should have expected either (*a*) τήνδε, acc. to λέγε, or (*b*) τῆσδε, as a direct quotation from the last verse: cp. Dem. or. 18 § 88 τίς ἦν...; ὑμεῖς, ὦ ἄνδρες 'Αθηναῖοι. τὸ δ' ὑμεῖς ὅταν λέγω, λέγω τὴν πόλιν. If (*e.g.*) ὑμῶν had pre-ceded ὦ ἄνδρες, Dem. would doubtless have said τὸ δ' ὑμῶν, or else ὑμᾶς δ'. Here,

CR. Lo, one of these maidens hath newly shown herself foolish, as the other hath been since her life began.

IS. Yea, O King, such reason as nature may have given abides not with the unfortunate, but goes astray.

CR. Thine did, when thou chosest vile deeds with the vile.

IS. What life could I endure, without her presence?

CR. Nay, speak not of her ' presence '; she lives no more.

IS. But wilt thou slay the betrothed of thine own son?

CR. Nay, there are other fields for him to plough.

IS. But there can never be such love as bound him to her.

CR. I like not an evil wife for my son.

but E has μέν τοι σοί: Brunck replaced μέντοι. **568** ἀλλὰ κτενεῖς MSS. Nauck writes οὐ μὴ κτενεῖς.—νυμφια (without acc.) L: νυμφεῖα r. **569** ἀρώσιμοι] In L an early hand has written ο above ω.—χάτέρων εἰσὶν MSS.: Dindorf, εἰσὶ χάτέρων. Nauck arranges vv. 569—574 as follows, bracketing 570 and 573 as spurious:— 569, 572, 571, 574; giving 572 and 574 to Ismene (with L). **571** υἱάσιν L:

however, no fair objection would remain if we had ἀλλὰ τὸ ἥδε μὴ λέγε, i.e. 'never use the word ἥδε about her,'—which makes the sense more general than if he said, ἀλλὰ τῆσδε μὴ λέγε, i.e. 'do not say (that you cannot live without) ἥδε.' The question, then, seems to resolve itself into this:—Wishing to give the more general sense just indicated, could the poet say ἥδε instead of τὸ ἥδε? To show that the art. was not always required in such quotation, it is enough to cite Ar. *Eq.* 21 λέγε δὴ μόλωμεν, by the side of τὸ μόλωμεν ib. 26. While, then, I cannot produce any exact parallel for this ἥδε, I think it reasonable to suppose that colloquial idiom would have allowed it. Those who deny this have two resources. (1) To point thus: ἀλλ' ἥδε μέντοι—μὴ λέγ'· i.e. instead of adding οὐκ ἔστιν ἔτι after μέντοι, he breaks off his sentence—'do not speak of her.' So Bellermann. (2) Semitelos reads ἀλλ' ἥδε μέν σοι μὴ λέγ' ὡς ἀρ' [for οὐ γὰρ] ἐστ' ἔτι, 'do not say that you have *her* any longer.' As to σοι, see cr. n. above. Neither of these readings gives such a forcible sense as the vulgate.

568 νυμφεῖα, sc. ἱερά, 'nuptials,' as *Tr.* 7 (but ib. 920 'bridal-chamber,' as in sing. below, 1205); here = νύμφην. Cp. Eur. *El.* 481 σὰ λέχεα, thy spouse: and so εὐνή, etc.—Having failed to win Creon's pity for herself, Ismene now appeals to his feeling for his son. Haemon's coming part in the play is thus prepared.

569 ἀρώσιμοι, a poet. form (y here), analogous to the epic forms of adjectives

in which a short vowel is lengthened for metre's sake (cp. on 492). Though the verb was ἀρόω, the adj. with the suffix σιμο would properly be formed from the subst. ἄροσις (cp. *O. C.* 27 n.). Suidas gives ἀρόσιμον κλῆμα· τὸ ἀροτριούμενον. For the metaphor cp. *O. T.* 1256 μητρώαν ...ἄρουραν, and ib. 1485, 1497: Lucr. 4. 1107.

570 οὐχ ὥς γ' ('Another marriage is possible for him'). 'No, not in the sense of the troth plighted between him and her,'—not such a union of hearts as had been prepared there. ἡρμοσμένα ἦν, impers., lit., 'as things had been adjusted'; cp. on 447: Her. 1. 112 ἡμῖν κακῶς βεβουλευμένα ἔσται: id. 6. 83 τέως μὲν δὴ σφι ἦν ἄρθμια ἐς ἀλλήλους. The choice of the word has been influenced by the Ionic and poet. use of ἁρμόζειν as = to betroth (ἐγγυᾶν): Her. 3. 137 ἁρμοσται (perf. pass. as midd.) τὴν Μίλωνος θυγατέρα...γυναῖκα, he has become engaged to her: Pind. *P.* 9. 127 ἁρμόζων κόρᾳ | νυμφίον ἄνδρα. Cp. 2 Epist. Cor. 11. 2 ἡρμοσάμην γὰρ ὑμᾶς ἑνὶ ἀνδρὶ παρθένον ἁγνήν.

571 υἱάσι, the regular Attic dat. plur. (as Plat. *Rep.* 362 E, Ar. *Nub.* 1001, etc.), from the stem υἱυ-, which furnished also the Attic nom. and gen. plur.; υἱεῖς, υἱέων; and the dual υἱῆ (or rather υἱεῖ, Meisterhans p. 63), υἱέοιν. The Attic forms of the sing. and the acc. plur. were taken from υἱο-, except that υἱέος, υἱεῖ were alternative forms for the gen. and dat. sing. Here L has the epic υἱάσιν, from a third stem, υἱ-, whence the Homeric forms υἷος, υἷι,

*ΑΝ. ὦ φίλταθ' Αἷμον, ὥς σ' ἀτιμάζει πατήρ.

ΚΡ. ἄγαν γε λυπεῖς καὶ σὺ καὶ τὸ σὸν λέχος.

*ΧΟ. ἦ γὰρ στερήσεις τῆσδε τὸν σαυτοῦ γόνον;

ΚΡ. Ἅιδης ὁ παύσων τούσδε τοὺς γάμους ἐμοί.   575

ΧΟ. δεδογμέν', ὡς ἔοικε, τήνδε κατθανεῖν.

ΚΡ. καὶ σοί γε κἀμοί. μὴ τριβὰς ἔτ', ἀλλά νιν
κομίζετ' εἴσω, δμῶες· ἐκ δὲ τοῦδε χρὴ
γυναῖκας εἶναι τάσδε, μηδ' ἀνειμένας.
φεύγουσι γάρ τοι χοἰ θρασεῖς, ὅταν πέλας   580
ἤδη τὸν Ἅιδην εἰσορῶσι τοῦ βίου.

υἱέσι r.   **572** The MSS. give this v. to Ismene.   The Aldine ed. (1502) and that of Turnebus (1553) first gave it to Antigone; and so Boeckh.—αἷμων L. αἷμον r.   **574** The MSS. give this verse to Ismene; Boeckh, to the Chorus. **575** ἐμοί L: ἔφυ r (including A).   κυρεῖ is Meineke's conject.; μόνος Nauck's, who also changes παύσων to λύσων.   **576** L gives this verse to the Chorus (not to Ismene, as has sometimes been stated).   The later MSS. are divided; most of them give it to Ismene.—ἔοικε] ἔοικεν L. Cp. 402.   **577** καὶ σοί γε κἀμοί] F. Kern

---

υἷα, υἷε, υἷες, υἷας: cp. Monro *Hom. Gr.* § 107.—The dat. of interest goes with **κακὰς γυναῖκας**, not with **στυγεῖ**: cp. Ar. *Nub.* 1161 πρόβολος ἐμός, σωτὴρ δόμοις, ἐχθροῖς βλάβη.

572 It is not of much moment that L, like the later MSS., gives this verse to Ismene.   Errors as to the persons occur not seldom in L (see, *e.g.*, cr. n. to *O. C.* 837, and cp. *ib.* 1737); and here a mistake would have been peculiarly easy, as the dialogue from v. 561 onwards has been between Creon and Ismene.   To me it seems certain that the verse is Antigone's, and that one of the finest touches in the play is effaced by giving it to Ismene. The taunt, κακὰς γυναῖκας υἱέσι, moves Antigone to break the silence which she has kept since v. 560: in all this scene she has not spoken to Creon, nor does she now address him: she is thinking of Haemon,—of the dishonour to *him* implied in the charge of having made such a choice, —ὡς ἀεὶ τὸν ὁμοῖον ἄγει θεὸς ὡς τὸν ὁμοῖον. How little does his father know the heart which was in sympathy with her own. This solitary reference to her love heightens in a wonderful degree our sense of her unselfish devotion to a sacred duty.   If Ismene speaks this verse, then τὸ σὸν λέχος in 573 must be, 'the marriage of which you talk' (like *El.* 1110 οὐκ οἶδα τὴν σὴν κλῆδον'), which certainly is not its natural sense.— **Αἷμον.** L has αἷμων.   Soph. would have

written ΑΙΜΟΝ: hence the tradition is subject to the same ambiguity as in ΚΡΕΟΝ.   The analogy of δαῖμον would probably have recommended the form in o.

573 ἄγαν γε λυπεῖς, 'Nay, thou art too troublesome,'—the impatient phrase of one who would silence another, as 589 (Ajax to Tecmessa) ἄγαν γε λυπεῖς· οὐ κάτοισθ', etc.: so *ib.* 592 πόλλ' ἄγαν ἤδη θροεῖς.

574 The MSS. give this verse to Ismene; but Boeckh is clearly right in giving it to the Chorus.   Ismene asked this question in 568, and Creon answered: she rejoined to this answer (570), and Creon replied still more bitterly.   She could not now ask her former question over again.   But there is no unfitness in the question being repeated by a new intercessor, since to ask it thus is a form of mild remonstrance.

575 ἐμοί, L's reading, is right.   Creon has been asked,—'Can you indeed mean to deprive your son of his bride?'   He grimly replies, 'I look to the Death-god to break off this match.'   The ἔφυ in the later MSS. was obviously a mere conjecture,—and a weak one.

576 This verse clearly belongs to the Chorus, to whom L assigns it.   The first words of the next verse show this.   Hermann objected that in similar situations the Chorus usually has two verses.   It is

AN. Haemon, beloved! How thy father wrongs thee!
CR. Enough, enough of thee and of thy marriage!
CH. Wilt thou indeed rob thy son of this maiden?
CR. 'Tis Death that shall stay these bridals for me.
CH. 'Tis determined, it seems, that she shall die.
CR. Determined, yes, for thee and for me.—(*To the two Attendants.*) No more delay—servants, take them within! Henceforth they must be women, and not range at large; for verily even the bold seek to fly, when they see Death now closing on their life.

[*Exeunt Attendants, guarding* ANTIGONE *and* ISMENE.— CREON *remains.*

conject. καὶ σοί γε κοινῇ. **578** ἐκ δὲ τοῦδε χρή L. The τοῦδε has been made from τασδε: whether the latter was originally τάσδε or τᾶσδε, or accentless, is doubtful, but the circumflex has been added by the corrector just over the o, perh. to avoid blotting in the erasure over υ. The correction ȣ had been written above before the letters ασ were altered in the text. The lemma of the schol. has ἐκ δὲ τᾶσδε. The later MSS. have ἐκ δὲ τοῦδε. **579** γυναῖκας εἶναι τᾶσδε (sic) μήδ᾽ ἀνειμένασ L. So the later MSS., but with τάσδε or τοῦδε (A): which latter shows the same tendency as L's

true that this is usually the case. But *O. T.* 1312 is enough to show that there was no rigid rule; why, indeed, should there be? And, here, surely, πλέον ἥμισυ ταυτόύ.—δεδογμένα (ἐστί), = δέδοκται: cp. on 570 ἡρμοσμένα, 447 κηρυχθέντα. Cp. Menander 'Αρρηφόρος 1. 3 δεδογμένον τὸ πρᾶγμ᾽· ἀνερρίφθω κύβος.

577 καὶ σοί γε κἀμοί, *sc.* δεδογμένα. It is settled, for both of us: *i.e.*, I shall not change my mind, and it is vain for thee to plead. The datives are ethic. We might also understand, 'settled *by* thee, as *by* me,'—alluding to the words of the Chorus in v. 211 and in v. 220. But I now feel, with Mr T. Page, that this would be somewhat forced.—We must not point thus: καὶ σοί γε. καί μοι μὴ τριβάς, etc. (so Semitelos). This would be more defensible if, in 576, σοί had stood with δεδογμένα: but, as it is, the vagueness of the latter confirms καὶ σοί γε κἀμοί. Bellermann, giving 576 to Ismene, adopts Kern's καὶ σοί γε κοινῇ ('yes, and she shall die with you').—μὴ τριβάς, *sc.* ποιεῖσθε: cp. Ar. *Ach.* 345 ἀλλὰ μή μοι πρόφασιν, ἀλλὰ κατάθου τὸ βέλος: *Vesp.* 1179 μή μοί γε μύθους.—νιν, plur., as *O. T.* 868 (masc.), *O. C.* 43 (fem.), *El.* 436 (neut.), etc.

578 f. ἐκ δὲ τοῦδε, κ.τ.λ. Compare 484 ἦ νῦν ἐγὼ μὲν οὐκ ἀνήρ, αὕτη δ᾽ ἀνήρ: 525 ἐμοῦ δὲ ζῶντος οὐκ ἄρξει γυνή: also 678 ff.

This much-vexed passage is sound as it has come down to us. Creon means: 'henceforth they must be *women*, and must not roam unrestrained.' The fact that a woman has successfully defied him rankles in his mind. Hence the bitterness of γυναῖκας here. The Attic notions of feminine propriety forbade such freedom as ἀνειμένας denotes. Cp. *El.* 516 (Clytaemnestra finding Electra outside the house) ἀνειμένη μέν, ὡς ἔοικας, αὖ στρέφει: Electra should be restrained, μή τοι θυραίαν γ᾽ οὖσαν αἰσχύνειν φίλους. So pseudo-Phocyl. 216 (keep a maiden in-doors), μηδέ μιν ἄχρι γάμων πρὸ δόμων ὀφθῆμεν ἐάσῃς. Ar. *Lys.* 16 χαλεπή τοι γυναικῶν ἔξοδος. The emphasis of γυναῖκας here is parallel with the frequent emphasis of ἀνήρ (as Eur. *El.* 693 ἄνδρα γίγνεσθαί σε χρή, a *man*). Cp. *O. C.* 1368 αἴδ᾽ ἄνδρες, οὐ γυναῖκες, εἰς τὸ συμπονεῖν.—All the emendations are weak or improbable. See Appendix.

580 f. χοὶ θρασεῖς. Remark how well the use of the masc. here suits the taunt conveyed in the last verse. πθλας (ὄντα)... ἀσορῶσι: cp. *O. C.* 29 πέλας γὰρ ἄνδρα τόνδε νῷν ὁρῶ: and see *ib.* 586 n.

582—625 Second στάσιμον. 1st strophe, 582—591, = 1st antistr., 593—603. 2nd strophe, 604—614, = 2nd antistr., 615—625. See Metrical Analysis.

στρ. α'. ΧΟ. εὐδαίμονες οἷσι κακῶν ἄγευστος αἰών.

2 οἷς γὰρ ἂν σεισθῇ θεόθεν δόμος, ἄτας

3 οὐδὲν ἐλλείπει, γενεᾶς ἐπὶ πλῆθος ἕρπον·   585

4 ὅμοιον ὥστε ποντίαις οἶδμα δυσπνόοις ὅταν

5 Θρήσσαισιν ἔρεβος ὕφαλον ἐπιδράμῃ πνοαῖς,

6 κυλίνδει βυσσόθεν κελαινὰν θῖνα, καί   590

7 δυσάνεμοι στόνῳ βρέμουσιν ἀντιπλῆγες ἀκταί.

ἀντ. α'.   ἀρχαῖα τὰ Λαβδακιδᾶν οἴκων ὁρῶμαι   593

2 πήματα * φθιτῶν ἐπὶ πήμασι πίπτοντ',   595

The sentence of death just passed on Antigone leads the Chorus to reflect on the destiny of her house, and on the power of fate generally.—When a divine curse has once fallen upon a family, thenceforth there is no release for it. Wave after wave of trouble vexes it. Generation after generation suffers. These sisters were the last hope of the race; and now an infatuated act has doomed them also. —What mortal can restrain the power of Zeus? Human self-will and ambition may seem to defy him, but he is drawing them on to their ruin.—Anapaests (626—630) then announce the approach of Haemon.

582 κακῶν ἄγευστος, act., cp. O. T. 969 ἄψαυστος ἔγχους n. Eur. Alc. 1069 ὡς ἄρτι πένθους τοῦδε γεύομαι πικροῦ. Her. 7. 46 ὁ...θεὸς γλυκὺν γεύσας τὸν αἰῶνα (having allowed men to taste the sweetness of life).

583 f. σεισθῇ θεόθεν, i.e. by an ἀρά (likened to a storm, or earthquake, that shakes a building): when a sin has once been committed, and the shock of divine punishment has once been felt. In the case of the Labdacidae the calamities were traced to the curse called down on Laïus by Pelops, when robbed by him of his son Chrysippus (O. T. p. xix.).—ἄτας οὐδὲν ἐλ-λείπει, (for these men, οἷς = τούτοις οἷς) no sort of calamity is wanting. Some join ἐλλείπει with ἕρπον, on the analogy of

παύεσθαι with part., 'never fails to go'; but this constr. is at least very rare. In a probably spurious ψήφισμα ἀρ. Dem. or. 18 § 92 we have οὐκ ἐλλείψει εὐχαριστῶν: but Xen. Mem. 2. 6 § 5 (adduced by Wecklein) is not an example, for there μὴ ἐλλείπεσθαι εὖ ποιῶν = 'not to be outdone in generosity.' Then in Plat. Phaedr. 272 B ὅ τι ἂν αὐτῶν τις ἐλλείπῃ λέγων = simply 'omit in speaking.'—γενεᾶς ἐπὶ πλῆθος. The phrase is bold, and somewhat strange; but I do not think that it is corrupt. γενεᾶς here is the whole race, not (as in 596) a generation of the race. The words mean literally, 'over a multitude of the race'; i.e., the ἄτη does not cease with the person who first brought it into the family, or with his generation, but continues to afflict succeeding generations. The collective noun γενεᾶς justifies the use of πλῆθος: as he might have said, ἀπογόνων πλῆθος. It is needless, then, to write γενεᾶν. We cannot understand, 'to the fulness of the race,' i.e. till the race has been exhausted.

586 f. ὅμοιον, adv.: Plat. Legg. 628 D ὅμοιον ὡς εἰ...ἡγοῖτό τις.—ποντίαις (see cr. n.) is far the most probable reading. The loss of the second ι, leaving ποντίας, would easily have brought in ἀλός, which the metre shows to be superfluous. In Greek poetry there is no objection to the three epithets with πνοαῖς: the whole phrase would be felt as meaning, 'stormy sea-

CH. Blest are they whose days have not tasted of evil. 1st
For when a house hath once been shaken from heaven, there strophe.
the curse fails nevermore, passing from life to life of the race;
even as, when the surge is driven over the darkness of the deep
by the fierce breath of Thracian sea-winds, it rolls up the black
sand from the depths, and there is a sullen roar from wind-
vexed headlands that front the blows of the storm.

I see that from olden time the sorrows in the house of 1st anti-
the Labdacidae are heaped upon the sorrows of the dead; strophe.

(the β from τ?) δ' ἀντιπλῆγες ἀκταί· L. So the later MSS. (βρέμουσιν for βρέμουσι
δ' Vat.). Bergk conject. δυσάνεμοι: Jacobs, δυσανέμῳ. **593 f.** Λαβδακιδᾶν] μ
deleted before β in L.—οἴκων] Seyffert conject. δόμων: Wecklein, κλύων or σκοπῶν.
—πήματα φθιμένων MSS. For φθιμένων Dindorf conject. φθιτῶν, comparing Eur.
Alc. 100, where φθιτῶν has become φθιμένων in some MSS. He also conjectured
πήματ' ἀλλ' ἄλλοις, which Wecklein receives. Seyffert, πήματ' ἐκφόντων.

winds from Thrace.' Construe: ὅταν
οἶδμα, when a surge, ποντίαις δυσπνν. Θρ.
πνοαῖς, driven by stormy sea-winds from
Thrace (instr. dat., cp. on 335 νότῳ), ἐπιδράμῃ ἐρεβος ὕφαλον, rushes over the
dark depths of the sea (lit., the darkness
under the surface of the sea). For δυσπνν.
πνοαῖς, cp. 502 n.: for Θρῄσσαισιν,
Aesch. *Ag.* 192 πνοαὶ δ' ἀπὸ Στρυμόνος
μολοῦσαι, *ib.* 654 Θρῄκιαι πνοαί (and 1418):
Il. 9. 5 (where the tumult in the breasts
of the Greeks is likened to a storm) Βορέης
καὶ Ζέφυρος, τώ τε Θρῄκηθεν ἄητον.

590 ff. κελαινάνθινα, the dark-coloured
mud or sand that the storm stirs up from
the bottom of the sea. θίς is masc. in
Homer, Ar., and Arist., and that was prob.
its usual gender. Soph. has it fem. again
in *Ph.* 1124, and so it is in later writers.
In the *Il.* θίς is always the sea-shore; in
Od. that is its regular sense, but once (12.
45) it means 'heap.' It is used as here
by Ar. *Vesp.* 696 ὥς μου τὸν θῖνα ταράτ-
τεις(my very depths). Verg. *G.* 3. 240 *at ima
exaestuat unda Vorticibus, nigramque alte
subiectat arenam.*—δυσάνεμοι should be
read. δυσάνεμον could not here be adv.
with ἐρέμουσιν, and must therefore be
epithet of θίνα, when it could mean only
τὴν ὑπὸ ἀνέμων ταραχθεῖσαν (schol.), *i.e.*
'stirred up by the storm,'—a strained
sense for it. Cp. Apoll. Rhod. 1. 593 ἀκτήν
τ' αἰγιαλὸν τε δυσάνεμον.—στόνῳ βρ.:
cp. 427.—ἀντιπλῆγες (only here) ἀκταί,
headlands which are struck in front, struck
full, by the waves; in contrast with παρα-
πλῆγες, 'struck obliquely': see *Od.* 5.
417 (Odysseus seeking a place to land) ἦν

που ἐφεύρω | ἠϊόνάς τε παραπλῆγας
λιμένας τε θαλάσσης ('shores where the
waves strike *aslant*'). Soph. was doubtless thinking of the Homeric phrase.—Not
(1) 'beating back the waves,' ἀντίτυποι:
nor (2) 'beaten again,'—*i.e.* by the ever-
returning waves. This last is impossible.
—Cp. *O. C.* 1240 where Oed. is likened
to a βόρειος...ἀκτὰ κυματοπλήξ. Oppian
Cyn. 2. 142 κρημνοῖσι καὶ ὑδατοπλήγεσιν
ἄκραις.

593 f. ἀρχαῖα, predicate: I see that,
from olden time, the house-troubles
(οἴκων πήματα) of the (living) Labdacidae are heaped upon the troubles of
the dead. The dead are now Laïus, Oedipus, and his two sons. ἀρχαῖα carries us
back to the starting-point of the troubles,
—the curse pronounced on Laïus by Pelops (cp. on 583).—ὁρῶμαι, midd., as in
Homer and Attic Comedy, but not in
Attic prose; which, however, used the
midd. περιορᾶσθαι (Thuc. 6. 103) and
προορᾶσθαι (Dem. or. 18 § 281, etc.).
Soph. has ὁρωμένη, midd., *Tr.* 306 (dial.);
and so, too, εἰδόμην *Ph.* 351 (dial.), etc.
Though οἴκων answers metrically to the
first two syllables of ἀγεύστος in 582, it
is not suspicious, because the second
syllable of the trochee can be irrational
(a long for a 'short': see Metr. Anal.
Conversely, φθιτῶν is metrically admissible, though its first syllable answers to
the second of ἐλλείπει in 585. This correction of φθιμένων is strongly confirmed
by the similar error of the MSS. in Eur.
Alc. 100 (see cr. n.).

3 οὐδ᾽ ἀπαλλάσσει γενεὰν γένος, ἀλλ᾽ ἐρείπει
4 θεῶν τις, οὐδ᾽ ἔχει λύσιν. νῦν γὰρ ἐσχάτας ὑπὲρ
5 ῥίζας <ὃ> τέτατο φάος ἐν Οἰδίπου δόμοις,   600
6 κατ᾽ αὖ νιν φοινία θεῶν τῶν νερτέρων
7 ἁμᾷ κόνις, λόγου τ᾽ ἄνοια καὶ φρενῶν ἐρινύς.

στρ. β'. τεάν, Ζεῦ, δύνασιν τίς ἀνδρῶν ὑπερβασία κατάσχοι; 605

597 ἐρείπει r, ἐρίπει L. Seyffert conject. ἐπείγει.   **599 f.** νῦν γὰρ ἐσχάτας
ὑπὲρ (ὅπερ L) | ῥίζας τέτατο φάος MSS.—Hermann proposed three different emen-
dations: (1) ὑπὲρ | ῥίζας δ τέτατο, to which the schol. points. (2) ὑπὲρ ῥίζας
ἐτέτατο, so that a new sentence begins with κατ᾽ αὖ. (3) ὅπερ | ῥίζας ἐτέτατο.
This last he preferred.—Nauck would change ὑπέρ into θάλος (acc. governed by
καταμᾷ). Keeping ὑπέρ, Theod. Kock and others would substitute θάλος for φάος.

596 f. **ἀπαλλάσσει**, releases (by ex-
hausting the malignity of the ἀρά) : so oft.
ἀπαλλάσσω τινὰ κακῶν, φόβου, etc.—γενεὰν γένος: cp. 1067 νέκυν νεκρῶν : Ai.
475 παρ᾽ ἦμαρ ἡμέρα.—The subject to ἔχει
(ἀλλ᾽ ἐρείπει θεῶν τις being parenthetical)
is 'the Labdacid house,' i.e. γενεά in the
larger sense (585), supplied from γενεὰν
just before. This is simpler than to supply
πήματα as subject.—λύσιν, deliverance
from trouble, as O. T. 911, Tr. 1171.
599 νῦν γὰρ ἐσχάτας κ.τ.λ. (1) The
first question is,—are we to read δ τέτατο
or ἐτέτατο? If ἐτέτατο, then the sentence
is complete at δόμοις. A new sentence
beginning with κατ᾽ αὖ would be intolerably abrupt: yet neither κᾆτ᾽ nor καὶ ταύταν
appears probable. This difficulty would
be avoided by changing ὑπέρ to ὅπερ: but
then ῥίζας φάος must mean, 'the comfort (or hope) afforded by the ῥίζα,'—a
strange phrase. And τέτατο confirms
ὑπέρ as well as φάος. I therefore prefer
δ τέτατο. (2) The next point concerns
νιν. Reading δ τέτατο, Wecklein still
refers νιν to ῥίζας, not to φάος, saying that
the constr. is as though ἃς ὑπὲρ ἐσχάτας
ῥίζας had preceded. This is a grammatical impossibility. With δ τέτατο, νιν can
refer only to φάος. Can this be justified?
Thus, I think. The ἐσχάτη ῥίζα of the
family is the last remaining means of pro-
pagating it. A light of hope (φάος) was
'spread above' this 'last root,'—as sunshine above a plant,—because it was
hoped that the sisters would continue the
race. The sisters themselves are, properly speaking, the ἐσχάτη ῥίζα. But as
the word ῥίζα can also have an abstract
sense, denoting the chance of propagation,
the sisters can here be identified with the
hope, or φάος, which shines above the ῥίζα.

In Greek this is the easier since φάος was
often said of persons, as Il. 18. 102 οὐδέ
τι Πατρόκλῳ γενόμην φάος, Eur. Hec. 841
ὦ δέσποτ᾽, ὦ μέγιστον Ἕλλησιν φάος. To
say καταμᾶν φάος (δόμων) is like saying,
'to mow down the hope of the race,'—in
this case, the two young lives. A further
reason against referring νιν to ῥίζα is that
the verb should then be, not καταμᾷ, but
ἐξημᾷ, as Ai. 1178 γένους ἅπαντος ῥίζαν
ἐξημημένος: a root is not 'mowed down,'
in such a case, but cut out of the ground.
The proposed change of φάος into θάλος,
though not difficult in a palaeographical
sense, is condemned by τέτατο, which
does not suit θάλος, but exactly suits φάος.
Cp. Ph. 831 τάνδ᾽ αἴγλαν ἃ τέταται τανῦν.
Od. 11. 19 ἀλλ᾽ ἐπὶ νὺξ ὀλοὴ τέταται δει-
λοῖσι βροτοῖσι: Hes. Op. 547 ἀὴρ πυροφό-
ρος τέταται μακάρων ἐπὶ ἔργοις (rich men's
fields): Theogn. 1077 ὀρφνη γὰρ τέταται.
Plat. Rep. 616 B διὰ παντὸς τοῦ οὐρανοῦ
καὶ γῆς τεταμένον φῶς. As to the proposed substitution of θάλος for ὑπέρ, (with
φάος retained,) it would be as violent as
needless.—For ῥίζας cp. Pind. O. 2. 46
ὅθεν σπέρματος ἔχοντα ῥίζαν: El. 765
πρόρριζον...ἔφθαρται γένος: Lucian Tyr.
13 πανωλεθρίᾳ παντὸς τοῦ γένους καὶ ῥίζό-
θεν τὸ δεινὸν ἅπαν ἐκκεκομμένον.

601 f. κατ᾽ αὖ...ἁμᾷ, = καταμᾷ αὖ,
'mows down in its turn' (not, 'otherwise
than we hoped'). In my first edition I
adopted the conjecture κονίς. Prof.
Tyrrell's able defence of the MS. κόνις
(Classical Review, vol. II. p. 139), though
it has not removed all my difficulties, has
led me to feel that more can be said for
that reading than I had recognised. I
now prefer, therefore, to leave κόνις in
the text, and to re-state here the arguments for and against it.

and generation is not freed by generation, but some god strikes them down, and the race hath no deliverance.

For now that hope of which the light had been spread above the last root of the house of Oedipus—that hope, in turn, is brought low—by the blood-stained dust due to the gods infernal, and by folly in speech, and frenzy at the heart.

Thy power, O Zeus, what human trespass can limit? 2nd strophe.

601 κατ'] κᾱτ' L, but a line has been drawn through the ^. The later MSS. have κᾶτ', κατ', κᾱτ' (V⁴), κᾱτ' (L²), or κατά νιν. Gaisford, writing κᾱτ' with Brunck and others, reads ὑπὲρ | ῥίζας ἐτέτατο (see last note).—καὶ ταύταν Semitelos. **602** ἀμᾷ L, ἀμᾷ r.—κόνις MSS. The conjecture κοπίς has been made by several scholars independently. Gaisford gives the priority, though doubtfully ('ni fallor'), to John Jortin (ob. 1770). Heath ascribes it to Askew. Reiske also suggested it. **604** τεάν] Triclinius conject. τὰν σάν: Wecklein, σὰν ἂν: Nauck, τίς σάν.—δύναμιν L, with ·σ· over μ from the first hand. **605** ὑπερβασίᾳ r. Meineke con-

---

(1) If κόνις be right, κόνις θεῶν τῶν νερτέρων is the dust, belonging (due) to the gods infernal, which Antigone strewed on her brother's corpse; it is φοινία, because the corpse was gory. The strongest point in favour of κόνις is that it is in harmony with the following words, λόγου τ' ἄνοια καὶ φρενῶν ἐρινύς. The whole sense then is: 'She, too—the last hope of the race—is now to die,—for a handful of blood-stained dust (i.e., for a slight, yet obligatory, act of piety towards her slain brother)—and for those rash words to Creon,—the expression of her frenzied resolve.' On the other hand, the objection to κόνις is the verb καταμᾷ, which implies the metaphor of reaping. (See Appendix.) The proposed version, 'covers,' is impossible, and, if possible, would be unsuitable. What we want is a verb meaning simply 'destroys,' or 'dooms to death.' Now it is true that Greek lyric poetry often tolerates some confusion of metaphor (see on v. 117, and cp. O. T. p. lviii): the question is whether this example of it be tolerable. Prof. Tyrrell holds that it is excused by the tumult of feeling in the mind of the Chorus. That is, the metaphor of a young life 'mowed down' is not completed by a mention of the agent, the Destroyer: it is swiftly succeeded in the speaker's thought by a dramatic image of the cause, Antigone sprinkling the dust, and defying Creon. This is conceivable; but it is at least extremely bold.

(2) If we read κοπίς, then καταμᾷ is appropriate, and φοινία also has a more evident fitness. The great objection is the want of unison with λόγου τ' ἄνοια καὶ φρενῶν ἐρινύς. If the τ' after λόγου means

'both,' the κοπὶς νερτέρων is the deadly agency as seen in the girl's rash speech and resolve: if the τ' means 'and,' it is an agency to which these things are superadded. On either view the language is awkward. This must be set against the gain in unity of metaphor.

It has further been urged against κοπίς that the word is too homely. This may be so; but we lack proof. κοπίς seems to have been a large curved knife, known to the Greeks chiefly as (a) a butcher's or cook's implement, (b) an oriental military weapon. It does not follow, however, that the effect here would be like that of 'chopper,' or of 'scimitar,' in English. The dignity of a word may be protected by its simplicity; and κοπίς is merely 'that which cuts.' Pindar was not afraid of homeliness when he described a chorus-master as a κρατήρ, or an inspiring thought as an ἀκόνα (cp. O. C. 1052 n.). Nicander could say, of the scorpion, τοίη οἱ κέντροιο κοπίς (Ther. 780). If κοπίς be right, the change to κόνις may have been caused, not by a misreading of letters, but by mere inadvertence,—the copyist having the word κόνις in his thoughts at the moment: it has already occurred frequently (247, 256, 409, 429).—See Appendix.

602 λόγου...ἄνοια, folly shown in speech (defining gen.),—Antigone's answer to Creon (450 ff.): cp. 562 (ἄνουν), 383 (ἀφροσύνη). φρενῶν ἐρινύς, an erinys of (or in) the mind: i.e. the infatuated impulse which urged Antigone to the deed is conceived as a Fury that drove her to her doom. Schol. ὅτι οἰστρηθεῖσα ὑπὸ τῶν ἐρινύων...τοῦτο τετόλμηκεν.

604 τεάν, epic and Ion. (Hom., Hes.,

8—2

2 τὰν οὔθ᾽ ὕπνος αἱρεῖ ποθ᾽ ὁ *πάντ᾽ ἀγρεύων,
3 οὔτε θεῶν *ἄκματοι μῆνες, ἀγήρως δὲ χρόνῳ
4 δυνάστας κατέχεις Ὀλύμπου μαρμαρόεσσαν αἴγλαν. 610
5 τό τ᾽ ἔπειτα καὶ τὸ μέλλον
6 καὶ τὸ πρὶν ἐπαρκέσει

ject. ὑπέρβασις (Pallis ὑπέρβιος) ἄν. Nauck, ἂν παρβασία.—κατάσχοι L, and so almost all the later MSS.: E seems to be alone in κατάσχῃ. **606** παντογήρωσ L, with gl. αἰώνιος above by S. The letters γηρ are underlined. παντογήρωσ was also read by the Scholiast. παντάγηρωσ A.—Bamberger conject. παντοθήρας. Schneidewin,

Her., Pind., etc.); admitted by Aesch. and Eur. in lyrics.—δύνᾶσιν: cp. 951. A poetical form used by Pind., Eur. (in dial. as well as in lyr.), etc.—κατάσχοι. Epic usage admits the optat. (without ἄν) where an abstract possibility is to be stated, as *Il.* 19. 321 οὐ μὲν γάρ τι κακώτερον ἄλλο πάθοιμι, 'for I could not (conceivably) suffer anything worse.' The Homeric instances are chiefly in negative sentences (*Od.* 3. 231 being a rare exception, ῥεῖα θεός γ᾽ ἐθέλων καὶ τηλόθεν ἄνδρα σαώσαι). Attic verse affords some certain examples,—all in negative sentences, or in questions when (as here) a negative answer is expected. So Aesch. *P. V.* 291 οὐκ ἔστιν ὅτῳ | μείζονα μοῖραν νείμαιμ᾽ ἢ σοί. Other instances are Aesch. *Ch.* 172, 595: *Ag.* 620: Eur. *Alc.* 52. Our passage is undoubtedly another genuine instance, and the attempts to alter it (see cr. n.) are mistaken. Attic prose, on the other hand, supplies no trustworthy example: in most of those which are alleged ἄν should be supplied. I have discussed this question in *O. C.*, Appendix on v. 170, p. 273.—Men may overstep their due limits: but no such ὑπερβασία can restrict the power of Zeus. He punishes the encroachment.

606 The MS. παντογήρως is unquestionably corrupt. Sleep, the renewer of vigour, could not be described as 'bringing old age to all.' Nor can the epithet be explained as 'enfeebling all,' in the sense of 'subduing them'; nor, again, as 'attending on all, even to old age.' The neighbourhood of ἀγήρως is not in favour of παντογήρως, but against it; in the case of παντοπόρος—ἄπορος (360), and of ὑψίπολις—ἄπολις (370), there is a direct contrast between the two words. Either πάντ᾽ ἀγρῶν or πανταγρεύς (see cr. n.) would be good, if οὔτ᾽ could be taken from the next verse, and added to this.

But οὔτ᾽ clearly belongs, I think, to the next verse,—as will be seen presently. Bamberger proposed παντοθήρας, or παντόθηρος. The former would be a subst. like ἰχθυοθήρας, 'fisherman,' ὀρνιθοθήρας, 'fowler': the latter (which I should prefer), an adj. like πολύθηρος, 'catching much' (Heliodorus 5. 18), εὔθηρος, 'having good sport.' παντόθηρος would suit the sense well. But its probability depends on the way in which we conceive the corrupt παντογήρως to have arisen. It is evident that the genuine ἀγήρως in the next line had something to do with it. It seems most likely that the eye of the transcriber who first wrote παντογήρως had wandered to ἀγήρως, and that by a mere inadvertence he gave a like ending to the earlier word. Now this might most easily have happened if the sixth letter of the earlier series had been Γ, but would obviously have been less likely if that letter had been Θ. I therefore think it more probable that παντογήρως arose from πάντ᾽ ἀγρεύων than from παντόθηρος. It is immaterial that the last four letters of the latter are nearer to the MS., since, on the view just stated, the transcriber's error arose from the fact that the consecutive letters ἀγ were common to ἀγρεύων and ἀγήρως, and that, from these letters onwards, he accidentally copied ἀγήρως. It may be added that such an error would have been easier with a separate word like ἀγρεύων than with the second part of a compound like παντόθηρος.—The verb ἀγρεύω, 'to catch' (common both in verse and in prose) is used by Soph. in fr. 507.—Soph. was thinking of *Il.* 14. 244 ff. (Ὕπνος speaking to Hera), ἄλλον μέν κεν ἔγωγε θεῶν αἰειγενετάων | ῥεῖα κατευνήσαιμι... | Ζηνὸς δ᾽ οὐκ ἂν ἔγωγε Κρονίονος ἆσσον ἰκοίμην, | οὐδὲ κατευνήσαιμ᾽, ὅτε μὴ αὐτός γε κελεύοι.

607 The MS. οὔτ᾽ ἀκάματοι θεῶν should answer metrically to 618 εἰδότι δ᾽

That power which neither Sleep, the all-ensnaring, nor the
untiring months of the gods can master; but thou, a ruler
to whom time brings not old age, dwellest in the dazzling
splendour of Olympus.

And through the future, near and far, as through the past,

πάντ' ἀγρευτάς. Wolff, πανταγρεύς. Wecklein, πάντ' ἀγρῶν (and formerly πάντ'
ἀφαυρῶν). Semitelos, πάντ' ἀγρώσσων. **607** οὔτ' ἀκάματοι θεῶν MSS. Hermann conject. οὔτε θεῶν ἀκμῆτοι. See Appendix. **608** The first hand in L
wrote ἀγήρως: an early corrector changed ι to σ. Most of the later MSS. have
ἀγήρως, but a few ἀγήρω. **612** ἐπαρκέσει] ἐπικρατεῖ Koechly, which Nauck

---

οὐδὲν ἔρπει. Far the best emendation
is οὔτε θεῶν ἀκμᾶτοι (Hermann ἀκμῆτοι). This supposes merely a transposition of two words, of which L affords
undoubted instances (cp. on 107), and the
very natural development of ἀκάματοι out
of the rarer form ἀκμῆτοι. For the latter
cp. *Hom. hymn. Apoll.* 520 ἀκμῆτοις δὲ
λόφον προσέβαν ποσίν. The word θεῶν
seems to me clearly genuine. Many recent editors have condemned it, because
Zeus is the marshaller of the seasons (*Il.*
2. 134 Διὸς μεγάλου ἐνιαυτοί, *Od.* 24. 344
Διὸς ὥραι, Plat. *Prot.* 321 A τὰς ἐκ Διὸς
ὥρας). How, then, could the poet say
that *Zeus* is not subdued by 'the months
of the gods'? The simple answer is that
the term θεῶν is not opposed to Zeus, but
includes him. Though Zeus (the Sky
Father) was more especially the ταμίας
ὡρῶν, that function can also be ascribed
to the gods collectively: see *e.g.* Plat.
Legg. 886 A οὐκοῦν, ὦ ξένε, δοκεῖ ῥάδιον
εἶναι ἀληθεύοντας λέγειν ὡς εἰσὶ θεοί;—
πῶς;—πρῶτον μὲν γῆ καὶ ἥλιος ἄστρα τε
τὰ ξύμπαντα καὶ τὰ τῶν ὡρῶν διακε-
κοσμημένα καλῶς οὕτως, ἐνιαυτοῖς τε
καὶ μησὶ διειλημμένα. Cp. *ib.* 809 D,
as illustrating another reason which made
the phrase θεῶν μῆνες so natural—the
fact, namely, that the ἑορταί were the
land-marks of the Calendar: τίνων δὴ πέρι
λέγομεν; ἡμερῶν τάξεως εἰς μηνῶν περιό-
δους καὶ μηνῶν εἰς ἕκαστον τὸν ἐνιαυτόν,
ἵνα ὧραι καὶ θυσίαι καὶ ἑορταὶ τὰ προσή-
κοντα ἀπολαμβάνουσαι ἑαυταῖς ἕκασται...
θεῶς μὲν τὰς τιμὰς ἀποδιδῶσι κ.τ.λ. And,
if θεῶν be genuine, then οὔτε belongs to
this verse, and we gain a fresh argument
against those emendations which would
append οὔτ' to v. 606: for οὔτ' | ἀκάματοι
θεῶν <νιν> is certainly not probable.
See Appendix.—All the immortals have
a *life* which is not worn out by those

months which they themselves control.
The distinction of Zeus is that his *su-
premacy* over gods and men is unalter-
able.—ἀκμᾶτοι, untiring in their course:
cp. *Il.* 18. 239 ἠέλιον δ' ἀκάμαντα : Eur.
fr. 597 ἀκάμας τε χρόνος.

608 f. I doubt whether the dat.
χρόνῳ could be instrumental or causal
here ('not made old *by* time'). It rather
seems to be an adverbial dat. of circumstance, 'not growing old with time' (as
time oes on). χρόνῳ oft. = 'at length'
(*O.* Cg437).—μαρμαρόεσσαν (only here)
=μαρμαρέαν. μαρμαίρω and its cognate
adj. are applied to any *sparkling* or *flashing* light (as of sun or stars, bright eyes,
gleaming metal). Cp. *Il.* 1. 532 αἴγλη-
αἰγλήεντος Ὀλύμπου. A. Blackwᵃll c
pares the language of St Paul in 1 Tim.
6. 15 ὁ μακάριος καὶ μόνος δυνάστης...φῶς
οἰκῶν ἀπρόσιτον.

611 f. τό τ' ἔπειτα (acc. of duration)
is what will immediately follow the *present*
moment (cp. Plat. *Parm.* 152 C τοῦ τε νῦν
καὶ τοῦ ἔπειτα), and is here distinguished
from τὸ μέλλον, the *more distant* future;
Plaut. *Pers.* 778 (quoted by Schneid.)
qui sunt, quique erunt (τὸ ἔπειτα), *quique
fuerunt, quique futuri sunt posthac* (τὸ
μέλλον). It is much as if we said, 'to-
morrow, and for all time.' Many have
compared Eur. *I. T.* 1263 τά τε πρῶτα |
τά τ' ἔπειθ' ἅ τ' ἔμελλε τυχεῖν: but even
if Seidler's ἅ τ', rather than ὅσ', be there
the true correction of the MS. ὅσα τ', the
parallelism is not strict, since τὰ ἔπειτα
would then mean 'what followed τὰ
πρῶτα,' not, 'what is to follow τὰ νῦν.'—
καὶ τὸ πρίν is usu. explained as a compressed form of ὥσπερ καὶ τὸ πρὶν ἐπήρκεσε:
but this is at least much bolder than the
examples which are brought to support it,
as Dem. or. 18 § 31 καὶ τότε καὶ νῦν καὶ ἀεὶ
ὁμολογῶ, which would be parallel only if

7 νόμος ὅδ'· οὐδὲν ἕρπει
8 θνατῶν βιότῳ *πάμπολύ γ' ἐκτὸς ἄτας.

ἀντ. β'. ἁ γὰρ δὴ πολύπλαγκτος ἐλπὶς πολλοῖς μὲν ὄνασις
ἀνδρῶν,   616
2 πολλοῖς δ' ἀπάτα κουφονόων ἐρώτων·
3 εἰδότι δ' οὐδὲν ἕρπει, πρὶν πυρὶ θερμῷ πόδα τις
4 προσαύσῃ. σοφίᾳ γὰρ ἔκ του κλεινὸν ἔπος πέφανται,   621
5 τὸ κακὸν δοκεῖν ποτ' ἐσθλὸν

adopts. **613** ἕρπει MSS.: ἕρπειν Heath: ἕρπων Boeckh. **614** πάμ|πολισ L.
The later MSS., too, have πάμπολις, but Camph. cites πάμπολῦν as written by the
first hand in one of them (Vat.), and corrected to πάμπολιν. πάμπολύ γ' Heath.
See Appendix. **616** ὄνησις L, the final σ made from ν by an early corrector.

it were καὶ νῦν καὶ ἀεὶ καὶ τότε ὁμολογῶ:
and νῦν τε καὶ πάλαι δοκεῖ (181) is irre-
levant, since πάλαι can take the pres. (279).
Rather, perh., ἐπαρκέσει, 'will hold good,'
means, 'will be found true,'—both in the
future, and if we scan the past.—For τὸ
before πρίν, cp. O. C. 180 ἔτι; προβίβαξε.
ἐπαρκέσει, will hold out, hold good, = διαρ-
κέσει: so only here, perhaps, for in Solon
fr. 5. 1 δήμῳ μὲν γὰρ ἔδωκα τόσον κράτος
ὅσσον ἐπαρκεῖ, we must surely read ἀπαρκεῖ,
with Coraës.

613 f. πάμπολύ γ' (Heath), for πάμπολις, is not only the best emendation,
but (in my belief) a certain one. I do
not know whether it has been noticed
that πάμπολῦν in one of the late MSS. (see
cr. n.),—a mere blunder for πάμπολις,—
forcibly illustrates the ease with which the
opposite change of πάμπολύ γ' into πάμπολις could have occurred. The νόμος, then,
is:—'Nothing vast comes to (enters into)
the life of mortals, ἐκτὸς ἄτας, free from
a curse (cp. ἔξω...αἰτίας, 445)'—without
bringing ἄτη. Cp. Plat. Rep. 531 D πάμπολυ ἔργον, Legg. 823 B πάμπολύ τι πρᾶγμα,
ib. 677 E γῆς δ' ἀφθόνου πλῆθος πάμπολυ.
Too much power, or wealth, or prosperity
—anything so great as to be μὴ κατ' ἄνθρωπον—excites the divine φθόνος: the
man shows ὕβρις, and this brings ἄτη.
Cp. Her. 7. 10 ὁρᾷς τὰ ὑπερέχοντα ζῷα
ὡς κεραυνοῖ ὁ θεὸς οὐδὲ ἐᾷ φαντάζεσθαι, τὰ
δὲ σμικρὰ οὐδέν μιν κνίζει; ὁρᾷς δὲ ὡς ἐς
οἰκήματα τὰ μέγιστα αἰεὶ καὶ δένδρεα τὰ
τοιαῦτα ἀποσκήπτει τὰ βέλεα; φιλέει γὰρ
ὁ θεὸς τὰ ὑπερέχοντα πάντα κολούειν.
Diog. L. 1. 3. 2 (Zeus) τὰ μὲν ὑψηλὰ

ταπεινῶν, τὰ δὲ ταπεινὰ ὑψῶν. Soph. fr.
320 καλὸν φρονεῖν τὸν θνητὸν ἀνθρώποις
ἴσα.—ἕρπει: cp. Ai. 1087 ἕρπει παραλλάξ
ταῦτα (come to men): for the dat., cp.
above, 186. The inf. ἕρπειν would be
admissible after οὐδέν, since this is not a
precept (like μὴ πλουτεῖν ἀδίκως), but a
statement of fact. In 706 L has ἔχει by
mistake for ἔχειν, and such errors are
frequent. And δοκεῖν in 622 might seem
to recommend ἕρπειν here. Yet ἕρπει
seems right. For this is not what the
νόμος says,—as δοκεῖν in 622 depends on
ἔπος πέφανται, and δράσαντι παθεῖν in
Aesch. Cho. 313 on μῦθος...φωνεῖ. The
constant fact, οὐδὲν ἕρπει, is the νόμος.
Cp. Ph. 435 λόγῳ δέ σ' ἐν βραχεῖ | τοῦτ'
ἐκδιδάξω· πόλεμος οὐδέν' ἄνδρ' ἑκὼν | αἱρεῖ
πονηρόν.—πάμπολις is impossible. For
the attempts to explain it, and for other
conjectures, see Appendix.

615—625 ἁ γὰρ δή κ.τ.λ. The γάρ
introduces an explanation of the law just
stated. 'No inordinate desire comes to
men without bringing ἄτη. For hope,
which can be a blessing, can also be a
curse, by luring a man to pursue forbidden things; and then he sins blindly, till
the gods strike him. The gods cause him
to mistake evil for good; and his impunity is of short duration.' Creon is destined to exemplify this. πολύπλαγκτος,
roaming widely—as a mariner over unknown seas—in dreams of the future.
Soph. was perh. thinking of Pind. O. 12.
6 αἵ γε μὲν ἀνδρῶν | πόλλ' ἄνω, τὰ δ' αὖ
κάτω ψεύδη μεταμώνια τάμοισαι κυλίνδοντ'
ἐλπίδες, 'at least, the hopes of men are

shall this law hold goo : Nothing that is vast enters into
the life of mortals withoud a curse.

For that hope whose wanderings are so wide is to many 2nd
men a comfort, but to many a false lure of giddy desires ; and anti-
the disappointment comes on one who knoweth nought till strophe
he burn his foot against the hot fire.

For with wisdom hath some one given forth the famous
saying, that evil seems good, soon or late,

ὄνασις Brunck.   **619** προσαύσῃ L, with ·αἱρει· (*i.e.* προσαίρει) written above
by an early hand.   The later MSS. have προσαύσῃ, προσψαύσῃ, προσαίρῃ, and
προσάρῃ.   **620** σοφίᾳ L, with ι written over a by a late hand.   σοφίας
r.   **621** πέφανται] In L the ν has been erased.   **622** ποτ'] Wecklein

---

oft tossed up and down, ploughing a sea
of vain deceits.'—πολύπλαγκτος might
also be 'act., 'causing men to err greatly';
but this is less fitting here.

616 πολλοῖς μὲν ὄνασις, by cheering
them, and inciting to worthy effort. This
clause is inserted merely for the sake of
contrast with the next.   When Greek
idiom thus co-ordinates two clauses, the
clause which we should subordinate to
the other is that which has μέν; as here,
'*though* a blessing to many.'   So *O. C.*
1536 (n.), εὖ μὲν ὀψέ δ', 'late, though
surely.'

617 ἀπάτα...ἐρώτων.   The gen. is best
taken as subjective, a cheating (of men)
by desires; *i.e.*, ἔρωτες ἀπατῶσι.   The
ἐλπίς *is* such an ἀπάτα, because it ends in
that.   If the gen. were subjective, the
sense would be ἐλπίς ἀπατᾷ ἔρωτας.   This
is equally possible, but hardly so natural.
In 630, ἀπάτας λεχέων, the gen. is neither
of these, but one of relation (a deceiving
of him about his marriage).   Cp. Hes.
Op. 460 νεωμένη οὔ σ' ἀπατήσει, when
ploughed again, the soil will not disap-
point thee.—κουφονόων: see on 342.

617 The ἀπάτα, or final frustration of
his desires, ἕρπει, creeps on him, οὐδὲν
εἰδότι, knowing nothing.   Others construe,
οὐδὲν ἕρπει εἰδότι, nothing comes to him
aware of it; *i.e.* he understands the true
meaning of nothing that happens to him.
This is somewhat forced; and that οὐδέν
is object to εἰδότι is confirmed by Antiphon or. 1 § 29 οἱ δ' ἐπιβουλευόμενοι
οὐδὲν ἴσασι πρὶν ἐν αὐτῷ ὦσι τῷ κακῷ γ'
ἤδη.   Cp. *Ai.* 964 τἀγαθὸν χεροῖ | ἔχοντες
οὐκ ἴσασι, πρίν τις ἐκβάλῃ.

619 πρὶν...προσαύσῃ.   Attic, like
epic, poetry can use simple πρίν, in-

stead of πρὶν ἄν (308), with subjunct.:
so *Ai.* 965 (see last n.), *Ph.* 917, *Tr.*
608, 946, etc.—προσαύσῃ (only here),
'burn against.'   The simple verb occurs
Od. 5. 490 ἵνα μή ποθεν ἄλλοθεν αὔοι (*sc.*
πῦρ), 'kindle.'   Attic had ἐναύω, 'kindle,'
and ἀφαύω, 'parch.'   The image here
seems to be that of a man who walks, in
fancied security, over ashes under which
fire still smoulders (cp. Lucr. 4. 927 *cinere
ut multo latet obrutus ignis*, Hor. *c.* 2. 1. 7
incedis per ignes Suppositos cineri doloso).
There was a prov., ἐν πυρὶ βέβηκας (Suidas, etc.).—πόδα: cp. Aesch. *Ch.* 697
ἔξω κομίζων ὀλεθρίου πηλοῦ πόδα: *P. V.*
263 πημάτων ἔξω πόδα | ἔχει (and so *Ph.*
1260 ἐκτὸς κλαυμάτων, Eur. *Her.* 109 ἔξω
πραγμάτων).—Some render προσαύσῃ
'bring to,' assuming an αὔω equiv. in sense
to αἴρω: but the evidence for this is doubtful: see Appendix.

620 f.   σοφίᾳ, modal dat., = σοφῶς:
cp. *El.* 233 εὐνοίᾳ γ' αὐδῶ: so ὀργῇ (*O. T.*
405), θυμῷ (*O. C.* 659), etc.—ἐκ του, *i.e.*
by some wise man of olden time:—not
like the οὐκ ἔφα τις in Aesch. *Ag.* 369 (alluding to Diagoras).   Cp. frag. adesp. 383
(schol. on *Tr.* 296) καὶ τοῦτο τοῦτος ἐστὶν
ἀνδρὸς ἔμφρονος, | ὅταν καλῶς πράσσῃ τις,
ἐλπίζειν κακά.   For similar γνῶμαι in
tragic lyrics, cp. Aesch. *Ag.* 750, *Ch.* 313.
—πέφανται: *Tr.* 1 λόγος μέν ἐστ' ἀρχαῖος
ἀνθρώπων φανείς: *O. T.* 525, 848.

622 f.   τὸ κακὸν δοκεῖν ποτ' κ.τ.λ.
The sense of ποτέ here is not 'sometimes,'
but 'at one time or another,' 'at length,'
as *Ph.* 1041 ἀλλὰ τῷ χρόνῳ ποτέ.   A moment arrives when he makes the fatal
error.   ἄτη (ἀάω), as the heaven-sent influence that leads men to sin, is properly
'hurt done to the mind.'   Milton, *Samson*

6 τῷδ᾽ ἔμμεν ὅτῳ φρένας

7 θεὸς ἄγει πρὸς ἄταν·

8 πράσσει δ᾽ ὀλίγιστον χρόνον ἐκτὸς ἄτας.   625

ὅδε μὴν Αἵμων, παίδων τῶν σῶν
νέατον γέννημ᾽· ἆρ᾽ ἀχνύμενος
τῆς μελλογάμου
τάλιδος ἥκει μόρον Ἀντιγόνης,
ἀπάτας λεχέων ὑπεραλγῶν;   630

ΚΡ. τάχ᾽ εἰσόμεσθα μάντεων ὑπέρτερον.
ὦ παῖ, τελείαν ψῆφον ἆρα μὴ κλύων
τῆς μελλονύμφου πατρὶ λυσσαίνων πάρει;

conject. τότ'. **623** ἔμμεν' L: ἔμμεν Brunck.   **625** ὀλίγωστον (sic) L, ωt having been made from σσ: the accent on ι is crossed out. ὀλιγοστὸν r. ὀλίγιστον Bergk. **626 f.** ἆρ' (sic) ἀχνύμενοσ | τῆσ μελλογάμου νύμφησ | τάλιδοσ ἥκει μόρον Ἀντιγόνησ L:

1676 Among them he a spirit of phrenzy sent, Who hurt their minds. Cp. βλαψί-φρων, φρενοβλαβής. Il. 19. 137 ἀλλ᾽ ἐπεὶ ἀασάμην, καί μευ φρένας ἐξέλετο Ζεύς. Theognis 403 σπεύδει ἀνήρ, κέρδος διζήμε-νος, ὅν τινα δαίμων | πρόφρων εἰς μεγάλην ἀμπλακίην παράγει, | καί οἱ ἔθηκε δοκεῖν, ἃ μὲν ᾖ κακά, ταῦτ᾽ ἀγάθ᾽ εἶναι, | εὐ-μαρέως, ἃ δ᾽ ἂν ᾖ χρήσιμα, ταῦτα κακά. Lycurgus in Leocr. § 92 οἱ γὰρ θεοὶ οὐδὲν πρότερον ποιοῦσιν ἢ τῶν πονηρῶν ἀνθρώπων τὴν διάνοιαν παράγουσι· καί μοι δοκοῦσι τῶν ἀρχαίων τινὲς ποιητῶν ὥσπερ χρησμοὺς γράψαντες τοῖς ἐπιγιγνο-μένοις ταῦτα τὰ ἰαμβεῖα καταλιπεῖν· ὅταν γὰρ ὀργὴ δαιμόνων βλάπτῃ τινά, | τοῦτ᾽ αὐτὸ πρῶτον, ἐξαφαιρεῖται φρενῶν | τὸν νοῦν τὸν ἐσθλόν, εἰς δὲ τὴν χείρω τρέπει | γνώμην, ἵν᾽ εἰδῇ μηδὲν ὧν ἁμαρτάνει. The schol. on our verse quotes an unknown poet's lines, ὅταν δ᾽ ὁ δαίμων ἀνδρὶ πορ-σύνῃ κακά, | τὸν νοῦν ἔβλαψε πρῶτον, ᾧ βουλεύεται. ('Quem Iuppiter vult perdere, dementat prius.' See n. in Appendix.)—The epic ἔμμεν (used also by Pind. and Sappho) occurs nowhere else in tragedy.

625 ὀλίγιστον, a superl. used not only in epic poetry but also by Attic writers (as Ar. and Plat.), is right here. The MS. ὀλιγοστόν cannot be defended by Ar. Pax 559 πολλοστῷ χρόνῳ, which is merely another form of πολλοστῷ ἔτει (Cra-tinus jun. Χείρ. 1); i.e. πολλοστός has its proper sense, 'one of many' (multesimus), and the χρόνος, like the ἔτος, is conceived as

the last of a series. So ὀλίγοστος χρόνος would mean, not, 'a fraction of time,' but, 'one in a small number of χρόνοι' or periods. In Arist. Metaph. 9. 1. 14 most MSS., and the best, have ὀλίγιστον...χρό-νον: while A^b (cod. Laur. 87. 12) is the only MS. cited in the Berlin ed. (p. 1053 a 9) for ὀλίγοστόν. And otherwise ὀλί-γοστός occurs only in later Greek, as Plut. Anton. 51 καταβὰς ὀλίγοστός, 'having gone to the coast with a small retinue'; Caes. 49 ὀλίγοστῳ τοσαύτην ἀμυνομένῳ πόλιν 'fighting so great a State with a small force.'—πράσσει...ἐκτὸς ἄτας, like πράσσει καλῶς: so πράσσειν κατὰ νοῦν (Plat. Rep. 366 B, Ar. Eq. 549). ἄτας is here 'calamity' (as in 584, 614), while in the last verse ἄταν is rather 'infatuation.' —Donaldson changed ἄτας here to ἄλ-γους, because the strophe (614) also ends with ἐκτὸς ἄτας. On the other hand Din-dorf ejects ἐκτὸς ἄτας from 614 (leaving a lacuna). But I believe ἐκτὸς ἄτας to be genuine in both places, as οὐδὲν ἕρπει also is both in 613 and in 618. We have to remember, first, that Soph. (like other ancient poets) easily tolerated repetition of words (see on O. C. 554); secondly, that tragic lyrics could admit refrains, and might, by a kindred instinct, permit such verbal echoes as these.

626 f. μήν instead of the usu. καὶ μήν (526).—νέατον, 'youngest and last,' Me-gareus being dead (1303): cp. 807 τὰν νεάταν ὁδόν; so 808, Ai. 1185. As applied

to him whose mind the god draws to mischief; and but for the briefest space doth he fare free of woe.

But lo, Haemon, the last of thy sons;—comes he grieving for the doom of his promised bride, Antigone, and bitter for the baffled hope of his marriage?

Enter HAEMON.

CR.   We shall know soon, better than seers could tell us.—
My son, hearing the fixed doom of thy betrothed, art thou
come in rage against thy father?

over τάλιδοσ S has written τῆs νύμφηs.   Triclinius omitted the words τῆs μελλογάμου
νύμφηs.   **630** λέχεων L.   **633** λυσσαίνων] Schol. in L, γρ. θυμαίνων.—
Meineke conject. δυσμενῶν: Semitelos, πατέρα δεννάσων.

---

to a person, νέατος could not be said of a sole survivor unless he was *also* the latest-born. γέννημ': cp. 471 n.—ἀχνύμενος with μόρον as internal acc.: cp. *Il.* 5. 361 ἄχθομαι ἕλκος.

628 In the MS. reading (see cr. n.) νύμφης is a gloss on τάλιδος: but τῆs μελλογάμου should be retained. Except in the lexicons, τάλις occurs only here and in a verse of Callimachus, αὐτίκα τὴν τάλιν παιδὶ σὺν ἀμφιθαλεῖ, quoted by the Schol., who says, τάλις λέγεται παρ' Αἰολεῦσιν ἡ ὀνομασθεῖσά τινι νύμφη. Hesychius has, τάλις· ἡ μελλόγαμος παρθένος καὶ κατωνομασμένη τινί· οἱ δὲ γυναῖκα γαμετήν· οἱ δὲ νύμφην. This shows that τάλις could mean, not only an affianced bride, but also a bride after marriage: just as νύμφη can mean either. The epithet τῆs μελλογάμου is not, then, superfluous; and τῆs μελλονύμφου in 633 is no argument against it. On the other hand τάλιδος, without the epithet, would have a crude effect. A passage in Pollux (3. 45) has been taken to prove that he had τῆs μελλογάμου in his text. It does not prove this,—nor the reverse. τῆs μελλογάμου in Pollux should be (as Semitelos saw) τὴν μελλόγαμον, and we should refer his words solely to v. 633. His point is simply that ἡ μελλόνυμφος i more correct than ἡ μελλόνυμφη.—Curtius connects τάλις with τέρ-ην, tender; θρόνα, flowers: Sanskrit *tár-una-s*, youthful, tender, *tál-uni*, girl, young woman. He supposes the first idea to be that of a plant sprouting or blossoming (cp. θάλος). This at least agrees well with what we know as to the usage of τάλις.

630 ἀπάτας (gen. sing.) λεχέων, a de-

ceit practised on him, a disappointment, in regard to his marriage. The gen. λεχέων is one of relation, helped, perhaps, by the idea of privation (as if ἀπάτη were ἀποστέρησις).

631—780 Third ἐπεισόδιον. Haemon vainly intercedes with his father. They quarrel, and the son abruptly leaves the scene (765). Creon then commands that Antigone shall at once be immured in a rocky vault.

631 μάντεων ὑπέρτερον = βέλτιον ἢ μάντεις ἴσασιν (and better, therefore, than they could tell us). Schol. ὁ λόγος παροιμιακῶς, ὁπότε μὴ στοχασμῷ χρώμεθα, ἀλλ' αὐτόπται τῶν πραγμάτων γινόμεθα. Eur. *H. F.* 911 ΑΓ. ὤλαστα τάν δόμοισι.—ΧΟ. μάντιν οὐχ ἕτερον ἕξομαι, 'I will not bring a seer, other than myself' (cp. *O. T.* 6), *i.e.* 'I need no seer to tell me that':— imitated by the author of the *Rhesus* 949 σοφιστὴν δ' ἄλλον οὐκ ἐπάξομαι, who also has 952 ἤδη τάδ'· οὐδὲν μάντεως ἔδει φράσαι. Cp. *O. C.* 403.

632 f. τελείαν announces that he will not yield.—ψῆφον: cp. 60.—ἆρα μή, like μῶν, 'can it be that...?' *El.* 446.—τῆs μελλονύμφου: for the gen., cp. Thuc. 1. 140 τὸ Μεγαρέων ψήφισμα, and n. on 11.—λυσσαίνων, the reading of the MSS., is a word not extant elsewhere, but as correctly formed as ὀργαίνω, χαλεπαίνω, etc. At first sight it seems too strong: λύσσα is 'raving.' But a certain vehemence of language characterises Creon (cp. 280 ff.). Instead of saying merely, 'have you come here in displeasure?', he says, 'have you come here to storm at me?' As σοὶ μέν shows, there is a tacit contrast with the sisters: he had described Ismene as λυσ-

√ ἦ σοὶ μὲν ἡμεῖς πανταχῇ δρῶντες φίλοι;

ΑΙΜΩΝ.

πάτερ, σός εἰμι· καὶ σύ μοι γνώμας ἔχων   635
χρηστὰς, ἀπορθοῖς, αἷς ἔγωγ' ἐφέψομαι.
ἐμοὶ γὰρ οὐδεὶς *ἀξιώσεται γάμος
μείζων φέρεσθαι σοῦ καλῶς ἡγουμένου.

ΚΡ. οὕτω γὰρ, ὦ παῖ, χρὴ διὰ στέρνων ἔχειν,
γνώμης πατρῴας πάντ' ὄπισθεν ἑστάναι.   640
τούτου γὰρ οὕνεκ' ἄνδρες εὔχονται γονὰς
κατηκόους φύσαντες ἐν δόμοις ἔχειν,
ὡς καὶ τὸν ἐχθρὸν ἀνταμύνωνται κακοῖς,
καὶ τὸν φίλον τιμῶσιν ἐξ ἴσου πατρί.
ὅστις δ' ἀνωφέλητα φιτύει τέκνα,   645
τί τόνδ' ἂν εἴποις ἄλλο πλὴν αὑτῷ πόνους

635 μοι] L has μου, the υ being joined to the following γ, as ι would not have been. μοι r. 637 ἀξίως ἔσται L. As the letters εσ are contracted into one character somewhat like ε, L's reading is even nearer than it looks in our type

σῶσαν (491). I therefore think λυσσαίνων genuine, and a finer reading than the variant noted in L, θυμαίνων. The latter word is used by Hesiod, and in Attic comedy. Some recent edd. place it in the text.

634 σοὶ μέν: cp. 498.—πανταχῇ δρῶντες, 'however I may act.' Ai. 1369 ὡς ἂν ποιήσῃς, πανταχῇ χρηστός γ' ἔσει. Her. 9. 27 πάντῃ γὰρ τεταγμένοι (wherever we may be posted) πειρησόμεθα εἶναι χρηστοί: id. 8. 110 πάντως ἕτοιμοι ἦσαν λέγοντι πείθεσθαι ('ready in every case').

635 f. σός: cp. O. C. 1323.—γνώμας ἔχων χρηστάς, having good counsels, ἀπορθοῖς (αὐτάς) μοι, thou settest them before me as rules. ἀπορθόω (a rare word) means, like ἀπευθύνω, (1) 'to straighten out,' and then (2) 'to guide in a straight course.' Plat. Legg. 757 E (praying the gods) ἀπορθοῦν τὸν κλῆρον πρὸς τὸ δικαιότατον, 'to direct the lot (for magistracies) in the best interests of justice.' Here the γνῶμαι are the κανόνες, regulae, which are to guide the youth's course: cp. fr. 430 ὥστε τέκτονος | παρὰ στάθμην ἰόντος ὀρθοῦται κανών. Eur. El. 52 γνώμης πονηροῖς κανόσιν ἀναμετρούμενος | τὸ σῶφρον.—Others understand: (1) ἀπορθοῖς γνώμας μοι, thou guidest my views, χρηστὰς ἔχων, having good views (of thine

own). Or (2) 'Having good views, thou guidest me,' supplying με with ἀπορθοῖς (like O. T. 104 ἀπευθύνειν πόλιν). But μοι would then be awkward. Cp. Plaut. Trin. 304 (a son to his father) sarta tecta tua praecepta usque habui mea modestia.

637 f. ἀξιώσεται, pass.; cp. 210, O. C. 581 δηλώσεται, O. T. 672 στυγήσεται (n.). ἀξ. μείζων φέρεσθαι, will be esteemed more important to win (cp. 439 ἥσσω λαβεῖν): so Plat. Theaet. 161 D ὥστε καὶ ἄλλων διδάσκαλος ἀξιοῦσθαι δικαίως, 'to be justly ranked as a teacher.' The same use is implied in Legg. 917 D ὁπόσης ἂν τιμῆς ἀξιώσῃ τὸ πωλούμενον (at whatever price he may value...).—L's reading, ἀξίως ἔσται, though tenable, seems slightly less probable, when we observe that this adv. is regularly used either (a) with gen., ἀξίως ἑαυτῶν, etc., or (b) absol., in such phrases as Thuc. 3. 40 κολάσατε...ἀξίως τούτους, 'according to their deserts.' (So O. T. 133 ἀξίως = 'as the case required.') Thus we could say, οὗτος ὁ γάμος ἀξίως ἔσται μείζων φ., 'will deservedly (= on its merits) be a greater prize.' But it is less natural to say, οὐδεὶς γάμος ἀξίως ἔσται μ. φ., 'no marriage will rightly be preferred,' etc., where ἀξίως becomes a mere equiv. for δικαίως or προσηκόντως. The change of ἀξιώσεται into ἀξίως ἔσται would

Or have I thy good will, act how I may?

HAE. Father, I am thine; and thou, in thy wisdom, tracest for me rules which I shall follow. No marriage shall be deemed by me a greater gain than thy good guidance.

CR. Yea, this, my son, should be thy heart's fixed law,—in all things to obey thy father's will. 'Tis for this that men pray to see dutiful children grow up around them in their homes,—that such may requite their father's foe with evil, and honour, as their father doth, his friend. But he who begets unprofitable children—what shall we say that he hath sown, but troubles for

---

to ἀξιώσεται, Musgrave's correction. late MS. (Dresden a, 14th cent.). grave and Schaefer conject. ἱστάναι. **645** φυτεύει MSS.: φιτύει Brunck. γρ. πέδας· ἵν' ᾖ, ἐμπόδιον, δεσμούς, κώλυμα τοῦ πράττειν ἃ βούλεται.

638 μείζων] μεῖζον is quoted from one **640** ὅπισθεν] ὅπιθεν L.—ἱστάναι] Musgrave and **643** ἀνταμύνονται L: ἀνταμύνωνται r. **646** πόνους] L has a marg. gl. by S,

---

have been the easier, since the ordinary fut. was ἀξιωθήσομαι.—σοῦ καλῶς ἡγουμ., (with μεῖζον), than thy good guiding: cp. Her. 1. 34 μετὰ δὲ Σόλωνα οἰχόμενον. —It is a mistake (I think) to detect a mental reserve in the participle ('than thy guiding, if, or when, it is good'). Haemon knows that his one chance of saving Antigone is first to mollify his father, and then to urge the argument from public opinion (688 ff.). His deference is unqualified.

639 γάρ in assent (O. T. 1117).—διὰ στέρνων ἔχειν, lit., 'to be disposed in one's breast,' = φρονεῖν, or διακεῖσθαι. The phrase differs in two points from others which seem like it. (1) The gen. with διά in such phrases regularly denotes a state or act of the mind, whereas στέρνων represents the mind itself. (2) ἔχειν in such phrases is always trans., the intrans. verb being εἶναι. Thus ἔχω τινά (or τι) δι' αἰσχύνης, αἰτίας, ὀργῆς, φυλακῆς, etc. But εἰμὶ δι' ἡσυχίης (Her. 1. 206), διὰ φόβου (Thuc. 6. 59), δι' ὄχλου (Ar. Eccl. 888). Here οὕτω, going with ἔχειν, shows that the verb is intrans.,—not trans., with ταῦτα understood.

640 (One ought to think thus),—that is, ὄπισθεν ἱστάναι τῆς πατρ. γνώμης, one ought to place oneself under the guidance of a father's counsel, πάντα, in all things (adv. neut. pl., 'O. T. 1197 etc.). Thus ἱστάναι depends on χρή,—the indefinite subject of ἔχειν (τινά) being continued with it; and the whole clause explains οὕτω. The image from a soldier posted behind his leader suits the military

tone in which Creon presently enforces the value of discipline (670). Cp. Plat. Rep. 471 D εἴτε καὶ ἐν τῇ αὐτῇ τάξει εἴτε καὶ ὄπισθεν ἐπιτεταγμένον. The phrase ὄπισθεν ἱστάναι τῆς γν. is a poetical equiv. for ἀκολουθεῖν τῇ γνώμῃ (Thuc. 3. 38).—We could also render,—'that all things rank second to a father's will': when ἱστάναι would depend on διὰ στέρνων ἔχειν as =νομίζειν. But ἱστάναι applies to the τάξις of persons more naturally than to the estimation of things: cp. Her. 9. 27 ἵνα δοκέει ἐπιτηδεότατον ἡμέας εἶναι ἑστάναι (in battle): and the constr. is also less simple. ἱστάναι (which Musgrave proposed) would suit that view better.

643 f. ὡς without ἄν, as 760, O. T. 359, and oft.—ἀνταμύνωνται, a neutral word: thus Thuc. 2. 67 τοῖς αὐτοῖς ἀμύνεσθαι, to retaliate; but 1. 42 τοῖς ὁμοίοις ἡμᾶς ἀμύνεσθαι, to reward: here κακοῖς defines it.—ἐξ ἴσου πατρί = ὥσπερ ὁ πατήρ (cp. 516).—O. C. 171 ἀστοῖς ἴσα χρὴ μελετᾶν.—The son's part is τοὺς αὐτοὺς ἐχθροὺς καὶ φίλους νομίζειν,—the definition of a ξυμμαχία as dist. from a merely defensive ἐπιμαχία, Thuc. 1. 44. Cp. 523 n.: Pind. P. 2. 83 φίλον εἴη φιλεῖν· | ποτὶ δ' ἐχθρὸν ἅτ' ἐχθρὸς ἐὼν λύκοιο δίκαν ὑποθεύσομαι.

646 f. ἄλλο is most simply taken as governed by φῦσαι, though, if we had ἤ instead of πλήν, Greek idiom would rather lead us to supply ποιῆσαι: see on 497, and cp. Ai. 125 οὐδὲν ὄντας ἄλλο πλὴν | εἴδωλ'. This is better than to make ἄλλο object to εἴπους ('what could one say of him,' etc.).—πόνους: cp. 533.—

φῦσαι, πολὺν δὲ τοῖσιν ἐχθροῖσιν γέλων·
μὴ νύν ποτ’, ὦ παῖ, τὰς φρένας <γ’> ὑφ’ ἡδονῆς
γυναικὸς οὕνεκ’ ἐκβάλῃς, εἰδὼς ὅτι
ψυχρὸν παράγκάλισμα τοῦτο γίγνεται,   650
γυνὴ κακὴ ξύνευνος ἐν δόμοις. τί γὰρ
γένοιτ’ ἂν ἕλκος μεῖζον ἢ φίλος κακός;
ἀλλὰ πτύσας ὡσεί τε δυσμενῆ μέθες
τὴν παῖδ’ ἐν Ἅιδου τήνδε νυμφεύειν τινί.
ἐπεὶ γὰρ αὐτὴν εἷλον ἐμφανῶς ἐγὼ   655
πόλεως ἀπιστήσασαν ἐκ πάσης μόνην,
ψευδῆ γ’ ἐμαυτὸν οὐ καταστήσω πόλει,
ἀλλὰ κτενῶ. πρὸς ταῦτ’ ἐφυμνείτω Δία
ξύναιμον· εἰ γὰρ δὴ τά γ’ ἐγγενῆ φύσει
ἄκοσμα θρέψω, κάρτα τοὺς ἔξω γένους.   660

648 μὴ νῦν L: μὴ νύν Aldus (μὴ τοι νυν A).—τὰς φρέναс ὑφ’ ἡδονῆσ L. The γ’ inserted after φρένας in some later MSS. was a conjecture of Triclinius. See

γέλων: cp. *Ei.* 1153 γελῶσι δ’ ἐχθροι: *Ai.* 79 οὔκουν γέλως ἥδιστος εἰς ἐχθροὺς γελᾶν; 961 οἱ δ’ οὖν γελώντων κἀπιχαιρόντων κακοῖς.
648 τὰς φρένας γ’. Recent edd. have usually scorned the simple insertion of γε, by which Triclinius healed the metre. But it should be noticed that γε may emphasise τὰς φρένας ἐκβάλῃς, and not merely τὰς φρένας: cp. 747: *O. C.* 1278 τοῦ θεοῦ γε προστάτην, where γε emphasises the whole phrase, not merely the word θεοῦ. The deprecatory force of γε, as seen in μὴ σύ γε (*O. C.* 1441 n.), also recommends it, even when we have not σύ. Cp. Eur. *Hipp.* 503 καὶ μή γε πρὸς θεῶν, εὖ λέγεις γάρ, αἰσχρὰ δέ, | πέρα προβῇς τῶνδ’. Without, then, thinking φρένας γ’ certain, I think it far more probable than the next best remedy, φρένας σύ γ’ ἡδονῇ. As to a third conjecture, σύ γ’ ἡδονῆς, the phrase οὕνεκα ἡδονῆς γυναικός (pleasure in her) would be very awkward. Some strange emendations have been proposed: see Appendix.—φρένας...ἐκβάλῃς, cast off the restraint of reason, as *O. T.* 611 φίλον... ἐσθλὸν ἐκβαλεῖν, *O. C.* 631 εὐμένειαν ἐκβάλοι (reject friendship). The first idea is that of *casting out* of house or land, banishing. Somewhat similar is Plat. *Crito* 46 B τοὺς δὲ λόγους, οὓς ἐν τῷ ἔμπροσθεν ἔλεγον, οὐ δύναμαι νῦν ἐκβαλεῖν (reject). Cp. 683.—ὑφ’ ἡδονῆς: *Ai.* 382

ἦ που πολὺν γέλωθ’ ὑφ’ ἡδονῆς ἄγεις. Here the word denotes sensuous impulse: cp. Eur. *Ph.* 21 ἡδονῇ δούς: Thuc. 3. 38 ἀκοῆς ἡδονῇ ἡσσώμενοι.
650 ψυχρόν, frigid, joyless: Eur. *Alc.* 353 ψυχρὰν μέν, οἶμαι, τέρψιν.—παραγκάλισμα: so *Tr.* 540 ὑπαγκάλισμα (of a wife); and so ἀγκάλισμα, ἐναγκάλισμα. The neuter gives a contemptuous tone. Cp. 320 λάλημα, 756 δούλευμα. Eur. *Or.* 928 τἄνδον οἰκουρήματα (of women), Aesch. *Ag.* 1439 Χρυσηίδων μείλιγμα (Agamemnon).
651 f. δόμοις. For the full stop after the 5th foot cp. *O. T.* 800.—ἕλκος, esp. an ulcer; said in *Il.* 2. 723 of a serpent's venomous bite; hence fitting here in ref. to the false friend, the ἔχιδνα in the house (531). So civil strife (στάσις ἔμφυλος) is described by Solon as πάσῃ πόλει...ἕλκος ἄφυκτον (4. 17).—φίλος is any one near and dear to us; the masc. is used, though the reference is to a wife, because the thought of domestic treason is put in the most general way: so (though with ref. to a woman) 464 κατθανών, 496 ἁλούς. Cp. Eur. *Alc.* 355 ἡδὺ γὰρ φίλους | κἂν νυκτὶ λεύσσειν, ὄντιν’ ἂν παρῇ χρόνον (Admetus speaking of his wife: we might read φίλος).
658 πτύσας, with loathing: Aesch. *P. V.* 1069 (speaking of treason) κοὐκ ἔστι νόσος | τῆσδ’ ἥντιν’ ἀπέπτυσα μᾶλλον.—ὡσεί

himself, and much triumph for his foes? Then do not thou, my son, at pleasure's beck, dethrone thy reason for a woman's sake; knowing that this is a joy that soon grows cold in clasping arms,—an evil woman to share thy bed and thy home. For what wound could strike deeper than a false friend? Nay, with loathing, and as if she were thine enemy, let this girl go to find a husband in the house of Hades. For since I have taken her, alone of all the city, in open disobedience, I will not make myself a liar to my people—I will slay her.

So let her appeal as she will to the majesty of kindred blood. If I am to nurture mine own kindred in naughtiness, needs must I bear with it in aliens.

Appendix. **656** τάσας L, πάσῃς Γ. **658** ταῦθ' L, with τ written above by an early hand. **659** τάτ' ἐγγενῆ (from ἐγγενῆ) L, with συγγενῆ written above by S. The later MSS. have τάτ' or (as A) τάδ' ἐγγενῆ.—Erfurdt restored τά γ'.

τε δυσμενῆ (οὖσαν), and as if she were a foe. For πτύσας connected by τε with an adj. in a different case, see n. on 381 σέ γ' ἀπιστοῦσαν ·. ἄγουσι ... καὶ ... καθελόντες. In El. 234 we have μάτηρ ὡσεί τις πιστά: but nowhere in Attic poetry do we find the epic and lyric use of ὡσεί τε as merely = ὡσεί (Il. 2. 780, Pind. 1. 44, etc.). And, as we have seen, it is needless to assume it here. Yet supposed difficulties about φίλοι and ὡσεί τε have led Nauck to propose that vv. 652—654 should be made into two, thus: γένοιτ' ἂν ἕλκος μεῖζον; ἀλλ' ἀποπτύσας | τὴν παῖδ' ἐν Ἅιδου τῆνδε νυμφεύειν μέθες.

654 νυμφεύειν here = γαμεῖσθαι, nubere, as 816. But it also = γαμεῖν, uxorem ducere: Eur. I. A. 461 Ἅιδης νιν, ὡς ἔοικε, νυμφεύσει τάχα.

656 f. ἀπιστήσασαν: cp. 219.—ψευθῆ: referring to his solemn and public declaration, 184—210.

658 κτενῶ. For the emphatic pause, cp. 72 θάψω, and n. on 46.—πρὸς ταῦτ', after an announcement of resolve, and before a defiant imperative, as O. T. 426, O. C. 455, El. 820, Aesch. P. V. 992, Ar. Ach. 959 etc. Similarly πρὸς οὖν τάδε, Ar. Nub. 1030.—ὑμνείτω, repeatedly invoke (a scornful word): cp. 1305, O. T. 1275 n.—Δία ξύναιμον: see on 487.

659 f. τά γ' ἐγγ. φύσει, those who, by birth, are relatives: for the place of the adverbial φύσει, cp. El. 792 τοῦ θανόντος ἀρτίως, Aesch. P. V. 216 τῶν παρεστώτων τότε. For the neut., instead of τοὺς ἐγγενεῖς, cp. Ph. 448 τὰ μὲν πανοῦργα καὶ παλιντρίβῆ...τὰ δέ | δίκαια καὶ τὰ χρηστ'.

—ἄκοσμα, unruly: so of Thersites, Il. 2. 213 ὃς ῥ' ἔπεα φρεσὶν ᾗσιν ἄκοσμά τε πολλά τε ᾔδη, | μάψ, ἀτὰρ οὐ κατὰ κόσμον, ἐριζέμεναι βασιλεῦσιν. Cp. 730.—θρέψω with predicative adj., as 1080, O. T. 98, etc.—κάρτα τοὺς ἔξω γ., sc. ἀκόσμους θρέψω. It is needless to supply a more general verb, like ποιήσω: the ruler's relation to his people justifies θρέψω: cp. O. T. 1 ὦ τέκνα. 'If I allow my own kindred to be unruly, I shall be obliged to tolerate unruliness in the citizens at large. For my authority as a ruler will be gone.'

661—671. Seidler transposes vv. 663—667, placing them after 6 1. The object is to bring vv. 668—671 into immediate connection with 662. In this there is one slight grammatical gain; since, as the vv. stand in the MSS., τοῦτον ...τὸν ἄνδρα (668) means, 'the man who acts thus' (viz., as described in vv. 666 f.). But the order given in the MSS. is right. The transposition obliterates one of the finest touches in the speech. Creon demands that the obedience of the citizen to the ruler shall be absolute (666 f.). And then he supplements this demand with a remark on the dignity of such obedience. The man who so obeys gives the best proof that he could also rule (668 ff.). Seidler destroys the point of vv. 668 ff. by placing them after 662.

The connection of thought in the whole passage—which is slightly obscured by compression—may be most clearly shown by taking the verses in small consecutive groups. (1) 659 f. If I tolerate disloyalty

ἐν τοῖς γὰρ οἰκείοισιν ὅστις ἔστ' ἀνὴρ
χρηστός, φανεῖται κἀν πόλει δίκαιος ὤν·
ὅστις δ' ὑπερβὰς ἢ νόμους βιάζεται,
ἢ τοὐπιτάσσειν τοῖς κρατύνουσιν νοεῖ,
οὐκ ἔστ' ἐπαίνου τοῦτον ἐξ ἐμοῦ τυχεῖν.   665
ἀλλ' ὃν πόλις στήσειε, τοῦδε χρὴ κλύειν
καὶ σμικρὰ καὶ δίκαια καὶ τἀναντία·
καὶ τοῦτον ἂν τὸν ἄνδρα θαρσοίην ἐγὼ
καλῶς μὲν ἄρχειν, εὖ δ' ἂν ἄρχεσθαι θέλειν,
δόρός τ' ἂν ἐν χειμῶνι προστεταγμένον   670
μένειν δίκαιον κἀγαθὸν παραστάτην.
ἀναρχίας δὲ μεῖζον οὐκ ἔστιν κακόν.
αὕτη πόλεις ὄλλυσιν, ἥδ' ἀναστάτους
οἴκους τίθησιν· ἥδε *συμμάχου δορὸς

663—667 Seidler, whom Nauck and others follow, places these five verses after 671. See comment. **664** Doederlein conject. ἤτοι 'πιτάσσειν.—The first hand in L wrote κρατύνουσιν νοεῖ. A later hand has made this into κρατοῦσιν ἐννοεῖ, the reading of some later MSS. (including A). **666** στήσειε. In L the final ε was added by S. **672** δὲ L, with ·γάρ· written above by S. Many of the later MSS. (including A) read γάρ. Stobaeus *Flor.* 43. 26 has δέ. **673** πόλισθ' L, with τ written above by S. The later MSS.

---

in my own relatives, I shall encourage it in other citizens. (2) 661 f. *For* (γάρ) only a man who is firm (χρηστός) where his own relatives are concerned will be found to uphold justice in the State (*i.e.* will have the authority necessary for doing so). (3) 663 f. Now, I recognise disloyalty in any one who breaks the law and defies the government, as Antigone has done. (4) 666 f. Instead of so doing, the citizen is bound to obey the government in everything. (5) 668—671. There is nothing slavish in that; on the contrary, it shows that the citizen is not only a good subject, but would, if required, be a good ruler ;—as he would also be a good soldier.—Then comes the general censure on unruliness (672—676). And then the conclusion :—I must vindicate my authority, and punish Antigone (677 —680).

663 f. ὑπερβάς, absol., having transgressed: *Il.* 9. 501 ὅτε κέν τις ὑπερβήῃ καὶ ἁμάρτῃ: so Plat. *Rep.* 366 A ὑπερβαίνοντες καὶ ἁμαρτάνοντες.—τοὐπιτάσσειν, prop. said of a master giving orders to slaves (*O. C.* 839): so ἐπιτάγματα are a despot's commands (Arist. *Pol.* 4. 4. 28). For the

art., cp. 78.—νοεῖ, as 44.—Antigone 'did violence to the laws' by her deed: she seemed 'to dictate to her rulers' when she proclaimed a law superior to theirs (450 ff.). Cp. 482 ff.

666 f. στήσειε: the optat. (instead of ὃν ἂν στήσῃ) puts the case in the most general way: any one whom she might conceivably appoint. Hence this optat. suits γνώμαι: cp. 1032: *Tr.* 92 τὸ γ' εὖ πράσσειν, ἐπεὶ πύθοιτο, κέρδος ἐμπολᾷ: *O. T.* 315 (n.), *ib.* 979.—καὶ τἀναντία, *i.e.* καὶ μεγάλα καὶ ἄδικα. So oft. in euphemisms, Thuc. 4. 62 ἀγαθὸν ἤ...τὰ ἐναντία: Plat. *Rep.* 472 C εὐδαιμονίας τε πέρι καὶ τοῦ ἐναντίου. Cp. Leutsch *Paroem.* App. 1. 100 κρεισσόνων γὰρ καὶ δίκαια κἄδικ' ἐστ' ἀκούειν: and the verse cited by schol. on Aesch. *P. V.* 75 δοῦλε, δεσποτῶν ἄκουε καὶ δίκαια κἄδικα.

668 f. τοῦτον...τὸν ἄνδρα refers to the indefinite subject of κλύειν in 666 :—the man who thus obeys. The looseness of grammatical connection would hardly be felt when the sense was so clear. Cp. 1035 (τῶν δ'). So in *O. C.* 942 αὐτούς refers to τὴν πόλιν in 939.—καλῶς...εὖ: for the change of word in the epanaphora

He who does his duty in his own household will be found righteous in the State also. But if any one transgresses, and does violence to the laws, or thinks to dictate to his rulers, such an one can win no praise from me. No, whomsoever the city may appoint, that man must be obeyed, in little things and great, in just things and unjust; and I should feel sure that one who thus obeys would be a good ruler no less than a good subject, and in the storm of spears would stand his ground where he was set, loyal and dauntless at his comrade's side.

But disobedience is the worst of evils. This it is that ruins cities ; this makes homes desolate; by this, the ranks of allies

---

have πόλεις τ' (as A), πόλεις δ' (L²), or πόλεις (V⁴). The choice is between πόλεις ὄλλυσιν, ἥδ' (Dindorf), and πόλεις τ' ὄλλυσιν ἥδ' (Nauck). L has ἥδ' here and in 674. ἥδ' is found in some later MSS. (V, Liv. a). See comment.
674 συμμάχηι L: σὺν μάχῃ r. Reiske and Bothe conjectured συμμάχου, which has been generally received. Held, κἢν μάχῃ. M. Schmidt, σὺν τροπῇ,

---

cp. *O. C.* 1501 σαφὴς μὲν ἀστῶν ἐμφανὴ δὲ τοῦ ξένου (n.).—ἂν with ἄρχειν (= ὅτι ἄρχαι ἂν) as well as ὅλλυιν.
670 f. δορὸς...χειμῶν. Eur. *Suppl.* 474 πολὺς κλύδων | ἡμῶν τε καὶ σοὶ ξυμμάχοις τ' ἐστὶ δορός.—προστεταγμένον, the regular term for placing soldiers at their posts: Thuc. 2. 87 ἔπεσθε, χώραν μὴ προλείποντες ᾗ ἂν τις προσταχθῇ.—παραστάτην, one who stands beside one in the ranks (as προστάτης in front and ἐπιστάτης behind): Xen. *Cyr.* 3. 3. 21 (the gods are invoked as) παραστάτας ἀγαθοὺς καὶ συμμάχους. The Attic ἔφηβος, on beginning, at eighteen, his term of service as a περίπολος, took an oath, οὐ καταισχυνῶ ὅπλα τὰ ἱερά [the arms given to him by the State], οὐδ' ἐγκαταλείψω τὸν παραστάτην ὅτῳ ἂν στοιχήσω (by whose side he should be placed): Stob. *Serm.* 43. 48. Thus for an Athenian audience this verse would be effective, and would seem peculiarly appropriate when addressed to the youthful Haemon.
672 πόλεις ὅλλυσιν, ἥδ' is far better and more spirited than πόλεις τ' ὅλλυσιν ἥδ': it is also strongly confirmed by the similar passage, 296 ff., where we have τοῦτο—τόδ'—τόδ', just as here αὕτη—ἥδ'... ἥδ'. When πόλεις had become, as in L, πόλις,—a corruption found also in Aesch. *Pers.* 489,—τ' may have been added for metre's sake. To ἥδ' itself there is no objection: it was certainly used in iambics by Soph. (fr. 253, fr. 503), no less than by Aesch. (*Cho.* 1025, *Eum.* 414),

and by Eur. (*Hec.* 313, *H. F.* 30).— Campb, reads πόλεις τ'...ἥδ', and regards the anacoluthon as making the lines 'more expressive.'
674 f. συμμάχου is a certain correction of L's συμμάχηι. The meaning is, 'Disobedience causes allied forces (σύμμαχον δόρυ) to break up in flight.' It turns union into disunion,—the hope of victory into defeat. With σὺν μάχῃ the sense would be, 'Disobedience, aiding the spear (of the foe), causes rout.' But this would represent disobedience as merely one cause of defeat,—an incident that turns the scale. It is evidently more forcible to represent it as breaking up an army which might otherwise have stood united and firm.—τροπὰς καταρρήγνυσιν, lit., *causes* rout *to break forth, i. e.* breaks up the army in rout. Cp. Athen. 130 c ὁ γελωτοποιὸς εἰσῆλθε...καὶ πολλοὺς κατέρρηξεν ἡμῶν γέλωτας, 'and *caused* shouts of laughter *to break forth* among us': (not, 'wreaked many witticisms upon us,'—as Casaubon took it.) The only peculiarity in the use of the verb is that it is here equiv. to ποιεῖ καταρρήγνυσθαι. We cannot compare Theocr. 22. 172 νεῖκος ἀναρρήξαντας, 'having broken *into* strife' (said of the parties to it), which is merely like ῥῆξαι φωνήν, etc.—τῶν δ' ὀρθουμένων (masc.), of those who have a prosperous course: Thuc. 2. 60 πόλιν...ὀρθουμένην, opp. to σφαλλομένην: 8. 64 ξυνέβη...τὴν πόλιν ἀκινδύνως ὀρθοῦσθαι. Cp. 163, 167.— τὰ πολλὰ σώματα, 'the greater number

τρόπας καταρρήγνῦσι· τῶν δ' ὀρθουμένων   675
σώζει τὰ πολλὰ σώμαθ' ἡ πειθαρχία.
οὕτως ἀμυντέ' ἐστὶ τοῖς κοσμουμένοις,
κοὔτοι γυναικὸς οὐδαμῶς ἡσσητέα.
κρεῖσσον γάρ, εἴπερ δεῖ, πρὸς ἀνδρὸς ἐκπεσεῖν,
κοὐκ ἂν γυναικῶν ἥσσονες καλοίμεθ' ἄν.   680
ΧΟ. ἡμῖν μέν, εἰ μὴ τῷ χρόνῳ κεκλέμμεθα,
λέγειν φρονούντως ὧν λέγεις δοκεῖς πέρι.
ΑΙ. πάτερ, θεοὶ φύουσιν ἀνθρώποις φρένας,
πάντων ὅσ' ἐστὶ κτημάτων ὑπέρτατον.
ἐγὼ δ' ὅπως σὺ μὴ λέγεις ὀρθῶς τάδε,   685
οὔτ' ἂν δυναίμην μήτ' ἐπισταίμην λέγειν·

with στίχας for τροπὰς in 675. **676** πειθαρχία] πιθαρχία L. **678** γυναικὸς]
'Lege γυναικῶν ex v. 680 et Eustathio p. 759, 39': Porson *Adv.* p. 172. But
Eustathius, *l.c.*, after quoting 677 correctly, proceeds, καὶ οὐ γυναικῶν ἡσσητέα·
ἀντὶ τοῦ ἀμυντέον καὶ ἀσσητέον. His point was the plur. For the rest, his memory
was inexact; see n. in Appendix on 292. **679 f.** Heimreich suspects both
these two verses. Bergk and Meineke reject 680. As Wecklein says (*Ars Soph.*

of lives,' differing from τοὺς πολλούς only
by bringing out the notion of personal
safety more vividly. Cp. *Ai.* 758 where
the masc. ὅστις follows τὰ...σώματα.—ἡ
πειθαρχία: called τῆς εὐπραξίας | μήτηρ
by Aesch. *Th.* 225. The schol. quotes
Il. 5. 531 αἰδομένων δ' ἀνδρῶν πλέονες σόοι
ἠὲ πέφανται.

677 ἀμυντέ', the impers. neut. plur.,
as Her. 9. 58 ἐκείνοισι ταῦτα ποιεῦσι οὐκ
ἐπιτρεπτέα ἐστί, ἀλλὰ διωκτέοι εἰσί: Thuc.
1. 86 τιμωρητέα, 88 πολεμητέα, 118 ἐπι-
χειρητέα, etc.: so *O. C.* 495 ὁδωτά. Cp.
447, 576. Eur. *Or.* 523 ἀμυνῶ δ', ὅσαπερ
δυνατός εἰμι, τῷ νόμῳ. Thuc. 1. 140 τοῖς
κοινῇ δόξασι βοηθεῖν.—τοῖς κοσμουμένοις
(neut.), the regulations made by οἱ κοσ-
μοῦντες, the rulers: meaning here, his
own edicts. For the act. κοσμεῖν, cp.
Her. 1. 59 (Peisistratus) ἔνεμε τὴν πόλιν
κοσμέων καλῶς τε καὶ εὖ. And for the
pass. thus used, *ib.* 100 ταῦτα μὲν κατὰ
τὰς δίκας ἐποίεε (Deïoces), τάδε δὲ ἄλλα
ἐκεκοσμέατό οἱ: 'and the following
regulations had also *been made* by him.'—
Another view (also noticed by the Schol.)
makes τοῖς κ. dat. οἱ κοσμούμενοι, 'the
rulers.' But (*a*) the only place which
might seem to favour this use of the midd.
is Thuc. 8. 24 (the Chians, the more they
prospered) τόσῳ καὶ ἐκοσμοῦντο ἐχυρώ-

τερον: but there the verb may well be
pass., 'the more securely was their government organised.' (*b*) As Creon is himself
at once ὁ ἀμύνων and ὁ κοσμῶν, it is more
natural that he should speak of his own
edicts than of 'the rulers.'—κόσμος was
said of a constitution, esp. oligarchical
(Thuc. 4. 76 μεταστῆσαι τὸν κόσμον καὶ ἐς
δημοκρατίαν...τρέψαι: 8. 72 μένειν ἐν τῷ
ὀλιγαρχικῷ κόσμῳ). The Cretan κόσμοι
were oligarchical magistrates, with military as well as civil powers (Arist. *Pol.*
2. 10).

678 κοὔτοι...ἡσσητέα: Ar. *Lys.* 450
ἀτὰρ οὐ γυναικῶν οὐδέποτ' ἔσθ' ἡττητέα |
ἡμῖν. (Cp. Milton, *Samson* 562 'Effemi-
nately vanquished.') Since ἡσσᾶσθαι is
only pass., its verbal in τέος can be only
pass.: as ἁλωτέον could mean only, 'one
must be taken.' But even in other cases
the verbal in τέος sometimes answers to
the pass., not to the act., sense of the
verb: as Xen. *Oec.* 7 § 38 ὅταν ἐκείνη
(the queen-bee) ἀπλίπῃ, οὐδεμία οἴεται τῶν
μελιττῶν ἀπολειπτέον εἶναι, ἀλλ' ἕπονται
πᾶσαι: *i.e.* ὅτι δεῖ ἀπολείπεσθαι (pass.),
'to be left behind': (for the stationary
bees could not be said ἀπολείπειν the
emigrant.)

679 f. δεῖ: for the pause, cp. 555.—
ἐκπεσεῖν) here absol., *to be displaced,*

are broken into headlong rout : but, of the lives whose course is fair, the greater part owes safety to obedience. Therefore we must support the cause of order, and in no wise suffer a woman to worst us. Better to fall from power, if we must, by a man's hand; then we should not be called weaker than a woman. +

CH. To us, unless our years have stolen our wit thou seemest to say wisely what thou sayest.

HAE. Father, the gods implant reason in men, the highest of all things that we call our own. Not mine the skill—far from me be the quest!—to say wherein thou speakest not aright;

---

em. p. 147), if 680 were condemned, 679 must go too.　**681** κεκλήμεθα L, but with gl. σεσυλήμεθα written above : κεκλέμμεθα r.—Hartung conject. τῶν φρενῶν : Schaefer, βεβλάμμεθα : whence Nauck, εἰ τι μὴ φρενῶν βεβλάμμεθα. **684** ὅσσ' L : ὅς r.—χρημάτων MSS.: but L has κτ written above by the first hand. —ὑπέρτατον L : ὑπέρτερον r.　**685** λέγημσ L : λέγεις r.—Heimreich would change

---

thrust out: oft. of dethronement (ἐκπ. τυραννίδος, ἀρχῆς, κράτους, Aesch.), or of exile (χθονός, O. C. 766).—κοὐκ ἄν...καλοίμεθ' ἄν : the doubled ἄν, as oft. in emphatic or excited utterances (O. T. 339 n.).—These two verses (like so many others) have been suspected merely because they are not indispensable. A defence is perhaps hardly needed. It is enough to remark that Creon's irritation under a woman's defiance (484, 525, 579) naturally prompts this further comment on the word γυναικός in 678. And the phrase γυναικῶν ἥσσονες (680) has a peculiar force as spoken to Haemon,—whom Creon afterwards taunts as γυναικὸς ὕστερον (746).

681 μέν : 498, 634.—τῷ χρόνῳ, by our age : cp. 729 τὸν χρόνον, 'my years': O. T. 963.—κεκλήμμεθα, are deceived : so 1218: Tr. 243 εἰ μὴ ξυμφοραὶ κλέπτουσί με.

682 δοκεῖς λέγειν φρονούντως περὶ (τούτων περὶ) ὧν λέγεις. At first sight it is natural to wish, with Herm., for δοκεῖς... ὧν λέγεις λέγειν πέρι. Cp. 1057 ἂν λέγῃς λέγων. But here it is fitting that λέγειν should have the prominence of the first place. And the undoubted harshness of the order may be partly excused by observing that ὧν λέγεις is practically equiv. to τούτων.

683 ff. θεοί. Creon had urged that filial piety demands the submission of the son's judgment to the γνώμη πατρῴα (640); and had warned Haemon against disregarding the voice of reason (648).

Haemon replies: 'Reason is the gift of the gods. I dare not suggest that your reasonings are wrong; but other men, too, may sometimes reason soundly. Now, I know what the Thebans are saying of your action; and, as a son devoted to your welfare, I ought to tell you.'—The tact and deference which mark this speech place Creon's αὐθάδεια in a stronger light.—κτημάτων : cp. 1050: O. T. 549: Her. 5. 24 κτημάτων πάντων ἐστὶ τιμιώτατον ἀνὴρ φίλος ξυνετός τε καὶ εὔνοος.

685 f. ἐγὼ δ' ὅπως : lit., 'I should not be able to say (and may I never be capable of saying!) in what respect (ὅπως) thou dost not say these things rightly.' He could not, if he would—and would not, if he could—impugn his father's reasonings. He only suggests that the case may have also another aspect, which Creon has not considered.—μὴ after ὅπως is generic, as after ὅς, ὅστις (691, 696): I could not say what point in thy argument is such as not to be true:—just as we could have, οὐκ οἶδα ὅ (or ὅ τι) μὴ ἀληθεύεις. The μή might be taken with ὀρθῶς ('how thou sayest otherwise than rightly'), but the order of words is against this. [It cannot be explained as substituted for οὐ through the influence of the optatives.]—μήτ' ἐπισταίμην. For this verb as = 'to be capable of,' cp. 472, Tr. 543 ἐγὼ δὲ θυμοῦσθαι μὲν οὐκ ἐπίσταμαι | νοσοῦντι κείνῳ. For the wish co-ordinated with the statement of fact, cp. 500: Tr. 582 κακὰς δὲ τόλμας μήτ' ἐπισταίμην ἐγὼ | μήτ' ἐκμάθοιμι, τάς τε τολμώσας στυγῶ : and ib. 143.

J. S. III.²   9

γένοιτο μέντἂν χἀτέρῳ καλῶς ἔχον.
σοῦ δ' οὖν πέφυκα πάντα προσκοπεῖν ὅσα
λέγει τις ἢ πράσσει τις ἢ ψέγειν ἔχει.
τὸ γὰρ σὸν ὄμμα δεινὸν ἀνδρὶ δημότῃ   690
λόγοις τοιούτοις οἷς σὺ μὴ τέρψει κλύων·
ἐμοὶ δ' ἀκούειν ἔσθ' ὑπὸ σκότου τάδε,
τὴν παῖδα ταύτην οἷ' ὀδύρεται πόλις,
πασῶν γυναικῶν ὡς ἀναξιωτάτη,
κάκιστ' ἀπ' ἔργων εὐκλεεστάτων φθίνει·   695
ἥτις τὸν αὑτῆς αὐτάδελφον ἐν φοναῖς
πεπτῶτ' ἄθαπτον μήθ' ὑπ' ὠμηστῶν κυνῶν
εἴασ' ὀλέσθαι μήθ' ὑπ' οἰωνῶν τινός·
οὐχ ἥδε χρυσῆς ἀξία τιμῆς λαχεῖν;

μὴ to δή, and omit v. 687. **687** χἀτέρῳ] Erfurdt conject. χἀτέρως or χἀτέρᾳ. The schol. in L has δυνατόν σε [not δυνατὸν δέ, as it has been reported] καὶ ἑτέρως καλῶς μεταβουλεύσασθαι. **688** σοῦ L, with ι written above by the first hand, and gl. in marg. by S, σὺ δ' οὐ πέφυκας. **690** τὸ γὰρ σὸν L: τὸ σὸν γὰρ r. **691** τέρψει] τέρψῃ L. Nauck rejects this verse. Autenrieth would place it before

687 καλῶς ἔχον (sc. τι: cp. O. T. 517 εἰς βλάβην φέρον), something good, some true thought, γένοιτο ἄν καὶ ἑτέρῳ, might come to (accrue to) another also. For γένοιτο cp. Plat. Symp. 211 D εἴ τῳ γένοιτο αὐτὸ τὸ καλὸν ἰδεῖν. (The phrase γένοιτο μέντἂν occurs also Ai. 86.)—Not: 'Yet it might be found well for another' (to say that you were wron). Haemon seeks to propitiate his father; but that purpose would scarcely be served by such a speech as this—'Being your son, I do not contradict you myself, *though I think that other people* might very reasonably do so.'

688 σοῦ δ' οὖν: 'but in any case (*i.e.*, whatever may be the worth of opinions different from yours) it is my natural part to watch on your behalf,' etc. For δ' οὖν cp. 722, 769; O. C. 1205 ἔστω δ' οὖν ὅπως ὑμῖν φίλον.—The gen. σοῦ is supported by the use of the gen. with προκήδομαι (741), προταρβῶ (83), προνοῶ, etc., and expresses the idea, 'in thy defence,' better than σοί would do. Cp. Eur. Med. 459 τὸ σὸν...προσκοπούμενος.—Herm. adopted the v. l. of the schol. in L, σὺ δ' οὐ πέφυκας, which Ellendt approves: but (a) πέφυκας is then less fitting, and (b) δ' οὖν commends the vulgate as genuine.—For the repeated τις, cp. Aesch. Eum. 889 μῆνιν τιν' ἢ κότον τιν'. Thuc.

4. 62 εἴ τῳ τι ἐστιν ἀγαθὸν ἢ εἴ τῳ τὰ ἐναντία. (Distinguish Eur. Or. 1218 ἦν τις,... | ἢ σύμμαχός τις ἢ κασίγνητος,—anyone,—be he ally or brother: and Andr. 733 ἔστι γάρ τις οὐ πρόσω | Σπάρτης πόλις τις, which, if sound, is a mere pleonasm.)

690 τὸ γὰρ σόν, not τὸ σὸν γάρ: so O. T. 671 τὸ γὰρ σόν, οὐ τὸ τοῦδ'· ib. 1024 ἢ γὰρ πρὶν...ἢ παιδία. In the case of σόν, at least, this order seems to strengthen, rather than diminish, the emphasis. ὄμμα: cp. O. T. 447 οὐ τὸ σὸν | δείσας πρόσωπον. Jeremiah i. 8 'Be not afraid of their faces.'—δημότῃ, the ordinary Theban citizen: cp. O. C. 78 n.

691 λόγοις τοιούτοις, causal dat.: thy face is terrible to the citizen *on account of* such words as shall displease thee: i. e. the citizen imagines the stern king's face growing darker at the sound of frank speech, and restrains his lips. (Cp. 509.) Doubts as to the dat. λόγοις τ. led Dindorf to suppose the loss of one verse (or more) after 690. Herwerden has suggested something like κοὐδείς ποτ' ἀστῶν ἐμφανῶς χρῆται, πάτερ, | λόγοις τοιούτοις κ.τ.λ. Nauck thinks that either v. 691 is wholly spurious, or that the words λόγοις τοιούτοις are corrupt. But, while the dat. is certainly bold—esp. with ἀνδρὶ δ. preceding it—it is (I think) quite within the possi-

and yet another man, too, might have some useful thought.
At least, it is my natural office to watch, on thy behalf,
all that men say, or do, or find to blame. For the dread of
thy frown forbids the citizen to speak such words as would
offend thine ear; but I can hear these murmurs in the dark,
these moanings of the city for this maiden; 'no woman,' they
say, 'ever merited her doom less,—none ever was to die so
shamefully. for deeds so glorious as hers; who, when her own
brother had fallen in bloody strife, would not leave him
unburied, to be devoured by carrion dogs, or by any bird:—
deserves not *she* the meed of golden honour?'

690, deleting the stop after ἔχει in 689.   695 δι' L: ἐπ' r.   696 αὐτῆς]
αὐτῆς L.   697 ℒ. μηθ'... μηθ' (*sic*) L: μηθ'... μηθ' r.—For ἄθαπτον μηθ',
Schneidewin proposed ἔθαπτεν μηθ': and Blaydes reads ἔθαψε, μηδ' (with μηδ'
in 698).—κυνῶν] In L a *v. l.* λόκων is noted by S.   699 τιμαῖσ L, with γρ.

bilities of classical idiom. We should
remember that Athenians were accustomed
to use a simple dat. (of 'time' or 'occasion') in speaking of festivals,—as τραγῳ-
δοῖs καινοῖs: cp. (*e.g.*) Plat. *Symp.* 174 A
χθὲς γὰρ αὐτὸν διέφυγον τοῖς ἐπινικίοις,
'I eluded him yesterday *when he was
holding* his sacrifice for victory.' So,
here, the dat. λόγοις τοιούτοις, though
properly causal, might sound to a Greek
ear like, '*at* such words,' *i. e.* 'when such
words are spoken.' The causal dat. in
391, ταῖs σαῖs ἀπειλαῖs, is similar. Cp.
also Thuc. 1. 84 εὐπραγίαιs...οὐκ ἐξυβρί-
ζομεν, where the notion, 'by reason of
successes,' is similarly blended with the
notion, 'in seasons of success.'—οἶs with
τέρψιs (cp. *O. C.* 1140, *Ph.* 460), κλύων
epexegetic. If, however, the order had
been κλύων τέρψιs, then οἷs might have
been for οὖs, by attraction. The μή is
generic ('such that not...'), cp. 696. For
the fut. midd. τέρψομαι (with pass. sense)
cp. fr. 612 ὅτου γε μὴ δίκαια τέρψεται,
and [Eur.] *Rhes.* 194. For the fut. ind.
after a relative with μή, cp. *O. T.* 1412 n.
—Nauck reads τέρψῃ (aor. midd.). This
rare aor. ἐτερψάμην is epic, as *Od.* 12. 188
τερψάμενος ('having had delight'). It is
not Attic, the Attic aor. in that sense
being ἐτέρφθην (*O. C.* 1140).

698 ℒ. ὑπὸ σκότου goes with ἀκούειν
more naturally than with ὀδύρεται, and
the sense is the same: *i.e.*, he is in the
σκότοs where the things are said: for the
gen., cp. 65 n., and *Tr.* 539 μίμνομεν μιᾶs
ὑπὸ | χλαίνης, which shows that we need

not here conceive the sounds as 'coming
from under' the darkness. Cp. Xen. *Cyr.*
4. 6. 4 κατέσχεν ὑπὸ σκότου τὸν φθόνον.
Eur. *Or.* 1457 ὑπὸ σκότου | ξίφη σπάσαν-
τεs. But ὑπὸ σκότῳ also occurs (Aesch.
Ag. 1030, Eur. *Ph.* 1214).

695 κάκιστ'... εὐκλεεστάτων: cp.
O. T. 1433 ἄριστος ἐλθὼν πρὸς κάκιστον.
Plat. *Apol.* 30 A τὰ πλείστου ἄξια περὶ
ἐλαχίστου ποιεῖται.—ἀπ' ἔργων, as their
result: *Ai.* 1078 πεσεῖν ἂν κἂν ἀπὸ σμικροῦ
κακοῦ.

696 ℒ. ἥτιs with causal force (*O. C.*
962); hence, too, the generic μήθ'...μήθ',
which belong to ἔασε (understood with
the second μήθ'), not to ἐλέσθαι: 'being
one who did not allow' (*quae non per-
miserit*).—αὐτάδελφον: cp. 1.—ἐν φοναῖs:
cp. 1314. The phrases ἐν φονῇσιν and
ἀμφὶ φονῇσιν are Homeric, and Her. uses
the former (with art., 9. 76 ἐν τῇσι φο-
νῇσι ἐόντας). The phrase ἐν φοναῖs is
used by Pindar, Aesch., Eur., and (in
parody) by Ar. But v. 1003 of this play—
the only play of Soph. which contains the
word—seems a solitary Attic instance of
φοναῖs without ἐν.

699 χρυσῆs, a general epithet for
what is brilliant or precious: thus Pind.
P. 3. 73 ὑγίειαν...χρυσέαν, and even (*O.*
10. 13) στεφάνῳ χρυσέαs ἐλαίαs (the
wreath of natural olive), as Olympia is
μάτηρ χρυσοστεφάνων ἀέθλων (*O.* 8. 1) in
a like sense. Cp. *O. T.* 157 ('golden'
hope), *O. C.* 1052 (the 'golden' bliss of
initiation).—There is no allusion to a
χρυσοῦs στέφανος.—λαχεῖν can take either

9—2

τοιάδ' ἐρεμνὴ σῖγ' ἐπέρχεται φάτις.　　　　700
ἐμοὶ δὲ σοῦ πράσσοντος εὐτυχῶς, πάτερ,
οὐκ ἔστιν οὐδὲν κτῆμα τιμιώτερον.
τί γὰρ πατρὸς θάλλοντος εὐκλείας τέκνοις
ἄγαλμα μεῖζον, ἢ τί πρὸς παίδων πατρί;
μή νυν ἓν ἦθος μοῦνον ἐν σαυτῷ φόρει,　　　705
ὡς φὴς σύ, κοὐδὲν ἄλλο, τοῦτ' ὀρθῶς ἔχειν.
ὅστις γὰρ αὐτὸς ἢ φρονεῖν μόνος δοκεῖ,
ἢ γλῶσσαν, ἣν οὐκ ἄλλος, ἢ ψυχὴν ἔχειν,
οὗτοι διαπτυχθέντες ὤφθησαν κενοί.
ἀλλ' ἄνδρα, κεἴ τις ᾖ σοφός, τὸ μανθάνειν　　710
πόλλ' αἰσχρὸν οὐδὲν καὶ τὸ μὴ τείνειν ἄγαν.
ὁρᾷς παρὰ ῥείθροισι χειμάρροις ὅσα
δένδρων ὑπείκει, κλῶνας ὡς ἐκσῴζεται·
τὰ δ' ἀντιτείνοντ' αὐτόπρεμν' ἀπόλλυται.
αὔτως δὲ ναὸς ὅστις ἐγκρατῆ πόδα　　　　715

καὶ στήλης in marg. by S.　τιμῆς r.　**701** ἐμοί made from ἐμοῦ in L.　**703** εὐκλείας MSS.: εὐκλείᾳ Johnson.　**705** After this v., Wecklein suspects the loss of a v. such as μηδ' ἀξίου τοὺς ἀλλόθεν λόγους παρείς.　**706** ὡς] Blaydes conject. δ or δ.—ἀλλ ο, from ἀλλ' δ, (not ἀλλ' δ,) L: ο and ω had been written above, but have

gen. or acc., the latter being more freq. (*O. C.* 450 n.). But here the inf. is rather epexegetic (cp. 1098 λαβεῖν), the gen. depending on ἀξία.

700 ἐπέρχεται, spreads *over* (the town). Cp. *Od.* 1. 299 οἷον κλέος Ἕλλαβε... | πάντας ἐπ' ἀνθρώπους. Cp. ὑφέρπειν, of secret rumour, *O. T.* 786 n.

703 f. θάλλοντος, prospering, as *Ph.* 419 μέγα | θάλλοντές εἰσι νῦν ἐν Ἀργείων στρατῷ.—μεῖζον εὐκλείας = μεῖζον ἢ εὐκλεια.—πρὸς παίδων, on their part, from their side: cp. *Tr.* 738 τί δ' ἐστίν, ὦ παῖ, πρός γ' ἐμοῦ στυγούμενον; We understand μεῖζον ἄγαλμά ἐστι τῆς ἐκείνων εὐκλείας. —The conjecture εὐκλείᾳ is attractive, (*a*) because θάλλω so oft. takes a dat. of respect, as Hes. *Op.* 234 (ἀγαθοῖσι), Pind. *O.* 9. 16 (ἀρεταῖσιν), etc.: (*b*) because the strong sigmatism of the verse is thus modified. But the words πρὸς παίδων confirm εὐκλείας, since with εὐκλείᾳ we should have expected παίδων alone. It is true that πατὴρ θάλλων εὐκλείᾳ could mean 'a father's fame' (cp. 638); but one could not have, πρὸς παίδων τί μεῖζον ἄγαλμα παίδων εὐκλείᾳ θαλλόντων;—

Triclinius wrongly joined εὐκλείας ἄγαλμα, thinking of εὐκλείας γέρας (*Ph.* 478) and στέφανον εὐκλείας μέγαν (*Ai.* 465).

705 f. νυν: cp. 524.—φόρει: Ar. *Eq.* 757 λῆμα θούριον φορεῖν: Eur. *Hipp.* 118 σπλάγχνον ἔντονον φέρων. So Shaksp. *Cymb.* 3. 4. 146 'if you could *wear* a mind | Dark as your fortune is': Caes. 5. 1. 113 'He *bears* too great a mind.'— ἦθος = a way of *thinking*: the inf. depends on it, as on 'do not *think.*' ὡς φὴς σύ, your way of speaking, = δ σὺ φής: cp. *O. C.* 1124 (n.) καί σοι θεοὶ πόροιεν ὡς ἐγὼ θέλω.—κοὐδέν, not καὶ μηδέν: it is merely oratio obliqua for ὅτι τοῦτο καὶ οὐδὲν ἄλλο ὀρθῶς ἔχει. The imperative μή...φόρει does not affect this: cp. *Ai.* 1085 καὶ μὴ δοκῶμεν δρῶντες ἃν ἡδώμεθα | οὐκ ἀντιτίσειν αὖθις ἃν λυπώμεθα. But καὶ μηδέν could also have stood here, since v. 705 could be regarded as equiv. to, 'do not feel confident that...': see n. on *O. T.* 1455.—τοῦτο, antecedent to ὡς φής, emphatically placed: cp. *O. T.* 385.

707 f. μόνος with φρονεῖν only.— ψυχήν: cp. 176. Theognis 221 ὅστις τοι δοκέει τὸν πλησίον ἴδμεναι οὐδέν, | ἀλλ'

Such is the darkling rumour that spreads in secret. For me, my father, no treasure is so precious as thy welfare. What, indeed, is a nobler ornament for children than a prospering sire's fair fame, or for sire than son's? Wear not, then, one mood only in thyself; think not that thy word, and thine alone, must be right. For if any man thinks that he alone is wise,—that in speech, or in mind, he hath no peer,—such a soul, when laid open, is ever found empty.

No, though a man be wise, 'tis no shame for him to learn many things, and to bend in season. Seest thou, beside the wintry torrent's course, how the trees that yield to it save every twig, while the stiff-necked perish root and branch? And even thus he who keeps the sheet of his sail

been erased.—φῂς] φῇσ L.—ἔχει L: ἔχειν Γ.   **707** αὐτὸς ἤ] αὐτῶν εὖ Priscian 17. 157.   **710** κεί τισ εἰ L: κεἰ τις ᾖ Γ (κἤν τις ᾖ A).   **711** ἄγαν] L has γαν in an erasure: the scribe had written μανθάν.   **712** παραρρείθροισι L.   **713** ἐκσώ̣ζεται L.   **715** αὔτως] οὔτως L, made from αὔτωσ.—ὅστις] ἅτισ L, with ὁσ written above

αὐτὸς μοῦνος ποικίλα ὄψε' (devices) ἔχειν, | κεῖνός γ' ἄφρων ἐστί, νόου βεβλαμμένος ἐσθλοῦ, | ἴσως γὰρ πάντες ποικίλ' ἐπισπάμεθα. Isocr. or. 3 § 43 joins Theognis, Phocylides as ἀρίστους...συμβίῳ τῷ τῶν ἀνθρώπων. They were read in schools. Hesiod and

709 οὗτοι after the collective ὅστις: Xen. Oec. 7. 37 ὅς ἂν κάμῃ τῶν οἰκετῶν, τούτων σοι ἐπιμελητέον πάντων.—διαπτυχθέντες, when laid open. Cp. Eur. Hipp. 984 τὸ μέντοι πρᾶγμ', ἔχον καλοὺς λόγους, | εἴ τις διαπτύξειεν, οὐ καλὸν τόδε. Andr. 330 ἔξωθέν εἰσιν οἱ δοκοῦντες εὖ φρονεῖν | λαμπροί, τὰ δ' ἔνδον πᾶσιν ἀνθρώποις ἴσοι. Also σκόλιον no. 7 in Bergk Poet. Lyr. (from Athen. 694 C, etc.) εἴθ' ἐξῆν ὁποῖός τις ἦν ἕκαστος | τὸ στῆθος διελόντ', ἔπειτα τὸν νοῦν | ἐσιδόντα, κλῄσαντα πάλιν, | ἄνδρα φίλον νομίζειν ἀδόλῳ φρενί. The image might be suggested by various objects,— a casket, tablets, fruit, or the like.—Cp. Shaks. Rom. 3. 2. 83 (of Romeo) 'Was ever book containing such vile matter So fairly bound?'—κενοί, sc. ὄντες: cp. 471.

710 f. ἄνδρα, subject to μανθάνειν, as O. T. 314 ἄνδρα δ' ὠφελεῖν κ.τ.λ.: for the place of τό, cp. 723, Tr. 65 σέ... | τὸ μὴ πυθέσθαι instead of τὸ σὲ μὴ πυθέσθαι.— καὶ...ξ: see O. T. 198 n.—τείνειν, absol., here, like τείνειν τόξον or τείνειν πόδα, 'to strain the cord too tight,'—to be overrigid in maintaining one's own views. This poet. use should be distinguished from the ordinary intrans. use of τείνω,

like τένδερε, 'to have a direction,' or 'take one's way' (Xen. An. 4. 3. 21 ἔτεινον ἄνω πρὸς τὸ ὄρος).

712 παρὰ ῥείθρ.: for ᾱ before initial ῥ, cp. O. T. 847 (ἐμὲ ῥέπον), O. C. 900 ἀπὸ ῥυτῆρος.—χειμάρροις, here a neut. adj., as Eur. Tro. 449 ὕδατι χειμάρρῳ: usu. ὁ χειμάρρους (sc. ποταμός). Tozer, Geo. Gr. p. 84: 'The numerous torrents (χειμάρροι) are the natural result of the configuration of the country, for the steep limestone mountains have but little of a spongy surface to act as a reservoir for the rain... It is especially at the time of the autumn rains that the greatest floods take place, and the sudden swelling and violent rush of the stream has furnished Homer with some of his finest similes.' (Il. 4. 452 ff., 16. 384 ff.: imitated by Verg. Aen. 2. 305 ff., 12. 523.)—Antiphanes (c. 380 B.C.) parodies these verses (fr. incert. 10: Athen. 22 F).

713 f. ὑπείκει. Cp. Babrius fab. 36: an oak, torn up by the roots, is being swept down by a boiling torrent, and asks the reeds how they have managed to escape; when a reed (κάλαμος) answers:—σὺ μὲν μαχομένη ταῖς πνοαῖς ἐνικήθης, | ἡμεῖς δὲ καμπτόμεσθα μαλθακῇ γνώμῃ, | τῶν βαιὸν ἡμῶν ἄνεμος ἄκρα κινήσῃ.—αὐτόπρεμνα = αὐτόρριζα, πρόρριζα; Il. 9. 541 χαμαὶ βάλε δένδρεα μακρὰ | αὐτῇσιν ῥίζῃσιν.

715 αὔτως, adv. from αὐτός (with 'Aeolic' acc.); see on O. T. 931.—ναός,

∨ τείνας ὑπείκει μηδέν, ὑπτίοις κάτω
∨ στρέψας τὸ λοιπὸν σέλμασιν ναυτίλλεται.
∨ ἀλλ᾽ εἶκε θυμοῦ καὶ μετάστασιν δίδου.
∨ γνώμῃ γὰρ εἴ τις κἀπ᾽ ἐμοῦ νεωτέρου
∨ πρόσεστι, φήμ᾽ ἔγωγε πρεσβεύειν πολὺ   720
∨ φῦναι τὸν ἄνδρα πάντ᾽ ἐπιστήμης πλέων·
∨ εἰ δ᾽ οὖν, φιλεῖ γὰρ τοῦτο μὴ ταύτῃ ῥέπειν,
∨ καὶ τῶν λεγόντων εὖ καλὸν τὸ μανθάνειν.
ΧΟ. ἄναξ, σέ τ᾽ εἰκός, εἴ τι καίριον λέγει,
∨ μαθεῖν, σέ τ᾽ αὖ τοῦδ᾽· εὖ γὰρ εἴρηται διπλᾶ.   725.

by first hand.—ἐγκρατῇ] ἐγκρατεῖ L, with η written above by first hand: ἐγκρα-
τῆι Γ.   717 τὸ λοιπὸν MSS.: Hermann conject. τὸ πλοῖον.—σέλμασι L.
718 θυμῶι L. So Ald., following Par. A, as usual. But θυμοῦ is in many of
the later MSS., including L³, V, V³ (first hand), V⁴, Aug. b, Dresd. a. See comment.

Doric for νεώς, allowed by tragedy even
in iambics, as *Ai.* 872, Aesch. *Th.* 62,
Eur. *Med.* 523: though νᾶες (953) and
ναΐ occur only in lyrics. So ναός, temple
(286), Ἀθάνα, κυναγός, ὁδαγός, ποδαγός
(1196): and even in Att. prose λοχαγός,
οὐραγός, ξεναγός.—ἐγκρατῆ, proleptic: cp.
475 περισκελῆ.—πόδα, the sheet: the πόδες
were ropes attached to the two lower cor-
ners of the sail, whence their name. Eur.
Or. 706 καὶ ναῦς γάρ, ἐνταθεῖσα πρὸς βίαν
ποδί, | ἔβαψεν, ἔστη δ᾽ αὖθις, ἢν χαλᾷ πόδα:
a ship dips when strained too hard by the
sheet (*i.e.* when the sheet is hauled too
taut), but rights again, if one slackens.
716 f. μηδέν, generic (such an one as
does not...).—κάτω στρέψας, sc. ναῦν,
easily supplied from ναός: for κάτω, cp.
527: for στρέφω = ἀναστρέφω, *O.C.* 1453.
Hermann's τὸ πλοῖον for τὸ λοιπόν is not
only needless, but spoils the force of the
phrase: 'thenceforth voyages,' is an ironical way of saying that the voyage comes
to an abrupt end: cp. 311.—σέλμασιν,
the rowers' benches: thus ὑπτίοις vividly
suggests the moment of capsizing.
718 εἶκε θυμοῦ, 'cease from wrath,'
lit., recede from it. The θυμός is conceived as ground from which he retires;
so θυμοῦ περᾶν = 'to go far in wrath,'
and is contrasted with εἴκειν: *O. T.* 673
στυγνὸς μὲν εἴκων δῆλος εἶ, βαρὺς δ᾽, ὅταν |
θυμοῦ περάσῃς. For the gen., cp. *Il.* 4.
509 μηδ᾽ εἴκετε χάρμης | Ἀργείοις: ib. 5.
348 εἶκε, Διὸς θύγατερ, πολέμου καὶ δηϊο-
τῆτος: Her. 2. 80 εἴκουσι τῇ ὁδῷ: id. 7.
160 ὑπείξομεν τοῦ ἀρχαίου λόγου: Ar. *Ran.*

790 ὑπεχώρησεν αὐτῷ τοῦ θρόνου. Eur.
has a somewhat similar phrase, *Hipp.* 900
ὀργῆς δ᾽ ἐξανεὶς κακῆς, ἄναξ | Θησεῦ, τὸ
λῷστον σοῖσι βούλευσαι δόμοις, where the
sense is, 'having remitted thy wrath,'
ἐξανεὶς [σεαυτὸν] ὀργῆς.—καὶ μετάστασιν
δίδου, 'and concede a change': allow our
pleading to change your mood. A change
in Creon's mood implies a change in the
whole situation. For the notions thus
blended in μετάστασιν here, cp. Alexis fr.
incert. 46 τῶν μετρίων αἱ μείζονες | λῦπαι
ποιοῦσι τῶν φρενῶν μετάστασιν: Andoc.
or. 2 § 18 οἴσειν ἐμέλλεν...τοῦ τότε παρόν-
τος κακοῦ μετάστασιν.—δίδου: a verb oft.
used of *concession* to the remonstrance of
friends: *Ai.* 483 παῦσαί γε μέντοι καὶ δὸς
ἀνδράσιν φίλοις | γνώμης κρατῆσαι: *Tr.*
1117 δός μοι σεαυτόν, μὴ τοσοῦτον ὡς
δάκνει | θυμῷ δύσοργος.—Others place a
comma or point at εἶκε, taking καί as =
'also'; 'yield, *also* permitting the wrath
to change' (with διδούς); or 'yield: also
permit,' etc. (an asyndeton, with δίδου).
On this view, either θυμῷ or θυμοῦ is possible. But the fatal objection to it is the
weakness of καί, whether the 'also' is
explained (*a*) as by Campbell (with δίδου),
—'if you are angry, be *also* placable'; or
(*b*) as by Wecklein (with διδούς)—'it is
possible not only to moderate one's passion, but *also* to desist from it,' which
implies that he might yield while still
angry.—See Appendix.
719 f. εἴ τις γνώμη πρόσεστι καὶ ἀπ᾽
ἐμοῦ ν. (ὄντος), *i.e.*, if I also, younger
though I am, can contribute a sound.

taut, and never slackens it, upsets his boat, and finishes his voyage with keel uppermost.

Nay, forego thy wrath; permit thyself to change. For if I, a younger man, may offer my thought, it were far best, I ween, that men should be all-wise by nature; but, otherwise—and oft the scale inclines not so—'tis good also to learn from those who speak aright.

CH. Sire, 'tis meet that thou shouldest profit by his words, if he speaks aught in season, and thou, Haemon, by thy father's; for on both parts there hath been wise speech.

and Appendix. **720** φήμ' L (not φῆμ'). **721** πλέω L: πλέων r. **725** αὖ τοῦδ'] αὐτοῦ δ' L.—διπλᾶι L. (The ι is certainly from the first hand.) διπλᾶ r. διπλῇ Hermann.

opinion. Cp. *O. C.* 291 τἀνθυμήματα | ...τἀπὸ σοῦ, the thoughts urged on thy part. *El.* 1464 τελεῖται τἀπ' ἐμοῦ. For the modest καί, cp. *O. T.* 1100 εἰ χρή τι κἀμέ...σταθμᾶσθαι: *Ph.* 192 εἴπερ κἀγώ τι φρονῶ.—If κἀπ' were taken as καὶ ἐπί, it must mean, 'in my case also.' Plat. *Rep.* 475 A ἐπ' ἐμοῦ λέγειν (to take me as an instance). In *El.* 1469 I formerly thus took κἀπ' ἐμοῦ θρήνων τύχῃ, but now think that there, too, it is καὶ ἀπό.—πρεσβεύειν = πρεσβύτατον εἶναι, to be the best thing: Eur. *Her.* 45 οἷσι πρεσβεύει γένος, whose birth has precedence (= the eldest): cp. *O. T.* 1365 (πρεσβύτερον) n.

721 φῦναι, should be by nature: Pind. *O. 9.* 107 τὸ δὲ φυᾷ κράτιστον ἅπαν (opposed to διδακταὶ ἀρεταί).—πάντ', adv.: *Tr.* 338 τούτων ἔχω γὰρ πάντ' ἐπιστήμην ἐγώ: *O. T.* 475 n.—The merit of listening to good advice is often thus extolled: Hes. *Op.* 291 οὗτος μὲν πανάριστος, ὃς αὐτὸς πάντα νοήσῃ· | ἐσθλὸς δ' αὖ κἀκεῖνος, ὃς εὖ εἰπόντι πίθηται. Her. 7. 16 ἴσον ἐκεῖνο, ὦ βασιλεῦ, παρ' ἐμοὶ κέκριται, φρονέειν τε εὖ καὶ τῷ λέγοντι χρηστὰ ἐθέλειν πείθεσθαι. Cp. Cic. *pro Cluentio* 31: Livy 22. 29.

722 εἰ δ' οὖν, sc. μὴ ἔφυ τοιοῦτος. This is better than to suppose that φιλεῖ γάρ has changed the form of the sentence (εἰ δ' οὖν τοῦτο μὴ ταύτῃ ῥέπει), since this elliptical εἰ δ' οὖν was a familiar Attic idiom: see Plat. *Apol.* 34 D εἰ δή τις ὑμῶν οὕτως ἔχει—οὐκ ἀξιῶ μὲν γὰρ ἔγωγε, εἰ δ' οὖν [sc. οὕτως ἔχει]—ἐπιεικῆ ἄν μοι δοκῶ πρὸς τοῦτον λέγειν: 'If any one of you is so disposed—I do not think that he ought to be so, but *suppose that he is*—I think that I might fairly say to him,' etc. Eur. *Hipp.* 507 εἴ τοι δοκεῖ σοι, χρῆν μὲν οὔ σ' ἁμαρ-

τάνειν· | εἰ δ' οὖν [sc. ἥμαρτες], πιθοῦ μοι ('you ought not to have erred,—but if you *have*'). So, without ellipse, Aesch. *Ag.* 1042 εἰ δ' οὖν ἀνάγκη τῆσδ' ἐπιρρέποι τύχης, 'but if one *should* be doomed to slavery' (then worthy masters are best). Eur. fr. 463 λύπη μὲν ἄτη περιπεσεῖν... | εἰ δ' οὖν γένοιτο, κ.τ.λ. Cp. δ' οὖν in 688 (n.).—τοῦτο...ταύτῃ: cp. *Ai.* 950 τάδ' ἔστιν τῇδε: Aesch. *P. V.* 511 οὐ ταῦτα ταύτῃ. μή is generic, going with ταύτῃ: in a way other than this.—ῥέπειν to incline (as the scale of a balance does): so Plat. *Legg.* 862 D τῇδε ῥέπει, *Tim.* 79 E ἐκείνῃ ῥέπον (to incline, or tend, in that direction).

723 καὶ τὸ τῶν εὖ λεγόντων μανθάνειν καλόν (ἐστι): for the place of εὖ, cp. 659: for that of τό, 710. The simple gen., as *O. T.* 545, etc.

724 Σ. σέ τ' doubled: cp. 1340, *O. T.* 637.—L's διπλᾶι really favours διπλᾶ rather than Hermann's διπλῇ: for ι subscript is oft. wrongly added or omitted (cp. 726 cr. n.); whereas ῃ was not likely to become ᾱ here. Either word is admissible; but I slightly prefer διπλᾶ, for this reason. It is true that the plur. of διπλοῦς in poetry usu. = simply 'two' (51, 1231, 1310, *O. T.* 20, 1135). But Soph. has at least one instance of the distributive sense ('two sets'), viz., *O. T.* 1249, where διπλοῦς = a twofold brood, *i.e.* Oed., and his children. (I do not add *O. T.* 288 διπλοῦς | πομπούς, taking it to mean merely 'two,' not 'two sets.') And in Attic prose the distributive use is not rare: thus in Plat. *Legg.* 722 D διπλοῖ... νόμοι are not 'two laws,' but 'two sets of laws.' We have, then, good warrant for διπλᾶ here as = 'two sets of arguments.'

ΚΡ. οἱ τηλικοίδε καὶ διδαξόμεσθα δὴ
  φρονεῖν ὑπ᾽ ἀνδρὸς τηλικοῦδε τὴν φύσιν;
ΑΙ. μηδὲν τὸ μὴ δίκαιον· εἰ δ᾽ ἐγὼ νέος,
  οὐ τὸν χρόνον χρὴ μᾶλλον ἢ τἄργα σκοπεῖν.
ΚΡ. ἔργον γάρ ἐστι τοὺς ἀκοσμοῦντας σέβειν;   730
ΑΙ. οὐδ᾽ ἂν κελεύσαιμ᾽ εὐσεβεῖν εἰς τοὺς κακούς.
ΚΡ. οὐχ ἥδε γὰρ τοιᾷδ᾽ ἐπείληπται νόσῳ;
ΑΙ. οὔ φησι Θήβης τῆσδ᾽ ὁμόπτολις λεώς.
ΚΡ. πόλις γὰρ ἡμῖν ἁμὲ χρὴ τάσσειν ἐρεῖ;
ΑΙ. ὁρᾷς τόδ᾽ ὡς εἴρηκας ὡς ἄγαν νέος;   735
ΚΡ. ἄλλῳ γὰρ ἢ 'μοὶ χρή *με τῆσδ᾽ ἄρχειν χθονός;
ΑΙ. πόλις γὰρ οὐκ ἔσθ᾽, ἥτις ἀνδρός ἐσθ᾽ ἑνός.

726 οἱ] In L, the first hand has written ἧι above οἱ. This was meant to indicate
a variant ἧ,—the ι being added by an error of a frequent kind (cp. 755 ἥισθ᾽).
Dindorf wrongly supposed that it was meant to indicate a correction of διπλᾶι in
715 into διπλῆι. In that case it would have been. written over or near διπλᾶι,
not at the beginning of v. 726.—διδαξόμεσθα δή] διδαξόμεσθ᾽ ἃ δεῖ Semitelos.
728 μηδὲν τὸ μὴ] μηδέν γ᾽ ὃ μὴ Tournier: μηδέν γε μὴ K. Walter.   729 τἄργα]

On the other hand, διπλῆ is strange
(though possible) as = 'in two ways,' *i.e.*
'on both sides.' It usu. means, 'doubly'
(Eur. *Ion* 760 κεἰ θανεῖν μέλλω διπλῆ);
or 'twice as much' (Plat. *Rep.* 330 C
διπλῆ ἢ οἱ ἄλλοι). So, here, it would
more naturally mean, 'twice over.'

726 f. καὶ with διδαξ., shall we *indeed*
be taught: *El.* 385 ἦ ταῦτα δή με καὶ βε-
βούλευνται ποιεῖν; *O. T.* 772 n. For διδαξ.
as pass., cp. 637.—δή, an indignant 'then':
the word ends a verse also in 923, *Tr.*
460, *Ph.* 1065, Eur. *Suppl.* 521, *Hipp.*
1093.—τὴν φύσιν, birth, and so age; *O.
C.* 1295 ὧν φύσει νεώτερος.

728 f. μηδέν, sc. διδάσκου: τὸ μὴ δίκ.
= ὃ μὴ δίκαιόν ἐστι: see on 360 οὐδέν...τὸ
μέλλον.—τὸν χρόνον, my years: cp.681.—
The change of τἄργα into τοὖργον (adopted
by Nauck) is no gain. The sing. is taken
as 'the cause' (which he defends). But
he means, 'you should consider, not my
age, but my conduct,—my merits': and
this is expressed by τἄργα, just as in *O. C.*
265 ὄνομα μόνον δείσαντες· οὐ γὰρ δὴ τό
γε | σῶμ᾽ οὐδὲ τἄργα τἀμά. Cp. Menander
fr. incert. 91 μὴ τοῦτο βλέψῃς, εἰ νεώτερος
λέγω, | ἀλλ᾽ εἰ φρονοῦντων τοὺς λόγους
ἀνδρῶν λέγω (*v. l.* φρονοῦντος...ἀνδρός:
Bentley, φέρω).

730 ἔργον. Haemon has asked that

his ἔργα may be considered. Creon asks
scornfully, 'Do you consider it an ἔργον—
something which you can urge in your
favour—to be the champion of a rebel?'
ἔργον would not have been thus used
alone, but for the desire to give τἄργα a
derisive echo. The Attic associations of
the word help, however, to explain this
use. Thus ἔργον meant (*a*) a thing *worth
doing*, as Ar. *Lys.* 424 οὐδὲν ἔργον ἐστάναι,
it is *no use*... (cp. *Ai.* 852); so οὐδὲν
προὄργου ἐστί, *non operae pretium est*: or
(*b*), one's allotted task, as Ar. *Av.* 862,
ἱερεῦ, σὸν ἔργον, θῦε. So here, without
meaning so much as 'achievement' (*El.*
689), it could mean, 'useful act,' 'worthy
task.'—τοὺς ἀκοσμοῦντας: so *Ph.* 387:
cp. above 660, 677.—σέβειν, as 511.

731 οὐδ᾽, not even: *O. C.* 1429 (n.)
οὐδ᾽ ἀγγελοῦμεν φλαῦρα. So far am I
from showing honour to evil-doers, that
I would not even wish others to do so.
Without directly denying that Antigone
can be described as ἀκοσμοῦσα, he denies
that she is κακή. This involves the whole
question between the divine and the
human law.

732 τοιᾷδε...νόσῳ, that of being κακή.
Others understand, τῷ εἰς τοὺς κακοὺς εὐσεβεῖν. But the sense of the dialogue
runs thus:—'C. Do you approve of honour-

CR. Men of my age—are we indeed to be schooled, then,
by men of his?

HAE. In nothing that is not right; but if I am young,
thou shouldest look to my merits, not to my years.

CR. Is it a merit to honour the unruly?

HAE. I could wish no one to show respect for evil-doers.

CR. Then is not she tainted with that malady?

HAE. Our Theban folk, with one voice, denies it.

CR. Shall Thebes prescribe to me how I must rule?

HAE. See, there thou hast spoken like a youth indeed.

CR. Am I to rule this land by other judgment than mine
own?

HAE. That is no city, which belongs to one man.

τοὔργον Hilberg. **781** οὐδ' ἄν] οὐ τὰν Schneidewin. **784** ἀμέ] ἄμε L.
785 τόδ'] In L an early hand has changed o to α. **786** ἄλλωι γὰρ ἢ (sic) μοι
χρή γε L. So (with χρή) most of the later MSS. Dobree's conject., ἄλλῳ γὰρ ἢ 'μοὶ
χρή ꞈμε, has been generally received.—Camph. cites ἄλλον γὰρ ἢ με from M⁴,=cod.
C. ₂ sup. in the Ambrosian Library at Milan, a 15th cent. MS. **787** ἀνδρὸς ἐσθ']
ἀνδρὸς ἐσθ' L.

---

ing law-breakers?—*H.* I should not dream
of honouring wrong-doers.—*C.* Is not she,
then, a wrong-doer?' Doubtless, Creon
could also say,—'Does not she, then,
honour wrong-doers (Polyneices)?' Here,
however, his point is that *she* is a rebel,—
not, that her brother was a traitor.—For
the fig. use of νόσος, cp. 1052, and n. on
653.—ἐπείληπται, attacked, as by a disease:
so the act., Thuc. 2. 51 (ἡ νόσος) δὶς...τὸν
αὐτὸν...οὐκ ἐπελάμβανε. (Distinguish the
sense of ἐπίληπτος in 406.)

788 Θήβης, possessive gen., not gen.
with ὁμόπτολις, which = 'of the same
city': the sense is, 'the united folk of
Thebes,'=the whole city, πάνδημος πόλις
(7). Cp. 693. The epic πτόλις is used
both in lyr. and in dial. by Aesch. and
Eur., but in neither by Soph.

784 ἡμῖν, plur. (instead of ἐμοί), combined with the sing. ἐμέ: cp. 1194: *Ai.*
1400 εἰ δὲ μή 'στι σοὶ φίλον | πράσσειν τάδ'
ἡμᾶς, εἶμ', ἐπαινέσας τὸ σόν: *Ph.* 1394
εἰ σέ γ' ἐν λόγοις | πείσειν δυνησόμεθα
μηδὲν ὧν λέγω (and *ib.* 1219 ff.): Eur.
H. F. 858 ἥλιον μαρτυρόμεσθα δρῶσ' ἃ
δρᾶν οὐ βούλομαι: *Ion* 391 κωλυόμεσθα μὴ
μαθεῖν ἃ βούλομαι.

785 ὡς ἄγαν νέος—despite the difference between your age and mine (726).

786 Dobree's με for γε is clearly right;
γε would throw a false emphasis on χρή
('Now, *ought* I to rule...?'): the sense
requires the stress to fall on ἄλλῳ ἢ 'μοί.

This dat. 'of interest' does not mean,
'for my own advantage' (or gain), but,
'to my own satisfaction,' *i.e.* 'according
to my own views.' Haemon has made
light of Creon's protest against dictation
from Thebes. Creon rejoins, 'What, am
I to rule Thebes in dependence on any
other judgment than my own?' In Eur.
Suppl. 410 Creon's herald says, πόλις γὰρ
ἧς ἐγὼ πάρειμ' ἄπο | ἑνὸς πρὸς ἀνδρός, οὐκ
ὄχλῳ, κρατύνεται.—For ἐμοὶ instead of
ἐμαυτῷ, cp. Plat. *Gorg.* 474 B ἐγὼ γὰρ δὴ
οἶμαι καὶ ἐμὲ καὶ σὲ...ἡγεῖσθαι.—Though
χρή γε is untenable, the dat. is no argument against it: χρή could be absolute,
the dat. being still a dat. of interest.
There is no certain Attic instance of
χρή with dat. In Eur. *Ion* 1317 τοῖσι
δ' ἐνδίκοις | ἱερὰ καθίζειν, ὅστις ἠδίκειτ',
ἐχρῆν, Dobree's τοὺς δέ γ' ἐνδίκους is needless: the sense is, 'in the interest of the
just, it was right,' etc. In Lys. or. 28 § 10
τοῖς ἄρχουσι τοῖς ὑμετέροις ἐπιδείξετε πότερον χρὴ δικαίους εἶναι, we should read
δικαίους, and just afterwards ὠφελομένους.
Xen. has δεῖ with dat. and infin., if the
text is sound in *An.* 3. 4. 35.

787 πόλις γὰρ οὐκ ἔσθ'. Cp. Arist.
Pol. 3. 16 περὶ δὲ τῆς παμβασιλείας καλου-
μένης,—αὕτη δ' ἐστὶ καθ' ἣν ἄρχει πάντων
κατὰ τὴν ἑαυτοῦ βούλησιν ὁ βασιλεύς,—
δοκεῖ δέ τισιν οὐδὲ κατὰ φύσιν εἶναι τὸ κύριον
ἕνα πάντων εἶναι τῶν πολιτῶν, ὅπου συνέστηκεν ἐξ ὁμοίων ἡ πόλις. For Plato, the

ΚΡ. οὐ τοῦ κρατοῦντος ἡ πόλις νομίζεται;
ΑΙ. καλῶς ἐρήμης γ' ἂν σὺ γῆς ἄρχοις μόνος.
ΚΡ. ὅδ', ὡς ἔοικε, τῇ γυναικὶ συμμαχεῖ.   740
ΑΙ. εἴπερ γυνὴ σύ· σοῦ γὰρ οὖν προκήδομαι.
ΚΡ. ὦ παγκάκιστε, διὰ δίκης ἰὼν πατρί.
ΑΙ. οὐ γὰρ δίκαιά σ' ἐξαμαρτάνονθ' ὁρῶ.
ΚΡ. ἁμαρτάνω γὰρ τὰς ἐμὰς ἀρχὰς σέβων;
ΑΙ. οὐ γὰρ σέβεις, τιμάς γε τὰς θεῶν πατῶν.   745
ΚΡ. ὦ μιαρὸν ἦθος καὶ γυναικὸς ὕστερον.
ΑΙ. οὐ τἂν ἕλοις ἥσσω γε τῶν αἰσχρῶν ἐμέ.
ΚΡ. ὁ γοῦν λόγος σοι πᾶς ὑπὲρ κείνης ὅδε.
ΑΙ. καὶ σοῦ γε κἀμοῦ, καὶ θεῶν τῶν νερτέρων.

739 καλῶσ· ἐρήμησγ' L: καλῶς γ' ἐρήμης Blaydes.   740 τῇ γυναικί] ταῖς γυναιξὶ
Tournier.   742 ὦ παγκάκιστε] ὦ παῖ κάκιστε in Plutarch's quotation (*Mor.* 483 c),
and so Porson wished to read (*Adv.* 172, Eur. *Or.* 301).   748 ὁρῶ] ὁρῶι L.
745 οὔ] Musgrave conject. εὖ.   747 οὐ κἂν L (meaning, doubtless, οὐκ ἂν, for
the κ ΄ of οὐκ is oft. thus detached in L, and joined to the next word): οὗ τἂν

τυραννίς is ἔσχατον πόλεως νόσημα, *Rep.*
544 C. Cic. *de Rep.* 3. 31 *ubi tyrannus
est, ibi...dicendum est nullam esse rem-
publicam.*

788 νομίζεται with gen., as *O. C.* 38
(n.).—In a different sense (and rather with
an allusion to demagogues) it is said in
Ph. 386 πόλις γὰρ ἐστι πᾶσα τῶν ἡγου-
μένων (like ἔστι τοῦ λέγοντος, *O. T.* 917).

789 καλῶς ἐρήμης γ' (L) is much
better than καλῶς γ' ἐρήμης (Blaydes and
Nauck): Soph. often thus adds γε to the
emphatic adj., as *El.* 365 οὐδ' ἂν σύ, σώ-
φρων γ' οὖσα: *ib.* 518 θυραῖαν γ' οὖσαν:
Ph. 811 οὐ μὴν σ' ἔνορκόν γ' ἀξιῶ θέσθαι.

740 Though at least one late MS.
(Paris E) has συμμαχεῖν, it is needless to
assume here the same mixed constr. as
Tr. 1238 ἀνὴρ δ' ὅδ', ὡς ἔοικεν, οὐ νεμεῖν
ἐμοὶ | φθίνοντι μοῖραν.

741 οὖν, indeed, in fact: cp. 489.—
προκήδομαι: cp. on προσκοπεῖν, 688.

742 ὦ παγκάκιστε: so Heracles to
his son Hyllus, *Tr.* 1124. Cp. *O. C.*
πλεῖστον...κάκιστος.—διὰ δίκης ἰὼν π 7 ΄3
engaging in controversy with him, b ΄ ΄ ΄
ing arguments with him. Thuc. 6 ΄ .60
ἀρνηθέντι διὰ δίκης ἐλθεῖν, to deny the
charge, and stand a trial. Xen. *An.*
1. 8 πάλιν αὐτοῖς διὰ φιλίας ἰέναι...
παντὸς πολέμου αὐτοῖς ἰέναι. So διὰ μάχης
(Her. 6. 9), δι' ἔχθρας (Eur. *Ph.* 479).—
Cp. Plut. *Mor.* 483 c (a brother, in a

brother's defence, ought to brave the displeasure of parents): αἱ δὲ ὑπὲρ ἀδελφοῦ
παρ' ἀξίαν κακῶς ἀκούοντος ἢ πάσχοντος
ἀντιδικίαι καὶ δικαιολογίαι πρὸς αὐτοὺς
(the parents) ἄμεμπτοι καὶ καλαί· καὶ οὐ
φοβητέαν ἀκοῦσαι (to have said to one) τὸ
Σοφόκλειον· ὦ παῖ κάκιστε (quoting this
v.)...καὶ γὰρ αὐτοῖς ἡ τοιαύτη δίκη (controversy) τοῖς ἐλεγχομένοις ποιεῖ τὴν ἧτταν
ἡδίω τῆς νίκης.

744 ἀρχάς, the king's powers or prerogatives, like κράτη (60, 166, 173): cp.
177, 797. Cp. Aesch. *Ch.* 864 ἀρχάς τε
πολισσονόμους | πατέρων θ' ἕξει μέγαν ὄλ-
βον (Orestes). Eur. *I. A.* 343 ἐπεὶ κατέ-
σχες ἀρχάς (Agamemnon).

745 οὐ γὰρ σέβεις: '(that plea is void),
for,' etc.: *i.e.* '*nay, but* thou dost not...'
Creon has asked, 'Do I wrong, when I
reverence my royal office?' Haemon
answers, 'Nay, there can be no such
reverence, when you dishonour the gods.'
A king rules by the divine grace. He
sins against his own office when he uses
his power to infringe the majesty of the
gods.—τιμάς, esp. sacrifices (as in this
case the offerings for the νέρτεροι): cp. *O.
T.* 909 n.

746 ὦ μιαρόν. In Haemon's last
words Creon hears an echo of Antigone's
doctrine—that the θεῶν νόμιμα rank above
the human king's edict (453). Hence
γυναικὸς ὕστερον, 'inferior to her,' rank-

CR. Is not the city held to be the ruler's?
HAE. Thou wouldst make a good monarch of a desert.
CR. This boy, it seems, is the woman's champion.
→ HAE. If thou art a woman; indeed, my care is for thee.
CR. Shameless, at open feud with thy father!
HAE. Nay, I see thee offending against justice.
CR. Do I offend, when I respect mine own prerogatives?
HAE. Thou dost not respect them, when thou tramplest on the gods' honours.
CR. O dastard nature, yielding place to a woman!
HAE. Thou wilt never find me yield to baseness.
CR. All thy words, at least, plead for that girl.
HAE. And for thee, and for me, and for the gods below.

Elmsley. [Porson on Eur. *Med.* 863 first pointed to the misunderstood crasis of τοι and ἄν as a source of MS. error, giving several examples; Elmsley on *Med.* 836 f. first applied the remark to this verse.]—The Aldine, following A and some other MSS., has οὐκ ἄν γ', and Brunck wrote οὐκ ἄν γ' ἕλοις κρείσσω με (for γε) τῶν αἰσχρῶν ποτέ.—οὐκ ἄν λάβοις Nauck.   **748** ὁ γοῦν] ὅ γ' οὖν L.

ing after her; so *Ai.* 1366, *Ph.* 181. Not, 'unable to resist her influence' (through love), as though it were γυναικὸς ἥσσον: a meaning which ὕστερος could not have. The general sense is, however, the same, —viz., that he ranks behind a woman, who leads him.

747 'I may be inferior to a woman, but at least you will never find me yielding to base temptations.' It would have been αἰσχρόν if he had allowed fear or self-interest to deter him from pleading this cause. (Cp. 509.) Cp. *Tr.* 489 ἔρωτος...ἥσσων: fr. 844 ἥσσων...ὀργῆς.—οὔ τᾶν is a certain correction of οὐκ ἄν (cp. *O. T.* 1445, 1469: *O. C.* 1351: *Tr.* 279: *Ai.* 456, 534, etc.). Against the weak conjecture οὐκ ἄν γ' is the repetition of γε: cp. on *O. C.* 387. Where τᾶν has been corrupted in our MSS., it has most often become τ' ἄν, sometimes γ' ἄν or δ' ἄν. But a change of οὔ τᾶν into οὐκ ἄν would also be easy in writing where, as in that of L, the κ of οὐκ was often attached to the next word (see cr. n.).—γε emphasises the whole phrase, ἥσσω τῶν αἰσχρῶν, not ἥσσω alone: cp. 648 n.

748 γοῦν: cp. *O. C.* 24 n. To plead her cause is to be ἥσσων τῶν αἰσχρῶν.

749 καὶ σοῦ γε. Creon is concerned, not merely as a king whose city will be punished by the gods, but as a man who is to be saved from incurring guilt.

750—757 Objections have been made

to the traditional order of these verses, chiefly in two respects. (1) 755 εἰ μὴ πατὴρ ἦσθ' is—it is argued—the strongest thing said by Haemon, and ought therefore to come immediately before Creon's final outburst, ἀληθές; (758). How could it be followed by merely so mild a phrase as μὴ κώτιλλέ με?—We may reply:— Haemon says that, *if* Creon were not his father, he *would have* thought him mad. It is to this that μὴ κώτιλλέ με refers, meaning, 'Do not seek to deceive me by an affectation of filial deference.' (2) 757 βούλει λέγειν τι is too mild a remark—it is said—to form the climax of provocation to Creon's anger. We may reply:—It is in substance, if not in form, such a climax, —for a father who holds that *unquestioning* obedience (640) is a son's first duty. It asserts Haemon's right to maintain his own views against his father's,—διὰ δίκης ἰέναι, as Creon put it (742). The traditional order seems, therefore, to be right.

Three modes of transposition have been proposed. (1) Enger puts 756 and 757 after 749. Then κώτιλλε (756) refers to Haemon's plea that he has his father's cause, and that of religion, at heart. We lose nothing by such a transposition; but neither do we gain.

(2) Donner (in his transl., ed. 1863) simply transposed verses 755 and 757, leaving the rest as they stand. For this

ΚΡ. ταύτην ποτ᾽ οὐκ ἔσθ᾽ ὡς ἔτι ζῶσαν γαμεῖς. 750
ΑΙ. ἥδ᾽ οὖν θανεῖται καὶ θανοῦσ᾽ ὀλεῖ τινά.
ΚΡ. ἦ κἀπαπειλῶν ὧδ᾽ ἐπεξέρχει θρασύς;
ΑΙ. τίς δ᾽ ἔστ᾽ ἀπειλὴ πρὸς κενὰς γνώμας λέγειν;
ΚΡ. κλαίων φρενώσεις, ὢν φρενῶν αὐτὸς κενός.
ΑΙ. εἰ μὴ πατὴρ ἦσθ᾽, εἶπον ἄν σ᾽ οὐκ εὖ φρονεῖν. 755
ΚΡ. γυναικὸς ὢν δούλευμα, μὴ κώτιλλέ με.
ΑΙ. βούλει λέγειν τι καὶ λέγων μηδὲν κλύειν;
ΚΡ. ἄληθες; ἀλλ᾽ οὐ, τόνδ᾽ Ὄλυμπον, ἴσθ᾽ ὅτι,
χαίρων ἐπὶ ψόγοισί δεννάσεις ἐμέ.

750 ποτ᾽ .. γαμεῖς.] πότ᾽ .. γαμεῖσ; L.   751 ἥδ᾽ οὖν L, and lemma schol.:
ἥδ᾽ οὖν vulg.: ἡ δ᾽ οὖν Hartung. Nauck conject. εἰ δ᾽ οὖν.   752 ἦ κἀπαπειλῶν. In L there has been an erasure at the letters απα, which are, however, by an early hand (the first, or S). The first hand had (I think) written ἦ
καὶ ἀπειλῶν. For an analogous error cp. O. C. 172 cr. n.   755 ἦσθ᾽] ἦσθ᾽ L.
Cp. 726.   757 κλύειν r, λέγειν L.—Wecklein conject. ψέγειν τι καὶ ψέγων μηδὲν

---

it may fairly be said that 757 comes very fitly after 754. On the other hand it seems to me that 756 does not aptly follow 757.

(3) Pallis arranges thus:—749, 756, 755, 754, 757, 750—753. Thus κενὰς γνώμας (753) becomes the last sting.— The fact is that, in a stormy altercation, we do not look for a closely logical texture and a delicately graduated crescendo. The MS. order is (to my mind) the best; but other arrangements are possible, and would be nearly as good.

750 Creon, instead of replying to v. 749, abruptly repeats his resolve. οὐκ ἔστιν ὡς ταύτην ἔτι ζῶσαν γαμεῖς (fut.) ποτέ, it cannot be that you shall ever wed her while she yet lives; i.e. she is to die at once, and can become your bride, if ever, only ἐν Ἅιδου (654). Cp. 1240.— ὡς for the more usual ὅπως: so Ph. 196 οὐκ ἔσθ᾽ ὡς οὐ.—The strange place of ποτέ is explained by the strong emphasis on ταύτην ('her, at any time, it is impossible that thou shouldest wed'). Soph. often admits bold arrangements of words (cp. O. T. 1245, 1251: O. C. 1428).

751 ἥδ᾽ referring to ταύτην (cp. 296 f.). At first sight ἡ δ᾽ is attractive; but that phrase is properly used with the imperat., and has a defiant or scornful tone (O. T. 669 ὁ δ᾽ οὖν ἴτω: Ai. 961 οἱ δ᾽ οὖν γελώντων: Ar. Ach. 186 οἱ δ᾽ οὖν βοώντων). The quiet ἥδ᾽ is more impressive here.— ὀλεῖ τινά, i.e. ἐμέ: Creon understands

him to mean σέ. As vv. 763 f. show, Haemon is resolved not to survive Antigone. But he has no thought of threatening his father's life: his frantic action at v. 1231 was a sudden impulse, instantly followed by remorse (1245). For the sinister τις, cp. Ai. 1138 τοῦτ᾽ εἰς ἀνίαν τοὔπος ἔρχεταί τινι. Ar. Ran. 552 ff. κακὸν ἥκει τινί...δώσει τις δίκην. Thuc. 4. 68 εἰ...μὴ πείσεταί τις, αὐτοῦ τὴν μάχην ἔσεσθαι.

752 ἦ ἐπεξέρχει καὶ ἐπαπειλῶν ὧδε θρασύς; Dost thou go the length of e'en threatening so boldly? The participial clause defines the manner of ἐπεξέρχει, and so is practically equiv. to ὥστε καὶ ἐπαπειλεῖν etc. The καί here belongs to the partic. (distinguish the composite ἦ καί in question, O. T. 368). Eur. Bacch. 1346 ἀλλ᾽ ἐπεξέρχει λίαν, (we have erred,) but thou goest too far (in vengeance). Cp. O. C. 438 τὸν θυμὸν ἐκδραμόντα μοι | μείζω κολαστήν.

754 κλαίων, as O. T. 401, 1152.— φρενώσεις, a poet. word, used by Xen. Mem. 4. 1. 5 τοὺς ἐπὶ πλούτῳ μέγα φρονοῦντας...ἐφρένου λέγων.

755 οὐκ εὖ φρονεῖν, as angrily refusing (754) to hear reason.

756 δούλευμα: cp. on 650.—μὴ κώτιλλέ με, 'do not seek to cajole me,'—referring to εἰ μὴ πατὴρ ἦσθ᾽, as expressive of filial respect. Creon means, 'do not pretend that you have any of the feelings with which a son ought to regard a father.'

CR. Thou canst never marry her, on this side the grave.

HAE. Then she must die, and _in death_ destroy another.

CR. How! doth thy boldness run to open threats?

HAE. What threat is it, to combat vain resolves?

CR. Thou shalt rue thy witless teaching of wisdom.

HAE. Wert thou not my father, I would have called thee unwise.

CR. Thou woman's slave, use not wheedling speech with me.

HAE. Thou wouldest speak, and then hear no reply?

CR. Sayest thou so? Now, by the heaven above us—be sure of it—thou shalt smart for taunting me in this opprobrious strain.

λέγειν.   **758** ἀληθες;] ἀληθέσ; L. (The first hand wrote merely a comma: S added the dot above it.) But in *O. T.* 350 (the only other instance in Soph.) L has ἀληθεσ (though without the note of interrogation).   **759** ἐπί] Dobree conject. ἔτι: Musgrave, ἐπιψόγοισι.—δεννάσεις] δ' ἐννάσεις L, the δ substituted by S for another letter (λ?). So in *Ai.* 243 L has δ' ἐννάζων: and in Theognis 1211 (Bergk) one MS. has δ' ἔνναζε.

Cp. Theognis 363 εὖ κώτιλλε τὸν ἐχθρόν (cajole)· ὅταν δ' ὑποχείριος ἔλθῃ, | τῖσαί νιν, πρόφασιν μηδεμίαν θέμενος: id. 851 Ζεὺς ἄνδρ' ἐξολέσειεν Ὀλύμπιος, ὃς τὸν ἑταῖρον | μαλθακὰ κωτίλλων ἐξαπατᾶν ἐθέλει. **757** λέγειν...κλύειν; do you wish to speak, and yet not to hear? λέγειν τι has a euphemistic tone ('to say something strong, or harsh'), like δρᾶν τι (*El.* 336), but the τι could hardly be represented in translation without exaggerating it. λέγειν καὶ ἀκούειν was a familiar phrase for fair discussion (Thuc. 4. 22 λέγοντες καὶ ἀκούοντες περὶ ἑκάστου ξυμβήσεσθαι: cp. *O. C.* 189). *El.* 628 πρὸς ὀργὴν ἐκφέρει, μεθεῖσά μοι | λέγειν ἃ χρῄζοιμ', οὐδ' ἐπίστασαι κλύειν: ib. 990 ἢ προμηθία | καὶ τῷ λέγοντι καὶ κλύοντι σύμμαχος. The words imply a claim of equality, and are also full of scorn: hence Creon's outburst. —Not: 'do you wish to taunt and not to be taunted in return?'—as if κλύειν = 'to have things said to one' (*Ai.* 1322 κλύοντι φλαῦρα συμβαλεῖν ἔπη κακά: *El.* 523 κακῶς δέ σε | λέγω κακῶς κλύουσα πρὸς σέθεν θαμά). **758** ἀληθες; the word which marks that Teiresias can no longer restrain his wrath against Oedipus (*O. T.* 350).—οὐ τόνδ' "Ολ., without μά: *O. T.* 660, 1088. Cp. *Ai.* 1389 Ὀλύμπου οὖδ' ὁ πρεσβεύων πατήρ: *O. C.* 1655.—ἴσθ' ὅτι, adverbial: cp. 276 n. **759** χαίρων, *impune*, as *O. T.* 363, *Ph.* 1299.—ἐπὶ ψόγοισι δεννάσεις, lit.,

revile me with (continual) *censures*: ψόγος is merely *censure*, fault-finding, not necessarily imp_ying offensive speech (cp. 680). δεννάζω, to reproach or revile: *Ai.* 243 κακὰ δεννάζων ῥήμαθ': [Eur.] *Rhes.* 925 (the Muse speaking of Thamyris) ὃς ἡμῶν πόλλ' ἐδέννασεν τέχνην. So Theogn. 1211 (if the verse be his, and not Anacreon's) μή μ' ἀφελῶς [ἀφίλωτ?] παίζουσα φίλους δένναζε τοκῆας, alluding to her saying that they had been slaves. Her. 9. 107 παρὰ δὲ τοῖσι Πέρσῃσι γυναικὸς κακίω ἀκοῦσαι δέννος μέγιστός ἐστι. This ἐπί with dat. is not merely 'with,' but implies a *continuing strain* of utterance: *El.* 108 ἐπὶ κωκυτῷ τῶνδε πατρῴων | πρὸ θυρῶν ἠχὼ πᾶσι προφωνεῖν: Eur. *Tro.* 315 ἐπὶ δάκρυσι καὶ | γόοισι τὸν θανόντα πατέρα... καταστένουσ' ἔχεις (thou art *ever* lamenting).—Others explain ἐπί as (a) 'in addition to,' which implies too sharp a contrast with δεννάσεις, esp. without καί: (b) 'with a view to,' *i.e.* 'in order to blame me.' Cp. Eur. *Ph.* 1555 οὐκ ἐπ' ὀνείδεσιν οὐδ' ἐπὶ χάρμασιν | ἀλλ' ὀδύναισι λέγω ('not *for* insult or spiteful joy, but *in* pain'). Here, however, that sense would be weak. —For Dobree's ἔτι, cp. Ar. *Plut.* 64 οὗτοι μὰ τὴν Δήμητρα χαιρήσεις ἔτι. It is plausible, and may be right. But I prefer ἐπὶ ψόγοισι, because (in the sense explained above) it is so fitting when an impatient man breaks off a dialogue which has irritated him throughout.

ἄγετε τὸ μῖσος, ὡς κατ' ὄμματ' αὐτίκα   760
παρόντι θνήσκῃ πλησία τῷ νυμφίῳ.

ΑΙ. οὐ δῆτ' ἔμοιγε, τοῦτο μὴ δόξῃς ποτέ,
οὔθ' ἥδ' ὀλεῖται πλησία, σύ τ' οὐδαμὰ
τοὐμὸν πρόσόψει κρᾶτ' ἐν ὀφθαλμοῖς ὁρῶν,
ὡς τοῖς θέλουσι τῶν φίλων μαίνῃ ξυνών.   765

ΧΟ. ἀνήρ, ἄναξ, βέβηκεν ἐξ ὀργῆς ταχύς·
νοῦς δ' ἐστὶ τηλικοῦτος ἀλγήσας βαρύς.

ΚΡ. δράτω, φρονείτω μεῖζον ἢ κατ' ἄνδρ' ἰών·
τὼ δ' οὖν κόρα τώδ' οὐκ ἀπαλλάξει μόρου.

ΧΟ. ἄμφω γὰρ αὐτὼ καὶ κατακτεῖναι νοεῖς;   770

ΚΡ. οὐ τήν γε μὴ θιγοῦσαν· εὖ γὰρ οὖν λέγεις.

ΧΟ. μόρῳ δὲ ποίῳ καί σφε βουλεύει κτανεῖν;

ΚΡ. ἄγων ἔρημος ἔνθ' ἂν ᾖ βροτῶν στίβος
κρύψω πετρώδει ζῶσαν ἐν κατώρυχι.

---

760 ἄγαγε L, ἄγετε r: ἄγ', ἄγε Wecklein.   761 θνήσκει L.   763 οὐδαμὰ]
οὐδαμᾶι L. Most of the later MSS. have οὐδαμᾶ, but Dresden a οὐδαμὰ, and Vat.
οὐδαμοῦ.   765 μαίνῃ] In L the first hand wrote μαίνηισ: another early hand,
deleting σ, wrote ε over α and ειϲ over ηι, thus indicating μαίνηι and μένεις (or
μενεῖς) as alternative readings. The later MSS. have μαίνῃ, μένεις, μενεῖς, μένῃς, or
μένῃ. The Schol. knew both μένῃς (which he explains first) and μαίνῃ.—ξυνών.
L has σ above ξ from first hand.   766 ἀνὴρ L, ἀνὴρ r.   767 βαρύς made

---

760 f. ἄγετε. The plur. is addressed
to the two πρόσπολοι who had ushered
the sisters into the house (578, κομίζετ'
ἔσω, δμῶες). So at 491 the plur. is used,
καλεῖτ'. And, in general, such orders
are usu. given in the plur., or by τις with
3rd pers. (as O. T. 1069). Cp. 931 τοῖσιν
ἄγουσιν. This is against Wecklein's ἄγ',
ἄγε. The objection to L's ἄγαγε is not
only the sing. number, but also the fact
that the 2nd aor. imperat. act. (and midd.)
of ἄγω does not seem to have been used
in Attic.—τὸ μῖσος: Ph. 991 ὦ μῖσος
(Odysseus): so μίσημα, στύγος, στύγημα.—
κατ' ὄμματ': Xen. Hier. 1. 14 οὐδεὶς...
ἐθέλει τυράννου κατ' ὀφθαλμοὺς κατηγορεῖν
(' to his face ').—παρόντι...πλησία. The
accumulation of words for ' presence '
marks his vehement anger: cp. Haemon's
pleonasm in 764, and O. T. 430.

762 ff. ἔμοιγε is placed as if it were
to be common to both the clauses (οὔτε...
τε), but the constr. changes: cp. El. 913
ἀλλ' οὐδὲ μὲν δὴ μητρὸς οὔθ' ὁ νοῦς φιλεῖ |
τοιαῦτα πράσσειν οὔτε δρῶσ' ἐλάνθανεν.—
For οὔτε followed by τε cp. O.C. 1397 (n.).

—οὐδαμά, neut. plur. adv.: this form is
required by metre in 830, as οὐδαμᾶ (Doric)
in 874: L always gives οὐδαμᾶι: see on
O. C. 1104.—ἐν ὀφθαλμοῖς, with them (the
instrumental ἐν, 962, 1003, 1201): an epic
phrase, Il. 1. 587 ἐν ὀφθαλμοῖσιν ἴδωμαι,
etc.: so oft. ἐν ὄμμασιν (Tr. 241).

765 ὡς: cp. 643.—τοῖς θέλουσι, i.e.
any who can endure it. Cp. the words
of Teiresias, 1087.—Haemon now finally
quits the scene. The deuteragonist is
thus set free for the parts of the Ἄγγελος
and the Ἐξάγγελος.

766 f. ἐξ ὀργῆς ταχύς, in haste caused
by wrath: cp. Il. 7. 111 μηδ' ἔθελ' ἐξ ἔριδος
σεῦ ἀμείνονι φωτὶ μάχεσθαι, out of mere
rivalry.—βαρύς, resentful: cp. O. T. 673
βαρὺς δ', ὅταν | θυμοῦ περάσῃς; so as epith.
of μῆνις (O. C. 1328) and ὀργή (Ph. 368).
The sense of βαρύ in 1251 is different.

768 μεῖζον ἢ κατ' ἄνδρα is said in
answer to their hint of fear:—let his passion touch the human limit, aye, or over-
pass it. O. C. 598 τί γὰρ τὸ μεῖζον ἢ κατ'
ἄνθρωπον νοσεῖς; For ἀνήρ = ἄνθρωπος, ib.
567.—ἰών: Ph. 351 εἰ τἀπὶ Τροίᾳ πέργαμ'

Bring forth that hated thing, that she may die forthwith in his presence—before his eyes—at her bridegroom's side!

HAE. No, not at my side—never think it—shall she perish; nor shalt thou ever set eyes more upon my face :—rave, then, with such friends as can endure thee. [*Exit* HAEMON.

CH. The man is gone, O King, in angry haste ; a youthful mind, when, stung, is fierce.

CR. Let him do, or dream, more than man—good speed to him !—But he shall not save these two girls from their doom.

CH. Dost thou indeed purpose to slay both?

CR. Not her whose hands are pure : thou sayest well.

CH. And by what doom mean'st thou to slay the other?

CR. I will take her where the path is loneliest, and hide her, living, in a rocky vault,

---

from βραχύσ in L. **769** τάδ' (*sic*) .. τάδ' L: τῷ δ' .. τῴδ' Dindorf.—μόρου L: μόρων Vat., V⁴. **770** αὐτὰ L: αὐτῷ Dindorf.—κατακτανῆναι (not κατακτῆναι) L: κατακτεῖναι r. **771** τήνδε (from τῆνδε) L, with γ above δ either from the first hand (so Duebner) or from an early corrector. The same hand has written οι above λέγεισ. Perh. εὖ γάρ ἀν λέγοις was a *v. l.* **773** ἀγων .. στίβοσ] Semitelos conject. ἀγκών .. στίβου.—ἐνθ' ἀν made from ἐνθα ἀν in L. **774** πετρώδη L with ει above η from the first hand.

αἱρήσοιμ' ἰών : *Ai.* 304 ὅσην κατ' αὐτῶν ὕβριν ἐκτίσαιτ' ἰών. So here it scornfully suggests some daring enterprise.

769 f. For δ' οὖν cp. 688, 722.—τὰ... τάδε: cp. 561 (τώ), *O. T.* 1472 (τοῖν), *O. C.* 1600 (τώ), *El.* 977 (τώδε τώ)—all fem.—Attic inscriptions of *c.* 450—320 B.C. present numerous instances of fem. dual τώ, τοῖν, τούτοιν, οἶν, but no instance of fem. dual τά, ταῖν, ταύταιν, or αἶν. (Meisterhans p. 50.) Hitherto the gen. and dat. ταῖν, ταῖνδε, ταύταιν have been retained even by those edd. who give τώ, τώδε, etc. (cp. *O. T.* 1462, 1504: *O. C.* 445, 859, 1149, 1290, etc.). But, so far as epigraphic evidence goes, the distinction is arbitrary.—καί with the whole phrase κατακτ. νεᾶς rather than with κατακτ. alone (for no minor penalty is in view): cp. 726.

771 θιγοῦσαν ; cp. 546.—γάρ οὖν : cp. 489, 741.

772 καί with βουλεύει ; (her doom having been fixed,) by what fate *do* you purpose to slay her? For καί thus following the interrog., cp. 1314. Aesch. *Ag.* 278 ποίου χρόνου δὲ καὶ πεπόρθηται πόλις; Eur. *Hec.* 515 πῶς καὶ νιν ἐξεπράξατ';—σφε=αὐτήν, Antigone: cp. 44 n.

773 ἔνθα = ἐκεῖσε ἔνθα, as *O. T.* 796: so *O. C.* 188 ἄγε...με... | ἵν' ἀν etc. Cp. *Ph.* 486 μή μ' ἀφῇς | ἔρημον οὕτω χωρὶς ἀνθρώπων στίβου.

774 πετρώδει...ἐν κατώρυχι, 'in a rocky cavern'; schol., ἐν ὑπογείῳ σπηλαίῳ. Verse 773 shows that Creon is not yet thinking of any special spot. And κατῶρυξ shows that he is not thinking of some merely natural grotto or cavern. This word, usu. an adj., here a subst., means a cavern, or chamber, excavated by man's hand: cp. Eur. *Hec.* 1002 χρυσοῦ παλαιαὶ Πριαμιδῶν κατώρυχες. So the place is described by κατασκαφής (891). The κατῶρυξ actually used was near the furthest and highest part of the plain, where Polyneices lay (1197). What, then, was the poet's conception? He seems to suppose the existence of tombs artificially constructed in the rocky πάγοι (411) which bordered on the Theban plain. In one of these tombs —chosen for the remoteness of its situation (773)—Antigone is to be immured. The general type of sepulchral chamber supposed here can be illustrated from actual remains which have been discovered in Greece: see below on vv. 1216 ff.

φορβῆς τοσοῦτον ὡς ἄγος μόνον προθείς, 775
ὅπως μίασμα πᾶσ᾽ ὑπεκφύγῃ πόλις.
κἀκεῖ τὸν Ἅιδην, ὃν μόνον σέβει θεῶν,
αἰτουμένη πού τεύξεται τὸ μὴ θανεῖν,
ἢ γνώσεται γοῦν ἀλλὰ τηνικαῦθ᾽ ὅτι
πόνος περισσός ἐστι τἀν Ἅιδου σέβειν. 780

στρ. ΧΟ. Ἔρως ἀνίκατε μάχαν, Ἔρως, ὃς ἐν κτήμασι πίπτεις,
2 ὃς ἐν μαλακαῖς παρειαῖς νεάνιδος ἐννυχεύεις,

775 ὡς ἄγος μόνον] Blaydes conject. ὅσον ἄγος φεύγειν, and many edd. have adopted ὅσον, while retaining μόνον. (Hartung, ὡς ἄγος φεύγειν.) Dindorf proposed: (1) ἔθος for ἄγος: (2) ὡς ἄγος φεύγειν μόνον | προθείς, ὅπως μίασμ᾽ ὑπεκφύγῃ πόλις: (3) ὡς ἄγος φεύγειν προθείς, deleting v. 776. Wecklein (Ars Soph. em. p. 27) suggested τρέπειν for μόνον. 776 ὑπεκφυγῃι L: ὑπεκφύγοι r. 778 του] τοῦ L. 779 γοῦν] γ᾽ οὖν L.

775 ὡς ἄγος μόνον, sc. εἶναι, so much as to be barely an expiation; only just enough to avoid the μίασμα. The conjectural change of ὡς into ὅσον (adopted by several edd.) would be necessary if the indic. ἐστί had to be supplied, since we could not say τοσοῦτον ὡς (instead of ὅσον) ἄγος ἐστί. That change is unnecessary, because it is the inf. εἶναι that is understood. Cp. Xen. An. 7. 3 § 22 ὅσον μόνον γεύσασθαι, and see n. on O. C. 790 for other instances where the inf. is expressed. The inf. is understood, as here, in Xen. An. 7. 8 § 19 ἔχοντες πρόβατα ὅσον θύματα (sc. εἶναι): so ib. 7. 3 § 20 ἔχων... ὅσον ἐφόδιον.—ἄγος was used by Soph. in his lost Phaedra to denote ἅγνισμα θυσίας (Hesych. 1. 63), i.e. 'an expiatory sacrifice' (cp. Aesch. Eum. 325 ἄγνισμα φόνου). In Aesch. Cho. 154 also ἄγος has been taken as = 'expiation,' but there it seems rather to be 'pollution.' Cp. the schol. here: ἔθος παλαιόν, ὥστε τὸν βουλόμενον καθειργνύναι τινὰ ἀφοσιοῦσθαι βραχὺ τιθέντα τροφήν, καὶ ὑπενδοὺν κάθαρσιν τὸ τοιοῦτο, ἵνα μὴ δοκῶσι λιμῷ ἀναιρεῖν· τοῦτο γὰρ ἀσεβές.—Curtius, Etym. 5th ed., § 118, would write ἅγος here. He distinguishes two roots. (1) ἀγ-, ἄγος, 'guilt,' ἀναγής, 'accursed': Sanskr. ǵr-as, 'vexation,' etc. (2) ἀγ-, ἅγος, 'consecration, sacrifice,' ἅγιος, etc.: Sanskr. jaǵ. On the other hand the analogy of piaculum suggests that ἄγος might combine the sense of 'expiation' with that of 'pollution.'

Creon's edict had announced that the transgressor would be publicly stoned to death (36). It is to this that the anxious question of the Chorus alludes (772). Creon had already said that Antigone's doom was to be κάκιστος (489). But now, at least, he feels that he cannot inflict such a death on the maiden, his kinswoman. She shall die, not by stoning, but by starvation. The choice is not prompted by cruelty, but simply by the desire to avoid physical violence.

The danger of a μίασμα—to be avoided by a dole of food—has no relation to the special circumstances,—Antigone's royal birth, and the nature of her offence. In the ancient belief, that danger existed whenever a person was put to death by starvation. Two notions were probably blended; (a) that, if a little food was given, the death was nature's work, not man's; (b) that the νέρτεροι claimed an indemnity for the usual ἐναγίσματα. So the Greeks put Philoctetes ashore on desolate Lemnos, —ῥάκη προθέντες βαιὰ καί τι καὶ βορᾶς | ἐπωφέλημα σμικρόν (Ph. 274). So, too, when a Vestal was to be buried alive, the small vault in the Campus Sceleratus was furnished with a couch, a burning lamp, and a small table, on which the dole was placed,—bread, olives, milk, and a jug of water (Plut. Num. 10).

776 πᾶσ᾽: cp. on 178. The sense is, 'in order that the whole city may not be defiled' (as it otherwise would be): μίασμ᾽ ὑπεκφύγῃ = μὴ μιανθῇ.

777 ὃν μόνον σέβει. Polyneices had come to destroy the shrines of the θεοί

with so much food set forth as piety prescribes, that the city
may avoid a public stain.   And there, praying to Hades, the
only god whom she worships, perchance she will obtain release
from death; or else will learn, at last, though late, that it is
lost labour to revere the dead.   [*Exit* CREON.

CH. Love, unconquered in the fight, Love, who makest havoc Strophe
of wealth, who keepest thy vigil on the soft cheek of a maiden ;

780 This v. was accidentally omitted from the text of L, and added in the
margin by the first hand.   **782** ὅς ῑ, ὅσṭ' L.—κτήμασι] For the conjectures,
see Appendix.

ἐγγενεῖς (199). By honouring him, and
Hades (519), she has dishonoured those
other gods
778 τὸ μὴ θανεῖν is acc. with τεύξεται:
cp. Aesch. *Ch.* 711 τυγχάνειν τὰ πρόσφορα:
O. C. 1106 (n.): fr. 814 καὶ τὰ καὶ τὰ
τυγχάνων. This comparatively rare constr.
has here been influenced by αἰτουμένη:
though it is unnecessary to refer the acc.
to the partic. only, or to understand, ' will
successfully ask.' See, however, Her. 5.
23 παρὰ Δαρείου αἰτήσας ἔτυχε...δωρεήν: 9. 109 πάντα γὰρ τεύξεσθαι αἰτήσασαν: where, in both instances, the acc.
depends on the partic. only.—We could
not well take τὸ μὴ θανεῖν here as = ὥστε
μὴ θανεῖν (like κωλύω τὸ μὴ ποιεῖν τι).
779 f. ἀλλὰ τηνικαῦτα : cp. 552.—
τάν, instead of τοὺς ἐν "Αιδου: 659.
781—**800** Third stasimon. Strophe
781—790 = antistr. 791—800.
After Creon's and Haemon's speeches,
the comment of the Chorus was in a neutral
tone (724). When Haemon departed in
anger, they spoke words implying that
allowance must be made for the heat of
youth (767). This beautiful ode is in a
kindred strain. If Haemon has sinned
against great θεσμοί—loyalty to country
and to father—at least he is under the
influence of a god whom none can withstand.
The pathos of the maiden's fate is
heightened by this plea for her lover.
When she is led in by the guards, on her
way to death, the Chorus avow that pity
works with them even as love with Haemon
(801—805). A perfect preparation is thus
made for the lyric dialogue between the
Chorus and Antigone (806—882).
781 ἀνίκατε μάχαν: *Tr.* 441 Ἔρωτι μέν
νυν ὅστις ἀντανίσταται, | πύκτης ὅπως ἐς
χεῖρας, οὐ καλῶς φρονεῖ. Eur. fr. 433
Ἔρωτα, πάντων δυσμαχώτατον θεόν. Plat.

Symp. 196 D καὶ μὴν εἴς γε ἀνδρίαν Ἔρωτι
οὐδὲ Ἄρης ἀνθίσταται· οὐ γὰρ ἔχει Ἔρωτα
Ἄρης, ἀλλ' Ἔρως Ἄρη.
782 ἐν κτήμασι πίπτεις, who *fallest
upon* men's possessions; who makest
havoc of their wealth and fortunes. Cp.
Od. 24. 526 ἐν δ' ἔπεσον προμάχοις, 'they
fell on the fore-fighters': so ἐμπίπτειν is
oft. said of the attacks of disease or passion.
Love makes men reckless of possessions:
it can bring ruin on great houses and
proud cities. Sophocles himself has given
us the best commentary: see *Tr.* 431,
referring to the capture of Oechalia by
Heracles, who loved Iolè, the daughter
of its king, Eurytus: ὡς ταύτης πόθῳ | πόλις δαμεῖη πᾶσα, κοὐχ ἡ Λυδία | πέρσειεν
αὐτήν, ἀλλ' ὁ τῆσδ' ἔρως φανείς. The
same thought is finely expressed by Eur.,
in a choral ode to Ἔρως, which this passage
has certainly helped to inspire (*Hipp.*
525 ff.): Ἔρωτα δέ, τὸν τύραννον ἀνδρῶν, |
...οὐ σεβίζομεν, | πέρθοντα καὶ διὰ πάσας | ἰόντα συμφορὰς | θνατοῖς, ὅταν
ἔλθῃ. Troy was sacked for the sake of
Helen,—ἑλέναυς, ἕλανδρος, ἑλέπτολις.
Medea betrayed her father's treasure to
Jason (cp. Eur. *Med.* 480). The *resistless
power* of Love is the central thought of
this ode. All that men prize most becomes his prey.—See Appendix.
783 f. ἐν μαλακαῖς παρειαῖς. Ion of
Chios (*ap.* Athen. 603 E) describes Soph. as
saying, ὡς καλῶς Φρύνιχος (the tragic poet,
flor. c. 490) ἐποίησεν εἴπας λάμπει δ'
ἐπὶ πορφυρέαις παρῇσι φῶς ἔρωτος.
Plut. *Mor.* 760 D σκότει τοίνυν...τοῖς
ἀρηίοις ἔργοις ὅσον Ἔρως περίεστιν, οὐκ
ἀργὸς ὤν, ὡς Εὐριπίδης ἔλεγεν, οὐδὲ ἀστράτευτος, οὐδ' ἐν μαλακαῖσιν [ἐννυχεύ]ων παρειαῖς νεανίδων.—ἐννυχεύεις, keepest thy
vigil: perh. here an image suggested by
a soldier's night-watch (like Horace's
pulcris excubat in genis, sc. Cupido, *C.*

3 φοιτᾷς δ᾽ ὑπερπόντιος ἔν τ᾽ ἀγρονόμοις αὐλαῖς·　785
4 καί σ᾽ οὔτ᾽ ἀθανάτων φύξιμος οὐδεὶς
5 οὔθ᾽ ἀμερίων * σέ γ᾽ ἀνθρώπων, ὁ δ᾽ ἔχων μέμηνεν.　790

ἀντ.　σὺ καὶ δικαίων ἀδίκους φρένας παρασπᾷς ἐπὶ λώβᾳ·
2 σὺ καὶ τόδε νεῖκος ἀνδρῶν ξύναιμον ἔχεις ταράξας·
3 νικᾷ δ᾽ ἐναργὴς βλεφάρων ἵμερος εὐλέκτρου　795
4 νύμφας, τῶν μεγάλων πάρεδρος ἐν ἀρχαῖς

785—790 L divides the vv. thus: φοιτᾷς δ— | τ᾽ ἀγρονόμοις— | καί σ᾽…ἀν|θρώ-πων…μέμηνεν.　786 τ᾽ ἀγρονόμοις] The first hand in L seems to have written πατρονόμοις.　789 ἐπ᾽ ἀνθρώπων L. So most of the later MSS., but Campb. cites ἀπ᾽ from Vat. (14th cent.). Nauck conject. σέ γ᾽ ἀνθρώπων: so also Blaydes (ed. 1859).　790 ὁ δ᾽] δδ᾽ L.　795 νικᾷ δ᾽ . . εὐλέκτρου. Two vv. in L, the second

4. 13. 8); cp. Xen. *An.* 6. 4. 27 ἐν δὲ τοῖς ὅπλοις ἐνυκτέρευον, and so νυκτοφυλακεῖν. Shaksp. *Rom.* 5. 3. 94 'beauty's ensign yet Is crimson in thy lips and in thy cheeks.' Gray, *Progress of Poesy* 1. 3. 16 'O'er her warm cheek and rising bosom move The bloom of young desire and purple light of love.'

785 f. ὑπερπόντιος: cp. 1301: so ἐκτόπιος (*O. T.* 1340), θαλάσσιος (*ib.* 1411), θυραῖος (*El.* 313), παράκτιος (Eur. *I. T.* 1424), etc. So Eur. fr. 434 ("Ερως) κἀπὶ πόντον ἔρχεται. Plut. *Mor.* 760 D quotes an unknown poet, on "Ερως:—πῦρ καὶ θάλασσαν καὶ πνοὰς τὰς αἰθέρος | περᾶν ἕτοιμος. Lucr. 1. 18 (Venus moves) *per maria ac montes fluviosque rapaces Frondi-ferasque domos avium camposque virentes.* —ἔν τ᾽ ἀγρ. αὐλαῖς. ἀγρόνομοι αὐλαί = dwellings in ἀγρὸς νεμόμενος, pastoral wilds: cp. 349 ἀγραύλου: *O. T.* 1103 πλάκες ἀγρόνομοι, upland pastures. *El.* 181 ἀκτὴ βούνομος, a shore on which oxen are pastured (cp. *O. T.* 26).—Some take the sense to be, 'Love conquers not man only, but fishes and wild beasts'; cp. fr. 856. 9 (Κύπρις) εἰσέρχεται μὲν ἰχθύων πλω-τῷ γένει, | ἔνεστι δ᾽ ἐν χέρσου τετρασκελεῖ γονῇ. (How could ὑπερπόντιος imply a visit to the fish?) Others find a reference to Paris carrying Helen over the Aegean, Aphrodite visiting Anchises in the pas-tures of Ida, etc. Rather the poet is merely saying, quite generally, how boundless is the range of Love.

787 f. οὔτ᾽ ἀθανάτων: *Tr.* 443 (of Love) οὗτος γὰρ ἄρχει καὶ θεῶν ὅπως θέλει: fr. 856. 13 (Κύπρις) τίν᾽ οὐ παλαίουσ᾽ ἐς τρὶς ἐκβάλλει θεῶν; Eur. fr. 434 Ἔρως γὰρ

ἄνδρας οὐ μόνους ἐπέρχεται, | οὐδ᾽ αὖ γυ-ναῖκας, ἀλλὰ καὶ θεῶν ἄνω | ψυχὰς χαράσ-σει.—σὲ…φύξιμός ἐστι, = σὲ δύναται φεύ-γειν. Cp. Aesch. *P. V.* 904 ὁ πόλεμος ἄπορα πόριμος: *Ag.* 1090 (στέγην) πολλὰ ξυνίστορα | …κακά: Xen. *Cyr.* 3. 3. 9 ἐπιστήμονες δ᾽ ἦσαν τὰ προσήκοντα: Isae. or. 5 § 26 ἐξαρνοί εἰσι τὰ ὡμολογημένα: [Plat.] *Alcib. II.* 141 D οἶμαι δέ σε οὐκ ἀνήκοον εἶναι ἔνια γε…γεγενημένα. Similarly with a subst., Plat. *Apol.* 18 B τὰ μετέωρα φρον-τιστής.

789 f. σέ γ᾽: for γε with the repeated σε, cp. *O. T.* 1101, *Ph.* 1116.—The MS. ἐπ᾽ could mean only, 'in the case of' (and so, 'among'): a use which is not ade-quately supported by Aristeid. *Pan.* 1. 96 μόνῃ τῇ πόλει ἐπὶ τῶν Ἑλληνικῶν, where he means, 'in the case of' (*i.e.*, 'so far as they are concerned'). Nor could ἐπ᾽ be an adverb ('moreover,' *O. T.* 181), as some take it.—ὁ δ᾽ ἔχων: Plat. *Phaedr.* 239 C ἀνὴρ ἔχων ἔρωτα.

791 f. ἀδίκους proleptic: cp. on 475: *Tr.* 106 εὐνάζειν ἀδακρύτων βλεφάρων πόθον (so that they shall not weep).— παρασπᾷς (cp. 298), a metaphor from a driver jerking his horses aside out of their course: *El.* 732 (the charioteer) ἔξω πα-ρασπᾷ (sc. τοὺς ἵππους), pulls them aside, out of the crowd of chariots. The word is fig. again in *O. C.* 1185 οὐ γάρ σε…πα-ρασπάσει | γνώμης, pluck thee from thy resolve.

794 ξύναιμον, not ξυναίμων, since νεῖ-κος-ἀνδρῶν forms one notion: cp. 862: *El.* 1390 τοὐμὸν φρενῶν ὄνειρον: *Ph.* 952 σχῆμα πέτρας δίπυλον: Aesch. *Eum.* 325 ματρῷον ἄγνισμα…φόνου.—ἔχεις with aor.

thou roamest over the sea, and among the homes of dwellers in the wilds; no immortal can escape thee, nor any among men whose life is for a day; and he to whom thou hast come is mad.

The just themselves have their minds warped by thee to Anti-wrong, for their ruin: 'tis thou that hast stirred up this present strophe strife of kinsmen; victorious is the love-kindling light from the eyes of the fair bride; it is a power enthroned in sway beside the eternal

beginning with ἵμερος.   **796** εὐλέκτρου] In L a letter (perh. ι) has been erased between ε and κ.   **798** πάρεδρος ἐν ἀρχαῖς MSS. In L the letters δρ are in an erasure, from ργ. The Schol. notes that some read παρέδρος, as Doric for παρέδρους. This indicates that he knew no other variant. See comment. and Appendix.

part.: cp. 22.—ταράξας, *excitasti.* Dem. or. 18 § 153 ἵν' εἰδῆτε ἡλίκα πράγματα ἡ μιαρὰ κεφαλὴ ταράξασα αὕτη δίκην οὐκ ἔδωκεν. In this sense later prose has also συνταράττω.

796 f. ἐναργής, 'clearly seen,' 'present to the lover's sight,' marks the vivid appeal to the senses, in contrast with the invisible and spiritual majesty of the θεσμοί which Love overrides. For ἐναργής as = 'before our eyes,' 'in bodily presence,' cp. *O. C.* 910; *Tr.* 11, 224.—βλεφάρων ἵμερος, love-influence from the eyes, εὐλέκτρου νύμφας, of the fair bride. Both genitives are possessive, but βλεφάρων goes more closely with ἵμερος, denoting the latter's source. Cp. 929: *O. C.* 729 ὀμμάτων... | φόβον...τῆς ἐμῆ ἐπεισόδου, fear, shown in your eyes (possess. gen.), of my entrance (objective gen.). In *Phaedr.* 251 B Plato describes ἵμερος as the desire infused into the soul by an emanation of beauty (κάλλους ἀπορροή) proceeding from the beloved, and received through the eyes of the lover (διὰ τῶν ὀμμάτων). So the soul is spoken of (*ib.* E) as ἐποχετευσαμένη ἵμερον, 'having refreshed herself with the love-shower' or 'effluence of beauty.' And ἵμερος itself receives fanciful derivations, as *ib.* 251 C, ἐκεῖθεν μέρη ἐπιόντα καὶ ῥέοντα, ἃ δὴ διὰ ταῦτα ἵμερος καλεῖται (*i.e.* from ἰέναι μέρη and ῥεῖν): while in *Crat.* 419 E it is explained by ἱμων ῥεῖ. The real origin of the word is prob. from rt. ἴς, 'wish,' whence ἰότητι, and 'Ἰσ-μήνη, *Desiderata.* Curt. § 617. Cp. Soph. fr. 430 (Hippodameia speaking of Pelops), τοιάνδ' ἐν ὄψει λίγγα θηρατηρίαν | ἔρωτος, ἀστραπήν τιν' ὀμμάτων, ἔχει (' such a subduing arrow of love, a lightning from the eyes'): Aesch. *Ag.*

742 μαλθακὸν ὀμμάτων βέλος, | δηξίθυμον ἔρωτος ἄνθος: *Suppl.* 1004 ὄμματος θελκτήριον | τόξευμ' ἔπεμψεν, ἱμέρου νικώμενος: Eur. *Hipp.* 525 Ἔρως, Ἔρως ὁ κατ' ὀμμάτων | στάζεις πόθον, εἰσάγων γλυκεῖαν | ψυχαῖς χάριν οὓς ἐπιστρατεύσῃ [*i.e.* 'on the eyes' of mortals: better ὁ...στάζων, or else ὃς ἀν'—.]—εὐλέκτρου, epithet of Κύπρις in *Tr.* 515. Cp. *Anthol. P.* 7. 649 εὐλεγχέος θαλάμου (happy nuptials).

797 πάρεδρος ἐν ἀρχαῖς. I leave these words in the text, without marking them as corrupt, because the case against them is not decisive, while no emendation is certain. But I strongly suspect them. If sound, they mean that the love inspired by the maiden's eyes is a power 'enthroned in sway by the side of the great laws.' The great laws are those 'unwritten' moral laws which most men feel and acknowledge (cp. on 454 f.); here, especially, the law of loyalty to country, the law of obedience to parents. In Haemon's case, love has shown that it is at least of equal force with these θεσμοί. For πάρεδρος, cp. *O. C.* 1267 Ζηνὶ σύνθακος θρόνων | Αἰδώς: *ib.* 1382 Δίκη ξύνεδρος Ζηνὸς ἀρχαίοις νόμοις. Pind. *O.* 8. 21 Διὸς ξενίου πάρεδρος | ...Θέμις. For ἐν ἀρχαῖς, Eur. *Andr.* 699 σεμνοὶ δ' ἐν ἀρχαῖς ἥμενοι κατὰ πτόλιν: *Or.* 897 ὃς ἂν δύνηται πόλεος ἐν τ' ἀρχαῖσιν ᾖ. Cp. also on 744.

The words answer metrically to φόξιμος οὐδείς (788). The first two syllables of πάρεδρος therefore represent a resolved long syllable. Pindar affords some instances of such resolution (see Appendix), and there is a probable example below (970 ἀγχίπολις Ἄρης, where see n.). But it is rare, and certainly unpleasing. As

10—2

5 θεσμῶν· ἄμαχος γὰρ ἐμπαίζει θεὸς Ἀφροδίτα.　799

νῦν δ᾿ ἤδη ᾿γὼ καὐτὸς θεσμῶν
ἔξω φέρομαι τάδ᾿ ὁρῶν, ἴσχειν δ᾿
οὐκέτι πηγὰς δύναμαι δακρύων,
τὸν παγκοίτην ὅθ᾿ ὁρῶ θάλαμον
τήνδ᾿ Ἀντιγόνην ἀνύτουσαν.　805

στρ. α΄. ΑΝ. ὁρᾶτ᾿ ἔμ᾿, ὦ γᾶς πατρίας πολῖται, τὰν νεάταν ὁδὸν
2 στείχουσαν, νέατον δὲ φέγγος λεύσσουσαν ἀελίου,
3 κοὔποτ᾿ αὖθις· ἀλλά μ᾿ ὁ παγκοίτας Ἅιδας ζῶσαν ἄγει

799 L divides thus: θεσμῶν· ἄμαχος γὰρ ἐμ|παίζει θεὸς Ἀφροδίτα.　**800** ἐμ-
παίζει] Blaydes conject. ἐμπαλει: Herwerden, ἐνστάζει.　**804** παγκοίταν L:

---

a whole, too, the phrase πάρεδρος ἐν
ἀρχαῖς is suspicious. A yet stronger objection is the strangeness of describing
the power which is *in conflict with* the
θεσμοί as their assessor, or peer, in sway;
an expression which would seem appropriate only if that power was working in
harmony with them; as when Eur. (*Med.*
843) spea s of σοφία παρέδρους...ἔρωτας, |
παντοίας ἀρετᾶς ξυνεργούς,—'the loves that
sit with wisdom, co-workers of all excel-
lence,'—these aspirations of the soul which
assist intellectual effort.

The best line of emendation yet suggested is that of Semitelos, who writes
ὥστε πέρα δρᾶν. He supposes that πέρα
δρᾶν became, first, πάρεδρον (ΠΕΡΑΔΡΑΝ—
ΠΑΡΕΔΡΟΝ). Then, πάρεδρον θεσμῶν seeming obscure, a marginal gloss ἐν ἀρχαῖς
was added. This gloss came into the
text, dislodging ὥστε: and πάρεδρον became πάρεδρος, to agree with ἵμερος. The
original sense, then, was: 'the ἵμερος pre-
vails, so that one transgresses the great
θεσμοί.' Cp. *El.* 1506 ὅστις πέρα πράσσειν γε τῶν νόμων θέλει. This suits, too,
the following lines: 'καὐτὸς (i.e., like Haemon) θεσμῶν | ἔξω
φέρομαι.—See Appendix.

800 ἐμπαίζει, 'wreaks her will' *in*
that contest which νικᾷ implies. We
find ἐμπαίζω with a dat. (1) of the object,
as Her. 4. 134 ἐμπαίζοντας ἡμῖν, 'mocking
us': (2) of the sphere, as Ar. *Th.* 975 χο-
ροῖσιν ἐμπαίζει, ' sports in dances.' The
ἐν of ἐμπαίζει here might also be explained
as (*a*) in the ἵμερος, or the βλέφαρα, *i.e.*
by their agency: or (*b*) 'on her victim.'
But the interpretation first given appears

simpler. (Cp. Vergil's absol. use of 'illu-
dere,' *G.* 1. 181, *Tum variae illudant
pestes.*)

801 f. καὐτὸς θεσμῶν ἔξω: *i.e.* like
Haemon, I also am moved to rebel against
Creon's sentence, and to take Antigone's
part.—φέρομαι, a proverbial image from
the race-course: Ar. *Ran.* 993 μόνον
ὅπως | μή σ᾿ ὁ θυμὸς ἁρπάσαι | ἐκτὸς οἴσει
τῶν ἐλαῶν, because some olives marked
the limits of the course at the end of the
race-course (schol. *ad loc.*), where the
chariots turned, and where the horses
were most likely to swerve or bolt. Plat.
Crat. 414 Β οὐ γὰρ ἐπισκοπεῖς ὥσπερ
ἐκτὸς δρόμου φερόμενον, ἐπειδὰν λείου ἐπι-
λάβωμαι (when I get on smooth ground).
Aesch. *P. V.* 883 ἔξω δὲ δρόμου φέρομαι
λύσσης | πνεύματι μάργῳ. Eur. *Bacch.*
853 ἔξω δ᾿ ἐλαύνων τοῦ φρονεῖν.—ἴσχειν δ᾿:
cp. 817 ἔχουσ᾿: 820 λαχοῦσ᾿, by the rule
of continuity (συνάφεια) in anapaestic
systems. In lyrics such elision is rarer
(see on 350).

803 πηγάς, not, the sources or springs,
but the streams, of tears : so *Tr.* 852
ἔρρωγεν παγὰ δακρύων, and oft.: cp. *O. C.*
479, where πηγάς = the water gushing from
the bowl. On the other hand in fr. 658
νυκτός...πηγάς = 'the sources of night' (the
west).

804 f. παγκοίτην. The question between Doric and Attic forms in tragic
anapaests cannot be decided by a rigid
rule. It depends on the presence or absence of a lyric character. Thus in 110 f.
the Doricisms are justified by the purely
lyric stamp of the anapaests. Here, Attic
forms are preferable. The lyric strains

laws; for there the goddess Aphrodite is working her unconquerable will.

ε ΛΜ   But now I also am carried beyond the bounds of loyalty, and can no more keep back the streaming tears, when I see Antigone thus passing to the bridal chamber where all are laid to rest.

AN.   See me, citizens of my 'fatherland, setting forth on my last way, looking my last on the sunlight that is for me no more; no, Hades who gives sleep to all leads me living *Kommc 1st strophe.*

παγκοίτην Wolff.   **809** λεύσουσαν L.   **810—816** L divides the vv. thus: κοθ-τοτ— | ᾿Αιδας— | τὰν— | ἔγκληρον— | τῷ μέ— | ὁμνήσεν .. νυμφεύσω.   **810** παγ-κοίτας] πάγκοινος Blaydes.   **811** ᾿Αιδας] ᾱιδασ L.

---

of Antigone are brought into finer relief by the different tone of the choral anapaests. Cp. 822, and see Appendix on 110.—Cp. *O. C.* 1578 (Death) τὸν αἰέ-νυπνον. The word θάλαμον here has ref. to its special sense, 'bridal-chamber': cp. 891 νυμφεῖον, 1207 παστάδα. So oft. in epitaphs on the unmarried; *Anthol. P.* 7. 489 (by Sappho) Τιμάδος ἅδε κόνις, τὰν δὴ πρὸ γάμοιο θανοῦσαν | δέ-ξατο Περσεφόνας κυάνεος θάλαμος. Kaibel *Epigrammata* 241 (on two young brothers) οἱ δισσοὶ σινόμαιμοι, ἰὼ ξένε, τῷδ᾿ ὑπὸ τύμβῳ | ἄψαυστοι τέκνων κείμεθα κου-ριδίων· | ᾿Ικέσιος κάγὼ νεαρὰν πληρούμενος ἥβαν |᾿Ερμιππος κρυερὸν τόνδ᾿ ἔχομεν θάλαμον.—ἀνύτουσαν with acc. of place, as *Ai.* 607 (ἀνύειν), *O. C.* 1562 (ἐξανύσαι): cp. 231.

806—943 Fourth ἐπεισόδιον. Antigone has now been brought out of the house by two of Creon's servants (οἱ ἄγοντες, 931) who are about to conduct her to her doom. She speaks of her fate to the Chorus, and they seek to comfort her,—while they intimate that she alone is to blame (853, 875). Creon enters (883); and, in obedience to his peremptory command, Antigone is presently led forth to death (943).

The structure of the κομμός (806—882) is as follows. 1st strophe (806—816) = 1st ant. (823—833). A system of choral anapaests (817—822) comes after the strophe, and a similar system (834—838) after the antistrophe.—2nd strophe (839—852) = 2nd ant. (857—871).—3rd str. (853—856) = 3rd ant. (872—875).—An epode forms the close (876—882). See Metrical Analysis.

806 f. νεάταν...νέατον 8f. In such an epanaphora μέν regularly precedes δέ

(as *O. T.* 25, 259; *O. C.* 5, 610, etc.); but there are numerous exceptions in Soph., as *O. C.* 1342 στήσω σ᾿ ἄγων, | στήσω δ᾿ ἐμαυτόν: *Ph.* 633 πάντα λεκ-τά, πάντα δὲ | τολμητά: *Tr.* 517 τότ᾿ ἦν χερός, ἦν δὲ τόξων πάταγος: *ib.* 1147 κάλει τὸ πᾶν μοι σπέρμα σῶν ὁμαιμόνων, | κάλει δὲ τὴν τάλαιναν ᾿Αλκμήνην.—νέατον, in contrast with αὖθις, is best taken as adv.: Eur. *Tro.* 201 νέατον τεκέων σώματα λεύσ-σω: cp. the adv. τελευταῖον (*O. T.* 1183), ἔσχατον (*O. C.* 1550), πανύστατον, etc.—κοὔποτ᾿ αὖθις, *sc.* ὀψομένη: *Ai.* 857 ῞Ηλιον προσεννέπω | πανύστατον δὴ κοὔποτ᾿ αὖθις ὕστερον.—Cp. the passage in Swinburne's *Erechtheus* where the maiden Chthonia, being about to die, speaks with the Chorus of Athenian Elders:—'People, old men of my city, lordly wise and hoar of head, | I, a spouseless bride and crownless, but with garlands of the dead, | From the fruitful light turn silent to my dark unchilded bed.'

810 παγκοίτας = ὁ πάντας κοιμίζων. *Ai.* 831 καλῶ θ᾿ ἅμα | πομπαῖον ῾Ερμῆν χθόνιον εὖ με κοιμίσαι. Blaydes conjectures πάγκοινος, very plausibly. Cp. *El.* 138 τόν γ᾿ ἐξ ᾿Αΐδα | παγκοίνου λίμνας. But these points may be noted. (1) Though we have had παγκοίτην so lately as in v. 804, such a repetition is no safe argument for spuriousness: see on 76. (2) The 2nd and 3rd syllables of παγκοίτας = καί νιν in 828, and πάγκοινος therefore gives a more exact correspondence; but this proves nothing, since a spondee and a trochee are equally admissible. (See Metr. Analysis.) (3) παγκοίτας is *here* a more expressive epithet than πάγκοινος ('receiving all'): eyes still bright with life and youth are to suffer the ἀτέρμονα νήγρετον ὕπνον.

4 τὰν Ἀχέροντος   812
5 ἀκτάν, οὔθ᾽ ὑμεναίων ἔγκληρον, οὔτ᾽ *ἐπινύμφειός
6 πώ μέ τις ὕμνος ὕμνησεν, ἀλλ᾽ Ἀχέροντι νυμφεύσω.

σν. α΄. ΧΟ. οὐκοῦν κλεινὴ καὶ ἔπαινον ἔχουσ᾽   817
ἐς τόδ᾽ ἀπέρχει κεῦθος νεκύων,
οὔτε φθινάσιν πληγεῖσα νόσοις
οὔτε ξιφέων ἐπίχειρα λαχοῦσ᾽,   820
ἀλλ᾽ αὐτόνομος, ζῶσα μόνη δὴ
θνητῶν Ἀΐδην καταβήσει.

ἀντ. α΄. ΑΝ. ἤκουσα δὴ λυγροτάταν ὀλέσθαι τὰν Φρυγίαν ξέναν
2 Ταντάλου Σιπύλῳ πρὸς ἄκρῳ, τὰν κισσὸς ὡς ἀτενὴς 825

814 ἐπινυμφίδιος MSS. (ἐπινυμφίδιος Vat.).   Dindorf conject. ἐπινύμφειος: Bergk,

---

811 f. ἄγει...ἀκτάν, a rare poet. constr. with ἄγω, as *Ph.* 1175 Τρῳάδα γᾶν μ᾽ ἤλπισας ἄξειν: Aesch. *Pers.* 861 νόστοι... | εὖ πράσσοντας ἄγον οἴκους (so Porson for ἐς οἴκους). Cp. *O. T.* 178 ἀκτὰν πρὸς ἑσπέρου θεοῦ.

813 ff. οὔθ᾽ ὑμεναίων...οὔτ᾽ ἐπινύμφειος...ὕμνος. The ὑμέναιος has not been sung by friends escorting bride and bridegroom to their home; nor has the ἐπιθαλάμιον been sung in the evening at the door of the bridal chamber. (1) For the procession-song, cp. *Il.* 18. 492 νύμφας δ᾽ ἐκ θαλάμων, δαΐδων ὕπο λαμπομενάων, | ἠγίνεον ἀνὰ ἄστυ· πολὺς δ᾽ ὑμέναιος ὀρώρει. Ar. *Pax* 1332 ff. gives a specimen, with the refrain Ὑμήν, Ὑμέναι᾽ ὦ. Cp. also *Av.* 1736. This was specially called the ἁρμάτειον μέλος (from the carriage conveying the newly-married couple), *Etym. M.* p. 145. (2) As to the ἐπιθαλάμιος (ὕμνος), or ἐπιθαλάμιον (μέλος), sung in the evening, see Phot. *Bibl.* p. 321 καὶ τὰ ἐπιθαλάμια δὲ τοῖς ἄρτι θαλαμευομένοις ἅμα οἱ ἤθεοι καὶ αἱ παρθένοι ἐπὶ τῶν θαλάμων ᾖδον. Extant specimens are Theocritus *Idyll.* 18 (for Helen and Menelaus), Catullus *Carm.* 61 and 62: for a burlesque, see Lucian *Symp.* 41. The word ὑμέναιος, though more specially denoting the procession-song, was a general term for a γαμήλιον ᾆσμα, and could denote the ἐπιθαλάμιος, in which Ὑμὴν ὦ Ὑμέναιε was the usual refrain (Theocr. 18. 58, Catull. 61. 4 etc.): so Pindar *P.* 3. 17

οὐδὲ παμφώνων ἰαχὰν ὑμεναίων, ἅλικες | οἷα παρθένοι φιλέοισιν ἑταῖραι | ἑσπερίαις ὑποκουρίζεσθ᾽ ἀοιδαῖς: Apollon. Rhod. 4. 1160 νυμφιδίαις ὑμέναιον ἐπὶ προμολῇσιν (threshold) ἄειδον. — οὔτε...ἔγκληρον,... οὔτε...ὕμνησεν: we expected οὔτε ὑμνηθεῖσαν: a finite verb is substituted for the second participial clause: cp. 255 f.: *O. C.* 348 πολλὰ μὲν...ἀλωμένη, | πολλοῖσι δ᾽...ἡγεῖται, with n. there on 351.

ἐπινύμφειος, Dindorf's correction of ἐπινυμφίδιος, is strongly supported by these facts. (1) In *O. C.* 1088 Soph. certainly used ἐπινικείῳ instead of the usual ἐπινικίῳ. Cp. above, 358, ἐναίθρεια. (2) In Aesch. *Cho.* 334 ἐπιτύμβιος (restored with certainty by Herm.) had been corrupted into ἐπιτυμβίδιος. Bergk's ἐπὶ νυμφείοις ('for crown of nuptials') is quite possible (cp. n. on 568); but an epithet for ὕμνος is decidedly preferable here. Bergk relies on the schol., λείπει θύραις ἢ κοίταις, which suggests that the Schol. read ἐπὶ νυμφιδίοις (or νυμφείοις); but, if this were so, the fact would have little weight. The corruption would have been easy.—Herm. Schütz defends ἐπινυμφίδιος as metrically possible. But, though it is possible that a logaoedic dactyl might replace a spondee here, the latter is at least better suited to the grave and mournful rhythm. The antistrophic verse (831) ends with παγκλαύτοις. So v. 816 ends with νυμφεύσω, and 833 with κατευνάζει.

816 Ἀχέροντι νυμφεύσω: cp. on 654.

to Acheron's shore; who have had no portion in the chant that brings the bride, nor hath any song been mine for the crowning of bridals; whom the lord of the Dark Lake shall wed.

CH. Glorious, therefore, and with praise, thou departest to that deep place of the dead: wasting sickness hath not smitten thee; thou hast not found the wages of the sword; no, mistress of thine own fate, and still alive, thou shalt pass to Hades, as no other of mortal kind hath passed.

AN. I have heard in other days how dread a doom befell ıst anti-our Phrygian guest, the daughter of Tantalus, on the Sipylian strophe. heights; how, like clinging ivy,

ἐπὶ νυμφείοις: Semitelos, ἐπὶ νυμφείαις, with εὐναῖς for ὕμνος. **819** φθιμάσι L.
822 θνατῶν ἀΐδαν L. Dindorf writes 'Αΐδην: others, "Αιδην.

---

820 ξιφέων (possessive gen.) ἐπίχειρα, 'the wages of swords,' i.e. the reward of strife with the sword,—viz. a violent death. The gen. after ἐπίχειρα always denotes that for which the reward is given, as Aesch. P. V. 318 ὑψηγόρου | γλώσσης, Ar. Vesp. 581 ταύτης (sc. τῆς δίκης), Plat. Rep. 608 C ἀρετῆς, [Dem.] Epist. p. 1484. 4 τῶν...πεπονημένων. Here, ξιφέων can hardly be a subjective gen., 'the reward which the sword gives'; though the meaning is the same. The ironical sense of ἐπίχειρα occurs in Attic prose as well as verse; Antiphon or. 1 § 10 ἡ μὲν διακονήσασα (in the murder) ἔχει τὰ ἐπίχειρα ὧν ἀξία ἦν (torture and death). Cp. El. 1382 τἀπιτίμια | τῆς δυσσεβείας. ξιφέων might be poet. plur. for sing., as in Eur. Andr. 812 ἐκ τε δεξιᾶς | ξίφη καθαρπάζουσιν, and Or. 1398 (cp. σκῆπ-τρα, etc.); but it is rather an ordinary plural.

821 f. αὐτόνομος, i.e. of your own free will. No one constrained her to do the act for which she suffers. She knew that death would be the consequence, and she chose it. The word is fitting, since she has set her laws (the θεῶν νόμι-μα) above Creon's. The implied contrast is with the helpless victims of disease or of war.—The word could not mean, 'by an ordinance peculiar to your case,' i.e. 'by the unique doom of a living death.' —δή strengthens μόνη, as Tr. 1063.—'Αΐδην seems preferable to "Αιδην in the paroemiac. Cp. on 804.—Acc. of motion, like δόμους στείχειν (O. C. 643).

823 ff. ἤκουσα δή. The Chorus has

said, 'No mortal's fate was ever like thine.' She continues: 'I have heard be-fore now (δή) how Niobe perished,—by a doom like mine.' To which the Chorus reply that Niobe was not a mere mortal (834).—The Theban princess remembers the fate of the Theban queen. Niobe, daughter of Tantalus, married Amphion, king of Thebes. She vaunted that she had borne many children, while Leto had borne only two. Wherefore those two, Apollo and Artemis, slew all her sons and daughters,—at Thebes, as said the Theban story; but Niobe returned to her old home at Mount Sipylus, and was there turned to stone. (Ovid, Met. 6. 310, represents her as carried to Sipylus after the change.) Νιόβη was the title of lost plays by Aesch. and Soph.—λυγρο-τάταν, adverbial: cp. 305 (ὅρκιος): Ai. 966 ἐμοὶ πικρὸς τέθνηκεν.—ξέναν, in rela-tion to Thebes; the foreign wife of the Theban king. Pindar wrote a παιάν on Niobe's marriage, and said that the Lydian ἁρμονία was first used at Thebes on that occasion. (Plut. de Mus. 15.)

825 Ταντάλου, gen. of parentage: cp. 486, Ai. 172 Διὸς Ἄρτεμις: 952 Ζηνὸς ἡ δεινὴ θεός. Tantalus, son of Zeus, had his royal seat on Mount Sipylus, which belonged to Phrygia in the older and larger sense of that term. In Aesch. Νιόβη (fr. 153) he describes his realm as extending 'twelve days' journey' from Sipylus westward to Ida.

Σιπύλῳ. Mount Sipylus is in the country once called Maeonia, and after-

3 πετραία βλάστα δάμασεν· καί νιν *ὄμβροι τακομέναν,
4 ὡς φάτις ἀνδρῶν,
5 χιών τ᾽ οὐδαμὰ λείπει, τέγγει δ᾽ ὑπ᾽ ὀφρύσι παγ-
    κλαύτοις   830
6 δειράδας· ᾇ με δαίμων ὁμοιοτάταν κατευνάζει.

827 ff. L divides the vv. thus: πετραία— | ὄμβρῳ— | ὡς φάτις— | τάκει (τέγγει)— | δειράδας— | δαίμων . . κατεινάζει. **828** ὄμβρῳ MSS. ὄμβροι Musgrave, which most edd. have received. Nauck, keeping ὄμβρῳ, changes χιών τ᾽ in 830 to αἰών

---

wards Lydia. It is a branch of the Tmolus range (N. of which stood Sardis), and extends in a N.W. direction to the Hermus. Magnesia 'ad Sipylum' was on that river's left bank. From a remote age volcanic forces were active in this region, known to the Greeks as the κατακεκαυμένη. Cp. Arist. *Meteor.* 2. 8 γενομένου σεισμοῦ τὰ περὶ Σίπυλον ἀνετράπη. A city called Tantalis, once situated at Sipylus, was said to have perished by an earthquake, which made a lake. Tantalus, like Niobe, is a type of prosperity plunged by ὕβρις into misery. Here, as in the case of Sodom and Gomorrah, some physical catastrophe was at the root of the tradition.—See on 831.

826 f. ἀτενής, prop. 'strained,' 'intent' (*e.g.* ἀτενὴς ὄψις), or 'intense' (as ἀτενεῖς ὀργαί): here it denotes the close embrace of the ivy. Cp. *hederae sequaces* (Persius *prol.*).—πετραία βλάστα δάμασεν, the 'growth of stone' (the process of petrifaction) 'subdued her,' *i.e.* passed gradually over her whole form: cp. Ovid, *Met.* 6. 301: Orba resedit | Exanimes inter natos, natasque, virumque, | Diriguitque malis. Nullos movet aura capillos. | In vultu color est sine sanguine: lumina maestis | Stant immota genis: nihil est in imagine vivi. | Ipsa quoque interius cum duro lingua palato | Congelat, et venae desistunt posse moveri. | Nec flecti cervix, nec bracchia reddere gestus, | Nec pes ire potest: intra quoque viscera saxumst. For αἶ in πετραία, cp. 1310 n.

828 ff. καί νιν ὄμβροι, κ.τ.λ. The poet is thinking of Niobe's petrified form among the lonely mountain-crags (*Il.* 24. 614 νῦν δέ που ἐν πέτρῃσιν, ἐν οὔρεσιν οἰοπόλοισιν, | ἐν Σιπύλῳ). 'The rain and the snow never leave her, as she pines with grief': *i.e.* she is amid the storms that visit snow-crowned Sipylus throughout the year.

By these words the poet wishes to call up a general image of bleak and storm-beaten solitude. Niobe's own weeping is then described by τέγγει δ᾽, etc. Now, if we kept the MS. ὄμβρῳ, that dat. would go closely with τακομέναν: 'as she melts, flows down, with rain' (or 'with water'), 'the snow never leaves her.' Thus τέγγει ...δειράδας would be anticipated, and in a prosaic manner; viz., by words suggesting that the appearance of weeping is due to water trickling down the rock. This is the true reason for preferring ὄμβροι to ὄμβρῳ. It is no argument against ὄμβρῳ that χιών τε would answer to τέγγει θ᾽ (for τε irregularly placed, cp. *O. T.* 258 n.). With ὄμβροι, θ᾽ could still follow τέγγει, but δ᾽ is better.—For the constr. ὄμβροι...χιών τ᾽ οὐ λείπει (verb agreeing in number with nearest subject) cp. 1132 f.: *O. C.* 7 στέργειν γὰρ αἱ πάθαι με χὠ χρόνος ξυνὼν | μακρὸς διδάσκει (n.). —χιών is taken by Wecklein as = 'snow-water' (Eiswasser). The only passage which seems to favour that sense is Eur. *Tro.* 1066 Ἰδαῖα...νάπῃ | χιόνι κατάρρυτα ποταμίᾳ, but there the adj. makes the difference: 'snow carried down streams' can be only 'snow-water.' In *Andr.* 215 Θρῄκην χιόνι τὴν κατάρρυτον means merely, 'on which snow falls thickly.' Cp. Quintus Smyrnaeus 1. 293 ὑπαὶ Σιπύλῳ νιφόεντι.—οὐδαμά: cp. 763.

831 τέγγει δ᾽ ὑπ᾽ ὀφρύσι...δειράδας. Though ὀφρύς and δειράς could be said of a mountain, Soph. is here thinking simply of the human form. παγκλαύτους (L) might be proleptic (cp. n. on ἀδίκους, 791), but παγκαλαύτοις is better, since ὀφρύσι seems to need an epithet.

The Niobe of Sipylus has usually been identified with a colossal rock-image on the N. side of the range. It is rudely carved in relief, within a rectangular niche on the face of a limestone cliff, and re-

the growth of stone subdued her; and the rains fail not, as men tell, from her wasting form, nor fails the snow, while beneath her weeping lids the tears bedew her bosom; and most like to hers is the fate that brings me to my rest.

(without τ'). He would, however, prefer οἴκτῳ to ὄμβρῳ. **830** οὐδαμᾶ] οὐδαμᾶι L. **831** τάκει θ' L: τέγγει θ' r. δ' for τ' Bothe.—παγκλαύτους L: παγκλαύτοις or παγκλαύστοις r.

---

presents a woman seated on a throne. (See Stark, *Niobe*, pl. 1, Leips. 1863: cp. Baumeister, *Denkm.* p. 1029). Prof. W. M. Ramsay, however, holds that this image is the 'very ancient' ἄγαλμα of Cybele mentioned by Paus. 3. 22. 4. In two respects it differs from the ancient accounts of the Niobe (quoted below): (a) it does not 'weep,'—for the rain-water drops from the front of the niche, clear of the figure; and (b) the likeness to a human form grows, instead of vanishing, as one approaches. (*Journ. Hellen. Studies* III. 61 ff., 1882.) This has been confirmed by another traveller, Herr Schweisthal (as reported in the *Berl. Phil. Wochenschr.*, May 28, 1887, p. 704). He finds the true Niobe at no great distance from the Cybele, but nearer Magnesia, and in the vicinity of a stream (the Jarikkaia) which Humann, in his 'Excursion into Sipylus' (1881), had already identified with the Achelous of *Il.* 24. 616. It is a natural phenomenon,—the semblance—as seen from a distance—of a draped woman, seated high on the rocks; she looks towards the right, and lifts her right arm, as if in lament.

The best ancient description is by a poet whose native place was in that neighbourhood,—Quintus Smyrnaeus (1. 293—306):—'Her streaming tears still fall from the heights of the rugged cliff; and in sympathy with her the sounding waters of the Hermus make lament, and the lofty peaks of Sipylus, over which the mist that shepherds dread floats evermore. A great marvel is she to passers by, because she is like a sorrowful woman, who mourns some cruel grief, and weeps without stint. Such verily seems the figure, when thou gazest at it from afar; but when thou drawest near, lo, 'tis but a sheer rock, a cliff of Sipylus' (φαίνεται αἰπήεσσα πέτρη, Σιπύλοιό τ' ἀπορρώξ). Nonnus was thinking of the effect *from the road*, when he wrote (2. 160), ἔσσομαι ὡς Νιόβη καὶ ἐγὼ λίθος, ὄφρα καὶ αὐτὴν |

λαΐνέην στενάχουσαν ἐποικτείρωσιν ὁδῖται. Pausanias, too, says that, at a certain distance from the cliff, δεδακρυμένην δόξεις ὁρᾶν καὶ κατηφῆ γυναῖκα, but that the illusion vanishes on a nearer approach (1. 21 § 3).

832 ὁμοιοτάταν, because the stone into which Niobe was changed may be likened to Antigone's rocky tomb: cp. *El.* 150 ἰὼ παντλάμων Νιόβα, σὲ δ' ἔγωγε νέμω θεόν, | ἅτ' ἐν τάφῳ πετραίῳ | αἰαῖ δακρύεις.—The Niobe in the Uffizi Gallery at Florence will occur to many as offering an ideal type of majestic sorrow and beauty not unworthy to be associated with Antigone, and yet suggesting a contrast no less than a resemblance; the contrast between the desolate mother, and the maiden who is going to join those whom she loves (897); between pride steadfast under divine anger, and the piety that has dared to offend man.

834—838 ἀλλά...θανούσαν. The Chorus desire to console Antigone. There is no element of reproof in their words here. She has likened herself to Niobe. 'And yet Niobe'—the Chorus say—'was a goddess, while thou art a mortal. But (καίτοι) it will be a great glory for thy memory that thy fate was as the fate of a goddess, in life and in death.' 'In life' (ζώσαν), and not only in death (θανούσαν), because Niobe, like Antigone, was in the fulness of her vitality when she met her doom. The moments of life through which Antigone is now passing are like the moments through which Niobe passed as she felt the beginning of the change into stone.—Why does Antigone rejoin, οἴμοι, γελῶμαι? Because her thought had been, 'my doom is terrible and miserable as Niobe's'; but the Chorus had answered, 'It is indeed glorious for thee to be as Niobe.' She had looked for present pity. They had comforted her with the hope of posthumous fame. —See Appendix.

σv. β΄. ΧΟ. ἀλλὰ θεός τοι καὶ θεογεννής,
    ἡμεῖς δὲ βροτοὶ καὶ θνητογενεῖς.   835
    καίτοι φθιμένῃ μέγα κἀκοῦσαι
    τοῖς ἰσοθέοις *σύγκληρα λαχεῖν
    ζῶσαν καὶ ἔπειτα θανοῦσαν.

στρ. β΄. ΑΝ. οἴμοι γελῶμαι. τί με, πρὸς θεῶν πατρῴων,
2 οὐκ *οἰχομέναν ὑβρίζεις, ἀλλ᾽ ἐπίφαντον;   840
3 ὦ πόλις, ὦ πόλεως πολυκτήμονες ἄνδρες·
4 ἰὼ Διρκαῖαι κρῆναι
5 Θήβας τ᾽ εὐαρμάτου ἄλσος, ἔμπας ξυμμάρτυρας ὕμμ᾽
    ἐπικτῶμαι,   845
6 οἷα φίλων ἄκλαυτος, οἵοις νόμοις

834 θεογγεννῆσ L (not θεογενῆσ, as Campb. gives it): the later MSS. vary between
θεογεννῆς and θεογενής. Wieseler conject. θεογενῆς: M. Schmidt, καὶ θεῶν γέννημ᾽:
Nauck, θείου τε γένους (and formerly καὶ θεοῦ γένης). **835** θνητογενεῖσ L.
836 φθιμένα L, with ω above α from the first hand. φθιμένῳ or φθιμέναν r.—
μέγ᾽ ἀκοῦσαι L: μέγα κἀκοῦσαι Seyffert: μέγα τἀκοῦσαι Wecklein. **837** τοῖσ
ἰσοθέοισ ἔγκληρα λαχεῖν L.—τοῖσι θεοῖσι σύγκληρα λαχεῖν Nauck (σύγκληρα Schaefer).
838 ζῶσαν .. θανοῦσαν. L has this v., which is also in most of the later MSS.;
but it is omitted by A, and consequently by the Aldine. Dindorf and others

834 θεός, sc. ἐκείνη μέν ἐστι (cp. 948).
The absence of a pron., to balance ἡμεῖς,
is unusual, but it is easy to carry on the
subject of τέγγει in 831. Niobe is of divine race, since her father was the son of
Zeus, and her mother the Pleiad Taygetè
(or Dionè, one of the Hyades). So in
Aesch. Νιόβη (fr. 157) her family is described as οἱ θεῶν ἀγχίσποροι (near kin),
...κοῦπω νιν ἐξίτηλον αἷμα δαιμόνων.—θεογεννής, god-begotten. The peculiarity is
that the word is formed directly from
γέννα, and not from the stem of the pass.
aor. in use: i.e., we should expect θεο-
γέννητος. But Pindar could coin θεότι-
μος (I. 5. 13) as=θεοτίμητος. Why, then,
should not a poet coin θεογεννής as=θεο-
γέννητος? It is of little moment that the
extant classical literature happens to present no strictly parallel compound with
γέννα (πονtoγεννής· and πρωτογεννής· being late Byzantine). θεογεννής occurs in
Orac. Sibyll. (5. 261), but is not classical.
The Schol.'s paraphrase, θειοτέρου γένους
τυγχάνουσα, is no token (as some fancy)
that he read a gen., such as θείου τε
γένους.
    836 καίτοι has an illative force, in-
troducing the next step in the reasoning:

cp. 949, O. T. 855.—L's φθιμένα should
p⁰b. be φθιμένῃ (see on παγκοίτην 804).
The variant φθιμένῳ (noted in L) is warrantable as the masc. of general statement (cp. 463): but it would be extremely harsh, when ζῶσαν..θανοῦσαν
refers to the same person.—κἀκοῦσαι,
'e'en to have it said of her' (καί meaning,
'even if there is no other comfort'). This
seems a little more expressive than τἀκοῦσαι (Wecklein), and also slightly more
probable palaeographically (cp. O. C. 172
cr. n.). The MS. μέγ᾽ ἀκοῦσαι is certainly
wrong, since a paroemiac could not begin
a new sentence. For ἀκούω (=λέγομαι,
audio) with inf., cp. Her. 3. 131 Ἀργεῖοι
ἤκουον μουσικὴν εἶναι Ἑλλήνων πρῶτοι.
    837 τοῖς ἰσοθέοις σύγκληρα, a lot
shared by demigods. Plut. Mor. 103 F χρὴ
γὰρ οὐ μόνον ἑαυτὸν εἰδέναι θνητὸν ὄντα τὴν
φύσιν, ἀλλὰ καὶ ὅτι θνητῷ σύγκληρός
ἐστι βίῳ καὶ πράγμασι ῥᾳδίως μεθιστα-
μένοις πρὸς τοὐναντίον: i.e. that one shares
the lot of humanity at large.—The decisive objection to the MS. reading ἔγκληρα is the sense of the adj.; for ἔγκληρος always means either (1) act., having
a share in, as Eur. I. T. 682 ἔγκληρον...
κασιγνήτην, 'heiress,'=ἐπίκληρον, and so

CH. Yet she was a goddess, thou knowest, and born of gods ; we are mortals, and of mortal race. But 'tis great renown for a woman who hath perished that she should have shared the doom of the godlike, in her life, and afterward in death.

AN. Ah, I am mocked! In the name of our fathers' gods, _{2nd strophe.} can ye not wait till I am gone,—must ye taunt me to my face, O my city, and ye, her wealthy sons? Ah, fount of Dircè, and thou holy ground of Thebè whose chariots are many; ye, at least, will bear me witness, in what sort, unwept of friends, and by what laws

reject it. But M. Seyffert defends it, and among recent edd. who retain it are Bellermann, Nauck, Wecklein, Pallis, Semitelos. **840** ὀλομέναν L: ὀλλυμέναν r. ὀθλομέναν Triclinius. οἰχομέναν J. F. Martin and Wunder. **843** πολυκτήμονσς Nauck. **844 f.** Διρκαίαι κρῆναι] Διρκαίαι καὶ κρῆναι L (by dittographia).—L divides the vv. thus: ἰὼ— | Θήβασ' | ξυμμάρτυρασ— | οἷα— | πρὸς ἔργμα—ἔρ|χομαι—ποταινίου. **846** ὑμμ'] ὑμμ' L.—ἐπικτώμαι] In the marg. of L, γρ. ἐπιβώμαι (by S). Bergk reads ὑμμ' ἐπιβώμαι with δύσμορα for δυσμόρῳ in 865: Blaydes, ὑμᾶς ἐπιβῶμαι, with δυσδαίμονι ib.—Musgrave conject. ἔτι κτώμαι.

Hipp. 1011: or (2) pass., included in one's κλῆρος, as *H. F.* 468 ἔγκληρα πεδία ...κεκτημένος ('by inheritance'). Here, ἔγκληρα was perh. partly due to a reminiscence of ἔγκληρον in 814.—The change of τοῖς ἰσοθέοις into τοῖσι θεοῖσιν, though easy, is needless. The epic ῑ of ἰσόθεος might well be allowed in tragic lyrics or anapaests, like the ᾱ of ἀθάνατος (cp. 339 n.): and Aesch. once uses it, *Pers.* 80 ἰσόθεος φώς. [But ἰσόθεος has ῑ in Eur. *Tro.* 1169, *I. A.* 626 (dial.), as ἰσόνειρον has in Aesch. *P. V.* 547.] Note that the MS. τοῖς ἰσοθέοις ἔγκληρα would have arisen more easily from ΤΟΙΣΙΣΟΘΕΟΙΣ-ΣΥΓΚΛΗΡΑ than from ΤΟΙΣΙΘΕΟΙΣΙΝΣΥΓ-ΚΛΗΡΑ.

838 ζῶσαν...θανοῦσαν. The constr., φθιμένῃ μέγα ἐστίν, ἀκοῦσαι ζῶσαν σύγκληρα λαχεῖν (instead of ζώσῃ), is not rare: cp. Xen. *An.* 1. 2 § 1 Ξενίᾳ τῷ Ἀρκάδι ἥκειν παραγγέλλει λαβόντα τοὺς ἄνδρας [though shortly before, παραγγέλλει τῷ Κλεάρχῳ λαβόντι ἥκειν]: *ib.* 3. 1. 5 συμβουλεύει τῷ Ξενοφῶντι ἐλθόντα εἰς Δελφοὺς ἀνακοινῶσαι: *ib.* 3. 2. 1 ἔδοξεν αὐτοῖς προφυλακὰς καταστήσαντας συγκαλεῖν τοὺς στρατιώτας. The dat. with the inf. is, in such cases, equally right, but the acc. sometimes excludes an ambiguity. (Cp. on *O. T.* 913.) *El.* 479 ὕπεστί μοι...κλύουσαν is not similar.—I can see no reason to suppose the loss of a verse. The fact that six anapaestic verses (817—822) follow the strophe proves

nothing. Cp. on 110 f., and Append. on 155 ff.

839 γελῶμαι: see on 834 ff. Cp. Job xvii. 2: 'Are there not mockers with me?'

843 πολυκτήμονες, an epith. which also implies εὐγενεῖς: cp. *O. T.* 1070 πλουσίῳ χαίρειν γένει. So these Theban elders are called κοιρανίδαι (940), and in *O. T.* 1223 ὦ γῆς μέγιστα τῆσδ' ἀεὶ τιμώμενοι: as Thebes itself, ἀγλααί (*O. T.* 153) and μεγάλαι (*ib.* 1203).

844 f. κρῆναι: so Polyneices appeals to Oed., πρὸς νύν σε κρηνῶν καὶ θεῶν ὁμογνίων (*O. C.* 1333, where see n.): and the dying Ajax invokes the κρῆναι of Troy (*Ai.* 862).—εὐαρμάτου: see n. on 148 f.—ἄλσος: cp. *El.* 5 (Argos) τῆι οἰστροπλῆγος ἄλσος Ἰνάχου κόρης, as the scene of Io's visitation by Hera. So Thebes is the 'sacred precinct' of Dionysus (cp. 154, 1137) and the other θεοὶ ἐγχώριοι.—ἔμπας, even if human sympathy fails me. Soph. has ἔμπας (= ὅμως) also in *Ai.* 122, 1338, and ἔμπα *ib.* 563 (dial.).

846 ὕμμ' (Aeolic and epic), as Aesch. *Eum.* 620: so dat. ὕμμι *O. C.* 247 (n.).—ἐπικτῶμαι, acquire, win: Aesch. *Eum.* 671 (ὅπως) καὶ τόνδ' ἐπικτήσαιο σύμμαχον, θεά. In this general sense the ἐπί is not inconsistent with what ἔμπας implies, viz. that she fails to win human sympathy.

847 οἷα: cp. on 823 (λυγροτάταν).—

7 πρὸς ἔργμα τυμβόχωστον ἔρχομαι τάφου ποταινίου·
δυστάνος
8 ἰὼ *βροτοῖς οὔτε νεκροῖς κυροῦσα 850
9 μέτοικος, οὐ ζῶσιν, οὐ θανοῦσιν.

στρ. γ'. ΧΟ. προβᾶσ᾽ ἐπ᾽ ἔσχατον θράσους
2 ὑψηλὸν ἐς Δίκας βάθρον
3 προσέπεσες, ὦ τέκνον, πολύ. 855
4 πατρῷον δ᾽ ἐκτίνεις τιν᾽ ἆθλον.

ἀντ. β'. ΑΝ. ἔψαυσας ἀλγεινοτάτας ἐμοὶ μερίμνας,
2 πατρὸς τριπόλιστον οἶκτον τοῦ τε πρόπαντος

848 ἔργμα L (with two dots over γ, indicating ἔρμα). This was the general reading, though V has ἔργμα, and Par. H (a copy of L) ἔρυμα. Schol. in marg. of L, ἔρμα, περίφραγμα. Brunck gave ἔργμα: Hermann, ἔρμα. 849 ποταινίου] ποταινείου (from ποτ' αἰνείου?) L, with ι over ει from the first hand. 851 οὔτ᾽ ἐν βροτοῖσιν οὔτ᾽ ἐν νεκρῶσιν | L. Triclinius changed βροτοῖσιν to βροτοῖς.—The antistr. v. is 870 κασίγνητε γάμων κυρήσας. Boeckh conject. βροτοῖς οὔτ᾽ ἐν νεκροῖς κυροῦσα (with κασίγνητος in 870): Seyffert, βροτοῖς οὔτε νεκροῖς κυροῦσα: and so Wecklein, but with ἰοῦσα. Emperius, οὔτ᾽ ἐν τοῖσιν ἔτ᾽ οὔτε τοῖσιν, which Heinrich Schmidt receives, adding γ' after δύστανος. Gleditsch, ἰὼ δύσποτμος | βροτῶν, οὐδὲ νεκρὸς νεκροῖσιν. Cp. on 869 f. 853 ἔσχατον] ἐσχάτου F. Kern, and so Bellermann. 855 πολὺν L: πολύ r. Dindorf (who,

φίλων ἄκλαυτος: cp. 1034: Ai. 910 ἄφαρκτος φίλων, and O. C. 1722 n.
848 ἔργμα τυμβόχωστον, an enclosure (prison) with a sepulchral χῶμα. The ἔργμα is the chamber in the rock, πετρώδης κατῶρυξ (774), in which she is to be immured: the χῶμα consists of the stones heaped up at the entrance, so as to close it: cp. 1216 ἁρμὸν χώματος λιθοσπαδῆ. For ἔργμα (εἴργω, to shut in) cp. Arist. Part. Anim. 2. 15. 1, where it is said that the eyelashes (βλεφαρίδες) protect the eyes, οἷον τὰ χαρακώματα ποιοῦσί τινες πρὸ τῶν ἐργμάτων, like the palings sometimes placed in front of fences (or hedges). The Berlin ed. (p. 958 b 18) there gives ἐργμάτων from the MSS. just as here L has ἔργμα, and as, conversely, MSS. of Pindar (I. 1. 27 etc.) give ἔργμα for ἔργμα=ἔργον. The old edd. of Arist. give ἐρυμάτων.—The reading ἔρμα (from ἐρείδω) = 'mound': C. I. 4599 ἐρισθενὲς ἔρμα θανοῦσιν: Kaibel Epigr. 1063. 4 κάγηραον ἔρμα. But this seems less fitting here than the notion of 'prison': cp. 886 περιπτύξαντες, 892 δείφρουρος.
849 ποταινίου, usu., 'recent,' 'fresh': here, 'of a new kind': cp. fr. 154. 5 ἡδο-

νὰς ποταινίους. A tomb destined for the dead is to receive the living (cp. 821).
851 Though every treatment of this verse must remain subject to doubt, far the most probable (to my mind) is Seyffert's modification of Boeckh's βροτοῖς οὔτ᾽ ἐν νεκροῖς κυροῦσα. This gives an exact correspondence·with 870, κασίγνητε γάμων κυρήσας, and there is every reason to think that 870 is sound. Further, the origin of L's reading is elucidated. The first οὔτε is omitted (Aesch. Ag. 532 Πάρις γὰρ οὔτε συντελὴς πόλις, cp. O. T. 239); and this poetical license might easily have led a corrector to suppose that the first οὔτε had been lost. Again, the loss of κυροῦσα would have been easy after νεκροῖς.
852 μέτοικος: cp. 868, 890: see on O. C. 934. It is her doom, ζῶσα τυμβεύειν (888). She is not a dweller with the living, because her abode is the grave; nor with the dead, because she lives.—The similar phrase—perhaps imitated from this—in Eur. Suppl. 968 f., οὔτ᾽ ἐν τοῖς φθιμένοις | οὔτ᾽ ἐν ζῶσιν ἀριθμουμένα (Musgrave κρινομένα) has no such special point: the Argive widows merely mean that their life is a living death.

I pass to the rock-closed prison of my strange tomb, ah me unhappy! who have no home on the earth or in the shades, no home with the living or with the dead.

CH.   Thou hast rushed forward to the utmost verge of 3rd daring; and against that throne where Justice sits on high thou strophe. hast fallen, my daughter, with a grievous fall. But in this ordeal thou art paying, haply, for thy father's sin.

AN.   Thou hast touched on my bitterest thought,—awaking 2nd anti-the ever-new lament for my sire and for all the doom given to strophe.

however, suspects a lacuna) conject. πάλιν: Schneidewin, ποδοῖν: Wolff, πόλει: Todt, πάθει: Seyffert, πολύς (as fem.): Bonitz, μόρῳ: Hartung, τάφῳ: Blaydes, μέγα. Wieseler points at τέκνον, joining πολύν with ἄθλον.   856 πατρῷον.. τιν' ἄθλον] Blaydes conj. πατρῴαν.. τιν' ἄταν: Seyffert, πατρῷον.. γένεθλον. —ἐκτείνεισ L, ἐκτίνεις Τ. Donaldson conj. ἐκτελεῖς: Pallis, ἐκτονεῖς.   857 ἔψαυσας] Blaydes writes ἔμψασας.   858 τριπόλιστον] Blaydes gives τριπόληστον: Hermann, τριπλοῖστον ('triplicatum'): Reiske, τριπτάλαιστον (with οἶτον): Bergk τρίπαλτον (with τε after πατρός).—οἶκτον L, and so the later MSS., though in L² (cod. Laur. 31. 10) the κ has been erased, and in V οἶτον is indicated as a variant. οἶκων in the lemma of L's schol. was doubtless a mere slip.   Brunck gave

853 ff. προβᾶσ'...πολύ: having advanced to the furthest limit of rashness, thou hast struck heavily (πολύ) against the lofty pedestal of Justice. We are to imagine the daring offender as going forward to a boundary where Justice sits enthroned, forbidding all further advance. Instead of pausing there, the rebel still rushes on, to cross the boundary—and, in doing so, dashes herself against the throne of the goddess. For βάθρον cp. Her. 1. 183 (a sitting statue of Zeus) καὶ τὸ βάθρον (pedestal) ᾧ καὶ ὁ θρόνος χρύσεός ἐστι. For προσέπεσες, Polyb. 1. 39 προσπεσόντες εἴς τινα βραχέα (having struck on some shallows—in sailing). Cp. Aesch. Theb. 409 μάλ' εὐγενῆ τε καὶ τὸν Αἰσχύνης θρόνον | τιμῶντα καὶ στυγοῦνθ' ὑπέρφρονας λόγους. Ag. 383 λακτίσαντι μέγαν Δίκας, βωμόν. Eum. 539 βωμὸν αἴδεσαι Δίκας, | μηδέ νιν κέρδος ἰδὼν ἀθέῳ ποδὶ λὰξ ἀτίσῃς. Solon fr. 4. 14 οὐδὲ φυλάσσονται σεμνὰ θέμεθλα Δίκης.—πολύ (adv.) = σφόδρα, violently.—Bellermann, adopting Kvičala's general view, and also Kern's ἰσχάτον, renders: 'having advanced, with extreme rashness (Dem. or. 18 § 17 οὔτε δικαίως οὔτ' ἐπ' ἀληθείας οὐδεμιᾶς εἰρημένα), to the lofty threshold (βάθρον) of Justice, thou hast fallen heavily down': i. e., 'while, with the utmost boldness, thou wert obeying the command of Justice, thou hast been

hurled to destruction.' But (1) προσέπεσες could not mean this: we must at least have κατέπεσες. (2) The Chorus feel pity, indeed, for Ant., and recognise the praise of piety, which she has won (817, 872). But they also regard her collision with the city's law as an act of frantic folly (λόγου τ' ἄνοια καὶ φρενῶν ἐρινύς, 603); and they presently tell her that she had left Creon no choice but to punish her (874). By Δίκη they understand the law of the State,—not those θεῶν νόμιμα which Ant. preferred to obey.

856 πατρῷόν τινα......ἄθλον, 'some ordeal inherited from thy sire' (v. 2); τινά softens a statement into a conjecture; it is perhaps the work of the fate which he bequeathed. This is better than to take τινά closely with πατρῷον as = 'of the paternal kind.'—ἐκτίνεις, art paying (to the fates which exact it), like ἐκτίνω δίκην, τίσιν, ἄποινα.

857 ff. μερίμνας, gen. sing.: οἶκτον, acc. depending on ἔψαυσας...μερίμνας as = ἐποίησάς με μεριμνᾶν: cp. El. 122 τίνα | τάκεις ὧδ' ἀκόρεστον οἰμωγὰν | τὸν πάλαι ἐκ δολερᾶς ἀθεώτατα | ματρὸς ἀλόντ' ἀπάταις Ἀγαμέμνονα, where τὸν...Ἀγαμέμνονα is governed by τίνα τάκεις...οἰμωγὰν as = τί οἰμώξεις; see other examples in n. on 211 f.   πατρός and πότμου are objective genitives with οἶκτον.—The objec-

8 ἁμετέρου πότμου κλεινοῖς Λαβδακίδαισιν. 861
4 ἰὼ ματρῷαι λέκτρων
5 ἆται κοιμήματά τ' αὐτογέννητ' ἐμῷ πατρὶ δυσμόρου
   ματρός, 865
6 οἵων ἐγώ ποθ' ἁ ταλαίφρων ἔφυν·
7 πρὸς οὓς ἀραῖος, ἄγαμος, ἄδ' ἐγὼ μέτοικος ἔρχομαι.
8 ἰὼ δυσπότμων κασίγνητε γάμων κυρήσας,
9 θανὼν ἔτ' οὖσαν κατήναρές με. 871

ἀντ. γ΄. ΧΟ. σέβειν μὲν εὐσέβειά τις,

οἶτον, which Dindorf and others adopt. **861** πότμου] δόμου Hartung and Blaydes. **863** ματρῷαι r: πατρῷαι L. Cp. 980. **864** ἆται] ἆται L.—κοιμήμματ' αὐτογενῆ | τ' L: κοιμήματά τ' αὐτογέννητ' r. Turnebus restored αὐτογέννητ'. **865** ἐμῷ L: ἀμῷ Triclinius, which gives a long syllable to correspond with the first syllable of ξυμμάρτυρας (846), but is unnecessary, since that syllable may be either long or short (see Metr. Anal.).—δυσμόρωι L: δυσμόρου r and schol.

tion to taking οἶκτον as acc. in apposition with ἔψαυσας...μερίμνας is that this would imply τό (σε) ψαῦσαι ἀλγ. ἐμοὶ μερίμνης οἶκτός ἐστιν: as Eur. Or. 1105 Ἑλένην κτάνωμεν, Μενέλεῳ λύπην πικράν, implies, τὸ Ἑλένην κτανεῖν Μενέλεῳ λύπη πικρά ἔσται: Aesch. Ag. 224 ἔτλα δ' οὖν | θυτὴρ γενέσθαι θυγατρός, γυναικοποίνων πολέμων ἀρωγάν, implies, τὸ θυτῆρα γενέσθαι ἀρωγή ἦν. Now, if we had, for instance, ἀνεμνήσθην μερίμνης, it is conceivable that οἶκτον, as acc. in appos., should mean οἶκτον ἀφορμὴν or ἔγερσιν. But when, as here, the subject of ἔψαυσας is distinct from the person who makes the lament, it seems impossible that οἶκτον should have this pregnant sense.—ἀλγ. μερίμνας is certainly not acc. plur. See on 546 and 961. No Greek hearer of these lyrics could take μερίμνας for anything but the usual gen. after ψαύω. If Soph. had intended the acc., he would at least have written ἀλγεινοτάταν...μέριμναν.—The interpretation given above would admit the reading οἶτον, 'doom,' which has, however, less authority (cr. n.). El. 166 τὸν ἀνήνυτον | οἶτον ἔχουσα κακῶν. But, as οἶτον πότμου is an impossible pleonasm, it would then be necessary to take τοῦ τε ...πότμου as depending on ἔψαυσας: for τριπόλιστον οἶτον could not be a parenthetic acc. in apposition with ἔψαυσας... μερίμνας ματρός. This would be very awkward. Further, οἶκτον is clearly the right word to introduce the lament ἰώ, etc., which actually follows.—τριπόλιστο-

τον (οἶκτον), a lament which has often been renewed; a thrice-told tale of sorrow. πολέω = to turn up the soil with the plough: ἀναπολέω, to plough anew: then fig., to 'go over the same ground' again. Pind. N. 7. 104 ταῦτά...τρὶς τετράκι τ' ἀμπολεῖν: Ph. 1238 δὶς ταῦτά βούλει καὶ τρὶς ἀναπολεῖν μ' ἔπη; No πολίζω as = πολέω occurs, but Pind. once has ἀναπολίζω as = ἀναπολέω (P. 6. 3). Similarly a poet might well use τριπόλιστος as if πολίζω existed. It is needless to write τριπόλητον. The epic adj. is τρίπολος.—κλεινοῖς Λαβδακίδαισιν, dat. of interest after πότμου, all the fate for (i.e. appointed for) us, the Labdacidae, instead of the possessive gen., κλεινῶν Λαβδακιδᾶν. Cp. Eur. Ph. 17 ὦ Θήβαισιν εὐίπποις ἄναξ. It is needless to explain the dat. by pressing the deriv. of πότμος from πίπτω ('what falls to one'). Cp. on 571, and on 865 (ἐμῷ πατρί).—ἁμετέρου (= ἡμῖν) is here joined with the dat. of interest, as the possessive pron. is oft. joined with the gen. of the pers. pron. (τἀμὰ δυστήνου κακά, O. C. 344).

863 ματρῷαι λέκτρων ἆται = ματρῴων λ. ἆται (see n. on 793), calamities of the mother's bed, i.e. springing from marriage with a mother. (So O. C. 526 γάμων . . ἄτᾳ.) For the plur. ἆται in this sense, cp. O. C. 1244, El. 215.—L's πατρῷαι ('calamities of my father's marriage') is possible, but less good, since (a) the epithet μητρῷα denotes the bed to which he came: cp. O. T. 976 καὶ πῶς

us, the famed house óf Labdacus. Alas for the horrors of the mother's bed! alas for the wretched mother's slumber at the side of her own son,—and my sire! From what manner of parents did I take my miserable being! And to them I go thus, accursed, unwed, to share their home. Alas, my brother, ill-starred in thy marriage, in thy death thou hast undone my life!

CH. Reverent action claims a certain praise for reverence; 3rd anti-strophe.

---

867 πρὸς οὖς.. ἔρχομαι] Two vv. in L, divided at ἆ|δ' ἐγώ. **869** ἴ. ἰὼ] ἰὼ ἰὼ L.—κασίγνητε γάμων κυρήσας] A separate v. in L.—Wolff read ἰὼ ἰὼ κάσις δυσπότμων γάμων κυρήσας, and in 851 (where see n.) ἰὼ δύστανος, οὔτ' ἐν βροτοῖς οὔτ' ἐν νεκροῖσιν. Bellermann suggests ἰὼ δυσπότμων ἰὼ γάμων κασίγνητε κύρσας = 851 ἰὼ δύστανοι γ' οὔτ' ἐν βροτοῖσιν οὔτ' ἐν νεκροῖσι.—For γάμων Morstadt conject. τάφων. **872** ἴ. σέβειν μὲν εὐσέβειά τις] Musgrave conject. μιν for μέν. Nauck, σέβειν μὲν εὐσεβὲς νεκρούς, οι σέβειν μὲν εὐσεβεῖς θέμις. M. Schmidt, σέβειν μὲν εὐσέβειά τις | κρείσσουτ· κράτος δ' ὅτῳ μέλει etc. Semitelos, σέβειν μὲν εὐσέβεια τοὺς | κάτω· κράτος δ' ὅτῳ μέλει etc.

τὸ μητρὸς λέκτρον οὐκ ὀκνεῖν με δεῖ; and (b) with πατρῴαι the explanation by ἐμῷ πατρί, etc., would have been less needed.

864 ἴ. κοιμήματα .. αὐτογέννητα .. ματρός, the mother's union with her own offspring; the adj. = μετὰ τοῦ αὑτῆς γεννήματος: cp. O. C. 1463 κτύπος .. διόβολος (= κτύπος τοῦ ἐκ Διὸς βέλους): Aesch. Eum. 212 ὅμαιμος (= συγγενοῦς) αὐθέντης φόνος.—ἐμῷ πατρί, dat. of interest, 'for my sire' (i.e. to his misery); the whole phrase being equiv. to, 'a mother's incestuous union with our father.' The dat. goes with the whole preceding phrase, not with αὐτογέννητα only ('incestuous in relation to him'), nor with κοιμήματα only ('sleep with him'). The latter, which Wecklein assumes, implies κοιμᾶσθαί τινι as = συγκ. τινί, an unproved constr.; for Hes. Th. 213 οὕτινι κοιμηθεῖσα θεὰ τέκε Νύξ ἐρεβεννή is of doubtful genuineness, and even there οὕτινι could go with τέκε.—δυσμόρου is far better than δυσμόρῳ: without it, the words could imply that only the father's sin merited pity.

866 ἴ. οἵων (masc.) ποτέ is exclamatory: 'from what manner of parents' (for the gen., cp. 38). The exclamatory οἷος is freq. in Soph. (cp. 1228, Tr. 997, etc.), and ποτέ strengthens it just as it strengthens the interrogative τίς or ποῖος (O. T. 754, Ph. 222, etc.). So the exclamatory οἷος is strengthened by ἆρα (Ai. 367, 920).—Most commentators make οἵων neut. relative to κοιμήματα: 'such

(wedlock) as that from which I sprang.' But ποτέ is fatal to this; for (a) it cannot here mean, 'in former days'; that would be too weak: (b) nor can οἵων ποτέ mean, 'of whatever kind they may have been'—like ὅστις ποτέ. Besides, the masc. οὖς most naturally refers to persons denoted by οἵων. I have therefore pointed at ματρός.—ἀραῖος, fem.: elsewhere this adj. is always of three terminations. So Attic tragedy uses κοινός, ποθεινός, πτωχός, φανερός, etc., as fem.: see O. C. 751 n.—μέτοικος: see on 852.

870 κασίγνητε. Polyneices. His marriage with Argeia, daughter of the Argive king Adrastus, was the seal of the armed alliance against Thebes, and thus the prime cause of Antigone's death (O. C. 378).—Not Oedipus. Such an allusion would be too repulsive here. In O. C. 535 ἀδελφεαί marks the climax of horror, and the word is wrung from unwilling lips. Further, as the doom of the whole race is in question (859), the brother is fitly mentioned.

871 θανὼν ἔτ' οὖσαν: so Electra says of her brother Orestes, ὥς μ' ἀπώλεσας θανών. Cp. on O. T. 1453.—κατήναρες. This act. aor. occurs in later poetry. The epic form of the compound is κατεναίρομαι, aor. κατενηράμην. Eur. uses the epic ἐναίρω, ἤναρον, but only in lyrics. Soph. has κατηναρισμένας (κατεναρίζω) in dial., Ai. 26.

872 σέβειν. 'Reverent action' (meaning her loyalty to Polyneices) 'is, in a

2 κράτος δ', ὅτῳ κράτος μέλει,
3 παραβατὸν οὐδαμᾷ πέλει,
4 σὲ δ' αὐτόγνωτος ὤλεσ' ὀργά.   875

ἐπ. ΑΝ.✓ἄκλαυτος, ἄφιλος, ἀνυμέναιος ταλαίφρων ἄγομαι
✓τάνδ' ἑτοίμαν ὁδόν.
✓οὐκέτι μοι τόδε λαμπάδος ἱερὸν
✓ὄμμα θέμις ὁρᾶν ταλαίνα·   880
✓τὸν δ' ἐμὸν πότμον ἀδάκρυτον
✓οὐδεὶς φίλων στενάζει.

ΚΡ.✓ἆρ' ἴστ', ἀοιδὰς καὶ γόους πρὸ τοῦ θανεῖν
✓ὡς οὐδ' ἂν εἷς παύσαιτ' ἄν, εἰ χρείη λέγειν;
✓οὐκ ἄξεθ' ὡς τάχιστα; καὶ κατηρεφεῖ   885
τύμβῳ περιπτύξαντες, ὡς εἴρηκ' ἐγώ,
✓ἄφετε μόνην ἔρημον, εἴτε χρῆ θανεῖν

874 οὐδαμᾶι L. 876 ff. L divides the vv. thus: ἄκλαυτος—| ταλαίφρων—| τάνδ'—| μοι—ὄμ|μα—ἐ|μὸν—| φίλων...στενάζει. For ταλαίφρων ἄγομαι τάνδ' ἑτοίμαν ὁδόν Dindorf writes ἔρχομαι τὰν πυμάταν ὁδόν. (Reiske had conjectured τάνδε πυμάταν ὁδόν.) Heinrich Schmidt places ταλαίφρων after ἄγομαι. 880 ταλαί-ναι L (not ταλαίνα). The final ι is from the first hand; but the word was first accented τάλαιναι, and then ταλαῖναι. 884 χρεί' ηι L: χρείη Dawes.—

sense, εὐσέβεια': i.e. though it is not complete εὐσέβεια—which the Chorus regard as including loyalty to the State's laws—yet, so far as it goes, it deserves praise of the same kind. Cp. 924 τὴν δυσσέβειαν εὐσεβοῦσ' ἐκτησάμην: by practising εὐσέβεια towards the dead, she had come to be thought, on the whole, δυσσεβής—as a law-breaker. The Chorus is here the apologist of Creon, and this concession is meant to emphasise the next sentence. Hence the purposed vagueness of σέβειν. The speaker avoids a direct reference to the peculiarly sacred and tender duty which Ant. had fulfilled. The proposed emendations (see cr. n.) would obliterate this touch.
873 f. κράτος δὲ οὐδαμᾷ παραβατὸν πέλει (τούτῳ), ὅτῳ κράτος μέλει: but an offence against authority cannot be permitted by him who has authority in his keeping. The antecedent to ὅτῳ, viz. τούτῳ, is an ethic dat., 'in his sight'; he must not look on and see the law broken. For this dat., cp. 904.—οὐδαμᾷ (Dor.): cp. 763.—For μέλει cp. 1335: Il. 2. 25

ᾧ λαοί τ' ἐπιτετράφαται καὶ τόσσα μέμηλεν. The Chorus echoes Creon's saying (677).
875 αὐτόγνωτος, act., deciding for oneself, αὐτὴ γιγνώσκουσα, like μεμπτός, 'blaming', ὕποπτος, 'suspecting', etc. (O. C. 1031 n.). Not pass., 'resolved upon' (i.e. here, 'adopted') 'by one's own choice,' as Ellendt takes it ('ultro susceptus'), and as the Schol. perh. did, who gives, αὐθαίρετος καὶ ἰδιογνώμων τρόπος.—ὀργά, disposition: see n. on 354 ff. (ὀργάς).
878 ἑτοίμαν, imminent, i.e. for which everything is prepared; Il. 18. 96 αὐτίκα γάρ τοι ἔπειτα μεθ' Ἕκτορα πότμος ἑτοῖμος: Plut. Mor. 706 C ἕτοιμον τὸ διαφθαρῆναι τοῖς μὴ βοηθοῦντα...τὸν λογισμὸν ἔχουσι (corruption is imminent for those who have not reason to aid them). Cp. 936.
879 τόδε λ. ἱερὸν ὄμμα=τῆσδε ἱερᾶς λαμπάδος ὄμμα (793 n.). Cp. Eur. I. T. 194 ἀλλάξας...| ἱερὸν...ὄμμ' αὐγὰς | ἅλιος. Ion 1467 ἀελίου δ' ἀναβλέπει λαμπ'σιν.
881 ἀδάκρυτον, predicate, with proleptic force: no friend mourns my fate,

but an offence against power cannot be brooked by him who hath power in his keeping. Thy self-willed temper hath wrought ⌣ thy ruin.

AN. Unwept, unfriended, without marriage-song, I am led *Epode.* forth in my sorrow on this journey that can be delayed no more. No longer, hapless one, may I behold yon day-star's sacred eye; but for my fate no tear is shed, no friend makes moan.

CR. Know ye not that songs and wailings before death would never cease, if it profited to utter them? Away with her—away! And when ye have enclosed her, according to my word, in her vaulted grave, leave her alone, forlorn—whether
she wishes to die,

Blaydes conject. παύσειεν for παύσαιτ' ἄν: but prints, by another conject., παύσαιτ' ἄν, εἰ 'ξείη, 'κχέων. Semitelos, προτοῦ λέγων | ὡς οὐδ' ἂν εἷς παύσαιτ' ἄν, εἰ χρείη θανεῖν. **885** ἄξεσθ' L, ἄξετ' r. **887** ἀφεῖτε μόνην L. Aldus (with A) has μόνην ἀφῆτ'. Most of the later MSS. have ἀφεῖτε, ἄφειτε, or ἀφῆτε: but for ἄφετε Vat. is cited. Blaydes, with Brunck, reads ἄπιτε μόνην, a *v. l.* noted in A.—χρὴ L: Dindorf conject. χρῇ: Hermann, εἰ χρῄζει: Nauck λῇ.

(and so it remains) unwept. Soph. has several instances of the predicative adj. thus added to a subst. which has the art. and possessive pron.; as *O. T.* 671 τὸ γὰρ σόν, οὐ τὸ τοῦδ', ἐποικτείρω στόμα | ἐλεινόν (n.): *El.* 1143 τῆς ἐμῆς πάλαι τροφῆς | ἀνωφελήτου. Cp. 791.

883 ⌞ ἆρ' ἔστι, ὡς, εἰ χρείη λέγειν ἀοιδὰς καὶ γόους πρὸ τοῦ θανεῖν, οὐδ' εἷς ἂν παύσαιτο (λέγων); The constr. would have been clearer with λέγων instead of λέγειν, but the latter has naturally been conformed to χρείη. The conject. παύσειεν is admissible (cp. *O. C.* 1751 παύετε θρῆνον, παῖδες), but unnecessary, and scarcely probable. Prof. Postgate's suggestion, that ἀοιδὰς καὶ γόους are objects to ἔστι, is tenable; but against it is the fact that in such cases the object of the principal verb is almost invariably the anticipated subject of the dependent clause (as *O. C.* 1197 γνώσει κακοῦ | θυμοῦ τελευτὴν ὡς κακὴ προσγίγνεται); as if here we had, ἆρ' ἔστ' ἀοιδὰς ὡς μακραὶ εἰσι; An object is very rarely so anticipated, as in Isae. or. 10 § 18, ἴσως οὖν ἄν τις...τὸν χρόνον ὑμῶν θαυμάσειε, πῶς τοτε πολὺν οὕτως εἰάσαμεν.—οὐδ' ἂν εἷς, more emphatic than οὐδεὶς ἄν: cp. *O. T.* 281 n.

885 οὐκ ἄξεσθ'. When the first of two or more commands is given by οὐ with fut. indic., that constr. is usually continued,

either (*a*) with καί, as Eur. *Andr.* 1066 οὐχ ὅσον τάχος | χωρήσεται τις...καί... λέξει...; or (*b*) with repeated οὐ, as Ar. *Lys.* 459 οὐχ ἕλξετ', οὐ παιήσετ', οὐκ ἀράξετε; Here a direct imperat. follows (887), and a note of interrogation must therefore be placed after τάχιστα.—κατηρεφεῖ, prop. 'roofed over,' ft. an epithet of a natural cave (*Od.* 13. 349 σπέος, Soph. *Ph.* 272 ἐν κ. πέτρᾳ), and in *El.* 381 of a chamber (στέγη) like this κατῶρυξ. The fact that Nauck wishes to change it into κατώρυχι (or κατωρυχεῖ) is a strong instance of μεταβολὴ πάντων γλυκύ.

886 περιπτύξαντες: see on 848 (ἔργμα). Cp. Eur. *Ph.* 1357 τειχέων περιπτυχαί. Kaibel *Epigr.* 468 λάϊνεος στήλη με πέριξ ἔχει.

887 χρῇ, wishes: 3rd pers. pres. ind. of χράω, with contraction into ῇ instead of ᾷ, as in διψῆν, ζῆν, κνῆν, πεινῆν, σμῆν, χρῆν (to give an oracle), χρῆσθαι, ψῆν. Schol., εἰ χρῄζει καὶ θέλει. If the nom. ζῶσα is sound, as it seems to be, in the next v., then χρῇ is certain: for εἰ χρῄζει has no probability. Only one other passage, however, gives unambiguous support to the forms χρῇς, χρῇ.—viz. Ar. *Ach.* 778, (the Megarian) οὐ χρῆσθα; σιγῇς, ὦ κάκιστ' ἀπολουμένα; 'will you not make a sound?' (οὐ θέλεις, sc. φωνεῖν;) There, indeed, Blaydes writes οὐ χρή τυ

εἴτ' ἐν τοιαύτῃ ζῶσα τυμβεύειν στέγῃ·
ἡμεῖς γὰρ ἁγνοὶ τοὐπὶ τήνδε τὴν κόρην·
μετοικίας δ' οὖν τῆς ἄνω στερήσεται. 890
AN. ὦ τύμβος, ὦ νυμφεῖον, ὦ κατασκαφὴς
οἴκησις ἀείφρουρος, οἷ πορεύομαι
πρὸς τοὺς ἐμαυτῆς, ὧν ἀριθμὸν ἐν νεκροῖς
πλεῖστον δέδεκται Φερσέφασσ' ὀλωλότων·
ὧν λοισθία 'γὼ καὶ κάκιστα δὴ μακρῷ 895
κάτειμι, πρίν μοι μοῖραν ἐξήκειν βίου.
ἐλθοῦσα μέντοι κάρτ' ἐν ἐλπίσιν τρέφω
φίλη μὲν ἥξειν πατρί, προσφιλὴς δὲ σοί,
μῆτερ, φίλη δὲ σοί, κασίγνητον κάρα·

---

888 ζῶσα τυμβεύειν L. The difficulty felt as to χρή in 887 is shown by two types of reading which appear in later MSS., viz. (1) ζῶσα τυμβεύει in A, R, etc.: (2) ζῶσαν τυμβεύειν in Vat., Aug. b, and a few other 14th cent. MSS. Triclinius wrote ζῶσα τυμβεύσει. Reiske conject. ζῶσαν ὑμνήσειν: Semitelos, ζῶσαν ὑμνῳδεῖν.—For τυμβεύειν Morstadt conject. νυμφεύειν. **891** In L the first hand

σιγῆν; but the MSS. are supported by the testimony of Suidas and Hesychius to χρῆς as = χρήεις. In the other four places where these forms are usu. read, they are not indispensable, χρή being possible; but in two, at least, they are much better than χρή, viz. El. 606 κήρυσσέ μ' εἰς ἅπαντας, εἴτε χρῇς κακήν, | εἴτε στόμαργον, κ.τ.λ.: and Ai. 1373 σοὶ δὲ δρᾶν ἔξεσθ' ἃ χρῇς. In the other two, χρή might well stand: Eur. fr. 910 πρὸς ταῦθ' ὅ τι χρὴ καὶ παλαμάσθω | καὶ πᾶν ἐπ' ἐμοὶ τεκταινέσθω: Cratinus Νόμοι fr. 2 νῦν γὰρ δή σοι πάρα μὲν θεσμοὶ | τῶν ἡμετέρων, πάρα δ' ἀλλ' ὅ τι χρῇς. Except in Ach. 778, the MSS. everywhere give χρή: and the variants in the next v. (see cr. n.) show that χρῇ was strange to the copyists, though known to the Scholiast.

888 ζῶσα τυμβεύειν, to live entombed. Elsewhere τυμβεύω = to entomb (Ai. 1063 σῶμα τυμβεῦσαι τάφῳ); or to bring as a funeral offering, El. 406 πατρὶ τυμβεῦσαι χοάς. Here it is intrans., = ἐν τύμβῳ εἶναι. Cp. σαλεύω, which means either (1) to put others on a σάλος,—to toss them: or (2) intrans., to be on a σάλος. So the intrans. θαλασσεύω = to be on the sea. παρθενεύω, which is trans. in classical Gk. ('to bring up a maiden'), is intrans. in Heliod. 7. 8 τὸ...παρθενεῦον τοῦ ἄστεος.—The conject. νυμφεύειν is not right. That taunt would be quite out of place

here. Creon says simply, 'I immure her,—I do not kill her; she can either die,—or live,—but in the tomb.'—στέγῃ, iron.: cp. El. 381 ζῶσα δ' ἐν κατηρεφεῖ | στέγῃ χθονὸς τῆσδ' ἐκτὸς ὑμνήσεις κακά, i.e. in a cave, or subterranean cell.

889 ἁγνοί: see on 775. His thought is: (1) she had warning: (2) no blood has been shed.—τοὐπὶ τήνδε, in what concerns her. In this phrase with the acc., ἐπί more often means, 'so far as depends on one': Eur. Hec. 514 ἡμεῖς δ' ἄτεκνοι τοὐπὶ σ': Or. 1345 σώθηθ' ὅσον γε τοὐπ' ἐμ': Thuc. 4. 28 (he told Cleon to try) τὸ ἐπὶ σφᾶς εἶναι (so far as the generals were concerned): Xen. Cyr. 1. 4. 12 ἄλλου τινὸς τὸ ἐπὶ σὲ ἀνάγκη ἔσται δεῖσθαι ἡμᾶς. In all these places ἐπί with dat. would equally suit the sense; but not so in this verse. Cp. 1348 τά γ' εἰς θεούς.

890 μετοικίας, cp. 852.—δ' οὖν, 688.—στερήσεται, 637.

891 f. ὦ τύμβος, nom. for voc.: cp. 379.—νυμφεῖον: cp. 1205.—κατασκαφῆς: see on 774.—ἀείφρουρος = ἣ ἀεὶ φρουρήσει με, not, ἣν ἐγὼ ἀεὶ φρουρήσω (like Aesch. P. V. 31 τήνδε φρουρήσεις πέτραν): cp. 886.

893 f. ἀριθμὸν...πλεῖστον: she thinks of Laïus, her father and mother, and her two brothers.—ἐν νεκροῖς with δέδεκται: the queen of the nether world has greeted them as they passed through the πολύξενοι

or to live a buried life in such a home. Our hands are clean as touching this maiden. But this is certain—she shall be deprived of her sojourn in the light.

AN. Tomb, bridal-chamber, eternal prison in the caverned rock, whither I go to find mine own, those many who have perished, and whom Persephone hath received among the dead! Last of all shall I pass thither, and far most miserably of all, before the term of my life is spent. But I cherish good hope that my coming will be welcome to my father, and pleasant to thee, my mother, and welcome, brother, to thee;

---

accented ᾱ—ᾱ—ᾱ. The first ω has been made ῳ. **892** ἀείφρουροσ L: αἰείφρουροσ r. **894** Φερσέφασσ' L (the first σ from ρ): Περσέφασσ' r. **895** λοίσθ' ἀγὼ L. (The accent on the first ι is faint.) The difference between the contracted αγ and εγ in L may be seen by comparing vv. 913, 916.

πύλαι to Hades (*O. C.* 1569 f.). So Oedipus is led by Ἑρμῆϊ ὁ πομπὸϊ ἥ τε νερτέρα θεὸϊ (*ib.* 1548). As ἡ ἀφανὴϊ θεὸϊ she is associated with Hades (*ib.* 1556).

Φερσέφασσα has L's support here. That form occurs also in Eur. *Helen.* 175, but Περσέφασσα in Aesch. *Cho.* 490. The *Il.* and *Od.* have only Περσεφόνεια. Φερσεφόνεια occurs in *Hom. hymn.* 13. 2. Pindar uses Φερσεφόνα. Plato attests that, in his day, the popular form was Φερρέφαττα, which he explains as the goddess of wisdom, who enables men φαρομένων ἐφάπτεσθαι, to grasp changing phenomena. People were afraid to utter the name Φερσεφόνη (*Crat.* 404 C). Attic inscr. of the 4th cent. B.C. give Περσεφόνη, Φερσεφόνη, Φερρέφαττα (Meisterhans pp. 36 ff.). MSS. have Φερσέφαττα (which should perh. be Φερρέφαττα) in Ar. *Ran.* 671, *Th.* 287. A vase ascribed to c. 435 B.C. gives ΠΕΡΣΟΦΑΤΑ (*sic*, Baumeister *Denkm.* p. 424). Welcker cites ΦΕΡΕΦΑΣΑ from an Agrigentine vase (*Götterl.* 1. 393). We may infer that Soph., c. 440 B.C., might have used either Περσέφασσα or Φερσέφασσα. The testimony of our oldest and best MS., L, may therefore be allowed to turn the scale.— In Περσεφόνη, the φον is certainly φαν, as in Ἀργειφόντηϊ, and this comes out more clearly in Περσέφασσα: cp. Τηλεφάσσα = Τηλεφάεσσα, Apollod. 3. 1. 1. The first part of the word is prob. φερ, φέρω; and the name meant originally, 'she who brings (vegetation) to the light.' The initial Π would then have been due to the following φ (cp. πέ-φυκα for φέ-φυκα).

The replacement of the initial φ may have been prompted by a wish to mitigate the δυσφημία of the name by avoiding an association with πέρθω.

895 f. κάκιστα, as a law-breaker (cp. 59): δή with superl., see 58 n.—μοῖραν... βίου: cp. 461. ἐξήκειν of time, as *Ph.* 199.

897 f. ἐν ἐλπίσιν τρέφω = ἐλπίζω. ἐν ἐλπίδι (or ἐλπίσιν) εἰμί was a common phrase. Cp. ἐν πόθῳ λαβεῖν τι (*O. C.* 1678).—φίλη μὲν ... προσφιλὴϊ δέ: cp. 669 καλῶϊ μὲν...εὖ δέ, n.

899 κασίγνητον κάρα. Eteocles. Whatever view may be taken of vv. 904—920, few would question the genuineness of 900—903: and if the latter are genuine, νῦν δέ shows that Polyneices is not meant here. She speaks first of those kinsfolk to whom she had rendered pious offices in the usual manner. Then she comes to him who is uppermost in her thoughts,—the brother whose case was different from that of the others. In v. 23 she spoke of the rumour that Eteocles had been duly buried. But nothing here implies her presence at his ἐκφορά. ἐλούσα κἀκόσμησα were acts preparatory to the πρόθεσιϊ. The χοαί could be rendered afterwards. She loved both brothers (cp. on 523). If father and mother were named here, without any mention of Eteocles, the omission would suggest that from *him* she could expect no welcome,—a contradiction of her real feeling (515). Further, the brevity of this reference to Eteocles heightens the effect of what follows.

ἐπεὶ θανόντας αὐτόχειρ ὑμᾶς ἐγὼ 900
ἔλουσα κἀκόσμησα κἀπιτυμβίους
χοὰς ἔδωκα· νῦν δέ, Πολύνεικες, τὸ σὸν
δέμας περιστέλλουσα τοιάδ᾽ ἄρνυμαι.
[καίτοι σ᾽ ἐγὼ ᾽τίμησα, τοῖς φρονοῦσιν, εὖ.
οὐ γάρ ποτ᾽ οὔτ᾽ ἂν εἰ τέκνων μήτηρ ἔφυν, 905
οὔτ᾽ εἰ πόσις μοι κατθανὼν ἐτήκετο,
βίᾳ πολιτῶν τόνδ᾽ ἂν ἠρόμην πόνον.
τίνος νόμου δὴ ταῦτα πρὸς χάριν λέγω;
πόσις μὲν ἄν μοι κατθανόντος ἄλλος ἦν,
καὶ παῖς ἀπ᾽ ἄλλου φωτός, εἰ τοῦδ᾽ ἤμπλακον· 910
μητρὸς δ᾽ ἐν Ἅιδου καὶ πατρὸς κεκευθότοιν
οὐκ ἔστ᾽ ἀδελφὸς ὅστις ἂν βλάστοι ποτέ.
τοιῷδε μέντοι σ᾽ ἐκπροτιμήσασ᾽ ἐγὼ
νόμῳ, Κρέοντι ταῦτ᾽ ἔδοξ᾽ ἁμαρτάνειν
καὶ δεινὰ τολμᾶν, ὦ κασίγνητον κάρα. 915

900—928 Dindorf rejects the whole of these 29 verses. **904** 'τίμησα] τίμησα L: cp. 457.—Lehrs rejects vv. 904—920. So Wecklein and Nauck. Nauck formerly omitted from νῦν in 902 to Κρέοντι in 914 inclusive (so that v. 902 should read, χοὰς ἔδωκα· ταῦτ᾽ ἔδοξ᾽ ἁμαρτάνειν); and in 916 changed διὰ χερῶν to δὴ Κρέων. **905** A. Jacob (*Quaest. Sophocleae*, 1821, p. 363) first condemned

---

900 f. ὑμᾶς. This play supposes Oedipus to have died at Thebes: see on 50.—**ἔλουσα κἀκόσμησα**: see nn. on *O. C.* 1602 f. λουτροῖς τέ νιν | ἐσθῆτί τ᾽ ἐξήσκησαν ᾗ νομίζεται. Cp. below, 1201. —**χοάς**: cp. 431.—**περιστέλλουσα**: here, of sprinkling the dust and pouring the χοαί: cp. the general sense of the word in *Ai.* 1170 τάφον περιστελοῦντε. More oft. of laying out the dead (like κοσμεῖν here, and συγκαθαρμόζειν in *Ai.* 922): *Od.* 24. 292 οὐδέ ἑ μήτηρ | κλαῦσε περιστείλασα. Verg. *Aen.* 9. 485 canibus date praeda Latinis | Alitibusque iaces: nec te tua funera mater | Produxi, pressive oculos, aut vulnera lavi, | Veste tegens.— **δέμας**: 205.

904—920 Few problems of Greek Tragedy have been more discussed than the question, whether these vv., or some of them, are spurious. Arist. (*Rhet.* 3. 16 § 9) quotes vv. 911, 912, and certainly had the whole passage in his text of Soph. The interpolation, then, if such it be, must have been made soon after the poet's death; and has been im-

puted to his son Iophon (ὁ ψυχρός), or some other sorry poet; or to the actors. I confess that, after long thought, I cannot bring myself to believe that Soph. wrote 905—912: with which 904 and 913—920 are in organic unity, and must now stand or fall. Some remarks will be found in the Appendix.

The main points (to my mind) are briefly these. (1) The general validity of the divine law, as asserted in 450—460, cannot be intelligibly reconciled with the limitation in vv. 905—907. (2) A still further limitation is involved in 911 f. She has buried her brother, not simply as such, but because, while he lived, he was an irreplaceable relative. Could she have hoped for the birth of another brother, she would not, then, have felt the duty to be so binding. (3) The composition of vv. 909—912 is unworthy of Sophocles.

904 'τίμησα (cp. 'φάνη, 457 n.), with εὖ (last word of v., as *O. C.* 642), I honoured thee rightly, τοῖς φρονοῦσιν, in the judgment of the wise; ethic dat. (25 n.): cp. 514.

for, when ye died, with mine own hands I washed and dressed you, and poured drink-offerings at your graves; and now, Polyneices, 'tis for tending thy corpse that I win such recompense as this.

→[And yet I honoured thee, as the wise will deem, rightly. Never, had I been a mother of children, or if a husband had been mouldering in death, would I have taken this task upon me in the city's despite. What law, ye ask, is my warrant for that word? The husband lost, another might have been found, and child from another, to replace the first-born; but, father and mother hidden with Hades, no brother's life could ever bloom for me again. Such was the law whereby I held thee first in honour; but Creon deemed me guilty of error therein, and of outrage, ah brother mine!

vv. 905—913 inclusive: and so Schneidewin, conjecturing in 914 Κρέοντι μέντοι, or μόνῳ Κρέοντι. Kvíčala condemns 905—911. **907** ἂν ἠρόμην г: ἀνηρόμην L. **911** κεκευθότοιν] βεβηκότων Arist. Rh. 3. 16 § 9. τετευχότων (τυγχάνω) Clemens Alex. Strom. 6, p. 747, 30.

---

906 ἐτήκετο, lay mouldering: Plat. Tim. 83 E ὅταν...τηκομένη σὰρξ ἀνάπαλιν εἰς τὰς φλέβας τὴν τηκεδόνα ἐξῇ. So tabum of corpses, Verg. Aen. 8. 487.
907 βίᾳ πολιτῶν. This was Ismene's phrase (79). Antigone had believed that the city was on her side (509). This has been noted as a mark of spuriousness in the verse. But it cannot (I think) be fairly claimed as such; for, since the Chorus had seemed to fail in sympathy (838), she had regarded herself as ἄφιλος (876) in Thebes.
908 πρὸς χάριν: see on 30.
909 ff. Cp. Her. 3. 119, which clearly supplied, not merely the thought, but the form, of these verses:—ἀνὴρ μέν μοι ἂν ἄλλος γένοιτο, εἰ δαίμων ἐθέλοι, καὶ τέκνα ἄλλα, εἰ ταῦτα ἀποβάλοιμι· πατρὸς δὲ καὶ μητρὸς οὐκέτι μοι ζωόντων, ἀδελφεὸς ἂν ἄλλος οὐδενὶ τρόπῳ γένοιτο. Arist. Rhet. 3. 16 § 9 (if you introduce a trait of character which will seem improbable, the reason of it should be added): ἂν δ' ἄπιστον ᾖ, τότε τὴν αἰτίαν ἐπιλέγειν, ὥσπερ Σοφοκλῆς ποιεῖ· παράδειγμα τὸ ἐκ τῆς Ἀντιγόνης, ὅτι μᾶλλον τοῦ ἀδελφοῦ ἐκήδετο ἢ ἀνδρὸς ἢ τέκνων· τὰ μὲν γὰρ ἂν γενέσθαι ἀπολόμενα [this = vv. 909, 910] μητρὸς δ' ἐν ᾅδου κ.τ.λ. (he then quotes 911 f., with βεβηκότων,—a mere slip of memory: see on 223).

Three points in these vv. are strange. (1) The gen. abs. κατθανόντος, for which a gen. has to be evolved from πόσις. The gen. of that word was not in Attic use ('mihi non succurrit exemplum ubi πόσεος aut πόσεως legatur,' Pors. Med. 906). Why was not ἀνδρός used? It looks as if the composer who made up these verses from Her. 3. 119 (see above) had sought to import a touch of tragic dignity by substituting πόσις for the historian's word, ἀνήρ. The gen. κατθανόντος cannot be taken (as some wish) with ἄλλος, 'different from the dead' (1). (2) ἀπ' ἄλλου φωτός. Why is it assumed that the first husband died before, or with, his child? The two hypotheses of loss should have been kept separate. We wanted something like καὶ παῖς ἂν ἄλλος, παιδὸς ἐστερημένη. (3) τοῦδ' means the first husband's child, but is most awkward.—As to οὐκ ἔστ' ἀδελφός κ.τ.λ., it may be somewhat inelegant; but it is not (as some urge) incorrect, since οὐκ ἔστιν ὅστις = οὐδείς.
918 ἐκπροτιμήσασ', 'having singled thee out for honour,'—with ref. to the supposed cases in which she would not have paid the burial rites. The double compound occurs only here,—as ἐξαφοράω only in O. C. 1648.

καὶ νῦν ἄγει με διὰ χερῶν οὕτω λαβὼν
ἄλεκτρον, ἀνυμέναιον, οὔτε του γάμου
μέρος λαχοῦσαν οὔτε παιδείου τροφῆς,
ἀλλ᾽ ὧδ᾽ ἔρημος πρὸς φίλων ἡ δύσμορος
ζῶσ᾽ εἰς θανόντων ἔρχομαι κατασκαφάς·]   920
ποίαν παρεξελθοῦσα δαιμόνων δίκην;
τί χρή με τὴν δύστηνον ἐς θεοὺς ἔτι
βλέπειν; τίν᾽ αὐδᾶν ξυμμάχων; ἐπεί γε δὴ
τὴν δυσσέβειαν εὐσεβοῦσ᾽ ἐκτησάμην.
ἀλλ᾽ εἰ μὲν οὖν τάδ᾽ ἐστὶν ἐν θεοῖς καλά,   925
παθόντες ἂν ξυγγνοῖμεν ἡμαρτηκότες·
εἰ δ᾽ οἵδ᾽ ἁμαρτάνουσι, μὴ πλείω κακὰ
πάθοιεν ἢ καὶ δρῶσιν ἐκδίκως ἐμέ.

ΧΟ. ἔτι τῶν αὐτῶν ἀνέμων αὐταὶ
ψυχῆς ῥιπαὶ τήνδε γ᾽ ἔχουσιν.   930
ΚΡ. τοιγὰρ τούτων τοῖσιν ἄγουσιν
κλαύμαθ᾽ ὑπάρξει βραδυτῆτός ὑπερ.
ΑΝ. οἴμοι, θανάτου τοῦτ᾽ ἐγγυτάτω
τοὔπος ἀφῖκται.
ΚΡ. θαρσεῖν οὐδὲν παραμυθοῦμαι   935
μὴ οὐ τάδε ταύτῃ κατακυροῦσθαι.

917 οὔτε τοῦ] οὗ τέ του L (του from τοῦ): Schneidewin conject. οὔτε πω.
920 θανάτων..κατασφαγᾶσ L: θανόντων..κατασκαφάς r. **922 f.** Nauck
rejects these two vv. **927** πλείω] Vauvilliers conject. μείω. **928** ἐνδίκως
L, with κ written above ν by S. **929 f.** ἔτι τῶν αὐτῶν ἀνέμων αὐταὶ | ψυχῆς
ῥιπαὶ τήνδε γ᾽ ἔχουσιν L. For αὐταί Erfurdt wrote αὐταί. Dindorf, thinking that
ψυχῆς was a gloss on ἀνέμων, and that αὐταί was afterwards added for metre's

916 διὰ χερῶν...λαβών, i.e., by forcible
arrest, as though I were a criminal. Cp.
O. C. 470 δι᾽ ὁσίων χειρῶν θιγών (='with'),
Aesch. Suppl. 193 (ἱκτηρίαι) ἔχουσαι διὰ
χερῶν.
917 ἀνυμέναιον: see on 814.
919 ἀλλ᾽: cp. on 810.—πρὸς φίλων
with ἔρημος (not with ἄγομαι), forsaken
on the part of my friends. The sense of
πρός in Ph. 1070 is similar, though there
it goes with the verb; ἢ καὶ πρὸς ὑμῶν ὧδ᾽
ἔρημος, ὦ φίλοι, | λειφθήσομαι δή...;
921 δαιμόνων δίκην, that which the
gods recognise (451), as distinguished
from the human δίκη (854) which she has
offended.
922 f. If the gods allow her to suffer

for obeying them, is it not vain for her to
invoke them?—βλέπειν εἴς τινα (for help),
as Ai. 398, 514, El. 959.—τίνα..ξυμ-
μάχων, what ally (of all conceivable allies)?
—ἐπεί γε δή: cp. Tr. 484 ἐπεί γε μὲν δή.
For the place of δή, cp. 726.—τὴν δυσσέβειαν, the repute of it; El. 968 εὐσέβειαν
ἐκ πατρὸς | θανόντος οἴσει: Eur. I. T. 676
καὶ δειλίαν γὰρ καὶ κάκην κεκτήσομαι: Med.
218 δύσκλειαν ἐκτήσαντο καὶ ῥᾳθυμίας:
Ion 600 γέλωτ᾽ ἐν αὐτοῖς μωρίαν τε λήψο-
μαι.
925 f. The gods are allowing her to
perish. But it does not follow that they
approve of her doom: for they are sometimes slow in punishing wrong (O. C.
1536). Hence the dilemma, introduced

And now he leads me thus, a captive in his hands; no bridal bed, no bridal song hath been mine, no joy of marriage, no portion in the nurture of children; but thus, forlorn of friends, unhappy one, I go living to the vaults of death.]

And what law of heaven have I transgressed? Why, hapless one, should I look to the gods any more,—what ally should I invoke,—when by piety I have earned the name of impious? Nay, then, if these things are pleasing to the gods, when I have suffered my doom, I shall come to know my sin; but if the sin is with my judges, I could wish them no fuller measure of evil than they, on their part, mete wrongfully to me.

CH. Still the same tempest of the soul vexes this maiden with the same fierce gusts.

CR. Then for this shall her guards have cause to rue their slowness.

AN. Ah me! that word hath come very near to death.

CR. I can cheer thee with no hope that this doom is not thus to be fulfilled.

---

sake, gives ἔτι τῶν αὐτῶν ἀνέμων μεταὶ | τήνδε γ' ἔχουσιν. **931** τοι γάρ τοι τούτων L. Dindorf conject. τοιγάρτοι καὶ: Wecklein, τοιγάρτοι νιν: Bothe, τοιγάρ τούτην r: τοῖσ L.——τούσιν r: τοῖσ L. **933 f.** ἐγγυτάτωι L.—Lehrs, with whom Nauck agrees, assigns these two vv. to the Chorus. **935 f.** L gives these two vv. to Creon: Boeckh, to the Chorus. The Scholiast recognises both views.

---

by ἀλλ' οὖν ('well then'). (1) If the gods approve of my doom, then, after suffering it, I shall become conscious (in the other world) that I have sinned. (2) But if they disapprove of it, and regard Creon as the sinner, then they will punish him at last. And I could wish him no sorer doom than mine.—ἐν θεοῖς: cp. 459.—ξυγγνοῖμεν = συνειδείημεν. Lys. or. 9 § 11 συνέγνωσαν δὲ καὶ αὐτοὶ σφίσιν ὡς ἠδικηκότες, 'became conscious that they had done wrong.' The word could also mean, ὁμολογήσαιμεν, 'confess': but in that sense it regularly takes either an inf., as Her. 1. 91 συνέγνω ἑωυτοῦ εἶναι τὴν ἁμαρτάδα: or a dependent clause, as Plat. Legg. 717 D ξυγγιγνώσκοντα ὡς εἰκότως...θυμοῖτ' ἄν.—παθόντες belongs more closely to the verb than does παθόντες: cp. Plat. Phaed. 70 A (ἡ ψυχὴ) διασκεδασθεῖσα οἴχηται διαπτομένη. For the tragic masc. plur., when a woman speaks of herself, cp. El. 399.

927 f. οὗτος, Creon: cp. 10.—μὴ πλέω, i.e. she will be content if they suffer ἴσα. She can imagine no worse fate. The tame conjecture μεῖω would not express

this bitter feeling.—καὶ δρῶσιν, do on their part: O. C. 53 n.

929 f. ἀνέμων-μεταὶ ψυχῆς, storm-gusts of the soul: both genitives are possessive: cp. 795 βλεφάρων-ἵμερος...νύμφας—Dindorf's expulsion of αὐταὶ | ψυχῆι (cr. n.) is unwarranted. ψυχῆς interprets the figurative sense; for αὐταὶ after τῶν αὐτῶν cp. n. on 155 ff. (νέοχμος νεαραῖσι).

931 f. τούτων, neut., causal gen. (O. T. 48). After τήνδε γ', this is better than ταύτην would be: τοιγάρτοι (whether with καὶ or with νιν) would be unpleasing.—κλαύμαθ': cp. 754: so Ph. 1260 ἐκτὸς κλαυμάτων.—ὑπὲρ = ἕνεκα (O. T. 165 n.). οἴμοι follows, but the change of person excuses the breach of synapheia: so O. C. 139 τὸ φατιζόμενον is followed by ἰώ, and ib. 143 πρέσβυς by οὐ.

933 f. This threat (to the guards) 'has come very near to death,' i.e., 'portends imminent death for me.' The phrase is not fig., 'is bitter as death to hear' (being a prelude to death).

935 f. Said by Creon, clearly—not by the Chorus. 'I can give thee no encouragement (οὐδέν adv.) to hope that

ΑΝ.. ὦ γῆς Θήβης ἄστυ πατρῷον
.. καὶ θεοὶ προγενεῖς,
ἄγομαι δὴ κοὐκέτι μέλλω··
.. λεύσσετε, Θήβης οἱ κοιρανίδαι,   940
.. τὴν *βασιλειδᾶν μούνην λοιπήν,
.. οἷα πρὸς οἵων ἀνδρῶν πάσχω,
.. τὴν εὐσεβίαν σεβίσασα.

στρ. α΄. ΧΟ. ἔτλα καὶ Δανάας οὐράνιον φῶς
        2 ἀλλάξαι δέμας ἐν χαλκοδέτοις αὐλαῖς·   945

987 γῆσ made from γῆ in L.   **989** δή is the reading of A: δὴ 'γὼ of L.   The
latter arose from the wish to make the paroemiac into a dimeter.   **940** οἱ] ὦ Pallis.
941 τὴν βασιλίδα μούνην λοιπήν L.   The correction βασιλειδᾶν, which recent edd. have
generally received, was first proposed by K. Winckelmann (Salzwedler Programm,
p. 30, 1852); afterwards by M. Seyffert, in his ed. (1865).   Triclinius conjectured

the doom is not to be ratified on this
wise' (i.e., by death). μὴ οὐ, not μή, on
account of οὐδέν(443 n.).—κατακυροῦσθαι,
pres. denoting what is to be; Ph. 113
αἱρεῖ τὰ τόξα ταῦτα τὴν Τρολαν μόνα. Attic
prose used κυροῦν or ἐπικυροῦν (γνώμην,
νόμον, ψήφισμα, etc.). Cp. Creon's peremptory word τελεῖαν in 632.—ταύτη
(722) combined with τάδε: cp. 39.
   938 θεοὶ προγενεῖς, ancestral, not
merely as protectors of the race, but also
as progenitors. She thinks esp. of Ares
and Aphrodite, the parents of Harmonia,
wife of Cadmus: Aesch. Theb. 135 σύ τ',
Ἄρης, πόλιν Κάδμου ἐπώνυμον | φύλαξαι
κήδεσαί τ' ἐναργῶς, | καὶ Κύπρις, ἅτ' εἶ
γένοις προμάτωρ, | ἄλευσον. Dionysus,
the son of 'Cadmean' Semele (1115), is
another of the deities meant. προγενής,
born before one, a poet. word, unfamiliar
to good Attic prose, but used by Aristotle
and later writers, usu. in comparat. (as
οἱ προγενέστεροι, 'those who have gone
before us'): so οἱ μεταγενέστεροι.
   939 δή = ἤδη (O. T. 968), as in καὶ
δή.—κοὐκέτι μέλλω, and am no longer
(merely) about to be led away: cp. O. C.
1074 ἔρδουσ' ἢ μέλλουσιν; Ph. 1255 κἀμέ
τοι | ταὐτὸν τόδ' ὄψει δρῶντα κοὐ μέλλοντ'
ἔτι. Meineke's conjecture μελλώ (=μέλ-
λησις, Aesch. Ag. 1356) was needless.—
Seyffert understands, 'I make no more
delay,'—said firmly and proudly: she
scorns to bring punishment on her guards
by detaining them longer. But this does
not suit ἄγομαι δή.

940 οἱ κοιρανίδαι, the Theban εὐπα-
τρίδαι of the Chorus: see on 843. The
nom. with art., instead of voc., = 'γε who
are princes of Thebes,' and so brings out
the implied reproach to their apathy.
This constr. usu. has a somewhat peremptory tone, as Plat. Symp. 218 B οἱ δὲ
οἰκέται...πύλας...τοῖς ὠσὶν ἐπίθεσθε. It is
different when a voc. precedes the art. and
partic., as Ar. Av. 30 ὦνδρες οἱ παρόντες
ἐν λόγῳ: cp. on 100 f.
   941 βασιλειδᾶν, i. e., of the race of the
Labdacidae. This correction of βασιλίδα
is certain. In Plat. Critias 116 C, τὸ τῶν
δέκα βασιλειδῶν γένος, the same corruption, βασιλίδων, occurs in the MSS.
Suidas has βασιλείδης· ὁ τοῦ βασιλέως
(where Küster wrongly proposed ὁ τοῦ
Βασιλείου). In adding the patronymic
suffix ιδα to a stem in ευ (βασιλευ), the ν
is dropped, as in the gen. plur. (βασιλέ-ων):
hence βασιλε-ίδης, βασιλείδης: cp. Πηλεί-
δης.—μούνην, ignoring Ismene; not in
bitterness (cp. on 559), but because she
feels that, in spirit at least, she herself is
indeed the last of the race. It is otherwise
when Oed. speaks of his daughters as his
only children (O. C. 895); and when Electra says that she is ἄνευ τοκέων (187),—
since Clytaemnestra is a μήτηρ ἀμήτωρ
(1154).
   943 εὐσεβίαν. Epic and lyric poetry
could substitute -ια for -εια in fem. nouns
from adjectives in -ης: so O. C. 1043
προμηθίας: Pind. P. 12. 4 εὐμαρία: Aesch.
Eum. 534 δυσσεβίας: Eur. H. F. 696·

AN. O city of my fathers in the land of Thebè! O ye gods, eldest of our race!—they lead me hence—now, now—they tarry not! Behold me, princes of Thebes, the last daughter of the house of your kings,—see what I suffer, and from whom, because I feared to cast away the fear of Heaven!

[ANTIGONE *is led away by the guards.*

CH. Even thus endured Danaë in her beauty to change the light of day for brass-bound walls; 1st strophe.

βασίλειαν: Bergk, Λαβδακιδᾶν: Doederlein, Οἰδιπόδα: Seidler and others, βασι-λῆδα. Emperius proposed λεύσσετε Θήβης τὴν κοιρανιδᾶν | μούνην λοιπήν, regarding τὴν βασιλίδα as a gloss. **943** εὐσέβειαν MSS.: εὐσεβίαν Triclinius, saying, οὕτω χρὴ γράφειν Ἰωνικῶς .. ἀλλὰ καὶ τὸ σεβίσασα ἀπὸ τοῦ σεβίζω ὀφείλεις λέγειν, which shows that his text had σεβήσασα. **944–954** L divides the vv. thus: ἔτλα— | ἀλλάξαι— | αὐλαῖσ— | τυμβήρει— | καίτοι— | καὶ Ζηνὸσ— | σκι γο-νὰσ— | ἀλλʼ ἁ— | οὔτʼ ἅν νιν— | οὐ πύργοσ— | κελαιναὶ .. ἐκφύγοιεν.

εὐγενίας. The motive was metrical convenience. Such forms are not Ionic, as Triclinius called them (cr. n.): thus Herod. used ἀληθείη, not ἀληθίη: though there are other cases in which Ionic substitutes ε for ει (as βαθέα, ἐπιτήδεοι, etc.).—σεβίσασα, of respecting a law or custom: so O. C. 636, Ai. 713 (θέσμια...σέβων).

944—987 Fourth stasimon. 1st strophe 944—954 = 1st antistrophe 955—965. 2nd str. 966—976 = 2nd antistr. 977—987. See Metrical Analysis.

As Antigone spoke the verses ending at 943, the guards were in the act of leading her forth. The choral ode may have begun before she had vanished; but she is not to be conceived as still present when she is apostrophised (949, 987).

A princess is about to be immured in a rocky cell. The Chorus remember three other royal persons who have suffered a like fate—Danaë, Lycurgus and Cleopatra. The only points which these cases have in common with Antigone's are the facts of noble birth and cruel imprisonment.

All four cases illustrate the same general truth—no mortal can resist fate. Danaë and Cleopatra were innocent; Lycurgus was guilty. But the Chorus do not mean to suggest Antigone's guilt or innocence; still less, to foreshadow the punishment of Creon. On this side, the ode is neutral, purely a free lyric treatment of the examples. Such neutrality suits the moment before the beginning of the περιπέτεια. Teiresias is soon to come.

944 f. Acrisius, the father of Danaë, was king of Argos. The oracle at Delphi told him that he was to be slain by his

daughter's son. He therefore immured the maiden in a chamber built for that purpose within the precincts of his house at Argos. Here Zeus visited her in the golden rain; she bore Perseus; and Acrisius sent mother and child adrift on the Aegean in a chest; but Zeus heard her prayer, and brought them safely to the island of Seriphus. Both Soph. and Eur. wrote a Δανάη: Soph. wrote also an Ἀκρίσιος.

καὶ Δανάας δέμας ἔτλα ἀλλάξαι οὐ-ράνιον φῶς: note the bold order of words, and cp. *Ph.* 598 f. (τίνος...πράγ-ματος). ἔτλα καί is a Homeric echo, from *Il.* 5. 382 ff. Aphrodite has been wounded by Diomede: her mother Dionè comforts her by saying that Ares, Hera, and Hades have also suffered wounds: τέτλαθι, τέκνον ἐμόν...| τλῆ μὲν Ἄρης... | τλῆ δʼ Ἥρη... | τλῆ δʼ Ἀΐδης. So here we have *three* examples—Danaë, Lycurgus, Cleopatra.—δέμας in periphrasis (*Tr.* 908) here suggests her youthful beauty.—ἀλλάξαι οὐρ. φῶς ἐν χαλκοδ. αὐλαῖς, 'to give up light, (so as to be) in a prison,' *i. e.* to *exchange* the light *for* the darkness of a prison. ἀλλάσσω τί τινος can mean either to give, or to take, one thing in exchange for another. When ἀλλάσσω is used absolutely, with ref. to place, it more naturally means 'to go to' (Eur. *Hec.* 483 ἀλλάξασʼ Ἀιδα θαλάμους), not, as here, 'to leave': but ἀμείβω is freq. in both senses. Cp. *Ph.* 1262 ἀμείψας... στέγας (having quitted them).

χαλκοδέτοις αὐλαῖς, 'a brass-bound dwelling': poet. pl. for sing., like δώματα, etc.: cp. 785. Pherecydes (*ap.* schol.

3 κρυπτομένα δ' ἐν τυμβήρει θαλάμῳ κατεζεύχθη·
4 καίτοι <καὶ> γενεᾷ τίμιος, ὦ παῖ παῖ,
5 καὶ Ζηνὸς ταμιεύεσκε γονὰς χρυσορύτους.   950
6 ἀλλ' ἁ μοιριδία τις δύνασις δεινά·
7 οὔτ' ἄν νιν *ὄλβος οὔτ' Ἄρης, οὐ πύργος, οὐχ ἁλί-
     κτυποι
8 κελαιναὶ νᾶες ἐκφύγοιεν.

ἀντ. α'. ζεύχθη δ' *ὀξύχολος παῖς ὁ Δρύαντος,   955
2 Ἠδωνῶν βασιλεύς, κερτομίοις ὀργαῖς,
3 ἐκ Διονύσου πετρώδει κατάφαρκτος ἐν δεσμῷ.

948 καὶ after καίτοι was added by Hermann. Wieseler conject. καίτοι γ' ἦν: as γεν follows, a scribe reading ΓΕΝΓΕΝ might easily omit γ' ἦν.—γενεᾶι L: γενεᾷ in Dresd. a was prob. either a late conject., or a mere error. (γέννα Aug. b, V⁴.)—Hartung conject. ἦν, ὦ παῖ (instead of ὦ παῖ, παῖ): and so Blaydes.   **950** χρυσορρύτουσ L: χρυσορύτους Triclinius.   **952** ὄλβοι Erfurdt: ὄμβρος MSS.

Apoll. Rhod. 4. 1091) describes it as 'a brazen chamber (θάλαμον...χαλκοῦν) made under ground, in the court-yard (αὐλῇ) of his house.' Paus. (2. 23. 7) says that he saw at Argos κατάγεων οἰκοδόμημα, ἐπ' αὐτῷ δὲ ἦν ὁ χαλκοῦς θάλαμος (made by Acrisius): i.e. the θάλαμος itself was above ground;—as Horace calls it turris aenea (C. 3. 16. 1). By the epithet χαλκοῦς the legend evidently meant to denote the strength and security of the prison,—as though the doors were of bronze. But it is very probable that this epithet original-ly came into the story through a remini-scence of a tomb (like the 'treasury of Atreus' at Mycenae), to the walls of which bronze plates had been nailed. (Cp. Introd. to Homer, ch. 11. § 25.) In Simonides fr. 37. 7 χαλκεογόμφῳ is said of the chest in which Danaë was sent adrift,—not of the θάλαμος.

946 τυμβήρει: cp. on 255.—κατε-ζεύχθη: was brought under the yoke, i.e., was strictly confined. Her. 8. 22 εἰ... ὑπ' ἀναγκαίης μέζονος κατέζευχθε ἤ ὥστε ἀπίστασθαι, if ye are in the bondage of a control too severe, etc. Cp. ζεύχθη, 955.

948 ff. τίμιος, sc. ἦν: cp. 834. Her-mann's καίτοι καὶ is preferable to Wie-seler's καίτοι γ' ἦν, because the doubled καὶ is forcible, while καὶ Ζηνός (without a previous καὶ) would be somewhat weak.—ταμιεύεσκε, as a precious charge. Cp. Aesch. Eum. 660 τίκτει δ' ὁ θρώ-

σκων: ἡ δ' (the mother) ἅπερ ξένῳ ξένη | ἔσωσεν ἔρνος. The iterative form occurs in only three other places of trag.: 963 Aesch. Pers. 656 ἴσκεν, Aesch. fr. 305 κλαί-εσκω.—χρυσορύτους, for metre's sake, like Ai. 134 ἀμφιρύτου: ρρ regularly follows a simple vowel, but ρ a diphthong (O. C. 469).—A bowl (κρατήρ) from Caere, of the 5th cent. B.C., shows the golden rain descending on Danaë; she is sitting on the bed in her chamber, and preparing to retire to rest. A second scene, on the same bowl, represents the moment when she is about to be placed, where Simonides imagines her, λάρνακι ἐν δαιδαλέᾳ. Both paintings are repro-duced by Baumeister (Denkm. p. 407).

951 ἁ μοιριδία τις κ.τ.λ. The pecu-liar place of τις makes it really equiv. to a parenthetic thought: 'the power of fate (whatever it may e) is a dread power.' So, while the general sense is what would be ordinarily given by ἁ μοιριδία δύνασις δεινά τις (δύνασίς) ἐστιν, the act-ual order of the words is more expressive. This is not merely an instance of τις preceding the adj. (as though τις δεινά stood for δεινά τις, cp. Ph. 519). Nor, again, is it strictly parallel with ὅταν δ' ὁ κύριος | παρῇ τις (O. C. 288), where art. and subst. precede; though it is similar.

952 f. οὔτ'...ὄλβος: wealth cannot buy off fate; arms cannot vanquish it; walls cannot keep it out; flight beyond sea cannot elude it.—Bacchylides fr. 36

and in that chamber, secret as the grave, she was held close prisoner; yet was she of a proud lineage, O my daughter, and charged with the keeping of the seed of Zeus, that fell in the golden rain.

But dreadful is the mysterious power of fate; there is no deliverance from it by wealth or by war, by fenced city, or dark, sea-beaten ships.

And bonds tamed the son of Dryas, swift to wrath, that 1st anti-king of the Edonians; so paid he for his frenzied taunts, strophe. when, by the will of Dionysus, he was pent in a rocky prison.

944—965 L divides thus: ζεύχθη— | 'Ηδωνῶν— | ὀργαῖσ— | πετρώδει— | οὕτω— | ἀνθηρόν .. κεῖνοσ— | ψαύων— | παύεσκε— | γυναῖκασ— | φιλαύλους .. μούσασ. **955** ὀξυχόλωσ MSS. (in L from ὀξυλόχωσ): ὀξύχολος Scaliger. **956** πετρώδει] ει made from η in L.

θνατοῖσι δ' οὐκ ἀφθαίρετοι | οὔτ' ὄλβοσ οὔτ' ἀκάματοι Ἄρησ οὔτε παμφθέρσησ στάσισ, | ἀλλ' ἐπιχρίμπτει νέφοσ ἄλλοτ' ἐπ' ἄλλαν | γαῖαν ἁ πάνδωρος αἶσα.—πύργοσ, city-walls, with their towers (*O. T.* 56).—οὔτ'...οὔτ', followed by οὐ...οὐχ : so even when only one οὔτε has been used, 249 n. **955** L ζεύχθη, was brought under the yoke. As κατεζεύχθη in 946 better suited the sense, 'was strictly confined,' so here the simple ζεύχθη better suggests the idea, 'was tamed by imprisonment.'— ὀξύχολος κ.τ.λ. = ὁ Δρύαντος ὀξύχολοσ παῖς: the adj. is epithet, not predicate. Verg. *Aen.* 3. 13 Terra procul vastis colitur Mavortia campis, | Thraces arant, acri quondam regnata Lycurgo. The 'Ηδωνοί, or 'Ηδῶνες (Thuc. 2. 99), occupied in historical times the part of Thrace E. of the Strymon and w. of the Nestus. In earlier times they had dwelt farther west, but had been driven eastward by the Macedonian conquest of Mygdonia. Dionysus, when he came from Asia with his new rites, was opposed by Lycurgus in Thrace, as by Pentheus at Thebes. The Λυκούργεια of Aeschylus is known from the schol. on Ar. *Th.* 135. This trilogy consisted of 'Ηδωνοί, Βασσαρίδες, Νεανίσκοι, with Λυκοῦργος as satyric drama. In *Il.* 6. 130 ff. Dionysus, pursued by Lycurgus, dives beneath the sea ; Thetis receives him ; and Zeus blinds Lycurgus. κερτομίοις ὀργαῖς, causal dat. with ἐζεύχθη; was subjugated by reason of the bursts of fury in which he reviled Dio-

nysus. For the dat., cp. 391, 691: *El.* 838 χρυσοδέτοις ἕρκεσι κρυφθέντα γυναικῶν, (Amphiaraus) buried alive, by reason of a woman's golden snares. ὀργαῖς might be general, 'moods' (355), but here has its special sense, though plur.: cp. Aesch. *Eum.* 848 ὀργὰς ξυνοίσω σοι. The dat. could be taken as a modal dat. with ὀξύχολος ('in,' or 'with,' his ὀργαί), but this is less good.—We could not take ζεύχθη...ὀργαῖς as = 'was enslaved to (his own) fierce moods.'—The recurrence of κερτομίοις in 961 is noteworthy, but not a ground for suspicion (76 n.): cp. 613 οὐδὲν ἕρπει with 618: and 614 ἐκτὸς ἄτας with 625. The idea of κερτόμιοις is mockery, or bitter jest: cp. *Ph.* 1235 κερτομῶν λέγεις τάδε; with the answer, εἰ κερτόμησίς ἐστι τἀληθῆ λέγειν. The word is illustrated by the whole scene in which Pentheus mocks and taunts Dionysus (Eur. *Bacch.* 451—514). So Aesch. fr. 59 made Lycurgus ask, ποδαπὸς ὁ γύνις; (whence comes this womanish youth?')

957 ἐκ Διονύσου, by his command (*O. C.* 67 n.). Lycurgus, having been driven mad by Dionysus, did many violent deeds, until at last the Edonians were commanded by an oracle to imprison him in a cave on Mount Pangaeus (Apollod. 3. 5. 1). He was afterwards torn asunder by wild horses (*ib.*), or devoured by panthers (Hyginus *Fab.* 132).—πετρώδει...δεσμῷ, the cave. Cp. Plat. *Legg.* 864 E ἐν δημοσίῳ δεσμῷ δεθείς. —κατάφαρκτος : for the spelling, cp. on 241.

4 οὕτω τᾶς μανίας δεινὸν ἀποστάζει
5 ἀνθηρόν τε μένος. κεῖνος ἐπέγνω μανίαις   960
6 ψαύων τὸν θεὸν ἐν κερτομίοις γλώσσαις.
7 παύεσκε μὲν γὰρ ἐνθέους γυναῖκας εὐιόν τε πῦρ,
8 φιλαύλους τ᾽ ἠρέθιζε Μούσας.   965

στρ. β'.   παρὰ δὲ Κυανεᾶν *πελάγει διδύμας ἁλὸς

960 ἀνθηρόν] Nauck conject. ἀτηρόν: Pleitner and Wolff, ἐνθηρον.—Schneidewin wrote ἀνθηρὸν τὸ μένος.   **961** ψαύων] Herwerden conject. χραίνων: M. Schmidt, θήγων: Nauck (formerly), θραύων: Mekler, σεύων.   **965** φιλαύλους L: φιλαύλους τ᾽ ι: φιλαύλους δ᾽ Seyffert, and so most recent edd.   **966—976** L divides the vv.

959 f. οὕτω, i.e., under the discipline of the rocky prison.—ἀνθηρόν, bursting into flower, hence, fig., exuberant, or at its height: cp. Plat. *Polit.* 310 D πέφυκεν ἀνδρία...κατὰ μὲν ἀρχὰς ἀκμάζειν ῥώμῃ, τελευτῶσα δὲ ἐξανθεῖν παντάπασι μανίαις: Aesch. *Pers.* 821 ὕβρις...ἐξανθοῦσ᾽. So oft. ἄνθος=ἀκμή, as *Tr.* 998 τόδ᾽ ἀκήλητον | μανίας ἄνθος.—ἀποστάζει =ἀπορρεῖ, 'trickles away,' so, 'gradually passes off.' The fig. use of ἀνθεῖν being so familiar, the change of metaphor in ἀποστάζει would hardly be felt. Wecklein, indeed, conceives that the poet is thinking of a tumour, which bursts when it has attained its full size. Unity of metaphor can be bought too dearly.—Others understand: 'so dread and exuberant is the rage that *flows from madness*': i.e., 'so dreadful was the excess of impiety into which L. had been led by his madness.' But here we look rather for some direct comment on his punishment. His abasement (ζεύχθη) is the theme of these verses. The reference to his crime comes later (962).

960 ff. ἐπέγνω τὸν θεόν, μανίαις ψαύων (αὐτοῦ) ἐν κ. γλώσσαις: he came to know the god, when in madness he assailed him with taunts. He had mistaken Dionysus for an effeminate mortal (see on 955 f.). Cp. *Od.* 24. 216 πατρὸς πειρήσομαι... | αἴ κέ μ᾽ ἐπιγνώῃ (recognise). ψαύω nowhere else takes an acc. in class. Greek (see on 546, 859), and it is unnecessary to regard this passage as a solitary example. Poetry, esp. lyric, allowed occasional boldness, and even harshness, in the arrangement of words (cp. 944: *O. T.* 1251 n.: *O. C.* 1428). Even in prose we could have (e.g.) ἐνίκησαν ἄφνω ἐπιπεσόν-

τες τοὺς πολεμίους, though the partic. could not govern an acc. Here the order is only so far bolder, that τὸν θεόν divides ψαύων from ἐν κ. γλώσσαις: as if, in our example, a second qualification of ἐπιπεσόντες (such as νύκτωρ) followed τοὺς πολεμίους. But, since the meaning of ψαύων is already indicated by μανίαις, we are not mentally straining forward for a clue to be given by ἐν κερτ. γλώσσαις. That is, we are not forced to bind the words, ψαύων τὸν θεόν, closely together in our thought, but can easily take the sentence as though it were pointed thus:—ἐπέγνω, μανίαις | ψαύων, τὸν θεόν, ἐν κερτ. γλώσσαις.—μανίαις, modal (rather than causal) dat. —ψαύων like καθαπτόμενος (ἀντιβίοις ἐπέεσσι, *Od.* 18. 415), but also suggesting profanation, — ἀθίκτον θιγγάνων. — ἐν = 'with' (764 n.).—γλώσσαις, a bold use of the plur., due to the fact that the sing., with an adj., could so easily be fig., e.g. κακὴ γλῶσσα = 'slander': so κερτόμιοι γλῶσσαι = 'taunts.'

963 f. παύεσκε: see on 950.—ἐνθέους γυναῖκας: the Maenads attendant on Dionysus, cp. 1128, 1150, *O. T.* 212, *O. C.* 680.—εὔιον...πῦρ, the torches which the Bacchanals swing while they raise the cry εὐοῖ. In *O. T.* 211 the god himself is εὔιος. Cp. Eur. *Bacch.* 307 (Dionysus by night on Parnassus) πηδῶντα σὺν πεύκαισι δικόρυφον πλάκα.

965 Μούσας. An interesting illustration is afforded by a sarcophagus in Baumeister's *Denkmaeler*, p. 837. At the centre of the group is the raging Lycurgus, with uplifted axe, about to slay the Dionysiac nymph Ambrosia, who cowers at his feet. A Fury is on each side of him, urging him on. To the right is Dionysus,—about to

There the fierce exuberance of his madness slowly passed away. That man learned to know the god, whom in his frenzy he had provoked with mockeries; for he had sought to quell the god-possessed women, and the Bacchanalian fire; and he angered the Muses that love the flute.

And by the waters of the Dark Rocks, the waters of the twofold sea, 2nd strophe.

thus : παρὰ— | διδύμασ— | ἀκταὶ— | ἠδ' ὁ θρηικῶν— | ἱν'— | δισσοῦσι— | εἶδεν— | τυφλωθὲν— | ἀλαὸν— | ἀραχθὲν— | χείρεσσι . . ἀκμαῖσι. **966** f. παρα δε (sic) κυανεων πελαγεων (note the accent) πετρων | διδύμασ ἀλὸσ L. Brunck omitted πετρῶν. For πελάγεων I conjecture πελάγει. See comment.

---

save the nymph by changing her into a vine; and behind him stand his followers. At the extreme left are three Muses—Urania, with globe; Clio, with roll; Euterpè, prob. with flutes. (Zoega seems clearly right in this explaining the three women: others have made them Moirae.)—The close relation of Dionysus with the Muses is marked by one of his Attic titles, Μελπόμενος (Paus. 1. 2. 5), as conversely Apollo had the title Διονυσόδοτος (id. 1. 31. 4). Muses were sometimes said to have nursed him. (Cp. Welcker, *Götterl.* 2. 611.)

The monuments relating to the myth of Lycurgus have been critically treated by Michaelis (*Annal. Inst.* 1871, pp. 248—270). The Italian vase-paintings follow a version different from that of Soph., viz. that the frenzy of Lycurgus was wreaked on his own son and wife. A large Neapolitan vase gives two pictures: in one, we see his murderous rage; in the other, Dionysus sits on his throne in calm majesty, stroking his panther.

966 Cleopatra is the third example. Her father was the wind-god, Boreas: her mother, the Athenian Oreithyia, whom he carried off to his wild home in Thrace. Cleopatra married Phineus, king of the Thracian Salmydessus, on the W. coast of the Euxine, not far from the entrance to the Bosporus. She bore him two sons. He afterwards put her away, and imprisoned her. Her imprisonment is not directly mentioned here : but cp. Diod. 4. 44, who says of Heracles, when serving with the Argonauts, τὴν Κλεοπάτραν ἐκ τῆς φυλακῆς προαγαγεῖν. Phineus then married Eidothea, sister of Cadmus. Eidothea put out the eyes of Cleopatra's two sons, and caused them also to be imprisoned.

It is the fate of Cleopatra herself which Soph. means to compare with Antigone's: this is plain from 986. The fate of the sons is made so prominent only because nothing else could give us so strong a sense of the savage hatred which pursued the mother.

Soph. supposes the outline of the story to be familiar. Cleopatra has already been divorced and imprisoned. The poet chooses the moment at which Cleopatra's sons are being blinded by Eidothea, with the sharp shuttle in her blood-stained hands. Ares, the god of cruel bloodshed, beholds with joy a deed so worthy of his Thracian realm.

The name of Cleopatra (like that of Capaneus, 133) is not mentioned. Two strophes are given to this theme, partly, perh., as having an Attic interest (982). Soph. wrote two plays called Φινεύς. We know only that Cleopatra's sons were there called Ὄαρθος (? Παρθένιος H. Weil) and Κράμβος: and that the subsequent blindness of Phineus was represented as a punishment of his cruelty (schol. Apoll. Rhod. 2. 178). Eidothea was mentioned by Soph. in his Τυμπανισταί (schol. on 980),—a play which perh. concerned the Dionysiac worship, since the τύμπανον (kettle-drum) was used in his ὄργια as well as in those of Cybelè. Another version called her Idaea, daughter of Dardanus.

παρὰ δὲ Κυανεᾶν πελάγει 8. ἁλός. For the double possessive gen., cp. 795, 929. πελάγει...ἁλός, as Eur. *Tro.* 88 πέλαγος Αἰγαίας ἁλός, the Homeric ἁλὸς ἐν πελάγεσσιν, etc. The rocky islets on the N. side of the entrance from the Euxine to the Bosporus were regularly called Κυάνεαι simply (without νῆσοι or πέτραι, Her. 4. 85). L's πετρῶν has long been recognised as a gloss. But Wieseler's change

2 ἀκταὶ Βοσπόριαι †ἠδ' ὁ Θρῃκῶν — ◡ —
3 Σαλμυδησσός, ἵν' ἀγχίπολις Ἄρης   970
4 δισσοῖσι Φινείδαις
5 εἶδεν ἀρατὸν ἕλκος
6 τυφλωθὲν ἐξ ἀγρίας δάμαρτος,
7 ἀλαὸν ἀλαστόροισιν ὀμμάτων κύκλοις,
8 *ἀραχθέντων ὑφ' αἱματηραῖς   975
9 χείρεσσι καὶ κερκίδων ἀκμαῖσιν.

968 ff. ἀκταὶ βοσπόριαι | ἠδ' ὁ θρῃκῶν σαλμυδησσὸσ | L. For ἠδ' (ἠδ' r) Triclinius wrote ἰδ'. Blaydes suggests ἰν' or καί: Semitelos τ' ἰδ'. After Θρῃκῶν, Boeckh supplies ἄξενος: Meineke, ἠἱών: H. Schütz, δύσχιμος.—ἰν' ἀγχἰπολια ἀρης L, with •ὀν• written over ἰν' by S. Of the later MSS., some (as A, V) have ἀγχί-πολις, others (as L², Vat., Vat. b, Aug. b, Dresd. a) ἀγχίπτολις. Dindorf

oi πελαγέων into σπιλάδων is also erroneous.

L's accent, πελάγων, points to the truth,—as similar small hints in that MS. have been found to do elsewhere also (cp. on 467; and *O. C.* 1113 n.). The correction, πελάγει, is so easy that it may well have occurred to others; but I have not met with it. It removes the difficulty (insuperable, to my mind) of παρά with the genitive here. Those who read κυανεᾶν σπιλάδων, or κυανέων πελαγέων, are forced to take παρά as = 'extending from the dark rocks (etc.) are the coasts.' But such a use is wholly unparalleled. As to 1123, see n. there. In Pind. *P.* 1 75 ἄρεομαι | πὰρ μὲν Σαλαμῖνος Ἀθαναίων χάριν = 'from Salamis' (i.e., by celebrating it). In Ar. *Ach.* 68 the Ravenna has ἐτρυχόμεσθα παρὰ Καύστριον | πεδίων ὁδοιπλανοῦντες, while other MSS. have διά (also with gen. plur.); but there παρὰ Καύστριον | πεδίον (Dindorf) is certain. In Pind. *P.* 3. 60 γνῶντα τὸ πὰρ ποδός, 'having learned one's nearest business' (cp. *P.* 10. 63), παρά has its normal sense,—'that which begins *from* one's foot,' = which is directly before one in one's path. The corruption of πελάγει into πελαγέων naturally followed that of Κυανεᾶν into κυανέων.

967 f. ἀκταὶ Βοσπόριαι, *sc.* εἰσί (cp. 948 n.). The Κυάνεαι are at the point where the coast of the Bosporus joins the western coast of the Euxine. The city Salmydessus stood just s. of the promontory of Thynias, about 60 miles N.W. of the entrance of the Bosporus, near the modern Midjeh. The name Salmydessus was given also to the tract of coast ex-

tending s. of the town.—After Θρῃκῶν a cretic has been lost (= -τον γοναν in 980). Boeckh supplies it with ἄξενος, which is at least simple and fitting. Cp. Aesch. *P. V.* 726 τραχεῖα πόντου Σαλμυδησσία γνάθος | ἐχθρόξενος ναύταισι, μητρυιὰ νεῶν. Schütz, referring to the schol. on 969, πέ-λαγος δέ ἐστι δυσχείμερον περὶ Θράκην, proposes δύσχιμος ('dangerous'), a word used by Aesch. and Eur., though not by Soph. But the want of a verb is somewhat awkward. Can the missing word be κλῄζεται? (Cp. *O. T.* 1451 n.: and for the sing., below, 1133.) Ships often grounded on the shallows (τέναγος) which stretched from Salmydessus into the Euxine. The Thracians had set up slabs (στῆλαι), marking off the coast into allotments for wrecking purposes. Before this was done, there had been much bloodshed between rival wreckers (Xen. *An.* 7. 5. 13).—The MS. †ηδ' cannot be right. A short syll. is required (= the last syll. of ἔχοντες in 980). In my first ed. I adopted ἰδ', the conjecture of Triclinius. Prof. Tyrrell remarks (*Class. Review* vol. II. p. 141) that ἰδέ is not elsewhere elided in classical poetry. As ἠδέ could be elided, that may be accidental. Still, it should be noted along with the other facts,—that ἰδέ occurs nowhere else in tragedy, and that the hiatus after Βοσπόριαι must be excused, as in epic verse, by the ictus before caesura (*Introd. to Homer* p. 194): cp. *Il.* 14. 175 ἀλειψαμένη, ἰδὲ χαίτας | πεξαμένη. On the whole, I now prefer to leave ἠδ', with an obelus. Either Βοσπόριαι καὶ ὁ or Βοσπόριαι θ' ὅ τε would be possible.

are the shores of Bosporus, and Thracian Salmydessus; where Ares, neighbour to the city, saw the accurst, blinding wound dealt to the two sons of Phineus by his fierce wife,—the wound that brought darkness to those vengeance-craving orbs, smitten with her bloody hands, smitten with her shuttle for a dagger.

(formerly) conject. ἀγχουρος. Seyffert, ἀρχέπολις. **972** ἀρατὸν] Hermann conject. ἀρακτὸν: Schneidewin, ἀραῖον. **973** τυφλωθὲν MSS.: ἀραχθὲν Wunder. **975** ἀραχθὲν ἐγχέων L: the later MSS. have either this or ἀραχθὲν ἀχέων. Seidler and Lachmann restored ἀραχθέντων. Nauck would prefer τυφλωθέντων here, and ἀραχθὲν in 973.

970 ἀγχίπολις Ἄρης. This reading (L's) agrees metrically with the antistrophe (981 ἀρχαιογόνων), if we suppose the 2nd and 3rd syllables of ἀγχίπολις to represent a resolved long syllable. Such a resolution is rare, but not unexampled: see on 798. We could avoid it by reading, with Gleditsch, ἀκταὶ Βοσπόριαι, ἵν' ὁ Θρηκῶν ἄξενος | Σαλμυδησσὸς Ἄρης τ' ἀγχίπολις. But (a) this does not explain how ᾗδ' came into the MSS.: and (b) it is evidently better to say, 'where Ares saw,' than, 'where Salmydessus and Ares saw.' The reference to the god's cruel joy would thus lose much of its force. If, on the other hand, ἀγχίπολις is read, then Ἄρης has ᾱ, and in 981 we must suppose the loss of a syllable after ἀρχαιογόνων. But such a loss is very improbable: that verse appears sound. Neither ἀγχουρος nor ἀρχίπολις has any likelihood.—Ares is 'neighbour to the city' of Salmydessus because his home is in Thrace (Il. 13. 301, etc.). There may also be a special reference to some local shrine. 'He saw the wound dealt': i.e., it was a deed such as he loves to see.

971 f. Φινεΐδαις, dat. of interest, with τυφλωθέν.—ἀρατόν, accursed, bringing a curse on the authors of the wound. In his dramatic treatment of the story, Soph. had connected this blinding of the sons with the punishment of blindness which the gods afterwards inflicted on Phineus himself (schol. Apoll. Rhod. 2. 178).—Ἕλκος τυφλωθέν. τυφλοῦν ἕλκος = to inflict a blinding wound. Cp. Ai. 55 ἔκειρε... φόνου, he dealt death by hewing down. Eur. Suppl. 1205 τρώσῃς φόνον, (wherever) thou dealest the death-wound. Verg. Aen. 11. 82 caeso sparsuros sanguine flammam (caedere sanguinem = to shed blood by cutting). In such pregnant idioms the special verb = a general verb plus the partic. of the special verb used

instrumentally: e.g., τυφλῶ ἕλκος = ποιῶ ἕλκος τυφλῶν.—ᾗ here = ὑπό of the direct agent: for, as κερκίδων indicates, she did it with her own hand. Distinguish ἐκ Διονύσου in 957 (by his order).

974 ἀλαόν...κύκλοις, sightless for the orbs, i.e., making them sightless. Cp. Pind. O. 1. 26 καθαροῦ λέβητος, the purifying cauldron.—ἀλαστόροισιν. The form ἀλάστορος was used by Aesch. as = ἀλάστωρ (fr. 87 πρευμενὴς ἀ., fr. 286 μέγαν ἀ.). The form may have been generally current, since Pherecydes used Ζεὺς Ἀλάστορος instead of Z. Ἀλάστωρ (Cramer Anecd. 1. 61). The blind orbs are ἀλάστοροι, 'avenging spirits,' in the sense that they mutely appeal to the gods for vengeance.—For the παρήχησις (O. T. 371) Wolff cp. Il. 6. 201 κὰτ πεδίον τὸ Ἀλήϊον οἶος ἀλᾶτο.

975 ἀραχθέντων. So ἀράσσω is used of Oed. striking his eyes with the περόναι (O. T. 1276).—ὑπό with dat. of the instrument, as in the epic ὑπὸ χερσὶ δαμῆναι, O. T. 202 ὑπὸ σῷ φθίσον κεραυνῷ.

976 κερκίδων, poet. plur. for sing., like βωμοί, σκῆπτρα, etc.—The κερκίς (κρέκω, to strike the web in weaving) was 'like a large netting needle' (Rich s.v. radius), 'rather longer than the breadth of the web.' It was used for two purposes. (1) As a rod with which to strike the threads of the woof, in order to condense them. The flat blade called σπάθη was a later substitute. In the modern loom this is done by the moveable bar called the 'batten.' (2) As a shuttle, i.e., an instrument for shooting the threads of the woof (κρόκη) from one side of the loom to the other, between the threads of the warp (στήμων). In the East weavers sometimes use a long reed for both these purposes. Eur. Tro. 198 οὐκ Ἰδαίοις ἱστοῖς κερκίδα δινεύουσ' ἐξαλλάξω ('no more,

ἀντ. β'.   κατὰ δὲ τακόμενοι μέλεοι μελέαν πάθαν   977
   2 κλαῖον, ματρὸς ἔχοντες ἀνύμφευτον γονάν·   980
   3 ἁ δὲ σπέρμα μὲν ἀρχαιογόνων
   4 ἄντασ' Ἐρεχθεϊδᾶν,
   5 τηλεπόροις δ' ἐν ἄντροις
   6 τράφη θυέλλαισιν ἐν πατρῴαις,
   7 Βορεάς, ἄμιππος ὀρθόποδος ὑπὲρ πάγου,   985
   8 θεῶν παῖς· ἀλλὰ κἀπ' ἐκείνᾳ
   9 Μοῖραι μακραίωνες ἔσχον, ὦ παῖ.

ΤΕΙΡΕΣΙΑΣ.

   Θήβης ἄνακτες, ἥκομεν κοινὴν ὁδὸν
   δύ' ἐξ ἑνὸς βλέποντε· τοῖς τυφλοῖσι γὰρ
   αὕτη κέλευθος ἐκ προηγητοῦ πέλει.   990
ΚΡ. τί δ' ἔστιν, ὦ γεραιὲ Τειρεσία, νέον;
ΤΕ. ἐγὼ διδάξω, καὶ σὺ τῷ μάντει πιθοῦ.

977—987 L divides thus: κατὰ δὲ— | μελέαν— | κλαῖον— | ἐχον|τεσ— | δὲ σπέρμα — | ἀντασ— | τηλεπόροισ— | τράφη— | βορεάσ— | θεῶν— | μοῖραι . . παῖ. 980 ματρὸς r, πατρὸσ L. Cp. 863. 981 f. Dindorf conject. ἀρχαιογόνοιο | . .

at the loom, will I send the shuttle flying across the warp').—Cp. Eur. *Hec.* 1170, where the women blind Polymestor with their brooches (πόρπαι = περόναι); and *O. T.* 1269 n.

977 f. κατά in tmesis, as *O. T.* 1198, *O. C.* 1689, etc.—κατατακόμενοι alludes to their imprisonment; cp. schol. on 980 τυφλώσασα τοὺς Κλεοπάτρας παῖδας ἐν τάφῳ καθείρξεν.—μέλεοι μελέαν: cp. 156: *O. T.* 479.

980 ματρὸς ἔχοντες ἀν. γονάν, having their origin from an unhappily-married mother. The epithet is made to agree with γονάν, not with ματρός, as in 793, νεῖκος-ἀνδρῶν ξύναιμον: *i.e.*, μητρὸς-γονή, mother-source, forms one notion. For γονάς ἔχειν cp. *O. C.* 972 δς οὔτε βλάστας πω γενεθλίους πατρός, | οὐ μητρὸς εἴχον. For ἀνύμφ., cp. Eur. *Tr.* 144 ἄλοχοι μέλεαι...καὶ δύσνυμφοι: *Hipp.* 757 κακονυμφοτάταν ὄνασιν ('to bless her with a marriage most unblest'). *O. T.* 1214 ἄγαμον γάμον.—The comma should not be placed after ματρός, which is inseparable from the following phrase. Without ματρός, the words ἔχοντες ἀνύμφευτον γονάν could still mean, 'born from one who was unhappily married,' but would be harsh and obscure. The word πάθαν

refers to their own fate. Then ματρὸς... γονάν supplements this by indicating that they mourn for their mother's fate also.

981 f. σπέρμα, acc. of respect; *Od.* 15. 267 ἐξ Ἰθάκης γένος εἰμί.—ἀρχαιογ.: *Ai.* 202 γενεᾶς χθονίων ἀπ' Ἐρεχθειδῶν.—ἄντασ' Ἐρ., attained unto them, could trace her lineage to them,—her mother Oreithyia being the daughter of Erechtheus. Remark that the acc. σπέρμα mitigates the boldness of ἄντασε, and also suggests its primary meaning—viz., that the genealogy is carried back to a point at which it *meets* the Erechtheid line. Cp. Her. 2. 143 (Hecataeus) γενεηλογήσαντί τε ἑωυτὸν καὶ ἀναδήσαντι τὴν πατριὴν ἐς ἑκκαιδέκατον θεόν.

983 τηλεπόροις, merely poet. for 'distant'; lit., to which it is a far journey. Not (I think), 'spacious' (*i.e.* 'in which one can go far'): nor, 'extending far into the mountains.' So in *Ai.* 564, τηλωπὸς οἰχνεῖ, the adj. is merely 'distant'; it has not its full sense, 'seen afar.' Boreas carried Oreithyia to a region of Thrace which the poets called 'Sarpedon' (we see the association with ἁρπάζω)—not, seemingly, the promontory called 'Sarpedonion,' on the s. coast, but in the wilds

Pining in their misery, they bewailed their cruel doom, those ₂nd
sons of a mother hapless in her marriage; but she traced her anti-
descent from the ancient line of the Erechtheidae; and in far-strophe.
distant caves she was nursed amid her father's storms, that child
of Boreas, swift as a steed over the steep hills, a daughter of
gods; yet upon her also the grey Fates bore hard, my
daughter.

Enter TEIRESIAS, *led by a boy, on the spectators' right.*

TE. Princes of Thebes, we have come with linked steps,
both served by the eyes of one; for thus, by a guide's help, the
blind must walk.
CR. And what, aged Teiresias, are thy tidings?
TE. I will tell thee; and do thou hearken to the seer.

Ἐρεχθείδα, reading ἀγχίπτολις in 970.   **984** θυίλλησιν MSS.   **987** ὦ παῖ]
Meineke conject. ὦ Ζεῦ: Bergk, ὦτα.   **990** ἐκ] Blaydes conject. ἦκ.

---

of Haemus. It is of this that Soph. is
thinking here: cp. fr. 575 ἡμεῖς δ' ἐν ἄντροις, ἔνθα Σαρπηδὼν πέτρα. That verse is
from the Τυμπανισταί, in which the story
of Cleopatra was noticed (cp. on 966); and
she was probably the speaker. Oreithyia
bore two sons to Boreas, Calais and
Zetes; and, besides Cleopatra, another
daughter, Chionê.

. **988** ἅμιππος, swift as horses. Cp.
O. T. 466 ἀελλάδων | ἵππων, 'storm-swift
steeds.' In prose ἅμιπποι = foot-soldiers
who, in the Boeotian army, were sometimes told off to run alongside the cavalry
(Thuc. 5. 57, Xen. *H.* 7. 5. 23). Cp.
Theogn. 715 ὠκύτερος δ' εἴησθα πόδας τα-
χεῶν Ἁρπυιῶν | καὶ παίδων Βορέω.—ὀρθό-
ποδος, steep. ὀρθόπους, 'erect upon one's
feet,' seems to be here merely a poet.
equiv. (suggested by metrical convenience)
for ὀρθός. This was the more natural,
since πούς, κνήμη, etc., were so oft. said
of mountains. In *O. T.* 866 ὑψίποδες,
said of the eternal νόμοι, differs from
ὀρθόπους here by implying movement
('of sublime range'). We need not,
then, explain ὀρθόπους as = ὀρθίοις τοῖς τοῦ
ἀναβαίνοντος ποσί.

988 f. κατ' ἐκείνῳ...ἔσχον = καὶ ἐκείνῃ ἔσχον, from the intrans. ἐπέχω as
='to direct (one's course) against a person,' 'to attack him': cp. *Od.* 19. 71
τί μοι ὧδ' ἐπέχεις κεκοτηότι θυμῷ; ('assail

me'): ib. 22. 75 ἐπ' αὐτῷ πάντες ἔχωμεν
('let us all have at him').—Others understand, 'extended even to her,' 'reached her,' which mars the personification.—
μακραίωνες: Aesch. *Eum.* 172 παλαι-
γενεῖς...Μοῖραι.

988—1114 Fifth ἐπεισόδιον. Teiresias denounces the divine wrath. Creon,
terror-stricken, hastens to bury Polyneices and to release Antigone.

988 f. ἄνακτες: cp. 843, 940.—86' ἐξ
ἑνὸς βλ., two seeing by the agency of
one (ἐκ as in 973): cp. *O. C.* 33 τῆς
ὑπέρ τ' ἐμοῦ | αὑτῆς θ' ὁρώσης. The
words would usu. mean, 'two seeing,
where only one saw formerly.' Cp. *O. C.*
1764, where the regular sense of πράσσειν
καλῶς, 'to fare well,' has not hindered
the poet from using it as = 'to do rightly.'

990 αὕτη κ., the blind have this
kind of walking appointed for them,—
viz., walking with the help of a guide.
αὕτη κ. = αὕτη ἡ κ. (*O. C.* 471): κέλευθος
is not predicate (like ταῦλαν in *O. C.*
88), as if the sense were, 'this (αὕτη for
τοῦτο) is walking for the blind,—viz. to
walk with a guide.' We do not need
the art. ἡ with ἐκ, because πέλει = not
simply 'is,' but, 'is possible.' Cp. *O. C.*
848 οὐκουν ποτ' ἐκ (by means of) τούτοιν
γε μὴ σκήπτροιν ἔτι | ὁδοιπορήσῃς (the
blind Oed.'s daughters).

991 τί δ' ἐστίν: cp. 20 n.

KP. οὔκουν πάρος γε σῆς ἀπεστάτουν φρενός.
ΤΕ. τοιγὰρ δι' ὀρθῆς τήνδ' *ἐναυκλήρεις πόλιν.
KP. ἔχω πεπονθὼς μαρτυρεῖν ὀνήσιμα.   995
ΤΕ. φρόνει βεβὼς αὖ νῦν ἐπὶ ξυροῦ τύχης.
KP. τί δ' ἔστιν; ὡς ἐγὼ τὸ σὸν φρίσσω στόμα.
ΤΕ. γνώσει, τέχνης σημεῖα τῆς ἐμῆς κλύων.
εἰς γὰρ παλαιὸν θᾶκον ὀρνιθοσκόπον
ἵζων, ἵν' ἦν μοι παντὸς οἰωνοῦ λιμήν,   1000
ἀγνῶτ' ἀκούω φθόγγον ὀρνίθων, κακῷ
κλάζοντας οἴστρῳ καὶ βεβαρβαρωμένῳ·
καὶ σπῶντας ἐν χηλαῖσιν ἀλλήλους φοναῖς
ἔγνων· πτερῶν γὰρ ῥοῖβδος οὐκ ἄσημος ἦν.
εὐθὺς δὲ δείσας ἐμπύρων ἐγευόμην   1005
βωμοῖσι παμφλέκτοισιν· ἐκ δὲ θυμάτων
Ἥφαιστος οὐκ ἔλαμπεν, ἀλλ' ἐπὶ σποδῷ

994 ναυκληρεῖσ L: ἐναυκλήρεις Valckenaer. **996** τύχη] Semitelos conject. κυρεῖς. Blaydes, νῦν ἀκμῆς ἐπὶ ξυροῦ. **998** σημεῖα τῆς ἐμῆς r: τῆς ἐμῆς σημεῖα L

993 f. οὔκουν...γε: cp. 321 n.—δι' ὀρθῆς, sc. ὁδοῦ. A rare instance of the fem. adj. in such a phrase with διά, which regularly takes a subst. (742 n.); but it follows the analogy of the freq. phrases with ἐκ, as ἐξ εὐθείας: Tr. 395 ἐκ ταχείας, 727 ἐξ ἑκουσίας: Thuc. 3. 92 ἐκ καινῆς: Her. 5. 116 ἐκ νέης, 6. 85 ἐξ ὑστέρης, 8. 6 ἐκ τῆς ἀντίης, etc.—ἐναυκλήρεις is right. The seer hopes, indeed, that the mischief can still be repaired (1025 ff.), but he thinks that Creon has made a disastrous mistake (1015). He could hardly say, then, δι' ὀρθῆς...ναυκλήρεις. Creon has only just become king; but he had formerly been regent for some years (cp. O. T. 1418). Aesch. has the verb in this fig. sense (Th. 652). Cp. 167 ὤρθου: O. T. 104 ἀπευθύνειν: ib. 923 κυβερνήτην.

995 πεπονθὼς ὀνήσιμα, ἔχω μαρτυρεῖν (πεπονθέναι). We could say, μαρτυρῶ σοι εὐεργετήσαντι (like σύνοιδα): but less well, μαρτυρῶ εὖ πεπονθώς. Cp. O. C. 1128 εἰδὼς δ' ἀμύνω τοῖσδε τοῖς λόγοις τάδε, with like emphasis on the partic., 'I have felt these benefits which I thus requite.'

996 φρόνει βεβώς, bethink thee that thou art placed. O. C. 1358 ἐν πόνῳ | ...βεβηκώς, n. Il. 10. 173 νῦν γὰρ δὴ πάντεσσιν ἐπὶ ξυροῦ ἵσταται ἀκμῆς, | ἢ μάλα λυγρὸς ὄλεθρος Ἀχαιοῖς, ἠὲ βιῶναι. Eur.

H. F. 630 ὧδ' ἔβητ' ἐπὶ ξυροῦ; Helen. 897 ἐπ' ἀκμῆς εἰμι κατθανόντ' ἰδεῖν.—τύχης, interpreting ξυροῦ, adds dignity and solemnity to the phrase.

997 ὡς, exclamatory. El. 1112 τί δ' ἔστιν, ὦ ξέν'; ὥς μ' ὑπέρχεται φόβος.

999 f. θᾶκον. Paus. (9. 16. 1) saw at Thebes, near the temple of Zeus Ammon, οἰωνοσκοπεῖον...Τειρεσίου καλούμενον. Near it was a shrine of Τύχη.—λιμήν, a place to which the birds came: schol. ὅρμος καὶ ἕδρα, ὅπου πάντα τὰ ὄρνεα προσέρχονται. Cp. Eur. Or. 1077 καὶ δῶμα πατρὸς καὶ μέγας πλούτου λιμήν ('receptacle'): Aesch. applied the same phrase to Persia (Pers. 250). Omens were taken, not only from the flight of birds, but also from the positions in which they settled,—from their sounds,—and from their mode of feeding. The λιμήν means a place to which they were lured by food, so that their συνεδρίαι (Aesch. P. V. 492), and the other signs, could be noted. Cp. Arist. H. A. 9. 1 ὅθεν καὶ τὰς διεδρίας καὶ τὰς συνεδρίας οἱ μάντεις λαμβάνουσι, διεδρα μὲν τὰ πολέμια τιθέντες, σύνεδρα δὲ τὰ εἰρηνοῦντα πρὸς ἄλληλα.—Herwerden conjectures οὐρανοῦ λιμήν, understanding a space of sky chosen as a field of augural observation (templum).

1001 f. κακῷ, ill-omened (O. C. 1433).

CR. Indeed, it has not been my wont to slight thy counsel.
TE. Therefore didst thou steer our city's course aright.
CR. I have felt, and can attest, thy benefits.
TE. Mark that now, once more, thou standest on fate's fine edge.
CR. What means this? How I shudder at thy message!
TE. Thou wilt learn, when thou hearest the warnings of mine art. As I took my place on mine old seat of augury, where all birds have been wont to gather within my ken, I heard a strange voice among them; they were screaming with dire, feverish rage, that drowned their language in a jargon; and I knew that they were rending each other with their talons, murderously; the whirr of wings told no doubtful tale.

Forthwith, in fear, I essayed burnt-sacrifice on a duly kindled altar: but from my offerings the Fire-god showed no flame;

(cp. comment. on 106). **999** ὀρνιθοσκόπον] Nauck conject. οἰωνοσκόπον.
1000 οἰωνοῦ] Herwerden conject. οὐρανοῦ. **1002** Wecklein conject. βεβαρβαρωμένως: Usener, βεβαρβαρωμένα.

—οἴστρῳ, 'gad-fly,' then fig., 'rage,' a word which often suggests divine stimulation: as Heracles asks, ποῦ δ' οἶστρος ἡμᾶς ἔλαβε; (Eur. *H. F.* 1144).—πλάζοντας, since φθόγγον ὀρνίθων = ὄρνιθας φθεγγομένους: *Il.* 17. 755 τῶν δ' ὥστε ψαρῶν νέφος ἔρχεται ἠὲ κολοιῶν | οὖλον κεκληγοντες: *Od.* 12. 181 ἀλλ' ὅτε τόσσον ἀπῆν (sc. ἡ νηῦς) ὅσσον τε γέγωνε βοήσας, | ῥίμφα διώκοντες.—βεβαρβαρωμένῳ. To the seer, the voices of birds were usually εὔσημοι (1021). Conversely the sound of a strange language is likened to the twittering of birds: Her. 2. 57 ἕως δὲ ἐβαρβάριζε (ἡ γυνή), ὄρνιθος τρόπον ἐδόκεέ σφι φθέγγεσθαι. Aesch. used χελιδονίζειν as = βαρβαρίζειν (fr. 440, cp. *Ag.* 1050).

1003 ἐν χηλαῖσιν, 'with' them: 764 n. —φοναῖς, an adverbial dat. of manner, 'murderously.' Cp. *O. C.* 1318 εὔχεται κατασκαφῇ | Καπανεὺς τὸ Θήβης ἄστυ δηώσειν πυρί, where the first dat. is one of manner, like φοναῖς here, and the second (instrumental) answers to ἐν χηλαῖσιν. Elsewhere the Attic use of the subst. is limited to the phrase ἐν φοναῖς (696 n.). The Schol. has φοναῖς ταῖς αἱμακτικαῖς: as though it were from an adj. φονός. So some recent edd. take it. Such an adj. could have come from the rt. φεν, but there is no trace of it.

1004 The feuds and friendships of birds (ἔχθραι τε καὶ στέργηθρα Aesch. *P. V.* 492) were among the signs noted by augurs. In this case there was a vague omen of bloodshed (φοναῖς), but no clear sign. The seer now sought further light by another mode of divination.—ἐμπύρων, sc. ἱερῶν, burnt-sacrifice; where the omen was given by the manner in which the fire dealt with the offering. Eur. *Suppl.* 155 μάντεις δ' ἐπῆλθες, ἐμπύρων τ' εἶδες φλόγα; *Phoen.* 954 ἐμπύρῳ χρῆται τέχνῃ. *I. T.* 16 εἰς ἐμπυρ' ἦλθε (had recourse to). This was ἡ δι' ἐμπύρων μαντεία, ignispicium, while ἱεροσκοπία = haruspicina, divination by inspecting entrails. In Aesch. *P. V.*, 488—499, vv. 488—492 concern ὀρνιθομαντεία: vv. 493—5, ἱεροσκοπία: and vv. 496—9, ἔμπυρα.—ἐγευόμην, proceeded to make trial of: *Tr.* 1101 μόχθων μυρίων ἐγευσάμην: Plat. *Rep.* 475 C ταντὸς μαθήματος γεύεσθαι.

1005 παμφλέκτοισι, fully kindled. Fuel was placed around the offerings on the altar, and ignited at several points. The epithet marks that the failure of the rite was not due to any negligence.—θυμάτων. The offering consisted of thighbones cut from a sheep (or ox), with some of the flesh adhering to them, and wrapped round with a double covering of fat. On the top of these thigh-bones were laid parts of the victim's intestines (σπλάγχνα), including the gall-bladder (χολή).

1007 Ἥφαιστος = πῦρ (n. on 110 ff.). It was a good sign if the fire at once seized on the offering, and blazed up in clear flames (Apoll. Rhod. 1. 436 σέλας... | πάντοσε λαμπόμενον θυέων ἄπο). It was

---

12—2

μυδῶσα κηκὶς μηρίων ἐτήκετο
κάτυφε κἀνέπτυε, καὶ μετάρσιοι
χολαὶ διεσπείροντο, καὶ καταρρυεῖς   1010
μηροὶ καλυπτῆς ἐξέκειντο πιμελῆς·
τοιαῦτα παιδὸς τοῦδ᾽ ἐμάνθανον πάρα
φθίνοντ᾽ ἀσήμων ὀργίων μαντεύματα·
ἐμοὶ γὰρ οὗτος ἡγεμών, ἄλλοις δ᾽ ἐγώ.
καὶ ταῦτα τῆς σῆς ἐκ φρενὸς νοσεῖ πόλις.   1015

1013 φθίνοντ᾽] Wecklein conject. φανέντ᾽: Semitelos φανθέντα, with Nauck's σεμνῶν for ἀσήμων.—μαντεύματα] Nauck μαγεύματα: M. Schmidt λατρεύματα.

a bad sign, if the fire was smothered in smoke, or played feebly around the flesh without consuming it. See Eur. *Ph.* 1255 μάντεις δὲ μῆλ᾽ ἔσφαζον, ἐμπύρους τ᾽ ἀκμὰς | ῥήξεις τ᾽ ἐνώμων, ὑγρότητ᾽ ἐναντίαν, | ἄκραν τε λαμπάδ᾽, ἢ δυοῖν ὅρους ἔχει, | νίκης τε σῆμα καὶ τὸ τῶν ἡσσωμένων: the seers 'were watching for *points* of flame, or for *breaks* in it,—such flickering as portends evil'; *i.e.*, they were watching to see whether it would blaze up or die down. The ἄκρα λαμπάς is prob. the highest point of the fire, which, if towards the right side, meant victory; if towards the left, defeat. So Statius, *Theb.* 10. 599, where Teiresias offers ἔμπυρα, and his daughter reports the signs to him (as the παῖς does here): *Sanguineos flammarum apices* (= ἐμπύρους ἀκμάς) *geminumque per aras* | *Ignem, et clara tamen mediae fastigia lucis* (= ἄκραν λαμπάδα) | *Orta docet: tunc in speciem serpentis inanem* | *Ancipiti gyro volvi* ('as if creeping on its way without an aim, the fire played timidly around the offering'). In Seneca *Oed.* 307 Teiresias asks, *Quid flamma? Larga iamne comprendit dapes?* | *Utrumne clarus ignis et nitidus stetit,* | *Rectusque purum verticem caelo tulit,* | *An latera circum serpit incertus viae,* | *Et fluctuante turbidus fumo labat?*

1008 f. The fat wrapped about the thigh-bones ought to have caught fire, when the flesh on the bones would have been burned, and the bones themselves calcined. But here there was no flame; the kindled fuel lay in smouldering embers (σποδός). The heat caused a fatty moisture to exude from the covering of the thigh-bones. Trickling forth on the embers, this moisture emitted smoke, and sputtered as it threw parti-

cles of the fat upwards. The gall-bladder, too, which lay on the top of the thigh-bones, instead of catching fire, was gradually inflated by the heat, till it burst, scattering the gall into the air. And now the melting of the fat which covered the thigh-bones had gone so far that it was no longer a covering, but merely a liquid that was streaming off them, while they themselves were left naked and intact. So utterly had the gods refused the offering.

μυδῶσα: cp. 410: *O. T.* 1278 φόνου μυδώσας σταγόνας.—κηκὶς μηρίων, a moisture exuding from them. For μηρία see on 1011. Cp. Aesch. *Cho.* 268 ἐν κηκῖδι τισσήρει φλογός, pitchy ooze of flame, *i.e.*, the funeral-fire of pine-wood from which pitch oozes. We might perh. join μηρίων ἐτήκετο, 'was distilled from them': but the other constr. is simpler, and τήκεσθαί τινος is not found elsewhere.—ἐτήκετο here = exuded: it goes with ἐπὶ σποδῷ (the embers of the fuel placed around the offering).—ἀνέπτυε, as particles of the fat crackled and were tossed upward at contact with the smouldering fire.

1010 χολαί. Arist. always uses the sing. χολή for the gall-bladder. In Plat. *Tim.* 82 E χολάς = 'kinds of bile,' the χολῆς εἴδη of 83 c. Here there was a metrical motive (διεσπείροντο) for the plur., which denotes not merely the gall-bladder, but also the gall dispersed from it. The gall-bladder, and the lobe of the liver, afforded omens, by colour and form, in ἱεροσκοπία (1005 n.): Aesch. *P. V.* 495 χολῆς λοβοῦ τε ποικίλην εὐμορφίαν: cp. Eur. *El.* 827 ff. But here, in ἔμπυρα, the χολή was simply a part of the burnt-offering,—added to the μηρία, because otherwise associated with divina-

a dank moisture, oozing from the thigh-flesh, trickled forth upon the embers, and smoked, and sputtered; the gall was scattered to the air; and the streaming thighs lay bared of the fat that had been wrapped round them.

Such was the failure of the rites by which I vainly asked a sign, as from this boy I learned; for he is my guide, as I am guide to others. And 'tis thy counsel that hath brought this sickness on our state.

1015 ταῦτα had been omitted in L, but the first hand has added it above the line.

---

tion. Cp: the unknown poet in Clemens Alex. *Strom.* p. 851 (it is vain to think that the gods rejoice) ὀστῶν ἀσάρκων καὶ χολῆς πυρουμένης. So, too, Menander *ap.* Athen. 146 E οἱ δὲ τὴν ὀσφὺν ἄκραν | καὶ τὴν χολὴν ὀστᾶ τ' ἄβρωτα τοῖς θεοῖς | ἐπιθέντες αὐτοὶ τἄλλα καταπίνουσ' ἀεί.

κατερρύει, running down, dripping, with the fat which was melting off them: schol. καταρρεόμενοι, καθυγραινόμενοι. This use of the adj. is parallel with a frequent use of the verb, as Eur. *Tro* 15 θεῶν ἀνάκτορα | φόνῳ καταρρεῖ: *Il.* 8. 65 ῥέε δ' αἵματι γαῖα: Eur. *Bacch.* 142 ῥεῖ δὲ γάλακτι πέδον, etc.—καταρρυεῖς could also mean, 'slipping down'; but it does not appear that the μηροί were displaced; they were merely bared.

1011 μηροί=μηρίων in 1008,—thigh-bones, with some flesh on them. μηρός is the ordinary word for 'thigh.' μηρία was the sacrificial word, denoting thigh-bones, with so much flesh as the sacrificer chose to leave upon them. The tendency to give the gods more bone than meat is noticed by the poets quoted on v. 1010 (ὀστῶν ἀσάρκων—ὀστᾶ ἄβρωτα), and by Hes. *Th.* 556 (where men offer ὀστέα λευκά to the gods,— as it is implied in the story there told, of Prometheus giving the worst parts of the ox to Zeus, and keeping the best for men. Since the bone was an essential part of the offering, μηρία cannot be merely, 'slices cut from the thighs.' In the Homeric phrase, κατὰ πίονα μηρία καίειν, the word means, like μηροί here, thigh-bones wrapped in fat, the κνίσῃ... μέλα συγκαλυπτά of Aesch. *P. V.* 496. In *Od.* 3. 456 ἐκ μηρία τάμνον | πάντα κατὰ μοῖραν, the phrase is equiv. to the μηροὺς ἐξέταμον of the *Il.* (1. 460 etc.); i.e., μηρία includes the bones. Only one ox is there in question, but πάντα = 'completely.' The Hom. μῆρα = μηρία (*Il.*

l. 464).—καλυπτῆς = 'which had been wrapped round them'; cp. *Il.* 21. 321 τόσσην οἱ ἄσιν καθύπερθε καλύψω, 'so thick a covering of silt will I lay on him.' This is better than to make the adj. active, 'covering,' like μεμπτός, 'blaming' (*Tr.* 446: cp. *O. T.* 969 n.). —πιμελῆς (πῖων), prop., soft fat (*adeps*), as dist. from στέαρ, stiff fat, tallow (*sebum*). The fat was laid in a double layer round the μηρία: *Il.* 1. 460 μηρούς τ' ἐξέταμον κατά τε κνίσῃ ἐκάλυψαν, | δίπτυχα ποιήσαντες. So human bones are wrapped δίπλακι δημῷ, *Il.* 23. 243.— ἐξέκειντο. lay outside of, *i.e.*, had been bared of, the fat.

1012 f. τοιαῦτα, adverbially with φθίνοντα: cp. 848 οἷα n.—ὀργίων μαντεύματα, 'oracles derived from rites,' —the predictions which he could have made if the rites had given him a sign. They gave none; and so his hopes of reading the future came to nought (φθίνοντα: cp. *O. T.* 906 φθίνοντα... | θέσφατα). Cp. *Tr.* 765 (where Heracles offers burnt sacrifice) ὅπως δὲ σεμνῶν ὀργίων ἐδαίετο | φλὸξ αἱματηρά.—ἀσήμων, not giving the φλογωτὰ σήματα (Aesch. *P. V.* 498) which burnt offerings can yield. Such signs might be good or evil, according to the aspects of the fire (cp. 1007 n.). But here the fire had refused to burn at all. Like the birds, these rites also had left him without any definite sign—though with a strengthened presentiment of evil.

1014 ἡγεμών. Cp. Statius *Theb.* 10. 603: the daughter of Teiresias describes the omens to him, *patriasque illuminat umbras.*

1015 ἐκ, of cause, as *O. C.* 620 ἐκ σμικροῦ λόγου. Cp. 957, 973.—φρενός, counsel, as 993.—νοσεῖ, *i.e.*, has incurred a μίασμα: cp. 1141.

βωμοὶ γὰρ ἡμῖν ἐσχάραι τε παντελεῖς
πλήρεις ὑπ' οἰωνῶν τε καὶ κυνῶν βορᾶς
τοῦ δυσμόρου πέπτωτος Οἰδίπου γόνου·
κᾆτ' οὐ δέχονται θυστάδας λιτὰς ἔτι
θεοὶ παρ' ἡμῶν οὐδὲ μηρίων φλόγα,   1020
οὐδ' ὄρνις εὐσήμους ἀπορροιβδεῖ βοάς,
ἀνδροφθόρου βεβρῶτες αἵματος λίπος.
ταῦτ' οὖν, τέκνον, φρόνησον. ἀνθρώποισι γὰρ
τοῖς πᾶσι κοινόν ἐστι τοὐξαμαρτάνειν·
ἐπεὶ δ' ἁμάρτῃ, κεῖνος οὐκέτ' ἔστ' ἀνὴρ   1025
ἄβουλος οὐδ' ἄνολβος, ὅστις ἐς κακὸν
πεσὼν ἀκεῖται μηδ' ἀκίνητος πέλει.
αὐθαδία τοι σκαιότητ' ὀφλισκάνει.
ἀλλ' εἶκε τῷ θανόντι, μηδ' ὀλωλότα

1016 f. παντελεῖς] In L εἰ has been made from η: over which ει had been written. So in 1017 πλήρεις from πλήρης.   1021 εὐσήμους] In L there has been an erasure of two (or three) letters after εὐ. Nauck conj. οὐδ' αἰσίους ῥοιβδοῦσιν ὄρνιθες βοάς.   1022 λίπος] Blomfield conject. λίβος.—Blaydes proposes (inter alia) ἀνδρ. βεβρῶτα σώματος λίπος, with δρνε' in 1021.   1025 ἁμάρτῃ L:

1016 βωμοί, the public altars of the gods, usu. raised on a base (κρηπίς) with steps (cp. 854, *O. T.* 182).—ἐσχάραι, portable braziers, used in private houses either for sacrifice to household deities (esp. Ἑστία), or for purposes of cooking. Harpocration *s.v.* quotes Ammonius of Lamprae (an Attic writer of the 1st cent. A.D., who left a treatise Περὶ βωμῶν καὶ θυσιῶν): ἐσχάραν φησὶ καλεῖσθαι τὴν μὴ ἔχουσαν ὕψος,...ἀλλ' ἐπὶ γῆς ἱδρυμένην. It stood on four legs, instead of having a pedestal like the βωμός (Ross *Inscrr.* 3. 52 ἐσχάραν τετράποδον). It was used in sacrifice to the ἥρωες, who, not being θεοί, had no claim to βωμοί: Pollux 1. 8 ἐσχάρα δ' ἰδικῶς δοκεῖ ὠνομάσθαι, ἐφ' ἧς τοῖς ἥρωσιν ἀποθύομεν.—παντελεῖς, in their full tale, 'one and all.' So ὁλόκληροι or ὁλοσχερεῖς could be used, where the notion was that of a total to which no unit was lacking.—Not, 'receiving ἱερὰ τέλεια'; nor, 'serving for all rites' (τέλη).

1017 f. πλήρεις (εἰσίν) are defiled, ὑπ' οἰων. κ. κυνῶν, by birds and dogs, βορᾶς τοῦ...Οἰδ. γόνου, with their food, (torn) from the son of Oed. This sense of πλήρης belongs also to πλέως and μεστός, but esp. to ἀνάπλεως, as to ἀναπίμπλημι. The fig. sense of πλήρεις might

here allow us to take ὑπό with βορᾶς, but it goes more naturally with the agents. For the gen. γόνου, describing the source or material of the βορά, cp. Aesch. *Ag.* 1220 κρεῶν...οἰκείας βορᾶς, food supplied by their own flesh (οἰκείας instead of οἰκείων: cp. above, 793). δυσμόρου, adverbially with πεπτῶτος, instead of δυσμόρως: cp. 823 λιγροτάταν ὀλέσθαι, n.— Two other constructions are possible. (1) τοῦ...γόνου, in appos. with βορᾶς: 'their food,—viz., the son': cp. 1040 βορὰν | φέρειν νιν. But this seems forced, when the reference is to dispersed morsels of his flesh. (2) τοῦ...γόνου as gen. absol., 'as,' or 'since,' he has fallen. Such a gen. absol., however, ought here to express not, 'as he has fallen,' but, 'as he has been left unburied.'

1019 κᾆτ', 'and then,' here = 'and so.' It usually means, 'and after that,' *i.e.*, 'and nevertheless' (*O. C.* 418).— θυστάδας, accompanying sacrifice: Aesch. *Theb.* 269 Ἑλληνικὸν νόμισμα θυστάδος βοῆς. Cp. *Il.* 9. 499 καὶ μὲν τοὺς (the gods) θυέεσσι καὶ εὐχωλῇς ἀγανῇσιν | λοιβῇ τε κνίσῃ τε παρατρωπῶσ' ἄνθρωποι | λισσόμενοι.

1021 f. ὄρνις, as *Il.* 24. 219; *El.* 149; Eur. *H. F.* 72, fr. 637: Ar. *Av.*

For the altars of our city and of our hearths have been tainted,
one and all, by birds and dogs, with carrion from the hapless
corpse, the son of Oedipus: and therefore the gods no more
accept prayer and sacrifice at our hands, or the flame of meat-
offering; nor doth any bird give a clear sign by its shrill cry,
for they have tasted the fatness of a slain man's blood.

Think then, on these things, my son. All men are liable to
err; but when an error hath been made, that man is no longer
witless or unblest who heals the ill into which he hath fallen,
and remains not stubborn. Self-will, we know, incurs the
charge of folly. Nay, allow the claim of the dead; stab not the

ἀμάρτοι ι.—οὐκ ἔστ᾽ L: οὐκέτ᾽ ἔστ᾽ ι.   **1027** ἀκεῖται MSS. ἀκῆται Wunder.—
ἄθνητος L: ἀκίνητος ι. Blaydes conject. ἀνίκητος or ἀνίατος: M. Schmidt, ἀνή-
κεστος.—πέλει L, with η written above by the first band.   **1029** τῷ θανόντι]
Heimsoeth conject. τῷ δέοντι: Nauck, τῷ φρονοῦντι: Wecklein, νουθετοῦντι:

168 (v. l. τίς ὅρνις οὗτος, a quotation
from tragedy: v. l. τίς οὗτος ὅρνις;). But
ὅρνις (Eur. Bacch. 1364, Ar. Av. 833,
etc.) is said to have been normal in Attic.
—The ruggedness of the rhythm gives a
certain impressive slowness, perhaps purposed. When an iambic verse has no
caesura in the 3rd or in the 4th foot, it
almost always has the 'quasi-caesura'
(elision) after the 3rd foot (as if εὐσήμους
were εὐφημοῦσ'). For other exceptions,
cp. Ai. 1091 Μενέλαε, μὴ γνώμας ὑποστή-
σας σοφάς: Ph. 101, 1064, 1369: Aesch.
Pers. 509 Θρῄκην περάσαντες μόγις πολλῷ
πόνῳ.—εὐσήμους: cp. on 1002.—βεβρῶτες, as if πάντες ὄρνιθες σιγῶσι had preceded. Cp. Her. 1. 87 ὡς ὥρα πάντα
μὲν ἄνδρα σβεννύντα τὸ πῦρ, δυναμένους
δὲ οὐκέτι καταλαβεῖν.—ἀνδροφθόρον. ἀν-
δρόφθορον αἷμα = ἀνδρὸς ἐφθαρμένου αἷμα:
cp. Ph. 208 αὐδὰ τρυσάνωρ: O. C. 711, n.
on αὔχημα σκιπτον.

1026 f. ἐπεί, instead of ἐπάν, with
subjunct.: O. C. 1225. The subject to
ἁμάρτῃ (ἀνήρ, or τις) is quickly supplied
by the next clause.—ἀνόλβος, of folly, as
Ai. 1156: so δύσποτμος, O. T. 888.

1027 ἀκεῖται. Il. 13. 115 ἀλλ᾽ ἀκεώ-
μεθα θᾶσσον· ἀκεσταί τοι φρένες ἐσθλῶν.—
ἀκίνητος: cp. O. T. 336 ἄτεγκτος. Plat.
Tim. 51 E τὸ μὲν ἀεὶ μετὰ ἀληθοῦς λόγου,
τὸ δὲ ἄλογον· καὶ τὸ μὲν ἀκίνητον πειθοῖ,
τὸ δὲ μεταπειστόν. Il. 15. 203 ἦ τι μετα-
στρέψεις; στρεπταὶ μέν τε φρένες ἐσθλῶν.

1028 αὐθαδία (poet. for αὐθάδεια),
self-will, incurs the reproach of σκαιότης
(for ἀφλισκάνει cp. 470). As δεξιός is a

quick-witted man, of flexible and receptive
mind, so σκαιός is one whose mental clum-
siness makes him unapt to learn. σκαιότης,
'ineptitude,' is often associated with igno-
rance and with inaccessibility to new ideas.
Cp. Plat. Rep. 411 E; one who omits to
cultivate his mind acts βίᾳ...καὶ ἀγριότητι,
ὥσπερ θηρίον..., καὶ ἐν ἀμαθίᾳ καὶ σκαιό-
τητι μετὰ ἀρρυθμίας τε καὶ ἀχαριστίας ζῇ.
Lys. or. 10 § 15 ἡγοῦμαι...τοῦτον...οὗτω
σκαιὸν εἶναι ὥστε οὐ δύνασθαι μαθεῖν τὰ
λεγόμενα. Ar. Vesp. 1183 ὦ σκαιὲ κἀπαί-
δευτε. So here σκαιότης expresses a stu-
pidity that is deaf to remonstrance.

1029 f. εἶκε τῷ θανόντι, 'make a
concession to the dead,' i.e., give him the
burial rites which are his due. It is not
as if he were a living foe, and prowess
(ἀλκή) could be shown by resisting his
claim. The words τῷ θανόντι have been
groundlessly suspected (see cr. n.).—
κέντει, stab. Cp. the scene in the Iliad
where the Greeks prick Hector's corpse
with their swords; Il. 22. 371 οὐδ᾽ ἄρα οἱ
τις ἀνουτητί γε παρέστη: and ib. 24. 421.
For κεντεῖν of cowardly or treacherous
wounding, cp. Ai. 1244 ἡμᾶς ἦ κακοῖς βα-
λεῖτέ που | ἦ σὺν δόλῳ κεντήσεθ᾽ οἱ λελειμ-
μένοι.—ἐπικτανεῖν, 'slay anew.' In comp.
with verbs of killing, ἐπί usu. = either 'in
addition' (O. C. 1733 ἐπενάριξον, n.), or
'over' a grave, etc., as usu. ἐπισφάττειν:
but cp. 1288: Diog. Laert. 2. 17 § 135
(Menedemus) Βίωνος...ἐπιμελῶς καταρέχ-
οντος τῶν μάντεων νεκροὺς αὐτὸς ἐπισφάττειν ἔλεγε. Cp. Ph. 946 ἐναίρων
νεκρόν.

κέντει. τίς ἀλκὴ τὸν θανόντ᾽ ἐπικτανεῖν; 1030
εὖ σοι φρονήσας εὖ λέγω· τὸ μανθάνειν δ᾽
ἥδιστον εὖ λέγοντος, εἰ κέρδος λέγοι.

ΚΡ. ὦ πρέσβυ, πάντες ὥστε τοξόται σκοποῦ
τοξεύετ᾽ ἀνδρὸς τοῦδε, κοὐδὲ μαντικῆς
ἄπρακτος ὑμῖν εἰμι, τῶν δ᾽ ὑπαὶ γένους 1035
ἐξημπόλημαι κἀμπεφόρτισμαι πάλαι.
κερδαίνετ᾽, ἐμπολᾶτε τἀπὸ Σάρδεων
ἤλεκτρον, εἰ βούλεσθε, καὶ τὸν Ἰνδικὸν
χρυσόν· τάφῳ δ᾽ ἐκεῖνον οὐχὶ κρύψετε,
οὐδ᾽ εἰ θέλουσ᾽ οἱ Ζηνὸς αἰετοὶ βορὰν 1040

Semitelos, θεσπίζοντι. **1030** ἐπικτανεῖν] The first hand in L had inadvertently written some other and longer word beginning with ἐπι.. κτανεῖν is in an erasure, which extends beyond it to the space of four or five letters. **1031 f.** μανθάνειν | δ᾽ ἥδιστον L. **1034 f.** κοὐδὲ μαντικῆς | ἄπρακτος ὑμῖν εἰμι τῶν δ᾽ ὑπαὶ γένους MSS. (ὑμῖν L). See comment. **1036** κἀμπεφόρτισμαι L, with κ written above μ by an early hand. The later MSS. are divided between κἀμ- and κἀκ-: A has the latter. **1037** τὰ πρὸ Σάρδεων L, with ὸν above τὰ from the first

1031 f. εὖ φρονήσας, having conceived kindly thoughts; a very rare use of the aor. part. in this sense, instead of εὖ φρονῶν. The aor. part. of φρονέω usu. means, (1) 'having come to a sound mind,' *O. T.* 649, and so Isocr. or. 8. § 141, εὖ φρονήσαντες: (2) 'having formed a project,' as Her. 7. 145: (3) in the pbrase τωὐτό (or τὰ αὐτά) φρονήσαντες, 'having come to an agreement,' Her. 1. 60, 5. 72.—**μανθάνειν δ᾽**: for the elision (ἐπισυναλοιφή) see *O. T.* 29 n.: and cp. above, 350.—**εἰ...λέγοι**: for the optative in the γνώμη, see 666 n. With ἥδιστον we supply ἐστί, as in *O. T.* 315.

1033 ὥστε = ὡς: *O.C.* 343.—**σκοποῦ**, sc. τοξεύουσι: the gen. as with στοχάζομαι: so *Il.* 4. 100 ὀΐστευσον Μενελάου: 14. 402 Αἴαντος δὲ πρῶτος ἀκόντισε. Cp. 241.

1034 f. κοὐδὲ μαντικῆς κ.τ.λ.: not even by seer-craft do ye leave me unattempted: in your plots against me ye resort even to seer-craft. Two points in this phrase are notable. (1) ἄπρακτος = 'not worked,' in the sense of, 'not plotted against.' πράσσειν oft. = 'to intrigue'; and 'to intrigue *against* one' might be expressed by πράσσειν περί τινος, or ἐπί τινι, though ἐπιβουλεύω τινί is the usu. phrase. But, while ἐπιβουλεύομαι had a personal pass. use ('to be plotted against'), we could not say πράσσονται,

'they are the objects of an intrigue.' ἄπρακτος is therefore bolder than its prose equivalent, ἀνεπιβούλευτος. Still, for poetry, it seems possible. (2) **μαντικῆς.** Such a gen., joined to a verbal adj. with a privative, more often denotes the agent, answering to a gen. with ὑπό after a pass. verb, or to the subject of an act. verb: cp. 847: *Tr.* 685 ἀκτῖνος...ἀθικτον (untouched *by* the ray). Here, the instrument, μαντική, is, in fact, personified as the agent: i.e., μαντικῆς does not correspond to the instrum. dat. in καὶ μαντικῇ πράσσετε περὶ ἐμοῦ, but to the nom. in καὶ μαντικὴ πράσσει περὶ ἐμοῦ ὑμῖν (ye have even seer-craft practising on me). An easier reading would be μαντικῇ. The instrumental dat. is often retained with the negative verbal; as Plat. *Symp.* 219 E χρήμασι... μᾶλλον ἄτρωτος ἢ σιδήρῳ: fr. com. anon. 52 ἀνεπιβουλεύτου φθόνου. But poetical usage seems to warrant μαντικῆς.—The conjecture ἄπρατος (see Appendix) would forestall the taunt which now forms the climax, ἐξημπόλημαι.

τῶν δ᾽ ὑπαὶ γένους, 'by the tribe of those men,'—the μάντεις implied in μαντικῆς. Creon, though he addresses Teiresias, is speaking as much to the Chorus as to him. If we read τῶν (without δ᾽), as relative, it would naturally

fallen; what prowess is it to slay the slain anew? I have sought thy good, and for thy good I speak: and never is it sweeter to learn from a good counsellor than when he counsels for thine own gain.

CR. Old man, ye all shoot your shafts at me, as archers at the butts;—ye must needs practise on me with seer-craft also;—aye, the seer-tribe hath long trafficked in me, and made me their merchandise. Gain your gains, drive your trade, if ye list, in the silver-gold of Sardis and the gold of India; but ye shall not hide that man in the grave,—no, though the eagles of Zeus should

hand. Notwithstanding the space after πρό, the scribe may have meant προσάρδεων to be one word, as it is in the lemma of the schol. But it is also possible that he merely forgot to accent πρό. Some of the later MSS. have τὸν πρὸ σάρδεων (as Vat.), others τὸν πρὸς σάρδεων (as A). Eustathius (p. 368. 30, 1483. 27) reads τὸν πρὸς Σάρδεων, which Brunck gave. Musgrave defended τὸν πρὸ Σάρδεων. Blaydes and Nauck restored τἀπὸ Σάρδεων. **1088** βούλεσθε made from βούλεσθαι L. **1040** οὐδ' εἱ] οὐ δὴ L.

refer to ὑμῖν: it could hardly refer to μαντικῆς. The conjecture of Semitelos, μαντικοῖς, would then be attractive. But such a substitute for μάντεις would be very strange. And, if we keep L's τῶν δ', the scornful demonstrative sufficiently interprets the reference to μάντεις.—ἰνταὶ in trimeters, as *El.* 711: Aesch. *Ag.* 892, 944, *Eum.* 417.—γένους: cp. 1055.—For other views of the passage, see Appendix.

1036 ἐξημπόλημαι. Creon means: 'The Thebans have bribed Teiresias to frighten me. He has taken their money. In return, he is to deliver me into their hands. I am like a piece of merchandise which has been sold for export, and put on board the buyer's ship.' Cp. 1063. Her. 1. 1 ἐξεμπολημένων (Ion.) σφι σχεδὸν πάντων, when they had sold off almost everything.—Neither ἐμφορτίζομαι nor ἐκφορτίζομαι occurs elsewhere, except that an old glossary (cited by Dind.) gives ἐξεφορτίσατο, *exoneravit* ('unladed'). In later Greek we find ἐμφοροῦσθαι ναῦν, ἐμφόρτος, and ἐκφοροῦν (both act. and midd.). Here, ἐμπεφόρτισμαι, the reading of the first hand in L, marks the completion of the sale by the delivery of the goods. The Schol. quotes Callimachus (fr. 529), ἐνεφόρτισέ με φόρτον.—The correction in L, ἀνεμφόρτισμαι, is far inferior. It would mean, 'unladed (as a cargo) from a ship': not, 'made into a cargo,' nor, 'exported as a cargo.'—In *Tr.* 537 there is a like association of ἐμπόλημα and φόρτος (though the passage is not other-

wise similar). Cp. Shaks. *Com. Err.* 3. 1. 72 'It would make a man mad as a buck, to be so bought and sold.'

1087 ἡ τἀπὸ Σάρδεων ἤλεκτρον: electron, or silver-gold, from the goldmines of Tmolus in Lydia, the range s. of Sardis. Croesus dedicated at Delphi a lion of refined gold (χρυσὸς ἄπεφθος), standing on a pedestal formed by 117 half-plinths, or ingots, of gold,—four being of refined gold, and the rest of this electron, or 'white gold' (λευκὸς χρυσός); Her. 1. 50. The celebrity of this ἀνάθημα in Greece helps to explain the poet's phrase. Stein on Her. *l.c.* shows that the ratio of silver to gold in electron was about 3 to 7. Pliny, who makes the ratio only 1 to 4, describes electron both as a natural blend of metals, and as an artificial product (*fit et cura,...addito argento*, 33. 80).—Paus. 5. 12 § 7 distinguishes the two senses of ἤλεκτρον, (1) silver-gold, (2) amber. The latter is the ἤλεκτρον of Herodotus (3. 115), and of *Od.* 15. 460, where a Phoenician brings a golden ὅρμος, —μετὰ δ' ἠλέκτροισιν ἔερτο ('strung with amber beads').—τἀπὸ is a certain correction of τὸν πρός (or πρό): in class. Greek ἤλεκτρον is always neut., as it is in Paus. also.—Ἰνδικὸν χρυσόν: Her. 3. 94 speaks of the Ἰνδοί as sending Dareius an annual tribute of 360 talents in gold dust (ψῆγμα).

1040 οἱ Ζηνὸς αἰετοί: *Il.* 24. 310 δς τε σοὶ αὐτῷ | φίλτατος οἰωνῶν, καὶ εὖ κράτος ἐστὶ μέγιστον. Pind. *P.* 4. 4 (the

φέρειν νιν ἁρπάζοντες ἐς Διὸς θρόνους,
οὐδ' ὡς μίασμα τοῦτο μὴ τρέσας ἐγὼ
θάπτειν παρήσω κεῖνον· εὖ γὰρ οἶδ' ὅτι
θεοὺς μιαίνειν οὔτις ἀνθρώπων σθένει.
πίπτουσι δ', ὦ γεραιὲ Τειρεσία, βροτῶν   1045
χοἰ πολλὰ δεινοὶ πτώματ' αἴσχρ', ὅταν λόγους
αἰσχροὺς καλῶς λέγωσι τοῦ κέρδους χάριν.
ΤΕ. φεῦ·
ἆρ' οἶδεν ἀνθρώπων τις, ἆρα φράζεται
ΚΡ. τί χρῆμα; ποῖον τοῦτο πάγκοινον λέγεις;
ΤΕ. ὅσῳ κράτιστον κτημάτων εὐβουλία;   1050
ΚΡ. ὅσῳπερ, οἶμαι, μὴ φρονεῖν πλείστη βλάβη.
ΤΕ. ταύτης σὺ μέντοι τῆς νόσου πλήρης ἔφυς.
ΚΡ. οὐ βούλομαι τὸν μάντιν ἀντειπεῖν κακῶς.
ΤΕ. καὶ μὴν λέγεις, ψευδῆ με θεσπίζειν λέγων.
ΚΡ. τὸ μαντικὸν γὰρ πᾶν φιλάργυρον γένος.   1055
ΤΕ. τὸ δ' ἐκ τυράννων αἰσχροκέρδειαν φιλεῖ.

1042 f. ὡς] ὡσ L.—τοῦτο μὴ τρέσας] Nauck conject. τοῦτο ταρβήσας. Blaydes,
τοῦτο δὴ τρέσας, if παρήσω be kept: but he gives τοῦτο μὴ τρέσας .. παρῶ τῳ (his
own conject.).   **1046** After αἴσχρ' two letters have been erased in L: the first

Delphian priestess) χρυσέων Διὸς αἰητῶν
πάρεδρος (the golden eagles on the ὀμ-
φαλός). Hor. *Carm.* 4. 4. 1 *ministrum
fulminis alitem.*
1042 f. οὐδ' ὡς, not even (I say) in
that case,—repeating the supposition, οὐδ'
εἰ θέλουσ'. Cp. *Il.* 9. 379 ff. οὐδ' εἴ μοι
δεκάκις τε καὶ εἰκοσάκις τόσα δοίη, | ...
οὐδέ κεν ὣς ἔτι θυμὸν ἐμὸν πείσει' Ἀγα-
μέμνων. *Od.* 22. 61 ff. οὐδ' εἴ μοι πατρώϊα
πάντ' ἀποδοῖτε | ...οὐδέ κεν ὣς ἔτι χεῖρας
ἐμὰς λήξαιμι φόνοιο.—Attic prose, too,
used καὶ ὡς, 'even in that case' (Thuc. 1.
44), οὐδ' ὡς (id. 1. 132), etc.—παρήσω.
οὐ μή, with the 2nd pers. fut. ind.,
prohibits; but with the 1st or 3rd pers.
it can be used in emphatic denial, though
the aor. subjunct. is more usual: *El.* 1052
οὐ σοι μὴ μεθέψομαί ποτε : see n. on *O. C.*
177. There is no reason, then, for suspecting the text (see cr. n.).
1044 θεοὺς μιαίνειν. Teiresias had
said that the altars were defiled (1016).
Creon replies that he will not yield,
even if birds fly with the carrion up to
the very throne of Zeus;—'*for no mortal
can pollute the gods.*' Campbell takes
this to be an utterance of scepticism,
like οὐκ ἔφα τις | θεοὺς βροτῶν ἀξιοῦσθαι
μέλειν (Aesch. *Ag.* 369),—anticipating
the Epicurean conception of gods who
are neither pleased nor angered by men.
This view seems to do some injus-
tice to the poet's dramatic psychology.
I read the words quite differently. The
most orthodox Greek piety held that 'no
mortal could pollute the gods.' See, for
example, Eur. *H. F.* 1232. Heracles,
having recovered sanity after slaying his
children, has covered his face, to hide it
from the holy light of the sun. Theseus
—who is a type of normal εὐσέβεια—
makes him uncover, saying,—τί δ'; οὐ
μαίνεις θνητὸς ὢν τὰ τῶν θεῶν. The sun-
god cannot be polluted by a mortal.
The idea of religious μίασμα was that a
mortal had contracted some impurity
which disqualified him for communion
with the gods. The tainting of an altar
cut off such communion by bringing
uncleanness to the very place where men
sought to be cleansed. Creon excitedly
imagines a seemingly worse profanation,
and then excuses his apparent impiety
by a general maxim which all would
admit:—'no man can pollute the gods.'

bear the carrion morsels to their Master's throne—no, not for
dread of that defilement will I suffer his burial:—for well I
know that no mortal can defile the gods.—But, aged Teiresias,
the wisest fall with a shameful fall, when they clothe shameful
thoughts in fair words, for lucre's sake.

TE.   Alas! Doth any man know, doth any consider...
CR.   Whereof? What general truth dost thou announce?
TE.   How precious, above all wealth, is good counsel.
CR.   As folly, I think, is the worst mischief.
TE.   Yet thou art tainted with that distemper.
CR.   I would not answer the seer with a taunt.
TE.   But thou dost, in saying that I prophesy falsely.
CR.   Well, the prophet-tribe was ever fond of money.
TE.   And the race bred of tyrants loves base gain.

hand had written αἰσχράν.   **1049** χρῆμα] Nauck conject. γνῶμα or ῥῆμα.
1051 πλείστη] πλείστηι L, made from πλήστη.   **1053** ἀντ' εἰπεῖν L.
1054 λέγω] λέγειν L, with ω written above by the first hand. Cp. O. T. 360.
1056 τὸ δ' ἐκ] Hartung conject. τὸ δ' αὖ: Bischopp and Seyffert, τὸ δέ γε.

'The sky-throne of Zeus is still more
sacred than his altar on earth: if defilement cannot reach him there, much less
here.' The sophism is of the kind with
which an honest but stubborn and wrong-
headed man might seek to quiet his
conscience. Creon reveres Zeus (304):
he feels for the majesty of the gods, and
refuses to believe that they can honour
the wicked (284 ff.). But his religious
sense is temporarily confused by his anger.

1046 πολλά, adv., = 'very,' with adj.:
O. C. 1514 n.

1047 καλῶς, = εὐπρεπῶς, in a bad
sense: Eur. Hipp. 505 τἀισχρὰ δ' ἢν
λέγης καλῶς: Thuc. 5. 89 μετ' ὀνομάτων
καλῶν. So Eur. Hec. 1191 τἀδικ' εὖ
λέγειν: cp. O. C. 807.

1048 ἆρ' οἶδεν κ.τ.λ. Instead of
being angered by Creon's bitter words,
Teiresias is communing with the mournful
thought which they suggest—the thought
of human folly. His sorrowful exclamation here is like his πάντες γὰρ οὐ φρονεῖτ'
in the scene with Oedipus (O. T. 328).

1049 τί χρῆμα; Cp. Eur. Hec. 754
(Hecuba having said, ἱκετεύω,) ΑΓ. τί
χρῆμα μαστεύουσα; So oft. in questions,
as Ai. 288, Ph. 1231.—πάγκοινον, a
sneer at the generality of the seer's
exordium. What aphorism is this to be?
But the seer's thought has a terribly
definite point, as Creon is soon to feel
(1066).

1050 f. κτημάτων: cp. 684.—ὅσῳπερ
with superl., as O. C. 743 n. By μὴ
φρονεῖν Creon hints that the seer's clever-
ness has outrun his prudence (1046).

1052 νόσου: cp. 732: πλήρης, 1017.

1053 In ἀντειπεῖν κακῶς, ἀντί quali-
fies the whole phrase: i.e., it means, 'to
revile in return,' ἀντιλοιδορεῖν, as ἀντι-
δρᾶν κακῶς (O. C. 1191) = ἀνταδικεῖν.

1054 καὶ μήν, 'and verily,' meaning
here, 'and yet,'—the adversative force
arising from the contrast between Creon's
profession and his practice. Cp. 221.—
λέγεις, sc. κακῶς τὸν μάντιν.—For the
metre, cp. 44, 502.

1055 γένος: 1035. Cp. Eur. I. A.
520 τὸ μαντικὸν πᾶν σπέρμα φιλότιμον
κακόν. Helen. 755 (of μαντική), βίου γὰρ
ἄλλως δέλεαρ ηὑρέθη τόδε, | κοὐδεὶς ἐπλού-
τησ' ἐμπύροισιν ἀργὸς ὤν,—i.e., the seer's
client is never enriched (though the seer
himself is).

1056 τὸ δ' ἐκ τυράννων. The text is
sound. Instead of saying, 'the race of
tyrants' (i.e., all the tyrants who exist),
he says, with more rhetorical force, 'the
race bred of tyrants,' i.e., the tyrants
whose progenitors have also been tyrants.
Thus ἐκ expresses that the love of 'base
gain' is hereditary. For τύραννος in the
bad sense, see O. T. 873 n.—αἰσχροκέρδειαν: not in the literal sense in which
Creon imputed it to his servants (313),
but in this, that Creon secures an un-

ΚΡ. ἆρ' οἶσθα ταγοὺς ὄντας ἂν λέγῃς λέγων;

ΤΕ. οἶδ'· ἐξ ἐμοῦ γὰρ τήνδ' ἔχεις σώσας πόλιν.

ΚΡ. σοφὸς σὺ μάντις, ἀλλὰ τἀδικεῖν φιλῶν.

ΤΕ. ὄρσεις με τἀκίνητα διὰ φρενῶν φράσαι.   1060

ΚΡ. κίνει, μόνον δὲ μὴ 'πὶ κέρδεσιν λέγων.

ΤΕ. οὕτω γὰρ ἤδη καὶ δοκῶ τὸ σὸν μέρος.

ΚΡ. ὡς μὴ 'μπολήσων ἴσθι τὴν ἐμὴν φρένα.

ΤΕ. ἀλλ' εὖ γέ τοι κάτισθι μὴ πολλοὺς ἔτι
τρόχους ἁμιλλητῆρας ἡλίου τελῶν,   1065
ἐν οἷσι τῶν σῶν αὐτὸς ἐκ σπλάγχνων ἕνα,

1057 λέγησ L, from λέγεισ. (The first hand has merely added strokes, denoting η, to the contracted character for ει, instead of altering the latter.)—λέγων] Keck conject. ψέγων. 1061 μόνον δὲ μὴ 'πὶ] μόνον δ' ἐπὶ L, with μὴ written above ἐπὶ by first hand. 1062 The first hand in L had placed a full stop at μέρος. The first

worthy personal triumph by trampling on religion and silencing just remonstrance (505 ff.). Such a triumph is an αἰσχρὸν κέρδος.

1057 f. ἆρ' οἶσθα λέγων ταγοὺς ὄντας ἃ ἂν λέγῃς; knowest thou that whatever it pleases thee to say is said of men who are rulers? λέγω τινά τι = to say something of him. ἃ ἂν λέγῃς is a scornful euphemism, implying that he indulges in random abuse. ταγούς: only here in Soph.: oft. in Aesch. (in P. V. 96 Zeus is ὁ νέος ταγὸς μακάρων); once in Eur., I. A. 269 (Adrastus). Here the word is not specially = στρατηγός (8), but simply = βασιλεύς.

1058 ἐξ ἐμοῦ: cp. O. T. 1221 ἀνέπνευσα ...ἐκ σέθεν.—ἔχεις σώσας, merely = σέσωκας (cp. 22). The rare position of ἔχεις might suggest the prose sense ('thou hast saved, and keepest'); but that position occurs where ἔχω is merely the auxiliary (794; Ai. 22 ἔχει περάνας).

1060 τἀκίνητα διὰ φρενῶν, = τὰ διὰ φρενῶν ἀκίνητα, those secrets in my soul which ought to be let alone. Cp. O. C. 1526 ἃ δ' ἐξάγιστα μηδὲ κινεῖται λόγῳ, n. For the place of the adv. διὰ φρενῶν, cp. 659 n.: for διά, 639 n.: Aesch. Th. 593 βαθεῖαν ἄλοκα διὰ φρενὸς καρπούμενος.

1061 κίνει: a word used esp. of sacrilege: Her. 6. 134 κινήσαντά τι τῶν ἀκινήτων (in a temple): Thuc. 4. 98 ὕδωρ...κινῆσαι (to profane, by secular use, water reserved for sacrifices).—μόνον δέ, sc. κίνει.—ἐπὶ κέρδεσιν, i.e., with a view to

receiving money from the Thebans for persuading me to bury Polyneices. So Oed. (O. T. 388) calls the seer, δόλιον ἀγύρτην, ὅστις ἐν τοῖς κέρδεσιν | μόνον δέδορκε.

1062 οὕτω γὰρ ἤδη: 'indeed, as matters stand (ἤδη), καὶ δοκῶ (λέξειν), I think that I shall speak thus—i.e., not for gain—so far as thou art concerned.' The seer, with grave irony, gives a new turn to Creon's phrase, μὴ ἐπὶ κέρδεσιν, and says that the admonition is superfluous. The message which he has to utter is fraught with no κέρδη—for Creon. For the plur. κέρδη in this general sense, cp. 1326. τὸ σὸν μέρος here = quantum ad te attinet: a sense quite as correct for it as the more usual quantum in te est (O. T. 1509, O. C. 1366, Tr. 1215). For καὶ emphasising δοκῶ (λέξειν), cp. 726. Creon's reply (1063) refers to the covert threat: 'say what thou wilt, thou shalt not shake my purpose.'—The choice lies between this view and that of the Scholiast, who makes the verse interrogative:—οὕτω νομίζεις, ὅτι ἐπὶ κέρδεσι λέγω; i.e., 'what, do I seem now—on thy part—to be speaking for money?' The points in favour of the Scholiast's interpretation are:—(a) The combination γάρ...καί (before the verb) suits an indignant question: cp. 770, Tr. 1124. (b) The tone of rising anger—which began at 1060—fitly preludes the outburst at 1064: cp. O. T. 343—350. But on the other hand:—(a) The indignation comes late, seeing that Creon has already used the same taunt four times (1036, 1047,

CR. Knowest thou that thy speech is spoken of thy King?

TE. I know it; for through me thou hast saved Thebes.

CR. Thou art a wise seer; but thou lovest evil deeds.

TE. Thou wilt rouse me to utter the dread secret in my soul.

CR. Out with it!—Only speak it not for gain.

TE. Indeed, methinks, I shall not,—as touching thee.

CR. Know that thou shalt not trade on my resolve.

TE. Then know thou—aye, know it well—that thou shalt not live through many more courses of the sun's swift chariot, ere one begotten of thine own loins

---

corrector (S) changed this into a mark of interrogation. **1064** πολλὰς L, with ·οὐ· above ά from first hand. **1065** τροχούς MSS.: τρόχους Erfurdt.—ἀμιλλητῆρας] Musgrave conject. ἀμιλλητῆρος.—ἡλίου τελῶν] Winckelmann conject. ἥλιον τελεῖν.

1055, 1059); not, indeed, in so directly personal a form, yet still openly enough. (b) Though the seer is angered (1085), it is dramatically better to conceive him as speaking here with a stern calmness. (c) It would be correct to say (e.g.) πέφασμαι λέγων, τὸ σὸν μέρος ('I have been represented as speaking..., so far as you could create such a belief'): but hardly, δοκῶ τὸ σὸν μέρος, as merely = δοκῶ σοί.— On the whole, then, the first view is best.—Others, which may be rejected, are:—(1) 'I think that I *shall* speak for your *good*.' But, if we are thus to supply ἐπὶ κέρδεσιν, and not οὐκ ἐπὶ κέρδεσιν, the verse must be interrogative. (2) 'So far as you are concerned, I do not expect to speak for my own profit'; i.e., I shall receive no thanks from you. (3) 'Do you really think that I shall find any satisfaction in speaking?'—i.e., it will be only pain for you, without advantage for me.

1063 ἴσθι ὡς μὴ ἐμπ., rest assured that thou art not to trade (1037) on my resolve; i.e., to make profit out of it (from the Thebans) by persuading me to surrender it. ὡς (which might have been absent) adds emphasis by marking the point of view at which he is to place himself. In such phrases it is more often added to a partic. in the accus., the object of the imperat. verb: Ph. 253 ὡς μηδὲν εἰδότ' ἴσθι μ' ὧν ἀνιστορεῖς: O. T. 848 n. But cp. Her. 1. 91 ἐπιστάσθω Κροῖσος ὡς ὕστερον...ἁλούς τῆς πεπρωμένης.—φρένα: cp. 993.

1064 ἀλλ' οὐ γέ τοι: 473 n.—μή ...τελῶν, that thou art not to accom-

plish, i.e., live through: μή is due to the imperat. κάτισθι (O. C. 78 n.). The easy correction, ἥλιον τελεῖν, has been received by some recent edd. (κάτισθι then has the constr. with inf., as 473 ἴσθι... πίπτειν). It may be right. But τελῶν, if not a usual phrase, is a natural one; and it is more impressive here to say, '*thou shalt not live through* many days,' than, 'the sun shall not fulfil many days.'— τρόχους = δρόμους, 'courses.' The MS. τροχούς = 'runners,' i.e., κύκλους, wheels. The authority for this Attic distinction goes back at least to the Augustan age: see Chandler § 332 n. 1 (2nd ed.), who cites Ammonius p. 137 τροχοὶ ὀξυτόνως καὶ τρόχοι βαρυτόνως διαφέρουσι παρὰ τοῖς Ἀττικοῖς. φησὶ Τρύφων (in the Augustan age) ἐν δευτέρᾳ περὶ Ἀττικῆς προσῳδίας. τοὺς μὲν γὰρ περιφερεῖς τροχοὺς ὁμοίως ἡμῖν προφέρονται ὀξυτονοῦντες· τρόχους δὲ βαρυτόνως λέγουσι τοὺς δρόμους. This passage helps to explain why our MSS. all give τροχούς here. When Ammonius wrote (towards the end of the 4th cent. A.D.) τρόχος, 'course,' was known only as an Atticism, while τροχός, 'wheel,' was a common word.—ἀμιλλητῆρας, racing, rapid: Eur. Or. 456 γέροντι δεῦρ' ἀμιλλᾶται ποδί. Xen. An. 3. 4. 44 ὥρμησαν ἀμιλλᾶσθαι ἐπὶ τὸ ἄκρον.—The Schol. explains, τοὺς ἀλλήλους διαδεχομένους, 'successive'; perh. taking the word to mean, 'competitors,' i.e., 'vying in swiftness.' But that does not warrant his version.

1066 ἐν οἶσι = ἐντὸς ὤν, i.e., before they have elapsed: cp. O. C. 619 n.— τῶν σῶν...ἐκ σπλάγχνων ἵνα, a strong

νέκυν νεκρῶν, ἀμοιβὸν ἀντιδοὺς ἔσει,
ἀνθ᾽ ὧν ἔχεις μὲν τῶν ἄνω βαλὼν κάτω,
ψυχήν τ᾽ ἀτίμως ἐν τάφῳ κατῴκισας,
ἔχεις δὲ τῶν κάτωθεν ἐνθάδ᾽ αὖ θεῶν   1070
ἄμοιρον, ἀκτέριστον, ἀνόσιον νέκυν.
ὧν οὔτε σοὶ μέτεστιν οὔτε τοῖς ἄνω
θεοῖσιν, ἀλλ᾽ ἐκ σοῦ βιάζονται τάδε.
τούτων σε λωβητῆρες ὑστεροφθόροι
λοχῶσιν, Ἅιδου καὶ θεῶν Ἐρινύες,   1075
ἐν τοῖσιν αὐτοῖς τοῖσδε ληφθῆναι κακοῖς.
καὶ ταῦτ᾽ ἄθρησον εἰ κατηργυρωμένος
λέγω· φανεῖ γὰρ οὐ μακροῦ χρόνου τριβὴ
ἀνδρῶν γυναικῶν σοῖς δόμοις κωκύματα.
ἐχθραὶ δὲ πᾶσαι συνταράσσονται πόλεις,   1080

1068 βαλὼν r: βάλλειν L, with ω above ει from first hand.   **1069** κατώκισασ L. κατοικίσας, the reading of some later MSS. (as E, L²), is adopted by Bothe, who omits τ᾽ after ψυχήν, and by Bergk, who places τ᾽ after ἀτίμως.   **1070** θεῶν] Semitelos conject. γόων, to go with ἄμοιρον.   **1078** τριβὴ L. The only trace of

fig. phrase, one whose life is nourished by thine own heart's blood,—the son begotten of thee. If the ref. were to the mother, σπλάγχνα could mean 'womb': cp. Kaibel *Epigr.* 691 ζωὴ δὲ πλείων μητρὸς ἐν σπλάγχνοις ἐμή (of a babe who died just after birth). So brothers and sisters are ὁμόσπλαγχνοι (511).

1067 νέκυν νεκρῶν: 596 n. The νεκροί are Polyneices and Antigone.— ἀντιδοὺς ἔσει, fut. perf.: cp. *O. C.* 816 n.

1068 ἀνθ᾽ ὧν here = ἀντὶ τούτων ὅτι, 'because': so Ar. *Plut.* 434. The phrase more often means 'wherefore' (*O. C.* 1295): cp. *O. T.* 264 n.—ἔχεις βαλὼν κάτω τῶν ἄνω (τινά), thou hast thrust to the grave (one) of the living. For the omission of τις after the partitive gen., cp. *El.* 1322 κλύω | τῶν ἔνδοθεν χωροῦντος.

1069 Bothe, omitting τι after ψυχήν, takes the latter with τῶν ἄνω, 'a life belonging to the upper world.' We could then read either (a) ἀτίμως...κατοικίσας, or (b) with Bergk, ἀτίμως τ᾽...κατοικίσας or κατῴκισας. But I prefer the MS. reading, because (a) τῶν ἄνω as = τῶν ἄνω τινά has a certain tone of solemnity and mystery which befits the utterance: (b) τῶν ἄνω... ψυχήν is somewhat weak: (c) the words ψυχήν τ᾽...κατῴκισας, both by rhythm and by diction, naturally form one clause,

—paraphrasing and interpreting the darker utterance in v. 1068.—Schütz takes ἀνθ᾽ ὧν as = ἀντὶ τούτων οὕς, and τῶν ἄνω as by attraction for τοὺς ἄνω: i.e., 'on account of those persons whom, being alive, thou hast entombed.' Kern, too, so takes ἀνθ᾽ ὧν, but makes τῶν ἄνω partitive ('on account of those among the living whom'); and so, I think, it must be on any view. But the parallelism of ἔχεις μέν...ἔχεις δέ plainly requires that ἀνθ᾽ ὧν should apply in the same sense to both clauses. Schütz, however, has to supply it with ἔχεις δέ in the changed sense of ἀντὶ τούτων (neut.) ὅτι.—For οἱ ἄνω = οἱ ἐν φάει, cp. 890: *Ph.* 1348 ὦ στυγνὸς αἰών, τί μ᾽ ἔτι δῆτ᾽ ἔχεις ἄνω | βλέποντα, κοὐκ ἀφῆκας εἰς Ἅιδου μολεῖν;—Some take τῶν ἄνω as = τῶν ἄνω θεῶν: 'one belonging to the gods above.' This is too forced.— ἀτίμως, ruthlessly: cp. *O. C.* 428, *El.* 1181.

1070 f. ἔχεις δέ = κατέχεις δέ. Since in ἔχεις μέν...ἔχεις δέ the rhetorical effect depends simply on the repetition (ἐπαναφορά), the change of sense is immaterial. —τῶν κάτωθεν θεῶν, possess. gen. with νέκυν, a corpse belonging to them. For κάτωθεν = κάτω, 521 n.—ἄμοιρον, without its due μοῖρα of burial rites: *Ai.* 1327 νεκρὸν ταφῆς | ἄμοιρον. Others take τῶν

shall have been given by thee, a corpse for corpses; because
thou hast thrust children of the sunlight to the shades, and
ruthlessly lodged a living soul in the grave; but keepest in this
world one who belongs to the gods infernal, a corpse unburied,
unhonoured, all unhallowed. In such thou hast no part, nor
have the gods above, but this is a violence done to them by
thee. Therefore the avenging destroyers lie in wait for thee,
the Furies of Hades and of the gods, that thou mayest be taken
in these same ills.

And mark well if I speak these things as a hireling. A
time not long to be delayed shall awaken the wailing of men
and of women in thy house. And a tumult of hatred against
thee stirs all the cities

---

a reading τριβῇ seems to be in A (τριβῆ). λόγου for χρόνου in E was probably a mere
oversight. **1080—1083** Wunder and Dindorf reject these four verses.
1080 ἐχθραί] Reiske conject. ἐχθρᾳ: Musgrave, ἐχθραῖς: Semitelos ἐχθραι .. συντα
ράσσουσιν.—συνταράσσονται] Bergk conject. συνταράξονται.

κ. θεῶν with ἄμοιρον: 'without a portion
in the gods below,' i.e., not admitted to
communion with them. But the phrase
is a strange one; and the leading thought
here is that the νέρτεροι are robbed of
one who belongs to them.—ἀκτέριστον
(1207), without offerings at the grave,
κτερίσματα (O. C. 1410): cp. 204.—ἀνό
σιον, 'unhallowed,' sums up the state of
the dead who has received no rites: cp.
545 n. Cp. Shaksp. Haml. 1. 5. 77 'Unhousel'd, disappointed, unanel'd' [without
sacrament—unprepared for death—without extreme unction].

1072 f. ἄν, sc. τῶν νεκρῶν, suggested
by νέκυν. Others make it neut., 'such
acts as these.' It cannot refer to οἱ
κάτωθεν θεοί.—βιάζονται, sc. οἱ ἄνω θεοί:
because it was an offence against the
pure οὐράνιοι θεοί to keep a μίασμα in
their presence. Cp. O. T. 1425 τὴν γοῦν
πάντα βόσκουσαν φλόγα | αἰδεῖσθ' ἄνακτος
Ἡλίου, and see n. there on 1427. The
subject to βιάζονται might, indeed, be
οἱ κάτωθεν θεοί, for Greek idiom is often
bold in such transitions: but the verb
suits a positive better than a negative
wrong.

1074 τούτων, neut., causal gen.: cp.
931 n.—λαμβάνηρες, though the subject
is fem.: so El. 850 ἵστωρ: Aesch. Ag.
111 χερὶ πράκτορι: ib. 664 τύχη...σωτήρ:
Suppl. 1040 θέλκτορι Πειθοῖ.—ὑστεροφθό
ρος, destroying after (though not, here,
long after) the crime. Aesch. Ag. 58 (Zeus)
ὑστερόποινον | πέμπει παραβᾶσιν Ἐρινύν.

Anthol. 12. 229 ὑστερόποιν' ἀξόμενοι Νέ
μεσιν.

1075 f. λοχῶσιν: El. 490 ὁ δεινοῖς
κρυπτομένα λόχοις | χαλκόπους Ἐρινύς.—
Ἅιδου καὶ θεῶν, possess. gen.; the Erinyes are their ministers, avenging their
wrongs: so oft. πατρός, μητρός, Ἐρινύες.
In El. 112 the Erinyes are σεμναί...θεῶν
παῖδες.—ληφθῆναι, inf. of result: cp. 64
ἀκούειν. The omission of ὥστε is somewhat bold, since the subject of the inf. is
not that of λοχῶσιν. Cp. O. C. 385 ἐμοῦ
θεοὺς | ὥραν τιν' ἕξειν ὥστε σωθῆναί ποτε.

1077 ff. κατηργ., prop., overlaid
with silver (Her. 1. 98); hence, fig.,
bribed. Cp. Pind. P. 11. 41 μισθοῖο συν
τίθεν παρέχειν | φωνὰν ὑπάργυρον (a word
prop. said of a gilded surface, with silver
below).—οὐ μακρ. χρόν. τριβή = a time
for which thou wilt not have long to wait.
Some, less naturally, make these words
a parenthesis with ἔσται understood, and
supply ταῦτα as subject to φανεῖ. Cp.
Ar. Ran. 156 θιάσους εὐδαίμονας | ἀν
δρῶν γυναικῶν.

1080—1083 The πόλεις are the
cities which had furnished contingents
to the Argive expedition against Thebes.
These cities are stirred with passionate
hatred against Creon by the tidings that
burial has been refused to their fallen
warriors. There is no direct allusion to
the war of the Epigoni,—the expedition
which the sons of the fallen chiefs led
against Thebes, and in which they destroyed it. Bergk's συνταράξονται might

ὅσων σπαράγματ᾿ ἢ κύνες καθήγνισαν
ἢ θῆρες, ἤ τις πτηνὸς οἰωνός, φέρων
ἀνόσιον ὀσμὴν ἑστιοῦχον ἐς πόλιν.
τοιαῦτά σου, λυπεῖς γάρ, ὥστε τοξότης
ἀφῆκα θυμῷ καρδίας τοξεύματα   1085
βέβαια, τῶν σὺ θάλπος οὐχ ὑπεκδραμεῖ./
ὦ παῖ, σὺ δ᾿ ἡμᾶς ἄπαγε πρὸς δόμους, ἵνα
τὸν θυμὸν οὗτος ἐς νεωτέρους ἀφῇ,
καὶ γνῷ τρέφειν τὴν γλῶσσαν ἡσυχωτέραν
τὸν νοῦν τ᾿ ἀμείνω τῶν φρενῶν ἢ νῦν φέρει.   1090

1081 σπαράγματ᾿] Seyffert conject. τὰ πράγματ᾿. Tournier, ἀπάργματ᾿ . . καθύ-
βρισαν.—καθήγνισαν MSS. Burton gave καθήγισαν (from which καθήγνισαν has been
made in V); and so most of the recent editors. Bellermann keeps καθήγνισαν.
1083 πόλιν] Nauck and Seyffert write πόλον (but in different senses): for other

suggest such an allusion; but the pres. συνταράσσονται is right. The reference is to the feelings which *now* agitate the cities. Those feelings are one day to produce the new war. Here the prophet notes them only as signs of a still distant storm. Having foretold a domestic sorrow for the father, he now foreshadows a public danger for the king.

It has been objected that the play contains no hint of burial having been denied to any one except Polyneices. This is not exactly the case: the phrase τῶν ἐχθρῶν κακά in v. 10 is such a hint. But it was unnecessary for the poet to state a fact which all his hearers would assume. Every one knew how Creon had refused burial to the Argives, and how Theseus had recovered their corpses by force of arms. In the *Supplices* of Eur. the Chorus consists of widows and mothers of the unburied warriors. No Athenian exploit was more famous (Her. 9. 27; Isocr. *Paneg.* § 52, *Encom. Helen.* § 31, *Panath.* § 168; Plat. *Menex.* 244; [Lys.] or. 2 §§ 4 ff.: [Dem.] or. 60 §§ 7 ff.). The war of the Epigoni, which was included in the epic *Thebais* (Paus. 9. 9 § 5), was dramatised both by Aesch. and by Soph. (ʼEπίγονοι).

Just as, in the *O. C.* (1410 n.), Soph. glances at the theme of his *Antigone*, so here he might naturally glance—however indirectly—at a later chapter of the Theban story,—whether his *Epigoni* already existed, or was still in the future. Dramatically, the reference is the more

fitting, since the legend represented Teiresias as still living, and still zealous for Theban welfare, when the Epigoni came.—For other views of the passage, see Appendix.

1081 ὅσων (fem.) σπαράγματα, mangled bodies *belonging* to them, as being the corpses of their citizens. The possessive gen. in this sense is quite justifiable, since σπαράγματα = σώματα ἐσπαραγμένα, just as πτώματα = σώματα πεπτωκότα. (It would be possible, but harsh, to make ὅσων masc., as = ἐπεὶ τοσούτων: cp. *O. C.* 263 n.)

L's καθήγνισαν = 'hallowed' them, in the sense of, 'gave burial rites to them': cp. Eur. *Or.* 40 μήτηρ πυρὶ καθήγνισται δέμας (has had the funeral rite of fire): *Suppl.* 1211 ὑπ᾿ αὐτῶν σώμαθ᾿ ἡγνίσθη πυρί. The *v. l.* καθήγισαν reaches the same meaning ('buried') by a different channel. καθαγίζω was properly 'to devote' or 'dedicate': Her. 1. 86 ἀκροθίνια ...καταγιεῖν θεῶν ὅτεῳ δή. Then, fig., to devote to the gods below by the funeral fire; Plut. *Anton.* 14 τὸ...σῶμα τοῦ Καίσαρος ἐν ἀγορᾷ καθαγίσαι ('solemnly burn'). Either καθήγνισαν or καθήγισαν, then, is admissible. But (apart from L's support) καθήγνισαν seems preferable on two grounds: (a) its primary sense lends force to the grim irony: (b) the funereal sense of καθαγίζω has only post-classical evidence.—Hesychius (καθαγίσω) says that Soph. used καθαγίζω, not in the sense of καθιερόω, but in that of μιαίνω :—a statement perh. founded on a misunderstanding

whose mangled sons had the burial-rite from dogs, or from wild
beasts, or from some winged bird that bore a polluting breath
to each city that contains the hearths of the dead.

Such arrows for thy heart—since thou provokest me—have
I launched at thee, archer-like, in my anger,—sure arrows, of
which thou shalt not escape the smart.—Boy, lead me home,
that he may spend his rage on younger men, and learn to
keep a tongue more temperate, and to bear within his breast
a better mind than now he bears. [*Exit* TEIRESIAS.

---

emendations see Appendix.
MSS.: ἡσυχαιτέραν Schaefer.
Herwerden, ἢ νῦν φέρει: F. W. Schmidt, τῶν γε νῦν φέρειν φρενῶν.

1089 L has τρέφειν, not στρέφειν.—ἡσυχωτέραν
1090 ἤ] ὧν Brunck.—Schneidewin, ἢ νῦν φέρει:

---

of καθήγισαν here. The Schol. read the
latter (μετὰ ἄγους ἐκόμισαν). But the fact
that L has καθήγισαν must be set against
these doubtful testimonies.—For the
irony, cp. *El.* 1487 πρόθες | ταφεῦσιν, ὧν
τόνδ᾽ εἰκὸς ἐστι τυγχάνειν (as Gorgias
called vultures ἔμψυχοι τάφοι, Longin. π.
ὕψους 3 § 2): Aesch. *Th.* 1020 ὑπ᾽ οἰωνῶν
... | ταφέντ᾽ ἀτίμως: Ennius *Ann.* 142
volturus crudeli condebat membra sepulcro:
Lucr. 5. 993 *viva videns vivo sepeliri vis-
cera busta.*

1088 ἑστιοῦχον...πόλιν, the city containing the ἑστίαι of those on whose flesh
the bird has fed. The sing. is used,
although several πόλεις are concerned,
since the case of one city is the case of
all. For the adj., cp. Aesch. *Pers.* 510
ἤκουσιν ἐκφυγόντες, οὐ πολλοί τινες, | ἐφ᾽
ἑστιοῦχον γαῖαν, 'the land of their homes.'
Eur. *Andr.* 283 ἑστιοῦχον αὐλάν, the
abode that contains his hearth. Here,
the word serves to suggest a pollution of
hearth and altar (1016). Pollution, in a
ceremonial sense, could be brought by
the ὀσμή, even without an actual transport of carrion. And it is only the birds
that are said to carry the taint.—See
Appendix on 1080 ff.

1084 ff. σοῦ, 'at thee,' with ἀφῆκα:
1033 n.—θυμῷ, modal dat.: 620 n.—
καρδίας τοξεύματα, heart-arrows, i.e.,
arrows for thy heart. Cp. Eur. *Hec.* 235
καρδίας δηκτήρια: *Med.* 1360 τῆς σῆς γάρ,
ὡς χρῆν, καρδίας ἀνθηψάμην.—Not, arrows
from my (angry) heart, like ὄμματος...
τόξευμα (Aesch. *Suppl.* 1004).—τῶν = ὧν:
cp. *O. C.* 747 n.

1087 ὦ παῖ. Cp. *O. T.* 444 ἄπειμι
τοίνυν· καὶ σύ, παῖ, κόμιζέ με.

1089 τρέφειν: cp. 660 n.—ἡσυχωτέραν, the MS. reading, has been prudently

retained by most of the recent edd. In
Plat. *Charm.* 160 A the MSS. give ὁ
ἡσυχώτατος, though two lines before they
give ὡς ἡσυχαίτατα. A grammarian in
Bekker *Anecd.* 98. 19 quotes ἡσυχώτερον.
In Aesch. *Eum.* 223 the MSS. give ἡσυχαιτέραν, and in Plat. *Phileb.* 24 C
ἡσυχαιτέρου. It is true that our MSS.
have no great weight on such a point,
and that, if the ω form had been the
current one in later Greek, it would have
been likely to oust an older form in αι.
But we see that sometimes, at least, the
MSS. could preserve the αι and the ω forms
side by side. It seems safer, then, to
suppose that the normal ω form and the
irregular αι form were both in Attic use,
than to assume that the αι form alone
was tolerated. The dictum of Thomas
Magister, (quoted by Dindorf,) p. 426
ἡσυχαίτερον· οὐχ ἡσυχώτερον, is indecisive
without more evidence than we possess.

1090 τὸν νοῦν...τῶν φρενῶν ἀμείνω
(τρέφειν) ἢ νῦν φέρει (αὐτόν). Cp. *Il.* 18.
419 τῇς ἐν μὲν νόος ἐστὶ μετὰ φρεσίν,
there is understanding in their breasts:
22. 475 ἐς φρένα θυμὸς ἀγέρθη, the soul
returned to her breast. The word φρήν
being thus associated with the physical
seat of thought and feeling, ὁ νοῦς τῶν
φρενῶν was a possible phrase. So trag.
adesp. fr. 240 (when divine anger visits
a man) ἐξαφαιρεῖται φρενῶν | τὸν νοῦν τὸν
ἐσθλόν. (Cp. 176 n. ad fin.)—φέρει
705 n.—If we took τῶν φρενῶν with
ἀμείνω, then ἢ must be changed to ὧν,
with Brunck. In so compact a clause,
ἢ could not be an irregular substitute
for ὧν. Nor could ἢ νῦν φέρει be an
epexegesis: 'better than his (present)
mind,—(that is, better) than he now
bears it.'

ΧΟ. ἀνήρ, ἄναξ, βέβηκε δεινὰ θεσπίσας·
    ἐπιστάμεσθα δ', ἐξ ὅτου λευκὴν ἐγὼ
    τήνδ' ἐκ μελαίνης ἀμφιβάλλομαι τρίχα,
    μή πώ ποτ' αὐτὸν ψεῦδος ἐς πόλιν λακεῖν.

ΚΡ. ἔγνωκα καὐτὸς καὶ ταράσσομαι φρένας·   1095
    τό τ' εἰκαθεῖν γὰρ δεινόν, ἀντιστάντα δὲ
    ἄτῃ πατάξαι θυμὸν ἐν δεινῷ πάρα.

ΧΟ. εὐβουλίας δεῖ, παῖ Μενοικέως, λαβεῖν.

ΚΡ. τί δῆτα χρὴ δρᾶν; φράζε· πείσομαι δ' ἐγώ.

ΧΟ. ἐλθὼν κόρην μὲν ἐκ κατώρυχος στέγης   1100
    ἄνες, κτίσον δὲ τῷ προκειμένῳ τάφον.

ΚΡ. καὶ ταῦτ' ἐπαινεῖς, καὶ *δοκεῖ παρεικαθεῖν;

1091 ἀνήρ] ἀνὴρ L.—After βέβηκε, ν has been erased in L. 1092 ἐπιστάμεσθα ι: ἐπιστάμεθα L. 1094 λακεῖν from λαβεῖν L. 1096 τό τ' εἰκαθεῖν..
ἀντιστάντα δὲ (without accent) L: the first hand has written τ above δε.—εἰκαθεῖν
Elmsley. 1097 ἄτῃ πατάξαι θυμὸν ἐν δεινῷ πάρα MSS.—Seyffert conject. ἐν
δεινοῦ πέρα (Musgrave had already proposed πέρα, and Martin δεινῶν or δεινοῦ
πέρα).—Wecklein, ἐπὶ δεινῷ πάρα.—Nauck, ἄτῃ παλαῖσαι δεινὰ καὶ δεινῶν πέρα.—
M. Schmidt, ἀντιστάντι δὲ | ἄτῃ, μαλάξαι θυμὸν ἐν δεινοῖς, πάρα.—Semitelos, ἄτῃ

1092 f. ἐξ ὅτου: cp. 12 n.—λευκὴν...
ἐκ μελαίνης. The words could mean
either: (1) 'since this hair which clothes
my head, once dark, has been white': or
(2) 'since this hair,—once dark, now
white,—has clothed my head,'—i.e., from
infancy. The first is the sense intended
here. There is a certain looseness of
expression, since the thought is, 'though
I am old, I can recall no such case';
whereas the period actually described
might be a comparatively short one. So
we can say, 'he has grown grey in the
service of his country,' meaning, 'he has
served it all his life.'—ἀμφιβάλλομαι: cp.
Rhianus (the elegiac poet of Crete,
c. 225 B.C.) Anthol. P. 12. 93 χαίρετε,
καλοὶ παῖδες, ἐς ἀκμαίην δὲ μόλοιτε | ἥβην,
καὶ λευκὴν ἀμφιέσαισθε κόμην. For the
1st pers. sing. following ἐπιστάμεσθα, see
734 n.

1094 μή. We might have had the οὐ
of oratio obliqua with λακεῖν, =ὅτι οὐκ
ἔλακε. But here we have μή, as after
πιστεύω and like verbs. So O. T. 1455
οἶδα, μήτε μ' ἂν νόσον | μήτ' ἄλλο πέρσαι
μηδέν (n.). Cp. O. C. 656 n., 797 n.
In such cases μή seems to add a certain
emphasis to the statement of fact (like
saying, 'I protest that I know no instance').—λακεῖν, infin. (instead of the

more usual partic.) after ἐπιστάμεσθα:
293 n. This verb is esp. used of prophecy: cp. Tr. 822 (where τοῦτος τὸ
θεσπρότον is subject to ἔλακεν): Aesch.
Ag. 1426 (of Clytaemnestra) περίφρονα δ'
ἔλακες. The ref. is esp. to the seer's
denunciation of Oedipus, and his command regarding Megareus (1303 n.).

1095 ἔγνωκα, I have noted it = I know
it well; more emphatic than οἶδα: cp.
O. C. 553 n.

1096 For τε...δέ, instead of τε...τε,
cp. Tr. 285 ταῦτα γὰρ πόσις τε σὸς |
ἐφεῖτ', ἐγὼ δὲ πιστὸς ὢν κείνῳ τελῶ: ib.
333 ὡς σύ θ' οἱ θέλεις | σπεύδῃς, ἐγὼ δὲ
τἄνδον ἐξαρκῆ τιθῶ. See also O. C.
367 n., 442 n.: Ph. 1312 f. Here, δέ is
accentless in L, and the first hand has
written τ above; but, if the genuine reading had been τε...τε, the change to τε...δέ
was not likely to occur; and the antithesis
makes δέ very natural. Cp. Aesch. Ag.
206 βαρεῖα μὲν κὴρ τὸ μὴ πιθέσθαι, | βαρεῖα
δ', εἰ τέκνον δαΐξω.

1097 f. ἄτῃ πατάξαι (170 n.) θυμόν,
to smite my proud spirit with a curse.
ἀντιστάντα implies that he is stationary:
the image is not, then, like that in 854
(ἐς Δίκας βάθρον | προσέπεσες). Rather the
ἄτη is to be conceived as sweeping down
on him, like the torrent which destroys

CH. The man hath gone, O King, with dread prophecies. And, since the hair on this head, once dark, hath been white, I know that he hath never been a false prophet to our city.

CR. I, too, know it well, and am troubled, in soul. 'Tis dire to yield; but, by resistance, to smite my pride with ruin— this, too, is a dire choice.

CH. Son of Menoeceus, it behoves thee to take wise counsel.

CR. What should I do, then? Speak, and I will obey.

CH. Go thou, and free the maiden from her rocky chamber, and make a tomb for the unburied dead.

CR. And this is thy counsel? Thou wouldst have me yield?

πατάξαι πημονήν ('to punish an outrage by injury') δεινοῦ πέρα. **1098** L has λαβεῖν, as Cobet and Campbell report; not λακεῖν, as Elmsley and Dübner. β and κ are somewhat alike in L, but β resembles our *u*, while the left-hand stroke of κ is always higher than 'the right-hand stroke. See 1094, where λακεῖν has been made from λαβεῖν. The difference is usually plain; nor is there any doubt here. L² agrees with L, but has λαχεῖν κρέον in marg.: E has λαχεῖν. A, with the other MSS., has κρέον. **1102** δοκεῖς MSS.: I conjecture δοκεῖ. Nauck, λέγεις, or με λῆς.—παρεικάθειν MSS.: παρεικαθεῖν Elmsley.

---

trees that resist it (712).—ἐν δεινῷ πέρα (=πάρεστιν), it is open to me, as the dreadful alternative; lit., as a thing in the region of τὸ δεινόν. For ἐν δεινῷ cp. *El.* 384 νῦν γὰρ ἐν καλῷ φρονεῖν ('tis opportune). Eur. *Her.* 971 οὐκοῦν ἔτ' ἐστὶν ἐν καλῷ δοῦναι δίκην: *I. A.* 969 ἐν εὐμαρεῖ τε (sc. ἐστί) δρᾶν: *Helen.* 1277 ἐν εὐσεβεῖ γοῦν νόμιμα μὴ κλέπτειν νεκρῶν ('tis a matter of piety). Here, the only peculiarity arises from the fusion of two propositions, viz. (1) πάρεστιν, and (2) ἐν δεινῷ ἐστιν. The phrase would have been clearer if ὂν had been added to ἐν δεινῷ: cp. 471 n. It may be noticed that elsewhere also Soph. uses πάρεστι and παρόν of an evil lot: *Ai.* 432 νῦν γὰρ πάρεστι καὶ δὶς αὐδῆσαι ἐμοί: *El.* 959 ἦ πάρεστι μὲν στένειν... | πάρεστι δ' ἀλγεῖν: *Ph.* 283 φέρουσαν οὐδὲν πλὴν ἀνιᾶσθαι παρόν. This is a point in favour of the traditional πέρα.—Seyffert's ἐν δεινοῦ πέρα would be excellent, were it not for ἐν, which cannot be justified by the use of εἰς with superlatives (*O. C.* 563 n.). Cp. [Dem.] or. 48 § 73 δεινόν, ὦ γῆ καὶ θεοί, καὶ πέρα δεινοῦ. Wecklein conjectures ἐπὶ (for ἐν) δεινῷ: 'by resisting, it is possible that, in addition to the difficulty (of resistance), I may incur calamity.' But, apart from the risk of calamity, there was nothing in

resistance that he could call δεινόν. There is no likelihood in conjectures which displace θυμόν, such as Nauck's (see cr. n.).

1098 The question between L's λαβεῖν, and the Κρέον of later MSS., is not an easy one to decide. If λαβεῖν is an error, then it must be explained by the scribe's eye having wandered to v. 1094. But it has not been noticed (I think) that the argument from v. 1094 is two-edged. There, the scribe of L wrote λαβεῖν, which was afterwards corrected to λακεῖν, either by his own hand or by another. It might be held, then, that he wrote λαβεῖν, by an error of the eye, in 1094, because his archetype had λαβεῖν in 1098. The ep-exegetic construction of the inf. (=ὥστε λαβεῖν αὐτήν, see examples on 489 f.) may have been a stumblingblock, leading transcribers to think it a redundant gloss; when Κρέον would have been the obvious resource. Everything considered, I prefer to retain λαβεῖν.

1100 f. κατώρυχος: 774 n.—κτίσον is here more than ποίησον, as it implies observance of solemn rites: cp. 1201 ff.: Aesch. *Cho.* 483 οὕτω γὰρ ἄν σοι δαῖτες ἔννομοι βροτῶν | κτιζοίατ'.

1102 I read the impers. δοκεῖ: 'and does it seem good (to you) that I should yield?' The dat. can be understood, as

ΧΟ. ὅσον γ᾽, ἄναξ, τάχιστα· συντέμνουσι γὰρ
θεῶν ποδώκεις τοὺς κακόφρονας βλάβαι.

ΚΡ. οἴμοι· μόλις μέν, καρδίας δ᾽ ἐξίσταμαι   1105
τὸ δρᾶν· ἀνάγκῃ δ᾽ οὐχὶ δυσμαχητέον.

ΧΟ. δρᾶ νυν τάδ᾽ ἐλθὼν μηδ᾽ ἐπ᾽ ἄλλοισιν τρέπε.

ΚΡ. ὧδ᾽ ὡς ἔχω στείχοιμ᾽ ἄν· ἴτ᾽ ἴτ᾽ ὀπάονες,
οἵ τ᾽ ὄντες οἵ τ᾽ ἀπόντες, ἀξίνας χεροῖν
ὁρμᾶσθ᾽ ἑλόντες εἰς ἐπόψιον τόπον.   1110
ἐγὼ δ᾽, ἐπειδὴ δόξα τῇδ᾽ ἐπεστράφη,
αὐτός τ᾽ ἔδησα καὶ παρὼν ἐκλύσομαι.

1105 καρδίαι L. Most of the later MSS. have καρδίας: but some καρδίᾳ (as A, L²), καρδίαν, or καρδία. In L there is an erasure before ἐξίσταμαι, the first hand having first written ἐξεπίσταμαι. Semitelos writes καὶ βίᾳ 'ξεπίσταμαι. (='have been taught' how to act). **1107** νῦν L. **1108** ἴτ᾽ ἴτ᾽] Triclinius conjecturally added the second ἴτ᾽. L has ἴτ᾽, as Elmsley read it: the rough breathing has been

___

in *Ph.* 526 ἀλλ᾽, εἰ δοκεῖ, πλέωμεν, and *ib.* 645. This correction is confirmed by Aesch. *Th.* 650 σὺ δ᾽ αὐτὸς ἤδη γνῶθι τίνα πέμπειν δοκεῖ, where L has δοκεῖ with an accent erased over the ο,—showing that the use of the impers. verb without a dat., seeming strange, had suggested δόκει (imperat.). There, some of the later MSS. have δοκεῖς. Here, L shares the error of the rest, and has δοκεῖς—generated, doubtless, from δοκεῖ by the same misapprehension as in Aesch. *l. c.* The decisive objection to δοκεῖς here is that it could mean only, 'art thou minded to yield?' (Aesch. *Ag.* 16 ὅταν δ᾽ ἀείδειν ἢ μινύρεσθαι δοκῶ); not, 'dost thou think it right that I should yield?'—παρεικαθεῖν: for the form, see on *O. T.* 651. **1108 f.** συντέμνουσι...τοὺς κ., cut them (*i.e.*, their careers) short, 'cut them off.' The compressed phrase, though not strictly correct, is natural.—ποδώκεις: cp. *Il.* 9. 505 ἡ δ᾽ Ἄτη σθεναρή τε καὶ ἀρτίπος: *Ai.* 837 Ἐρινῦς τανύποδας (who are ταχεῖαι, *ib.* 843): *O. T.* 418 δεινόπους ἀρά.—βλάβαι, 'harms,' 'mischiefs,' with ref. to the primary sense of βλάπτω, to disable, or stop: *Il.* 6. 39 (horses) ὄζῳ ἔνι βλαφθέντε μυρικίνῳ, 'caught in' a tamarisk branch: Aesch. *Ag.* 120 (a hare) βλαβέντα λοισθίων δρόμων, 'stopped' from running further. The βλάβαι θεῶν cannot, however, be properly regarded as personified beings; and therefore we should not write Βλάβαι. In Aesch. *Eum.* 491 εἰ κρατήσει δίκα τε καὶ βλάβα |

τοῦδε μητροκτόνου, where some write Δίκα—Βλάβα, the sense is, 'if the cause and the wrong (=the wrongful cause) of Orestes shall prevail.'—κακόφρονας: for the ō before φρ, cp. 336 n. **1105 f.** μόλις μέν (ἐξίστ.), ἐξίστ. δέ: cp. Eur. *Ph.* 1421 μόλις μέν, ἐξέτεινε δ᾽ εἰς ἧπαρ ξίφος: Ar. *Nub.* 1363 κἀγὼ μόλις μέν, ἀλλ᾽ ὅμως ἠνεσχόμην.—ἐξίσταμαι καρδίας, resign my cherished resolve: Plat. *Phaedr.* 249 D ἐξιστάμενος...τῶν ἀνθρωπίνων σπουδασμάτων, καὶ πρὸς τῷ θείῳ γιγνόμενος. This use of καρδία was suggested by the similar use of θυμός, with which Homer associates it as the seat of desire or passion (*Il.* 13. 784 νῦν δ᾽ ἀρχ᾽, ὅππῃ σε κραδίη θυμός τε κελεύει): thus πληροῦσα θυμόν (Eur. *Hipp.* 1328) = πληροῦσα ἐπιθυμίαν.—τὸ δρᾶν, acc. of inner object, defining the concession: *Ph.* 1252 ἀλλ᾽ οὐδέ τοι σῇ χειρὶ πείθομαι τὸ δρᾶν.—δυσμαχητέον: *Tr.* 492 θεοῖσι δυσμαχοῦντες. **1107** ἐπ᾽ ἄλλ. τρέπε = ἄλλοις ἐπίτρεπε: Aesch. *Eum.* 434 ἢ κἀπ᾽ ἐμοὶ τρέψειτ᾽ ἂν αἰτίας τέλος; ('would ye commit the decision of the charge to me?') This is 'tmesis' in the proper sense,—where the prep. determines the special sense of the verb: cp. *Il.* 8. 108 οὓς ποτ᾽ ἀπ᾽ Αἰνείαν ἑλόμην = ἀφειλόμην. **1108** ὡς ἔχω, *i.e.*, forthwith: 1235: *Ph.* 819 δέξαι θανάσιμόν μ᾽ ὅπως ἔχω.—στείχοιμ᾽ ἄν, optat. with ἄν expressing a fixed resolve: *O. T.* 343 οὐκ ἂν πέρα φράσαιμι: *O. C.* 45 οὐχ...ἂν ἐξέλθοιμ᾽ ἔτι.—ἴτ᾽ ἴτ᾽. The rhythm given by the tri-

CH. Yea, King, and with all speed ; for swift harms from the gods cut short the folly of men.

CR. Ah me, 'tis hard, but I resign my cherished resolve, —I obey. We must not wage a vain war with destiny.

CH. Go, thou, and do these things ; leave them not to others.

CR. Even as I am I'll go :—on, on, my servants, each and all of you,—take axes in your hands, and hasten to the ground that ye see yonder! Since our judgment hath taken this turn, I will be present to unloose her, as I myself bound her.

questioned, but is certain. The later MSS. have ἴτ, or (as A) οἴτ'. Nauck conject. εἶ or ἀλλ': Mekler, ὥτ'. **1111** δόξαι τῆδ' (sic) ἐπεστράφην L: δόξα τῆδ' ἐπεστράφη r. The corruption in L (shared by L² and V⁴) evidently arose from failure to perceive that τῆδ' was an adverb. **1112** αὐτός τ' ἔδησα] Semitelos conject. αὐτὸς πέθησας.

---

brach suits this agitated utterance. εἶ' would be no improvement (see cr. n.). ··

1109 οἱ τ' ὄντες οἱ τ' ἀπόντες, one and all. This was doubtless a familiar phrase: cp. 40 n. El. 305 τὰς οὔσας τέ μοι | καὶ τὰς ἀπούσας ἐλπίδας διέφθορεν. Plaut. Trin. 360 comedit quod fuit quod non fuit.—δέξασθ. In Xen. An. i. 5. 12 the ἀξίνη is used by one who is ξύλα σχίζων. Here it has usually been supposed that the ἀξῖναι were to cut wood for the burning of the corpse. But no regular πυρά was made; the remains of the corpse were burned with νεοσπάδες θαλλοί, branches freshly plucked from the trees in the plain (1201). On the other hand, some implement was needed to raise the τόμβος ὀρθόκρανος of earth (1203). It seems, then, as if Soph. referred to some kind of axe which could serve like the γενῦς of v. 249 (n.). No tool was used to break open Antigone's tomb; the stones were dragged away (1216).

1110 ἐπόψιον, pass., looked-upon, beheld, from here: hence = φανερόν (schol.), 'in view.' Cp. O. C. 1600 εἰς προσόψιον | πάγον, the hill which was in view. —As Creon speaks, he points with his hand in a direction to the left of the spectators. The region meant is the furthest and highest part of the Theban plain (1197), where the body of Polyneices still lay. In the πάγοι adjacent to it was the rocky tomb of Antigone (774 n.).—Hermann assumed the loss of some vv. after 1110, in which Creon described the ἐπόψιος τόπος,—explaining that he would first bury Polyneices, and then free Antigone. But what need

was there for this, when he was himself to accompany his servants? Besides, his men, like all the other Thebans, might be supposed to know the place meant; and the Chorus had already said what was to be done there. Equally baseless is Bergk's theory that vv. 1111 —1114 are an interpolation, designed to fill a gap in the original text. See the notes on them. Dindorf agrees with Bergk only so far as to suspect vv. 1111, 1112.

1111 ἐγὼ δ'. The sense is not: 'do you go and bury Polyneices, while I release Antigone.' Creon takes part in both acts (1196 ff.). But at this moment his foremost thought is of saving Antigone. If she dies, his son must die (1066). Therefore, while he glances at the burial-rites by telling his men to bring axes, he describes his own part by his most urgent task,—the release.— ἐπεστράφην, prop., 'turned round'; as a person faces about. Eur. Alc. 187 καὶ πολλὰ θάλαμον ἐξιοῦσ' ἐπεστράφη. τῆδ', this way, in this direction (O. C. 1547).

1112 αὐτός τ' ἔδησα κ.τ.λ. = ὥσπερ αὐτὸς ἔδησα, οὕτω καὶ αὐτὸς παρὼν ἐκλύσομαι. The co-ordination (parataxis) of clauses by τε...καί, as elsewhere by μέν... δέ, is peculiarly Greek. Cp. O. T. 419 βλέποντα νῦν μὲν ὄρθ', ἔπειτα δὲ σκότον (= dark then, though now thou hast sight): O. C. 853 οὔτε νῦν καλὰ | δρᾷς, οὔτε πρόσθεν εἰργάσω (= thou art not doing well now, as neither didst thou formerly): ib. 1202 (οὐ καλὸν) αὐτὸν μὲν εὖ | πάσχειν, παθόντα δ' οὐκ ἐπίστασθαι τίνειν (while receiving benefits, to be incapable of re-

δέδοικα γὰρ μὴ τοὺς καθεστῶτας νόμους
ἄριστόν ᾖ σῴζοντα, τὸν βίον τελεῖν.'

στρ. α'. ΧΟ. πολυώνυμε, Καδμείας νύμφας ἄγαλμα,   1115
2 καὶ Διὸς βαρυβρεμέτα
3 γένος, κλυτὰν ὃς ἀμφέπεις
4 Ἰταλίαν, μέδεις δὲ
5 παγκοίνοις Ἐλευσινίας   1120

1114 σῴζοντα τὸν βίον] τὸν βίον σῴζοντα L.   1115—1125 L divides
thus: πολυώνυμε— | νύμφας— | βαρυβρεμέτα— | κλυτὰν— | Ἰτάλειαν .. παγκοίνους— |
δημοῦσ— | ὦ βακχεῦ— | ναίων— | ῥέεθρον— | τ' ἐπὶ .. δράκοντοσ | .   1115 Καδ-
μείας] Dindorf writes Καδμεῖας, and in 1126 διλόφοιο for διλόφου.—νύμφας ἄγαλμα

quiting them). Here, the rhetorical effect
of the idiom is to place the two acts in
bolder contrast. The middle ἐκλύομαι and
the active ἐκλύω (Aesch. *P. V.* 326) are
equivalent in poetry. They do not differ
as λύω (said of the captor) from λύομαι (of
the ransomer).—Nauck and others take
the words figuratively; 'As I have made
the tangle, I will unravel it' (cp. 40 n.).
This is surely wrong. See on v. 1111.

1113 f. δέδοικα μή...ᾖ: cp. *O. T.* 747
δεινῶς ἀθυμῶ μὴ βλέπων ὁ μάντις ᾖ. In
both these places, 'I fear lest...' means 'I
shrewdly suspect that ..,' and δέδοικα μή
might therefore be followed by pres.
indic., which expresses a fear that
something is now going on (cp. 278 n.
Ar. *Nub.* 493 δέδοικα...μὴ πληγῶν δέει).—
τοὺς καθεστ. νόμους, the laws established
by the gods,—the θεῶν νόμιμα of 454 f.—
σῴζοντα...τὸν βίον τελεῖν = σῴζειν ἕως ἂν
τελευτήσῃς: but the turn of phrase chosen
unconsciously foreshadows Antigone's
fate.

1115—1154 This ὑπόρχημα, or
'dance-song,' takes the place of a fifth
stasimon. The Chorus hopes that Creon
may be in time to save Antigone, and
that his sin against the dead may be
expiated without disaster. Hence this
strain, full of gladness, invoking the
healing presence (1144) of the bright and
joyous god who protects Thebes. The
substitution of a ὑπόρχημα for a stasimon
is used with a like dramatic purpose in
other plays. (1) *O. T.* 1086—1109: the
Chorus hopes that Oedipus may prove to
be of Theban birth. (2) *Ai.* 693—717,
a joyous invocation of Pan, the Chorus
believing that Ajax has indeed repented.
(3) *Tr.* 633—662: the Chorus joyously
anticipates the return of Heracles. In

each of these cases the beginning of the
end is near.

1st strophe 1115—1125 = 1st antistr.
1126—1136: 2nd str. 1137—1145 = 2nd
antistr. 1146—1154. See Metrical Analysis.

1115 f. πολυώνυμε, *i.e.*, worshipped
by various special titles in different places.
The reference of the epithet to local
rituals is well brought out by Theocr. 15.
109 (Aphrodite) πολυώνυμε καὶ πολύναε.
Most of the greater deities are called
πολυώνυμοι by the poets; but the word is
peculiarly suitable to Dionysus, owing to
the manner in which his cult was inter-
woven with other cults; thus in relation to Demeter he was Ἴακχος; to the
Muses, Μελπόμενος; to Hades, Ζαγρεύς.
Dionysus was distinctively πολυειδής καὶ
πολύμορφος (Plut. *Mor.* 389 c). Upwards of sixty titles given to him can be
enumerated (see Preller, *Griech. Mythol.*).
—Καδμείας. We should not write Καδμεῖας, and διλόφοιο in 1126, with Dindorf.
Nor is it necessary to place νύμφας after
ἄγαλμα, with Nauck. See Metrical Analysis.—ἄγαλμα, glory: Aesch. *Ag.* 207
τέκνων...δόμων ἄγαλμα.—νύμφας, bride,
young wife. Semele, daughter of Cadmus
and Harmonia, was beloved by Zeus, and
was ensnared by Hera into praying him
that he would come to her in the same
guise as to Hera. He came to her, therefore, armed with his thunderbolts, and
amid lightning, which destroyed her. She
was great with child, and Zeus saved her
son, Dionysus. βαρυβρεμέτα (for the ῠ,
cp. 336 n.) alludes to this story. Ov. *Met.*
3. 298 (Jupiter, bound by his own oath,
grants Semele's prayer): *ergo maestissi-
mus altum | Aethera conscendit, nutuque
sequentia traxit | Nubila; quis nimbos*

My heart misgives me, 'tis best to keep the established laws, even to life's end.

CH.   O thou of many names, glory of the Cadmeian bride, 1st offspring of loud-thundering Zeus! thou who watchest over strophe. famed Italia, and reignest, where all guests are welcomed, in the sheltered plain of Eleusinian

---

MSS.: ἄγαλμα νύμφας Nauck.   1119 Ἰτάλειαν L: Ἰταλίαν r.—R. Unger conject. Ἰκαρίαν (also suggested by Erfurdt): Bergk, Κιδαλίαν: M. Schmidt, Φιγαλίαν: Seyffert, φυταλίαν.—μέδεισ from μηδείσ L.   1120 παγκοίνουσ L. The first hand sometimes writes υσ very like ισ: but normally it makes this distinction, that υ is joined to the σ, while ι is not; so in κόλποισ, 1121.

---

immixtaque fulgura ventis | Addidit, et tonitrus, et inevitabile fulmen.

1119 The traditional reading, Ἰταλίαν, may be supported by these considerations. (1) Southern Italy, the seat of so many Greek colonies, was pre-eminently associated with the cultivation of the vine; and Sophocles has himself used the name which expresses that fact: Triptolemus fr. 538 Οἰνωτρία τε πᾶσα καὶ Τυρσηνικὸς | κόλπος Λιγυστική τε γῆ σε δέξεται. (2) The opening words of the ode, Καδμείας νύμφας ἄγαλμα, claim Thebes as the birth-place of Dionysus. Though Italy, then, is mentioned before Eleusis, Parnassus and Euboea, that precedence has not the effect of representing Italy as the head-quarters of the Dionysiac worship. Rather the mention of Italy just after Thebes serves to exalt the Theban god by marking the wide range of his power. And this reference to a distant country well suits the immediately following παγκοίνοις, expressing that Eleusis receives votaries from every part of the Greek world. (3) Athenian colonists founded Thurii, on the site of Sybaris, in 444—3 B.C.,—only two or three years before the probable date of this play. Thus, just at this time, the Athenian mind had been turned towards Southern Italy, and the allusion would strike a chord of sympathy in the audience. It may be worth remembering that the poet himself would naturally have felt a more than common interest in the new home of his friend Herodotus.

The only worthy rival of Ἰταλίαν is the conjecture Ἰκαρίαν. This was the name of a deme in the N. E. of Attica, picturesquely situated in an upland valley bounded on the N. by the mountain-chain ('Aphorismo') which shuts in the plain of Marathon, and on the s. by Pentelicus. The site—at a place called 'Dionyso'—is proved by local inscriptions, found by members of the American School in 1888. The story was that, when Dionysus first entered Attica, he was received at Icaria by Icarius, whom he taught to make wine. Icaria was associated with the earliest celebrations of the rural Dionysia (thus the ἀσκωλιασμός, or dancing on greased wine-skins, was said to have been introduced by Icarius himself), and with the infancy of Attic drama in both kinds,—as it was also the birth-place of Thespis, and, at a later time, of the comic poet Magnes. Inscriptions and other remains show that, in the 5th century B.C., it was the seat of an active Dionysiac worship, with dramatic performances. These discoveries remind us that Sophocles might well have called Icaria κλυτάν. Prof. A. C. Merriam further points out that, in literature, the legend of Icaria is often associated with that of Eleusis (American School at Athens: Seventh Annual Report, 1887—88, p. 96). To Statius, Theb. 12. 619 (Icarii Celeique domus), may be added Apollod. 3. 14. 7, Lucian De Salt. 39 f., Nonnus 27. 283 ff., etc. But these facts remain: (1) Ἰταλίαν is also suitable, and is in all the MSS.: (2) it widens the range ascribed to the god's power: (3) a corruption of Ἰκαρίαν into Ἰταλίαν is not one to which the letters would readily lend themselves, and would have been the less likely to occur because Icaria was familiarly associated with Dionysus.

1120 f. παγκοίνοις, welcoming guests from every quarter to the Eleusinian Mysteries: schol. ἐν οἷς πάντες συνάγονται διὰ τὰς πανηγύρεις. Cp. El. 138 ἐξ Ἀΐδα παγκοίνου λίμνας. Pind. O. 6. 63

6 Δηοῦς ἐν κόλποις, Βακχεῦ, Βακχᾶν
7 ὁ ματρόπολιν Θήβαν
8 * ναιετῶν παρ' ὑγρὸν
9 Ἰσμηνοῦ ῥεῖθρόν <τ'> ἀγρίου τ' ἐπὶ σπορᾷ δρά-
κοντος·   1124

ἀντ. α'. - σὲ δ' ὑπὲρ διλόφου πέτρας στέροψ ὄπωπε
2 λιγνύς, ἔνθα Κωρύκιαι
3 στείχουσι Νύμφαι Βακχίδες,

1121 Δηοῦς] δηιοῦσ L.   1122 ὦ βακχεῦ· βακχᾶν μητρόπολιν L. Herm. deleted
ὦ: Musgrave added ὁ before μητρόπολιν.—ματρόπολιν Dindorf.   1128 f. ναίων
παρ' ὑγρὸν ἰσμηνοῦ | ῥέεθρον L (the second ρ of ῥέεθρον from ν). Dindorf restored
ναιετῶν. Triclinius gave ὑγρῶν .. ῥεέθρων (Hermann ῥείθρων). I conjecture ὑγρὸν ..
ῥεῖθρόν τ'.   1126—1186 L divides thus: σὲ δ'— | στέροψ...ἐν|θα— | στείχουσι— |
κασταλείασ τε— | σε νυσαίων— | κισσήρεισ— | πολυστάφυλοσ— | ἀμβρότων— | θηβαίασ
...ἀγυιάσ. | 1126 διλόφου MSS.: διλόφοιο Dindorf (cp. on 1115).   1127 f. ἐν|θα

πάγκοινον ἐς χώραν (Olympia).—κόλποις, recesses, i.e., the sheltered Thriasian plain, enclosed by hills,—Aegaleos on the E., Cithaeron on the N., and the Kerāta range on N. w. and w. Cp. Ar. Ran. 373 ἐς τοὺς εὐανθεῖς κόλπους λειμώνων (where, though the scene is in Hades, the allusion is to the Initiated visiting Eleusis). So Pind. O. 9. 87 Νεμέας... κατὰ κόλπον: ib. 14. 23 κόλποις παρ' εὐδόξου Πίσας. This is better than to refer κόλποις to the Bay of Eleusis, whose shores are the λαμπάδες ἀκταί of O. C. 1049 (where see nn.).—Ἐλευσίνίας: on the ῑ, see n. on this v. in Metr. Analysis. Δηοῦς = Δήμητρος: Hom. h. Dem. 47 πότνια Δηώ. In this connection the proper name of the god was Ἴακχος (1152), a young deity who was represented as the son of Cora (or of Demeter); cp. O. C. 682 n. Indeed, Arrian expressly distinguishes the Eleusinian Iacchus from the Theban Dionysus, An. 2. 16 § 3: Ἀθηναῖοι Διόνυσον τὸν Διὸς καὶ Κόρης σέβουσιν...καὶ ὁ Ἴακχος ὁ μυστικὸς (the chant of the initiated) τούτῳ τῷ Διονύσῳ, οὐχὶ τῷ Θηβαίῳ, ἐπᾴδεται. But, as Welcker remarks (Götterl. 2, p. 543), Dionysus was the general name, often substituted for the special title.
1122 Βακχεῦ. The omission of ὦ before this word, and the addition of ὁ before ματρόπολιν, are conjectural (cr. n.). But they are certainly right; for the antistrophic words (1133) answering to Βακχεῦ—Θήβαν, are χλωρά τ' ἀκτὰ | πολυστάφυλος πέμπει, which are unques-

tionably sound.—ματρόπολιν: cp. O. C. 707 n. Thebes is the 'mother-city' of the Bacchants, as being the city of Semele and the native place of Dionysus. It was the place at which the Dionysiac cult, coming from Asia Minor by way of Thrace, first established itself in Greece Proper. From Thebes the cult was propagated to Delphi, and associated with the worship of Apollo. See Eur. Bacch. 306. Cp. O. T. 210 n., Tr. 510.
1128 f. L has ὑγρὸν...ῥέεθρον, not ὑγρῶν...ῥεέθρων, which was merely a conjecture of Triclinius. And the use of παρά with the genit. is not only un-exampled (see n. on 966), but here, at least, wholly unintelligible. Metre requires, however, that a long syllable (answering to the first syll. of Θηβαίας in 1135) should precede ἀγρίου. I obtain this by adding τ' after ῥεῖθρον. The second syll. of ὑγρόν, as the last of a verse, is common. παρά with acc. is correct in ref. to a river, the notion being that his abode extends along its banks: cp. El. 184 ὁ παρὰ τὸν Ἀχέροντα θεὸς ἀνάσσων: Xen. An. 4. 3 § 1 τοῦ πεδίου τοῦ παρὰ τὸν Κεντρίτην ποταμόν: ib. § 6 ἐστρατοπεδεύσαντο παρὰ τὸν ποταμόν. For the position of τ', cp. O. T. 258 n., O. C. 33 n. The sing. ῥεῖθρον is not less suitable than the plur.: cp. Aesch. Pers. 497, P. V. 790. For the epithet ὑγρόν, cp. Od. 4. 458 (Proteus) γίγνετο δ' ὑγρὸν ὕδωρ, 'running water.'—Ἰσμηνοῦ: see n. on 103 f.
1128 ἐπὶ σπορᾷ δρ., 'over the seed

Deô! O Bacchus, dweller in Thebè, mother-city of Bacchants, by the softly-gliding stream of Ismenus, on the soil where the fierce dragon's teeth were sown!

Thou hast been seen where torch-flames glare through 1st anti-smoke, above the crests of the twin peaks, where move the strophe. Corycian nymphs, thy votaries,

κωρύκιαι νύμφαι | στείχουσι βακχίδες L. Blaydes places νύμφαι after στείχουσι. Dindorf gives νύμφαι στίχουσι (Hesych. στίχουσι· βαδίζουσι, πορεύονται. στίχωμεν· πορευθῶμεν, βαδίσωμεν). Pallis, στείβουσι νύμφαι. Rauchenstein, Κωρύκιον | νύμφαι νέμουσι. M. Schmidt, Κωρύκιαι | γνυφαί ('glens') τ' ἔχουσι Βακχίδες. (Hesych. explains γνυφή by νάπη.) Seyffert, ἔνθα Κωρυκίας | γνυφάς τ' ἔχουσι Βακχίδες. So Keck, but with νάπας τ' for γνυφάς τ', and Semitelos with εὐνάς τ'.

---

of the dragon,' *i.e.*, on the ground where Cadmus sowed the dragon's teeth, from which the ancestors of the Cadmeans sprang. Hence the Thebans are called σπαρτοὶ ἄνδρες (*O. C.* 1534 n.). The place where Cadmus sowed the teeth was shown on the s. side of Thebes, near the Ἠλεκτραι πύλαι (Paus. 9. 10. 1).—Not, '(ruling) over the dragon's seed,' as if σπορᾷ meant the Thebans.

1126 f. The general sense is: 'and on the heights of Parnassus thou holdest thy revels by night amid the Corycian Nymphs, who brandish torches.'—διλόφου πέτρας: *i.e.*, two πέτραι, each with a λόφος (cp. 146 διρατεῖς λόγχας, n.): two peaks, one of which stands on each side of a great recess in the steep cliffs above Delphi,—the cliffs called Φαιδριάδες, 'gleaming,' from their splendour in the morning sunshine (cp. Eur. *Ion* 86 ff.). These cliffs are about 2000 ft. above sea-level. The easternmost of the two peaks was called 'Τάμπεια: the westernmost, perh. Ναυπλία, but this is doubtful. Neither of them is the summit of Parnassus. That summit, called Λυκώρεια, rises high above them (about 8000 ft. above the sea). Misunderstanding διλόφου, the Roman poets gave a wrong impression by their 'biceps Parnassus,' which Lucan brings out when he says (5. 72) 'Parnassus gemino petit aethera colle.'

By ὑπὲρ διλόφου πέτρας Soph. means the high ground above these two lower peaks, but below the summit of Parnassus. This high ground is what Eur. calls the διόρνυφος πλάξ (Eur. *Bacch.* 307). It consists of uplands stretching about 16 miles westward from the summit,

and affording pasturage, interspersed with firs, and with pieces of arable land: wheat, oats, and barley are now grown there. These uplands were the scene of a Dionysiac τριετηρίς, a torch-festival, held every second year, at the end of winter, by women from the surrounding districts; even Attic women went to it (Paus. 10. 4. 3). Cp. Lucan 5. 73 *Mons Phoebo Bromioque sacer, cui numine misto | Delphica Thebanae reserunt trieteria Bacchae:* and Macrobius *Sat.* 1. 18. 3. Here, however, the poet alludes, not to the human festival, but to supernatural revels.

λιγνύς is a smoky flame, such as a resinous pine-torch gives; στέροψ finely expresses the lurid and fitful glare flashing through the smoke.—ὄπωπε, gnomic perf., 'hath (oft) seen thee': *i.e.*, when the Nymphs brandish their torches, Dionysus is in the midst of them. It was the popular belief that dancing fires could be seen by night on Parnassus, when the god was holding his revels. Eur. *Ion* 716 (Parnassus) ἵνα Βάκχιος ἀμφιπύρους ἀνέχων πεύκας | λαιψηρὰ πηδᾷ νυκτιπόλοις ἅμα σὺν Βάκχαις: cp. *ib.* 1125: *Bacch.* 306: *Phoen.* 226: *I. T.* 1243.

Κωρύκιαι...Νύμφαι: Nymphs who haunt the Κωρύκιον ἄντρον and its neighbourhood. The name is from κώρυκος, 'a wallet' (and so, a hollow thing), and was given also to a cave on the Cilician coast. The Parnassian cave is near the top of a hill on the high table-land which lies at the base of the central cone,—about 7 miles N. E. of Delphi, and as many N. W. of Aráchova. It is a large stalactite cavern, consisting of an outer chamber of some 200 ft. in length, and an inner one

4 Κασταλίας τε νᾶμα.   1130
5 καί σε Νυσαίων ὀρέων
6 κισσήρεις ὄχθαι χλωρά τ' ἀκτὰ
7 πολυστάφυλος πέμπει,
8 ἀμβρότων ἐπέων
9 εὐαζόντων, Θηβαίας ἐπισκοποῦντ' ἀγυιάς·   1135

στρ. β'.   τὰν ἐκ πασᾶν τιμᾷς ὑπερτάταν πόλεων
2 ματρὶ σὺν κεραυνίᾳ·
3 καὶ νῦν, ὡς βιαίας ἔχεται   1140
4 πάνδαμος πόλις ἐπὶ νόσου,
5 μολεῖν καθαρσίῳ ποδὶ Παρνασίαν ὑπὲρ κλιτὺν
6 ἢ στονόεντα πορθμόν.   1145

1130 κασταλείασ L, with ϊ above ει from the first hand.   1134 ἀμβρότων L: ἀβρότων Turnebus.—ἐπέων] Hartung conj. ἐπετῶν (Pallis, ἐπετᾶν).   1135 Θηβαίασ L. Θηβαίας Hermann (=1124 ων ἀγρίου τ').   1137—1145 L divides thus: τὰν— | ὑπερτάταν— | ματρὶ— | καὶ νῦν— | ἔχεται— | ἐπὶ— | καθαρσίῳ— | ὑπέρ...πορθμόν. | 1137 L τὰν ἐκ πασᾶν τιμᾶσ | ὑπερτάταν πόλεων L. The second α of ὑπερτάταν seems to have been ω: and some letters have been erased above the line. Dindorf conject. τὰν ἔκπαγλα τιμᾷς | ὑπὲρ πασᾶν πόλεων. Blaydes τὰν ἐξ ἀπασᾶν |

---

of about 100 ft.; the greatest breadth is about 200 ft., and the greatest height, 40. In 480 B.C., when the Persians were coming, many of the Delphians took refuge in it (Her. 8. 36). An old place of sacrifice can still be seen in it; and an inscription found there shows that it was sacred Πανὶ καὶ νύμφαις (C. I. G. 1728). Aesch. Eum. 22 σέβω δὲ νύμφας, ἔνθα Κωρυκὶς πέτρα | κοίλη, φίλορνις, δαιμόνων ἀναστροφή.
The simple transposition, στείχουσι νύμφαι for νύμφαι στείχουσι, satisfies the metre, and is far more probable than the change of στείχουσι into στίχουσι,—a form which, though noticed by Hesychius, is not known to have been used by any Attic writer of the classical age.
1130 Κασταλίας τε νᾶμα, sc. ὀπωπέ σε. The Κασταλία is a stream which flows from a fissure in the high cliffs above Delphi. It issues near the easternmost of the two peaks (1126 ff., n.),—that which was called Τάμπεια: and bounds in cataracts, down a precipitous channel, to Delphi, where its water was used for all sacred purposes. Below Delphi it joins the Pleistus (Aesch. Eum. 27). It is now called Ἅγιος Ἰωάννης. It is fitly mentioned here, since it rises on the edge

of the highlands which form the scene of the revels.
1131 καί σε Νυσαίων. And from Nysa in Euboea thou comest to visit Thebes, with thy followers who cry εὐοῖ. The Euboean Nysa was imagined near Aegae (famous for its temple of Poseidon), on the w. coast of the island, opposite Anthedon. Cp. Stephanus Byz. and Hesych. s.v. Νῦσα. That word. prob. denoted a moist and fertile place: Welcker would refer it to a lost νύω from rt. νυ (νέω) Götterl. I. 439. 'Dionysos' was 'the Zeus of Nysa' (Preller Myth. I. 549). Legend placed a Nysa in Thrace (Il. 6. 133), Macedonia, Thessaly, Boeotia, Naxos, Caria, Lydia, Cilicia, Arabia, Aethiopia, Libya, India, and even at Parnassus. In a fragment of the Thyestes Sophocles beautifully describes a wondrous vine of Euboea, which puts forth leaves and bears fruit in the same day: fr. 235 ἔστι γάρ τις ἐναλία | Εὔβοιἀ αἶα· τῇδε βάκχειος βότρυς | ἐπ' ἦμαρ ἔρπει, κ.τ.λ.
1132 κισσήρεις ὄχθαι, ivy-clad hills. Usually ὄχθη = a river-bank, ὄχθος = a hill: so Ph. 726 Σπερχειοῦ...παρ' ὄχθαις, and just afterwards (729) Οἴτας ὑπὲρ ὄχθων. But the distinction is not always observed; nor need we suspect our MSS.;

hard by Castalia's stream.

Thou comest from the ivy-mantled slopes of Nysa's hills, and from the shore green with many-clustered vines, while thy name is lifted up on 'strains of more than mortal power, as thou visitest the ways of Thebè:

Thebè, of all cities, thou holdest first in honour, thou, and thy mother whom the lightning smote; and now, when all our people is captive to a violent plague, come thou with healing feet over the Parnassian height, or over the moaning strait! ^{2nd} strophe.

ὑπερτιμᾷς πόλεων. Wecklein proposed (*Ars Soph. em.* p. 76) τὰν ἔκπαγλα τιμᾷς | ὑπερτιμᾷς πόλεων, but in his ed. (1874) has τασᾶν instead of τιμᾷς. **1140** καὶ νῦν L. Tournier conject. καιρός. **1141** πάνδημος L: πάνδαμος Dindorf.—Boeckh added ἀμά before πόλις, in order to obtain a metrical correspondence with the MS. text of the antistrophic verse, 1150: but see n. there.—ἐπὶ] Musgrave conject. ὑπό. **1144** παρνησίαν L: Παρνασίαν r.

---

for the fact was noticed in antiquity (schol. on Aratus *Phaenom.* 33). Thus Pind. *P.* 1. 64 ὄχθαις ὕπο Ταϋγέτου: Eur. *Suppl.* 655 Ἰσμήνιον πρὸς ὄχθον.—The κισσός was to Dionysus what the δάφνη was to Apollo. The crowning with ivy (κίσσωσις) was a regular incident of his fesitvals: he was called κισσεύς, κισσοκόμης, κισσοχαίτης. Cp. Alciphron *Epist.* 2. 3 § 10 μὰ τὸν Διόνυσον καὶ τοὺς Βακχικοὺς αὐτοῦ κισσούς. Ov. *F.* 3. 767 hedera est gratissima Baccho.

1132 πολυστάφυλος: cp. *Il.* 2. 537 Χαλκίδα τ' Εἰρέτριάν τε πολυστάφυλόν θ' Ἰστίαιαν. As Histiaea, afterwards Oreus, was on the N. coast, we may suppose that the Homeric epithet—here borrowed by Soph.—would have been at least equally applicable to other parts of the island.—κόραν, agreeing with nearest subject: 830 n.

1134 f. The words ἀμβρότων ἐπέων answer metrically to ναιετῶν παρ' ὑγρόν (1123). There is no metrical reason, then, for altering the MS. ἀμβρότων, with Turnebus, to ἀβρότων. Cp. *O. T.* 158 ἄμβροτε Φάμα. There is no certain instance of ἄβροτος in Tragedy. Cp. Pind. *P.* 4. 299 ἀμβροσίων ἐπέων, 'divine strains.' Here the epithet suggests the mystic power of the invocation.—εὐάζοντων: see on εὔιον, 964: 'while divine chants resound with the cry evoe'; i.e., while the bacchants escort thee on thy way to Thebes with chants of praise. The conjecture ἐπετᾶν is neat, but needless.

1137 f. τὰν ἐκ πασᾶν. There is no reason, metrical or other, for suspecting

the MS. reading here. See on 1146. τάν, Θήβαν, implied in Θηβαίας: cp. 668, 1072.—For ἐκ ('chosen out of') cp. 164: ὑπερτάταν, proleptic; cp. Eur. *I. A.* 573 μείζω πόλιν αὔξει: Plat. *Rep.* 565 c τοῦτον τρέφειν τε καὶ αὔξειν μέγαν.

1139 κεραυνίᾳ, destroyed by the lightning of Zeus: see on 1115 f. Works of art frequently associate Dionysus with his mother. Thus a fragmentary vase-painting shows him introducing her to Olympus (Welcker, *Alte Denkm.* III. pl. 13). On coins she is sometimes enthroned beside him. See Baumeister, *Denkm.* p. 443.

1140 f. ἔχεται ἐπὶ βιαίας νόσου, is captive to a violent (=a most grievous) plague. The νόσος is the divine anger which Thebes has incurred (1015). ἐπὶ νόσου seems to be like ἐπ' εἰρήνης ('in time of peace' *Il.* 2. 797), ἐπὶ σχολῆς (Aeschin. or. 3 § 191): i.e., the prep. expresses the continuing presence of the νόσος, and the whole phrase strictly means, 'the city is in distress, under the prevalence of a malady.' (We could scarcely compare ἐπὶ ξύλου, and suppose a metaphor from a rack or cross; cp. n. on 308 f.) Musgrave's ὑπό (for ἐπί) is tame. For ἔχεται cp. Plat. *Legg.* 780 B ὑπὸ πολλῆς ἀπορίας ἐχομένοις. There is only a verbal likeness to Her. 6. 11 ἐπὶ ξυροῦ γὰρ ἀκμῆς ἔχεται (are poised) ἡμῖν τὰ πρήγματα.—For βιαίας cp. n. on 1310 δειλαίος. The text is sound, without Boeckh's conjectural insertion of ἀμά before πόλις: see on 1150.—πάνδαμος: cp. on 7.

1143 ff. μολεῖν: infin. for imperat.: cp. n. on 150 ff.—καθαρσίῳ: Dionysus

ἀντ. β.   ἰὼ πῦρ *πνειόντων χοράγ᾽ ἄστρων, νυχίων
2 φθεγμάτων ἐπίσκοπε,
3 παῖ Διὸς γένεθλον, προφάνηθ᾽,
4 *ὦναξ, σαῖς ἅμα περιπόλοις   1150
5 Θυίαισιν, αἵ σε μαινόμεναι πάννυχοι χορεύουσι
6 τὸν ταμίαν Ἴακχον.

1146—1154 L divides thus: ἰὼ— | χοραγέ— | φθεγμάτων— | παῖ— | προφά-
νηθι— | σαῖσ— | θυϊάσιν— | πάννυχοι— | χορεύουσι . . Ιακχον. | 1146 f. ἰὼ πῦρ
πνεόντων | χοραγέ ἄστρων· καὶ νυχίων | L. (So the later MSS., some with χοράγ᾽.)
For πνεόντων, Brunck gave πνειόντων. Hermann, inserting τῶν before πῦρ, made
πνεόντων a spondee. He also deleted καὶ before νυχίων.—Wolff: ἰὼ πύρπνων
ἄστρων χοραγέ καὶ νυχίων. (So Campbell, but with ὦ πῦρ πνεόντων.)—Semitelos: ἰὼ

was often invested with the attributes of
the Purifier and Healer, as καθάρσιος,
ἀλεξίκακος, ἀκέσιος, etc. Cp. Athen. 22
E, and 36—37. This was one aspect of
the Delphian cult which associated him
with Apollo.—κλιτόν – –, as Tr. 271:
but – –, Od. 5. 470 ἐς κλιτὺν ἀναβάς.
Here, the last syll. of the verse being
common, ὑν stands for ὑν. —πορθμόν, the
Euripus, between Euboea and Boeotia.
At Chalcis (Egripo) it is only 40 yards
across.—στονόεντα refers to the noise of
wind and water in the strait, with its
constantly changing currents. Strabo 9.
403 περὶ δὲ τῆς παλιρροίας τοῦ Εὐρίπου
τοσοῦτον μόνον εἰπεῖν ἱκανόν, ὅτι ἑπτάκις
μεταβάλλειν φασὶ καθ᾽ ἡμέραν ἑκάστην καὶ
νύκτα. Livy (28. 6) explains this by the
squalls from the hills. Cp. Lucan's description of the Euripus, 5. 234, Arctatus
rapido fervet qua gurgite pontus.
    1146 f. πνειόντων, Brunck's simple
correction of πνεόντων, heals the metre.
The MS. reading in 1137 f. is above all
reasonable suspicion; and these verses
now agree with them. It is a sin against
all critical method to make violent
changes in 1137 f.—as Dindorf (followed
by Wecklein) does—in order to keep the
short syllable of πνεόντων here. Hermann's argument against πνειόντων, which
has deterred editors from admitting it, was
strangely weak. He said that the first
syllable of the epic πνείω never occurs
with ictus (i.e., in arsis); and that, if the
tragic poets had used that form, they
would at least not have put an ictus on
the πνει. But Homer repeatedly has
πνοῇ with ictus on the 1st syll. (as first

word of the verse): and as πνοιή to πνοή,
so is πνείω to πνέω. It is plain, therefore, that the Homeric absence of ictus
from the πνει of πνείω was purely an
accident of convenience in composition,
—the phrases being μένεα πνείοντες. ζε-
φυρίη πνείουσα, ἠδὺ μάλα πνείουσαν, πνείει
τε καὶ ἕρπει, etc. We need not dwell,
then, on the fact which makes a second
fallacy in the argument,—viz. that the
ictus on πνει here is only equal to that
which falls on ονr (see Metr. Anal.).
Tragic lyrics teem with epic forms and
phrases. ζάω was at least as familiar a
word as πνέω. Yet twice in lyrics Soph.
has ventured to use the epic ζώω: El.
157 οἷα Χρυσόθεμις ζώει: O. C. 1213
ζώειν. Is it, then, reasonable to suppose
that the poet, requiring – – – instead of
– – –, would have hesitated to use the
familiar epic form πνειόντων? Nor is
this all. In Aesch. Cho. 621 the MSS.
give πνέονθ᾽ ἁ κυνόφρων ὕπνῳ: where
πνέονθ᾽ ἁ = σύμμετρον in the strophe (610),
and the 1st syllable is (pace Hermanni)
necessarily long, being that of a spondee
(or trochee): Heath's correction, πνείονθ᾽,
is therefore certain.
    Other conjectures are: (1) ἰὼ πύρπνων
ἄστρων χοραγέ καὶ νυχίων (G. Wolff).
The objection is that the contracted πύρ-
πνους and πύρπνοον do not justify πύρπνων
for πυρπνόων: cp. Eur. Med. 478 ταύρων
πυρπνόων ἐπιστάτην. (2) ὦ (for ἰὼ) πῦρ
πνεόντων χοραγέ καὶ νυχίων (Campbell).
Here πνεόντων is a spondee. But such
a synizesis seems very improbable. Remark, too, that L's χοραγέ ἄστρων does
not warrant us in supposing that ἄστρων

O thou with whom the stars rejoice as they move, the
stars whose breath is fire; O master of the voices of the night;
son begotten of Zeus; appear, O king, with thine attendant
Thyiads, who in night-long frenzy dance before thee, the giver
of good gifts, Iacchus!

2nd anti-
strophe.

πῦρ πⲛλλόντων χοράγ', ἄστρων νυχίων | φθεγμάτων. Cp. on 1149. 1148 φθεγ-
μάτων] φεγγάτων Gleditsch, on a former conject. of Nauck's. 1149 ταί
διὸς L. In order to obtain a long syll. (=νῦν 1140), Pallis proposes Διὸς ταί :
Seyffert, ταί Δίον : Bothe, ταί Ζηνός.—Semitelos writes, ἐπισκόπει | γᾶν, Δρούς
γένεθλον. 1150 προφάνηθι ναξίαισ L. Bergk restored προφάνηθ', ὦναξ.—
Musgrave had given προφάνηθ', ὦ Ναξίαις. See on 1141. 1152 θυιάσιν L:
Θυίαισιν Boeck .

originally preceded χοραγέ. Neglect of
elision is frequent in L: thus, to take
one play only, the *O. C.* supplies these
examples : 266 τἀμά· ἐπεί : 694 ἔστιν δὲ
οἴαν : 883 τἀδε. ὕβρις : 915 κύρια ὧδε :
1026 θηρῶντα ἡ τύχη : 1210 ἴσθι, ἐάντερ.
The deletion of καὶ before νυχίων is also
warranted by instances in which καὶ has
been thrust into L. Here, the καὶ would
decidedly enfeeble the passage.

χοράγ' ἄστρων. The sympathetic joy
of the elemental powers—stars, moon, and
sea—was especially associated with those
night-festivals in which Dionysus bore
his mystic character, as the young Ἴακχος
of the Eleusinian ritual, the companion
of Demeter and Cora (n. on *O. C.* 682 ff.).
See Eur. *Ion* 1078 ff., where the reference is to the Dionysus of the Great Mysteries at Eleusis : ὅτε καὶ Διὸς ἀστερωπὸς
| ἀνεχόρευσεν αἰθήρ, | χορεύει δὲ Σελάνα |
καὶ πεντήκοντα κόραι | Νηρέος. Hence
this crowning strain, which begins by
greeting him as χοραγὸς ἄστρων, fitly closes
with his Eleusinian name—νυχίων φθεγμάτων, the songs, or wild cries, of his
worshippers. Eur. *Bacch.* 485 (Pentheus)
τὰ δ' ἱερὰ νύκτωρ ἢ μεθ' ἡμέραν τελεῖς;—
ΔΙ. νύκτωρ τὰ πολλά· σεμνότητ' ἔχει σκό-
τος. Plut. *Mor.* 291 A mentions, as
Boeotian festivals of Dionysus, the Ἀγρι-
ώνια and Νυκτέλια,—ὦν τὰ πολλὰ διὰ
σκότους δρᾶται. Ar. *Ran.* 340 (the Chorus
of the Initiated) ἔγειρε φλογέας λαμπάδας
ἐν χερσὶ τινάσσων, | Ἴακχ', ὦ Ἴακχε, | νυκ-
τέρου τελετῆς φωσφόρος ἀστήρ.

1149 ταί Διὸς=καὶ νῦν ὡς (1140),
but is sound, since the second syllable
may be either long or short (see Metr.
Anal.).

1150 ἄναξ is a certain correction of

L's ναξίαισ. The latter, *i. e.*, Ναξίαις,
may be rejected for two reasons. (1) vv.
1140 f. (καὶ νῦν—ἐπὶ νόσου) are clearly
sound, and the weak addition of ἀμά before πόλις is a pure guess, based on the
supposed genuineness of Ναξίαις here.
(2) Naxos was, indeed, peculiarly associated with Dionysus, through Ariadne's
story, and in other ways (Diod. 5. 50 ff.,
Plin. *N. H.* 4. 12. 22): but, here, Ναξίαις,
as the epithet of his followers, would be
inappropriate, since he is to visit Thebes
either from Parnassus or from Euboea
(1143 f.).

1152 f. Θυίαισιν (θύω, to sacrifice),
female votaries of Dionysus,—here, his
attendant Nymphs (*O. C.* 679 n.),—not
human worshippers. The pediment of
the temple at Delphi represented Dionysus with the Thyiads, and a setting sun
(Stephani, *Compt. rend.*, 1860, vol. 3 pp.
77 ff.). Similar names were Βάκχαι,
Λῆναι, Μαινάδες (this properly a general
epithet); and, in Macedonia, Κλώδωνες,
Μιμαλλόνες (Plut. *Alex.* 2). Plut. *Mor.*
389 C quotes some words of a thyiad
song, εὔιον ὀρσιγύναικα μαινομέναις Διόνυσον ἀνθέοντα τιμαῖς. In Elis a Dionysiac
festival was called τὰ Θυῖα (Paus. 6. 26.
1). Cp. Catull. 64. 255 ff.: Verg. *Aen.* 4.
301 ff.—χορεύουσι with acc. of the god,
as Pind. *I.* 1. 7 Φοῖβον χορεύων. Cp.
κόπτομαι, τίλλομαι, τύπτομαι with acc. of
person mourned.

1154 ταμίαν, dispenser (of their fortunes): cp. Plat. *Rep.* 379 E ὡς 'ταμίας'
ἡμῖν Ζεὺς 'ἀγαθῶν τε κακῶν τε τέτυκ-
ται.'—Ἴακχον : see on χοράγ' ἄστρων
(1146).

1155—1352 Exodos. The threefold
catastrophe. Creon's remorse.

ΑΓΓΕΛΟΣ.

Κάδμου πάροικοι καὶ δόμων ᾽Αμφίονος,   1155
οὐκ ἔσθ᾽ ὁποῖον στάντ᾽ ἂν ἀνθρώπου βίον
οὔτ᾽ αἰνέσαιμ᾽ ἂν οὔτε μεμψαίμην ποτέ.
τύχη γὰρ ὀρθοῖ καὶ τύχη καταρρέπει
τὸν εὐτυχοῦντα τόν τε δυστυχοῦντ᾽ ἀεί·
καὶ μάντις οὐδεὶς τῶν καθεστώτων βροτοῖς.   1160
Κρέων γὰρ ἦν ζηλωτός, ὡς ἐμοί, ποτέ,
σώσας μὲν ἐχθρῶν τήνδε Καδμείαν χθόνα,
λαβών τε χώρας παντελῆ μοναρχίαν,
ηὔθυνε, θάλλων εὐγενεῖ τέκνων σπορᾷ·
καὶ νῦν ἀφεῖται πάντα. τὰς γὰρ ἡδονὰς   1165
ὅταν προδῶσιν ἄνδρες, οὐ τίθημ᾽ ἐγὼ

1156 στάντ᾽ ἂν] Nauck conject. πάντ᾽ ἄν: Meineke, ἂν τιν᾽: Semitelos, ὅτῳ σινόστ᾽ ἀν. 1157 ἂν from ἀμ, with an erasure after it, L. 1160 καθεστώτων] Blaydes conject. ἐφεστώτων. 1161 ὡς ἐμοί, ποτέ] ὡς ἐμοί ποτε L. 1162 μὲν] Hartung conject. γάρ. 1163 λαβών τε] λαβόντε L. 1164 After θάλλων, τε has been erased in L. 1165 ff. τὰς γὰρ ἡδονὰς | ὅταν προδῶσιν ἀνδρὸς οὐ τίθημ᾽ ἐγώ· L. Then follows v. 1168 πλούτει τε. So too the later MSS. Athenaeus 7. 280 C supplies verse 1167, quoting 1165—1171 thus: τὰς γὰρ ἡδονὰς | ὅταν προδῶσιν ἄνδρες, οὐ τίθημ᾽ ἐγώ | ζῆν τοῦτον, ἀλλ᾽ ἔμψυχον ἡγοῦμαι νεκρόν. | πλούτει τε . . . πρὸς τὴν ἡδονήν. In 12. p. 547 C he quotes the same verses in the same

---

1155 δόμων goes with Κάδμου also: cp. O. T. 417 μητρός τε καὶ τοῦ σοῦ πατρός: O. C. 1399 κελεύθου τῆς τ᾽ ἐμῆς δυσπραξίας. Cadmus founded Thebes; at a later time, Amphion (Niobe's husband) and his brother Zethus built a wall round it (Apoll. Rhod. 1. 740 ff.). The Thebans are πάροικοι (neighbours) δόμων, as dwelling around the Καδμεία, the Theban acropolis which was the seat of Cadmus (cp. O. T. 20 n.).

1156 f. οὐκ ἔστι (τοιοῦτος ἀνθρώπου βίος), ὁποῖον οὔτ᾽ αἰνέσαιμ᾽ ἂν ποτε οὔτε μεμψαίμην στάντα: there is no kind of human life that I would ever praise, or complain of, as fixed. The partic. στάντα has a causal force, giving the ground for the praise or blame. Prosperity may seem secure, or misery irremediable; but no condition can be regarded as really stable (στάσιμον). Soph. has given us a perfect comment on στάντα (which Nauck calls 'undoubtedly' corrupt) in fr. 786, and it is strange that it should have escaped notice:—ἀλλ᾽ οὑμὸς ἀεὶ πότμος ἐν πυκνῷ θεοῦ | τροχῷ κυκλεῖται, καὶ μεταλλάσσει φύσιν· | ὥσπερ

σελήνης δ᾽ ὄψις εὐφρόνας δύο | στῆναι δύναιτ᾽ ἂν οὔποτ᾽ ἐν μορφῇ μιᾷ,—cannot *remain fixed* in one phase.—βίον is the antecedent drawn into the clause and case of the relative: O. C. 56 ὃν δ᾽ ἐπιστείβεις τόπον | ...καλεῖται etc.: ib. 907 νῦν δ᾽ οὔσπερ αὐτὸς τοὺς νόμους εἰσῆλθ᾽ ἔχων.—The only other tenable view would be: οὐκ ἔστι (βίος τοιοῦτος στὰς) ὁποῖον αἰνέσαιμ᾽ ἄν: there is no life so situated that I could praise it. On this view, στάντα would cohere closely with ὁποῖον, having been attracted into the acc. like βίον itself. This is not impossible; but, if this were the construction, I should wish to read ὁποίᾳ: cp. Ai. 950 οὐκ ἂν τάδ᾽ ἔστη τῇδε μὴ θεῶν μέτα.

1160 μάντις...τῶν καθεστώτων, a prophet *about* them,—i. e., one who can say how long they will last. The conjecture ἐφεστώτων ('imminent'), which Nauck receives, is decidedly wrong for two reasons. (1) Though we find Κῆρες ἐφεστᾶσιν, etc., the perf. *part.* was regularly used as it is in Ai. 1072 τῶν ἐφεστώτων (masc.) κλύειν 'to obey the *rulers*'; and here a Greek would rather have sup-

Enter MESSENGER, *on the spectators' left hand.*

ME. Dwellers by the house of Cadmus and of Amphion, there is no estate of mortal life that I would ever praise or blame as settled. Fortune raises and Fortune humbles the lucky or unlucky from day to day, and no one can prophesy to men concerning those things which are established. For Creon was blest once, as I count bliss; he had saved this land of Cadmus from its foes; he was clothed with sole dominion in the land; he reigned, the glorious sire of princely children. And now all hath been lost. For when a man hath forfeited his pleasures, I count him not

words. Eustathius p. 957. 17 quotes τὰς γὰρ ἡδονὰς | ὅταν προδῶσιν ἄνδρα (*sic*), οὐ τίθημ' ἐγώ, and remarks that, after these words, τὰ ἀκριβῆ ἀντίγραφα have the verse, ἦν τοῦτον, ἀλλ' ἔμψυχον ἡγοῦμαι νεκρόν. If his statement did not rest merely on Athenaeus, then, in the 12th cent., a century after L was written, there were MSS. extant which could have corrected it here; yet all our MSS. share its defect. This point should be noticed as favouring the view that all our MSS. come from L. The edition of Turnebus (Paris, 1553) was the first which incorporated v. 1167.—See Appendix.

posed the sense to be, 'no one in authority is a prophet.' (2) The point is that things may seem established, and yet he unstable.

1161 δὴ ἐμοί: *Ai.* 396 ἔρεβος ὦ φαεννότατον ὡς ἐμοί: cp. *O. C.* 20 n.

1162 ff. σώσας...ἐχθρῶν: the gen. as after λύω. Ἐλευθερόω: *Ph.* 919 σῶσαι κακοῦ: Eur. *Or.* 779 σωθῆναι κακῶν.— The regular constr. would have been ἦν ἤλπισεν, σώσας μὲν χθόνα, λαβὼν δὲ μοναρχίαν. For δέ, τε has been substituted, as in *Tr.* 1012 πολλὰ μὲν ἐν πόντῳ κατά τε ὄρια πάντα καθαίρων: *Ph.* 1056 πάρεστι μὲν | Τεῦκρος,... | ἐγώ θ': ib. 1136 ὁρῶν μὲν αἰσχρὰς ἀπάτας, | στυγνόν τε φῶτ'. Then in the second clause, λαβών τε, a new finite verb, ηὔθυνε, has been inserted, with the result that λαβών now begins a new sentence. Cp. 815 ὕμνησεν, n.— συντελής, complete; Plat. *Legg.* 698 A ἡ συντελής...ἐλευθερία: cp. 737 n.—ηὔθυνε: cp. 178, 167: *O. T.* 104 ἀπευθύνειν πόλιν. The temporal augment for verbs beginning with ευ is attested by Attic inscr. of c. 403–321 B.C. (Meisterhans, p. 78).—ηὔγανε, not εὐγανῶν: 793 n.

1164 ἀφεῖται πάντα, all has been given up,—has slipped from his grasp, and been lost. Cp. Her. 8. 49 ἡ γὰρ Ἀσσυρίη ἀπεῖτο ἤδη (to the Persians). The perf. pass. of ἀφίημι is always pass. in sense, usu. meaning either 'set free'

(as Isocr. or. 17 § 11), or, 'left free' (Plat. *Critias* 117 C, of open ground), or 'permitted' (Thuc. 5. 91). The only apparent instance of ἀφεῖμαι as a perf. midd. is Dem. or. 23 § 157 τοῦ μὲν τιμωρεῖσθαι τὸν Χαρίδημον ἀφεῖσθαι, ἀποστεῖλαι δ' ὑπόσπονδον. But there, as ἀποστεῖλαι suggests, we must surely read the 2nd aor. midd. ἀφέσθαι, which was frequent in this sense (Plat. *Gorg.* 458 C, etc.). If ἀφεῖται were midd. here, we should require πάντων: cp. Thuc. 2. 60 τοῦ κοινοῦ τῆς σωτηρίας ἀφίεσθε.

1166 προδῶσιν. προδιδόναι ἡδονάς could not mean merely, 'to *resign*' one's joys. It necessarily implies a fault on the loser's part; and it is precisely because Creon had committed such a fault that I believe προδῶσιν to be sound. The man accused of taking a bribe to break the law was described at 322 as ἐπ' ἀργύρῳ... τὴν ψυχὴν προδούς. Our word, 'to forfeit,' *i.e.*, 'to lose by one's own fault,' seems fairly to represent the shade of meaning which distinguishes προδιδόναι ἡδονάς from ἀπολλύναι ἡδονάς. Creon's joys—the life of his son, and the good opinion of his subjects—have been sacrificed by him to the indulgence of stubborn self-will. Athenaeus, who twice quotes this passage (cr. n.), shows that c. 200 A.D. it was read as above: he is our oldest and best source for it. L's ἀνδρὸς must be con-

ἦν τοῦτον, ἀλλ' ἔμψυχον ἡγοῦμαι νεκρόν.
πλούτει τε γὰρ κατ' οἶκον, εἰ βούλει, μέγα,
καὶ ζῆ τύραννον σχῆμ' ἔχων· ἐὰν δ' ἀπῇ
τούτων τὸ χαίρειν, τἄλλ' ἐγὼ κἀπνοῦ σκιᾶς   1170
οὐκ ἂν πριαίμην ἀνδρὶ πρὸς τὴν ἡδονήν.
ΧΟ. τί δ' αὖ τόδ' ἄχθος βασιλέων ἥκεις φέρων;
ΑΓ. τεθνᾶσιν· οἱ δὲ ζῶντες αἴτιοι θανεῖν.
ΧΟ. καὶ τίς φονεύει; τίς δ' ὁ κείμενος; λέγε.
ΑΓ. Αἵμων ὄλωλεν· αὐτόχειρ δ' αἱμάσσεται.   1175
ΧΟ. πότερα πατρῴας ἢ πρὸς οἰκείας χερός;
ΑΓ. αὐτὸς πρὸς αὑτοῦ, πατρὶ μηνίσας φόνου.
ΧΟ. ὦ μάντι, τοὔπος ὡς ἄρ' ὀρθὸν ἤνυσας.

1168 πλούτει from πλουτεῖ L. βούλει is accentless in L, with an erasure above it. 1169 ζῇ] ζῆι L: ζῇ r (with gl. ζῆθι in V). 1170 ί. ἐγώ] Tournier proposes to write ἄγω, and to delete v. 1171.—πριαίμην ἀνδρί] Gleditsch conject. ποιοίμην πάντα.

sidered in connection with the fact that L (like our other MSS.) omits v. 1167. L has a point at προδῶσιν, and its reading was (I suspect) understood thus: 'when (men) forfeit their pleasures, I do not count that the part of a man' (i.e., of one who can be really said to live). Hence I do not think that L's ἀνδρός really confirms Seyffert's conjecture, καὶ γὰρ ἡδοναὶ | ὅταν προδῶσιν ἀνδρός, 'when a man's pleasures fail.' For this use of προδιδόναι, cp. Her. 7. 187 οὐδέν μοι θώυμα παρίσταται προδοῦναι τὰ ῥέεθρα τῶν ποταμῶν (that they failed = ἐπιλιπεῖν): id. 8. 52 τοῦ φράγματος προδεδωκότος, the barricade having failed (them). Xenophanes fr. 1. 5 ἄλλος δ' οὗτος ἕτοιμος, ὃς οὐποτέ φησι προδώσειν. So with acc., [Dem.] or. 52 § 13 τὸν ὀφθαλμὸν αὐτὸν προδιδόντα (his eye-sight failing him). Yet here the phrase would seem a strange one. And if ἀνδρός was older than ἀνδρός, as we have reason to believe that it was, that fact would confirm the genuineness of τὰς γὰρ ἡδονάς.—See Appendix.

οὐ τίθημι with inf., as oft. with the midd. τίθεμαι; Plat. Phaed. 93 C τῶν οὖν τιθεμένων ψυχὴν ἁρμονίαν εἶναι. Cp. El. 1270 δαιμόνιον αὐτὸ τίθημ' ἐγώ.

1167 For ζῆν, ζών has been proposed: but the Epic and Ionic ζώς does not occur in Attic.—τοῦτον after the plur. as, conversely, ὅστις is followed by οὗτοι (709 n.), and νέκυν by ὧν (1072).—ἔμψ. νεκρόν: cp.

Ph. 1018 ἄφιλον, ἔρημον, ἄπολιν, ἐν ζῶσιν νεκρόν.

1168 ί. πλούτει...ζῆ, the hypothetical imperat.: Antiphon fr. 130 (ap. Stob. Flor. 68. 37) φέρε δὴ καὶ παῖδες γενέσθωσαν· φροντίδων ἤδη πάντα πλέα. Dem. or. 20 § 14 οὐδὲ γὰρ εἰ πάνυ χρηστόν ἐσθ', ὡς ἐμοῦ γ' ἕνεκα ἔστω, βελτίων ἐστὶ τῆς πόλεως τὸ ἦθος.—εἰ βούλει: Plat. Rep. 432 Α τοὺς ἰσχυροτάτους καὶ τοὺς μέσους, εἰ μὲν βούλει, φρονήσει, εἰ δὲ βούλει, ἰσχύϊ. For the form ζῆ, cp. Eur. I. T. 699 ἀλλ' ἕρπε καὶ ζῆ καὶ δόμους οἴκει πατρός. But Anthol. P. 11. 57 πῖνε, γέρον, καὶ ζῆθι (by Agathias, c. 550 A.D.): and so ib. 10. 43 (author uncertain).—σχῆμα, outward show, dignity, pomp: Plat. Legg. 685 C τὸ τῆς ἀρχῆς σχῆμα...οὐ σμικρόν.

1170 τὸ χαίρειν: Ai. 555 ἕως τὸ χαίρειν καὶ τὸ λυπεῖσθαι μάθῃς. Aesch. Eum. 301 ἔρρει, τὸ χαίρειν μὴ μαθών ὅπου φρενῶν: ib. 423 ὅπου τὸ χαίρειν μηδαμοῦ νομίζεται. For the thought, cp. Simonides fr. 71 τίς γὰρ ἁδονᾶς ἄτερ θνατῶν βίος ποθεινὸς ἢ ποία τυραννίς; | τῆς δ' ἄτερ οὐδὲ θεῶν ζαλωτὸς αἰών: where ἡδονή is as general as τὸ χαίρειν here. More often, however, the sentiment refers to sensuous ἡδοναί: cp. Mimnermus fr. 1 τεθναίην ὅτε μοι μηκέτι ταῦτα μέλοι: Antiphanes fr. incert. 51 (it is foolish to disparage ἔρως), εἰ γὰρ ἀφέλοι τις τοῦ βίου τὰς ἡδονάς, | καταλείπετ' οὐδὲν ἕτερον ἢ τεθνηκέναι.—καπνοῦ σκιᾶς: gen. of price

as living,—I hold him but a breathing corpse. Heap up riches in thy house, if thou wilt; live in kingly state; yet, if there be no gladness therewith, I would not give the shadow of a vapour for all the rest, compared with joy.

CH. And what is this new grief that thou hast to tell for our princes?

ME. Death; and the living are guilty for the dead.

CH. And who is the slayer? Who the stricken? Speak.

ME. Haemon hath perished; his blood hath been shed by no stranger.

CH. By his father's hand, or by his own?

ME. By his own, in wrath with his sire for the murder.

CH. O prophet, how true, then, hast thou proved thy word!

1175 αὐτόχειρ] Meineke conject. ἀρτίχειρ. **1177** φόνου] φόνωι L, with ου above from first hand.—Herwerden conject. γόνος: Keck, κόρης.

(nom., καπνοῦ σκιά). *Ph.* 946 οὐδ' οἶδ' ἐναίρων νεκρὸν ἢ καπνοῦ σκιάν, | εἴδωλον ἄλλως. Aesch. fr. 390 τὸ γὰρ βρότειον σπέρμ' ἐφ' ἡμέραν φρονεῖ, | καὶ πιστὸν οὐδὲν μᾶλλον ἢ καπνοῦ σκιά. So Soph. fr. 12 ἄνθρωπός ἐστι πνεῦμα καὶ σκιὰ μόνον. Cp. Pind. *P.* 8. 95 σκιᾶς ὄναρ | ἄνθρωπος. Aesch. *Ag.* 839 εἴδωλον σκιᾶς.

1171 πριαμένῳ ἀνδρί. After a verb of buying or receiving, the dat. of interest denotes the person who has the thing taken off his hands: Ar. *Ach.* 812 πόσου πρίωμαί σοι τὰ χοιρίδια; *Il.* 15. 87 Θέμιστι δὲ καλλιπαρῄῳ | δέκτο δέπας.—πρὸς τὴν ἡδ., *compared with* it: fr. 327. 4 κᾶστι κρέα τὰ χρήματα | θνητοῖσι τἆλλα δεύτερ': Eur. fr. 96 ἀλλ' οὐδὲν ηὐγένεια πρὸς τὰ χρήματα. Suppose that one could buy either (1) wealth and power without joy, or (2) joy without wealth and power; in comparison with (2), (1) would be worth nothing.—Not, '*in exchange for* pleasure,' like Plat. *Phaed.* 69 A ἡδονὰς πρὸς ἡδονὰς... καταλλάττεσθαι: for the price is expressed by καπνοῦ σκιᾶς.

1172 f. βασιλέων = τυράννων, the royal house. *Tr.* 316 μὴ τῶν τυράννων; is she of the royal stock?—αἴτιοι θανεῖν, instead of τοῦ θανεῖν: Antiphon or. 5 § 23 ἐγὼ αἴτιος ἦν πεμφθῆναι ἄγγελον.—As vv. 1186 ff. show, Eurydicè is supposed to be in the act of opening the palace-door, to come out, when she overhears evil tidings. If she is supposed to have fainted (1188) immediately on hearing the general announcement in v. 1173,

then her request in v. 1190 is the more natural. Possibly the spectators were allowed to catch a glimpse of her through the partly opened doors; though the Chorus announce her only at 1180.

1174 φονεύει = ὁ φονεύς ἐστιν: cp. *O. T.* 437 τίς δέ μ' ἐκφύει βροτῶν (is my sire), where see n.—ὁ κείμενος: cp. Aesch. *Eum.* 590 οὐ κειμένῳ πω τόνδε κομπάζεις λόγον.

1175 αὐτόχειρ could mean either 'by a kinsman's hand,' or 'by his own hand.' See n. on 56 αὐτοκτονοῦντε. Hence such compounds sometimes receive a further definition, as *Ai.* 841 αὐτοσφαγεῖς | πρὸς τῶν φιλίστων ἐκγόνων. But in Aesch. *Eum.* 336 αὐτουργίαι, without any such addition, = 'murders of kinsfolk.' G. Wolff ought not, however, to have compared Xen. *H.* 6. 4. 35, ἀποθνῄσκει αὐτοχειρίᾳ μὲν ὑπὸ τῶν τῆς γυναικὸς ἀδελφῶν, βουλῇ δὲ ὑπ' αὐτῆς ἐκείνης, i.e., 'by the deed of their hands' (cp. above, v. 306), 'though at her instigation.' Attic prose does not use αὐτόχειρ or αὐτοχειρία in the pregnant poetical sense (a slayer, or a slaying, of kinsfolk), but merely in the general sense, 'doing with one's own hands,' etc. See Plat. *Legg.* 872 B: *ib.* 865 B, etc.

1177 f. φόνου, causal gen.: 931 (τούτων) n.—ὀρθὸν ἤνυσας, hast fulfilled it, so that it comes right (cp. 1136, n. on ὑπερτάταν): *O. T.* 506 πρὶν ἴδοιμ' ὀρθὸν ἔπος: cp. *ib.* 853. *O. C.* 454 (μαντεῖα) ἁμοὶ Φοῖβος ἤνυσέν ποτε.

ΑΓ. ὡς ὧδ' ἐχόντων τἆλλα βουλεύειν πάρα.

ΧΟ. καὶ μὴν ὁρῶ τάλαιναν Εὐρυδίκην ὁμοῦ   1180
δάμαρτα τὴν Κρέοντος· ἐκ δὲ δωμάτων
ἤτοι κλύουσα παιδὸς ἢ τύχῃ πάρα.

ΕΥΡΥΔΙΚΗ.

ὦ πάντες ἀστοί, τῶν λόγων ἐπῃσθόμην
πρὸς ἔξοδον στείχουσα, Παλλάδος θεᾶς
ὅπως ἱκοίμην εὐγμάτων προσήγορος.   1185
καὶ τυγχάνω τε κλῇθρ' ἀνασπαστοῦ πύλης
χαλῶσα, καί με φθόγγος οἰκείου κακοῦ
βάλλει δι' ὤτων· ὑπτία δὲ κλίνομαι
δείσασα πρὸς δμωαῖσι κἀποπλήσσομαι.

1179 τἆλλα βουλεύειν] Blaydes conject. τῶνδε βουλεύειν: Martin, τἆλλα μου κλύειν: Wecklein, τἆλλα συμβάλλειν. 1182 πάρα] Brunck conject. περᾷ. 1183 ὦ πάντες] Blaydes conject. ὤνακτες: Heimsoeth, ἄνωθεν (with ῥημάτων for τῶν λόγων): Hense, γέροντες.—τῶν λόγων L: τοῦ λόγου γ' A. 1184 θεᾶς] Nauck conject. βρέτας: Dorschel (ap. Wolff) σέβας. Semitelos, Παλλάδ' ὡς θεᾶν.

1179 δέ with the gen. absol. (cp. 1063 n.) marks the point of view which is to be taken: 'in the certainty that matters stand thus.' πάρεστι βουλ. τὰ ἄλλα, 'ye may consider of the rest': i.e., such are the facts; it only remains to deal with them as may seem best. βουλεύειν, to form plans, decide on a course of action, O. T. 619: τὰ ἄλλα, adverbial acc. of respect, 'as to what remains,' instead of περὶ τῶν ἄλλων (Ai. 551 τὰ δ' ἄλλ' ὁμοίως).—ὧδ' ἐχόντων, neut. gen. abs., without a subject: Ai. 981 ὡς ὧδ' ἐχόντων... | πάρα στενάζειν: El. 1344 τελουμένων εἴποιμ' ἄν: Aesch. Pers. 170 πρὸς τάδ', ὡς οὕτως ἐχόντων τῶνδε, σύμβουλοι λόγου | τοῦδέ μοι γένεσθε, Πέρσαι. Thuc. I. 116 ἐσαγγελθέντων ὅτι...νῆες...πλέουσιν.

1180 καὶ μὴν: 526 n.—Εὐρυδίκην: anapaest in 5th place: cp. 11 n. Schol.: Ἡσίοδος Ἡνιόχην αὐτὴν καλεῖ· ἵκετο δ' εἰς Κρέοντα καὶ Ἡνιόχην [ταύτην ἔπλον, sc. Heracles: Scut. 83].—ὁμοῦ= ἐγγύς: Ar. Pax 513 καὶ μὴν ὁμοῦ 'στιν ἤδη. Soph. has it also as a prep.: Ai. 767 θεοῖς... ὁμοῦ=σὺν θ.: in Ph. 1218 νεὼς ὁμοῦ=πέλας νεώς.

1182 κλύουσα παιδός: gen. of connection, 'about' him: O. C. 307 κλύων σοῦ (n.), hearing of thee.

1183 ὦ πάντες ἀστοί, said to the

Chorus and the Messenger, as representing the Thebans generally. In Eur. I. T. 1422 Thoas says ὦ πάντες ἀστοί, not to the Chorus (of Greek women), but to the Tauri as represented by his attendants. So, too, in Ar. Eccl. 834 ὦ πάντες ἀστοί is said to an imaginary body of Athenian citizens, represented by two men on the stage. In Lys. 638 the Chorus say ὦ πάντες ἀστοί to the audience.

1184 f. Παλλάδος προσήγορος εὐγμάτων answers to Παλλάδα προσαγορεύω εὐγματα: i.e., the first gen. is objective, while the second represents an 'inner' accus. A combination of genitives was easily tolerated by Greek idiom: cp. 795 βλεφάρων ἵμερος...νύμφας (n.): Xen. Cyr. 8. 3. 19 δεόμενοι Κύρου ἄλλος ἄλλης πράξεως. προσήγορος, active, as O. T. 1338: it is passive ib. 1437, Ph. 1353.—The shrine to which Eurydicè was going may be imagined as one of the two Παλλάδος ναοί at Thebes mentioned in O. T. 20 (n.). She was anxious to do her part in seeking to propitiate the angry gods (1019).—So Iocasta comes forth from the house to offer prayers at the altar of Apollo Λύκειος (O. T. 919), and Clytaemnestra at that of Apollo προστατήριος (El. 637).

1186 f. τυγχάνω τε...καὶ...βάλλει: just as she was loosing the bolt, she heard

ME. These things stand thus ; ye must consider of the rest.
CH. Lo, I see the hapless Eurydicè, Creon's wife, approaching ; she comes from the house by chance, haply,—or because she knows the tidings of her son.

Enter EURYDICÈ.

EU. People of Thebes, I heard your words as I was going forth, to salute the goddess Pallas with my prayers. Even as I was loosing the fastenings of the gate, to open it, the message of a household woe smote on mine ear : I sank back, terror-stricken, into the arms of my handmaids, and my senses fled.

1185 ὅπως] Wolff conject. ὅμμ' ὡς.   1186 τε L, with γ written above τ by the first corrector S, (not, I think, by the first hand:) some of the later MSS. have γε: L² has δέ.   1189 δμωαῖσι] In L, S has written •εσ• over αἶ (i.e., δμώεσσι).

---

the sound (cp. 1172 f. n.). For the temporal parataxis with τε...καί, cp. Xen. *An.* 1. 8 § 1 ἤδη τε ἦν ἀμφὶ ἀγορὰν πλήθουσαν καὶ πλησίον ἦν ὁ σταθμός: so *ib.* 4. 2. 12, 4. 6. 2, *Cyr.* 1. 4. 28. So with καί alone, *O. T.* 718 n.

κλῆθρα χαλῶσα πύλης ἀνασπαστοῦ, loosing the bolts of the door, so that it should be opened (proleptic, cp. 475, 881). For the fem. of the verbal in -τός, see *O. T.* 384 n.—κλῆθρα, 'bolts,' are bars of wood drawn across the doors inside, and held by staples or sockets (πυθμένες *O. T.* 1261) in the door-posts (σταθμοί). Such bars were usu. called μοχλοί, but even in prose we find the more general word κλῆθρα: Xen. *An.* 7. 1. 17 διακόπτοντες τὰς θύρας τὰ κλεῖθρα ἀναπεταννύουσι τὰς πύλας. There, as here, the plur. κλῆθρα, referring to only one gate, indicates that more than one bolt was used; so, too, Ar. *Lys.* 310 κἂν μὴ καλούντων τοὺς μοχλοὺς χαλῶσιν αἱ γυναῖκες, | ἐμπιμπράναι χρὴ τὰς θύρας. Cp. Aesch. *Cho.* 878 πύλας | μοχλοῖς χαλᾶτε, open the door by (withdrawing) the bars. Eur. *Med.* 1314 χαλᾶτε κλῇδας. Plut. *Pelop.* 11 ἀνοῖξαι καὶ χαλάσαι τὰς θύρας.

ἀνασπαστοῦ. These doors opened inwards. ἐπισπᾶν θύραν meant to shut the door after one, in going out. Cp. Xen. *H.* 6. 4. 36 ὡς δ' εἰσῆλθον, ἐπισπάσασα τὴν θύραν ἔχετο τοῦ ῥότρου (Thebe's object was to shut her brothers into the room, till they had killed Alexander of Pherae): 'when they had entered, she, [having gone out and] shut

the door, held the knocker,'—the ῥόπτρον being a metal ring on the outside of the door, which also served as ἐπισπαστήρ or handle (cp. Her. 6. 91). Plut. *Dion* 57 οἱ μὲν ἔξω τὰς θύρας ἐπισπασάμενοι κατεῖχον. (In *O. T.* 1244 πύλας...ἐπιρράξασα is said of Iocasta, within the room, shutting the doors; but they, too, opened inwards, see *ib.* 1261 ff.) Hence ἀνασπᾶν θύραν, 'to draw it back,' is the opposite of ἐπισπᾶν, and means 'to open it' (from within). That phrase was not actually current, ἀνοιγνύναι being the common word; but the poetical ἀνασπαστός here implies it. Polyb. 5. 39. 4 is not rightly compared : there, ὡς ἀνασπάσοντες...τὰς πυλίδας, 'intending to wrench the gates open,' from outside: cp. id. 2. 5. 5 *fin.*... γεφύρας ἀνασπάσαντες τὰς σανίδας, 'having torn up the floor of the bridge.'

φθόγγος, the Messenger's words. She had fainted before hearing more, perhaps, than vv. 1172 f., where see n.—οἰκεῖου, domestic (affecting her family): cp. 1249. —Distinguish οἰκ. πάθη (*Ai.* 260), οἰκ. ἄτας (*El.* 215) as = 'caused by oneself.'

1188 δι' ὥτων: *El.* 737 ὀξὺν δι' ὥτων κέλαδον ἐνσείσας θοαῖς | πώλοις: cp. *O. T.* 1386 f.—πρὸς δμωαῖσι, with κλίνομαι: a use of the dat. with πρός which has epic precedent, as *Il.* 20. 420 λιαζόμενον προτὶ γαίῃ, sinking to earth: *ib.* 21. 507 τὴν δὲ προτὶ οἷ | εἷλε πατὴρ Κρονίδης, took her to his arms: cp. *O. T.* 1302 n.—ἀποπλήσσομαι, as = λιποψυχῶ, only here: Hippocr. uses it of apoplexy.

14—2

ἀλλ' ὅστις ἦν ὁ μῦθος αὖθις εἴπατε·   1190
κακῶν γὰρ οὐκ ἄπειρός οὖσ' ἀκούσομαι.
ΑΓ. ἐγώ, φίλη δέσποινα, καὶ παρὼν ἐρῶ,
κοὐδὲν παρήσω τῆς ἀληθείας ἔπος.
τί γάρ σε μαλθάσσοιμ' ἂν ὧν ἐς ὕστερον
ψεῦσται φανούμεθ'; ὀρθὸν ἀλήθει' ἀεί.   1195
ἐγὼ δὲ σῷ ποδαγὸς ἑσπόμην πόσει
πεδίον ἐπ' ἄκρον, ἔνθ' ἔκειτο νηλεὲς
κυνοσπάρακτον σῶμα Πολυνείκους ἔτι·
καὶ τὸν μέν, αἰτήσαντες ἐνοδίαν θεὸν
Πλούτωνά τ' ὀργὰς εὐμενεῖς κατάσχεθεῖν,   1200
λούσαντες ἁγνὸν λουτρόν, ἐν νεοσπάσιν
θαλλοῖς ὃ δὴ 'λέλειπτο συγκατήθομεν,
καὶ τύμβον ὀρθόκρανον οἰκείας χθονὸς
χώσαντες, αὖθις πρὸς λιθόστρωτον κόρης

1193 παρείσω L, with η above ει from S.   1194 ἐς ὕστερον] ἐσύστερον L.
1195 ἡ ἀλήθει' L: ἀλήθει' Hermann.   1197 πεδίον ἐπ' ἄκρων (sic) L. The
later MSS. have either πεδίον ἐπ' ἄκρων (as V), or πεδίον ἐπ' ἄκρον (as A).   Pallis,

1192 f. καὶ παρὼν ἐρῶ, κοὐδὲν
παρήσω: I both will speak as one who
was present, and will omit nothing: i.e.,
as my knowledge is full, so shall the story
be told without reserve. For the parataxis, cp. 1112: El. 680 κἀπεμπόμην
πρὸς ταῦτα καὶ τὸ πᾶν φράσω: Tr. 626
ἐπίσταμαί τε καὶ φράσω σεσωσμένα. For
παρών as partic. of the imperfect, cp.
166 σέβονται (n.). Verses 1192—1195
form the dramatic apology for a trait
which is manifestly open to criticism,—
viz., the fulness of harrowing details
communicated by the Messenger to this
unhappy mother, who has only just recovered from a swoon. (See esp. 1231
—1239.)
    1194 f. ὧν = τούτοις ὧν: Xen. Mem.
1. 2. 6 διαλέγεσθαι παρ' ὧν λάβοιεν τὸν
μισθόν, to converse with any who might
pay them. Cp. 35 n.—ὧν with ψεῦσται
(=fabricators), as one could say, ταῦτα
ἐψεύσαντο. For φανούμεθ' after the sing.
verb, cp. 734 n.—ὀρθόν, not ὀρθή: O. T.
542 n.: O. C. 592.
    1196 ποδαγός, Doric (cp. 715 ναῦς, n.),
'guide,' as Eur. Ph. 1715 σύ μοι ποδαγὸς
ἄθλια γενοῦ (Oed. to Antigone). Plat.
Legg. 899 A has ποδηγεῖν as = 'to guide.'
—The word is usu. taken here as merely

padissequus, 'attendant.' But the sense
of 'guiding' is essential to it.   Creon had
indicated the region (1110), but he need
not be supposed to know the spot where
the body lay, or even the exact situation
of Antigone's tomb. ἑσπόμην, 'attended,'
is compatible with guiding.
    1197 πεδίον...ἄκρον = the furthest part
of the plain.   Near this part were the
πάγοι on which the watchers sat (411),
and Antigone's tomb was in one of those
πάγοι (774 n.).   Thebes had hills to the
N. of it, and stood on a low spur which
they throw out southward (117 ff., n.).
The ἄκρον πεδίον, then, is the plain's
northern edge, where it touches the lower
slopes of the hills.   The 'furthest' was
thus also the highest part.—νηλεές, passive: O. T. 180.
    1198 κυνοσπάρακτον: cp. 206, 1017.
Antigone had paid the rites while the
corpse was still intact (257), and in this
sense is said to have saved it from birds
and dogs (697: cp. 467).
    1199 f. τὸν μέν, as opposed to Antigone:
but instead of τῆς δὲ νυμφείου, etc., we
have a change of construction (1204 αὖθις
κ.τ.λ.).—ἐνοδίαν θεόν, Hecatè, who was
conceived as a wandering goddess, haunt-
ing the places where roads met, and where

But say again what the tidings were ; I shall hear them as one who is no stranger to sorrow.

ME. Dear lady, I will witness of what I saw, and will leave no word of the truth untold. Why, indeed, should I soothe thee with words in which I must presently be found false? Truth is ever best.—I attended thy lord as his guide to the furthest· part of the plain, where the body of Polyneices, torn by dogs, still lay unpitied. We prayed the goddess of the roads, and Pluto, in mercy to restrain their wrath ; we washed the dead with holy washing ; and with freshly-plucked boughs we solemnly burned such relics as there were. We raised a high mound of his native earth ; and then we turned away to enter the maiden's nuptial chamber with rocky couch,

---

πάγων ἐπ' ἄκρων. **1200** πλούτωνά τ' ὀργᾶς from πλούτωνά τ' ὀργᾶς L.—κατασχέθειν L : κατασχεθεῖν Elmsley. **1202** δὴ λέλειπτο L : cp. on 539.

---

offerings were left for her. (Τριοδῖτις, Trivia: Theocr. 2. 36 ἁ θεὸς ἐν τριόδοισι.) Sophocles in his 'Ριζοτόμοι gave an incantation by Medea, invoking Helios and Hecatè (fr. 490, schol. Apoll. Rhod. 3. 1214): Ἥλιε δέσποτα καὶ πῦρ ἱερόν. | τῆς εἰνοδίας Ἑκάτης ἔγχος, | τὸ δι' Οὐλύμπου πωλεῦσα φόρει (which she bears when she moves through the sky, as Selenè), | καὶ γῆς ναίουσ' ἱερὰς τριόδους, | στεφανωσαμένη δρυΐ καὶ πλεκταῖς | ὠμῶν σπείραισι δρακόντων. The last two lines refer to a custom of representing her as crowned with serpents, and with chaplets of oak-leaves. Creon invokes her along with Pluto (Hades, O. T. 30 n.), because on earth she represented the χθόνιοι. As ἐνοδία, she was more especially associated with Hermes ἐνόδιος and ψυχοπομπός: hence she was sometimes called ἄγγελος. —θεόν, fem., as 834: O. C. 1548 ἡ... νερτέρα θεός, ib. 1556 τὰν ἀφανῆ θεόν (Persephone). Cp. ib. 683 n.—τόμενάς, proleptic: 881 n.—κατασχεθεῖν: cp. on 1102.

1201 f. λούσαντα ἀγν. λουτρόν (cognate acc.): cp. on 901.—ἐν, 'with,' of the instrument: 764 (n.), 962, 1003.—θαλλοῖς, from the ὕλη πεδὰς close by (420).—Boeckh thought that olive-boughs were meant, citing a νόμος ap. [Dem.] or. 43 § 71 ἐὰν μὴ (ἐλαίᾳ)...ἐπὶ ἀποθανόντα δέῃ χρήσασθαι. But that, surely, does not refer to a τυφά. The olive, like the laurel, was used for other purposes connected with the dead,—viz., in crowning the corpse

for the πρόθεσις (cp. schol. Eur. Ph. 1626), and in decking the κλίνη on which the corpse was laid (Ar. Eccl. 1030).—ὃ δὴ = ὃ τι δήποτε, implying that much of the body had been destroyed. Cp. Her. 1. 160 ἐπὶ μισθῷ ὅσῳ δή· οὐ γὰρ ἔχω τοῦτό γε εἰπεῖν ἀτρεκέως.—λέλειπτο: cp. 457 'φάνη n.—συγκατήθομεν. The σύν here is perh. not merely 'completely,' but implies the collecting of dismembered pieces : as συγκατακαίω regularly = to burn something 'along with' something else (Xen. An. 3. 2. 27). Like ἀνεβαίνομεν (1205), this is the imperf. of consecutive action ('proceeded to burn,' = 'next burned').

1203 τύμβον. If the Homeric usage was followed, when the flesh had been burned the bones would be washed with wine or oil, wrapped in fat, and placed in an urn (λάρναξ). The urn having been deposited in a grave (κάπετος), the τύμβος (or σῆμα) would be raised over it. Cp. Introd. to Homer, ch. II. § 33.—ὀρθόκρανος, lit., with head erect, so = 'high': cp. ὑψικάρηνος, ὑψίλοφος (of hills). From κρᾶν (κρανίον) we have also βούκρανος, ταυρόκρανος.—οἰκείας, 'native,'—a thing pleasing to the dead: so in O. C. 406 Oed. asks, ἦ καὶ κατασκιῶσι Θηβαίᾳ κόνει; The father's prophecy for his sons was fulfilled: of their father-land they obtained ὁπόσαν καὶ φθιμένοισιν κατέχειν (Aesch. Th. 731: cp. O. C. 789).

1204 f. αὖθις answers to τὸν μέν (1199), as in 167 τοῦτ' αὖθις to τοῦτο μέν.

νυμφεῖον Ἄιδου κοῖλον εἰσεβαίνομεν.　　1205
φωνῆς δ᾽ ἄπωθεν ὀρθίων κωκυμάτων
κλύει τις ἀκτέριστον ἀμφὶ παστάδα,
✓ καὶ δεσπότῃ Κρέοντι σημαίνει μολών·
τῷ δ᾽ ἀθλίας ἄσημα περιβαίνει βοῆς
ἕρποντι μᾶλλον ἆσσον, οἰμώξας δ᾽ ἔπος　　1210
ἵησι δυσθρήνητον· ὦ τάλας ἐγώ,
ἆρ᾽ εἰμὶ μάντις; ἆρα δυστυχεστάτην
κέλευθον ἕρπω τῶν παρελθουσῶν ὁδῶν;
παιδός με σαίνει φθόγγος. ἀλλά, πρόσπολοι,
ἴτ᾽ ἆσσον ὠκεῖς, καὶ παραστάντες τάφῳ　　1215
ἀθρήσαθ᾽, ἁρμὸν χώματος λιθοσπαδῆ
δύντες πρὸς αὐτὸ στόμιον, εἰ τὸν Αἵμονος

1208 μολών] L has αθ written above ολ by S: this variant μαθών is in the text of some later MSS. (as V). **1209** ἄσημα] Nauck conject. ἄχημα.—περιβαίνει] Schaefer conject. περισαίνει: Wunder, περιπολεῖ. **1212** ἆρ᾽ L.—εἰμί] L has the second ι in an erasure: εἰ μή had been written. **1215** παραστάντες .φ. τάφωι L.

For αὖθις as = 'afterwards,' cp. *Ai.* 1283, *Tr.* 270.—λιθόστρωτον, 'with floor of stone,' here suggests, 'affording no couch but one of stone,' in contrast with a real νυμφεῖον, which contains a λέχος εὔστρωτον... | χλαίνησιν μαλακῆς ἐστρωμένον (*Hom. hymn. Ven.* 157 f.).—κόρης νυμφεῖον-Ἄιδου, the maiden's death-bower: cp. 795 n., 929.
1206 κωκυμάτων, the word used by Teiresias (1079): here, as usu., for the dead: cp. 28, 204. 1302: so κωκυτός, *Ai.* 851 etc.—Cp. *El.* 683 ὀρθίων κηρυγμάτων.
1207 ἀκτέριστον ἀμφὶ παστάδα, near (*i.e.* from the quarter of) the bridal-chamber where no funeral-rites had been paid; *i.e.*, where Antigone had been made the bride of Death, without even such honours as befitted such nuptials. For ἀκτέριστος cp. 1071 n. The word παστάς seems to be here used simply as a poetical equivalent for θάλαμος. There is probably no reference to pillars of rock (natural or artificial) in the τάφος. On the uses of παστάς, see Appendix.
1209 ἀθλίας...ἄσημα βοῆς, indistinct sounds, consisting in an ἀθλία βοή: *i.e.*, as he drew nearer, the sounds resolved themselves into the mournful cry of a human voice. The genit. is thus a 'defining' one. Cp. *O. C.* 923 n. φωτῶν

ἀθλίων ἱκτήρια (suppliant objects consisting in unhappy persons). Below, in 1265, the form of ὤμοι ἐμῶν ἄνολβα βουλευμάτων is analogous, but the gen. is there partitive (see n.). Here, βοῆς could, indeed, be possessive ('sounds belonging to, *i.e.*, forming part of, a cry'). But the perspective of the description is better kept by the other view of the genitive, which supposes that a sound, ambiguous at a distance, defines itself as we approach.
—περιβαίνει, with dat. instead of the normal acc.; this dat. denotes the person interested, *i.e.*, here affected through the senses: *O. C.* 372 εἰσῆλθε τοὺς τρὶς ἀθλίους ἔρις (n.): *Tr.* 298 ἐμοὶ γὰρ οἶκτος... εἰσέβη. For the image, cp. *O. C.* 1477 ἀμφίσταται | διαπρύσιος ὄτοβος: *Od.* 6. 122 ὥς τέ με κουράων ἀμφήλυθε θῆλυς ἀϋτή.
1210 f. μᾶλλον ἆσσον: cp. Aesch. *Th.* 673 μᾶλλον ἐνδικώτερος: Eur. *El.* 222 μᾶλλον ἐχθίους: Plat. *Legg.* 781 A λαθραιότερον μᾶλλον καὶ ἐπικλοπώτερον.—ἔπος (= θρῆνον) δυσθρήνητον: see n. on 7.—ὦ τάλας: cp. *O. T.* 744 n.
1213 f. τῶν παρελθουσῶν: cp. 100 f. κάλλιστον...τῶν προτέρων, n.—σαίνει, 'greets my ear.' As σαίνω was properly said of a dog wagging its tail or fawning so it could be said of a sight or a sound

the caverned mansion of the bride of Death. And, from afar off, one of us heard a voice of loud wailing at that bride's unhallowed bower ; and came to tell our master Creon.

And as the King drew nearer, doubtful sounds of a bitter cry floated around him ; he groaned, and said in accents of anguish, 'Wretched that I am, can my foreboding be true? Am I going on the wofullest way that ever I went? My son's voice greets me.—Go, my servants,—haste ye nearer, and when ye have reached the tomb, pass through the gap, where the stones have been wrenched away, to the cell's very mouth,—and look, and see if 'tis Haemon's

---

The meaning of this φ is simply (I think) that the scribe's eye had caught the word φθορὰν in 1224. Having written φ, he judged it simpler to leave it (with dots) than to change it by erasure into τ. **1216** ἀθρήσαθ', ἁρμὸν] Semitelos conject. ἀθρεῖτε, θαλάμων.—χώματος] Seyffert conject. χάσματος: Tournier, θώματος.—λιθοσπαδῆ. In L, ι has been erased after ῆ. Cp. on 726.

---

which *appeals for recognition* by vividly striking our senses. Like *arridere*, the word usually implied a sensation of pleasure (*O. C.* 319 n.). But it could also denote, as here, a recognition attended by pain. So in Eur. *Hippol.* 862 f., where Theseus recognises the seal on the tablets left by his dead wife, he says τύποι...προσσαίνουσί με.

1215 εἰκός, adverbial: cp. 823, 847: *Tr.* 937 ἐρημία βᾶσ'.

1216 ἁρμὸν χώματος λιθοσπ., an opening in the stones heaped up at the entrance, made by dragging some of them away. Cp. 848 ἔργμα τυμβόχωστον. Haemon, in his frenzy of despair, had broken into the tomb by wrenching away part of this rude wall-work. The gap remained as he had made it. He had reached the spot only a short time before Creon (cp. on 1223).

ἁρμὸν. The word ἁρμός means, (1) a *fastening*: Eur. *Med.* 1315 ἐκλύεθ' ἁρμούς, undo the fastenings of the doors: (2) the *chink* between two things which are joined together: so in Plut. *Alex.* 3 a furtive *listener* is described as τῷ τῆς θύρας ἁρμῷ προσβαλὼν (τὴν ὄψιν), 'having put his eye to the chink in the door.' So here ἁρμός is an *aperture*, just wide enough to admit of a man going through (cp. δύντες).— ἁρμὸς (with its derivatives ἁρμοῖ, ἁρμόζω, ἁρμονία), and ἀρπεδόνη (or ἀρπεδών), 'rope,' are connected with the causative form of the root ar, ar-pajā-mi, 'to fasten': see Curt. *Etym.* § 488.

1217 στόμιον. Having passed through the gap, they will find themselves in a narrow passage. They are to go along this passage to the very mouth (στόμιον) of the sepulchral chamber into which it opens.

The kind of tomb which the poet here imagines is perhaps best represented, in Greece, by the rock-tombs of Nauplia, and of Spata in Attica. These consist of chambers worked horizontally into the rock, and approached by a passage or δρόμος, answering to that which Creon's men have to traverse before they reach the στόμιον of the tomb. The general type seems to have been determined by that of the more elaborate domed tombs, such as the so-called 'Treasury of Atreus' at Mycenae, which, like these ruder copies, were entered by a δρόμος. Indeed, the Nauplia tombs indicate a rough attempt to reproduce the dome (θόλος). [See Helbig, *Das Homer. Epos aus den Denkm. erläutert*, p. 53, with the sources quoted there in nn. 5, 6.]

The phrase λοίσθιον τύμβευμα (1220) might suggest a recess *within* the principal chamber, like that in the 'Treasury of Atreus'; but it is simpler to take it as merely 'the furthest part of the tomb.' We may observe that the words κατῶρυξ (774) and κατασκαφής (891) are sufficiently explained if we suppose that the δρόμος leading to the chamber sloped downwards from the entrance.

φθόγγον συνίημ', ἢ θεοῖσι κλέπτομαι.
τάδ' ἐξ ἀθύμου δεσπότου *κελευσμάτων
ἠθροῦμεν· ἐν δὲ λοισθίῳ τυμβεύματι
τὴν μὲν κρεμαστὴν αὐχένος κατείδομεν,
βρόχῳ μιτώδει σινδόνος καθημμένην,
τὸν δ' ἀμφὶ μέσσῃ περιπετῆ προσκείμενον,
εὐνῆς ἀποιμώζοντα τῆς κάτω φθορὰν
καὶ πατρὸς ἔργα καὶ τὸ δύστηνον λέχος.
ὁ δ' ὡς ὁρᾷ σφε, στυγνὸν οἰμώξας ἔσω
χωρεῖ πρὸς αὐτὸν κἀνακωκύσας καλεῖ·
ὦ τλῆμον, οἷον ἔργον εἴργασαι· τίνα
νοῦν ἔσχες; ἐν τῷ συμφορᾶς διεφθάρης;

1218 Reiske conject. *φόβοισι κλέπτομαι*: Tournier, *θεοῖσι βλάπτομαι*. **1219** *τάδ' ἐξ ἀθύμου*] Nauck reads *ὀξυθύμου*, ascribing that conject. to J. P. Pompe van Meerdervoort, and referring to Naber *Mnem. nov.* 9. 219 f.—Heath conject. *τάδ' οὖν ἀθύμου*: Pallis, *τάδ' οὐκ ἄθυμοι*: Seyffert, *τάδ' ἐξ ἑτοίμου*: Semitelos, *τάδ' εἰκάθοντες*.—*κελεύσμασιν* MSS. Dindorf writes *κελεύμασιν*, the form given by L in Aesch. *Pers.* 397, *Ch.* 751. Burton conject. *κελευσμάτων*. **1222** *μιτώδει*] The first

1218 **θεοῖσι**: dat. of agent with *pres. pass.*: see n. on 503 ff.—**κλέπτομαι**, am deluded: 681 n.—Cp. *O. C.* 316 ἢ γνώμη πλανᾷ;

1219 The simple correction, **κελευσμάτων** for *κελεύσμασιν*, is (I think) certainly right. Cp. Aesch. *Pers.* 397 ἔπαισαν ἅλμην βρύχιον ἐκ κελεύσματος (and similarly Eur. *I. T.* 1405): Her. 6. 50 ἔλεγε δὲ ταῦτα ἐξ ἐπιστολῆς τῆς Δημαρήτου.

With **κελεύσμασιν**, we have only two tolerable resources. (1) To join *κελεύσμασιν ἐξ ἀθύμου δεσπότου*, 'orders given by him.' But, though *τοῖς ἐξ ἀθ. δεσπ. κελεύσμασιν* could be defended by *τὴν ἐξ ἐμοῦ δυσβουλίαν* (95), the phrase without the article is very strange. In phrases which might appear similar, it will be found that a verb has influenced the use of *ἐκ* with gen.: thus *Ai.* 137 *σὲ δ' ὅταν*... | *λόγος ἐκ Δαναῶν κακόθρους ἐπιβῇ*: Aesch. *Ag.* 1366 *ἦ γὰρ τεκμηρίοισιν ἐξ οἰμωγμάτων* | *μαντευσόμεσθα τἀνδρὸς ὡς ὀλωλότος*; here, however, it is impossible to take *ἐξ ἀθύμου δεσπότου* with *ἠθροῦμεν*, and to make *κελεύσμασιν* a mere epexegesis ('looked, at our master's instigation, *i.e.*, by his command').

(2) The alternative is to amend **ἐξ ἀθύμου**. Only one correction is probable, viz. **ὀξυθύμου**. The decisive objection to this is the sense. It could mean only, 'swift to wrath,' like *ὀξύχολος* (955). It could not mean merely, 'agitated' (by alarm). But Creon is no longer proud or fierce; he has been humbled: his late words (1211 ff.) expressed only grief and fear.

Dindorf writes **κελεύμασιν**, holding this to be the older Attic form (cr. n.). The fact appears to be that both *κέλευμα* and *κέλευσμα* are well attested in our MSS. of some authors: and there is no evidence from inscriptions. As regards the verb, Lobeck (on *Ai.* 704) remarks that, while *ἐκελεύσθην* is far commoner than *ἐκελεύθην*, *κεκέλευμαι* and *κεκέλευσμαι* are both well attested for the best age. But Veitch's statement on this point is more accurate. While *ἐκελεύθην* is extremely rare in classical Greek, *κεκέλευμαι* is nearly (if not quite) unknown to it. It would be very rash, then, to affirm that Soph. must have used the non-sigmatic form of the noun.

1221 **αὐχένος**: the gen. of the part, as with verbs of seizing, etc.: Arist. *H. A.* 9. 50. 7 *ὅταν κρεμάσωσι (τὰς ὗς) τῶν ὀπισθίων ποδῶν*: so *κρεμῶμεν* with gen., Ar. *Plut.* 312: *Il.* 17. 289 (*τὸν*) *ποδὸς ἕλκε*: *Od.* 3. 439 *βοῦν δ' ἀγέτην κεράων*.

1222 **μιτώδει**, thread-like, *i.e.*, formed by a thread-wrought fabric (the *σινδών*), and not, as usual, by a cord. *μίτρος* (ὁ),

voice that I know, or if mine ear is cheated by the gods.'

This search, at our despairing master's word, we went to make; and in the furthest part of the tomb we descried *her* hanging by the neck, slung by a threadwrought halter of fine linen; while *he* was embracing her with arms thrown around her waist,—bewailing the loss of his bride who is with the dead, and his father's deeds, and his own ill-starred love.

But his father, when he saw him, cried aloud with a dread cry, and went in, and called to him with a voice of wailing:— 'Unhappy, what a deed hast thou done! What thought hath come to thee? What manner of mischance hath marred thy reason?

---

hand in L wrote μιτωίδη, adding ει above the η. S inserted ρ between τ and ω, and accented ω, but without deleting the accent on ι. A few of the later MSS. have μιτρώδει, either in the text (as V⁴), or as a correction (V¹, V²): it is also the Aldine reading. **1226** στιγνὸν L, with ν above γ from an early hand. **1226** οἷον] τοῖον L. **1229** συμφορᾶς (not ξ-) L.

---

the thread of the warp: Eur. *I. T.* 817 ὕφηνα καὶ τόδ' εἶδος εὐμίτοις πλοκαῖς (I wrought this scene, too, with threads deftly woven).—σινδόνος. σινδών (prob. from Ἰνδ-, *Sind*) was a general term for a smooth, fine texture, as βύσσος was the specific word for a kind of fine linen: Her. 2. 86 describes mummies as swathed σινδόνος βυσσίνης τελαμῶσι (where see Stein). Thuc. 2. 49. 4 τῶν πάνυ λεπτῶν ἱματίων καὶ σινδόνων. Diog. Laert. 6. 90 tells of an Athenian (*c.* 300 B.C.) being reprimanded by the ἀστυνόμοι for luxuriousness, ὅτι σινδόνα ἠμφίεστο.—Antigone used her veil (κάλυμμα: cp. Ar. *Lys.* 532).

1223 Haemon has thrown his arms around her waist (ἀμφὶ μέσσῃ περιπετῆ), embracing her (προσκείμενον), where she hangs lifeless. But verses 1236—1240 require us to suppose that Antigone's body is then stretched on the ground. We are left to understand that Haemon, while uttering his lament (1224 f.), has lifted the corpse, so as to extricate it from the noose, and has laid it down. Cp. *O. T.* 1266 (where Oed. finds Iocasta hanging), χαλᾷ κρεμαστὴν ἀρτάνην.—μέσσῃ: cp. 1236: fr. 235. 5 (iambics). Eur. has this form only in lyr.; Aesch. nowhere.—περιπετῆ, act.; but pass. in *Ai.* 907 ἔγχος περιπετές ('on which he fell'), unless I am right in suspecting that there we should read, τόδ' ἔγχος περιπετοῦς κατηγορεῖ, 'shows that he

fell upon it.' Cp. *O. C.* 1620 ἐπ' ἀλλήλοισιν ἀμφικείμενοι, n.

1224 f. εὐνῆς...τῆς κάτω, his bride who is dead. Cp. Eur. *Tro.* 831 αἱ μὲν εὐνάς (husbands), αἱ δὲ παῖδας, | αἱ δὲ ματέρας γεραιάς. It would be awkward to understand, 'the ruin of his marriage, (which is to be only) in the world below.'—πατρὸς ἔργα: he does not know that Creon is listening.—λέχος, marriage, as in 573. This word, too, could mean 'bride' (*Ai.* 211): it is v. 1224 that decides our version.

1226 σφε, Haemon: 44 n.—στυγνόν, bitter,—the notion of 'sad,' 'gloomy,' coming from that of 'hateful': cp. Moschus 3. 68 καὶ στυγνοὶ (*tristes*) περὶ σῶμα τεὸν κλαίουσιν Ἔρωτες.

1228 f. οἷον ἔργον: i.e., Haemon's forcible entrance into Antigone's tomb.—τίνα νοῦν ἔσχες; lit., 'what thoughts hast thou conceived?'—the aor. meaning, as usu., not 'had,' but 'came to have.' So *El.* 1013 f. νοῦν σχὲς...εἰκαθεῖν, '*form* the purpose to yield': ib. 1465 νοῦν ἔσχον, ὥστε συμφέρειν τοῖς κρείσσοσιν.—ἐν τῷ συμφορᾶς, by what manner of calamity: i.e., 'what cruel god hath deprived thee of thy reason?' *Ai.* 314 κἀνήρετ' ἐν τῷ πράγματος κυροῖ ποτε: *Ph.* 174 ἐπὶ παντὶ τῷ χρείας: Eur. *Helen.* 1195 ἐν τῷ δὲ κεῖσαι συμφορᾶς;—διεφθάρης, mentally: *Il.* 15. 128 μαινόμενε, φρένας ἠλέ, διέφθορας: Eur. *Helen.* 1192 διέφθαρσαι φρένας;

ⱽἔξελθε, τέκνον, ἱκέσιός σε λίσσομαι.   1230
ⱽτὸν δ᾽ ἀγρίοις ὄσσοισι παπτήνας ὁ παῖς,
ⱽπτύσας προσώπῳ κοὐδὲν ἀντειπών, ξίφους
ⱽἕλκει διπλοῦς κνώδοντας· ἐκ δ᾽ ὁρμωμένου
ⱽπατρὸς φυγαῖσιν ἤμπλακ᾽· εἶθ᾽ ὁ δύσμορος
ⱽαὑτῷ χολωθείς, ὥσπερ εἶχ᾽, ἐπεντᾱθεὶς   1235
ἤρεισε πλευραῖς μέσσον ἔγχος· ἐς δ᾽ ὑγρὸν
ἀγκῶν᾽ ἔτ᾽ ἔμφρων παρθένῳ προσπτύσσεται·
καὶ φυσιῶν ὀξεῖαν ἐκβάλλει ῥοὴν
λευκῇ παρειᾷ φοινίου σταλάγματος. ⁿ ᵈˣ ᵖ
ⱽκεῖται δὲ νεκρὸς περὶ νεκρῷ, τὰ νυμφικὰ   1240

1232 ἀντειπών ὅλωσ L, with ξίφουσ written above ὅλωσ by the first hand.
The final ν of ἀντειπών has been made from ο, and δ has been written above
the line, by the first hand.—Wecklein thinks that ὅλωσ came from κολεῶν [rather
κολεοῦ] written over ξίφους: but ἕλκει did not require such explanation.—
Seyffert conject. βέλους: Dindorf, ἔτος.—Nauck thinks the whole verse spurious.
1234 εἶθ᾽ ὁ] In L the first hand wrote εἰ δύσμοροσ: S made εἰ into εἶθ᾽ ὁ.
1235 αὑτῷ] αὐτῶι L.   **1236** μέσσον] Nauck conject. πηκτόν: Pallis, δισσὸν.

1230 f. ἱκέσιος, adverbial: cp. 1215
ὠκεῖς, n. He extends his right hand in
supplication.—ὄσσοισι: Aesch. admits
ὄσσοις, and Eur. both ὄσσοις and ὄσσων,
in iambics no less than in lyrics.—παπτήνας: with an acc. this verb usu. ='to
look around *for*,' as *Il.* 4. 200.
1232 πτύσας προσώπῳ. Haemon is
momentarily insane with despair and rage:
the very words αὑτῷ χολωθείς, 1235,
indicate the transport of frenzy which
these verses were meant to depict. Nothing could do more violence to the language, or more injury to the dramatic
effect, than the Scholiast's theory that
πτύσας προσώπῳ has a merely figurative
sense, 'with an expression of loathing on
his face.' When the figurative sense of a
word (like πτύσας) is to be marked by a
qualifying addition (like προσώπῳ), that
addition must not be such as equally to
suggest the literal sense. Thus a social-
ist riot might be called 'a fire not of
Hephaestus' (Eur. *Or.* 621); but it
would not be equally happy to describe it
as 'a fire kindled by the tables of the
rich.' πτύσας προσώπῳ, instead of ἐπι-
πτύσας προσώπῳ (πατρός), is merely an
instance of the boldness with which
poetry could use a simple dative to express the object to (or against) which an
action is directed. Such a dat. is often
equivalent to (*a*) ἐπί with dat., (*b*) ἐπί,

πρός, or εἰς, with acc.,—in various re-
lations, and with various shades of meaning. Thus we have such phrases as κακοῖς
γελῶν (*Ai.* 1042)=κακοῖς ἐπεγγελῶν: *Ph.*
67 λύπην…'Αργείοις βαλεῖς=ἐμβαλεῖς: Eur.
Suppl. 322 τοῖς κερτομοῦσι γοργὸν ὡς ἀνα-
βλέπει, how she looks up sternly *at* her
revilers: *Il.* 7. 101 τῷδε δ᾽ ἐγὼν αὐτὸς
θωρήξομαι, against him: *ib.* 23. 635 δι
μοι ἀνέστη, against me: and below 1236
ἤρεισε πλευραῖς=ἐπήρεισε. Prose would
have πτύσας εἰς (or ἐπὶ) πρόσωπον.
1233 f. διπλοῦς κνώδοντας ξίφους, his
cross-hilted sword. κνώδοντες are the two
projecting cross-pieces at the point where
the hilt joins the blade. The hilt (κώπη)
of the Greek sword had no guard, nor
had it always the cross-pieces; but these,
when used, served partly to protect the
hand. The κνώδοντες, or cross-hilt, can
be seen on some of the swords given by
Guhl and Koner, p. 244, fig. 277 (*a, d*).
The cross-hilt was sometimes simply a
straight cross-bar; sometimes the side
next the hand was rounded. Cp. Silius
Italicus *Pun.* 1. 515 *pressumque ira simul
exigit ensem,* | *Qua capuli statuere morae.*
—κνώδων (κυάω, ὀδούς) meant properly
any tooth-like prong or spike: see Xen.
Cyneg. 10. 3, where boar-spears (προβόλια)
have κνώδοντας ἀποκεχαλκευμένους στι-
φρούς, stout *teeth* forged of bronze, projecting from the shaft a little below the

Come forth, my child·! I pray thee—I implore!' But the boy
glared at him with fierce eyes, spat in his face, and, without
a word of answer, drew his cross-hilted sword:—as his father
rushed forth in flight, he missed his aim;—then, hapless one,
wroth with himself, he straightway leaned with all his weight
against his sword, and drove it, half its length, into his side;
and, while sense lingered, he clasped the maiden to his faint
embrace, and, as he gasped, sent forth on her pale cheek the
swift stream of the oozing blood.

Corpse enfolding corpse he lies; he hath won his nuptial

1238 ροὴν L. The schol. in L has: τὴν πνοὴν τοῦ φοινίου σταλάγματος ἐκβάλλει
τῇ λευκῇ αὐτῆς παρειᾳ, ὅ ἐστιν, αἷμα ἐξέπνευσεν. The last words show that
πνοὴν was not a slip for ροὴν, but was in the Scholiast's text. Most of the later
MSS. (including A) have πνοὴν: but a few have ροὴν (as L², V, V⁴, Aug. b).—
Blaydes conject. σφαγὴν, and ἐμβάλλει for ἐκβάλλει. **1240** περὶ νεκρῶι L:
but it does not follow that the scribe meant the two words to form one.

---

bead (λόγχη). In *Ai.* 1025, τοῦδ' αἰόλου
κνώδοντος, 'this gleaming spike,' is the
end of the sword-blade projecting through
the body of Ajax. So in Kaibel *Epigr.*
549· 11 (an epitaph of the 1st cent. A.D.)
φασγάνου κνώδοντι = 'with the point (not,
'edge') of the sword': the ref. is to
thrusting, not cutting.—The Scholiast
wrongly explains διπλοῦς κνώδοντας by
διπλᾶς ἀκμάς, 'double edge.' This interpretation was obviously suggested by
διπλοῦς (since a sword is often called
δίστομον or ἀμφήκες), while the true sense
of κνώδων was not accurately remembered:
thus the Schol. vaguely calls it τὸ ὀξὺ τοῦ
ξίφους.

ἐκ δ' ὁρμ., tmesis: cp. 427.—φυγαῖσιν,
dat. of manner (620 n.). The poet. plur.
of φυγή, when it does not mean 'remedies'
(304), usu. means 'exile' (Eur. *El.* 233).
The gen. might be absol., but is more
simply taken with ἤμπλακ'.

Haemon, in his madness, meant to
kill his father. He had harboured no
such purpose before (see on 753); and
his frantic impulse is instantly followed
by violent remorse. Arist. (*Poet.* 14)
observes that it is not conducive to a properly tragic effect (οὐ τραγικόν, ἀπαθές)
if a person contemplates a dreadful act,
and then desists from it, in the light of
sober thought or fuller knowledge: διόπερ
οὐδεὶς ποιεῖ ὁμοίως εἰ μὴ ὀλιγάκις (such in-
cidents in Tragedy are rare), οἷον ἐν Ἀν-
τιγόνῃ Κρέοντα ὁ Αἵμων. It need not be
assumed that Arist. meant to censure
Sophocles; it is more natural to suppose

that he cited the exception as one justified
by the circumstances. But it should
further be noticed that Aristotle was not
accurate in taking this incident as the
exception which illustrated his rule. For
Haemon did not abandon his dreadful
purpose; he was simply foiled by his
father's flight. And then, in swift remorse, he actually did τῶν ἀνηκέστων τι.

1285 ff. ὥσπερ εἶχ': cp. 1108.—
ἐπεντανθείς, lit., 'stretched,' or 'strained,'
against the sword: i.e., pressing his right
side against the point of the sword, which
at the same time he drove home with his
right hand.—πλευραῖς, used as though
ἤρεισε were ἐπήρεισε: cp. Pind. *P.* 10.
51 ἄγκυραν ἔρεισον χθονί. For the verb
cp. Eur. *Andr.* 844 (ξίφος) ἀπόδος,...ἵν'
ἀνταίαν | ἐρείσω πλαγάν.—μέσσον, pre-
dicative, denoting the point up to which
he drove it in: *Ai.* 899 κεῖται κρυφαίῳ
φασγάνῳ περιπτυχής.—ἔγχος = ξίφος: *Ai.*
95, 658, etc.—ἐς δ' ὑγρὸν ἀγκῶν', since
π. προσπτύσσεται = παρθένον λαμβάνει:
cp. the beautiful lines in Eur. *Ph.* 1439
(the dying Eteocles): ἤκουσε μητρός, κά-
πιθεὶς ὑγρὰν χέρα | φωνὴν μὲν οὐκ ἀφῆκεν,
ὀμμάτων δ' ἄπο | προσεῖπε δακρύοις.

1238 φυσιῶν, breathing hard: ροὴν
is governed by ἐκβάλλει only. But in
Aesch. *Ag.* 1389 the compound governs
the acc.: κἀκφυσιῶν ὀξεῖαν αἵματος σφα-
γὴν | βάλλει μ' ἐρεμνῇ ψακάδι φοινίας
δρόσου.—ροὴν is plainly right: the bad
variant, πνοὴν, was perh. suggested by
φυσιῶν.

τέλη λαχὼν δείλαιος ἔν <γ'> Ἀιδου δόμοις,
δείξας ἐν ἀνθρώποισι τὴν ἀβουλίαν
ὅσῳ μέγιστον ἀνδρὶ πρόσκειται κακόν. .

ΧΟ. τί τοῦτ' ἂν εἰκάσειας; ἡ γυνὴ πάλιν
φρούδη, πρὶν εἰπεῖν ἐσθλὸν ἢ κακὸν λόγον.   1245

ΑΓ. καὐτὸς τεθάμβηκ'· ἐλπίσιν δὲ βόσκομαι
ἄχη τέκνου κλύουσαν ἐς πόλιν γόους
οὐκ ἀξιώσειν, ἀλλ' ὑπὸ στέγης ἔσω
δμωαῖς προθήσειν πένθος οἰκεῖον στένειν.
γνώμης γὰρ οὐκ ἄπειρος, ὥσθ' ἁμαρτάνειν.   1250

ΧΟ. οὐκ οἶδ'· ἐμοὶ δ' οὖν ἥ τ' ἄγαν σιγὴ βαρὺ
δοκεῖ προσεῖναι χἡ μάτην πολλὴ βοή.

ΑΓ. ἀλλ' εἰσόμεσθα, μή τι καὶ κατάσχετον
κρυφῇ καλύπτει καρδίᾳ θυμουμένῃ,
δόμους παραστείχοντες· εὖ γὰρ οὖν λέγεις·   1255
καὶ τῆς ἄγαν γάρ ἐστί που σιγῆς βάρος.

1241 ἐν γ' Ἀιδου] ἐν αἴδου L, with most of the later MSS.: but L², with a few others, has εἰν. Brunck wrote ἐν Ἀιδου. Heath conject. ἐν γ': Vauvilliers, εἰς Ἀιδου δόμους: Semitelos, Ἐνοδίας δόμοις: Mekler, ἐν σκότου δόμοις: Nauck, ἐν γαίας μυχοῖς.   **1245** ἡ was omitted by the first hand in L, and added by S. **1248** ἀξιώσειν] Pallis conject. ἀξιοῦν χεῖν: Burges, ὀξὺν ἥσειν: Blaydes, ἐξανήσειν:

1241 τέλη, rites: O. C. 1050 n.—ἐν γ' Ἀιδου. Though εἰν occurs nowhere else in tragic iambics, it might fairly be defended, in a ῥῆσις of epic colour, as a reminiscence of the Homeric εἰν Ἀιδαο. But I decidedly prefer Heath's ἐν γ' ('in that world, though not in this'), because it adds point and pathos to what would otherwise be a somewhat tame statement of fact. Cp. 750. For another (probable) loss of γε in this play, cp. 648. For ἐν γε, cp. O. T. 1380 ἐν γε ταῖς Θήβαις: O. C. 153 ἐν γ' ἐμοί: Ph. 685 ἴσος ἐν γ' ἴσοις: Eur. fr. 349 ὡς ἐν γ' ἐμοὶ κρίνοιτ' ἂν οὐ καλῶς φρονεῖν.
1242 δείξας...τὴν ἀβουλίαν: for the constr., cp. .n. on 883 f. For δεικνύναι said of a warning example, see El. 1382 καὶ δεῖξον ἀνθρώποισι τἀπιτίμια | τῆς δυσσεβείας οἷα δωροῦνται θεοί: cp. O. T. append. on 622 ff.
1243 πρόσκειται: cp. 94 n.
1244 ς΄ τί τοῦτ' ἂν εἰκάσ., sc. εἶναι: what wouldst thou conjecture this to be (or, to mean)? The optat. ending used here was the usual one in Attic: cp. O. T.

843 n.—ἐσθλὸν ἢ κακόν: cp. on 40.— A silent exit is similarly a prelude to disaster in the case of Deianeira (Tr. 813). Iocasta, too, quits the scene, not, indeed, without a word, yet with a reticence which is called σιωπή (O. T. 1075).
1246 τεθάμβηκ': cp. O. C. 1140 θαυμάσας ἔχω (n.): and so oft. τεθαύμακα.— βόσκομαι: cp. fr. 863 ἐλπὶς γὰρ ἡ βόσκουσα τοὺς πολλοὺς βροτῶν.
1247 ς΄ γόους...ἀξιώσειν = to think them ἄξιοι, i.e., meet. This use of ἀξιόω is freq. in regard to persons, as Ai. 1114 οὐ γὰρ ἠξίου τοὺς μηδένας (esteem them). On the other hand, ἄξιος, as applied to actions, oft. = 'proper,' 'becoming': as Ar. Eq. 616 νῦν ἄρ' ἄξιά γε πᾶσίν ἐστιν ἐπολολύξαι. But, if ἀξιοῦν τινα could mean, 'he thinks a person estimable,' poetry, at least, could surely say, ἀξιοῖ τι, 'he thinks a thing proper.' The text, then, seems sound.—ὑπὸ στέγης: for the gen., cp. 692 n.
1249 προθήσειν governs πένθος: στένειν is epexeg. (for them to mourn): cp. 216 n. She will 'set the grief before

rites, poor youth, not here, yet in the halls of Death; and he hath witnessed to mankind that, of all curses which cleave to man, ill counsel is the sovereign curse.

[EURYDICĒ *retires into the house.*

CH. What wouldst thou augur from this? The lady hath turned back, and is gone, without a word, good or evil.

ME. I, too, am startled; yet I nourish the hope that, at these sore tidings of her son, she cannot deign to give her sorrow public vent, but in the privacy of the house will set her handmaids to mourn the household grief. For she is not untaught of discretion, that she should err.

CH. I know not'; but to me, at least, a strained silence seems to portend peril, no less than vain abundance of lament.

ME. Well, I will enter the house, and learn whether indeed she is not hiding some repressed purpose in the depths of a passionate heart. Yea, thou sayest well: excess of silence, too, may have a perilous meaning. [*Exit* MESSENGER.

Semitelos, ἐξαύσεν. **1250** Blaydes conject. ἄμοιρος for ἄπειρος: Semitelos, δεινῶν for γνώμης. Meineke, Dindorf and Nauck reject the verse. **1251** ἐμοὶ δ'] ἐμοι δ' L: ἐμοιγ' Brunck.—σιγὴ from σιγῆ L. **1253** ἀλλ'] Pallis conject. τάχ'.— κατάσχετον] Musgrave conject. κατὰ σκότον. **1254** θυμουμένηι L: a line has been drawn through the ι. Some of the later MSS. have θυμουμένη. **1255** ἐστὶ τοῦ] Bergk conject. ἔσθ' ὅπου. Nauck suspects the verse (*Jahr. f. Philol.*, 65. 250).

---

them' by making a lament, after which her handmaids, sitting around her, will wail in chorus. *Il.* 24. 746 (Andromache has bewailed Hector,) ὣς ἔφατο κλαίουσ'· ἐπὶ δὲ στενάχοντο γυναῖκες. | τῇσιν δ' αὖθ' Ἑκάβη ἁδινοῦ ἐξῆρχε γόοιο.

1250 γνώμης...οὐκ [ἄπειρος. The reading has been unjustly suspected. γνώμης, 'judgment,' or 'discretion,' is here regarded as an influence moulding the character from without. The phrase means, then, 'not uninformed by discretion,'—not unversed in its teachings. Cp. Plat. *Rep.* 519 B τοὺς ἀπαιδεύτους καὶ ἀληθείας ἀπείρους, 'uninformed by truth.'

1251 f. δ' οὖν: 688 n.—προσεῖναι: so oft. of attendant circumstances (or of characteristic attributes): *Tr.* 150 τοῦ λόγου δ' οὐ χρὴ φθόνον, | γύναι, προσεῖναι. —Cp. 790.

1252 f. εἰσόμεσθα, μή τι...καλύπτει, 'we shall know (about our fear) lest (μή) she is concealing,' i.e., whether we are right in fearing that she conceals something. As Goodwin says (*Moods and Tenses*, § 46, N. 5a), this passage is one

of the most favourable to the view that μή has an *interrogative* force, and yet here also μὴ καλύπτει plainly expresses a fear. The pres. *indic.* is used, because the fear is strictly present; there is no thought that the thing feared can possibly be prevented. Before assuming that μή could have the force of εἰ οὐ ('whether not'), we should require an example in which the clause with μή, after a verb like οἶδα, expressed something which is not *feared* (but hoped; or else regarded with neither fear nor hope). As if here we had, εἰσόμεσθα μὴ ζήσειν ἔτι μέλλει. Cp. 278 n. The use of μή in *direct* question (*O. C.* 1502) is, of course, elliptical: *e.g.*, μὴ οὕτως ἔχει; comes from (δέδοικα) μὴ οὕτως ἔχει.—καὶ ('indeed') goes with the whole phrase κατάσχετον...καλύπτει: cp. 770 n. —κατάσχετον, a poet. word, here = 're-pressed' (cp. *El.* 1011 κατάσχες ὀργήν): usu., 'possessed' (by a god, or by passion), like κάτοχος.

1255 δόμους παραστείχοντες, advancing into the house: Eur. *Med.* 1137 παρῆλθε νυμφικοὺς δόμους.

ΧΟ. καὶ μὴν ὅδ' ἄναξ αὐτὸς ἐφήκει
μνῆμ' ἐπίσημον διὰ χειρὸς ἔχων,
εἰ θέμις εἰπεῖν, οὐκ ἀλλοτρίαν
ἄτην, ἀλλ' αὐτὸς ἁμαρτών.　　　　　　　　1260

στρ. α΄. ΚΡ. ἰὼ
2 φρενῶν δυσφρόνων ἁμαρτήματα
3 στερεὰ θανατόεντ'·
4 ὦ κτανόντας τε καὶ
5 θανόντας βλέποντες ἐμφυλίους·
6 *ὤμοι ἐμῶν ἄνολβα βουλευμάτων.　　　　1265
7 ἰὼ παῖ, νέος νέῳ ξὺν μόρῳ,
8 αἰαῖ αἰαῖ,
9 ἔθανες, ἀπελύθης,
10 ἐμαῖς οὐδὲ σαῖσι δυσβουλίαις.

στρ. β΄. ΧΟ. οἴμ' ὡς ἔοικας ὀψὲ τὴν δίκην ἰδεῖν.　　1270

ΚΡ. οἴμοι,
2 ἔχω μαθὼν δείλαιος· ἐν δ' ἐμῷ κάρᾳ

1259 f. ἀλλοτρίαν | ἄτην] Musgrave conject. ἀλλοτρίας | ἄτης. 1261—1269 L divides thus: ἰὼ — | ἁμαρτήματα — | θανατόεντ' — | θανόντας — | ἐμφυλίους — | ἰὼ μοι — | βουλευμάτων — | ἰὼ παῖ — | αἰ αἰ — | ἔθανες — | ἐμαῖς ... δυσβουλίαις. 1263 κτανόντας τε καὶ are written as a single word in L, καὶ being denoted by a contraction. 1265 ἰώ (not ἰὼ) μοι L, with the other MSS.: ὤμοι

1257 καὶ μὴν: 526.—**ἐφήκει**:—Ai. 34 καιρὸν δ' ἐφήκεις.—The Messenger now goes into the palace. The same actor returns at 1277 as ἐξάγγελος.

1258 μνῆμ', as the epithet ἐπίσημον shows, means that the son's corpse is a memorial of the father's unwisdom.—διὰ χειρός: cp. 916.

1259 f. εἰ θέμις εἰπεῖν (cp. O. C. 1556), because it is a heavy charge against the King, that he has caused his son's death.—ἄτην, in apposition with μνῆμα: the corpse is an ἄτη, because the death was caused by Creon's infatuation. ἀλλοτρίαν here answers to οἰκεῖος as = 'caused by oneself' (cp. on 1187).—ἁμαρτών is causal: he is bringing a corpse, not through the fault of others, but because he himself has erred. For the partic. in the nom., opposed to a clause of different form, cp. Dem. or. 23 § 156 εἰδεν, εἴτε δή τινος εἰπόντος εἴτ' αὐτὸς συνείς. See also 381 f.

1261—1347 This κομμός is composed of four strophes and four anti-

strophes, which correspond as follows. (1) 1st strophe 1261—1269 = 1st antistr. 1284—1292. (2) 2nd str. 1271—1277 = 2nd ant. 1294—1300. (3) 3rd str. 1306—1311 = 3rd ant. 1328—1333. (4) 4th. str. 1317—1325 = 4th ant. 1339—1347.

The lyric strophes and antistrophes are divided from each other by iambic tri-meters, spoken by the Chorus or by the Messenger.—See Metrical Analysis.

1261 φρενῶν δυσφρόνων: 502 n. Cp. Aesch. Th. 874 ἰὼ ἰὼ δύσφρονες, 'misguided ones.' More often, δύσφρων = 'gloomy,' or 'malignant.'—στερεά, with ref. to his own αὐθάδεια, cp. 1028, 714. So Plat. Polit. 309 B τὸ στερεὸν ἦθος. Cp. Ai. 925 ἔμελλες χρόνῳ | στερεόφρων ἄρ' ὦδ' ἐξανύσειν κακὰν | μοῖραν.

1263 f. ὦ...βλέποντες. Like Antigone (937), Creon now calls the Theban Elders to witness. Cp. n. on 162—210. —κτανόντας refers to Creon himself (for the plur., cp. 10), as θανόντας to

Enter CREON, *on the spectators' left, with attendants, carrying the shrouded body of* HAEMON *on a bier.*

CH. Lo, yonder the King himself draws near, bearing that which tells too clear a tale,—the work of no stranger's madness,—if we may say it,—but of his own misdeeds.

CR. Woe for the sins of a darkened soul, stubborn sins, fraught with death! Ah, ye behold us, the sire who hath slain, the son who hath perished! Woe is me, for the wretched blindness of my counsels! Alas, my son, thou hast died in thy youth, by a timeless doom, woe is me!—thy spirit hath fled,— not by thy folly, but by mine own!

Kommos
1st stroph

CH. Ah me, how all too late thou seemest to see the right!

CR. Ah me, I have learned the bitter lesson! But then, *2nd strophe.*

Turnebus. 1266 ξὺν μόρῳ] ξυμμόρωι L. 1267 αἰ αἰ αἰ L: αἰαῖ αἰαῖ
Dindorf. 1268 ἀπελύθης] Keck conject. ἀπεσύθης. 1270 ἰδεῖν] L has γρ.
ἔχειν in marg. from S.—Pallis conject. μαθεῖν. 1271—1277 L divides thus:
οἴμοι | ἔχω— | θεὸσ— | ἔπαισεν— | οἴμοι, λακπάτητον— | φεῦ φεῦ] ἰὼ πόνοι .. δύστονοι.

Haemon: for the ταρήχησις, cp. *Ph.* 336 ὁ κτανών τε χὠ θανών.—ἐμφυλίους = συγγενεῖς: cp. *O. T.* 1406 αἷμ᾽ ἐμφύλιον (n.): *O. C.* 1385 γῆς ἐμφυλίου, 'the land of thy race.'

1260 ἐμῶν ἀνολβα βουλευμάτων, the unhappy (counsels) among my counsels (partitive gen.); *i.e.*, the unhappiness involved in my counsels. See on 1209. This poetical periphrasis has the effect of making the idea expressed by ἀνολβα stand out with a quasi-substantival force, and so is slightly stronger than ὤμοι ἐμὰ ἄνολβα βουλεύματα. It would be possible, but it is neither requisite nor fitting, to supply ἁμαρτήματα (1261) with ἄνολβα, placing only a comma at ἐμφυλίους.— Ἰὼ ἄνολβος, of folly, cp. 1026.

1266 νέος νέῳ ξὺν μόρῳ, 'young, and by an untimely death,' is a pleonasm, but a natural one. The schol. explains νέῳ by καινοτρεπεῖ ('a death of a strange kind'). This sense is possible (cp. Aesch. *Suppl.* 712 ἀπροσδοκήτους τούσδε καὶ νέους λέγων), but is far less fitting here. νέῳ ξὺν μόρῳ, suggesting the thought that his years had been few, recalls Andromache's lament,—ἄνερ, ἀπ᾽ αἰῶνος νέος ὤλεο (*Il.* 24. 725).

1268 ἀπελύθης: cp. 1314, where the midd. aor. has the same sense. In later Greek ἀπολύεσθαι and ἀπόλυσις came to be used of any 'departure': thus in Polyb. 3. 69 τὴν ἀποχώρησιν…ἐποιοῦντο is presently varied to ἐποιοῦντο τὴν ἀπόλυσιν. Here, however, the word has a distinctly poetical colour, and suggests the release of ψυχή from σῶμα,—though without the feeling expressed by the words, ἀπολύεις τὸν δοῦλόν σου…ἐν εἰρήνῃ (St Luke ii. 29). A fragment of Plutarch (Wyttenbach, p. 135) attests a familiar use of ἀπολύεσθαι and ἀπόλυσις with reference to death. Eustathius quotes this v., and v. 1314, in support of a like statement (p. 548, 52).

1269 ἐμαῖς οὐδὲ σαῖσι. οὐδέ here = καὶ οὐ: cp. 492. The negative form would be οὐκ ἐμαῖς ἀλλὰ σαῖς (*El.* 1470).

1272 ff. ἔχω μαθών = μεμάθηκα (21 n.), though here with a slightly stronger emphasis than that of an ordinary perf.: 'I have fully learned.'—No change is required in 1273. The soundness of the metre is confirmed by the antistrophic verse (1296), which is free from suspicion. Construe: ὁ δὲ θεὸς ἐν τῷ ἐμῷ κάρα ἔπαισέ με, μέγα βάρος ἔχων. Three points claim

3 θεὸς τότ᾽ ἄρα τότε μέγα βάρος μ᾽ ἔχων
4 ἔπαισεν, ἐν δ᾽ ἔσεισεν ἀγρίαις ὁδοῖς,
5 οἴμοι, λακπάτητον ἀντρέπων χαράν.   1275
6 φεῦ φεῦ, ὦ πόνοι βροτῶν δύσπονοι.

ΕΞΑΓΓΕΛΟΣ.

ὦ δέσποθ᾽, ὡς ἔχων τε καὶ κεκτημένος,   1278
τὰ μὲν πρὸ χειρῶν τάδε φέρων, τὰ δ᾽ ἐν δόμοις
ἔοικας ἥκειν καὶ τάχ᾽ ὄψεσθαι κακά.   1280

1278 θεὸς τότ᾽ ἄρα τότε μέγα βάρος μ᾽ ἔχων MSS.—Erfurdt places θεὸς after τότ᾽ ἄρα. Meineke would write με μέγα βάρος for μέγα βάρος μ᾽. Enger (followed by Nauck) gives τότε θεὸς τότ᾽ ἄρα μέγα βάρος ἔχων. **1275** λακπάτητον] In L the first hand omitted the last three letters; S has added them above the line.—A has the *v. l.* λεωπάτητον (with γρ. λαοπάτητον), prompted by the wish to make an iambic senarius. Another *v. l.* was λαξπάτητον, or λὰξ πατητὸν (λαξ πατητὸν E). **1276** ὦ πόνοι]

notice. (1) The place of με. This was possible, because μέγα βάρος, without ἔχων, could have stood as an adverbial cognate acc.: hence ἔχων is rather a superfluity than a word for which the ear was waiting. Greek poetry (esp. lyric) often has bold arrangements of words: cp. 944, 960 (n). (2) μέγα βάρος ἔχων = σφόδρα βαρὺς ὤν. Cp. 300: *O. C.* 24. 249 γῆρας | λυγρὸν ἔχεις: *ib.* 1. 368 ὕβριν ἔχοντες. (3) ἐν δ᾽ ἐμῷ κάρᾳ might have been followed by ἐνήλατο, or the like; but, ἔπαισε being used, the enclitic με was required to make it clear. The charge of redundancy would be just only if ἐμῷ were followed by ἐμέ.—For the image, cp. 1345: Aesch. *Ag.* 1175 δαίμων ὑπερβαρὴς ἐμπίτνων: and see *O. T.* 263 n. Triclinius understood the blow on the head to mean a disordering of the intellect (ἀντὶ τοῦ, ἐξέστησε τὰς ἐμὰς φρένας). But it is simply a poetical picture of the fell swoop with which the god descended on his victim,—taking possession of him, and driving him astray. Perhaps ἐμβρόντητος helped to suggest the other view. For the form of the dat. κάρᾳ, cp. *O. C.* 564.—ἐν δ᾽ ἔσεισεν, tmesis (420).—ἀγρίαις ὁδοῖς: cp. Pind. *P.* 2. 85 ἀλλ᾽ ἄλλοτε πατέων ὁδοῖς σκολιαῖς, in paths of guile.

1275 λακπάτητον, proleptic (475). The form λαξπάτητον, which Eustathius treats as the normal one (adding, ὅ τινες .. διὰ τοῦ κ γράφουσιν), is defended by Ellendt. He thinks that the κ form came

from correctors who supposed that ξπ was an impossible combination for Attic Greek. We find, indeed, ἐξπηχυστί Soph. fr. 938, and the 'Attic' forms ἔξπουν, ἔξκλινον, ἐξμέδιμνον (*O. T.* 1137 n.). But, though λαξπάτητον may well have been admissible, it is evident that the κ form would be recommended by ease of pronunciation. The compound occurs only here.—ἀντρέπων, as though it were an altar, a statue, or a fair building. Cp. Aesch. *Ag.* 383, *Eum.* 539 (quoted on 853 ff.).—For the apocope of ἀνά in comp., cp. *O. C.* 1070 ἄμβασιν, *Tr.* 528 ἄμπνει, *ib.* 839 ἄμμιγα, *Ai.* 416 ἄμπνοάς (all lyr.). In *Tr.* 396 (dial.) Herm. conjectured κἀννεώσασθαι for καὶ νεώσασθαι. It is unknown whether ἀγχαξ (fr. 883) occurred in lyr. or in dial. Cp. *Introd. to Homer*, Appendix, p. 197.

1276 φεῦ φεῦ, ὦ. The hiatus is excused by the pause.—πόνοι .. δύσπονοι: cp. 502 n.

1278 ὡς ἔχων τε καὶ κεκτημένος. Creon is actually touching (or helping to support) his son's corpse (1258 διὰ χειρὸς ἔχων, 1297 ἔχω μὲν ἐν χείρεσσιν). And meanwhile his wife lies dead within the house. The Messenger therefore says that Creon has come as one who both *has in hand* (ἔχων), and *has in store* (κεκτημένος). ἔχων is explained by τὰ μὲν πρὸ χειρῶν .. φέρων, and κεκτημένος by τὰ δ᾽ ἐν δόμοις. Cp. Plat. *Theaet.* 197 B οὐ τοίνυν μοι ταὐτὸν φαίνεται τῷ κεκτῆσθαι τὸ ἔχειν. οἷον εἰ ἱμάτιον πριάμε-

methinks, oh then, some god smote me from above with crushing weight, and hurled me into ways of cruelty, woe is me,—overthrowing and trampling on my joy! Woe, woe, for the troublous toils of men!

Enter MESSENGER *from the house.*

ME. Sire, thou hast come, methinks, as one whose hands are not empty, but who hath store laid up besides; thou bearest yonder burden with thee; and thou art soon to look upon the woes within thy house.

ἰὼ πόνοι L. **1278** ΕΞΑΓΓΕΛΟΣ] The designation in L is οἰκέτης here, and at v. 1282: ἄγγελος at vv. 1293, 1301, 1312, 1315. **1279** πρὸ χειρῶν] προχειρῶν L.—τάδε] ταδέ (not τὰ δέ) from ταδε, L.—τὰ δ᾽ ἐν δόμοισ L first hand. A corrector has made τὰ δ᾽ into τάδ᾽. **1280** τάχ᾽ L. Some of the later MSS. have τά γ᾽ (as A), others τάδ᾽ (as V⁴).—ὄψεσθαι] ὄψεσθε L. Dindorf states (after Dübner) that the final ε has been made by a late hand into αι: but (as can be seen in the autotype facsimile, p. 63 B) there has been no such attempt at correction.—See comment.

νόε τις καὶ ἐγκρατὴς ὢν μὴ φοροῖ, ἔχειν μὲν οὐκ ἂν αὐτόν αὐτό, κεκτῆσθαι δέ γε φαῖμεν. So ib. 198 D; the chase after knowledge has a view either to (a) τὸ κεκτῆσθαι, possession, or (b) τὸ ἔχειν, holding, ready for use, that which is already possessed,—ἣν ἐκέκτητο μὲν πάλαι, πρόχειρον δ᾽ οὐκ εἶχε τῇ διανοίᾳ. Cp. *Rep.* 382 B (men do not like) τῇ ψυχῇ περὶ τὰ ὄντα ψεύδεσθαί τε καὶ ἐψεῦσθαι καὶ ἀμαθῆ εἶναι καὶ ἐνταῦθα ἔχειν τε καὶ κεκτῆσθαι τὸ ψεῦδος: where ψεύδεσθαι answers to ἔχειν τὸ ψεῦδος,—to be deceived at a given time on a given matter; and ἐψεῦσθαι to κεκτῆσθαι τὸ ψεῦδος, —the settled incapacity for apprehending realities. In *Crat.* 393 A he says that ἄναξ and ἕκτωρ mean the same thing; οὐ γὰρ ἄν τις ἄναξ ᾖ, .. δῆλον .. ὅτι κρατεῖ τε αὐτοῦ καὶ κέκτηται καὶ ἔχει αὐτό (where ἕκτωρ has suggested both verbs).— The point of the phrase here is missed when it is taken as merely, ' possessing sorrows in the fullest sense of possession.'
1279 f. πρὸ χειρῶν: cp. Eur. *Tro.* 1207 καὶ μὴν πρὸ χειρῶν αἵδε σοι σκυλευμάτων | Φρυγῶν φέρουσι κόσμον (they are carrying robes, ib. 1220). *I. A.* 36 δέλτον τε γράφεις | τήνδ᾽ ἣν πρὸ χειρῶν ἔτι βαστάζεις. Thus the phrase means merely, 'visible in the hands,' without implying that the hands are outstretched. —τάδε, with adverbial force, 'yonder': so 155, 386, 526, 626, 805, 868, 1257.
τὰ δ᾽ ἐν δόμοις κ.τ.λ. The regular constr. would have been, ἔοικας ἥκειν ὡς ἔχων τε καὶ κεκτημένος,—τὰ μὲν πρὸ χειρῶν

τάδε φέρων, τὰ δ᾽ ἐν δόμοις τάχ᾽ ὀψόμενος. The present form has arisen thus. (1) Since τὰ μὲν .. φέρων interprets ἔχων, the poet wished it to come immediately after ἔχων τε καὶ κεκτημένος. (2) ἔοικας ἥκειν, although thus postponed, ought still to have been followed by τάχ᾽ ὀψόμενος. But the place of ἔοικας in the long sentence now prompted the change of τάχ᾽ ὀψόμενος into καὶ τάχ᾽ ὄψεσθαι. The sentence, as it stands, would have seemed less boldly irregular to the Greek ear than it does to us, because Greek idiom so readily permitted the change of a second participial clause into a clause with a finite verb. (Cp. 256 ἐπῆν: 816 ὑμνήσῃ.) Thus there would be nothing unusual in the following:—ἥκεις, τὰ μὲν φέρων, τὰ δὲ ἔοικας τάχα ὄψεσθαι. Here, instead of ἥκεις, we have ἔοικας ἥκειν, and the place of ἔοικας has led to ἥκειν and ὄψεσθαι being linked by καί.
Since τὰ δ᾽ ἐν δόμοις is governed by ὀψόμενος only, the words ἥκειν καὶ form a parenthesis, being equivalent to ἥκων. This is a rare constr., and alleged examples should be scrutinised before acceptance (cp. 537 n.); but there are some undoubted instances. Cp. Xen. *H.* 7. 3. 7 ὑμεῖς τοὺς περὶ Ἀρχίαν ... (οὐ ψῆφον ἀνεμείνατε, ἀλλὰ) ὁπότε πρῶτον ἐδυνάσθητε ἐτιμωρήσασθε. Thuc. 6. 78 ἐξ ἧς (κρατεῖν δεῖ ἢ) μὴ ῥᾳδίως ἀποχωρεῖν. Plat. *Legg.* 934 E διδασκέτω (καὶ μανθανέτω) τὸν .. ἀμφισβητοῦντα. [Lys.] *In Andoc.* § 33 ἐπιτιμᾷ (καὶ ἀποδοκιμάζει) τῶν ἀρχόντων τισί. *Anthol. P.* 7. 664 Ἀρχίλοχον

ΚΡ. τί δ᾽ ἔστιν αὖ κάκιον * ἐκ κακῶν ἔτι;
ΕΞ. γυνὴ τέθνηκε, τοῦδε παμμήτωρ νεκροῦ,
δύστηνος, ἄρτι νεοτόμοισι πλήγμασιν.

ἀντ. α΄. ΚΡ. ἰώ,

2 ἰὼ δυσκάθαρτος Ἅιδου λιμήν,   1284

3 τί μ᾽ ἄρα τί μ᾽ ὀλέκεις;   1285

4 ὦ κακάγγελτά μοι

5 προπέμψας ἄχη, τίνα θροεῖς λόγον;

6 αἰαῖ, ὀλωλότ᾽ ἄνδρ᾽ ἐπεξειργάσω.

7 τί φής, ὦ παῖ, τίνα λέγεις μοι νέον,

1281 τί δ᾽ ἐστιν (sic) αὖ κάκιον ἢ κακῶν ἔτι; L.—J. Pflugk (whom Schneidewin follows) conject., τί δ᾽ ἔστιν; ἢ κάκιον αὖ κακῶν ἔτι; So Emperius, but with ἤ.— Reiske, τί δ᾽ ἔστιν αὖ; κάκιον ἢ κακῶν ἔτι; So Wecklein and Bellermann.— Canter, τί δ᾽ ἔστιν αὖ κάκιον ἐκ κακῶν ἔτι; So Brunck and Hermann.—Herm. also proposed, κάκιον ὄν κακῶν ἔτι; which Schütz prefers.—G. H. Müller, τί δ᾽ ἔστι δὴ κάκιον αὖ κακῶν ἔτι;—Blaydes, τί δ᾽ ἔστιν αὖ κάκιον ἢ τὰ νῦν ἔτι;— Heiland (Progr. Stendal. 1851) would delete the verse, so that the five vv. (1278—80, 1282 f.) might answer to 1301—1305. Mekler agrees with him.   1282 τέθ-νηκεν L.—Nauck conject. τέθνηχ᾽, ἢ τοῦδε γεννήτωρ νεκροῦ: Semitelos, τέθνηκ᾽ ἐκ τοῦδε πημάτων νεκροῦ: Pallis, μήτηρ τέθνηκεν τοῦδε παμμόρου νεκροῦ.

(καὶ στᾶθι καὶ) εἴσιδε. Others, indeed, take καὶ τάχα as = 'full soon,' and ὄψεσ-θαι as depending on ἥκειν: 'thou seemest to have come in order to see full soon,' etc. This final inf. is tenable (O. T. 198 n.). But I know no example of καὶ τάχα as = 'full soon,' like καὶ μάλα, καὶ λίαν, etc. And, even if it were possible, it would here be weak.—See Appendix.

1281 τί δ᾽ ἔστιν. In order to form a judgment on this difficult verse, a careful scrutiny of Sophoclean usage is required. (1) The reading closest to the MSS. would be, τί δ᾽ ἔστιν αὖ; κάκιον ἢ κακῶν ἔτι; This involves merely a change of punctuation, and of accent (ἤ for ἢ). But it suggests these difficulties. (a) The interrogative ἤ occurs about 50 times in Soph.: and in every instance it is the first word of the interrogative clause. Only a vocative sometimes precedes it, as O. C. 1102 ὦ τέκνον, ἤ πάρεστον; so ib. 863, Ph. 369. Eur., indeed, does not always observe this rule: El. 967 τί δῆτα δρῶμεν; μητέρ᾽ ἤ φονεύσομεν; In Eur. Hec. 1013 I should point thus, ποῦ δῆτα; πέπλων ἐντὸς ἤ κρύψασ᾽ ἔχεις; (ἤ Valckenaer for ἤ). But, if we read κάκιον ἢ κακῶν ἔτι here, it would be a solitary departure from the practice of Soph., as seen in fifty other

examples. (b) The formula τί δ᾽ ἔστι (cp. on v. 20) occurs 21 times in Soph. (including Ph. 733, where the MSS. give τί ἔστι without δ᾽) as a question complete in itself. But there is not one instance of τί δ᾽ ἔστιν αὖ; which is, indeed, ill-suited to the rhythm of the tragic senarius. (2) Transposing αὖ and ἤ, we could read, τί δ᾽ ἔστιν; ἤ [or better, ἤ] κάκιον αὖ κακῶν ἔτι; But: (a) if this had been the original order, it is most improbable that ἤ and αὖ would have changed places, as they have done in the MSS. The sense would have been perfectly clear, whereas with αὖ...ἤ it is obscure. (b) The prominent place of αὖ in the MSS. is confirmed by many like instances: e.g. 1172: O. C. 1500 τίς αὖ παρ᾽ ὑμῶν κοινὸς ἠχεῖται κτύπος; Ph. 1089 τίπτ᾽ αὖ μοι τὸ κατ᾽ ἦμαρ ἔσται; ib. 1263 τίς αὖ παρ᾽ ἄντροις θόρυβος ἵσταται βοῆς;

(3) Canter gave, τί δ᾽ ἔστιν αὖ κάκιον ἐκ κακῶν ἔτι; The change of ἐκ to ἤ would have been peculiarly easy before initial κ (ΚΑΚΙΟΝΕΚΑΚΟΝ for ΚΑΚΙΟΝΗΚΑΚΟΝ). For ἐκ, cp. Tr. 28 ἀεί τιν᾽ ἐκ φόβου φόβον τρέφω. Il. 19. 290 ὥς μοι δέχεται κακὸν ἐκ κακοῦ αἰεί. Eur. Ph. 371 ἀλλ᾽ ἐκ γάρ ἄλγους ἄλγος αὖ σὲ δέρκομαι]...ἔχουσαν. On the grounds stated above, I prefer this

CR. And what worse ill is yet to follow upon ills?

ME. Thy queen hath died, true mother of yon corpse—
ah, hapless lady!—by blows newly dealt.

CR. Oh Hades, all-receiving, whom no sacrifice can appease! *1st anti-*
Hast thou, then, no mercy for me? O thou herald of evil, *strophe.*
bitter tidings, what word dost thou utter? Alas, I was already
as dead, and thou hast smitten me anew! What sayest thou,
my son? What is this new message that thou bringest—

1284—1292 L divides thus: ἰὼ ἰὼ — δυσκάθαρ|τος — ὀλέκεισ | ἰὼ— | προ-
πέμψασ— | αἰαῖ— | τί φησ— | σφάγιον— | γυναικεῖον ... μόρον. | **1284** In L
the first hand wrote χο before these vv.; a later hand changed it to κρε. **1286** ἰὼ
L: ὦ ῑ. **1287** λόγον] In L the first hand wrote λόγων, and then changed
it to λόγων: a later hand has made λόγον. **1288** αἰαῖ] αἰ αἰ L.—ἀνδρ']
ἀνδρα L. Cp. on 1147. **1289** τί φησ ὦ παῖ· τίνα λέγεις μοι νέον λόγον L.—
R. Enger, omitting λόγον with Seidler, reads ὦ τίν' αὖ for ὦ παῖ τίνα, which
Wecklein receives. Nauck prefers παῖ; τίν' αὖ.—Donaldson, τί φής; τίνα λέγεις
νέον μοι νέῳ, which Dindorf adopts. And so Schütz would read, only with the
MS. λόγον (followed by a note of interrogation) instead of νέῳ.

reading. The comparat. **κάκιον** means
merely that the sum of his misery will
be greater: not that he can conceive a
calamity sorer than his son's death. Cp.
O. T. 1364 f. εἰ δέ τι πρεσβύτερον ἔτι
κακοῦ κακόν, | τοῦτ᾽ ἔλαχ᾽ Οἰδίπους.

1282 f. **παμμήτωρ**: schol. ἡ κατὰ
πάντα μήτηρ: true mother; whose grief
for her son would not suffer her to survive
him; and whose act shows the same
passionate temperament as his. Contrast
μήτηρ ἀμήτωρ (*El.* 1154). παμμήτωρ usu.
=ἡ πάντων μήτηρ (n. on 338). Cp.
παμβασιλεία as ='monarchy in the fullest
sense' (n. on 737).—νεοτόμ.: adj. compounded with a word cognate in sense to
the subst.: cp. 7 n. ἄρτι ('a moment
ago') gives precision to the less definite
νεοτόμοισι: *Tr.* 1130 τέθνηκεν ἀρτίως
νεοσφαγής (cp. *Ai.* 898): Plat. *Legg.* 792 E
τῶν ἀρτίων νεογνῶν.

1284 δυσκάθαρτος "Αιδου λιμήν
(nom. for voc., 1211). The 'haven'
or 'receptacle' of Hades,—that nether
world in which he receives the dead
(810, 893)—is 'hard to be appeased,' in
the sense that Hades is ever demanding
fresh victims. The life of Haemon has
already been exacted by Hades as a
penalty for the offence of Creon against
the νέρτεροι. But even this atonement
(κάθαρμα) has not proved enough. δυσκάθαρτος is used here as if one could say
καθαίρειν (for Ἰλάσκομαι) θεόν: but that
constr. does not occur. Cp. *O. C.* 466
καθαρμόν...δαιμόνων (n.), such an atone-

ment as belongs (is due) to them. Plat.
Rep. 364 E λύσεις τε καὶ καθαρμοὶ ἀδικημά-
των.—For λιμήν cp. 1000: *Ant. P.* 7.
452 μνήμονες Εὐβούλοιο σαόφρονος, ὦ παρι-
όντες, | πίνωμεν· κοινὸς πᾶσι λιμὴν 'Αΐδης.

1286 f. **κακάγγελτα** is equiv. to two
distinct epithets, κακά and ἀγγελλόμενα,
so that the whole phrase='tidings of
dire woes.' Cp. 146 δικρατεῖς λόγχας
(n.).—προπέμψας, said to the ἐξάγγελος,
as the *herald* of the tidings. This use of
προπέμπω comes from its sense of 'escort-
ing' (*O. C.* 1667): we should not compare *El.* 1155 φί μας λάθρα προὔπεμπες οὐδ
φανούμενος | τιμωρὸς αὐτός ('didst send
forth,' from thy secret place of exile);
nor, again, *Ph.* 1205 βελέων τι προπέμψατε
('produce,' 'furnish'): but rather *Ph.*
1265 μῶν τί μοι νέα | πάρεστε πρὸς κακοῖσι
πέμποντες κακά;

1288 ἐπεξεργάσω: see on 1030.
1289 ff. ὦ παῖ, said to the Messenger.
It has been objected that, at such a
time, Creon could not use those words
except with reference to Haemon (as in
1266, 1340). From a modern literary
point of view, the objection is just. But
we should remember how very familiar ὦ
παῖ actually was as a mode of address,
whether by elders to juniors, or by masters
to slaves. Here it is used, not as to a
slave, but merely as to a younger man;
there is in it a certain pathetic appeal for
sympathy. (Cp. ὦ παῖ, ὦ τέκνον, as said
by the Messenger to Oed. in *O. T.*
1008, 1030.) Enger's conjecture, ὦ τίν'

15—2

༳8 αἰαῖ αἰαῖ,   1290
‵9 σφάγιον ἐπ' ὀλέθρῳ
‵10 γυναικεῖον ἀμφικεῖσθαι μόρον;

ΧΟ.‵ ὁρᾶν πάρεστιν· οὐ γὰρ ἐν μυχοῖς ἔτι.

ἰντ. β'. ΚΡ.‵ οἴμοι,
‵2 κακὸν τόδ' ἄλλο δεύτερον βλέπω τάλας.   1295
‵3 τίς ἄρα, τίς με πότμος ἔτι περιμένει;
‵4 ἔχω μὲν ἐν χείρεσσιν ἀρτίως τέκνον,
‵5 τάλας, τὸν δ' ἔναντα προσβλέπω νεκρόν.
‵6 φεῦ φεῦ μᾶτερ ἀθλία, φεῦ τέκνον. /   1300

ΕΞ.‵ ἥδ' *ὀξυθήκτῳ βωμία περὶ *ξίφει

1290 αἰ αἰ αἰ L: αἰαῖ αἰαῖ Dindorf.   1291 ἐπ' ὀλέθρῳ] ἐπολέθρωι L.   1293 L
gives this v. to the ἄγγελος. (Cp. on 1301.) Erfurdt first assigned it to the
Chorus.   1294—1300 L divides thus: οἴμοι | κακὸν— | τίσ ἄρα— | ἔχω— |
τάλασ— | προσβλέπω— | φεῦ φεῦ .. τέκνον. | 1297 τέκνον] Wecklein writes
νεκρόν.   1298 τὸν δ' ἔναντα] L has τάδ' ἐναντία· | προσβλέπω νεκρόν: but in the

αὖ (instead of ὦ παῖ τίνα), has not much
palaeographical probability. It gives,
indeed, a closer correspondence with
1266. But the form of dochmiac which
the MS. reading gives here is equally
correct. (See Metr. Analysis.) Seidler
was certainly right in omitting λόγον (see
cr. n.): and that remedy suffices.

Construe : τίνα νέον σφάγιον γυναικεῖον
μόρον λέγεις ἀμφικεῖσθαί μοι ἐπ' ὀλέθρῳ,
'what new death,—the bloody death of a
woman,—dost thou describe as heaped
on destruction (i.e., superadded to Haemon's death), for my sorrow (μοι)?' (Cp.
595 πήματα φθιτῶν ἐπὶ πήμασι πίπτοντ'.)
γυναικεῖον = γυναικός: cp. Aesch. Pers.
8 νόστῳ τῷ βασιλείῳ.—The notion expressed by ἀμφικεῖσθαι ἐπ' ὀλέθρῳ seems
to be, strictly, that of death entwined
with death, like corpse embracing corpse
(1140). The verb ἀμφικεῖσθαι prop.='to
be set around' (as a wall round a city).
Perhaps the bold phrase here was partly
prompted by the fact that persons embracing each other could be described
(O. C. 1620 n.) as ἐπ' ἀλλήλοισιν ἀμφικείμενοι. I prefer this view.

But another version is possible, if μοι
is taken with ἀμφικεῖσθαι: 'besetting
me,' ἐπ' ὀλέθρῳ, for (my) ruin. Cp. 1285

τί μ' ὀλέκεις; For ἐπί, cp. Thuc. 4. 86 οὐκ
ἐπὶ κακῷ, ἐπ' ἐλευθερώσει δέ. The difficulty is that ἀμφικεῖσθαι cannot well be
said of one sorrow (Eurydice's death),
and that, therefore, we have to evolve
from the epithet νέον the notion of a
circle of woes of which this μόρος is one.
Thus the image would be much more
obscurely expressed than that in Ai. 351,
ἴδεσθέ μ' οἷον ἄρτι κῦμα φοινίας ὑπὸ ζάλης |
ἀμφίδρομον κυκλεῖται, ('behold what a
surge hath but now burst around me and
hemmed me in, under stress of a deadly
storm,') where Ajax is sitting in the
midst of the carnage which he has
wrought. It is altogether improbable
that ἀμφικεῖσθαι alludes to Eurydice's
corpse having been brought (by the ἐκκύκλημα) into such a position that Creon
stood between it and Haemon's. See
1298, where Creon speaks of her as being
ἔναντα.

1294 ὁρᾶν πάρεστιν. The corpse
of Eurydice, and probably also the altar
at which she fell (1301), are now shown
to the spectators by means of the ἐκκύκλημα. The precise mechanism of this
contrivance is unknown; but the texts
leave no doubt as to its general nature. It
was a small stage, with space enough for

woe, woe is me!—of a wife's doom,—of 'slaughter· heaped on slaughter?

CH.   Thou canst behold : 'tis no longer hidden within.

[*The doors of the palace are opened, and the corpse of* EURYDICE *is disclosed.*]

CR.   Ah me,—yonder I behold a new, a second woe! What destiny, ah what, can yet await me? I have but now raised my son in my arms,—and there, again, I see a corpse before me! Alas, alas, unhappy mother! Alas, my child!   ^{removed}

2nd anti-strophe.

ME.   There, at the altar, self-stabbed with a keen knife,

---

marg. S has written, γρ. τόνδ' (*sic*, not τὸν δ') ἔναντα.   **1801** ἦδ' (*sic*) ὀξύθηκτος ἡ δὲ βωμία πέριξ L. Arndt conject. ἦδ' ὀξυθήκτῳ βωμία περὶ ξίφει. For βωμία, he afterwards proposed πτώσιμος. See Appendix.

---

three or four persons; and was low enough to admit of an actor stepping off it with ease. It was pushed on through the central stage entrance, and was usually brought sufficiently far forward to allow of actors entering or making their exit behind it. Here, the corpse of Eurydice is evidently in full view of the house (cp. 1299). Soph. has used the ἐκκύκλημα in two other plays: *El.* **1458** (the corpse of Clytaemnestra, with Orestes and Pylades beside it); and in *Aj.* 344 (Ajax in his tent among his victims). See Albert Müller, *Gr. Bühnenalterthümer*, pp. 142 ff. (1886).

Recent explorations in the Dionysiac theatre at Athens have given rise to a theory that, until Lycurgus completed the theatre (*c.* 330 B.C.), there was no permanent raised stage or proscenium. Even if this could be proved, it would still, however, remain certain that some such expedient as the ἐκκύκλημα was used in the fifth century B.C. This is proved by the texts of Aesch., Soph., and Eur., as well as by the two scenes of Ar. where the tragic ἐκκύκλημα is parodied (*Ach.* 408—479; *Thesm.* 95—238). Ar. has the words ἐκκυκλεῖν and εἰσκυκλεῖν. Wecklein thinks that the ἐκκύκλημα was employed when a part of the interior of the house was to be disclosed, but the ἐξώστρα when merely a single object was to be shown; and that the ἐξώστρα was used here (*N. Jahrb.* 1870, vol. 101, p. 572:

Philol. 31. 451). The meaning of ἐξώστρα is, however, doubtful.

1297 χείρεσσιν (976), though in an iambic verse, is excused by the lyric character of the whole κομμός. Eur. once admits it in dial., *Alc.* 756 ποτῆρα δ' ἐν χείρεσσι κίσσινον λαβών, where Monk needlessly proposed ποτήριον δ' ἐν χεροῖ.

1298 ἔναντα: an epic form, sometimes admitted in Attic poetry. Eur. *Or.* 1478 (lyr.) ἔναντα δ' ἦλθεν | Πυλάδης. Ar. *Eq.* 342 τῷ καὶ πεπαθὼς ἀξιοῖς ἐμοῦ λέγειν ἔναντα; Triclinius gave here the Hellenistic form ἔναντι (St Luke i. 8), which seems to be confined to the LXX., Apocrypha, and N.T.; see n. by Moulton in his ed. of Winer's Grammar, p. 591 (8th Engl. ed.).

1301 ἦδ': he indicates the dead body of Eurydice, now made visible by the ἐκκύκλημα.—Arndt's first emendation is given in the text. His later substitution of πτώσιμος for βωμία was not an instance of second thoughts being wiser. The altar meant is that of Ζεὺς Ἑρκεῖος in the αὐλή of the house (487). The objection made to βωμία here is to the effect that one could say βῶμος ἐφέζεται or ἵσταται, but not βῶμος ποιεῖ τι: *i.e.*, that the verb must refer directly to the assuming of the position denoted by βῶμος. It is quite true that this is usually the case; Eur. *Suppl.* 93 βωμίαν ἐφημένην: O. T. 32 ἐζόμεσθ' ἐφέστιοι: and cp. above, 785 f. But here βωμία is not merely an adverbial

λύει κέλαινὰ βλέφαρα, κωκύσασα μὲν
τοῦ πρὶν θανόντος Μεγαρέως κλεινὸν *λάχος,
αὖθις δὲ τοῦδε, λοίσθιον δὲ σοὶ κακὰς
πράξεις ἐφυμνήσασα τῷ παιδοκτόνῳ.　　　　1305

στρ. γ´. ΚΡ. αἰαῖ αἰαῖ,
　2 ἀνέπταν φόβῳ. τί μ᾽ οὐκ ἀνταίαν
　3 ἔπαισέν τις ἀμφιθήκτῳ ξίφει;
　4 δείλαιος ἐγώ, *αἰαῖ,　　　　　　　　1310
　5 δειλαίᾳ δὲ συγκέκραμαι δύᾳ.

1302 λύει] Bergk conject. μύει: Wieseler, κλήει.—κελαινὰ] λ from ν in L. **1303** κλεινὸν λέχος MSS. Seyffert conject. κεινὸν λέχος. Bothe, κλεινὸν λάχος (Blaydes, αὐτὸν λάχος; Semitelos, καινὸν λάχος). Pallis, κλεινὸν δέμας. Gleditsch, κλεινὸν σθένος. Meineke, κλεινὸν τέλος. **1304** δὲ σοὶ] δέ σοι L.—For σοὶ Pallis writes σὰς. **1305** πράξεις] Nauck conject. φράς: Heimsoeth, βάξεις. **1306** αἰαῖ αἰαῖ] αἰ αἰ αἰ αἰ (from αἰ) L. **1307—1311** L divides thus: ἀνέπταν— | τί μ᾽ οὐκ— | ἔπαισεν— |

---

word, to be taken closely with λύει. It is rather an instance of an adj. used with the force of a participle, and virtually equivalent to βωμία στᾶσα: i.e., it means, 'having taken her place at the altar,' she slew herself. Cp. *O. C.* 83 ὡς ἐμοῦ μόνης πέλας (sc. οὔσης): and see above on 471. Further: even if it were necessary to bind βωμία closely with λύει, it would be bold to say that poetry could not permit this slight modification in the ordinary use of the word, when we remember how free was the adverbial use of adjectives in poetry (e.g., *Ai.* 217 νύκτερος Αἴας ἀπελωβήθη).

ξίφει. A sacrificial knife, which lay on the altar. Cp. Eur. *Alc.* 74 (Death speaks) στείχω δ᾽ ἐπ᾽ αὐτήν, ὡς κατάρξωμαι ξίφει. For the prep. cp. *Ai.* 828 πεπτῶτα τῷδε περὶ νεορράντῳ ξίφει.

Next to Arndt's, the best conjecture seems that of Blaydes, ᾗδ᾽ ὀξυθήκτῳ σφαγῖδι βωμία πέρι. In favour of Arndt's we may observe:—(a) the MS. πέριξ (a word not used by Soph., and nowhere common) was not likely to have originated from πέρι alone: whereas it could easily arise from περὶ ξίφει, if ἴφει had been blotted or lost. (b) The MS. ἧδε (or ἢ δὲ) is just the kind of feeble make-shift which is sometimes found in the MSS., where a verse had come down in a mutilated state: see, e.g., on *O. T.* 943 f., 1264 f.—For other conjectures, see Appendix.

1302 λύει κελαινὰ βλέφαρα, allows her eyes to close in darkness. λύει re-laxes: the eyelids are deprived of power to remain open. The phrase has been suggested by the epic λῦσε δὲ γυῖα, λύντο δὲ γυῖα, etc., and seems quite intelligible; though, doubtless, it would have been more natural to say κλήει, as Soph. has done in fr. 640, βλέφαρα κέκληται. In [Eur.] *Rhes.* 8 we have λῦσον βλέφαρα γοργωπὸν ἕδραν, of opening the eyes; but that has no bearing on the different use here. Wolff brings what at first sight is a perfect parallel: *Anthol. P.* 3, 11 ἀνθ᾽ ὧν ὄμματ᾽ ἔλυσε τὰ Γοργόνος ... Περσεύς. But unfortunately neither he nor Bellermann has observed the meaning. It is not, 'caused the Gorgon's eyes to close,' but, 'uncovered the Gorgon's head.' The epigram refers to Perseus bringing Medusa's head to Seriphos, and therewith petrifying Polydectes, who had married Danaë, and sent her son on his perilous mission.—The objection to this is that elsewhere the verb has these usages:—(1) intrans., ὄμματα λύεται, the eyes close, or λύομεν, we shut our eyes; (2) trans., as *Anth. P.* 9. 558 ὕπνον κόρας (with the post-classical ᾶ), causes to close.' That is, there is no classical example of such a phrase as λύει ὄμματα, she shuts her eyes.

1303 Μεγαρέως. Cp. Aesch. *Theb.* 474 Μεγαρεύς, Κρέοντος σπέρμα, τοῦ σπαρτῶν γένους, where he is one of the Theban ...

she suffered her darkening eyes to close, when she had wailed for the noble fate of Megareus who died before, and then for his fate who lies there,—and when, with her last breath, she had invoked evil fortunes upon thee, the slayer of thy sons.

CR. Woe, woe! I thrill with dread. Is there none to strike me to the heart with two-edged sword?—O miserable that I am, and steeped in miserable anguish!

3rd
strophe.

δειλαιοσ— | δειλαίᾳ ... δόᾳ. | **1807** ἀνταίαν] L has γρ. καιρίαν in the margin, from S. **1810** δείλαιοσ. ἐγώ φεῦ φεῦ MSS. In L the first hand had written συγκέκραμαι δόαι (from the next v.) immediately after ἐγώ. Those words have been erased, and φεῦ φεῦ written in their place; not (I think) by a later hand, but by the first scribe himself. The error was, indeed, one which could not escape him.—For φεῦ φεῦ, Erfurdt conject. αἰαῖ (=the second ἴτω in 1332): Gleditsch repeats ἐγώ. **1811** In L δειλαίαν has been made from δειλαία.

---

warriors who guard the gates : his patriotic death is foreshadowed *ib.* 477 θανὼν τροφεῖα πληρώσει χθονί. The story is thus told by Eur. (*Phoen.* 930—1018), who calls him Menoeceus. While the Argives are pressing Thebes, Creon and Eteocles send for Teiresias. The seer says that Ares is wroth, because Cadmus of old slew the god's offspring, a dragon (or serpent?) which had its lair outside the walls. One of the Cadmean race, sprung from the dragon's teeth, must die to appease him. Now, Creon and his two sons are the only pure-bred σπαρτοί left. And Haemon is married. The seer therefore suggests that Menoeceus should die. Menoeceus pretends that he means to fly to Delphi. Creon leaves the scene, in order to provide him with money for the journey. Menoeceus then rushes to the top of a tower on the walls, where he cuts his throat, and falls into the dragon's former den (σηκὸν ἐς μελαμβαθῆ | δράκοντος, *Ph.* 1010, see n. above on 411). Statius, who also calls him Menoeceus, tells the story in *Theb.* 10. 589—782, and, like Eur., makes the son practise a pious fraud in order to hinder his father from preventing the sacrifice.—κλεινὸν λάχος: cp. Eur. *Ph.* 1013, where he says, στείχω δὲ θανάτου δῶρον οὐκ αἰσχρὸν τόλει | δώσων, νόσου δὲ τήνδ' ἀπαλλάξω χθόνα. Statius *Th.* 10. 670 where Virtus says to Menoeceus, *rape nobile fatum.* λάχος is freq. in poetry, and is used by Xen. The MS. λόχος would be forced as an allusion to the dragon's den (θαλάμαι, Eur. *Ph.* 931, or σηκός, *ib.* 1010) into which the corpse fell.

And it could not here be a general word for 'grave.'
1804 l. κακὰς πράξας = δυσπραξίας. A solitary instance of the plur. in this sense; as, conversely, *Tr.* 879 is the only instance of the sing. πρᾶξις as = 'mode of doing,' instead of 'fortune' (*O. C.* 560 n.). In Eur. *El.* 1305 κοιναὶ πράξεις, κοινοὶ δὲ πότμοι, the sense is, 'actions.' But the peculiarity here does not warrant a suspicion (see cr. n.). It is equally exceptional, the other way, when πράσσειν καλῶς means 'to act well' (*O. C.* 1764 n.).— δεψμνήσ. = ἐπαρασαμένη: cp. 658 n.
1807 l. ἀνέτταν, aor. referring to a moment just past; we should use the pres.: cp. *O. C.* 1466 ἔπτηξα θυμόν: *Ai.* 693 ἔφριξ' ἔρωτι περιχαρὴς δ' ἀνεπτόμην: cp. *O. T.* 337 n. The act. aor. ἔπτην is once used in lyrics by Aesch. (*P. V.* 555 προσέπτα), and once by Eur. (*Med.* 440, ἀνέπτα). It is a poetical form, but occurs in late prose (Arrian, Lucian, etc.).— φόβῳ, with fear of the curses invoked by Eurydicè.—ἀνταίαν, *sc.* πληγήν (*O. C.* 544 n.), a blow which strikes one full on the breast: *El.* 195 παγχάλκων ἀνταία | γενύων ὡρμάθη πλαγά: Eur. *Andr.* 844 ἴν' ἀνταίαν | ἐρείσω πλαγάν. But διανταία = a thrust which passes through the body : Aesch. *Cho.* 639 ξίφος | διανταίαν ὀξυπευκὲς οὐτᾷ.
1810 l. δείλαιος, but in 1311 δειλαίᾳ with αἰ: cp. *O. C.* 443 οἱ τοῦ πατρὸς τῷ πατρί: *ib.* 883 ἆρ' οὐχ ὕβρις τάδ'; ὕβρις: *Ph.* 296 ἀλλ' ἐν πέτροισι πέτρον: *ib.* 827 ὕπν'...ὕπνε (with ῠ in the first place, but ῠ in the second): *El.* 148 ὃ Ἴτυν, αἰὲν Ἴτυν ὀλοφύρεται.—The following are a

ΕΞ. ὡς αἰτίαν γε τῶνδε κἀκείνων ἔχων
⁀πρὸς τῆς θανούσης τῆσδ᾽ ἐπεσκήπτου μόρων.
ΚΡ. ποίῳ δὲ κἀπελύσατ᾽ ἐν φοναῖς τρόπῳ;
ΕΞ. παίσασ᾽ ὑφ᾽ ἧπαρ αὐτόχειρ αὐτήν, ὅπως   1315
⁀παιδὸς τόδ᾽ ᾔσθετ᾽ ὀξυκώκυτον πάθος.

τρ. δ´. ΚΡ. ὤμοι μοι, τάδ᾽ οὐκ ἐπ᾽ ἄλλον βροτῶν
2 ἐμᾶς ἁρμόσει ποτ᾽ ἐξ αἰτίας.
3 ἐγὼ γάρ σ᾽ ἐγὼ ἔκανον, ὦ μέλεος,
4 ἐγώ, φάμ᾽ ἔτυμον. ἰὼ πρόσπολοι,   1320
5 ἄγετέ μ᾽ ὅ τι *τάχιστ᾽, ἄγετέ μ᾽ ἐκποδών,
6 τὸν οὐκ ὄντα μᾶλλον ἢ μηδένα.

ΧΟ. κέρδη παραινεῖς, εἴ τι κέρδος ἐν κακοῖς·
βράχιστα γὰρ κράτιστα τἀν ποσὶν κακά.

1313 μόρων] μόρων L. The later MSS. have μόρων, μόρῳ (as A), or μόρων (as Aug. b and T). **1314** ἐν φοναῖς] L has εἰς φονάσ written by S above ἐν φοναῖς. **1317** ὤμοι MSS. (ὥ μοι μοι L). Erfurdt gave ἰώ μοι for the sake of closer metrical agreement with 1339, ἄγοιτ᾽ ἄν.—ἐπ᾽ ἄλλον] Pallis conject. ἐπ᾽ ἄλλῳ. **1319** ἐγὼ γάρ σ᾽ ἐγὼ ἔκανον ὦ μέλεοσ L, with most of the later MSS.: but Aug. b has ἔκτανον, and so the Aldine. Hermann inserted a second σ᾽ after ἐγώ. Nauck proposes ἐγὼ γάρ σ᾽ ἔκτανον, ὦ μέλεος, and in 1341 σέ τ᾽ αὖ τάνδ᾽· οὐδ᾽ ἔχω, ὦ μέλεος.

---

few among many instances of αἱ before o: 827 πετραία: 1131 Νυσαίων: 1140 βιαίας: *Od.* 20. 379 ἔμπαιον: Tyrt. 10. 20 γεραιούς: Aesch. *Suppl.* 385 (lyr.) ἰκταίου (Dind. ἰκτίου): Eur. *El.* 497 (dial.) παλαιόν. For the repetition cp. 379, 977.—συγκέκραμαι, 'blended with' anguish, *i.e.* steeped in it: (Whitelaw: 'Fulfilled with sorrow, and made one with grief.') Cp. *Ai.* 895 οἴκτῳ τῷδε συγκεκραμένην, 'her soul is steeped in the anguish of that wail': Ar. *Plut.* 853 οὕτω πολυφόρῳ συγκέκραμαι δαίμονι, where the words just before, ὡς ἀπόλωλα δείλαιος (850), might suggest that the parody glanced at our passage.

1312 f. ὡς αἰτίαν...ἔχων, as being responsible for, = ὡς αἴτιος ὤν. So Aesch. *Eum.* 579 Apollo, defending the accused Orestes, says, αἰτίαν δ᾽ ἔχω | τῆς τοῦδε μητρὸς τοῦ φόνου, I am responsible for (not, 'am accused of') the deed. In this sense of the phrase, ἔχω = παρέχω: cp. Thuc. 2. 41 ἀγανάκτησιν ἔχει, gives cause of resentment; id. 2. 61 ἔχει αἴσθησιν, makes itself felt. But in prose αἰτίαν ἔχω usu. = 'to bear the *blame*' for a thing,

i.e. to *be held* responsible for it: Her. 5. 70 εἶχον αἰτίην τοῦ φόνου τούτου: Plat. *Apol.* 38 C ὄνομα ἕξετε καὶ αἰτίαν...ὡς Σωκράτη ἀπεκτόνατε.—τῶνδε...μόρων, that of Haemon: κἀκείνων, that of Megareus (1303 f.). For the plur., cp. *El.* 205 τοὺς ἐμὸς ἴδε πατὴρ | θανάτους αἰκεῖς.—ἐπεσκήπτου, wast denounced. In Attic law ἐπισκήπτομαί τινι (midd.) meant, to take proceedings against a witness for perjury (ψευδομαρτυριῶν): Isae. or. 5 § 9 πρὶν ἐπεξελθεῖν οἷς ἐπεσκήψατο τῶν μαρτύρων. The rare pass. occurs in Plat. *Legg.* 937 B ἐὰν δούλη ἐπισκηφθῇ τὰ ψευδῆ μαρτυρῆσαι.

1314 κἀπελύσατ᾽, quitted life: see on 1268 ἀπελύθης. For καί, cp. 772 n.— ἐν φοναῖς: 696 n.

1315 f. ὑφ᾽ ἧπαρ, expressing movement, 'home to' it: cp. *Tr.* 930 ὁρῶμεν αὐτὴν ἀμφιπλῆγι φασγάνῳ | πλευρὰν ὑφ᾽ ἧπαρ καὶ φρένας πεπληγμένην. Eur. *Or.* 1063 παίσας πρὸς ἧπαρ φασγάνῳ.—ὀξυκώκυτον, by the household (cp. 1079): she, herself heard the news in silence (1256).

1317 f. τάδ᾽ οὐκ ἐπ᾽ ἄλλον βροτῶν ἁρμόσει ποτέ, the guilt can never fit (= be

ME. Yea, both this son's doom, and that other's, were laid to thy charge by her whose corpse thou seest.

CR. And what was the manner of the violent deed by which she passed away?

ME. Her own hand struck her to the heart, when she had learned her son's sorely lamented fate.

CR. Ah me, this guilt can never be fixed on any other of mortal kind, for my acquittal! I, even I, was thy slayer, wretched that I am—I own the truth. Lead me away, O my servants, lead me hence with all speed, whose life is but as death! *4th strophe.*

CH. Thy counsels are good, if there can be good with ills; briefest is best, when trouble is in our path.

1320 ἐγὼ φάμ' ἔτυμον L. Semitelos conject. ἐγώ, φαμί, σύννομ'. **1322 f.** ἀγετέ μ' ὅτι τάχος, ἄγετέ μ' ἐκ ποδῶν (sic, not ἐκποδών) L. Unless the οι of τάχος is lengthened before the pause, the dochmiac requires either (a) a long syllable there, or (b) the addition of one short. Hence (a) Erfurdt proposed τάχιστ' instead of τάχος. Many edd. receive this. Enger, ἄγ' ἄγεθ' ὅτι τάχοι μ', ἀπάγετ' ἐκποδών. Meineke, ἄγετέ μ', ὅτι τάχος μ' ἀπάγετ' ἐκποδών. Pallis, ἄγετέ μ' ὅτι τάχος, τίθεσθέ μ' ἐκποδών. (b) Schöne, ἀπάγετέ μ' ὅτι τάχος, ἄγετέ μ' ἐκποδών. **1327** βράχιστα γὰρ κράτιστα] In L, S notes a v. l., κράτιστα γὰρ τάχιστα.

---

fixed upon) another man, ἐξ ἡμᾶς αἰτίας, (being transferred) from my responsibility, —i.e., so as to leave me blameless. For the intrans. ἁρμόσει, cp. O. T. 902 (n.), El. 1293. ἐκ here is not for ἀπό, but is used as if we had, οὔποτε ἐξ ὑπαιτίου ἀναίτιος φανοῦμαι (cp. Tr. 284 ἐξ ὀλβίων ἄζηλον εὑροῦσαι βίον). Thus ἐξ ἐμᾶς αἰτίας is really a compressed way of saying, 'by change from a state of things in which the αἰτία (blame) was mine.'

1319 f. μέλεος: for the nom., cp. 1211.—φάμ' ἔτυμον, i.e., this is the simple truth: I was virtually, though not actually, his slayer.

1322 ὅ τι τάχιστ'. This (Erfurdt's) emendation seems the simplest and best cure for the metre (see cr. n.). It is worth noticing that Soph. has this phrase in a closely similar passage, O. T. 1340 ἀπάγετ' ἐκτόπιον ὅ τι τάχιστά με. He has ὅσον τάχος thrice, and ὡς τάχος eight times, but ὅ τι τάχος nowhere else.

1325 τὸν οὐκ ὄντα μᾶλλον ἢ μηδένα, one who exists no more than a nonentity. In μηδένα, μή has its generic force: one who is such as to be a mere cipher. Cp. Ai. 1114 οὐ γὰρ ἠξίου τοὺς μηδένας. O. T.

1019 καὶ πῶς ὁ φύσας ἐξ ἴσου τῷ μηδενί; (dat. of ὁ μηδείς,—he who is μηδείς in respect to consanguinity). Here τὸν μηδέν would have been equally fitting: cp. Ai. 1231 ὅτ' οὐδὲν ὢν τοῦ μηδέν (the dead) ἀντέστης ὕπερ.—Postgate suggests (Trans. Cambridge Phil. Soc., 1886, p. 58) that this use of the oblique cases of μηδείς in sing., and of οὐδείς and μηδείς in plur., may have come from an attraction of the neuter by the masc. article: e.g., τοὺς μηδένας from τοὺς μηδέν. We do not find ὁ μηδείς. When it became declinable, the phrase could dispense with the article; e.g., τὸν μηδέν could be simply μηδένα.

1326 f. κέρδη: the plur. more often refers to money (1061); but cp. El. 767 ἦ δεινὰ μέν, κέρδη δέ.—τὰ γὰρ ἐν ποσὶ κακὰ κράτιστα (ἐστι) βράχιστα (ὄντα): instead of, κράτιστόν ἐστι τά...κακὰ βράχιστα εἶναι. For the personal constr., cp. O. T. 1368 κρείσσων γὰρ ἦσθα μηκέτ' ὢν ἢ ζῶν τυφλός, and n. ib. 1061. For the omission of ὄντα, cp. the oracle in κίνει Καμάρυσαν· ἀκίνητος γὰρ ἀμείνων (sc. οὖσα), ap. Stephanus Byz. s. v. Καμάρινα. —τὰν ποσίν, before our feet, claiming

ἀντ. γ΄. ΚΡ. ἴτω ἴτω,

φανήτω μόρων ὁ κάλλιστ᾽ *ἔχων   1329

ἐμοί, τερμίαν ἄγων ἀμέραν,

ὕπατος· ἴτω ἴτω,

ὅπως μηκέτ᾽ ἆμαρ ἄλλ᾽ εἰσίδω.   1333

ΧΟ. μέλλοντα ταῦτα· τῶν προκειμένων τι χρὴ

πράσσειν· μέλει γὰρ τῶνδ᾽ ὅτοισι χρὴ μέλειν.   1335

ΚΡ. ἀλλ᾽ ὧν ἐρῶ μέν, ταῦτα συγκατηυξάμην.

ΧΟ. μὴ νυν προσεύχου μηδέν· ὡς πεπρωμένης

οὐκ ἔστι θνητοῖς συμφορᾶς ἀπαλλαγή.

1330 ἔχων Pallis: ἐμῶν MSS.   **1333** ἆμαρ ἀλλ᾽ L.   **1336** ἐρῶ L. .The
later MSS. have ἐρῶ μὲν (V ἐρῶμεν). Bothe writes ἐρῶμεν. Schneidewin, ἐρῶμαι.
F. W. Schmidt, ἐρῶ 'γώ. Dindorf, ἐρῶ, τοιαῦτα. Seyffert, ἐρῶ γ᾽, ἄπαντα. Blaydes,
ἐρῶ γε τυγχάνειν κατηυξάμην.—Nauck thinks that ἐρῶ ταῦτα is right, and that in 1314
we should perh. read καλύσετ᾽ for κἀπελύσατ᾽ the schol. there having τίνι τρόπῳ, φησίν,

---

immediate attention. Cp. Eur. *Alc.* 739
ἡμεῖς δέ, τοῖν ποσίν γάρ οἰστέον κακόν, |
στείχωμεν, ὡς ἂν ἐν πυρᾷ θῶμεν νεκρόν.
So Pind. *P.* 8. 32 τὸ δ᾽ ἐν ποσί μοι τράχον,
my present theme.

1329 ff. μόρων ὁ κάλλιστ᾽ ἔχων. I
have adopted ἔχων, a conjecture of Pallis
for ἐμῶν, on the following grounds.
(1) The phrase μόρων ἐμῶν could mean
nothing but, 'of all fates possible for
me.' This, however, is most strange.
In 1313 μόρων meant 'violent deaths':
so Aescl². *Th.* 420 αἱματηφόρους μόρους.
Hence it has been proposed to render
μόρων ἐμῶν here, (a) 'the deaths caused
by me': as Hermann, 'veniat caedium
per me factarum suprema, exoptatissime
mihi ultimum diem adducens.' (b) Figuratively, 'the many deaths that I have
died'; cp. 1288 ὀλωλότ᾽ ἄνδρ᾽ ἐπεξειργάσω.
But neither version is tolerable. (2) Triclinius proposed to make ἐμῶν fem., and
to take it with τερμίαν: when it would
at least be necessary to write ἐμᾶν (sc.
ἀμερᾶν). But, either with ἐμῶν or with
ἐμᾶν, the relation of ὁ κάλλιστ᾽...ἄγων to
the gen. μόρων is exceedingly awkward.
'That one among fates which *best* brings
my last day,' cannot be explained as an
equivalent for, 'that best of fates which
brings it'; *i.e.*, for μόρων ὁ κάλλιστος, ὁ...
ἄγων.
Both these difficulties (which to me
seem insuperable) are removed by read-

ing μόρων ὁ κάλλιστ᾽ ἔχων, the best
of fates. ἔχων could have been
changed to ἐμῶν, either by conjecture or
by accident, is shown by v. 575, where
at the end of the verse L has the probably
true ἐμοί, while other MSS. have ἔφυ. (If
κύπει is right in 467, and ξίφει in 1301,
these, too, are instances of final words
corrupted.) A question of **punctuation**
remains. The comma might follow either
ἔχων or ἐμοί. I prefer the latter. Cp.
Ai. 394 ἰὼ σκότος, ἐμὸν φάος, | ἔρεβος ὦ
φαεννότατον, ὡς ἐμοί.

1332 ὕπατος, an emphatic repetition
of ὁ κάλλιστ᾽ ἔχων,—'supreme of fates,'—
far best. It has been usual to take ὕπατος here as 'last.' But neither ὕπατος
nor ὑπέρτατος ever bears that sense in
classical Greek. Pindar often uses ὕπατος as 'best,' but never as 'last': *O.* 1.
100, *P.* 6. 42 and 10. 9, *N.* 10. 32. In
post-classical poetry ὕπατος sometimes
means 'last,' but that use was imitated
from the Lat. *supremus* and *summus.*
Thus in an epitaph on an Italian, a certain Aelius, Apollonides writes (*Anthol.*
P. 7. 233), νοῦσον ὅτ᾽ εἰς ὑπάτην ὤλισ-
θανε, τέρμα τ᾽ ἄφυκτον | εἶδεν. Whether
the Apollonides of the Anthology was or
was not he of Nicaea, who dedicated to
Tiberius a commentary on Timon's Σίλ-
λοι (Diog. Laert. 9. 109), at least he belonged to that age. This is proved by
his words in *Anthol. P.* 9. 287, Ἡελίου

CR. Oh, let it come, let it appear, that fairest of fates, for me, that brings my last day,—aye, best fate of all! Oh, let it come, that I may never look upon to-morrow's light! *cp. Ced.*

CH. These things are in the future; present tasks claim our care: the ordering of the future rests where it should rest.

CR. All my desires, at least, were summed in that prayer.

CH. Pray thou no more; for mortals have no escape from destined woe.

ἐλύετο ..;).—L here gives the temporal augment in συγκατηυξάμην. So *Ph.* 1019 L bas πόξάμην: *Tr.* 610 ηὔγμην: *ib.* 764 κατηύχετο. An Attic inscr. of 361 B.C. gives ηὔχθαι (Meisterhans, p. 78). **1337** προσεύχου] One MS. of the 14th cent. (Aug. b) has κατεύχου, which Benedict had conjectured.

νῆσον ὅτ' εἶχε Νέρων, alluding to the residence of Tiberius at Rhodes (*c.* 6 B.C.—2 A.D.). The epigram was written after Tiberius had been adopted by Augustus in 4 A.D., as he is called Ζῆνα τὸν ἐσσόμενον, and perhaps after he had come to the throne (14 A.D.). It would be interesting to know whether ὕπατος as = 'last' can be carried back beyond the Roman, or later Alexandrian, age; I can find no trace of it.

1334 ς. μέλλοντα, belonging to the future. To Creon's wish for death the Chorus replies, in effect, 'Sufficient unto the day is the evil thereof.'—τῶν προκειμένων: the duties which lie immediately before us; meaning here especially the obsequies of the dead.—For τι cp. *O. C.* 500 ἀλλ' ἐν τάχει τι πράσσετον.—τῶνδ' = τῶν μελλόντων.—ὅτοισι χρὴ μέλειν, *i.e.*, τοῖς θεοῖς. Cp. *Ph.* 1036 θεοῖσιν εἰ δίκης μέλει, | ἔξοιδα δ' ὡς μέλει γε.

1336 ἐρῶ μέν: for μέν cp. n. on 11. It merely gives a slight emphasis to ἐρῶ.—συγκατηυξάμην: κατά expresses that the prayer is solemn; σύν, that it sums up his desires. (For this force of σύν cp. 1201.) Cp. *O. C.* 585 ἐνταῦθα γάρ μοι κεῖνα συγκομίζεται ('by that boon I reap all the rest').—Nauck thinks that L's reading, ἀλλ' ἂν ἐρῶ, ταῦτα συγκατηυξάμην, is sound, and that in the corresponding verse, 1314, we should perh. read, τοίῳ δὲ κάλλιστ' (for κατελύσατ') ἐν φοναῖς τρόπῳ; He refers to the scholium on 1314: τίνι τρόπῳ, φησίν, ἐλύετο, καὶ ἐφέρετο εἰς φονάς; ἀντὶ τοῦ, ποίῳ τρόπῳ εἰς φόνον ἔπεσεν; Now, this does not point, I think, to the Scholiast's having ἐλύετο in his text, though it suggests that he had εἰς φονάς. He used the simple

verb in his paraphrase in order to bring out the literal sense (as he took it) of ἀπελύσατο. This is shown by ἐφέρετο and ἔπεσεν: he understood, 'she was set free (as a runner in a race is dismissed from the starting-post), and rushed (ἐφέρετο) to bloodshed.'—Further, the origin of L's reading is manifest. ἐρῶ μὲν had become ἐρῶμεν (as it actually is in at least one later MS.). Then the plur. ἐρῶμεν seemed too harsh with the sing. συγκατηυξάμην immediately following (though, in fact, it would have been quite defensible, cp. 734 n.), and was changed to ἐρῶ. Semitelos would read with L here, and yet leave 1314 unaltered. He refers to *Ai.* 905 where L has τίνος ποτ' ἆρ' ἔπραξε χειρὶ δύσμορος corresponding with 951 ἄγαν ὑπερβριθὲς ἄχθος ἤνυσαν. But there ἔπραξε is surely corrupt: Hermann gives ἔρξε, and Wecklein ἔπαθε.

1337 προσεύχου, without θεοῖς or θεούς. Cp. *Her.* 1. 48 ὡς τὸ ἐκ Δελφῶν ἤκουσε, αὐτίκα προσεύχετό τε καὶ προσεδέξατο.—Campbell thinks that 'the rationalism of the day appears in this advice of the Chorus.' But such an interpretation ill accords with the tone of the Chorus, which presently insists on the duty of piety towards the gods (1348). Nor does it seem in harmony with the pervading spirit of the poet's work. Rather Creon is exhorted to recognise, with pious resignation, the fixity of the divine decrees. Cp. the closing words of the *Oed. Col.*, ἀλλ' ἀποπαύετε μηδ' ἐπὶ πλείω | θρῆνον ἐγείρετε· | πάντως γὰρ ἔχει τάδε κῦρος. Brunck compared *Aen.* 6. 376 (Aeneas to Palinurus in the shades) *Desine fata deum flecti sperare precando.*

ἀντ. δ. ΚΡ. ἄγοιτ' ἂν μάταιον ἄνδρ' ἐκποδών,

2 ὅς, ὦ παῖ, σέ τ' οὐχ ἑκὼν *κατέκανον,   1340

3 σέ τ' *αὖ τάνδ', ὤμοι μέλεος· οὐδ' ἔχω

4 πρὸς πότερον ἴδω, πᾷ *κλιθῶ· πάντα γὰρ

5 λέχρια τὰν χεροῖν, τὰ δ' ἐπὶ κρατί μοι   1345

6 πότμος δυσκόμιστος εἰσήλατο.

ΧΟ. πολλῷ τὸ φρονεῖν εὐδαιμονίας

πρῶτον ὑπάρχει· χρὴ δὲ τά γ' εἰς θεοὺς

μηδὲν ἀσεπτεῖν· μεγάλοι δὲ λόγοι   1350

1339—1346 L divides thus: ἄγοιτ'— | ὅς, ὦ παῖ— | ὅς, σέ τ'— | ὅπᾶ— | πάντα— | λέχρια— | πότμος...εἰσήλατο. | **1339** ἐκποδών] ἐκ ποδῶν L, with μ above κ from first hand. **1340** σέ τ' τ: σέ γ' L.—κατέκτανον MSS.: κατέκανον Wilhelm Schneider: κάκτανον Hermann: ἔκτανον Musgrave. **1341** σέ τ' αὐτάν L: σέ τ' αὖ τάνδ' Seidler. L has ὅς before σέ τ', doubtless by inadvertent repetition from 1340: Hermann deleted it. **1342** l. ὅπᾶ: πρὸς πρότερον ἴδω πᾶ καὶ θῶ | L. For πρότερον, some of the later MSS. (including A) have πότερον. For καὶ θῶ, Musgrave conjectured

1339 ἄγοιτ' ἄν, an entreaty: cp. *O. C.* 725. The opt. with ἄν had a different tone in 444.—μάταιον here expresses rash folly: cp. *O. T.* 891 ματᾴζων: *Tr.* 565 ματαίαις χερσί.

1340 l. κατέκανον is the best, as it is the simplest, emendation of κατέκτανον (see cr. n.). Though the pres. κατακαίνω is not classical, the aor. is frequent: Xen. uses it (*An.* 3. 1. 2, etc.).—σέ τ' αὖ τάνδ' is a certain correction of σέ τ' αὐτάν. Here the latter would be like saying, 'and actually *thee*,'—as if the slaying of Haemon had been comparatively venial. It cannot be naturally explained as meaning, 'the mother with the son.'

1342 l. πρὸς πότερον...πάντα γάρ. The reading of this verse cannot be certainly determined. The traditional text (see cr. n.) exceeds the metre. My own view is as follows:

(1) The MS. ὅπα should be struck out. It evidently came in from the margin, having been a gloss on πᾷ, meant to show that πᾷ κλιθῶ is not a direct question, but depends on οὐδ' ἔχω. Retaining ὅπα, we should have to suppose a double question: 'nor do I know in what direction, (or) to which thing, I am to look.' This is not only very awkward, but very weak. The hiatus after ἔχω, though not unexampled, is at least another point against ὅπα.

(2) L has πάντα γάρ in a line by itself: but, considering the caprices of lyric division in that MS. (as in the rest), we cannot urge that fact as a hint of interpolation. If ὅπα was a spurious addition to 1342, then πάντα γάρ might easily have been carried over. Again, the words πάντα γάρ are not indispensable; yet the effect of λέχρια τὰν χεροῖν, without them, would be rather oddly abrupt. Therefore we are by no means warranted (I think) in ejecting πάντα γάρ.

(3) κλιθῶ, for καὶ θῶ, is certain. On this last point there is now a general agreement.—The resulting dochmiac differs from that in 1320 only by the 'irrational' long (the ω of ἴδω) for short (the first of ἔτυμον): and this is admissible. See Metrical Analysis.—Other views are noticed in the Appendix.

πρὸς πότερον, i.e., to the corpse of Haemon at his side, or to that of Eurydicè in front of him (1297 ff.).—ἴδω, deliberative subjunct. in the indirect question, depending on οὐκ ἔχω: cp. n. on *O. T.* 71.—πᾷ κλιθῶ, in what direction I am to lean, i.e., where I am to find any support: my son and my wife have fallen: all my fortunes lie in ruin. πᾷ here answers to the dat. after κλίνομαι when it means 'to lean against' a thing, as *Od.* 6. 307 (she sits) κίονι κεκλιμένη.—Not merely,

CR. Lead me away, I pray you; a rash, foolish man; who ^{4th anti}
have slain thee, ah my son, unwittingly, and thee, too, my wife— ^{strophe,}
unhappy that I am! I know not which way I should bend my
gaze, or where I should seek support; for all is amiss with that
which is in my hands,—and yonder, again, a crushing fate hath
leapt upon my head.

[*As* CREON *is being conducted into the house,
the Coryphaeus speaks the closing verses.*

CH. Wisdom is the supreme part of happiness; and reverence towards the gods must be inviolate. Great words

κλιθῶ, ὅτῳ was first omitted by Seidler. See Appendix. **1844 f.** λέχρια τάδ' ἐν
χεροῖν L, and so most of the later MSS.: for τάδ', Aug. b and Dresd. a give τά τ'.
Brunck gave λέχρια τὰν χεροῖν: Kayser, λέχρια τὰ πρὸ χεροῖν. **1847—1858** These
six verses are rejected by Fr. Ritter. **1849** τά τ' εἰσ θεοὺσ L. For τά τ'
Triclinius gave τά γ'.—Dindorf writes χρὴ δ' ἐι τὰ θεῶν: Blaydes, χρὴ δ' ἐι τοὺτ
θεοὺτ: also conjecturing (as Wecklein does, *Ars Soph. em.* p. 167) χρὴ δὲ τὰ πρὸτ
θεοὺτ.

'whither I am to betake myself,' ποῖ
τράπωμαι; This is shown by λέχρια.

1844 f. λέχρια τὰν χεροῖν. τὰν seems
right (see cr. n.): the MS. τάδ' ἐν would
come from ΤΑΕΝ. Creon is still touching the corpse of Haemon. The phrase
τὰ ἐν χεροῖν would mean, figuratively,
'the matters with which I am engaged'
(so ἔχων τι ἐν χερσί, Her. 1. 35). Here,
the words take a dramatic force from
their literal sense. 'All is amiss with
that which I handle.' Creon has, indeed, mismanaged the work which his
hands found to do; and the proof of it is
the corpse which he is touching. λέχριος
= 'slanting,' 'oblique.' As ὀρθός means
either 'straight' or 'upright,' so λέχριος
can mean either 'moving sideways' (*O. C.*
195), or, 'not upright,' 'slanting.' Cp.
πλάγιος, the ordinary prose equiv. of
λέχριος, which has the second sense in
Philemon Ἀγύρτης 5 σχήματα | πλάγι'
ἐστὶ τἄλλα, τοῦτο δ' ὀρθὸν θηρίον, (man
alone is *erect*, while other creatures (*i.e.*
quadrupeds) are bent earthward (cp. Sal-
lust, *Cat.* 1 pecora quae natura *prona...
finxit*). So, here, λέχρια means primarily
'awry':—τὰ πράγματα οὐκ ὀρθῶς ἔχει. Cp.
Shaksp, *Rich. II.* 2. 4. 24 *And crossly to
thy good all fortune goes.* But it is further
tinged with the sense of 'prone,' applicable to the corpse. The Scholiast

here has usu. been understood as explaining λέχρια by πλάγια καὶ πεπτωκότα.
But he meant only πλάγια to explain
λέχρια, while πεπτωκότα referred to πότμος...εἰσήλατο: this is clear (I think) from
his whole phrase, πλάγια καὶ πεπτωκότα,
τὰ μὲν ἐν χερσί, τὰ δὲ ἐπὶ τῇ κεφαλῇ.

τὰ δ' ἐπὶ κρατί μοι κ.τ.λ., while on the
other hand: for the adverbial τὰ δ', see
O. T. 666 n. These words refer to the
deaths of Eurydice and Antigone, as τὰ
ἐν χεροῖν referred to the death of Haemon.
It is quite possible to read τάδ', as
= 'thus'; but then τὰ ἐν χεροῖν would
denote *all* his woes, and so we should
lose the dramatic blending of a literal
with a figurative sense.—εἰσήλατο: cp.
on 1271 f.

1847 f. εὐδαιμονίας πρῶτον, the most
important element in it. Cp. Plat. *Rep.*
389 D σωφροσύνης δέ, ὡς πλήθει, οὐ τὰ
τοιάδε μέγιστα, ἀρχόντων μὲν ὑπηκόους
εἶναι, κ.τ.λ.—τὰ γ' εἰς θεούς: cp. 889 n.:
O. T. 706 (n.) τό γ' εἰς ἑαυτόν. *Ph.* 1441
εὐσεβεῖν τὰ πρὸς θεούς.—For the sentiment,
cp. 1050 f.

1849 f. μεγάλοι...λόγοι: cp. 127 n.
—For the position of τῶν ὑπεραύχων, cp.
944 f. Δαναὸς...δέμας.—πληγὰς...ἀποτί-
σαντες, as the price: cp. Her. 2. 65
ἀποτίνει ζημίην (a fine). So *ib.* 5. 56
οὐδεὶς ἀνθρώπων ἀδικῶν τίσιν οὐκ ἀποτείσει.

μεγάλας πληγὰς τῶν ὑπεραύχων
ἀποτείσαντες
γήρᾳ τὸ φρονεῖν ἐδίδαξαν.

1851 Nauck would place μεγάλας πληγὰς after τῶν ὑπεραύχων. Semitelos thinks

---

1852 γήρᾳ, without a prep.: so Eur. *Hec.* 203, etc.: but this is poetical, prose

of prideful men are ever punished with great blows, and, in old age, teach the chastened to be wise.

that the two latter words may have crept in from a gloss, 'ἀντὶ τῶν ὑπεραύχων,' on μεγάλοι λόγοι.

---

preferring ἐν γήρᾳ, ἐν τῷ γήρᾳ, or ἐπὶ γήρως.—ἐδίδαξαν, gnomic aor. (709).—τὸ φρονεῖν, so soon after 1347: cp. on 76, 625 (ἐκτὸς ἄτας), 956 (κερτομίοις).

APPENDIX.

Verses 2 f. ἆρ' οἶσθ' ὅ τι Ζεὺς τῶν ἀπ' Οἰδίπου κακῶν
ὁποῖον οὐχὶ νῷν ἔτι ζώσαιν τελεῖ;

The view taken in the commentary—that ὅ τι is subject to ἐστί understood—seems to have been first proposed by W. Schneider, then by Neue; it was·advocated by Bonitz (*Beiträge* II. 17); and it is now received by Bellermann. What is new in my note, so far as I know, is the attempt to show how associations of colloquial idiom may have helped to soften the apparent harshness, and, more especially, to excuse the hyperbaton of Ζεύς. Here, at any rate, we approach the root of the difficulty which these verses present. The ultimate question is,—how much irregularity would the spoken language of the day have tolerated in such a sentence? We do not know: we can but study the evidence of contemporary analogies.

At one time I inclined to the only theory which dispenses with the assumption of irregularity. This consists in taking τελεῖ with both clauses: ἆρ' οἶσθ' ὅ τι Ζεὺς τῶν...κακῶν (τελεῖ), ὁποῖον οὐχὶ νῷν ἔτι ζώσαιν τελεῖ; Then,—τελεῖ being, in this case, better regarded as *fut.*,—the sense would be, 'what will Zeus fulfil, which he will not fulfil *while we live*!'—that condition being emphasised by the form of the sentence. Grammatically, this is blameless. Cp. Plat. *Legg.* p. 710 D πάντα σχεδὸν ἀπείργασται τῷ θεῷ, ἅπερ (sc. ἀπεργάζεται) ὅταν βουληθῇ διαφερόντως εὖ πρᾶξαί τινα πόλιν: where the relative clause, expressing the condition, ὅταν βουληθῇ...πόλιν, is parallel with our gen. absol., νῷν ἔτι ζώσαιν. If the τελεῖ after ζώσαιν stood after κακῶν, the parallelism of form would be complete: except, indeed, that the Platonic sentence is a little bolder, since it is natural to supply ἀπεργάζεται (or ἀπειργάσατο) rather than ἀπείργασται. Yet, admissible as this construction is, it is undoubtedly harsh. And that harshness—especially at the outset of the play—is a strong argument against it.

Two other interpretations have been suggested by those who take ὅ τι as a pronoun. (*a*) ὁποῖον is resumptive of ὅ τι. 'Knowest thou *what* evil,—*what sort of* evil,—he does not fulfil?'—an emphatic pleonasm. The Scholiast seems to have acquiesced in this:—εἶπεν δὲ διττῶς· πρῶτον μὲν ὅ τι, ἔπειτα δὲ ὁποῖον, ἀρκοῦντος θατέρου. But this seems weak; and it is certainly jerky. Others modify this view by taking οὐχί with ὁποῖον *only:* 'Knowest thou what of the ills—nay, what *not*—is being fulfilled by Zeus,' etc. But, 'knowest thou *what* of the ills...' (ὅ τι *without* οὐχί) would have implied, not *less* than her meaning, but the *reverse* of it. (*b*) Two questions are combined in ὅ τι ὁποῖον (as in τίς πόθεν εἶ;)—'what, (*and*) of what kind?' This view, proposed by Zehlicke (Greifsw. 1826), has been rightly rejected by A. Boeckh (*Ueber die Ant.* p. 175).—Wecklein's comment is, 'ὅ τι ὁποῖον, *quid quale,* welches Leid, wie es immer heissen mag': *i.e.*, 'what woe,—of whatever sort it may be.' I do not see how the words could yield this sense.

If we read ὅτι, the conjunction, then ὁποῖον is substituted for the direct ποῖον. 'Knowest thou that Zeus fulfils—what not?' In favour of this, we might, perhaps, suggest two points. (1) The double question, being somewhat awkward, may have made it easier to slide into the irregular relative construction with ὁποῖον. (2) The familiarity of the combination οἶδ᾽ ὅτι—strongly illustrated by its use as an adverbial parenthesis (275 n.)—may have made it easier to treat οἶσθ᾽ ὅτι, after some intervening words, as if ὅτι did not exist. On the other hand, the harshness of the construction is aggravated by the shortness of the sentence. We cannot compare *O. T.* 1401, where the MSS. give ἆρά μου μέμνησθ᾽ ὅτι | οἷ᾽ ἔργα δράσας ὑμῖν εἶτα δεῦρ᾽ ἰὼν | ὁποῖ᾽ ἔπρασσον αὖθις; For there —even if ὅτι is kept—it is obviously impossible that μέμνησθ᾽ ὅτι οἷα δράσας, etc., should be a fusion of μέμνησθ᾽ ὅτι τοιαῦτα δράσας with μέμνησθ᾽ οἷα δράσας: the alternative—to treat οἷα and ὁποῖα as exclamatory— though not (to my mind) tolerable, would be a less evil: but clearly ὅτι should there be τι. It has been suggested, indeed, that ὁποῖον is not substituted for ποῖον, but is itself a direct interrogative. This has been supported by the analogy of ὁπότερος in direct question. Plat. *Lysis* 212 C ναί· ὁπότερος οὖν αὐτῶν ποτέρου φίλος ἐστίν; Heindorf there cites *Euthyd.* 271 A ὁπότερον καὶ ἐρωτᾷς, ὦ Κρίτων; *Rep.* 348 B ὁποτέρως οὖν σοι...ἀρέσκει; Let it be assumed that the readings are sound in those places. Still, there is at least no similar instance of ὁποῖος: nor is ὁποῖον here the *first word* of a direct question.

The proposed emendations are all unsatisfactory. They are of three classes.

(1) Those which alter v. 2, leaving v. 3 untouched.—Bothe: ἆρ᾽ οἶσθά τι Ζεύς.—Meineke: ἆρ᾽ οἶσθα δὴ Ζεύς.

(2) Those which alter v. 3, leaving v. 2 untouched.—Dindorf: ἐλλεῖπον for ὁποῖον.—Paley: οὐκ ἔσθ᾽ ὁποῖον οὐχὶ νῷν ζώσαιν τελεῖ (*Journ. Phil.* x. p. 16). He thinks that ἔτι was a gloss (due to the frequency of its combination elsewhere with ζῆν), and that, when ἔτι had crept into the text, οὐκ ἔσθ᾽ was erroneously omitted.—Blaydes: ἢ ποῖον, or τὸ λοιπόν, for ὁποῖον.

(3) Those which change, or transpose, words in both verses.— Heimsoeth (*Krit. Stud.* i. 211): ἆρ᾽ οἶσθά πού τι τῶν ἀπ᾽ Οἰδίπου κακῶν | ὁποῖον οὐ Ζεὺς νῷν ἔτι ζώσαιν τελεῖ;—Nauck: ἆρ᾽ οἶσθ᾽ ὅ τι Ζεὺς

νῶν ἔτι ζώσαιν τελεῖ | ὁποῖον οὐχὶ τῶν ἀπ' Οἰδίπου κακῶν; As Moriz Schmidt says, this would naturally mean, 'Knowest thou what Zeus fulfils for us, which does not belong to the woes from Oedipus?'— Moriz Schmidt (1880): ἆρ' ἴσθ' ὅ τι Ζεὺς τῶν ἀπ' Οἰδίπου κακῶν—ἔοικεν οὐχὶ νῶν ἔτι ζώσαιν τελᾶν; He prefers ἴσθ' to οἶσθ' on the ground that, after the latter, ὅτι would naturally be taken as the conjunction. (But cp. Plat. *Theaet.* 197 D κατασκευάζομεν οὐκ οἶδ' ὅ τι πλάσμα.) The origin of ὁποῖον was, he supposes, a marginal gloss ὁποιονδήποτε, referring to κακῶν.—Semitelos compresses the two vv. into one: ἆρ' οἶσθ' ὅ τι Ζεὺς οὐχὶ νῶν ζώσαιν τελεῖ;

4 **οὔτ' ἄτης ἄτερ.** It is difficult to avoid the conclusion that we have to choose between two views. One is that the words ἄτης ἄτερ are sound, but that there has been some confusion of negatives. I shall return presently to this theory, which has lately been gaining ground in Germany. The other view is that the words ἄτης ἄτερ conceal a corruption, but that the process which led to it can no longer be traced.

It must never be forgotten—it is indeed the capital condition of sound criticism here—that οὔτ' ἄτης ἄτερ was already the traditional reading in the time of Didymus, *c.* 30 B.C.[1] The practice of writing explanations, 'glosses,' in the margin of MSS. was common in the later age to which our MSS. belong; but we are not entitled to suppose that it existed in the earlier Alexandrian age, from which the MSS. of 30 B.C. had come down. Therefore we cannot assume, as Porson did, that ἄτερ arose from a marginal gloss ἀτηρ᾽, *i.e.* ἀτηρόν, representing the *sense* of some other word or phrase which originally stood in the text. Again: it is possible that ἄτης ἄτερ arose from a dittographia, ἄτης ἄτης, and that the word which originally followed ἄτης bore no likeness to ἄτερ. But this also would be a bold assumption. And, apart from such hypotheses, we can only be guided by the letters of οὔτ' ἄτης ἄτερ. No reading can claim to be more than a guess, unless it is such that a mis-writing of it might have generated those words.

This distinction between the clue of sense and the clue of writing at once sets aside a large number of conjectures. Among the rest, which suit the letters, not one, I think, suits the context. If, then, the words οὐκ ἄτης ἄτερ are corrupt, they probably arose by some accident, or series of accidents, of another kind than mere mis-writing. And if this is so, we may chance, indeed, to hit the truth by a conjecture; but we can no longer prove it.

The attempts to explain οὔτ' ἄτης ἄτερ *without* supposing a confusion of negatives have only a historical interest, and can be briefly dismissed. (1) Triclinius suggested two versions, both of which make ἄτερ an adverb, = χωρίς. (*a*) 'There is nothing painful, there is no excepted form of ἄτη (lit., nothing of ἄτη, apart),...that I have not seen'; *i.e.*, ἄτερ = ἄτερ ὄν. (*b*) 'Nothing painful, no sort of ἄτη, ἄτερ (ἐστί), *is apart*,' *i.e.*

---

[1] Schol. in L: Δίδυμος φησὶν ὅτι ἐν τούτοις τὸ ἄτης ἄτερ ἐναντίως συντέτακται τοῖς συμφραζομένοις· λέγει γὰρ οὔτως· οὐδὲν γάρ ἐστιν οὔτε ἀλγεινόν, οὔτε ἀτηρόν, οὔτε αἰσχρὸν ὃ οὐκ ἔχομεν ἡμεῖς. ἄτης ἄτερ δέ ἐστι τὸ ἀγαθόν.

'is absent.'—(2) Seidler: 'There is nothing painful, there is no shame or dishonour (such as can come) *without guilt*' (ἄτης ἄτερ), i.e., 'no *un-merited* shame or dishonour.'—(3) Boeckh: 'There is nothing painful, nor—*leaving aside the curse upon our race* (ἄτης ἄτερ)—is there any shame or dishonour that I have not seen.' Thus the parenthesis, ἄτης ἄτερ, refers to the fatal deeds and woes of the Labdacidae, while αἰσχρόν and ἄτιμον refer to the dishonouring of Polyneices by Creon.—(4) A modification of the last view would give the parenthesis a more general sense; 'nor—*leaving aside the ruin of our fortunes*—is there any disgrace or dishonour.'

The theory that the poet himself was betrayed into an error by the accumulation of negatives deserves to be very carefully weighed. As a general rule, mistakes of the kind which people easily make in hurried or involved speaking have a somewhat larger scope in the ancient classical texts than in days when a writer's proof-sheets are revised for press,—with close criticism in prospect. Yet modern literature is by no means free from them; and, in particular, the multiplication of negatives has always been apt to cause irregularities,—even in short sentences. Abbott (*Shaksp. Grammar* § 405) quotes Ascham's *Schole-master*, 37, 'No sonne, were he never so olde of yeares, might not marry': Shaks. *C. of E.* 4. 2. 7, 'First he denied you had in him no right'; etc. Bellermann brings two German instances (both from good writers, and in short sentences): Lessing's *Emilia Galotti* II. 6: 'Wie wild er schon war, als er nur hörte, dass der Prinz dich *nicht ohne Missfallen* gesehen!' And in a letter from Schiller to Goethe (Nov. 23, 1795): 'Da man sich *nie bedacht* hat, die Meinung über meine Fehler zu *unterdrücken*.' It is true that, in these examples, the irregularity consists in having a negative too much, while in Sophocles we should have to suppose a negative too little. Still, since two negatives precede the first οὔτ', the origin of the error would be similar[1].

The simplest form of the confusion-theory is to suppose that Sophocles wrote οὐδὲν γὰρ οὔτ' ἀλγεινὸν οὔτ' ἄτης ἄτερ | οὔτ' αἰσχρὸν οὔτ' ἄτιμόν ἐσθ', κ.τ.λ., meaning, 'there is nothing either painful or *not* without ἄτη,' etc.,—instead of οὔτ' οὐκ ἄτης ἄτερ. Another form of it is that advocated by Hermann Schütz (*Sophokleische Studien*, 1886), pp. 6 ff., who would point thus: οὐδὲν γὰρ οὔτ' ἀλγεινὸν οὔτ' ἄτης ἄτερ | οὔτ' αἰσχρὸν οὔτ' ἄτιμόν ἐσθ', etc. He understands: 'Nothing is not-painful or free from ἄτη.' Setting out, like Hermann, from the fact that οὐδὲν οὐκ ἀλγεινόν ἐστι means πάντα ἀλγεινά ἐστι, he supposes that the poet meant to say, οὐδὲν γὰρ οὐκ ἀλγεινὸν οὐδ' ἄτης ἄτερ ἐστί, but, wishing to co-ordinate the clauses, slid into the incorrect οὔτ' ...οὔτ'. That is, we have to suppose that οὔτ' ἀλγεινόν = οὔτ' οὐκ ἀλγεινόν. But I much prefer the simpler view first stated, for these reasons. (*a*) It is much easier to suppose that the influence of a *preceding* οὔτε should

---

[1] In Thuc. 7. 75 § 4 οὐκ ἄνευ ὀλίγων (ἐπιθειασμῶν) used to be explained as a like error, for οὐκ ἄνευ οὐκ ὀλίγων. But this seems impossible. Nor can ὀλίγων be explained (with Classen) as = 'in a faint voice.' Either ἄνευ or ὀλίγων (probably the latter) is corrupt.

have caused a *second* οὔτε to be used instead of οὔτ' οὐκ, than it is to suppose that the first οὔτε should have been so used. (*b*) It seems clear that the words from οὐδὲν to ἀτιμόν ἐσθ' formed a single sentence. The sense is greatly weakened by having a point after ἄτερ. (*c*) In v. 5 we should then require οὐδ'...οὐδ', unless we assumed a further inaccuracy in the use of οὔτ'...οὔτ'.

The negatives will supply a solution of a different kind if, instead of supposing they were originally confused, we suppose that the *second* οὔτε has been corrupted, from οὐκ or from οὐδ'. With οὐκ ἄτης ἄτερ the sense would be, ' Nothing either painful—not without ἄτη—or shameful,' etc. The ἄλγος, or mental anguish, was not unattended by ἄτη, external calamity. With οὐδ' ἄτης, the only difference would be that the clause would then be linked to ἀλγεινόν : ' Nothing either painful (and not harmless), or shameful,' etc. Cp. *O. T.* 1282 στεναγμός, ἄτη, θάνατος, αἰσχύνη, κακῶν | ὅσ' ἐστὶ πάντων ὀνόματ', οὐδέν ἐστ' ἀπόν. The great attraction of this remedy is that it changes only one letter; the drawback is the somewhat forced sense.

We may now consider the conjectural emendations of ἄτης ἄτερ. Apart from the hypothesis of a marginal gloss or of a dittographia, the letters of ἄτης ἄτερ are our only safe guides. Mr E. Maunde Thompson has kindly given me the aid of his palaeographical learning and skill in an attempt to find some approximate limits for the corruption. We have to start from the fact that no variant seems to have been known in 30 B.C. About 230 B.C. Ptolemy Euergetes had acquired for Alexandria a standard text of the dramatists which had been written at Athens about 330 B.C.[1] If the words οὐκ ἄτης ἄτερ stood in the text of 330 B.C., inscriptions supply the only form of writing by which the possibilities of change can certainly be measured. But it is otherwise if the text of 330 B.C. had a different reading, and if οὐκ ἄτης ἄτερ arose after that text had been brought to Alexandria. The papyri of the Ptolemaic age give Greek writing of the 2nd century B.C. It is a beautiful linked handwriting, firm and yet easy,—quite unlike the formally carved letters on contemporary stone. Such a handwriting presupposes at least a century of development. We may therefore believe that the forms of letters in the papyri of 250 B.C. were essentially the same as in those of 150 B.C. Now, one trait of the Ptolemaic writing is the well-marked distinction between letters which rest on the line, and letters which go below it. Thus the tails of φ and ρ are long, so that there was small chance of any confusion between such letters and, for instance, θ and ο. Hence, if we suppose ἄτης ἄτερ to have been a Ptolemaic corruption from a Ptolemaic archetype, we must, at any rate, be reluctant to part with ρ : while, on the other, we must hesitate to introduce φ. The letter τ could have come from λ (written somewhat awry), or, more easily, from γ, or π. The form of the Ptolemaic ς was such that, if ἄτη had been written with a mere linking-stroke (-) after it, a careless scribe might have evolved ἄτης.

---

[1] See the Introduction to the Laurentian MS. of Sophocles, part II., pp. 13 f., where I have collected and examined the authorities.

A final -ον might have been represented by a contraction, or else lost by accident. Hence Ptolemaic writing would explain how ἄτης ἄτερ might have arisen (*e.g.*) from ἄτης πέρ(α), or ἄτην περῶν, or ἀλάστορον: but not from ἄτην φέρον, or ἄτην ἄγον, or ἀτηφόρον. It may be added that ε was usually large in proportion to ο, and that a confusion between them, though quite possible, is so far less probable. The subjoined transcript (made by Mr Thompson) shows how οὔτ' ἄτης ἄτερ would have appeared in a Ptolemaic MS. of *c.* 250 B.C. :

It must always be remembered that these data are relevant only if we suppose the corruption to have taken place at Alexandria later than about 250 B.C. They cannot be safely used if the Ptolemaic copies were merely repeating an older Attic blunder; for we do not know how far the Attic handwriting of the 4th cent. B.C. resembled the Ptolemaic.

I subjoin a classified list of the conjectures known to me.

1. Conjectures which retain οὔτ' ἄτης, but change ἄτερ.—Robinson Ellis : ἀτάρ, = *sed vero*, 'nay,' with cumulative force.—Wecklein (*Ars Soph. em.* p. 70): πέρα.—London ed. of 1722 : μέτα.—Porson : ἔχον. —Hermann : γέμον.—Sallier and Bothe : ἄπερ.—Bergk : ὅπερ (omitting verse 5).—In the *Journal of Education* (May 1, 1888) Prof. L. Campbell remarked that I have made 'no reference to one [view], which, but for the abrupt transitions which it involves, would be at least plausible,— supposing vv. 4—6 to be an apostrophe to the shade of Œdipus, and reading οὔτ' ἄτης, πάτερ.' It had escaped the memory of my friendly critic that it was I myself who suggested this emendation, in a letter written to him in the spring (I think) of 1886. I mentioned it also to Mr E. M. Thompson; but I did not care to print it in my first edition : and I record it now, only to show that it was not overlooked.—The conjecture of Buchholz, given below (under ' 5.'), was not then known to me.

2. Conjectures which keep ἄτερ, but change ἄτης.—Koraes : ἄγης [what is ἄγης ἄτερ is ἄζηλον].—Ast : ἄκους.

3. Changes of ἄτης ἄτερ into two other words.—Brunck : ἄτην φέρον or ἀτηρὸν αὖ.—Donaldson : ἄτην ἄγον.—Musgrave : ἄτῃ σαγέν ('loaded with calamity').—Semitelos : ἀτήρ' ἄπερ.—Blaydes : ἀτηρὸν οὔτ'.—Pallis : ἄγαν βαρύ.—Hartung : ἀτηρὸν ὧδ'.

4. Changes of ἄτης ἄτερ into one word.—Johnson : ἀάατον ('noxium'). —Brunck : ἀτήριον [implying ἀτήρ, from ἄω, contracted for ἀάω, as λυτήριος implies λυτήρ].—Dindorf : ἀτήσιμος [as if formed, through ἄτησις, from ἀτάομαι].—Pallis : ὑπερβαρές.—Blaydes :—ἀτηφόρον, ὀλέθριον, or δύσφορον, or δυσχερές.—ἀλάστορον had occurred to me, but it seems impossible that it should have been used as = ἄλαστον. Cp. on. v. 974.

5. Conjectures which change both οὔτ' and ἄτης ἄτερ.—Buchholz : οἶδ' ἄτλης, πάτερ.—Moriz Schmidt : ἐσθ' ὁποιονοῦν.

23 ff. 23 Ἐτεοκλέα μέν, ὡς λέγουσι, σὺν δίκῃ
24 χρησθεὶς δικαίᾳ καὶ νόμῳ κατὰ χθονὸς
25 ἔκρυψε τοῖς ἔνερθεν ἔντιμον νεκροῖς.

The attempts to correct this passage have been of two classes : I. those which disturb the present number of verses : II. those which are confined to verbal emendation.

I. 1. Wunder, whom several editors have followed, rejected verse 24. Such a theory fails to explain the origin of that verse. And the result is intrinsically bad. The honours paid to Eteocles are then dismissed too curtly. It is indispensable to the coming contrast that they should be described with some emphasis.

2. The latter objection applies equally to compressions of vv. 23, 24 into a single verse. This verse has been variously shaped. A. Jacob proposed Ἐτεοκλέα μὲν σὺν δίκῃ κατὰ χθονός. Instead of σὺν δίκῃ, Kayser suggests ὡς νόμος, Dindorf ὡς λόγος, Schneidewin ᾗ (or ἥ) δίκη, and Kolster (*Philol.* v. 223) ὡς νόμῳ. Pallis gives Ἐτεοκλέα μὲν σὺν δίκῃ τε καὶ νόμῳ.

3. F. Kern supposes the loss of one or more verses after v. 23. This, of course, opens indefinite possibilities as to the origin of χρησθεὶς δικαίᾳ in 24.

II. 1. Among the merely verbal emendations, the simplest are those which change only χρησθείς.—For this word, Moriz Seyffert proposed χρηστός.—F. W. Schmidt, χρηστοῖς [adopted by Bellermann, as meaning, ' just, *in the sight of the good*' ; and by Wecklein, as ' meet *for patriots*'].—Nauck, κρίσα.

2. Changes of χρησθεὶς δικαίᾳ.—Wiesler proposed χρηστὸς δίκαια, with a comma after δίκῃ, so that δίκαια should be in appos. with the sentence.—Hermann Schütz (*Jahr. f. kl. Philol.*, 1876, p. 176) proposed χρῆσθαι δικαίων. In the note on 23 f. I suggest that this emendation would be improved by the further change of καὶ νόμῳ into τῷ νόμῳ. In his *Sophokleische Studien* (Gotha, 1886), p. 11, I find that Schütz himself now proposes this improvement. [Engelmann would read νῦν (for σὺν) δίκῃ | χρῆσθαι δικαίων καὶ νόμῳ.]—John W. Donaldson, in his ed. (1848), first conjectured προσθεὶς δίκαια, which he placed in the text. The same emendation was afterwards made by Jul. Held (*Observv.* p. 3, Schweidnitz, 1854).—Wecklein (*Ars Soph. em.* p. 107) proposes μνησθεὶς δίκης δὴ (or δικαίων).

3. A few emendations are of larger scope.—Moriz Schmidt :—Ἐτεοκλέα μέν,—πιστός, ὡς λέγει, δίκης | κρίσει δικαίᾳ κἀννόμῳ,—κατὰ χθονὸς | ἔκρυψε etc.—Semitelos : Ἐτεοκλέα μέν, ὡς λέγουσιν, ἔνδικον | κρίνας, δικαίῳ καὶ νόμῳ κατὰ χθονὸς | ἔκρυψε.

After my commentary on vv. 23 f. had been printed, I discovered that the conjecture σὺν δίκης | χρήσει had been made before, —viz., by Gerh. Heinrich Müller, in his *Emendationes et interpretationes Sophocleae* (Berlin, 1878), p. 51; and that Madvig had thought of σὺν τύχης (for δίκης) χρήσαι. In one respect, however, I have not been anticipated,—viz., in the statement of the considerations by which the emendation was suggested to me, and by which it may be defended. Even if it should find little acceptance, still many students will probably feel that this is a case where we have to choose between gentle remedies,—among which σὺν δίκης χρήσαι may ask a hearing,— and violent remedies which part company with the tradition. It may well be, of course, that the fault really lies deeper—and beyond discovery now.

110 ff. Some edd. change γᾷ (110), γᾶν, ὑπερέπτα (113) to the forms in η, because no other Doric forms occur in these anapaests. Anapaests held an intermediate place between dialogue and lyrics proper. According to the context in which they occur, they are sometimes more nearly akin to the former, and sometimes to the latter. Now, in the lyrics of Attic Tragedy the Doric α was a conventional mark of lyric style. The question of retaining it in any given set of anapaests must therefore be governed by the consideration just stated, and cannot be settled by an inflexible rule. In this passage the anapaests are essentially part of the choral song ; and the Doric forms γᾷ, γᾶν, ὑπερέπτα, are therefore appropriate. They serve to maintain the continuity of lyric character. It is otherwise with the anapaests spoken by the Chorus just after the third stasimon (801—805), and in the following kommos (815—822). There, it is evident that the anapaests have the tone of dialogue rather than of lyrics ; they are intended to afford a relief, or a contrast, to the lyrics before and after them. (Cp. n. on 804 f.) In them, accordingly, it seems clearly best to write παγκοίτην (804), and θνητῶν Ἀίδην (822). Some cases occur elsewhere which are on the border-line ; but, as a general rule, it is not difficult to decide. The MSS. almost invariably give the Doric forms in anapaests, which the transcribers regarded as following ordinary lyric usage.

138 ff.   εἶχε δ' ἄλλᾳ τὰ μέν, |
              ἄλλα δ' ἐπ' ἄλλοις, κ. τ. λ.

This, Erfurdt's reading, is a very gentle correction of L's εἶχε δ' ἄλλᾳ τὰ μὲν ἄλλᾳ τὰ δ' ἐπ' ἄλλοις, and has the peculiar merit of suggesting how the vulgate arose,—viz., by a confusion between ἄλλᾳ, ἄλλα on the one hand, and between τὰ μέν, τὰ δέ on the other. Dindorf's objection to the short μέν at the end of the verse is obviated by the pause (cp. on 1276). And, since the immediately preceding words, βακχεύων κ.τ.λ., have indicated the threats of Capaneus, the reference in τὰ μέν is perfectly clear. The irony of εἶχε δ' ἄλλᾳ is also tragic. It is surprising, then, that Erfurdt's correction has not found more general acceptance.

The other emendations fall under three heads. (1) Those which keep at least one ἄλλᾳ.—Hermann : εἶχε δ' ἄλλᾳ μὲν ἄλλᾳ· τὰ δ' ἐπ' ἄλλοις.—Emperius : εἶχε δ' ἄλλᾳ μὲν ἄλλ', | ἄλλα δ' ἐπ' ἄλλοις. —

Wecklein: εἶχε δ' ἄλλᾳ τὰ τοῦδ', | ἄλλα δ' ἐκ' ἄλλοις. [So in ed. 1874: formerly εἶχε δ' ἄλλᾳ τάδ' ἄρ', *Ars Soph. em.* p. 12.]—Hense: εἶχε δ' ἄλλᾳ τάλαντ'· | ἄλλα δ' ἐπ' ἄλλοις.—Musgrave: εἶχε δ' ἄλλᾳ τὰ δεῶν'· | ἔθλα δ' ἐπ' ἄθλοις.—G. Wolff: εἶχε δ' ἄλλᾳ τὰ Διός· | ἄλλα δ' ἐπ' ἄλλοις. (2) Those which change ἄλλᾳ into another part of ἄλλος.—Seyffert: εἶχε δ' ἄλλος τὰ μέν· | ἄλλα δ' etc.—Semitelos: εἶχε δ' ἄλλους δέον· | ἄλλα δ' ἐπ' ἄλλοις. (3) Those which change ἄλλᾳ into some other word or words.—Blaydes: εἶχε ταύτᾳ τὰ μέν, | ἄλλα δ' ἐπ' ἄλλοις.—Gleditsch: εἶλε τόνδ' ἄδε μοῖρ'· | ἄλλα δ' etc.—Kayser: ἔσχε δ' Ἅιδα λαχάν· | ἄλλα δ' etc. [Nearer to the letters than either of these would be εἶχε δ' αὖδ' αἶσά νιν, — the pause excusing the short νιν, as it excuses μέν.]

155 ff. The traditional text has:

155 ἀλλ' ὅδε γὰρ δὴ βασιλεὺς χώρας
156 Κρέων ὁ Μενοικέως νεοχμὸς
157 νεαραῖσι θεῶν ἐπὶ συντυχίαις
158 χωρεῖ· τίνα δὴ μῆτιν ἐρέσσων
159 ὅτι σύγκλητον τήνδε γερόντων
160 προὔθετο λέσχην
161 κοινῷ κηρύγματι πέμψας;

Verse 156, now a tripody, must be either shortened to a monometer, or lengthened to a dimeter. Taking the first alternative, Dindorf omits νεοχμός, while Hartung omits Μενοικέως, reading Κρέων ὁ νεοχμὸς νεαραῖσι θεῶν|. Bergk would omit Κρέων ὁ Μενοικέως and also θεῶν, rea ing (with νεοχμοῖς for νεαραῖσι) νεοχμὸς νεοχμοῖς ἐπὶ συντυχίαις. But it seems far more probable that the verse should be lengthened to a dimeter, by supplying one anapaest or its equivalent (see comment. on 155 ff.).

When this has been done, one difference still remains between this system of anapaests and that in vv. 141—147; viz., that the monometer. v. 160, answers to a dimeter, v. 146. Such a discrepancy seems to have been permissible. There is no ground for thinking that the correspondence between anapaestic systems was necessarily of the same precision as that between lyric strophes, while there is some evidence the other way. Thus the anapaestic system in 110—116 is, according to the most probable text, shorter by a monometer than that in 127—133. This small difference of detail was quite compatible with a general regularity of effect in such systems (cp. note on vv. 100—161, p. 27).

Many critics, however, have required a rigidly complete correspondence with 141—147. They have therefore supplied the metrical equivalent of three anapaests. The supplements are shown by brackets. (1) Erfurdt: [τῆσδ' ἄρτι] Κρέων ὁ Μενοικέως [παῖς | φανθεὶς] νεοχμὸς νεαραῖσι θεῶν.—(2) Hermann: [ὃς τῆσδε] Κρέων [παῖς] ὁ Μενοικέως | [νεοχμὸς] νεοχμὸς νεαραῖσι θεῶν.—(3) Boeckh: Κρέων ὁ Μενοικέως, [νέον εἴληχὼς | ἀρχήν,] νεοχμὸς νεαραῖσι θεῶν.—(4) Wolff: Κρέων ὁ Μενοικέως, νεοχμὸς [νεοχμῶς | ταγὸς ταχθείς,] νεαραῖσι θεῶν.—(5) Wecklein: Κρέων ὁ Μενοικέως [οἴκων ἔξω | ταγὸς] νεοχμὸς νεαραῖσι θεῶν.—Moriz Schmidt and Herm. Schütz take a like view, but leave a lacuna.

292 λόφον δικαίως εἶχον, ὡς στέργειν ἐμέ. The following are the passages in which Eustathius refers to this verse. On *Il.* 10. 573: παρὰ Σοφοκλεῖ τὸ ὑπὸ ζυγῷ νῶτον εὐλόφως φέρειν. On *Od.* 5. 285: τῷ Σοφοκλεῖ ἐν τῷ κάρα σείοντες οὐδ' ὑπὸ ζυγῷ νῶτον εὐλόφως εἶχον. Cp. also on *Od.* 10. 169 ὁ τραγικὸς Οἰδίπους (an oversight for Κρέων) φησὶ τῶν τινας πολιτῶν μὴ ἐθέλειν ὑπὸ ζυγῷ νῶτον εὐλόφως φέρειν. On *Il.* 23. 508 νῶτος εὐλοφος παρὰ Σοφοκλεῖ. The very way in which these references are made suffices to show how preposterous it is to re-write the verse in accordance with them. G. Wolff has brought together a number of instances in which Eustathius has made similar slips. For example:—(1) *El.* 66, δεδορκότ' ἐχθροῖς ἄστρον ὡς λάμψειν ἔτι, cited on *Il.* 2. 135 δεδορκὼς ἄστρον ὡς λάμψειν: (2) *O. T.* 161 κυκλόεντ' ἀγορᾶς θρόνον εὐκλέα, cited on *Il.* 24. ι Σοφοκλῆς που κυκλόεντα θῶκον ἀγορᾶς εὐκλεῆ: (3) *ib.* 1035 δεινόν γ ὄνειδος cited on *Il.* 17. 105 καλόν γ' ὄνειδος: (4) *Ai.* 445 φωτί, cited on *Il.* 6. 367 ἀνδρί: (5) *ib.* 1219 ἄκραν, cited on *Il.* 6. 397 ἱερήν. Such instances, which could easily be multiplied, detract nothing from the merit of Eustathius in his proper field ; they merely show that his incidental literary references were usually made from memory, and that his memory was not infallible. We cannot treat his quotations as if they possessed a critical value for the texts of authors to whom he casually alludes. So much is equally true of Aristotle.

318 L here has τί δαὶ ῥυθμίζεις. δαί, a colloquial form of δή, is not read in any other passage of Soph., but is supported by L in Aesch. *P. V.* 933 (where τί δ' ἂν should be read), and *Cho.* 900 (where Porson rightly gave ποῦ δή). As Ar. and Plato show, δαί was commonly used in short phrases expressing surprise, like τί δαί; πῶς δαί; τί δαὶ λέγεις; etc. In this verse δαί is clearly unsuitable, while on the other hand δέ constantly follows τί in such questions. The Triclinian gloss, διὰ τὸ μέτρον, suggests that δέ was changed to δαί by a corrector who did not know that δέ could be long before ῥ. In Plat. *Gorg.* 474 c where τί δὲ δὴ αἴσχιον is right, some MSS. have τί δαὶ δή : and in many other places δαί seems to have supplanted δέ or δή. (In Ar. *Ach.* 912, however, the metre permits δαί, which some edd. have changed to δέ.) Porson on Eur. *Med.* 1008 says, 'assentior Brunckio δαί e tragicis eximenti'; but the case of Eur. is different from that of Aesch. or of Soph. Thus in *Ion* 275 (τί δαὶ τόδ';) it is quite possible that the colloquial style of the passage should have led Euripides to prefer δαί. Each passage in which the MSS. ascribe δαί to him should be tested by our sense of the degree in which, there, he meant to reproduce the language of every-day life.

340 Here, as in 509, I have preferred the spelling ὀλῶ to ἐλῶ, though without regarding it as certain. Cobet (*Var. Lect.* 361) pronounces confidently for ἰλῶ, though without convincing reasons. The fact is that the MS. evidence is small in amount and doubtful in quality; and there is no epigraphic evidence. In Eur. fr. 544, οὐρὰν δ' ὑπίλασ', the MSS. of Athen. 701 B give ὑπήλασ' or ὑπήκας: those of Aelian *De Nat. An.* 12. 7 give ὑπήλλασ' or ὑπίλλασ'. Erotianus (gloss. Hippocr.

p. 378) gives ὑπείλλει. See Nauck, *Fragm. Trag.* p. 420; and cp. Schweighäuser on Athen. *l. c.* (vol. 8, p. 366). In Plat. *Tim.* 40 B εἰλλομένην and ἰλλομένην are among the various readings of the MSS. (others being these same forms aspirated, and εἱλομένην, εἱλουμένην, εἱλουμένην): so, again, *ib.* 76 B, 86 E. In Arist. *De Cael.* 2. 13 the Berlin editors (p. 293 *b* 31) give ἴλλεσθαι, as also *ib.* 14 (p. 296 *b* 26), noting εἰλεῖσθαι as a *v. l.* in the first passage, and εἰλεῖσθαι in the second. Here, the corruption in L, ἀποτρύετ' ἀπλομένων, arose from ΑΠΟΤΡΥΕΤΑΙΙΛΟΜΕΝΟΝ (ἀποτρύεται ἰλομένων), Π having been substituted for the doubled iota, Π. This passage, then, must be added to the testimony for ἴλλω *versus* εἴλλω. So, too, must ἐπίλλουσιν (L) and ὑπίλλουσι (A, with other MSS.), in 509. In Ar. *Nub.* 762, where most MSS. have εἶλλε, the Ravenna has ἴλλε. This last seems the most significant of all the facts which can be gathered from the MSS. That is, there is no testimony for εἴλλε which can fairly be set against this. There is no instance in which εἴλλε is supported by a manuscript excelling the other MSS. of the same author as much as the Ravenna excels the other MSS. of Aristophanes. I cannot, therefore, concur with Mr Rutherford (who does not notice *Ant.* 340 and 509, or Arist. *De Caelo* 2. 13) in thinking that 'the evidence for the spelling εἴλλω is...much greater than that for ἴλλω' (*New Phryn.*, p. 90). I should rather have thought that the MS. evidence, so far as it goes, is slightly in favour of ἴλλω. It is true that our MSS. sometimes wrongly changed ει to ι, as in ἔτισα for ἔτεισα: but, in regard to ἴλλω, we have to consider whether the doubling of λ might not have induced a weakening of the initial diphthong into ι.

350 f. λασιαύχενά θ' ἵππον ἕεται ἀμ | φίλοφον ζυγόν L.—The emendations may be divided into two classes.

I. The following retain ἀμφίλοφον ζυγόν, either as acc. or nom.

(i) Brunck: ὑπάξεται for ἕεται. This would be the simplest remedy. But the future tense is impossible. In this context, nothing but a present tense would be endurable. The gnomic aor. ὑπήγαγεν (Blaydes) must also, therefore, be rejected. It is, indeed, too far from the letters to be probable. (ii) Gustav Jacob: ὁπλίζεται ('Man fits the horse with a yoke'). This is now received by Bellermann, who formerly proposed ἐθίζεται (also with double acc.). He compares ἀμφιέννυμί τινά τι, etc. (iii) Dindorf: ἀέξεται, 'ut iugum equos ἀέξεσθαι dicatur, qui iugo adhibito dociliores et sollertiores redduntur' (*i.e.*, the yoke 'improves' the horse !)—(iv) G. Wolff: ἴσας ἄγει ('having put the yoke on the horse, he leads him').—(v) Campbell: ὑφέλκεται.—(vi) Blaydes, in his text, ὀχμάζει ὑπ'.

II. In the following, ἀμφίλοφον ζυγόν is modified.—(i) Schöne and Franz, ὀχμάζεται ἀμφὶ λόφον ζυγῷ (so Wecklein), or ζυγῶν (so Donaldson). Receiving ὀχμάζεται, (ii) Schneidewin, ἀμφιλοφῶν ζυγόν, (iii) Kayser, ἀμφιλόφῳ ζυγῷ, (iv) Blaydes, *inter alia*, ἀμφιβαλὼν ζυγόν.—(v) Schütz, ἐφέζεται ἀμφὶ λόφον ζυγῶν.—(vi) Seyffert, ἀνάσσεται ἀμφιλόφῳ ζυγῷ.—(vii) Semitelos, κρατεῖ δὲ μηχαναῖς ἀγραύλους | θῆρας ὀρεσσιβάτας, λασιαύχενά θ' | ἵππον, ὃν ἐξετέ ἀμφὶ λόφον ζυγοῖ.—(viii) Pallis, λασιαύχενόν θ' | ἵππον ζεύξατ' ἐν ἀμφιλόφῳ ζυγῷ.

466 f. L gives εἰ τὸν ἐξ ἐμῆς | μητρὸς θανόντ' ἄθαπτον ἠισχόμην νέκυν. The later MSS. have ἠισχόμην (ᾐσχόμην), ἠνσχόμην, ᾐσχόμην, ἰσχόμην, ἠνεσχόμην, or ἠνειχόμην. Leaving aside the mere corruptions, ἠισχόμην and ᾐσχόμην, we see that the other MS. readings represent two different kinds of endeavour to amend the passage. One was ἰσχόμην: along with which we might have expected to find ἐσχόμην: and, in fact, ἐσχόμην and ᾐσχόμην were the readings known to Eustathius (p. 529. 20, on *Il.* 5. 120). The other assumed the aor. or imperf., of ἀνέχομαι, contracted or uncontracted.

Hermann, who thought ἰσχόμην defensible ('non spernendum'), adopted ἐσχόμην. He took it, seemingly, in the sense of ἠνεσχόμην. This, as all would now admit, is impossible. Brunck adopted the portentous ἠνεχόμην from Pierson. Dindorf defends ἠνσχόμην as = ἠνεσχόμην: but see comment. Most of the other emendations assume either (1) ἠνεσχόμην, or (2) ἀνεσχόμην.

(1) Blaydes: μητρὸς θανόντ' ἄθαπτον ὄντ' ἠνεσχόμην.—Nauck: παρ' οὐδέν· ἀλλ' ἄθαπτον εἰ τὸν ἐξ ἐμῆς | μητρὸς πατρός τε τὸν θανόντ' ἠνεσχόμην.—Tournier: παρ' οὐδέν· ἄλγος δ' ἦν ἄν, εἰ τὸν ἐξ ἐμῆς | μητρὸς πατρός τε μὴ ταφέντ' ἠνεσχόμην.—Pallis, more boldly still, assumes the double compound: εἰ τὸν ἐξ ἐμῆς | μητρὸς φανέντ' (or τραφέντ') ἄθαπτον ἐξηνεσχόμην.

(2) G. Wolff: εἰ τὸν ἐξ ἐμῆς | μητρός θ' ἑνός τ' ἄταφον ἀνεσχόμην νέκυν.—Seyffert: εἰ τὸν ἐξ ὁμῆς | μητρὸς θανόντ' ἄταφον ἀνεσχόμην νέκυν. —Moriz Schmidt: παρ' οὐδέν· ἀλλ' ἄλγιστ' ἄν, εἰ τὸν ἐξ ἐμῆς | ταφέντ' ἄθαπτον ὦδ' ἀνεσχόμην νέκυν (understanding χειρός with ἐμῆς).

Any reader who will consider these conjectures will find, I think, that they justify the remarks made in my note on this passage.

578 f. ἐκ δὲ τοῦδε χρὴ | γυναῖκας εἶναι τάσδε—The following emendations have been proposed. (1) Dindorf: εὖ δὲ τάσδε χρὴ | γυναῖκας ἷλαι μηδ' ἀνειμένας ἐᾶν. So Meineke, but with εἷρξαι instead of ἷλαι Herwerden (*Obs. cr. in fragm. Com.* p. 134) improves this to εἷρξαι. And Nauck accordingly gives εὖ δὲ τάσδε χρὴ | γυναῖκας εἷρξαι μηδ' ἀνειμένας ἐᾶν. He would prefer, however, to place ἐᾶν *before* ἀνειμ., with Madvig (*Adv.* 1. 216). (2) Bergk adopts the insertion of ἐᾶν and the omission of τάσδε in 579, but would refrain from further change: ἐκ δὲ τοῦδε χρὴ | γυναῖκας εἶναι μηδ' ἐᾶν ἀνειμένας. The change of subject for the infinitives would, however, be very harsh. (3) Seyffert: εὖ δετὰς δὲ χρὴ | γυναῖκας εἶναι τάσδε μηδ' ἀνειμένας. Engelmann substituted ἐκδετὰς for εὖ δετάς. This is one of those conjectures which are taking at first sight, but which reflection condemns. δετός occurs only in the subst. δετή, a faggot. Nor were the royal maidens to be put in bonds; they were merely to be detained in the house.

601 f κατ' αὖ νιν...ἀμᾷ κόνις. The primary sense of ἀμᾶν was probably 'gather': the special sense 'cut,' 'mow,' was derived from the gathering of crops. The passages in which the verb occurs are of three classes. (1) Those which refer to reaping or mowing, and which therefore throw no light on the question whether 'gather' or 'cut' was the original notion. (2) Those which require the sense 'gather': as *Il.* 24. 165 (κόπρον) καταμήσατο χερσὶν ἑῇσιν, 'heaped it up' on himself: imitated by Josephus, *Bell. Iud.* 2. 21. 3 καταμώμενοι τῆς κεφαλῆς κόνιν. *Od.* 5. 482 εὐνὴν ἐπαμήσατο, 'heaped up a couch': *ib.* 9. 247 (γάλα) ἐν ταλάροισιν ἀμησάμενος, 'having collected.' (3) Those which require the sense, 'cut': as *Il.* 3. 359 (and 7. 253) διάμησε χιτῶνα. *Od.* 21. 300 ἀπ' οὔατα... | ῥῖνάς τ' ἀμήσαντες.

If, however, the MS. κόνις is retained in v. 602, the fact that καταμᾷ originally meant 'gathers in,' and only secondarily 'cuts down,' will not help to obviate the confusion of metaphor; for the metaphor is still borrowed from the gathering of the harvest.

Some critics have proposed to translate καταμᾷ 'covers.' Now, the version 'covers' would be suitable only if the φοινία θεῶν τῶν νερτέρων κόνις were the dust of the grave which is to hide Antigone: whereas it surely means the dust, due to the νέρτεροι, which she sprinkled on her brother's gory corpse. But how could καταμᾷ mean 'covers'? Prof. Lewis Campbell says:—'As καταμᾶσθαι κόνιν is 'To cover oneself with dust,' so, by a poetical inversion, the dust may be said καταμᾶν, 'To cover,' or 'Sweep out of sight.'" But καταμᾶσθαι κόνιν derives the sense, 'to cover oneself with dust,' only through its literal sense of 'heaping up dust for (or on) oneself.' Does, then, 'poetical inversion' allow us to say, κόνις καταμᾷ με, when we mean, καταμῶμαι κόνιν? On this point I can only repeat what I said in my first edition (commentary on vv. 601 f.);—"'Poetical inversion' has its limits. 'He pulls down a pail of water upon himself.' This operation would not be correctly described by saying, 'the pail of water pulls him down.''

In the *Journal of Education* (May 1, 1888) Prof. Campbell suggests, however, another explanation, different from the 'poetical inversion'; viz., that ἀμάω may be 'a homonym with more than one meaning.' That is, besides the rt. ἀμα, 'gather,' there may have been another ἀμα, meaning 'cover.' To this we can only reply that the sense 'gather' (with its derivative 'cut,' 'mow') suffices everywhere else, and that this one passage seems inadequate ground for assuming another root with a different sense. As to the Homeric ᾱ in the act. ἀμάω, Mr Leaf (on *Il.* 18. 34) has pointed out that it occurs only under ictus, and therefore lends no support to the hypothesis of two distinct verbs.

With regard to the usage of the word κονίς, a few words may be added in supplement to the commentary. (1) Ar. fr. 184, κοπίδι τὰν μαγαρικάν, is enough to indicate that, if the kitchen use of the implement was the most familiar to Athenians, other kinds of κοπίς were also known to them. (2) The military κοπίς, as used by some orientals, occurs in Xen. *Cyr.* 2. 1. 9, where Cyrus describes the ordinary equipment of the Persian nobles called ὁμότιμοι as θώραξ,...γέρρον..

κοπὶς δὲ ἢ σάγαρις εἰς τὴν δεξιάν. Again, in *Cyr.* 6. 2. 10, the Asiatic troops of Cyrus are armed with ἀσπίς, δόρυ, and κοπίς. That the blade of the κοπίς was of a curved form is shown by its being distinguished from the Dorian σφαγίς, of which the blade was straight: cp. Eur. *El.* 811, 837. It is unknown whether the military κοπίς was a small curved sword, like a scimitar, or a curved blade on a long handle, like a 'bill.' At any rate the fact that it was current in Attic prose as the name of a warlike weapon tends to show that, for Attic ears, it cannot have been a word of such homely sound as 'chopper'; and Euripides, at least, did not think it out of keeping with the tone of a tragic ῥῆσις. (3) The image of Death thus armed might be illustrated by Eur. *Or.* 1398 ὅταν αἷμα χυθῇ κατὰ γᾶν ξίφεσιν | σιδαρέοισιν Ἀιδα. Eur. fr. 757 βίον θερίζειν ὥστε κάρπιμον στάχυν. Apoll. Rh. 3. 1186 Ἄρεος ἀμώοντος. Hor *Ep.* 2. 2. 178 *metit Orcus | grandia cum parvis.*

606 f. L has ὁ παντογήρω | οὔτ' ἀκάματοι θεῶν. These words answer metrically to 617 f. -νόων ἐρώτων | εἰδότι δ' οὐδὲν ἕρπει. The conjectures have followed one of two courses, according as παντογήρω is (1) retained, or replaced by a metrical equivalent: (2) replaced by – ᴗ –, while οὔτ' is brought back from v. 607.

(1) Hermann: ὁ παντογήρως | οὔτε θεῶν ἄκμητοι. [He afterwards preferred, ἀκάματοι θεῶν οὔ.] The Doric ἄκματοι should, however, be written. Schneidewin conjectured οὔτ' ἐτέων ἄκματοι.—Heath and Brunck had proposed a simple transposition (with οὐδέ), οὐδὲ θεῶν ἀκάματοι. But ἄκματοι is metrically better, and would most easily have arisen from ἀκάματοι. For the form, cp. *Hom. hymn. Ap.* 520, ἄκμητοι δὲ λόφον προσέβαν ποσίν. It is unnecessary, then, to write οὔτε θεῶν ἀκμῆτες, with Blaydes.—Dindorf: ὁ παντογήρως | οὔτ' ἄκοποι θεῶν νιν.— Neue, whom Hartung follows: ὁ παντογήρως | ἀκάματοί τε θεῶν οὔ.— Nauck (omitting θεῶν): ὁ παντογήρως | οὔτ' ἀκάμαντες.

(2) Donaldson: ὁ παγκρατὴς οὔτ' | ἀκάματοι θέοντες. So Wolff, but with ὁ πανταγρεύς.—Wecklein desires a verb in the place of θεῶν: as ὁ πάντ' ἀγρῶν, οὔτ' | ἀκάματοι φθίνουσιν. He also thought of φθεροῦσιν. Mekler prefers σκεδῶσιν.

613 f. The MSS. give οὐδὲν ἕρπει | θνατῶν βιότῳ πάμπολις ἐκτὸς ἄτας. On πάμπολις the Schol. has, ὁ κατὰ πᾶσαν πόλιν ἕρπων νόμος, ὅ ἐστι, πάντες ἄνθρωποι. Triclinius took the sense to be: 'the law never (οὐδέν as adv.) comes (= is never applicable to) the life of men, in any of their cities, without ἄτη': *i.e.*, when any mortal thinks to rival the sovereignty of Zeus, he incurs ἄτη. This interpretation, which tortures the language without fitting the context, requires no refutation. Boeckh reads ἕρπων. Receiving this, Prof. Campbell explains:—'This principle (the sovereignty of Zeus) will last the coming time, and the time to come, as well as the time past, never swerving, as it moves onward, from calamity to the life of mortals in all their cities.' Are we, then, to understand that the attitude of mortals towards the sovereignty of Zeus has been, and

will be, *everywhere and always*, such as to bring down divine wrath?
There are other difficulties; but this suffices.

Wecklein, adopting Heath's πάμπολύ γ' in his text, conjectures πλημμελὲς (*Ars Soph. em.* p. 47), which D'Ooge receives. It means 'nothing wrong,' *i.e.*, nothing out of harmony with the sovereignty of Zeus. But πάμπολύ γ' is far better in this general maxim, and is also far nearer to the letters.—Hartung, admitting Lange's παντελῶς, reads οὐδέν' ἕρπειν| θνατῶν βίοτον παντελὲς ἐκτὸς ἄτας, 'that no mortal life performs its course to the end (παντελὲς adv.) without ἄτη.'—Schneidewin sought a similar sense by reading οὐδὲν ἕρπει | θνατῶν βίοτον τὸν πολὺν ἐκτὸς ἄτας, *i.e.*, 'no mortal (οὐδὲν = οὐδεὶς) goes through the greater part of life without ἄτη.' Pallis: οὐδέν' ἕρπειν | θνατῶν βίοτου πρὸς τέλος ἐκτὸς ἄτας.—Bergk invented a form παμπήδὴς as = παμπήδην ('altogether').

619 προσαύσῃ. The following are the principal pieces of evidence for an αὔω = αἴρω. (1) Alcman fr. 94 τὰν Μῶσαν καταύσεις. Eustathius explains this by ἀφανίσεις: cp. Ar. *Nub.* 972 τὰς Μούσας ἀφανίζων. (2) Hesychius: καταῦσαι· καταυλῆσαι [κατανλῆσαι Lobeck], καταδῦσαι. (3) Pollux 6. 88 ἐξαῦσαι τὸ ἐξελεῖν. (4) *Etym. M.* p. 346. 58 gives ἐξαυστήρ as 'a flesh-hook,' for taking meat out of the pot (= κρέαγρα). Lobeck (on *Ai.* 805, p. 296 f., 3rd ed.) would add the *v. l.* προσάρῃ [and προσαίρῃ] here, regarding them as glosses on the true sense of προσαύσῃ. But it is surely far more probable that προσάρῃ and προσαίρῃ were merely conjectures, (generated, probably, by a corruption,) which sought to give a clear and simple word, suited to the context. And, on the other hand, two things are certain,—viz., that προσαύω could mean to 'burn against,' and that such a sense is specially fitting here. It may be granted that there was an αὔω = αἴρω, but there is no proof that an Attic writer would have used αὔω, or any compound of it, in that sense. And there is one piece of evidence the other way. Pollux (see above) quotes ἐξαῦσαι as = 'to take out,' from αὔω = αἴρω: yet it is known that an Attic writer used ἐξαῦσαι as = 'to roast,' from αὔω 'to kindle': Plat. com. Ἑορταί fr. 9 τὸ δὲ ὀπτῆσαι ἐξαῦσαι (*ap.* Eustath. p. 1547. 48, on *Od.* 5. 490, αὔοι).

622 The Greek verses given in the note, ὅταν δ' ὁ δαίμων, κ.τ.λ., were probably the original of 'Quem Iuppiter vult perdere, dementat prius.' They are cited, with this Latin verse added in brackets, by James Duport (Regius Professor of Greek at Cambridge, 1639—1654) in his *Gnomologia Homerica* (Cambridge, 1660), p. 282. He is illustrating *Od.* 23. 11, μάργην σε θεοὶ θέσαν. Joshua Barnes, in the 'Index prior' to his Euripides (Camb., 1694), has, 'Deus quos vult perdere, dementat prius, incerta v. 436.' On that verse itself, p. 515, another version is given, viz., 'At quando numen miserias paret viro, Mens laesa primum.' And in the margin he cites 'Franciados nostrae' v. 3, 'certe ille deorum | Arbiter ultricem cum vult extendere dextram | Dementat prius.' It was suggested to me that the line 'Quem Iuppiter' etc. had first appeared in Canter's Euripides. I have looked through both

the editions, but without finding it. His duodecimo ed. (Antwerp, 1571) has an appendix of 16 pages, 'Euripidis sententiae aliquot insigniores breviter collectae et Latinis versibus redditae': but 'Quem Iuppiter' is not among them. His folio ed. (of 1614) does not seem to contain it either. Publius Syrus 610 has 'stultum facit fortuna quem volt perdere.' This shows that part of the line, at least, was familiar *circ.* 50 B.C. The use of *dementat* as = *dementem facit* proves, of course, a post-classical origin.

648 The older MSS. have τὰς φρένας ὑφ' ἡδονῆς. Triclinius wrote φρένας γ'—rightly, I think (see comment.). Critics have proposed various other remedies, which may be classified thus. (1) Changes confined to ὑφ'. Hermann, πρὸς ἡδονῆς: Blaydes, δι' ἡδονήν: Hertel, σύ γ' ἡδονῆς (Meineke, σύ γ' ἡδονῇ): Seyffert, χύθ' ἡδονῆς (*i.e.* χυτά, adv., as = 'at random,' *temere*). (2) Larger changes.—Kayser, φιληδίᾳ for ὑφ' ἡδονῆς.—Stürenburg, κακόφρονος (do.).—Wecklein, τῶν φρενῶν ὑφ' ἡδονῆς |...ἐκπέσῃς.—Semitelos, μὴ νῦν ποτῶ[ποτάομαι—'be fluttered'], παῖ, τὰς φρένας, μήθ' [*imo* μηδ'] ἡδονάς, | κ.τ.λ.—Pappageorgius, removing the note of interrogation after γέλων in 647, writes γέλων | ὑφ' ἡδονῆς· μὴ νύν ποτ', ὦ παῖ, τὰς φρένας, against metre.

718 L gives ἀλλ' εἶκε θυμῶι καὶ μετάστασιν δίδου. For θυμῷ, several of the later MSS. have θυμοῦ. Porson was content to propose ἀλλ' εἶκε θυμόν, comparing *O. C.* 1178 τάδ' εἰκαθεῖν, etc. Hermann conjectured, ἀλλ' εἶκε, θυμῷ καὶ μετάστασιν διδούς, 'sed cede, irae etiam intermissionem faciens.' (He does not say how he understood καί, which he renders by the equally ambiguous *etiam*.) Afterwards, while adhering to this text and punctuation, he preferred to retain δίδου with Gaisford; 'quae est per asyndeton instantius precantis oratio.'—Dindorf: ἀλλ' εἶκε, καὶ θυμῷ μετάστασιν δίδου. (So Pallis, but with θυμοῦ.)

The bolder treatments of the verse have usually been directed against θυμῷ or θυμοῦ. Schneidewin: ἀλλ' εἶκε δή μοι, or ἀλλ' εἶκέ θ' ἡμῖν. —Martin: ἀλλ' εἶκε μύθῳ. (So Nauck.)—Meineke: ἀλλ' εἶκε δήμῳ. (He afterwards acquiesced in εἶκε θυμῷ as = 'yield in thy mind,' but then desired καὶ μετάστασιν τίθου as = μετάστηθι.)—Mekler: ἀλλ' εἶκε καὶ σύ. —Mr J. G. Smith suggests, ἀλλ' εἴ γε θυμοῖ: this is ingenious, but the γε is unsuitable.

782 ἐν κτήμασι πίπτας. These words have provoked a curious variety of interpretation and of conjecture. Besides the version defended in my note, the following have been proposed. (1) 'Love attacks rich men.' (Hermann: 'Non videtur mihi dubitari posse quin κτήματα pro opulentis ac potentibus dixerit.') 'Love attacks cattle': κτήμασι = κτήνεσι (Brunck). (3) 'Love falls on his slaves,' *i.e.* falls on men, so as to enslave them,—κτήμασι being proleptic. This was Schneidewin's view, who compared Lucian *Dial. Deor.* 6. 3 where Hera describes Zeus as ὅλως κτῆμα καὶ παιδιὰ τοῦ Ἔρωτος. But surely it is one thing for Hera to say that Zeus is 'the very chattel and play-thing of Love,' and quite another thing to suppose that Sophocles here meant to say, ' Love falls upon his chattels.' κτῆμα, in this sense, suits humorous prose, but not elevated poetry.

The conjectures have been numerous. (1) Keeping the rest, instead of κτήμασι Dindorf proposes λήμασι (1860 Oxon. 3rd ed.), or ἐν τ' ἀνδρῶν (1863 Leipsic 4th ed.): Blaydes, σώμασι (or νώνισι as a trisyll.): Hartung, στήθων: Meineke, δέμασι: Musgrave, σχήμασι (*titulos dignitatesque invadis*). Seyffert, βλήμασι. (2) Some would change the verb, with or without changing κτήμασι. Blaydes: εἰν ὄμμασι παίζεις (or -ιν ἴζεις). He also mentions an old conject., εἰν ὄμμασιν ἵππῃ ('*harmest through the eyes*'?).—Pallis: ἐν δέργμασιν ἴζεις.—Semitelos: ἐν κτήμασι τίκτει ('art born amid wealth').

797 f. τῶν μεγάλων πάρεδρος ἐν ἀρχαῖς | θεσμῶν. If πάρεδρος is sound here, the first two syllables are equivalent to the first long syllable of a dactyl. The following examples are furnished by Pindar. In each case I give the antistrophic verse along with the verse in which the example occurs. The example itself is printed in thicker type.

(1) *Ol.* 10 (11).

1st epode v. 17

καὶ χάλκ|εος Ἄρ|ης| τράπε δὲ | Κύκν|εια μάχ|α καὶ ὑ|πέρβ|ιον ∧ ||

2nd ep. v. 40

οὐ πολλ|ὸν ἴδε | πατρ|ίδα πολ·ὺ | κτέανον ὑπ|ὸ στερε|ῷ πυρ|ὶ ∧ ||

(2) *Pyth.* 11.

1st strophe v. 4 ματρὶ | πὰρ Μελί|αν χρυσί|έων | ἐς ἄδυτ|ον τριπόδ|ων ∧ ||
1st antistr. v. 9 ὄφρα | Θέμιν ἱερ|ὰν Πυθ|ῶν|ά τε καὶ | ὀρθοδίκ|αν

(3) *Nem.* 7.

4th str., v. 70 Εὐ|ξεν|ίδα πάτρ|αθε | Σώ|γενες ἀπ|ομνύω ∧ ||
4th antistr., v. 78 κολλ|ᾷ χρυσὸν | ἔν τε | λευκ|ὸν ἐλέφ|ανθ᾽ ἁμᾷ ∧ ||

[Here, ξεν|ῐδᾰ πᾱτρ=ᾳ χρῠσὸν. This is a very rare instance of ῠ in the subst., though χρῠσεος is frequent.]

(4) *Isthm.* 3.

4th str., v. 57 θεσπεσί|ων ἐπέ|ων λοιπ|οῖς ἀθ|ύρειν ||
4th ant., v. 63 ἐρνεῖ | Τελεσι|άδᾳ. τόλμ|ᾳ γὰρ | εἰκὼς ||

In the third and fourth of these examples, it will be observed that the resolution of the long syllable into ∪ ∪ has the special excuse of a proper name.

836—838 L gives the verses thus:

836 καίτοι φθιμένα [with ω over a] μέγ᾽ ἀκοῦσαι
837 τοῖς ἰσοθέοις ἔγκληρα λαχεῖν
838 ζῶσαν καὶ ἔπειτα θανοῦσαν.

The following opinions on this passage claim notice. (1) Hermann, omitting v. 838, transposed the two other verses thus :—

καίτοι φθιμένῳ τοῖς ἰσοθέοις
ἔγκληρα λαχεῖν μέγ᾽ ἀκοῦσαι.

Thus the pivot of his criticism was the belief that μέγ᾽ ἀκοῦσαι, being sound, should close a paroemiac. So Dindorf, too, formerly gave the passage (3rd ed. Oxon., 1860). [In his 6th Leipsic ed. (cur. Mekler, 1885) it is, καίτοι φθιμένῳ τοῖσι θεοῖσιν | σύγκληρα λαχεῖν μέγ᾽ ἀκοῦσαι.] Bergk also rejects 838. (2) G. Wolff refers to the schol. on 834 : καρτερεῖν σε χρή, ὡς καὶ ἡ Νιόβη ἐκαρτέρησεν, καίτοι θειοτέρου γένους τυγχάνουσα. Ταντάλου γὰρ ἦν τοῦ Διός.—Παραμυθούμενος αὐτήν, θεὸν φησὶ τὴν Νιόβην. Hence Wolff inferred that the Schol. read a verse, now lost, in which Antigone was exhorted to be patient (καρτερεῖν). He suggested σὲ δὲ καὶ τλῆναι πρέπον ὡς κείνην, to come immediately before ζῶσαν καὶ ἔπειτα θανοῦσαν. He also changed the full stop after θνητογενεῖς to a comma, and καίτοι to καὶ τῷ. The obvious reply to Wolff's theory is that the Schol.'s paraphrase, καρτερεῖν σε χρή, etc., refers to what the Chorus *suggests*,—not, necessarily, to what it *says*,— 'Niobe was a goddess, and you are a mortal' (and mortals expect suffering : therefore, if she was patient, you well may be so).

(3) Wecklein, too, assumes the loss of a verse. In 836 f. he reads

καίτοι φθιμένῳ μέγα τἀκοῦσαι
τοῖσι θεοῖσιν σύγκλημα λαχεῖν,

and indicates a lacuna between these verses and ζῶσαν καὶ ἔπειτα θανοῦσαν. His grounds are not G. Wolff's, but merely (*a*) the unsatisfactory sense, (*b*) the fact that at vv. 817 ff. we have six, and not five anapaests. [On this point, see Appendix on 155 ff.] Nauck's view is similar.

(4) Bellermann is disposed to agree with those who, like Hermann, Dindorf, and Bergk, reject 838. He remarks : 'Besonders auffallend ist ζῶσαν, da im *Leben* Antigones und Niobes keinerlei Ähnlichkeit gefunden werden kann.' This objection I venture to think that I have answered ; see n. on 834—838, p. 153.

(5) Semitelos gives :—

καί τῳ φθιμένων θαῦμά γ᾽ ἀκοῦσαι
τοῖσι θεοῖσίν σ᾽ ἔγκληρα λαχεῖν
ζῶσαν καὶ ἔπειτα θανοῦσιν,

i.e., 'Many among the dead will marvel to hear that in *life* thou didst win the same lot as a goddess (Niobe), and afterwards (after thy death) the same lot as the dead.' Are the dead to marvel, then, at the appearance among them of one who had seemed to be lifted out of the ranks of ordinary mortals ?

904—920 This famous passage affords one of the most interesting exercises for criticism which can be found in ancient literature. Is it indeed the work of Sophocles? Or was it interpolated, after his death, by his son Iophon? The anonymous Life of Sophocles records a statement by the biographer Satyrus[1] (*c.* 200 B.C.) that the poet died in the act of reading the *Antigone* aloud. It has been suggested that he may then have been employed in revising the play, with a view to reproducing it; and that Iophon, in completing the task, may have brought in these verses. Another possibility is that they were due to the actors, whose innovations Lycurgus sought to check as early as *c.* 330 B.C. At any rate these verses were recognised in the text of Sophocles at the time when Aristotle composed his *Rhetoric*,—*i.e.*, not later than *c.* 338 B.C.

The first impression which the passage tends to produce is well described in the simple and direct words of Goethe, as reported by Eckermann. 'In the course of the piece, the heroine has given the most admirable reasons for her conduct, and has shown the noble courage of a stainless soul; but now, at the end, she puts forward a motive which is quite unworthy of her, ('ganz schlecht,') and which almost borders on the comic.' And then Goethe expresses the hope that scholars will prove the passage to be spurious.

Among those who think it genuine, few, perhaps, would say that it is good. A large majority would allow that, at the best, it requires some apology. The question comes to this:—Can the faults of the passage, as they appear to a modern taste, be excused by a peculiarity in ancient modes of thought? Or are they such as to make it inconceivable that any great poet, ancient or modern, should have embodied the passage in a work of art?

At v. 458 Antigone said that she had buried her brother, in defiance of Creon's edict, because she deemed that no mortal 'could override the unwritten and unfailing statutes of heaven.' 'Not through dread of any human pride could I answer to the gods for breaking these.' 'The justice that dwells with the gods below' (451) requires that rites should be paid to the dead by the living; and, among the living, that duty falls first upon the kinsfolk. This is a perfectly intelligible principle; and everything else that Antigone says or does is in harmony with it. But here she startles us by saying that she would *not* have braved Creon, and obeyed the gods, if it had been merely a husband or a child that had been lying unburied. Yet her religious duty would have been as clear—on her own principle—in those cases as in this. Would she have been prepared, then, to suffer that punishment beyond the grave which she formerly professed to fear (459)? Or does she now suppose that the gods would pardon a breach of the religious duty in any case except that of a brother? Whichever she means, her feet slip from the rock on which they were set; she suddenly gives up that which, throughout the drama, has been the immovable basis of her action,—the universal and unqualified validity of the divine law.

---

[1] See *O. C.* p. xli.

But this is not all. After saying that she would not have thus buried husband or child, she adds this explanation. 'The husband lost, another might have been found, and child from another, to replace the first-born; but, father and mother hidden with Hades, no brother's life could ever bloom for me again.' She has not buried even her brother, then, simply because he was her brother; but because he was her last brother, and there could not now be any more. The inference is that, if Polyneices had not been a relative unique in his own kind, she might have thought twice. This astonishing view is at once explained by the origin of the verses which contain it (909—912). They are a tolerably close metrical version—and a very poor one, too—of the reason given by the wife of Intaphernes for saving her brother rather than her husband or one of her children. (Her. 3. 119: see comment. on 909 ff.)

Now, the 'primitive sophism' employed by the wife of Intaphernes, and the tendency to exalt the fraternal tie, are things which we may certainly recognise as characteristic of that age. And it is true that Aeschylus has some quaint subtleties of a similar kind: as when Apollo defends Orestes on the ground that a man's mother is not, properly speaking, his parent (*Eum.* 658); and when Athena votes for Orestes because she herself had had no mother at all (736).

But all that is beside the question here. We have to ask ourselves:— In adopting the argument used by the wife of Intaphernes, could a great poet have overlooked the absurdities involved in transferring it from the living to the dead? Moriz Seyffert suggests an excuse, to this effect:— 'She means that, if she had not buried him, she would not have had his love when (in the course of nature) she joined him in the world below.' But such a motive would have been independent of the fact that no other brother could be born to her. And another brother—also dear to her—was already in the world of the dead (cp. 899 n.). The plain fact is that the composer who adapted the words from Herodotus was thinking only of the rhetorical opportunity, and was heedless of everything else. Remark particularly verse 908, which prefaces the four verses paraphrased from the historian:—τίνος νόμου δὴ ταῦτα πρὸς χάριν λέγω; There is a certain tone of clumsy triumph in that, strongly suggestive of the interpolator who bespeaks attention for his coming point. The singularities of diction in vv. 909—912 have been noticed in the commentary.

The considerations which have been stated above render it incredible to me that Sophocles should have composed vv. 905—912: with which v. 913 on the one side, and v. 904 on the other, closely cohere. A. Jacob,—who, in 1821, first brought arguments against the genuineness of the passage,—was content to reject vv. 905—913. And Schneidewin, sharing his view, proposed μέντοι (or μόνῳ, to precede Κρέοντι) for νόμῳ in v. 914. The sequence would then be,

904 καίτοι σ' ἐγὼ 'τίμησα τοῖς φρονοῦσιν εὖ.
914 Κρέοντι μέντοι ταῦτ' ἔδοξ' ἁμαρτάνειν, κ.τ.λ.

But v. 904 has thoroughly the air of a preface to a specific self-justification. If it was followed merely by the statement, 'Yet Creon thought me wrong,' both v. 904 and v. 914 would be very weak. Again, it is evident that v. 913 could not directly follow v. 903, since the νόμος mentioned in 914 would not then have been stated. Now observe, on the other hand, how fitly v. 921 would follow 903 :—

$$\tau \grave{o} \ \sigma \grave{o} \nu$$
903 δέμας περιστέλλουσα τοιάδ᾿ ἄρνυμαι.
921 ποίαν παρεξελθοῦσα δαιμόνων δίκην;

Verse 921 is in every way worthy of Sophocles; nor does any just suspicion rest on 922—928. I agree, then, with those who define the interpolation as consisting of vv. 904—920.

In conclusion, it will be proper to state the principal arguments (not already noticed) which have been used to defend the authenticity of the passage.

(1) Bellermann's defence (in the Wolff-Bellerm. ed., pp. 83 f.) is, perhaps, the most ingenious. He argues, in effect:—She does not give up her original motive,—the religious duty. But she feels that this duty has degrees, answering to degrees of relationship. No one could be held bound to *give his life* in order to bury a stranger; and so, from the zero point, the scale of obligation rises, till it becomes strongest in the case of a brother. Here, then, as everywhere, her sole motive is the divine command. She merely says :—'I can imagine breaking that command in any case—yes, in a husband's or in a child's —*sooner than* in the case of this brother.' This is psychologically natural. The duty which occupies us at a given moment is apt to seem the most imperative; and the mind seizes on every thought that can enforce it. It does not follow that, if the supposed cases had been real, Antigone would then have acted as she now imagines. She knew the feelings of a sister; she had never known those of wife or mother.

To this I should reply :—The sliding-scale-theory of the religious duty here involves a fallacy, from the Greek point of view. Greeks distinguished between the obligation in respect to θυραῖοι and in respect to οἰκεῖοι. A husband and child are on the same side of that line as a brother. [In Her. 3. 119 οἰκήιοι is the term which comprehends all three relationships.] It is true that, if the dead had been a mere stranger, she could not have been deemed ἐναγής (cp. 255 f. n.) for declining to bury him at the cost of her own life. But her duty towards husband or child would have been the same in kind as her duty towards her brother. Besides, Bellermann's subtlety invests the crude and blunt sophistry of the text with an imaginative charm which is not its own. If the psychological phase which he supposes in the heroine had been expressed by the poet, such an expression must have preserved the essential harmony between her recent and her present attitude of mind.

Thudichum[1] also holds that Antigone is still loyal to her former principle. But now—so near to death, and condemned by all—she wishes to declare, in the most impressive manner, how overmastering was the sense of religious duty which she obeyed. It was not through insolence that she defied the State. She would have deferred to it in almost any imaginable case—but here she could not.—This is in general accord with Bellermann's view, but differs from it in giving the passage a more external character;—one of self-defence rather than of self-communing; and that is no gain, either in dignity or in pathos.

(2) Boeckh and Seyffert, in their editions of the play, take a bolder line. They agree in thinking that Antigone has abandoned the lofty ground on which she had formerly justified her action.

Boeckh concedes that this passage 'destroys the grandeur of her conduct.' She has now attained to a perception that she did wrong in breaking Creon's law. And, at the moment when that noble illusion fails her, 'the poet permits her to catch at such support as sophistry can lend to despair.'

Seyffert's conception is more refined; it is, in fact, related to Boeckh's much as the harmonising theory of Bellermann is related to that of Thudichum. She had acted, says Seyffert, from an elevated sense of religious duty. She finds herself condemned by all. The enthusiasm of her religious faith has been chilled; she is helpless and hopeless; her troubled thoughts fall back on the one thing of which she still feels sure,—the deep human affection which bound her to her brother.

Now, of Seyffert's view we may say, first, what has been said of Bellermann's,—that it is an idealising paraphrase of a crude text. But there is a further and yet graver objection,—one which applies alike to Seyffert and to Boeckh. After this disputed passage, and at the very moment when she is being led away to death, she says:— 'If these things are pleasing to the gods, when I have suffered my doom, I shall come to know my sin; but if the sin is with my judges, I could wish them no fuller measure of evil than they, on their part, mete wrongfully to me.' (925 ff.) Here the poet identifies his heroine, in one of her latest utterances, with the principle on which the catastrophe turns. Creon *is* punished by the gods; and his punishment is the token that they approve of Antigone's conduct. In the very last words which she speaks she describes herself as τὴν εὐσεβίαν σεβίσασα. (943.) Thus, in two different places—both of them subsequent to the suspected passage—she stands forth distinctly as the representative of the great law which had inspired her act. Is it probable—would it be endurable—that at a slightly earlier moment,—in vv. 905—912,—she should speak in the tone of one to whom that divine law had proved a mockery and a delusion,—who had come to feel that thence, at least, no adequate vindication of her conduct could be derived,—and who was

---

[1] *Jahresbericht d. Gymn. z. Büdingen.* Schulj. 1857—8, pp. 33 ff., quoted by Semitelos, p. 600.

now looking around her for such excuse, or such solace, as could be
found on a lower range of thought and feeling?

No; if this passage is to be defended at all, it must be defended from
such a point of view as that taken by Bellermann, not from that of
Seyffert or of Boeckh. Goethe's wish can never be fulfilled. No one
will ever convince every one that this passage is spurious. But every
student of the *Antigone* is bound to reflect earnestly on this vital
problem of the text,—the answer to which must so profoundly affect our
conception of the great drama as a whole.

966 f. Wieseler's conjecture, παρὰ δὲ κυανεᾶν σπιλάδων (for πελαγέων)
διδύμας ἁλός, published in 1857 (*Ind. Lectt. Götting.* p. 10), has been
received by some editors. Bergk proposed Κυανεᾶν σπιλάδας, to avoid
παρά with the genitive, which is, indeed, an insuperable objection to
σπιλάδων: but then, with the change of case, the probability of the
emendation is still further diminished.

Other readings are:—Wecklein, παρὰ δὲ κυανέων (*sic*) σπιλάδων διδύμας
πέτρας (for ἁλός). | Meineke, παρὰ δὲ κυανέων τεναγέων διδύμας ἁλός, com-
paring Scymnus Perieget. 724 εἶτ᾽ αἰγιαλός τις Σαλμυδησσὸς λεγόμενος |
ἐφ᾽ ἑπτακόσια στάδια τεναγώδης ἄγαν.—Hartung alters more boldly:—
παρὰ δὲ Κυανέων (*sic*) διδύμαις ἁλὸς | ἀκταῖς Βοσπορίαις Θρῃκῶν Ἄρης |
Σαλμυδήσιος ἀγχιπτόλεμος.

1034 f. The MSS. give κοὐδὲ μαντικῆς | ἄπρακτος ὑμῖν εἰμι τῶν δ᾽ ὑπαὶ
γένους.

(1) For ἄπρακτος, H. Stephanus conjectures ἄπρατος: Nauck, ἄγευστος: Pallis, ἄτρωτος or ἄπληκτος.

(2) The words τῶν δ᾽ ὑπαὶ γένους have given rise to many conjectures, which, as I cannot but think, are unnecessary. Brunck is content
with τῶν for τῶνδ᾽, and Blaydes with τῶν γένους ὑπα. But others have
sought to obtain the sense, 'and by my kinsmen': thus Hermann, τῶν
δ᾽ ὑπ᾽ ἐγγενῶν· Dindorf (omitting εἰμί) τῶν δὲ συγγενῶν ὑπο: Schneidewin,
τῶν δ᾽ ὑπ᾽ ἐν γένει: Nauck, τοῖσι δ᾽ ἐν γένει. Donaldson, again, proposes
τῶν ὑπ᾽ ἀργύρου. Seyffert, γόνους (for γένους), to be taken with ἐξημπόλημαι: *i.e.*, 'by whom I have long since been relieved of my son' ('who
have long since alienated my son's loyalty from me'!).—Wolff strangely
proposed μῶν for τῶν δ᾽.—Moriz Schmidt supposes that either two or
four verses for the Chorus have been lost after 1032. Then πρέσβυ in
1033 would be said by Creon to the Chorus, not to Teiresias. He also
thinks that one verse of Creon's has dropped out after 1034.

1080—1083 Boeckh denies that there is any reference, direct or
indirect, to the war of the Epigoni. He takes the verses as merely stating
a general axiom: 'All cities, becoming hateful [ἐχθραί, to the gods], are
convulsed by calamity,'—when dogs, etc., defile their altars with carrion.
This, surely, robs the seer's words of all force and point. Schneidewin,
agreeing with Boeckh, takes ἐχθραί as 'hateful to the Erinyes' (1075).
Semitelos, favouring the same view, amends thus: ἔχθραι [the subst., for

ἐχθραί, adj.] δὲ πᾶσαι συνταράσσουσιν πόλεις, *i.e.*, 'intestine factions.'—
Kvíčala would place verses 1080—1083 immediately after v. 1022, when
ἐχθραί, as 'hateful *to the gods*,' would be interpreted by the neighbouring
θεοί in 1020.

Erfurdt, with whom Hermann agrees, supposes a reference to the
war of the Epigoni. My commentary has shown how far, and in what
sense, I think that view correct. Wex finds an allusion to the war made
by Athens on Thebes, in order to enforce burial of the Argives. But
then, as Herm. says, Athens must have been specially indicated.

In 1081 Seyffert writes τὰ πράγματ' for σπαράγματ', with καθῆγισαν,
understanding, 'Hostile to thee, all the cities will be [Bergk's συνταρά-
ξονται] in tumult, whose *affairs* have been polluted by birds,' etc., that
carry pollution ἑστιοῦχον ἐς πόλον (for πόλιν), 'to the region near the
altars.' His idea was that the affairs of the cities would be impeded by
unfavourable auspices.—Nauck also conjectures ἑστιοῦχον ἐς πόλον, but
refers it to the birds:—'the sky that contains their homes,'—the πόλος
that is their πόλις (Ar. *Av.* 179).—Other emendations of πόλιν are the
following. Dobree (*Adv.* 2. 31), σποδόν: Blaydes, δόμον, πέδον, πυράν,
or φλόγα: Wieseler, πάλην as = τέφραν, σποδόν.—Schneidewin would
write ἐς φλογοῦχον ἑστίαν (or ὀμφαλόν): Semitelos, ἄστεως ἐς ὀμφαλόν,
comparing Pind. fr. 45. 3.

1165 f. τὰς γὰρ ἡδονὰς | ὅταν προδῶσιν ἄνδρες.—The conjectures are
of two classes, according as they retain τὰς γὰρ ἡδονάς, or require καὶ γὰρ
ἡδοναί. (1) Blaydes proposes τὰς γὰρ ἡδονὰς | ὅταν προδῷ τις, ἄνδρ' ἔτ'.
Mekler, τὰς γὰρ ἡδονὰς | ὅταν προδῷ σῶμ' ἀνδρός. Both these use the
verb in the same sense as if we retained προδῶσιν ἄνδρες. The only
object, then, is to avoid the plur. ἄνδρες before τοῦτον: but the plur. is
quite admissible.—Herm. Schütz suggests τὰς γὰρ ἡδονὰς | ὅταν προῶσιν
ἄνδρες. The act., though much rarer in this sense than the midd., is
defensible: cp. Thuc. 8. 32 τὰς ναῦς...προήσειν. But the open οω is
unexampled in tragic dialogue, though we find open οε (as in αὐτοέντης,
προείπας). I had thought of παρῶσιν ('remit,' then, 'give up,' *O. C.*
1229 n.), but now believe προδῶσιν to be sound.—(2) Wecklein ὅταν γὰρ
ἡδοναὶ | βίον προδῶσιν ἀνδρός.—Semitelos: καὶ γὰρ ἡδοναὶ | ὅτου προδῶσιν
ἀνδρός ('when a man's pleasures take flight').—Hartung (omitting 1167):
καὶ γὰρ ἡδοναὶ | οὖς ἂν προδῶσιν, ἄνδρας οὐ τίθημ' ἐγώ.—Seyffert's reading
has been noticed in the commentary.

1207 In the history of the word παστάς two points, at least, are clear.
(1) Writers of the 5th and 4th centuries B.C. used the word to denote
a portico, or a corridor, supported by pillars. In Her. 2. 148 παστάδες
are pillared corridors dividing, and connecting, the groups of chambers
in the Labyrinth near Lake Moeris. In Her. 2. 169 παστάς is a structure like a gallery, or cloister, built on to one side of an open court
(αὐλή) in a temple. Doors opened from the παστάς into a sepulchral
chamber. In Xen. *Mem.* 3. 8. 9 παστάδες are the open porticoes,
or verandahs, of dwelling-houses, which receive the winter sunshine.
(2) The word παστάς was especially associated with the θάλαμος or bed-

room of a married couple. In Eur. *Or.* 1371 a Phrygian slave escapes from Helen's apartments in the house of Menelaus by climbing παστάδων ὑπὲρ τέρεμνα, *i.e.* over the roof-beams above the colonnade or peristyle (παστάδες) of the women's court. Theocritus (24. 46) uses παστάς as = θάλαμος,—the bed-room of Amphitryon and Alcmenè: ἀμφιλαφὴς δ' ἄρα παστὰς (the wide chamber) ἐνεπλήσθη πάλιν ὄρφνης. So παστός in Lucian *Dial. Mort.* 23. 3 : νεανίαν, οἷος ἦν ἐκ τοῦ παστοῦ (as he came forth from the bridal chamber).

Then the word is often *joined with* θάλαμος in epitaphs on young brides or maidens: *Anthol. P.* append. 248 οὔπω νυμφείου θαλάμου καὶ παστάδος ὥρης | γευσαμένην: *ib.* 9. 245 δυσμοίρων θαλάμων ἐπὶ παστάσιν οὐχ Ὑμέναιος | ἀλλ' Ἀίδης ἔστη πικρογάμου Πετάλης (by Antiphanes, 1st cent. B.C.). So παστός, Kaibel *Epigr.* 468 ἐκ δέ με παστῶν νύμφην κάιχ (sic) θαλάμων ἥρπασ' ἀφνῶς Ἀίδας.

The three last passages suggest that παστάς was *a part* of the θάλαμος, which could stand poetically for the whole. But what part? We might suppose, an external portico. Against this, however, is the fact that the παστός is once, at least, placed definitely *within* the θάλαμος, as though it were a synonym for the marriage-bed: *Anthol. P.* 7. 711 χρύσεων παστὸς ἔσω θαλάμων. Possibly it was some arrangement of pillars specially associated with the interior of the θάλαμος,—whether in a recess containing the bed, or otherwise.

Here, I believe that the poet used παστάς simply for θάλαμος, without reference to any columnar character of the rocky tomb.—The word is probably compressed from παραστάς (pilaster, *anta*): thus παραστάδες can mean, 'a vestibule' (Eur. *Ph.* 415), as παστάς also can (*Anth.* 6. 172).

1279 f.   τὰ μὲν πρὸ χειρῶν τάδε φέρων, τὰ δ' ἐν δόμοις
        ἔοικας ἥκειν καὶ τάχ' ὄψεσθαι κακά.

The following conjectures illustrate the difficulties which some critics have felt here. (1) Musgrave proposed, τὰ μὲν πρὸ χειρῶν, τὰ δ' ἐφορῶν, τά γ' ἐν δόμοις | ἔοικας ἥκων κύντατ' ὄψεσθαι κακά. He understood: '(having) one sorrow in thy hands (viz., Haemon's corpse), and *giving charge concerning* another [viz., concerning Antigone's body, which Creon had consigned to the guards], thou art likely, on arrival, to see most cruel woes in thy house.' He compared Eur. *Suppl.* 807 τὰ κύντατ' ἄλγη κακῶν (the idea of 'cruel,' or 'ruthless,' coming from that of 'shameless,' as in ἀναιδής, *improbus*).—(2) Brunck: φέρεις for φέρων, and ἥκων for ἥκειν, so that καὶ τάχ' = '*full* soon.'—(3) Semitelos adopts Brunck's changes and makes some others,—thus: τὰ μὲν πρὸ χειρῶν τάδε φέρεις, ἃ δ' ἐν δόμοις | εἴακας, ἥκων καὶ τάχ' εἰσόψει κακά. [He does not explain εἴακας, but perh. intended it to mean, 'hast permitted to happen.']—(4) Hartung: φέρειν for φέρων. He understands: 'thou seemest to bear some woes in thy hands, and to have come (in order) full soon (καὶ τάχ') to see the woes in the house.'—(5) Blaydes adopts φέρεις, and also changes ἥκειν καὶ into εἰσήκων.—(6) Wieseler (*Lectionskatal.*, Götting. 1875—6) proposes ἔοικώθ' ἥκεις for ἔοικας ἥκειν: meaning by ἐοικότα woes that have naturally resulted from Creon's acts.—(7) Wex rejects v. 1280, ἔοικας ἥκειν καὶ τάχ᾽ ὄψεσθαι κακά. He supposes that the Messenger's speech was interrupted, after the word δόμοις (1279), by Creon's hurried question, τί δ᾽ ἐστιν etc. The forged verse was designed to complete the unfinished sentence.—It is obvious that the easiest mode of smoothing the construction would be simply to transpose vv. 1279 f. Then τὰ μὲν πρὸ χειρῶν τάδε φέρων, τὰ δ᾽ ἐν δόμοις would be a case of parataxis (like that in 1112), = ὥσπερ τὰ πρὸ χειρῶν, οὕτω καὶ τὰ ἐν δόμοις. But neither this nor any other change is necessary.

1301 With regard to the traditional reading, ἥδ᾽ ὀξύθηκτος ἥδε βωμία πέριξ, it is generally admitted that the first of the two epithets will not bear the figurative sense, 'with keen resolve.' Hence the conjectures have followed one of three courses.

(1) To read ὀξυθήκτῳ instead of ὀξύθηκτος, and introduce a subst. in the dat., meaning 'knife' or 'sword.' The readings of Arndt and Blaydes have been noticed in the commentary. Gleditsch, with much less probability, suggests ἡ δ᾽ ὀξυθήκτῳ φασγάνῳ περιπτυχής.

(2) To retain ὀξύθηκτος, making the knife the subject of the sentence. Thus Hermann: ἥδ᾽ ὀξύθηκτος οἶδε βωμία πτέρυξ: 'yonder keenly-whetted altar-knife knows (how she perished)':—the Messenger points to the knife, lying near the body. For πτέρυξ, 'blade,' cp. Plut. *Alex.* 16 ὥστε τῶν πρώτων ψαῦσαι τριχῶν τὴν πτέρυγα τῆς κοπίδος.— Hermann further supposes that, after v. 1301, something has been lost. He infers this from the scholium,—ὡς ἱερεῖον περὶ τὸν βωμὸν ἐσφάγη, παρὰ τὸν βωμὸν προπετής,—because it has the appearance of an attempt to explain a defective text.—Donaldson, adopting πτέρυξ, places the lacuna after βλέφαρα,—not, as Hermann does, after 1301. He also differs from Hermann in supposing that the Scholiast read something now lost. Hence, with the scholium for guide, he conjectures:—ἡ δ᾽ ὀξύθηκτος ἥδε βωμία πτέρυξ | λύει κελαινὰ βλέφαρα [προσπίπτει δ᾽ ἐκεῖ | σφάγιον ὅπως βωμοῖσι,] κωκύσασα μέν, etc.

(3) To substitute ὀξύπληκτος for ὀξύθηκτος.—Thus Seyffert: ἴδ᾽, ὀξύπληκτος ἥδε φοινίαν ἀπρίξ | λύει etc.: 'lo, this woman, sharply smitten with a deadly blow (φοιν., sc. πληγήν), from a tightly-clutched weapon (ἀπρίξ),' etc.—Wecklein (*Ars Soph. em.* p. 74): ἥδ᾽ ὀξύπληκτος βῆμα βώμιον πέριξ ('at the altar steps').—Hartung: ἡ δ᾽ ὀξύπληκτος βωμία περιπτυχής, 'crouching at the altar' ('um den Hausesheerd geschmiegt'), —to represent the Schol.'s προπετής.—Pallis: ἥδ᾽ ὀξύπληκτος ἡμιν οἰκείᾳ χερί.

1342 f. The traditional reading is ὅπα πρὸς πότερον [πρότερον L] ἴδω, πᾷ καὶ θῶ· πάντα γὰρ | λέχρια τάδ᾽ [or τά τ᾽] ἐν χεροῖν.

Verse 1342 is a dochmiac dimeter. But we cannot assume that the dochmiacs answered, syllable by syllable, to those in the strophic verse, 1320. Here, as often in dochmiacs, conjecture is rendered more uncertain by the fact that a dochmiac dimeter admitted of so many different forms. [A clear and accurate synopsis of all the forms in use is given by Schmidt, *Rhythmic and Metric*, p. 77.] It will simplify a study of the various treatments applied to this passage, if we note that they represent three different ideas, viz. :—

(1) πάντα γάρ is to be kept, but without ejecting anything else from v. 1342. Therefore the strophic v., 1320, must be enlarged. Brunck and Boeckh take this view. So, in 1320, Brunck doubles πρόσπολοι, while Boeckh there writes (provisionally), προσπολοῦντες ἀγετέ μ' ὅ τι τάχος, ἀγετέ μ' ἐκποδών. This view is metrically unsound, since it breaks the series of dochmiac dimeters.

(2) πάντα γάρ is to be kept, but something else is to be omitted, in order that v. 1342 may be a dochmiac dimeter.—Seidler first proposed to omit ὅπα, which seems to me the right course. The strong argument for it is that, while the omission of ὅπα makes the metre right, we can also show how ὅπα first came in: it had been a gloss on πᾷ (see comment.). Bellermann is of the same opinion.—Others, keeping ὅπᾳ, preserve πάντα γάρ by some different expedient. Thus Wunder: ὅπᾳ πρὸς πότερον ἴδω· πάντα γάρ.—Kayser: ὅπᾳ πρὸς πότερα κλιθῶ· πάντα γάρ. This is approved by a writer in the *Athenaeum* (May 5, 1888), who thinks that ἴδω πᾷ may have arisen from ΡΑ ΟΠΑΙ, and that the MS. reading is due to the blending of ὅπᾳ πρὸς πότερα κλιθῶ with a v. l., πρὸς ὁπότερον ὅπᾳ κλιθῶ.—Bergk: ὅπᾳ πρότερ' ἴδω καὶ θῶ· πάντα γάρ.—Blaydes : πρὸς πότερον πρότερον ἴδω· πάντα γάρ.—Hermann : πᾷ θῶ, ὅπᾳ πρότερον ἴδω. πάντα γάρ.—Gleditsch : ὅπᾳ πρόστροπος κλιθῶ· πάντα γάρ.

(3) πάντα γάρ is to be omitted. This was first recommended by Nauck. Wecklein writes, ὅπᾳ πρὸς πότερον ἴδω, πᾷ κλιθῶ· and brackets πάντα γάρ.—Pallis : ὅποι πρῶτον ἴδω, ὅπα καὶ κλιθῶ.—G. H. Müller : ὅπᾳ προσπέσω· ἰώ, πᾷ κλιθῶ;—Semitelos : ὅπᾳ πρὸς πότερον ἴδω καὶ κλιθῶ· | λέχρια πάντα γὰρ τάδ'· ἐπὶ κρατί μοι etc.,—omitting ἐν χεροῖν, and assuming that πάντα γάρ has been wrongly transposed.

INDICES.

I. GREEK.

The number denotes the verse, in the note on which the word or matter is illustrated. When the reference is to a *page*, p. is prefixed to the number.)(means, 'as distinguished from.'

βαρύς, resentful, 767
βασιλείδης, formation of, 941
βασιλεῖς, a royal family, 1172
βαστάζω, 216
βεβαρβαρωμένος, said of birds, 1002
βέλη, of frost, or of rain, 358
βιώσιμος and βιωτός, 566
βλάβαι θεῶν, 1104
βλέπειν εἴς τινα, for help, 923
βλέφαρον = ὄμμα, 104
βουλεύω, uses of, 278, 1179
βώμιος, adverbial use of, 1301
βωμοί and ἐσχάραι, 1016

Γ

γάρ in assent, 639
γὰρ οὖν, 489
γε added to an emphatic adj., 739
,, deprecatory force of, 648
,, emphasising a whole phrase, 213
,, emphasising a whole clause, 648
,, lost in the MSS., 648, 1241
,, with repeated pron. (σέ...σέ γε), 789 f.
γε μέντοι, 233, 495
γενεᾶς ἐπὶ πλῆθος, sense of, 585
γενῇς, 249
γέννημα, offspring, 471
γένος, 'tribe' (said scornfully), 1035
γεραίρω, 368
γήρᾳ, without prep., 1352
γλῶσσαι, said of one man, 961
γνῶμαι in tragic lyrics, 620
γνώμης ἄπειρος, 1250
γονὴν ἔχειν τινός = γεγονέναι ἐκ τινος, 980
γοῦν emphasising a pronoun, 45
γυνή, emphatic, a true woman, 579

Δ

δ' οὖν, 688, 890, 1251
δαί and δή, p. 250
δέ added to οὕτω, after a simile, 426
,, introducing an objection, 518
,, irregularly follows τε, 1096
,, = ἀλλά, 85
δεδραγμένος, 235
δεικνύναι, of warning example, 1242
δεινά, τά, senses of, 332
δέμας, of a corpse, 205

δέμας Δανάας = fair Danaë, 944
δεννάζω, 759
δεξιόσειρος, 140
δέον, ἐς, 386
δεσμός, a prison, 957
δή added to ὅταν, 91
,, added to relat. pron., 1202
,, at the end of a verse, 726
,, with μόνος, etc., 58, 821, 895
,, = ἤδη, 939
δηλοῖ ὠμός, for δηλοῖ ὠμὸς ὤν, 471
δηλόω with partic. in nomin., 20
δῆτα in assent, 551
Δηώ = Δημήτηρ, 1121
διὰ δίκης ἰέναι τινί, 742
διὰ μέσου construction, the, 537
διὰ στέρνων ἔχειν, 639
διὰ φρενῶν, 1060
διὰ χερῶν λαβών, 916; cp. 1258
διαπτυχθέντες, said of men, 709
διασκεδαννύναι νόμους, 287
διδάσκομαι, midd., sense of, 356
διδόναι μετάστασιν, 718
δίκαιός εἰμι with infin., 400
δίκελλα, 250
Δίκη, the, of the νέρτεροι, 451
δίκη δαιμόνων, 921
διπλοῦν ἔπος, 53
διπλοῦς, senses of, 14 : distributive use of, 725
διπλῇ, adv., use of, 725
δίχα, adv. or prep., 164
δοκεῖ (impers.), corrupted to δοκεῖς, 1102
δορί and δόρει, 195
δράκων, meaning of, 126
δυοῖν...δύο, 13
δύσαυλος, 358
δυσκάθαρτος, 'hard to appease,' 1284
δυσμαχητέον, 1106
δυσσέβεια = the *repute* of impiety, 924
δυσχείρωμα, 126

E

ἐάν τε καὶ [ἐὰν] μή, 327
ἐγγενεῖς θεοί, 199
ἔγκληρος, senses of, 837
ἔγνωκα, 'I have come to know,' 1095
ἔγχος = ξίφος, 1236

τις omitted after partitive genit., 1068

,, omitted (θνητὸς ὢν δυστυχεῖ), 455

,, repeated (λέγει τις ἢ πράσσει τις), 689

,, with 2nd of two clauses, where it affects both, 257

τις εἷς instead of εἷς τις, 269

τὸ ἐπὶ τῇνδε, *quod ad eam attinet*, 889

τὸ μή with inf., instead of simple μή, 27, 535, 544

τὸ σὸν μέρος, adv., senses of, 1062

τοῖος introducing a reason, 124

τοιοῦτος, adverb., 'in such wise,' 1012

τοῖς, τοῖς δέ, the one side,...the other, 557

τοτέ...ἄλλοτε, 367

τοῦτο μέν, followed by ἔπειτα δέ, 61 : by τοῦτ' αὖθις, 167

τρέφω with predicative adj. (ἄκοσμα), 660

τριπόλιστος, 858

τροπαῖος Ζεύς, 143

τρόχος)(τροχός, 1065

τυγχάνω with acc., 778

τυμβεύειν, intrans., 888

τυμβήρης, 255

τύπτω, how far in Attic use, 171

τυραννίς, allusions to, 506

τύραννος with a bad sense, 1056

τυφλῶ ἕλκος, 971 ff.

Υ

ῠ before βρ, 1116

ὑγρός, epith. of water, 1123

ὑγρός, 'nerveless,' 1237

υἱέσι, the Att. dat. pl. of υἱός, 571

ὑμέναιος)(ἐπιθαλάμιος, 813

ὄμμα, 846

ὕν and ὗν in κλιτόν, 1143

ὑπαί, in iambics, 1035

ὕπατος, class. use of, 1332

ὑπέρ = ἕνεκα, 932

ὑπερβάς, absol., 663

ὑπεροπλία, with ῑ, 130

ὑπερπόντιος φοιτᾷς, 785

ὑπέρτερον = πλέον, 16

ὑπερτρέχω, fig., to prevail over, 455

ὑπήνεμος, 411

ὑπίλλω, 509

ὑπό with acc. (ὑφ' ἧπαρ), 1315

,, with dat. of instrument, 975

ὑπό with dat., rare in Attic prose, 65

,, ,, gen. (οἱ ὑπὸ χθονός), 65

ὑπὸ σκότου, 692; cp. 1248

ὑπόρχημα, substituted for a stasimon, 1115

ὕστερός τινος,)(ἥσσων τινός, 746

ὑστεροφθόρος, 1074

ὑφειμένη, 'lurking,' 531

ὑψίπολις, 370

Φ

φαίνεσθαι, pass., of old sayings, 621

φαίνομαι with adj., without ὤν, 177

φάος, fig. use of, 599

φάρξαι, spelling of, 241, cp. 957

φέρειν with partitive gen., 537

,, = φέρεσθαι, 464

φέρεσθαι, epexegetic of μείζων, 638

Φερσέφασσα, 894

φεύγω = to plead in defence, 263

φημί, accentuation of, 561

φίλος (masc.), said of a wife, 652

φοναῖς, ἐν, 696

φονάω, 117

φορεῖν ἦθος, 705

φρενοῦν, 754

φροντίσας, how used, 1031

φυγαί, means of escape, 363

φύξιμος, governing acc., 786

φύσις, one's age, 727

Χ

χαίρειν, τό, joy, 1170

χαλκόδετοι αὐλαί, 945

χάριν, πρός, 30

χάριν τόλμης, 'on account of' it, 371

χείμαρρος, as adj., 712

χείρεσσι, in iambics, 1297

χελιδονίζειν = βαρβαρίζειν, 1001

χιών, as = 'snow-water,' doubtful, 829

χθές and ἐχθές, 456

χοαί to the dead, 431, 901 : when poured by Antigone, 429

χολή and χολαί, 1010

χοραγὸς ἄστρων, of Dionysus, 1147

χορεύω θεόν, in his honour, 1153

χρή with dat., no certain Attic example of, 736

II. MATTERS.

infin., epexegetic, 165, 216, 439, 638, 699, 1098, 1249

,, instead of partic., after ἐπίσταμαι, 293: after οἶδα, 473

,, of consequence (without ὥστε), 64

,, of result, without ὥστε, 1076

,, with art., as acc. of inner object (πείθομαι τὸ δρᾶν), 1105

interpolation, p. liii

Ion, p. ix, n. 1; p. 5; meets Sophocles, p. xliii

Ionicisms in dialogue, 86, 308

ironical form of threat, 310

Isocrates, on the growth of civilisation, 354

Italy, southern, and Dionysus, 1119

iterative form (-εσκον), 949

ivy, in cult of Dionysus, 1132

L

language, origin of, in the Eleatic view, 354

last word of verse corrupted, 1329

laughter, malicious, 647

Laurentian MS., noteworthy readings of, 386; errors as to persons in, 571; its errors sometimes point to the true reading, 467, 966; neglect of elision in, 1147; relation of, to other MSS., p. lii

laws, the 'unwritten,' 454

logaoedic verse, p. lvi

lots, mode of drawing, 396

Love, the invincible god, 781

'love thy friends,' etc., 643

Lycurgus, the Thracian, 955 ff.; in art, 965

M

Maenads, 963

masc. gender used in a general statement, though referring to a woman, 464, 479, 580, 652

masc. partic. after neut. (or fem.) subject, 341

,, subst. as fem. adj., 1074

mattock, 250

Megareus, death of, 1303

Mendelssohn's Antigone music, p. xli

metaphor, not consistently sustained, 117

middle forms, poetical, 351, 593

Mimnermus, p. ix, n. 1

monarchy, absolute, 737

,, of heroic age, how depicted by Tragedy, p. xxiv

mules for ploughing, 341

Muses, associated with Dionysus, 965

N

names, proper, puns upon, 110

,, ,, of 1st or 3rd decl., 198

Naxos, and Dionysus, 1150

negatives, confusion arising from several, 244

neuter adj. with partitive genit. (πρῶτον εὐδαιμονίας), 1347

,, adj. with art., and genit. (as τὸ θρασὺ τῆς γνώμης), 365

,, instead of masc. (οὐδὲν λόγων ἀρεστόν), 500, 659, 780

,, noun (λάλημα), used scornfully, 310

Niobe, 823 ff., 834

nominative for voc., 228 f., 379, 891

,, in quotation ('ἥδε' μὴ λέγε), 567

number, coincidence or contrast of (δυοῖν ...δύο, δύο...μίαν), 13, 55, 170

Nysa in Euboea, 1131

O

oaths, pleonastic phrases concerning, 394

Oedipus, end of, how conceived here, 50, 900

Olympus, brightness of, 609

optat. of wish, co-ordinated with a statement of fact, 686

,, instead of subjunct. with ἄν, in universal statement, after a primary tense (χρὴ κλύειν, ὃν πόλις στήσειε), 666, 1032

,, with ἄν, in giving leave, 80; scornfully, 444

,, with ἄν, of fixed resolve, 1108

,, ,, ,, in entreaty, 1339

,, without ἄν, of the conceivable, 605

ordeal by fire, etc. 265

synizesis of μή, 33; other cases of, 95, 152

synonym used, instead of repeating a word (καλῶς μέν...εὖ δέ), 669, 898

T

Tantalus, 825

technical Attic words, admitted in poetry, 160

temples, 'peripteral,' etc.: votive offerings in, 285

temporal clause as object (μισῶ, ὅταν), 495

Theban rivers, the, 104

Thebans, 'the dragon's seed,' 126, cp. 1125

Thebes, the 'seven-gated,' 100; 'rich in chariots,' 149; 'mother-city' of Bacchants, 1122

Theognis, an echo of, 707

Thrace, stormy winds from, 587

Thucydides, illustration from, 189

Timocreon on Themistocles, 297

tmesis of ἐκ, 427, 1233; of ἐν, 420, 1274; of ἐπί, 986, 1107; of κατά, 977; of σύν, 432

tombs in the rocks near Thebes, 774; Antigone's, how conceived, 1217

torrents in Greece, 712

torture used to extract confession, 309

tribrach in 2nd foot of verse, 29

tribrach in the 5th place of trimeter, 418

transpositions of words in L, 29, 106, 607, 1129

trilogy—a term not strictly applicable to the *O. T., O. C.,* and *Ant.,* p. xlix

'tyrannis,' the, of the historical age, tinges the picture of monarchy in Attic drama, p. xxiv

V

vase-paintings relating to Antigone, p. xxxix

verb agrees in number with nearest subject, 830, 1133

  ,, finite, substituted for a participial clause, 256, 813 f., 1163

  ,, pregnant use of (τυφλῶ ἕλκος=ποιῶ ἕλκος τυφλῶν), 971 ff.

  ,, understood with μόλις μέν, 1105

verbal in -τέος, answers to pass. sense of verb, 678

  ,, ,, ,, impers. neut. pl., 677

verse without caesura or quasi-caesura, 1021

viper, imagery from the, 531

W

weaving, implements for, 976

women, domestic seclusion of, 579

Z

zeugma of verb, 442

CAMBRIDGE: PRINTED BY C. J. CLAY, M.A. AND SONS, AT THE UNIVERSITY PRESS.

SOPHOCLES. PART I. OEDIPUS TYRANNUS.

Second Edition. Demy 8vo. 12s. 6d.

Notices of the Press.

'The appearance of the first volume of a complete edition of Sophocles, by Professor Jebb, is an event of interest, not only to classical students, but to all who care for literature. No living English scholar unites in himself so many of the qualities which, for our generation, form the ideal of classical scholarship. He has the passion for beauty, the feeling for style and literary expression, the artistic enthusiasm of the Italian Renaissance....Professor Jebb is gifted with a sympathetic insight into Greek idiom and the latent capacities of the language. He has a remarkable and, so far as I know, a unique, faculty of infusing poetry into grammar, of leading his readers, through particles, moods, and tenses, vividly to realise the dramatic situation and enter into the feelings of the speaker. Under his guidance we seem not so much to be engaged in a work of logical analysis or of skilful dissection as to be following a vital process of growth and of construction.'—Professor S. H. BUTCHER, in the *Fortnightly Review.*

'Of his explanatory and critical notes we can only speak with admiration. Thorough scholarship combines with taste, erudition, and boundless industry to make this first volume a pattern of editing.'—*The Times.*

'We get in one compact volume such a cyclopædia of instruction, such a variety of helps to the full comprehension of the poet, as not so many years ago would have needed a small library, and all this instruction and assistance given, not in a dull and pedantic way, but in a style of singular clearness and vivacity.'—*The Athenæum.*

'An edition which marks a definite advance, which is whole in itself, and brings a mass of solid and well-wrought material such as future constructors will desire to adapt, is definitive in the only applicable sense of the term, and such is the edition of Professor Jebb. No man is better fitted to express in relation to Sophocles the mind of the present generation.'—*The Saturday Review.*

'We have no hesitation in saying that for any scholar, and indeed, for many who cannot claim to be scholars, but still "have a little Greek," to read their *Sophocles* again with Professor Jebb's help at hand, so unfailing, so admirable as it is, will be a treat of the very highest kind. It is very seldom that a scholar and critic of the largest attainments has also great literary ability. This rarest of combinations is found in Professor Jebb, and the result is eminently satisfactory.'—*The Spectator.*

'Some fourteen or fifteen years ago, a series of classical editions for the use of schools appeared under the title of *Catena Classicorum.* The series was very well received, and many of the editions fulfilled the promise with which it started. Unquestionably the best books of the series were Mr Jebb's *Ajax* and *Electra* of Sophocles, which really made an epoch in school editions...In our opinion, Professor Jebb's *Oedipus Tyrannus* deserves to be, in the same way, a model for the higher classical editions....The faculty for criticism in most cases coexists with the faculty for interpretation; for the two depend on the same qualities—namely, accurate grammatical knowledge, and keen insight into the mind of antiquity. Professor Jebb is well known to possess both these qualities in an eminent degree.'—*Journal of Education.*

'At last we come to the commentary: and here we must repeat that Professor Jebb's power of delicately disentangling and firmly grasping the fine shades of use and meaning of the Greek words strikes us as most masterly. We may not always agree: but he never flinches or shirks a difficulty: he notices a hundred things which are usually passed over: and his range of illustration is surprising, both from its width and its aptness. In short his *method* is consummate: if we differ, it is Professor Jebb, we find, who has sometimes supplied the materials and evidence. And above all, in threading the mazes of this most intricate of authors he never blurs a point: he is always most admirably clear.'—*The Oxford Magazine.*

SOPHOCLES. PART II. OEDIPUS COLONEUS.

Demy 8vo. 12s. 6d.

'Der zweite Band dieser willkommenen Sophoklesausgabe verfolgt dasselbe Ziel wie die erste, eine gründliche, sachgemässe Interpretation der Dichterworte. Ich brauche des Herausgs. Gelehrsamkeit und guten Geschmack, sein feines grammatisches Verständniss, seine liebevolle, von allem Conventionalismus befreite Hingabe an das Individuum des Dichters, an seine Art zu denken und zu reden, nicht von neuem zu rühmen; das beste Zeugniss für den Commentar, der noch zu Ausführlichkeit gegenüber dem ersten Bande gewonnen hat, scheint mir der Umstand zu sein, dass durch ihn die Echtheit der überlieferten Schreibung an vielen Stellen festgestellt wird: gar manche Conjectur, so hoffe ich, wird für immer aus den Sophoklesausgaben verschwinden.'—G. KAIBEL in the *Deutsche Litteraturzeitung*, Nr. 21 (May 22, 1886).

'Dem ersten Teile der neuen Sophokles-Ausgabe...schliesst sich der vorliegende zweite Band würdig und mehr als würdig an. Alle Fragen, welche die Kritik, Erklärung und ästhetische Auffassung des Ödipus auf Kolonos berühren, sind mit Einsicht und Geschmack und nicht ohne Anregung neuer Gesichtspunkte behandelt, und das Lob, welches man dem ersten Teile spenden konnte, gebührt dem zweiten um so mehr, als die Verwertung der anderweitigen Litteratur eine ausgedehntere ist.'—
N. WECKLEIN in the *Neue Philologische Rundschau*, No. 25 (Dec. 11, 1885).

'Das Buch enthält eine sehr gründliche Arbeit eines gelehrten Philologen. Sein Studium ist allen zu empfehlen, welche sich einmal gründlich philologisch mit Sophokles beschäftigen wollen.'—C. SCHMELZER in the *Berliner Philologische Wochenschrift*, No. 46 (Nov. 13, 1886).

'Sie bietet sehr viel, und fördert in vielfacher Weise die Kritik und die Exegese.'—
Jahresbericht, vol. 46 (1887).

'Ich hoffe in meinen späteren Werken beweisen zu können, mit welcher freudigen Begeisterung ich ein Werk studirt habe, das so viele neue Gesichtspunkte eröffnet, und durch Anschaulichkeit wie Schärfe seiner Erläuterungen ausgezeichnet ist.'—
J. H. HEINRICH SCHMIDT, in the Preface to vol. IV. of his *Synonymik der Griechischen Sprache* (1886).

'It remains only to say that all who are interested in classical scholarship and literature will look forward with impatience to the completion of this incomparable edition.'—*Athenæum*, May 22, 1886.

'Upon the appearance of the *Oedipus Tyrannus* we spoke of this edition as definitive in the only applicable sense, as marking a distinct advance and bringing materials which all future editors would be careful to adopt. After reading the *Oedipus Coloneus* we are inclined to say that this praise was put too low. A classic like Sophocles will be read by each generation from their own point of view and illustrated by their own lights; but, though there cannot be a final interpretation of such work, there can be, for a particular language, a permanent basis of interpretation; and such, we think, Professor Jebb will be found to have furnished to the English students and interpreters of Sophocles.'—*Saturday Review*, Aug. 14, 1886.

'We have not space enough to point out in detail the numberless felicities of explanation and illustration to be found in these notes; but any one who glances through a few pages for himself will allow that no English commentary on Sophocles, or on any other Greek author, can compare with this in all-round merit.'—*Cambridge Review*, May 2, 1886.

'High as was the level of interpretation attained in the Commentary on the Oedipus Tyrannus, in this edition it is higher still. It is not easy to say whether Professor Jebb is better in explanation or in illustration. In their combination, at any rate, he is so successful that we rarely differ from him without an inward acknowledgment—the highest compliment that we can pay an editor—that he may be right...We have referred incidentally to the Introduction. It is not less satisfactory than the rest of the work. It shows the same learning, at once wide and minute, the same power of combination and presentation, the same literary tact and skill... Professor Jebb's acquaintance with the literature of his subject is exhaustive, and his appreciation of the labours of his predecessors is at once just and generous...In the interests of Sophoclean studies and English scholarship alike, we wish the work, of which this is an instalment, a swift and successful completion. It is one of which Professor Jebb's countrymen may well be proud.'—*Journal of Education*, Sept. 1, 1886.

'Such work as this is worth waiting for, so well considered, so complete, we are almost disposed to say, so final is it. Its merits are due to a happy combination of fine literary taste and a thorough mastery of Greek scholarship. An editor so equipped renders to students a service that can hardly be estimated; there are many to whom this volume will, as did its predecessor, the edition of the *Oedipus Tyrannus*, give a quite new insight into the genius of Sophocles, as also into the greatness of the Greek drama.'—*Spectator*, April 17, 1886.

SOPHOCLES. PART III. THE ANTIGONE.

Demy 8vo. 12s. 6d.

'Der dritte stattliche Band der Sophoklesausgabe von dem tüchtigen Hellenisten Jebb, der jüngst bei Gelegenheit des Universitätsjubiläums von Bologna in einer herrlichen Pindarischen Ode einen glänzenden Beweis seiner Beherrschung der griechischen Sprache gegeben hat, zeichnet sich durch die gleichen Vorzüge aus wie die beiden ersten Bände und bietet eine Zusammenfassung alles dessen, was für die Kritik und Erklärung der Antigone wichtig ist, woraus der Verf. sich mit Geschmack und sicherem Urteil seinen Text und seine Auffassung der einzelnen Stellen zu gestalten weisz. Am meisten gefällt die Unbefangenheit, mit welcher der Verf. die Überlieferung und die verschiedenen Ansichten der Gelehrten behandelt. Er verteidigt die handschriftlichen Lesarten niemals mit Scheingründen; er ist andrerseits einem leichtfertigen Verlassen der Überlieferung abhold, und zwar nicht blosz in Bezug auf andere, sondern auch auf sich, indem er mit eigenen Konjekturen sehr sparsam und vorsichtig ist: er prüft alles, was andere vorgebracht haben, und behält das Beste.'— Dr WECKLEIN in the *Berliner Philologische Wochenschrift*, 12 Jan., 1889.

'Seitdem die hellenische Gesellschaft zu London 1885 das Facsimile des La veröffentlicht hat, kann jeder paläographisch geschulte Philolog die Lesarten der

NOTICES OF THE PRESS.

Handschrift selbst kontrollieren, Abweichungen früherer Kollationen lösen und verbreitete Irrtümer berichtigen. So hat nun Professor Jebb in seinen schon früher erschienenen Ausgaben des Oedipus Coloneus und Oedipus Tyrannos (2. Aufl.) und in dieser Antigoneausgabe die Lesarten des La so vollständig und genau wie möglich angegeben und schafft dadurch eine Sophoklesausgabe, so wichtig für die Kritik, wie es seiner Zeit die dritte Auflage der Oxforder Sophoklesausgabe Dindorfs war.'—H. MÜLLER in *Neue Philologische Rundschau*, July 7, 1888.

'Professor Jebb's edition of Sophocles is already so fully established, and has received such appreciation in these columns and elsewhere, that we have judged this third volume when we have said that it is of a piece with the others. The whole edition so far exhibits perhaps the most complete and elaborate editorial work which has ever appeared.'—*Saturday Review*, April 7, 1888.

'This edition marks the highest level yet attained by Sophoclean criticism, whether regarded on the side of literary workmanship or of exact scholarship, and when completed will be a monument of the best classical learning of this generation.'—*Scotsman*.

'In an edition so distinguished by accurate perception and fine analysis, it is almost superfluous to say that the critical part of the work has been excellently done, for in reality interpretation and criticism when carried to the highest point meet and coalesce. The more thorough the interpretation, the less need will there be for conjectures, which often—even the most attractive—have their origin in a lack of insight into the meaning of the text, or an impatience of the attention requisite to grasp it. The text before us is certainly the best text of the *Antigone* yet given to the world. Yet it might on the whole be called conservative. We may safely say that never is a reading of the MSS. condemned unheard. No conjecture, however specious, finds its way into the text until the editor has satisfied himself that the MS. tradition is certainly erroneous.'—Prof. TYRRELL in *Classical Review*, Vol. II. p. 138 (May, 1888).

'Professor Jebb's keen and profound sympathy, not only with Sophocles and all the best of ancient Hellenic life and thought, but also with modern European culture, constitutes him an ideal interpreter between the ancient writer and the modern reader. His Introduction, which deals with the plot, motive, and psychology of the play, is in itself a singularly pleasing composition.'—*Athenæum*, May 5, 1888.

'It would be difficult to praise this third instalment of Professor Jebb's unequalled edition of Sophocles too warmly, and it is almost a work of supererogation to praise it at all. It is equal, at least, and perhaps superior in merit to either of his previous instalments; and when this is said, all is said. Yet we cannot refrain from formally recognising once more the consummate Greek scholarship of the editor, and from once more doing grateful homage to his masterly tact and literary skill and to his unwearied and marvellous industry.'—*Spectator*, June 2, 1888.

'We have unquestionably, in this edition of Sophocles, so far as it has proceeded, a splendid example of the work which can be done by the English school of classics at its best; and we have no doubt that the rest of the edition will confirm the judgment which must be pronounced by all competent critics on the treatment of the three great Theban dramas.'—*Quarterly Review*. (April, 1890.)

C. J. CLAY AND SONS,
CAMBRIDGE UNIVERSITY PRESS WAREHOUSE,
AVE MARIA LANE.

Printed by BoD™in Norderstedt, Germany